AF600097

THE CHRONOLOGY OF REVOLUTION

THE CHRONOLOGY OF REVOLUTION

COMMUNISM, CULTURE, AND CIVIL SOCIETY IN TWENTIETH-CENTURY BRITAIN

BEN HARKER

UNIVERSITY OF TORONTO PRESS
Toronto Buffalo London

Toronto Buffalo London
utorontopress.com

ISBN 978-1-4875-0739-8 (cloth)
ISBN 978-1-4875-3616-9 (EPUB)
ISBN 978-1-4875-3615-2 (PDF)

Library and Archives Canada Cataloguing in Publication

Title: The chronology of revolution : communism, culture, and civil society in twentieth-century Britain / Ben Harker.
Names: Harker, Ben, author.
Description: Includes bibliographical references and index.
Identifiers: Canadiana (print) 20200346172 | Canadiana (ebook) 20200346180 | ISBN 9781487507398 (cloth) | ISBN 9781487536169 (EPUB) | ISBN 9781487536152 (EPUB)
Subjects: LCSH: Communist Party of Great Britain – History – 20th century. | LCSH: Communism – Great Britain – History – 20th century. | LCSH: Political parties – Great Britain – History – 20th century.
Classification: LCC JN1129.C62 H37 2021 | DDC 324.241/09750904 – dc23

University of Toronto Press acknowledges the financial assistance to its publishing program of the Canada Council for the Arts and the Ontario Arts Council, an agency of the Government of Ontario.

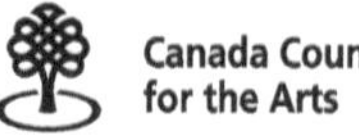

For Rosa

Contents

List of Illustrations ix

Acknowledgments xi

List of Abbreviations xiii

Introduction 3

1 The Chronology of Revolution, 1920–1940 13

2 Constructive Communists, 1940–1947 38

3 The British Road to Socialism, 1947–1956 76

4 The Struggle for Renewal, 1956–1968 109

5 The Spectre of Eurocommunism, 1968–1979 149

Conclusion 201

Notes 207

Index 351

Illustrations

Party propaganda machine, 1920s 14
Communist Pioneers in Birmingham, 1920s 14
Home Front journal, 1942 44
Second Front rally, Trafalgar Square, 1942 45
Student recruitment leaflet, 1946 64
The British Road to Socialism (1951) 79
Communist-refashioned billboard advertising *Mighty Joe Young* (1949) 98
Barbara Niven addressing a street meeting, early 1950s 101
Activist selling *Arena* at Sadler's Wells, London, 1951 102
Communists protest against racism in Notting Hill, late 1950s 127
Communists in Ilford basking in the reflected glory of the Soviet Sputnik launch, 1957 130
Communists with membership cards, 1958 130
Arnold Kettle, Alan Bush, Lindsay Anderson, and John Berger, 1960s 134
Young Communist League activists in Manchester during the December 1963 by-election 139
The Beatles in *Challenge*, December 1963 142
Handbill for *The Trend* Young Communist League recruitment drive, 1967 143
Poster for Communist Women's Struggle event, London, 1975 160
Poster for Communist University of London, 1977 169
Granada Television filming the 1977 Congress for *Decision: British Communism* 189
The Communist Party stall at the Glastonbury Festival, 1984 198

Acknowledgments

The research for this book was generously supported by a British Academy Small Grant (2010), a Jackson Brothers Beinecke Library Fellowship (Yale University, 2013), and an AHRC Leadership Fellowship (2016–17), 'Wars of Position: Communism and Civil Society' (AH/NOO/2903/1). The latter involved a collaboration with the People's History Museum, Manchester, and its in-house Labour History Archive and Study Centre (LHASC). Special thanks to all the staff there, especially Cath Birchall, Chris Burgess, James Darby, Jenny Mabbott, Julic Parry, Simon Sheppard, Darren Treadwell, Mark Wilson, and to all those involved in the project's two conferences, 'Loyal Dissidents' (2016) and 'Wars of Position: Marxism and Civil Society' (2017), especially Phil O'Brien. I am grateful to the University of Manchester for funding for the book's indexing. The book would have taken even longer to write without the support of Emily Weygang. Warmest thanks to her and to my mother Janet Harker and sister Kate Harker. Thanks to colleagues and friends in Manchester and beyond for conversations about the project and judicious reading of sections of the manuscript: David Alderson, Francesca Billiani, John Callaghan, Daniela Caselli, Laura Chrisman, Catherine Clay, John Connor, Madeleine Davis, Kristin Ewins, Francis King, Keith Gildart, David Hobbs, Masashi Hoshino, Kevin Morgan, Glyn Salton-Cox, Stan Smith, Elinor Taylor, Emily Weygang, and Matthew Worley. Thanks are not enough for Dani Caselli, with whom even chronological revolutions in dark times seem possible.

I was very well served by the anonymous readers whose criticisms and suggestions have, I hope, resulted in a better book. It has been a pleasure to have worked with editors of the calibre of Stephen Shapiro and Robin Studniberg throughout. Many thanks to freelancer Barry Norris for superb copy editing and to staff at the University of Toronto Press for all their hard work in bringing the book to publication. I am grateful to the Communist Party Archive Trust and the LHASC for permission to reproduce the images, all of which come from their collections. Every effort was made to discover and contact the photographers who took the photographs included; if anyone believes they should be credited, University of Toronto Press and the author will be happy to do so in future printings or editions of the book. Thanks are due to many archives and libraries for all their assistance, notably: the Beinecke and Stirling Libraries, Yale (New Haven); the National Archives, British Library, Marx Memorial Library and Theatre Workshop Archive at the Theatre Royal, Stratford East (London); the Modern Records Centre (Warwick); the History Centre (Hull); the Bodleian Library and Ruskin College Library (Oxford); the Special Collections of the University Libraries of Birmingham, East Anglia, Leeds, Nottingham, Salford and Sussex; the National Library of Australia (Canberra); the Working Class Movement Library (Salford); and the BBC Written Archives (Caversham).

Abbreviations

ABCA	Army Bureau of Current Affairs
ABT	Association of Building Technicians
ACTT	Association of Cinematograph, Television and Allied Technicians
AEU	Amalgamated Engineering Union
AIA	Artists International Association
AScW	Association of Scientific Workers
ATO	Architects' and Technicians' Organisation
AUEW	Amalgamated Union of Engineering Workers
CEMA	Council for Education in Music and the Arts
CPGB	Communist Party of Great Britain
CUL	Communist University of London
ENSA	Entertainments National Service Association
IMF	International Monetary Fund
JPC	Joint Production Committee
LBC	Left Book Club
LGSM	Lesbian and Gays Support the Miners
LPC	Local Party Committees
LPO	London Philharmonic Orchestra
NCC	National Cultural Committee
NCLC	National Council of Labour Colleges
NEAC	National Educational Advisory Committee
NUM	National Union of Mineworkers
NUS	National Union of Students
NUT	National Union of Teachers
PCF	Parti communiste française
PCI	Partito Comunista Italiano
SCR	Society for Cultural Relations with the USSR
TASS	Technical, Administrative and Supervisory Section
TGWU	Transport and General Workers Union

TUC	Trades Union Congress
UCATT	Union of Construction, Allied Trades and Technicians
UCL	University College London
UCS	Upper Clyde Shipbuilders
ULF	United Labour Federation
WEA	Workers' Educational Association
WFSW	World Federation of Scientific Workers
WLM	Women's Liberation Movement
WMA	Workers' Music Association
YCL	Young Communist League

THE CHRONOLOGY OF REVOLUTION

Introduction

A great deal was expected of the Communist Party of Great Britain (CPGB, 1920–91) by the Soviet leaders who inspired its formation. Trotsky hoped that the new party, situated in the world's first industrialized nation, might be the vanguard of the 'the destinies of all mankind,' and break the link in imperialism's chain.[1] Far from forming a vanguard for the global proletariat, the party was never even a mass party in the home of the world's oldest labour movement: membership peaked at 56,000 during the Second World War; at the time, the Labour Party had 235,000 members, the Parti communiste française (PCF) had 290,000 and the Partito Comunista Italiano (PCI) 1,771,000.[2] The British party was never a significant force, theoretically or politically, in the international Communist movement. Even at its post-war height, it was too marginal in national political life to warrant a place in Stalin's Cominform. Electorally, it would never share the spoils of the much larger 'Eurocommunist' parties in the 1970s.[3] With just 8,000 members by 1989, it ignominiously dissolved itself two years later.[4]

The Chronology of Revolution: Communism, Culture, and Civil Society in Twentieth-Century Britain puts new questions to the party's history. It is a recuperative analysis of failure, produced at a moment when capitalism faces systemic crisis and the Left, making uneven advances, returns seriously to questions about socialist renewal and strategy.[5] For some in these debates, history is just that, and twentieth-century Communist Parties in particular the nightmare from which the twenty-first-century Left needs to awaken, being irrelevant to facing the future or the formulation of new conceptions, as we know all they ever were. Rejecting the form and function of those parties, runs the logic, is a precondition for reinscribing communism into what Alain Badiou calls the 'ideological sphere.'[6] This study, by contrast, is undergirded by three key convictions. First, capitalism is inherently incapable of 'the incorporation of all its people, *as whole human beings*,' and the transition to socialism remains an ethical imperative: the choice is still socialism or barbarism.[7] Second, some version of the party form remains indispensable to democratic socialist advance in mass democracies, where parties function as what Chantal Mouffe terms 'symbolic markers allowing people to situate themselves in the social world and to give meaning to their lived experiences.'[8] Third, despite their manifold corruptions, degenerations, and failures, the Communist Parties remain an unavoidable antecedent in mass anticapitalist struggle in the West, which still need working through and beyond in both the everyday and psychological senses. For the sake of historical precision, the study concentrates on the failure of a single party that the Bolsheviks themselves saw as a case testing the possibility of socialist revolution in the developed West.[9] The study's analytical frame, however, lends itself to broader and comparative application, as it focuses on the underanalysed disjunction between the Communist Parties of the 'new type' attached to the Third International and the evolving forms of developed Western capitalism that proved resistant to their incursions.[10] The concept of Stalinism, I argue – 'an ideology of a revolutionary elite which ... degenerated into a bureaucracy' – is a fundamentally *necessary* tool with which to analyse this failure, but it is not *sufficient* for doing so, and can by no means grasp all that these parties were or all the reasons they failed.[11] The study widens the usual analytical focus, seeing failure as rooted in three interlocking and inherited politico-theoretical problems facing Communist Parties in the developed West. Schematically these can be designated as economic, political, and 'cultural,' or relating to civil society. Although inextricably related to and reinforced by Stalinism, the British party's failure to identify and transcend these problems was not reducible to Stalinism, nor was it by any means unique to that party.

The First Two Problems

The usual period frame for analysing the international Communist movement is Eric Hobsbawm's 'short twentieth century' (1914–91), the years between the First World War and the end of the USSR – 'a coherent historical period that has now ended.'[12] This flatters the Communist movement by positioning it at the century's dynamic core. Read instead in the *longue durée* of the capitalism that it came into being to overcome, twentieth-century Communism looks almost immediately out of time. The mass working-class unrest between 1918 and 1920 – 'the only period,' as Donald Sassoon notes, 'during which it was not unrealistic to assume that a "revolution in the West" was on the agenda' – was over by the time Lenin drafted his famous 'Twenty-one Conditions' of membership of the Comintern at its Second Congress in July-August 1920.[13] That the Communist Parties were born too late to benefit from the convulsions that ushered them into being is evident from their sorry record in revolution: with the exception of the short-lived Hungarian Soviet Republic and the People's Republic of Mongolia, no new communist regimes were created between the wars.[14]

Most of the international Communist movement's life (1920–90) coincided not with wars and revolutions in the developed West, but with the longest capitalist boom in history, which ran from the late 1940s to 2008 and reached its height in the quarter-century following 1950, a period in which the US economy doubled in size, the British, West German, and Italian economies quadrupled, and the Japanese boomed tenfold.[15]

One core and abiding problem of the international Communist movement, I argue, was its fundamental underestimation of the resilience of capitalism and its supporting structures and ideologies. According to independently minded Soviet economist Nikolai Kondratieff, capitalism could best be analysed in terms of long phases of rise, decline, and reconfiguration, a framework according to which the twentieth-century Communism born of the Russian Revolution was itself a symptom of the disintegration of the third 'long cycle' of industrial capitalism, which was launched in the 1890s, foundered at the end of the First World War, and terminated in the Great Depression.[16] Bolshevik attacks on Kondratieff's unconscionable theories of capitalism's capacity for survival through mutation culminated in his execution under the Stalin regime in 1938, a liquidation which firmly buried his insights from Communist consciousness.[17] Naturally preferred by Communists for whom the Russian Revolution was the historical fulcrum of class struggle was the theory extracted by the Comintern from Lenin's *Imperialism: The Highest Stage of Capitalism* (1916), which envisaged not what Kondratieff called *Long Cycles of the Conjuncture* (1926), but a single cycle. Imperialism, by this reckoning, was the crescendo of 'moribund capitalism.'[18] This catastrophist analysis formed a compelling, constitutive framework of Third International Communism, strongly coloured by optimism of the intellect. A recurring theme of this study is the powerful pull of the 'final crisis' mindset on the British party, which saw no need for an economics committee analysing a self-evidently doomed capitalism until 1943, and for whom imminent crisis remained doxa well into the 1960s.[19] A particular focus is the party's inability to make sense of the Keynesian moment – what Wolfgang Streeck calls the 'state-administered ... welfare-state capitalism of the three post-war decades.'[20]

As that inability implies, the catastrophist bent of the party's underpowered economic analysis compounded and concealed another major theoretical weakness in the Marxist tradition bequeathed to Third International Communism: the absence of deep analysis of the structures of the bourgeois democratic state with which Communism had to contend in the West – especially representative democracy as a form of class rule. Marx wrote little about such political structures.[21] Lenin registered the crucial historical difference between West and East, notably in *What Is to Be Done?* (1902) and *'Left Wing' Communism – An Infantile Disorder* (1920), but his definition of the bourgeois state as 'a special machine for the suppression of one class by another' in his talismanic *The State and Revolution* (1917) did little to differentiate between the diverse temporalities and traditions of bourgeois states.[22] This gap impeded serious analysis of the specific combinations of compulsion, consent, and coercion that defined the representative bourgeois democratic state in the advanced capitalist countries. At this point, 'political' questions – the failure of parties to analyse and respond to the structures of representative democracy, which is my second key focus – shade into my third and most substantial concern: 'culture,' or civil society, as a location of class power and its reproduction in developed societies, and communist theoretical and organizational responses to it. This needs teasing out more fully.

The Chronology of Revolution

From the outset, while capitalism and its political superstructures remained insufficiently analysed, there was always in Third International Communism an uneasy sense that 'culture,' in the broad sense of a way of life, mattered more in consolidating and stabilizing class power in the industrialized and largely literate and enfranchised West than in Russia, and that different modes of organization might be required in response. In July 1924, for instance, Trotsky echoed Lenin in arguing that making a revolution in Britain would be more difficult than in Russia – Trotsky predicted one in 'five or ten years' – but the building of socialism would be proportionately easier.[23] The key difference on both counts was 'culture,' first as an impediment to socialism – as a means through which the ruling class blocked oppositional consciousness – then as a facilitator, an inheritance in and through which socialism could be constructed rapidly and efficiently.[24] In placing such emphasis on the relationship between 'culture' and class power in the developed world, Trotsky gestured towards the possibility of a fundamentally different revolutionary chronology there, one grounded in the fact that the structures, practices, and intellectuals that mediated between rulers and ruled mattered a great deal and that the right kind of interventions in these fields might be a prerequisite for revolutionary advance. But despite the gesture – and it was one made more strongly the following year, when Trotsky argued that revolution in Britain would be a 'gradual process' requiring 'serious preparatory activity' – there was no detailed formulation of such a strategy.[25] The emphasis instead was on economic catastrophism and political insurrectionism on the Soviet model: 'smashing, breaking up and demoralizing the enemy forces' and the 'seizure of power.'[26] The only culture that counted here was 'Leninism,' 'the product and consummation of all man's previous culture,' at once its apex and cutting edge.[27] Defining culture *as* Leninism collapsed it back into politics in the sense of seizing the state, and left no more to be said about it for now. But *after* Leninist revolution, Trotsky embellished, the cultural question would re-emerge in far more encouraging circumstances. The 'gigantic store' of human culture currently possessed by the British bourgeoisie would be received like a birthright by the proletariat, resourcing it to forge beyond the underdeveloped and largely illiterate Soviet Union in socialist construction within a generation.[28] 'Do your duty,' he imagined telling British comrades who had often needed chiding in the past, 'we, with you, shall win together!'[29]

From the outset, the place in class rule and revolutionary strategy of what Trotsky capaciously called 'culture,' I argue, would be a tension, sometimes open, sometimes hidden, in Communist Parties in the developed world. This 'cultural' problem was enmeshed in questions of the economics and politics of mass societies, but also distinct from them. It would rumble away in debates within British Communism, as elsewhere, in the 1920s and 1930s and come to the fore in the Popular Front years, with the imperative to territorialize and transform national cultures in the face of fascist advance. These questions would find their most significant Communist theoretical elaboration in Antonio Gramsci's 'Prison Notebooks,' composed between 1929 and 1935 and published in Italian between 1948 and 1951 and sporadically in other European languages in the quarter-century after that.[30] Gramsci's text, which would have a powerful effect on its belated translation into English in 1971, addressed why the October Revolution failed to spread to Western countries, and what alternative strategies were necessary there. The central theme was precisely what Trotsky called 'culture' and its role in class power, both ruling and oppositional. Gramsci engaged with the earlier Comintern debates, including Trotsky's contribution and Lenin's insistence on the difficulty of beginning a revolution in the advanced countries, and developed the analysis in what he saw as a Leninist spirit.[31] Where Trotsky had talked about 'culture,' Gramsci preferred 'civil society,' a term with a complex pre-history[32] that he revived in order to register the mechanisms of political power in parliamentary or constitutional states and the difficulties, as Ellen Meiksins Wood later put it, 'of supplanting a system of class domination in which class power has no visible point of concentration in the state but is diffused throughout society and cultural practices.'[33] For Gramsci, civil society was the complex ensemble of 'private' social and cultural institutions and activities outside the State and judiciary, a sphere to which intermediaries or 'intellectuals' were crucial.[34] In Russia, Gramsci noted in a well-known passage that echoed and finessed Trotsky's analysis, 'the State was everything' and civil society 'primordial and gelatinous.' In modern Western democracies, by contrast, ruling classes did not rule only by coercion, but also by consent, with civil society forming a front line of 'trenches' and 'permanent fortifications' in the ongoing struggle to establish and maintain hegemony.[35] To a degree proportionate to a nation's level of development, civil society was, for Gramsci, therefore key in the ruling class's ability to rule. Developing the military imagery, he identified as essential for the revolutionary party long 'wars of position' – something like Trotsky's untheorized 'serious preparatory activity' – across civil society to build for a rising class the moral, social, and intellectual authority necessary to occupy the trenches and make a direct challenge for power.[36] For Gramsci, revolution – in the deep sense of a transition from one mode of production to another – was in the West a long process involving the creation and consolidation of a new hegemony for a different order of society. This long-haul process or 'war of position' was ongoing, and needed to be differentiated from the act of seizing state power – a 'war of manoeuvre,' a necessary but not sufficient part of the process. Received assumptions about the chronology of revolution – seize the state, build socialism – needed to be rethought.[37] But although he was notionally committed to conceiving 'the doctrine of hegemony as a complement to the theory of State-as-force,' Gramsci's fragmentary writings did not progress beyond sometimes contradictory military metaphors in describing the actual processes of transition between wars of position and manoeuvre: indeed, they had so little to say about the latter that they would lend themselves later to readings that reduced politics to wars of position, or even to Cultural Studies.[38] The ultimate implication of the analysis was nonetheless clear: a fundamentally different strategy and, crucially, a new type of party were required.

Writing under the eyes of the prison censors, Gramsci was also sparing in detail about the type of broadened 'modern Prince' or mass communist party necessary to 'proclaim' and 'organize' these wars. Nonetheless, the belated impact of these fragmentary writings on the Communist movement lay in their uncanny familiarity, rather than their radical novelty or shocking revelation.[39] Gramsci's prison writings resonated precisely because they systematized ideas long implicit and often suppressed in Communist discourse and practice, spelling out what Communism had always, at some level, half-known about class, culture, and consciousness as far back as the early 1920s, but had never formulated amidst a Communist culture confident in looming capitalist crisis, unseasonally inclined to insurrectionism, and distorted from the late 1920s by the calcifying orthodoxy of Stalinism. The struggle to explain the blockage to revolutionary advance in developed societies, to develop a theory and practice of Communist modes of activism at the level of civil society, and to imagine or prefigure an alternative or expanded organizational form in which they could be integrated into class struggle was a recurrent but overlooked story in Communist Parties in the West and beyond.

A central concern of this study is how that struggle played out in Britain. A key claim is that ambivalences, hesitations, and dissident positions around 'civil society,' which interleaved with assumptions about the capitalist economy and its political superstructures, proved a key fault line in twentieth-century British Communism. Looking back, these hesitations represent an instance of how, as Jodi Dean puts it, Communist Parties were never identical with their official orthodoxies – which, like most ideologies, were both enabling and restrictive – but were always 'ruptured, incomplete, irreducible,' and, as such, remain 'pregnant with the unrealized potentials of the past.'[40] In terms of civil society, the practice of the British party, like that of other national parties, was surprisingly wide, cutting across science, publishing, the arts, architecture, education at all levels, popular culture, and, belatedly, debates about 'race,' gender, and the sexual division of labour.[41] Through much of its history, the party established a 'cultural' presence out of proportion to its tiny membership or levels of political representation and one which greatly exceeded that of other, much bigger parties of the Left, including the electorally focused Labour Party. Just as important, what was achieved in these spheres was often wider than the party's official theories, program, or line.[42] This disjunction between what it was often actually doing and what it said it was doing – put differently, its inability to assimilate some of its most effective work into coherent strategy – was closely related to another key concern of this study: the debilitating domination of a 'base-superstructure' theoretical model. This model saw the economic as primary and culture as derivative, legitimating the party's subordination of its cultural work and professional and intellectual strata to industrial work and 'proletarian' party discipline. These constitutive and abiding frameworks, which sidelined culture with their gendered, workerist hierarchies, more often reproduced than challenged the broader culture's own patriarchy and anti-intellectualism. They constituted interventions in civil society as, by definition, marginal to the core identity, priorities, and practices of a 'Bolshevized' party.

This study is recuperative in that it restores that history to view, analysing in depth those exceptional moments when these key hierarchies were overturned and notions of cultural struggle were tolerated and even promoted by the party leadership, especially the Popular Front period (1935–38/9), the period of late and post-war reconstruction (1942–47), and the so-called Battle of Ideas against American imperialism (1947–56). I probe tensions between activism and official ideology and between the party's intellectual stratum and its more traditionally minded leadership. I also uncover unlicensed intellectual and political formations, what I call cultural countercurrents within British Communism – sometimes valued, sometimes marginalized by the leadership – that expressed in theoretical terms the logic of Trotsky's hesitation, prefigured or amplified elements of Gramsci's insights, and struggled to see and constitute 'civil society' as a significant locus of politics and work there as a precondition for advance. These currents thought through the relationship between such work and more obviously 'political' practices, sporadically unsettling and sometimes directly confronting the opposition between 'politics' and 'cultural work' as official Communist orthodoxy understood it. The internal splits and debates within Communism that these currents shaped – and that are often lost to history – about what the party should do in civil society and how that related to economic and political struggles might seem like mere infighting. Actually, these divisions remain alive, for at these moments a different party was faintly foreshadowed, and they comprise a small but significant archive for analysis in terms of debates about the form and function of the party in the present and future. For however peripheral, *sotto voce*, or marginalized by the leadership, these challenges were made by those who – unlike well-known former Communist intellectuals of the British New Left, including E.P. Thompson (1924–93) and Raymond Williams (1921–88) – remained fundamentally committed to thinking about the chronology of revolution in the West and to developing the idea of 'the party,' seeing it as an indispensable vector of historical transformation. As such, although often overlooked, the thought of diverse figures – including Freda Utley (1898–1978), Tom Wintringham (1898–1949), Jack Lindsay (1900–90), Bill Warren (1935–78), Pat Devine, and Beatrix Campbell – is relevant to debates about the form and function of the party today as the Left rediscovers hegemonic socialist politics. Books, including Nick Srnicek and Alex Williams' *Inventing the Future: Postcapitalism and a World Without Work* (2016) compellingly argue that 'the contemporary left should reclaim modernity, build a populist and hegemonic force,' and aspire to 'construct a new future oriented politics capable of challenging capitalism at the largest scales.'[43] Although clear on what is to be done – aligning with Gramsci and refuting the Leninist revolutionary chronology of 'building dual power with a revolutionary party and overthrowing the state' – this new work has less to say about the agents of such processes and nothing about antecedent currents that attempted these strategies and failed.[44] Standing behind this study is the conviction that such new theoretical work would be enriched by greater historical understanding of the often-forgotten attempts and failures to construct such forces in the past in and through Communist movements and parties – processes that, as Mike Makin-Waite has recently argued, remain resonant and open to critique and development at a moment when so much of the Communist life-world has passed into history.[45]

Outline of the Book

This is an interdisciplinary study whose core is theoretical and that synthesizes political theory and empirical and narrative historiography with close analysis of key documents and cultural moments. To analyse in detail Communist responses to specific conjunctures, the study is structured chronologically, with the long chapters divided into sections examining particular debates, episodes, and spheres of work. Gramsci famously stated that to write the history of 'the party means in fact to write the general history of the country.'[46] To write the history of the party's work in 'civil society' – used here as what Perry Anderson calls a necessary 'practico-indicative concept, to designate all those institutions outside the boundaries of the State system proper' – one also needs, by definition, to write a history of the nation's civil society.[47] So, as well as being an institutional history that analyses the party's 'cultural' interventions, committees, structures, personnel, debates, publications, and policies, the study necessarily looks outward, analysing the interface between the party and the broad culture and the ways in which this interface focused discussions and revealed tensions around the question of the form and function of the party and the chronology of revolution in the West. Often, this messy interface was a matter of what was *not* seen. Literary critic Fredric Jameson argues that cultural texts have a 'political unconscious,' a fundamental, if often barely registered, position in relation to history's heartbeat: the class struggle.[48] Standing behind my analysis is the conviction that Jameson's formula can productively be reversed in relation to political movements and parties: these possess a cultural unconscious, a set of unscrutinized and usually unrecorded assumptions, beliefs, prejudices, and impulses about the culture in which they operate. The study reads the Communist Party's cultural unconscious, which ultimately determined its field of operations and shared more with mainstream culture than the party would have owned, especially in terms of patriarchy, anti-intellectualism, and deeply ingrained convictions about the intrinsic value of 'high' culture.

The study's period focus is also distinct. The richest historical analysis of British Communism produced to date focuses on the years of the Comintern (1920–43), and is fundamentally concerned with disentangling the core-periphery relationships between Moscow and the party's headquarters in King Street, London.[49] My primary focus falls later, on the point at which the party's immanent out-of-time-ness becomes most visible: the long-haul struggle to negotiate the lengthy post-war boom and the compromise formation of 'welfare capitalism,' a period of profound economic, demographic, technological, social, and cultural change. I argue that, after the dissolution of the Comintern in 1943, the British party, like other national Communist Parties, was thrown back on its own resources, and required to navigate the national terrain and map the road to socialism in Britain. The absence of direct guidance from the Soviet Union laid bare the extent of the party's former dependency; its theoretical gaps around capitalist resilience, the bourgeois state, and civil society now bit deepest. To gain the most from the lessons contained in this failure, the book's coverage thickens as we get closer to the present, culminating in the key moment of the mid- to late 1970s, a period in which many on the Left are detecting instructive parallels with our own moment.[50]

Chapter One moves briskly over some well-chronicled terrain, analysing abiding tensions between dominant conceptions of the party as a machine for the seizure of the state and often-forgotten countercurrents that always stressed the importance of the broader struggle across civil society and that culminated in the Popular Front moment (1935–38/9), when the party line sanctioned Communists to bring their concerns to bear on wide spheres of civil society. The more detailed analytical narrative begins with Chapter Two (1940–47), and focuses on the party's divided political responses to the processes of post-war reconstruction. The central argument here is that, theoretically underpowered, the party was unable to reorient and reinvent itself to capture, consolidate, and develop the significant work being done by activists across the economy in wartime factories and in civil society (Women's Parliaments, science, the arts, education, architecture, debates about state support for culture). Chapter Three (1947–56) registers the unsurprising Cold War constraints on party conceptions, but focuses centrally on the party's failure to grapple meaningfully – theoretically and organizationally – with the actually existing political structures of Britain through which it was committed to working in the post-war period and whose transformation was central to the always-hazy visions of its post-war program, *The British Road to Socialism* (1951). Chapter Four (1956–68) analyses the now-ageing party's failure to renew itself culturally and intellectually in a bewildering decade in which, despite some new energies, the traditions of the past weighed like a nightmare on the brains of the living, and the censorious and culturally conservative party struggled to read an emerging culture whose watchwords were experimentation on the frontiers of 'high' and 'low' and in which a key agent was 'youth.' The last chapter (1968–79) analyses the party's agonized search for renewal in the context of the 'new social movements,' especially third-wave feminism, and draws to a close with what Hobsbawm called the halting of the 'forward march of labour,' a period which saw the falling off of working-class militancy and trade union density and the ascendancy of neoliberalism.[51] Here I argue that positions that had been countercultural and oppositional since the beginning of British Communism achieved a belated, conscious articulation in the mid- to late 1970s with the assistance of Gramsci's newly translated *Selections from the Prison Notebooks*. The failure, I argue, to institute these as central to the party's identity and strategy in the process of the overhaul of *The British Road to Socialism* in 1977 represented at once both a culmination and a terminus. After this, the party had little new to say, and my treatment of its death throes is accordingly brief. I strive, however, to shun the condescension of posterity. A basic assumption is that the problem the party ran up against in the late 1970s – to imagine the form and function of a revolutionary party properly implanted in civil society and whose counter-hegemonic work there was meaningfully integrated with struggle in 'political' and 'industrial' spheres –still has not been solved. The party's bitterly contested and ultimately doomed eleventh-hour struggle to reinvent itself in this way is unprecedented in the history of the British Left in its partial confrontation of problems that remain politically live, as I argue in the Conclusion. In the present, as in the past, we are haunted by what Stuart Hall called 'the absent ghost' of the 'party' in Gramsci's sense: 'the proclaimer and organiser of an intellectual and moral reform' geared towards 'the realisation of a superior, total form of modern civilization.'[52]

1
The Chronology of Revolution, 1920–1940

'World revolution,' wrote Lenin in April 1920, 'powerfully stimulated and accelerated by the horrors, vileness and abominations of the world imperialist war' was developing with 'splendid rapidity' and assuming 'a wonderful variety of changing forms.'[1] In Britain, there was as yet no Communist Party, but he detected a 'powerful and rapidly growing Communist movement,' and wanted to see a Communist Party created from these elements.[2] Political advice and funds alike were dispensed through the new Communist International, formed the previous January.[3] The idea of what future party general secretary, Harry Pollitt (1890–1960), called a 'realistic and practical' party in the Bolshevik model was the powerful magnet that attracted representatives from various socialist organizations to the Communist Unity Convention at the Cannon Street Hotel, London, in late July 1920.[4] There was naturally consensus among the 160 delegates assembled – representing the British Socialist Party, the Socialist Labour Party, groups within the Independent Labour Party, and local organizations – around what Lenin called the 'cardinal principles' required for affiliation to the International. The 5,125 members who signed up with the new party that August and at the subsequent convention the following January unanimously regarded the Soviet system as superior to parliamentarianism, and affirmed the principle of the dictatorship of the proletariat.[5] The correct Communist strategy regarding Britain's political institutions and traditions – elections, parliamentary democracy, the Labour Party – was soon settled from Moscow under the rubric of the 'United Front' line: Communists should work through existing structures to expose their hollowness.[6] From the outset, however, questions of revolution's chronology and how Communists should respond to civil society hovered awkwardly on the edge of discussions, with early national debates unwittingly echoing those within the Comintern about the challenge of extending revolution to a Western context where insurrectionary approaches seemed so far doomed to failure.[7] Long before Gramsci's 'Prison Notebooks,' leading British Communist William Paul (1884–1958) had

Party propaganda machine, 1920s. CP Picture Archive, Box 8, NMLH 2000, 10.316/4.

Communist Pioneers in Birmingham, 1920s. CP Picture Archive, Box 73.

richly described the ideological work performed by civil society – including the media, the press, the church, education, theatre, and popular culture – and identified the need for revolutionaries to struggle against capitalism in 'every strand of the social fabric.'[8] Such work was not, however, coherently defined or assimilated in a party confidently structured around an insurrectionist strategy in an era of wars and revolutions.[9]

A Machine for Revolution

According to the dominant discourse, society was a 'bourgeois dictatorship' in which the 'key organs of education and propaganda' lay 'under capitalist control'; Parliament merely veiled class power 'by an appearance of popular consent which is rendered unreal by the capitalist control of the social structure.'[10] This 'Leninist' vision came fundamentally to determine the shape of the international Communist movement through the so-called Bolshevization of the Communist Parties in 1922–23, to which Rajani Palme Dutt (1896–1974) was central in Britain. 'Our task is not to create some propagandist society or revolutionary club,' he and Pollitt – the Communist Party of Great Britain's coming men – wrote in their Bolshevization blueprint, *Report on Organization*, formally adopted by the party in 1922.[11] The insurrectionist tide of 1917–20 had now receded, but the new type of party was geared firmly towards capturing the apparatus of the state itself – for Lenin, a machine whose function was class subordination.[12] The party would be a proletarian machine for revolution more powerful than the bourgeois one. There was no hesitation about 'the main field of activity': the point of production – the 'factory or workshop' – was 'the real unit' of working-class strength, and thus of Communist politics in which 'cells' were to be established and from which proletarian power was to be built to challenge bourgeois class rule on the Leninist model of 'dual power.'[13] Despite Comintern advice that the revolutionaries needed to operate on three fronts – political, industrial, and educational – simultaneously, and that the industrial and educational – the latter, in particular – mattered as much as the political, broader civil society in general was sidelined.[14] Culture, in this document – the most important in the party's history – featured only as tantalizing bait ('concerts, dances, plays, tea parties, outings and other recreations') to draw to the machine 'sympathisers' remote from the industrial front line, especially women, youth, and children.[15] This steely insularity soon restructured all spheres of the party in ways that boosted centralized efficiency, but pulled it away from civil society and made it susceptible to bureaucratic degeneration, despite the document's soon-forgotten emphasis on 'open controversy' and 'free discussion.'[16] The Executive Committee was partitioned into organizational and political bureaus presiding over a plethora of special committees, none of which was concerned with civil society. More tightly controlled Local Party

Committees (LPCs), or 'Locals,' divided into subgroups, replaced general area branches, and an ethos of discipline and hypermilitancy was cultivated. A probation period was introduced, 'a disciplinary measure calculated to enhance the prestige of full membership' and to sift out the wayward or insufficiently dedicated.[17] A 'complete break with the old Socialist traditions of ineffectiveness' was enacted at every level, down to the Socialist Sunday Schools movement, which had reached its peak of influence in the pre-war period and which the party initially had supported.[18] Around 500 Communist offspring between the ages of nine and fourteen were now weaned from 'Love and Justice' and drilled as 'active fighters in the Communist movement,' producing their own journal and rehearsing their roles as leading cadres through administrative duties, public oratory, paper sales, and the organization of school protests and strikes.[19] The Young Communist League (YCL), which ran the Children's Sections and ideally functioned as a bridge between it and the adult party, was also firmly cast in the 'Bolshevized' image of the latter,[20] having, if anything, even less place for 'cultural faddists and intellectual idlers' than did the senior party.[21] For the rest of the party's life, this vision of the party as a machine would function as a forbidding 'Leninist' superego in discussions of its form and function – the true model against which deviations could be measured.

Intellectuals

For Gramsci, analysing the reproduction of class power in the West at a moment of defeat in the early 1930s, the emphasis was very different. The key group were those intermediaries or 'intellectuals' who organized production, religion, and culture, defining, adapting, and diffusing the ideas of the ruling order so that they could be understood, accepted, and lived by all. Through the work of intellectuals, Gramsci argued, what was actually historically specific in societies came to be experienced by the masses as inscrutably natural. The capture of this group was therefore crucial for the taking of power.[22]

This same emphasis was present in very early discussions within British Communism. Inimical to the Bolshevization vision, however, it was very soon erased. At the dawn of the party, for instance, suffragist Sylvia Pankhurst (1882–1960), of the Workers' Socialist Federation, had insisted that the nascent Communist Party in a non-revolutionary period needed fresh ideas more than 'a rigidity of discipline,' and defied the Comintern's rules governing national parties, refusing to relinquish control of her 10,000-circulation newspaper, the *Workers' Dreadnought*.[23] Facing down what she called a 'spice of brutality' in the name of editorial autonomy, she was expelled in September 1921, and was viewed with suspicion from thereon.[24] The young party's talk of welding the intelligentsia and workers into a united party was quickly a distant memory.[25] Post-Bolshevization, the only intellectuals who mattered were those, like Dutt, willing to shed their former selves and 'the remnants of bourgeois culture' to serve the party machine.[26] The core group that had already taken this course was miniscule as a percentage of the predominantly proletarian party's tiny membership, although more significant in terms of its future leadership. It included Dutt, an Anglo-Swedish doctor's son who had been sent down from Balliol for his open support of the Bolshevik Revolution; Andrew Rothstein (1898–1994), the Oxford-educated son of an émigré Lithuanian Jewish Bolshevik, who would likewise serve on the Central Committee; Robin Page Arnot (1890–1986), a former Fabian socialist; and the Trinity-educated Emile Burns (1889–1972), who would later join the Central Committee and spend many years in the 'agit-prop' Department correcting theoretical heterodoxy.[27] That the party's proletarian ethos and gruelling discipline repelled potential professional recruits was taken as proof of its imperviousness to the 'middle-class intellectuals' and 'careerists' who knew nothing of 'the everyday struggles of the masses on the industrial field' and had allegedly wrecked the Labour Party.[28] Certainly considered of little use to the revolution's machine were the university educated and, by extension, the professional spheres in which they worked. Post-Bolshevization, such figures were seen as at best ineffectual and at worst an outright danger, being contaminated by bourgeois culture – 'a hindrance' to working-class freedom – and too enmeshed in the old regime ever to keep pace with the 'shock of reality' in revolutionary situations.[29] When the Soviets at the Comintern's Fifth World Congress of 1924 asked the British delegation what had been done to attract and coordinate intellectual and professional workers, the unusually independently minded response was that they had done nothing at all.[30]

'Intellectualism' was a dirty word even in the notional 'United Front' period, when the ratio of graduates to workers changed very little.[31] It naturally remained so during the aggressive proletarianism of the Third Period 'class against class' line (1928–35), driven by the Comintern's catastrophist analysis that capitalist economic crisis, inter-imperialist wars, and possible attacks on the Soviet Union were brewing 'gigantic class battles' and renewed revolutionary opportunity that the Communist Parties should lead alone.[32] Intellectuals were disciplined with new vigour, and the term applied negatively even to Local Party Committees in small northern towns that stuck with older habits of comradely discussion.[33] There was, Dutt emphasized with shrill italics in a notorious article intended to set the record straight, '*no special work and role of Communists from the bourgeois intellectual strata*,' an edict from which he would never much waver and which retained a considerable charge even during the Popular Front period and sometimes especially among self-flagellating intellectuals wracked by class guilt.[34] Then, as in the past and future, a key assumption was that this stratum, prone to 'wearing sandals and looking "arty,"' risked discrediting the party in the eyes of the respectable working class, and should be kept in check through party activism.[35] In short, through the 1920–41 period, shifts in attitudes to civil society and intellectuals would, for the leadership at least, remain essentially a matter of strategic and sometimes incremental modification of core assumptions according to the party line. The overwhelmingly proletarian British party was an acute case in this respect, but by no means unique: as Geoff Eley puts it, the 'Third International was cramped and unsympathetic for intellectuals, bluntly and aggressively intolerant of critical theoretical work.'[36] The model of the party as a machine and its hierarchies was fixed: it could accommodate an expansion of work in civil society, but was not fundamentally changed by such tactical broadening. The chronology of revolution required the building of the party, the creation of dual power that would prefigure the dictatorship of the proletariat, and the seizure of the state. In terms of the party's attitude to intellectuals, the rhythm would be one of alternative laxity (United Front, Popular Front) and tightening (Third Period, Nazi-Soviet Pact period). There would be differences around the priority accorded to work in civil society, especially during the Popular Front years, but there was palpable relief among more seasoned Communists when the onset of a new 'imperialist war' reactivated Leninist lessons about war, civil war, and revolutionary opportunity.[37] The core conviction remained that the machine was both necessary and sufficient.

Gender Trouble

The dominant logic, however, was never the only story. Pulling through the Communist Party were countercurrents rooted in alternative conceptions of class power and revolutionary strategy that variously exceeded, challenged, and resisted dominant conceptions. These currents insisted on the significance of culture, civil society, and intellectuals for the reproduction of class power, and, in so doing, sometimes implicitly and sometimes explicitly gestured towards a different type of party attuned to conditions in the West.

One early fault line concerned gender and feminism. Like Sylvia Pankhurst, a number of Communist suffragists saw the sexual division of labour as a crucial means of capitalism's capacity to reproduce itself. They duly took very seriously the Comintern's early commitment to confront not only wage slavery, but also 'domestic family dependence.'[38] Although encouraged initially by such radical tones, and by a younger generation of militants who seemed unencumbered by the 'dead clothes' of their elders, they soon came to find the party's line on gender little more advanced than that of preceding socialist organizations. They were frustrated that discussion of gender was short-circuited by the confident assumption that patriarchy was an appendage of capitalism that would wither away with Soviet-style revolution.[39] Helen Crawfurd (1877–1954) regretted that 'the urgency and importance' of work challenging patriarchy 'was far from appreciated,' while rank-and-file members cited party inertia on 'the woman question' in early resignation letters.[40] Dora Montefiore (1851–1933), a former

Women's Political and Social Union activist and the only woman on the new party's executive, found her talents and experiences sidelined by the party, and her abilities were lost to British Communism when she emigrated. Another significant feminist, Stella Browne (1880–1955), had left by 1923, unsuccessful in her attempts to persuade her comrades that gender equality was a precondition of communism and not a superstructure that would arise automatically with it.[41] From the beginning, there was a deep synergy between the party's patriarchal assumptions that, in the image of the machine, venerated the male industrial militant worker while failing to analyse the sexual division of labour that stood behind such figures, and its anti-intellectualism – 'intellectual' meaning unmanly (bourgeois, soft-handed, 'old school tie,' often homosexual). Both were instances of how the party mirrored the dominant culture more than it would have owned. In terms of political organization, this cast of thought allowed the party's limited early efforts to engage working-class women to wither still further.[42] As I argue in Chapter Five, it would not be until the 1970s that basic attitudes which saw the sexual division of labour as a secondary form of oppression and feminism as divisive of the class struggle would be seriously challenged.

Unruly Educators

Other early differences around attitudes to civil society centred on education. These were expressed most forcefully by wife-and-husband writers and translators Cedar Paul (1880–1972) and Eden Paul (1865–1944), metropolitan intellectuals with strong European connections well respected in the new party on the strength of their long-standing commitment to the Left.[43] They argued that the key contradiction of developed capitalism was not private ownership of socialized production. Rather, it was the system's inability to educate workers sufficiently for mass production and its technologies – through civil society (schools, cinema, the pulpit, and the press) – *without* also equipping them to 'look beyond the bourgeois ideology' and its exploitative economic and social relations.[44] The central opportunity and key task for Communists in such societies, as they saw it, was therefore an educative and ideological one, a question of popular consciousness: to equip the working class to recognize and reject such ideology – a conviction reinforced by their eager following of Soviet and international debates about 'proletarian culture' during the early 1920s.[45] Although frequently whimsical, the Pauls' writings of the early 1920s pre-empted many later 'cultural' controversies in resisting base-superstructure determinism – which held that ideas were a secondary manifestation determined by economic structures, a model that would be used to hold intellectuals in check – and in insisting that ideas were themselves a force 'acting and reacting on the material conditions of production' and shaping 'the quasi-omnipotent force of creative revolution.'[46] The Pauls were active in the Plebs League and the National Council of Labour Colleges (NCLC), an expansive and trade union–backed network of adult education catering to 15,000 students.[47] Here they advocated 'independent working-class education' focusing on key subjects that would 'render the worker's mind immune to bourgeois ideology' (economics, geography, history, biology, sociology, psychology, politics).[48] They duly concerned themselves with teaching, writing, and translating the necessary works of philosophy and political economy.[49] Regarding education as a key location of politics and the creation of alternative socialist educational practices as crucial for Communist political advance in the West, in the autumn of 1922 the Pauls were central to a movement to form a new 'organization' within the young CPGB committed to developing education in and beyond the party in line with these priorities.[50] A discouraging response from the Executive Committee warned that 'the time was not ripe for anything of the kind,' reflecting the official position that such cultural initiatives would have to wait.[51] Although the party had little to say about civil society or culture, its guiding assumptions about the chronology of revolution were clear. Culture, like patriarchy, was a derivative superstructure secondary to the economic base. Cultural transformation was not a precondition of revolutionary advance, but would follow from it.[52] Until 'the conquest of power' – which would occur independently of the cultural sphere – cultural matters were 'subordinate to political expediency.'[53]

Pre-Bolshevization, the party had identified the NCLC as the natural hub of revolutionary educational advance with which it should work.[54] Post-Bolshevization, as the Pauls increasingly found, it sought to co-opt this apparatus into the party machine, attacking its people and publications as an 'alien' influence peddling unscientific Marxism and impeding the development of 'the real revolutionary movement' among the British working class.[55] Many of those now considered useless by Dutt and opportunists by Pollitt resigned their memberships, a process that exiled a group for whom civil society, educational empowerment, and the raising of working-class consciousness were key to advance.[56] Deeply frustrated by the Bolshevized party's increasingly inward attitude to the existing networks of adult education, some Communist educationalists of divided loyalties retaliated, accusing the party leadership of ruthlessness, sectarianism, and damaging the cause of workers' education.[57] Educationalist Frank Horrabin (1884–1962) and the Pauls went further, directly challenging the Communist movement's narrowing conception of the revolutionary process by translating and publishing in the July 1925 issue of the NCLC journal *Plebs* an article, 'How shall we prepare for revolution?' by dissident French Marxist Robert Louzon (1882–1976), which had appeared five months earlier in his journal, *La Révolution prolétarienne*.[58] The article presented what Horrabin termed 'a powerful plea for the recognition of different spheres of work in the pre-revolutionary period' by following through the logic of Trotsky's earlier hesitation around the need for a broader approach in the West.[59] Echoing Gramsci's early 1920s newspaper articles that substantially finessed Soviet 'proletcult' positions in emphasizing the proletariat's need to win 'intellectual power,' Louzon provocatively queried whether the militarized and Bolshevized model of the party, 'indispensable for the success of an insurrection,' was adequate to the task of preparing the working class for revolution, especially in Western Europe, with its developed civil society.[60] Here, he argued, the task was also to produce 'new values' or 'an aggregate of ideas, wishes, and social forms antagonistic to those of the dominant class' upon which 'the new society' could be built.[61] For Louzon the Bolshevizing Communist movement, fixed upon a vanguardism that sat uneasily with the official United Front line, was failing to conceptualize and coordinate a broader range of interventions across civil society, and was desensitizing and isolating itself in the process.

The argument touched a nerve in the British party, which was too small, struggling, and anti-intellectual to have engaged substantially with the debates about Soviet cultural policies that animated sister European parties.[62] Those who expressed any agreement with Louzon fell under immediate suspicion, including one party member and NCLC educationalist activist who was disciplined after approvingly quoting Louzon in a public debate at the *Plebs* 1925 summer school.[63] Another activist who persisted in expressing such 'idealist' views was expelled slightly later after seeking to reach out to kindred theoretical deviants.[64] More immediately, Louzon's article was instantly and tetchily rebutted by the party leadership via Willie Gallacher (1881–1965), whose riposte, 'How not to prepare for revolution,' dismissed Louzon and those who agreed with him as 'liquidationists' who were doing capitalism's dirty work in undermining the Soviet Union.[65]

Reading on Sundays

'Bolshevization' and its rhetoric strengthened the party's identity by intensifying its insularity. The party press was in turn transformed in line with the new machine's tempo, as *Report on Organization* demanded '*a newspaper* of the working class and not a small magazine of miscellaneous articles with a Communist bias.'[66] The broad-based weekly, the *Communist*, had enjoyed a circulation of 60,000 under a succession of editors, including the former *Daily Herald* typographer Francis Meynell (1891–1975).[67] Now accused of 'tickling the public' rather than coordinating party activity, the *Communist*'s latest incarnation, currently edited by the party's foremost organic intellectual, Tommy Jackson (1879–1955), was supplanted in February 1923 by Dutt's *Workers' Weekly*, a 'real workers' newspaper' that aspired to be 'to the English workers what *Pravda* has been to the Russian workers.'[68] Dutt's paper prided itself on sharing no features with the 'middle-class' ones, by which he meant the dominant culture in which workers lived their lives.[69] Gone were the cartoons, cultural coverage, historical features on radical history, and contributions from non-party members. The model was instead the type of agitational paper prescribed by the Third Congress of the Comintern. Civil society was nowhere. Industry, politics, and Parliament alone were analysed through the 'telegraphic style' said to be preferred by Lenin, a format also used in the plethora of Communist factory papers produced at the local level.[70]

As Horrabin and the Pauls had signalled, however, such Duttian zeal was in tension with the official Comintern line, the 'United Front' tactic of preparing for revolution by working with and through the existing labour movement.[71] In cultural terms, the tension was expressed most powerfully through the *Sunday Worker*, a newspaper edited by Central Committee member William Paul, launched in March 1925 in the image of broader tactics. The paper soon became the de facto organ of the National Left Wing Movement, which aimed to challenge Labour's ban on Communists and to realign the Labour Party with the rank and file.[72] The *Sunday Worker* would prove an important publication through which different Communist visions of revolution's chronology were expressed. For some, to 'spend time talking about art and culture' was self-evidently pointless, as neither could 'come into the Workers' lives' until power was taken.[73] Such voices boomed through the paper, especially at moments when levels of industrial militancy appeared to legitimate more traditional dual-power tactics. But the paper's dominant mode reactivated William Paul's ideas about the need to make interventions across 'every field of social activity.[74] Unwittingly, it gestured towards Gramsci's view that the revolutionary newspaper potentially prefigured the 'modern Prince' or ideal Communist Party as an immanent party which covered, in textual terms, the national economic, political and educational terrain that the actual party would need to territorialize at the level of organization and influence.[75] Reaching a circulation of 85,000, the paper's effect was to draw Communism back into hesitant but fuller engagements with the broader culture and civil society tentatively begun by the pre-Bolshevization *Communist*.[76]

A woman's page was entrusted to now former Communist Winifred Horrabin, which debated questions of gender and class in a period when the party's own organization of a women's section was making at best minimal headway, despite the detailed recommendations in the Bolshevization document.[77] The paper also bucked the insular trend in adult education, defying the party line, affirming the NCLC, and commissioning contributions from educational activists no longer in the party (the Horrabins, Ellen Wilkinson, the Pauls, Mark Starr).[78] Although sometimes mocked for being 'as dilettantish as any capitalist yapper' by those who cast themselves as embodiments of proletarian rectitude,[79] the *Sunday Worker* read the culture in the spirit of the more nuanced proletcult positions, which had argued for Communism's 'precise knowledge and transformation of the culture created by the entire development of mankind.'[80] The paper was duly committed to challenging anti-intellectualism, to developing working-class cultural levels, and to assuming cultural, intellectual, and moral authority in defending 'all that is beautiful and inspiring in art and culture' from the ravages of capital and reaction.[81] Significant here was the arts page, co-edited by multilingual Oxford graduate, novelist, and critic Ralph Fox (1900–37) and Tommy Jackson, who had already expressed his scorn about the narrowing of discussion in the Bolshevized party.[82] Those debates on class, culture, and consciousness conspicuously absent in British communism's early years were now given space in the *Sunday Worker*'s pages, including a sympathetic review of Trotsky's *Literature and Revolution* (1924) – whose author was rapidly becoming international Communism's most notorious *persona non grata* – while Jackson's and Fox's own articles worked within the traditions of working-class autodidacticism, to which they, like Cambridge economist Maurice Dobb (1900–76), remained quietly committed.[83] As one appreciative reader wrote, the arts page was 'an education in itself' that 'helped me and my mates to understand good books which would otherwise have been closed.'[84]

The *Sunday Worker* also provided a space and function for sympathetic cultural figures who had formerly been unable to envisage a role for themselves in party work, including the composer Rutland Boughton (1878–1960), who was appointed music editor, and joined the party in February 1926.[85] Committed to retrieving music from what he saw as its degenerated capitalist function as 'sense ticklers of the wealthy,' he wrote over twenty articles for the paper over a four-year period and instituted an important motif of British Communism's subsequent cultural world: the preservation and development of folksong – 'shanties, drinking songs, songs of labour' – as a workers' culture seen to be relatively uncorrupted by the culture industry.[86] Central to Boughton's sometimes whimsical vision was the active promotion of participatory cultural forms that engaged workers as both producers and audience, and were therefore seen to counter the passivity allegedly imposed by high and mass culture alike. His optimistic plan for a national network of working-class cultural organizations formed in the paper's image across civil society – drama societies, choirs, bands, study groups – was solidly at odds with the party's priorities, but he nevertheless brought into Communism's orbit the 15 London choirs and 520 singers of the London Labour Choral Union, an organization he had co-formed with recently elected Labour MP Herbert Morrison the year before.[87] Soon these choirs would share members with the Workers' Theatre Group, formed in the summer of 1926 when the *Sunday Worker* brokered an alliance between the party, existing London-based leftist theatre groups, the cultural wing of the NCLC, and the earnestly titled but largely inert Council for Proletarian Art, formed on the party's cultural fringes two years earlier.[88] Theatre was a natural sphere of activity given the low overheads involved, the labour movement's established traditions of theatrical endeavour, and the availability of Soviet and German models enthusiastically chronicled in the paper's pages. Theatrical turns, moreover, were common at party socials and fundraisers.[89] Very much a cultural expression of the *Sunday Worker*'s ethos and moment, the Workers' Theatre Group was soon optimistically rebranded as the Workers' Theatre Movement, and began staging small-scale productions.[90]

One strand of the *Sunday Worker*'s remit was therefore cultural transmission to the educationally marginalized on the basis that knowledge was power and that the working class could not advance without it. Another strand was the critical reading of inter-war mass culture – altogether shunned by Dutt's paper – which increasingly shaped the textures of everyday working-class experience. Here British Communism began to think seriously about the ideological function of the modern cultural apparatus, its effect on working-class consciousness, and its potential relevance to emancipatory politics. Hollywood cinema was predictably damned for its 'incursions of capitalist dope into working class mentality,' and Rudolph Valentino was brushed aside as a morbid symptom of 'American super-capitalism.' But the general analysis was more supple, registering counterimpulses and contradiction even in the Hollywood system – notably in Charlie Chaplin's underdog appeal and connections with the Left.[91] And in a period when the British Broadcasting Company was making its controversial transition to a monopoly national public broadcasting corporation – it received its charter in 1926 – the *Sunday Worker*'s reports of Soviet media developments informed the paper's analysis. Here the paper differentiated between radio's use – as a medium solidifying definitions of a national culture – and its international potential as a vector of communication and radicalization, 'making it possible for peoples of the earth to learn the tastes, desires and ambitions of each other.'[92] Elsewhere, too, the *Sunday Worker* aligned Communism with technological modernity, drawing upon the print innovations briefly deployed by Helen Crawfurd and Tommy Jackson for the British section of the Berlin-based Internationale Arbeiter Reliefe (Workers' International Relief) in their *Soviet Russia Pictorial* (1923–4) and *Workers' International Pictorial* (1924–5)[93] in the name of becoming a fully fledged 'Labour *pictorial* newspaper,' a version of which was achieved thirteen years later in the form of *Picture Post*.[94] Limited budgets prevented the *Sunday Worker* from ever becoming the pictorial paper it initially aspired to be. On a smaller scale, instructing readers how to compose photographs, and then printing the best of them, began to make the case for a technically savvy grassroots media.[95] The paper here grasped the significance of new sites of political contestation in an age of emerging media, outflanking the *Daily Herald* in innovative energy, if not in sales (the latter sold 300,000 copies at the beginning of the 1920s, 2 million at the end).[96] The contrast could not have been greater between the radical inventiveness of the *Sunday Worker* and the metallic instrumentality of its successor, the *Daily Worker*, launched in the image of the 'class against class' line in January 1930. Dutt considered the paper's pilot issue, which strategically mirrored the mass circulation *Daily Herald*, an 'insult to every Communist,' a theme to which he would warm frequently in this period.[97] His agitational *Workers' Weekly*, rather than the now-withdrawn *Sunday Worker*, would be the de facto model for the new party daily. The implied reader was the enlightened, clean-living, and class-conscious proletarian militant Dutt often invoked to ward off discussions about the efficacy of party propaganda.[98] Actually existing workers, with their proclivities for what Dutt called 'capitalist sport' – betting and other forms of 'pleasure after a day's graft' – were disregarded, even when they wrote letters of protest about the absence of football and racing in the paper's pages.[99] In part a bold initiative in the spirit of 'class against class' revolutionary confidence, whose production and distribution networks certainly galvanized party identity, the *Daily Worker* was virtuously detached from the broader culture and civil society. Its dismal circulation of 10,000 measured the extent of the party's isolation in a period when membership had dropped by three-quarters since the General Strike's influx, and bumped along below 3,000 for the whole of the paper's first year, reaching an unprecedented low of 2,500 in November 1930.[100]

What Is to Be Done?

The critique of narrowing conceptions, initiated by the Pauls, was reopened at the turn of the 1930s by Freda Utley (1898–1978), a journalist, writer, and London University graduate who had joined the CPGB in 1927.[101] Possessing confidence to criticize the party on the strength of a spell in Moscow working for the Comintern, she strayed far beyond her brief in a review of the latest volume of Lenin's *Collected Works* in the party journal.[102] Reading the newly translated writings of the *Iskra* period that culminated in *What Is to Be Done?* (1902), Utley encountered here a Lenin at odds with party 'Leninism,' and presumed to distinguish between the two. Drawing attention to Lenin's argument that workers unassisted could attain only trade union consciousness, and that intellectuals were crucial to impart socialist consciousness, she challenged the party's economism – the conviction that working-class radicalization would dependably follow capitalist crisis – the marginalization of its intellectual stratum, and the neglect of theoretical training at all levels of party life, prescribing 'hard intellectual labour combined with practical activity' for what she saw as the weakest and most amateur party in advanced Europe.[103] Unrepentant when chastized for mechanically applying Lenin's teachings from 1902 to modern Britain, she elaborated rather than retracted her argument, echoing the earlier arguments of the Pauls and Louzon in insisting that the intellectual work of shaping radical consciousness increased rather than decreased in the context of developed societies, with their mass communications and expanded civil society mediating between rulers and ruled.[104] Now publicly taken to task for her 'attack on the Party leadership, and THEREFORE ON THE PARTY LINE' she was officially and decisively corrected three times in print, the third time by the Political Bureau, which confusingly branded her, with the assistance of quotations from Stalin's writings, as both a 'Left' spontaneist sectarian and a right opportunist.[105]

These themes were soon picked up by Maurice Dobb, appointed as lecturer in Economics at Cambridge in 1924 and unusual in having joined the party before his graduation. Back in the early 1920s, the idea of being a Communist student had made little sense given the emphasis on the industrial proletariat, as the small group of future Communist intellectuals gathered to talk about Communism in Dobb's Pembroke room at Cambridge recognized, jokily calling themselves 'Spillikins' to signal an appropriately ironic awareness of their distance from the front line.[106] Through the 1920s, Dobb dutifully subscribed to the idea that this was a party of a new type that could do without 'mere pure-milk-of-the-world theorists' like them and that 'science and research' were secondary to political struggle, rather than meaningful sites of it.[107] His thinking about the subordination of intellectuals was very different a decade later, however, in the context of economic crisis and the collapse of the second Labour government when not only Utley but Labour Party intellectuals G.D.H. Cole and E.N. Brailsford were turning to Lenin's *What Is to Be Done?* for guidance.[108] As Dobb was well placed to know, even Bloomsbury was now wondering whether 'far more radical measures of Marxism were necessary' to arrest reaction and war.[109] Dobb was keenly aware of the emerging rival networks of leftist thought outflanking his anti-intellectual party.[110] He knew that climbing party membership, which more than doubled between the collapse of the Labour government in late August 1931 and the end of the year,[111] was bringing a party presence to spheres of national life – medicine, engineering, architecture, the law – with which it was previously unconcerned.[112] Well placed as a Cambridge don to judge the receptiveness to Marxism among the young intelligentsia, Dobb's typically wide-ranging interventions across educational and media networks – the academy, the Labour Research Department, adult education, public lecturing, BBC broadcasting, newspaper articles – provided abundant evidence of what might be done by Communists to bring Marxist perspectives to bear on the broader culture.[113] He revisited his former conviction about revolution's chronology and his previous insistence that intellectual work should be subordinate to political expediency before the revolution.[114] For him, the new cultural mood, the party's marginality, and the weakness of its Marxism now converged to raise once more the question first asked by the Pauls and Boughton about Communism's making coordinated interventions in civil society and cultural life. Dobb proposed in 1931 that the party should form a Section of Intellectual Workers along recent Soviet lines.[115] It should be organized centrally by the party, structured around intellectual specialisms, and supported by a new, broad-based, party-run theoretical Marxist journal.[116]

Dobb's proposal was firmly rejected, however, and he himself held in check through a series of public attacks reminiscent of those recently made on Utley. But the leadership was gradually coming to recognize that ground was being lost, and was soon tolerating something like the types of specialist cultural activity recently forbidden.[117] This first took the form of *Cambridge Left*, a broad journal set up at the centre of student Communism by future Mass Observation co-founder Charles Madge (1912–96) and very like the one Dobb had proposed twelve months earlier; its first issue appeared in the summer of 1933.[118] The keynote in discussions about Communism and intellectual life was now struck not by Dutt – involved in instituting the policy that all books written by Communists should be centrally screened for deviations – but by another former Spillikins member and rising intellectual star, the now Cambridge lecturer in structural crystallography, J.D. Bernal (1901–71).[119]

In 'The Scientist and the World Today,' a *Cambridge Left* essay that marked a turning point in British Communist discourse on revolution's chronology and in his own hitherto fluctuating commitment, Bernal dutifully registered the earlier discourse that intellectual work was secondary to party activism.[120] But that obligatory line of argument was now subordinate to a larger claim that related immediately to science, but readily lent itself to wider interpretation. Intellectual labour was itself, Bernal argued, a force for social transformation that Communist modernity, and its scientifically minded and now rapidly industrializing workers' state, needed above all.[121] Emboldening such an affirmation of Communist-oriented intellectual work was the well-documented Second International Congress of the History of Science and Technology, held in London in June and July 1931, at which Bernal, Cambridge University student activist David Guest (1911–38), and Imperial College mathematics professor Hyman Levy (1889–1975) heard the copious expositions of the Soviet delegation.[122] That event and a subsequent trip to the Soviet Union had done much to dislodge for Bernal and some of his associates the prevailing Communist common sense about the secondary status of intellectual work.[123] For if the function of science was to decode the real world with a view to transforming it, then there was a natural synergy between science and Communism, the latter being both a science of society and the ultimate telos of the human enlightenment to which true science was forever striving.[124] In a crisis conjuncture in which science's once-enlightening force was allegedly being captured by capital, imperialism, nascent fascism, and a booming arms trade, it now seemed increasingly possible to Bernal and his associates to be a Communist in part *by* being a pioneering scientist in whom implicit assumptions about science's true, emancipatory function were made conscious and explicit.[125] The resonant point was not only that Communism, science, and culture possessed a natural radical synergy, but that as 'bourgeois' culture degenerated into barbarism, Communists had to become both a political and intellectual vanguard. Such recently proscribed views about the need for Communists to build cultural and intellectual prestige through providing intellectual leadership, although not meaningfully integrated into party identity or strategy, were fast becoming accepted across the party's rising cadres – notably among students – and building contradictions for the future.

The Dimitrovian Turn

The party's first formalized program, *For Soviet Britain*, adopted in February 1935, held true to the traditional Leninist emphasis: the bourgeois state was a machine of class rule, imperialism the highest stage of moribund capitalism. Familiar remedies were proposed: dual power grounded in workers' councils, insurrection, mutinous 'workers in uniform,' and the future reconfiguration of economic and social relations under the dictatorship of the proletariat. The transformation of civil society would wait until after the revolution, at which point 'the best means of education and culture' would be 'handed over' to the workers' councils and Trade Unions for administration.[126] A new note was sounded within the text, however, reflecting the preceding countercurrents and the Bernallian analysis. The complexity of the social terrain was emphasized. The strategic significance of 'technical and professional workers' in developed capitalist societies was noted. A version of Bernal's argument that 'capitalism' was 'going too slow for science,' impeding its dynamism with market anarchy, was registered.[127] Tom Wintringham (1898–1949) had already gone further, escalating such positions into a call for a different strategy, arguing that international anticolonial struggles in Ireland, China, and India had demonstrated the benefits of broader class alliances, and that, closer to home, British Communists needed to engage more constructively with the 'petty bourgeois' class stratum, 'capitalism's chief social medium of influence over the working class,' currently in turmoil.[128] It was a swelling imperative towards broadening British Communism's base and strategy eventually endorsed with the new line of the Comintern unveiled by incoming Comintern General Secretary Georgi Dimitrov's widely reported and rapidly published address to the Seventh World Congress in August 1935.[129]

In one of the decade's powerfully talismanic political texts, Dimitrov, the hero of the Reichstag trial, remapped the advance to socialism in a conjuncture defined by spreading fascism. Fascism, in an analysis central to 1930s Communism and widely influential beyond it, was defined as capitalism's last stand – the form of 'open terrorist dictatorship' to be imposed when the existing form of 'class domination,' bourgeois democracy, no longer served capital's interest.[130] The final 'substitution,' Dimitrov claimed, would follow a period in which the ground would be cleared through the erosion of democracy and the implementation of 'reactionary measures,' a process he already detected happening in Britain in the anti–working-class policies pursued by the National Government.[131] It was therefore necessary for Communists to move beyond 'class against class' sectarianism – the mistakes of the previous line were tacitly acknowledged – and to build three tiers of alliances: core 'united front' alliances within the working class, a broader antifascist national alliance 'against the liquidation of bourgeois-democratic liberties,' and an international 'joint struggle against the approaching danger of imperialist war.'[132] The mechanisms of the bourgeois state – scantily theorized by Lenin in *State and Revolution* – now received greater analysis by Dimitrov in a conjuncture where the choice the working class faced was not 'between proletarian dictatorship and bourgeois democracy, but between bourgeois democracy and fascism.'[133] The bourgeois state, Dimitrov registered, contained within it 'the democratic gains which the working class had wrested in the course of years of stubborn struggle': the right to strike, legal status for trade unions, the right of assembly, franchise, freedom of the press.[134] These should be defended from fascist encroachment.

The new line was never merely defensive, however, but a strategy for socialist advance towards familiar long-term objectives: the building of the party on democratic centralist principles, the 'mass political strike,' the creation of soviets, revolution, the dictatorship of the proletariat, and the 'final emancipation' of Communism.[135] The difference was that a range of preparatory stages around broadening fields of struggle was now considered essential.[136] A more flexible approach to revolution's chronology was now needed, Dimitrov argued, which distinguished between social democratic governments ('an instrument of class collaboration') and united front governments ('an instrument of collaboration between the revolutionary vanguard of the proletariat and anti-fascist parties').[137] The latter, if committed to revolutionary demands – 'control of production, control of the banks, disbanding of the police' – could represent a key stage in the transition to proletarian revolution in the Leninist vein.[138]

This was a major shift, as Dimitrov conceded, and the overcoming of Communism's own reflexes around the chronology of revolution was identified as a precondition of success. Previously, Communists had seen themselves as disciplined sections of an international army primed to lead insurrections against their respective states with guidance from the Comintern. Now, nations and their political structures, civil societies, cultural traditions, and national stories were identified as central terrains of fascist advance, and hence of Communism's active resistance and potential advance. Communism must 'acclimatise itself' in each country and work with the masses 'as they are,' not as they 'should like them.' They should find a '*common language*' with the actually existing working class in order to overcome the party's isolation from the masses and broader allies.[139] This meant territorializing national identity and narratives, with Communism positioning itself as the heir and defender of progressive national traditions and as the saviour of the 'culture of the people,' imperilled by 'the shackles of decaying monopoly capitalism.'[140] Like this emphasis on the preservation and development of such structures and traditions, the importance of alliances – the report stressed the significance of the peasantry, women, intellectuals, and youth – naturally upgraded the status of civil society in Communist discourse by designating a rich cultural and social terrain in which Communists should create such bonds.[141] In particular, Dimitrov stressed the importance of 'non Party class bodies' in factories, among the unemployed, in urban and rural communities, and in fields of 'cooperative work' and 'cultural activity.'[142]

The Comintern had now unveiled a strategy that registered the limitations of insurrectionism in current conditions, especially in developed countries, and that overlapped substantially with that intimated in Gramsci's as yet unpublished 'Prison Notebooks' (Gramsci's close comrade Togliatti was an assistant to Dimitrov).[143] The report was rapidly translated, published as a twopenny pamphlet, and loudly affirmed in the party press, and Dimitrov almost instantly passed into Communist mythology, requiring due commemoration.[144] It legitimated in Britain, as elsewhere, currents long latent but buried by the authoritative heft of the Bolshevik machine. Much that had been implicit in the critique of the Pauls, Utley, Dobb, and Bernal and in initiatives like the *Sunday Worker* around the need for broader conceptions of politics had now been affirmed by the Comintern. The new line's effect was to animate hitherto marginalized intellectuals – a swelling stratum in the first half of the 1930s – and to ratify the struggles across civil society for which many, including the premature Popular Fronter Wintringham, had long argued.[145]

The effects were rapid as the party looked outward, turning to engage with the spheres of civil society where its work had previously been conflicted and tentative. Its media efforts were broadened and a new journal, *Discussion*, created as a non-sectarian, alliance-building venture pledging not to 'ram an "official" point of view down its readers' throats.'[146] The revamped *Daily Worker* now looked more to the mass-circulation *Daily Express* than to *Pravda* for inspiration, excising its forbidding hammer-and-sickle masthead and thickening its cultural coverage with features, photographs of celebrities, a controversial beauty page, and previously forbidden betting tips in pursuit of what newly recruited Fleet Street reporter Claud Cockburn (1904–81) called 'more hustle, modernity and snappy popular journalism.'[147] Alarmed that the likes of Virginia Woolf were now contributors, Moscow heard a babel of voices in which the Communist 'system' was lost, but sales rose sharply to 50,000 per day (higher Saturday sales brought the weekly circulation to 377,000), close to the pre-war *Daily Herald* often invoked as a model.[148] Party membership more than doubled between February 1936 (7,000) and the end of 1938 (18,000), 810 members being recruited on the day of the party's carefully choreographed 'March of English History' through central London on 20 September 1936. The party was soon congratulating itself in Dimitrovian terms for 'learning to speak to English workers in a language they understand.'[149]

As Dimitrov counselled, Popular Front Communists became adept at exerting politico-cultural influence through 'non-party' bodies and front organizations in civil society, whether bookshops,[150] a refashioned publishing house, Lawrence & Wishart,[151] literary and scientific periodicals *Left Review* (1934–38) and *Modern Quarterly* (1938–39), or the Left Book Club (LBC), which sold two million books within three years, and by April 1939 had attracted 57,000 members – treble the membership of the middlebrow Book Society – organized across 1,500 reading groups.[152] Here the party was working with the grain of inter-war British culture and its modern institutions and cultural habits. New front organizations were also created on the French Popular Front model, notably For Intellectual Liberty, which championed democratic government and civil liberties, and supported interned and exiled German intellectuals,[153] and the Workers' Music Association (WMA), which pulled together eight existing organizations to promote socialist music making.[154] 'Class against class'–period cultural organizations were developed and broadened, including Kino Films, which now extended its reach beyond Communist circles in the capital, bringing Soviet and German feature films and alternative newsreels about British politics and the Spanish Civil War to around 100,000 viewers in 1936 and 200,000 in 1938.[155] The Artists International Association (AIA, formerly Artists International),[156] Unity Theatre,[157] and Marx House were all broadened,[158] the premises of all three providing hubs of educational and cultural activity. Dimitrov had stressed the importance of 'mobilising the masses of toiling women.'[159] The party's fundamental approach to feminism held: sex war was not class war; feminism divided the working class; patriarchy, like religion, would fade away with capitalism. But the party now firmed up its women's organization to maximize its influence, permitting activists to work with feminist groups, where they played a leading role in creating and running front organizations, notably the Women's Committee Against War and Fascism, which launched a journal, *Woman Today*, in September 1936.[160] Like rigid attitudes to feminism, party discourse on religion was relaxed in the name of building alliances around antifascism and peace.[161] Equivalent collaborative impulses compelled Communists to work through existing bodies previously regarded as impervious to progressive influence. The BBC was analysed with a new sophistication by Communists including Charles Madge, who saw in it a national apparatus available for radical recoding.[162] It was also penetrated in a period of regional expansion with disconcerting ease by Communists and fellow-travellers, particularly in the North Region, from where surprisingly radical programs were broadcast that challenged dominant national narratives and foregrounded working-class concerns.[163] Communist numbers grew on campuses. Oxford's October Club had two hundred members by 1934, and individual Cambridge colleges now had Communist cells of between twenty-five (Downing) and fifty (Trinity).[164] The party's increased commitment to its student stratum was duly signalled by the appointment of Jack Cohen (1906–68) as national student organizer in 1936.[165] The separatist zeal that had led to the formation of a rival Federation of Student Societies was dropped and its sections reaffiliated to the long-standing and broad United Labour Federation (ULF), which had 3,000 members by 1937.[166] The new strategy in student work of open, broad campaigning, in which building alliances around Popular Front ideas took priority over narrow party recruitment, proved effective at all levels.[167] By early 1939 the Communist-dominated Cambridge University Socialist Club had 1,000 members – 20 per cent of the total undergraduate cohort and double the 1936 figure.[168] Inside the ULF, Communist student activist Brian Simon (1915–2002) was involved in shaping Labour Party educational policy,[169] and was elected vice-president of the National Union of Students (NUS) in July 1938 and president the following year.[170]

When party leader Willie Gallacher visited Cambridge in 1934, he had told the students, 'if you have a vocation, it's pointless to run away to factories': the party needed 'good scientists, historians and teachers.'[171] Newly graduated Communists fanned out into professional life, bringing Dimitrovian perspectives to bear on spheres of civil society hitherto untouched by their party. Communist architects energized the Modern Architectural Research Group, founded in 1933 with its commitment to 'a future which must be planned, rather than a past which must be patched up.'[172] In 1935 this cohort formed the Architects' and Technicians' Organisation (ATO), which divided its energies between broad Popular Front work (supporting antifascism and Aid for Spain), practical activism and advocacy (providing surveyors, advice, and legal assistance for working-class families), and educational work, notably by mounting the 1936 exhibition, 'Working-Class Housing.'[173] ATO soon controlled the key architects' union, the Association of Architects, Surveyors and Technical Assistants.[174] Communist scientists, meanwhile, captured the Association of Scientific Workers, a moribund organization in 1932 whose national Executive Committee Bernal had joined in 1934. By the end of the decade, infused by the energies of the scientific Left, first in Cambridge and, increasingly, in London, where key figures (Bernal, Levy, J.B.S. Haldane) had taken professorships, its membership more than doubled to 1,319, and would double again within the next two years.[175] The work of Communist schoolteachers, the party's largest and still expanding white-collar cohort,[176] was an exemplar of broadened horizons at the level of civil society, as party educational discourse advanced beyond reflex encomia of Soviet school systems or assumptions that teachers were merely pawns in the game of capitalist oppression.[177] Educational processes were now seen as a 'fruitful sphere of activity,' and Communist teachers – often the most dynamic elements in both the LBC and the thousand-strong Teachers' Anti-War Movement[178] – unwittingly echoed Gramsci in identifying school education as a powerful source of a hegemony and resistance.[179] They debated pedagogy, produced textbooks suffused with Popular Front politics, and, like the architects and scientists, made significant gains within the key unions, with future National Union of Teachers (NUT) president G.C.T. Giles elected to the union's Executive Committee in 1937 and Nan MacMillan (1906–2002) as president of the National Union of Women Teachers in 1939.[180] Some of these Popular Front cultural initiatives have been mapped by historians and biographers.[181] Their legacies are traced in the chapters that follow.

Minds, Chains

Dimitrov's broad-brush report was pulled between a rhetoric of Communist strategy breaking with the past and one of narrower 'tactical orientation'; in the absence of a developed, theorized account of the chronology of revolution more detailed and nationally specific than the one he provided, there was space for a spectrum of interpretation and views.[182] The status of the Popular Front reorientation meant very different things to Communists. Some, like Dutt saw it as a temporary adjustment, necessary, as Eric Hobsbawm put it, 'to get the golf ball of revolution out of the bunker … after which the game would go on as before';[183] others found themselves as Communists within its framework. That the new line compelled many fellow-travelling intellectuals to overcome their hesitation and take party cards is well known: novelist Sylvia Townsend Warner (1893–1978) and her poet and journalist partner Valentine Ackland (1906–69) were among those who joined in 1935, while poet Cecil Day Lewis (1904–72) and composer Alan Bush (1900–95) signed up in 1936.[184] Overall, the Popular Front turn in Britain crystallized Communist countercurrents into a new and legitimate cultural formation within the party, to which the questions of nation, civil society, culture, popular consciousness, and revolutionary strategy were central.[185] A catalytic figure was again Wintringham, a 'terrific driving force' moved to poetry by the example of Dimitrov and sharply attuned to the model of the PCF,[186] 'Paris-Moscow' now being his politico-geographical coordinates.[187] Other key intellectuals were novelist and playwright Montagu Slater (1902–56), already a member, and Popular Front–period recruits poet Randall Swingler (1909–67), novelist and classicist Jack Lindsay (1900–90), and Edgell Rickword (1898–1982), the poet and a former editor of the *Calendar of Modern Letters*. The gravitational point for the group's distinctly Dimitrovian politico-cultural concerns was another journal, the organ of the British Section of the Writers' International, *Left Review*, launched in October 1934, and what Lindsay called 'a rallying point for the whole movement.'[188] That the leadership kept a close eye on a journal considered insufficiently proletarian was a mark of the enduring tensions.[189] But the most sophisticated thinking in the British party now came from the journal and its milieu, especially from Rickword, who joined the CPGB in 1936, would edit *Left Review* at the height of its influence (1936–37), and was rapidly promoted through the party's cultural structures into a quasi-official spokesperson on cultural questions.[190]

A key articulation of Rickword's thinking came in the concluding essay in a symposium, *The Mind in Chains: Socialism and the Cultural Revolution* (1937), edited by Day Lewis, which gathered many *Left Review* contributors.[191] Here, Rickword countered Dutt, echoed Dimitrov, and argued that Communism's habitual marginalization of intellectuals in the name of an alternative 'proletarian culture' reproduced, rather than challenged, bourgeois society's own 'isolation of the intellectuals from the masses of the people.'[192] And repeating Freda Utley's earlier apostasy in distinguishing between Lenin's writings and Communism's authorized version of Leninism, Rickword quoted Lenin's 'On Proletarian Culture' (1920), which emphasized the need for creative Marxism to assimilate and refashion the cultural past. Culture here was not accumulated bourgeois booty to be seized in the heat of revolution and distributed by workers' councils and trade unions, but an epistemology – 'the inherited solution of vital problems to the importance of society' – essential for perceiving and knowing 'the world as it is.'[193] Cast in these terms, culture and labour were 'mutually dependent aspects of the production process,'[194] culture being a type of general intellect enabling production – 'the tremendous creation and recreation of life going on in factory, mine and farm' – although a combination of factors made it difficult to recognize it as such.[195] In particular, the differentiated specialisms of the modern capitalist life-world, combined with the fetishistic commodity form and the structural class inequalities that made only a gatekeeping leisure class 'cultured,' accentuated the abstraction of culture from ordinary life ('culture' thus appeared 'an independent activity').[196] Rather, what created a 'flourishing culture' was mass 'participation in the constructive work of society,' the precondition for which – mass literacy – had been fulfilled by capitalism ('society can now afford that all its members shall be intellectuals).'[197] These arguments overcame the opposition between culture and production, intellectual and worker, within which discussions on culture, including those within party discourse, remained caught. They also undermined the idea of the 'Leninist' party delivering the state and turning culture over to the working class for future use, as detailed in *For Soviet Britain*. For Rickword, like Gramsci, revolution's chronology needed rethinking: the 'struggle for power' was at some level always substantially cultural, being 'decided long before there is any question of barricades.'[198] The ongoing assimilation and transformation of culture – what Gramsci called 'winning intellectual power' – was therefore not secondary to politics, but a prerequisite for socialist advance.[199] The question of whether the existing form of the party was adequate to these very different operations was implicit in Rickword's argument, although it remained undeveloped, and Dimitrov naturally had not dwelt on the discrepancies between the new tasks of Communism and its established organizational structures. For Rickword, prefigurative intimations of cultural assimilation and collaboration – such as the mutually enriching collaborations of socialists artists and scientists on documentary films about malnutrition, or antiwar activism – indicated what was necessary and possible, and anticipated what he elsewhere called 'the new struggle, the cooperative and constructive effort' of building 'a socialist society.'[200]

Such thinking was temporarily countenanced by the leadership in the months following Dimitrov's address and the Popular Front electoral breakthroughs in France and Spain, with Wintringham tasked to present a report on party work, 'Among the Intellectual and Professional Sections of the Middle Class.'[201] It always rubbed, however, against core impulses and dominant conceptions, as debates in the journal *Discussion* revealed. Jack Lindsay affirmed the Dimitrovian strategy of situating Communism within a narrative of struggle for expanded freedom; others detected in such formulations opportunism, backsliding, and 'confusing the vanguard with democratic illusion.'[202] As so often, the question of the status of intellectuals within the party was a conduit for broader questions around the party's identity and historical role. Valentine Ackland argued that worker-intellectual divisions and hierarchies needed to be revisited in the context of modern, literate, mass societies, where the print media were central to the struggle.[203] The more traditionally minded resisted any such revisionism, prescribing 'patient, steadfast and faithful carrying out of the practical work allotted' for intellectuals inclined to get above themselves.[204] Such mistrust of 'arty,' 'collarless,' and 'unshaven' intellectuals was emboldened once more as the tensions inherent in the Dimitrovian strategy – building national credibility through alliances *and* defending the Soviet Union – were forced into view by the deteriorating political climate. Those most committed to Popular Front positions found themselves marginalized in a darkening political context shadowed not only by fascist advance, but also by the Moscow Show Trials (August 1936, January 1937), the splintering of the Popular Front in France, and Communist *realpolitik* as the war deteriorated in Spain – a period defined by tightening Comintern control and the return of more traditional conceptions.[205] The faltering of Popular Front politics in 1938–9 was a moment whose central text was not Dimitrov's Report but Stalin's *History of the Communist Party of the Soviet Union / Bolsheviks / Short Course* (1939), a book whose very structure folded theoretical Marxism squarely into the substantially airbrushed story of the inexorably advancing 'Leninist' party, and became what E.P. Thompson later called 'the fundamental "education" text of communists from Stalingrad to Cardiff and Calcutta to Marseilles,' 'a gigantic historical fabrication' conceived to induce 'military mental habits.'[206] The leadership of the British party would play its own part in the erasure of awkward Soviet history, suppressing John Reed's eyewitness account of the Russian Revolution, *Ten Days that Shook the World* (1919), a text in which Trotsky eclipsed Stalin.[207] The party apparatus would be fully mobilized to import the *Short Course* into Britain in 10,000-copy consignments and to promote it through intense recruitment and educational drives as infallible wisdom to be 'consulted again and again when new problems have to be faced.'[208] But for the *Left Review* group, whose making as Communists was inseparable from the promises and problems of Popular Frontism, the multiple provocations of the Dimitrov report and the questions it asked without fully answering would remain the theoretical cornerstone. There are grounds to see some of their late 1930s work as a Dimitrovian antidote to Stalin's toxicity, and the leadership clearly regarded it as such.[209] The case should not, however, be overstated. Theirs was never a coherent cultural opposition or ideologically pure countercurrent untainted by Stalinism. Like Wintringham, Rickword praised Stalin in print, was ultimately loyal, and never escalated the logic of his insights into dissent.[210] A conflicted Swingler colluded in the contraction of the Popular Front *Daily Worker*'s broad cultural coverage, which had briefly revived the spirit of the *Sunday Worker* and in which his circle of Popular Front Communists had reason to take satisfaction.[211] Lindsay defended the Moscow trials in the pages of *Tribune*.[212] The formation was collectively cowed by what Thompson called 'not only a formal structure but also a psychological structure among Communist intellectuals,' a superego of 'Bolshevik' anti-intellectualism buttressed by the anti-intellectualism of British culture with which the party shared more than it believed.[213] The formation was also depleted at the end of the 1930s by expulsions (Wintringham in July 1938), disillusionment (Cecil Day Lewis, Charles Madge), and the deaths of former and potential allies in Spain (David Guest, Ralph Fox, John Cornford, Christopher Caudwell).[214] For all that, it remained, theoretically and culturally, the most advanced point of twenty years of Communist countercurrents around revolutionary strategy and civil society. The group published historical novels,[215] anthologies,[216] cultural criticism,[217] and historiography – most notably, A.L. Morton's enduring *A People's History of England* (1938), the foundational scene of the Party's Historians' Group.[218] It produced live events, including Swingler and Alan Bush's mass pageant, *Music and the People*, staged at the Royal Albert Hall on 1 April 1939, where Paul Robeson led a choir of 500, with 10,000 in attendance.[219] The group also set up Fore Publications, a mass-circulation press venture that was Dimitrovian to the core;[220] publications included Jack Lindsay's *England My England: A Pageant of the English People* (1939), which sold 80,00 copies.[221] Such activities always exceeded the leadership's narrow Popular Front conceptions, and briefly brought a version of Communism's Dimitrovian turn to the fore of British cultural life. When George Orwell claimed that, in the second half of the 1930s, 'the central stream of English literature was more or less directly under Communist control,' he was referring to the *Left Review* formation.[222] He exaggerated, but Lindsay and Rickword had certainly succeeded where Dutt had failed in creating a rapport with Britain's foremost socialist intellectual, J.B. Priestley, who praised their *A Handbook of English Freedom* (1939) in the *Daily Worker*.[223] Initially an expression of Popular Front enthusiasm, this formation soon became a beleaguered location of cautious resistance against narrowing conceptions that struggled to sustain the broken tradition which stood behind it.[224] Nonetheless, it would take forward unresolved questions about nation, state, civil society and the chronology of revolution into the wartime and post-war period.

2
Constructive Communists, 1940–1947

'Never before have we had such political capital,' wrote Harry Pollitt as the end of the war came into view.[1] Party membership reached its all time peak of 56,000 in 1942–3, touching a quarter of the Labour Party's individual membership.[2] In 1945 the Communist Party had over 200 local councillors, two Members of Parliament, and the *Daily Worker* was selling over 100,000 copies per day.[3] Impressively wide-ranging initiatives were mobilized between 1941 and 1947. To a degree overlooked in the standard national histories, the party played a role in the planning and practice of national reconstruction, its Popular Front structures providing the foundations for this work.[4] The spheres in which it was most active were wartime economic production, the wartime 'cultural upsurge,' science, architecture, and education. One function of this chapter is to reconstruct that work. A key argument, however, is that a number of interpenetrating factors – theoretical lacunae, the international situation, intellectual dependency on the Soviet Union, party structure and hierarchies, entrenched mindsets, cultural conservatism – combined to block the party from fully recognizing what it was achieving, and from reconfiguring its identity or formulating a coherent strategy to facilitate advance from 'a better Britain today' to 'a Socialist Britain tomorrow' at a moment when the 1943 dissolution of the Comintern licensed more independence.[5] Rather, the devolutionary momentum of the international Communist movement in these years exposed the party's theoretical weaknesses, throwing it back on resources it lacked and revealing the degree to which it had been ill prepared by the movement of which it was a part for formulating a strategy for advancing to socialism in a developed industrial democracy. In particular it lacked insight into capitalism's flexibility and capacity for self-stabilization, the mechanisms of the bourgeois state, and the role of civil society in the reproduction of class power. As a result, the significant and overlooked achievements enabled by this more constructive turn were sporadic, barely coordinated, tentative, and more quickly reversed by the Cold War than they might have been. The historical pressure on the party at this moment was great, and its scope for advance fundamentally restricted by the Labour Party's historical hostility to it. Other Communist Parties – notably the French and the Italian, both riding high on the basis of moral authority accrued through leading wartime resistance – proved more flexible, and other perspectives were available to the British one than those that dominated. Historians have been attentive to those Communists bewildered by 'revisionism,' who called in these years for a return to more confrontational class politics.[6] Forgotten proto-Gramscian voices argued at the time for a broader conception of the party, for a meaningful discussion of strategy, for deeper analysis of the bourgeois state and the crucial relationship between civil society and class power and, more practically, between the Communist Party and the Labour Party. I conclude the chapter by analysing what they said and presenting them as a strong articulation of the countercurrents that had existed since the CPGB's formation.

Cultural Upsurge

The celebrity-peppered cultural world of 1930s British Communism is well known, but the party's cultural influence was higher in and through the wartime 'upsurge' of popular participation in exhibitions, theatre, and factory concerts chronicled by Jack Lindsay in his best-selling overview, *British Achievement in Art and Music* (1945).[7] Paradoxically, the party's strong grassroots presence in this moment owed much to the fragmentation of Popular Front–period cultural networks in the wake of the Nazi-Soviet pact with which the last chapter concluded. In a period when the Left Book Club split acrimoniously, Communist streetcorner speakers were barracked, and *Daily Worker* sellers spat at and showered with the contents of chamber pots, necessity proved the mother of invention.[8] The focus shifted from grandiose Popular Front themes – culture's place in revolution, the contestation of reactionary national narratives, the need to provide leadership in literary, artistic, and scientific spheres – to the more basic business of retaining and recruiting members from the cultural world, especially in London, where 40 per cent of the party membership lived.[9] The party line now focused on fomenting and channelling wartime discontent, and worked from January 1941 through the People's Convention, a front organization whose charter stressed wartime living conditions, trade union rights, secure air raid provision, and friendship with the Soviet Union.[10] At a moment when concert halls, dance halls, West End theatres, and cinemas were closed by bombing, blackout, and call-up, musicians were targeted by the party, especially the 3,000 estimated to be unemployed in London.[11] The key figures in Popular Front cultural Communism had been the writers gathered around *Left Review*. In the early war years, its strength was predominantly musical, with 54 in the party musicians' fraction by October 1941 and 180 a year later – the WMA's new premises in Newport Street forming an organizational hub.[12] Core activists included composers Alan Bush (1900–95), Christian Darnton (1905–81), and Benjamin Frankel (1906–73), singers and musicians Martin Lawrence and Geraldine Peppin, and dance band leaders and musicians Ivor Mairants (1908–98), Van Phillips, and Lew Stone (1898–1969).[13] These Communists worked to recruit and build influence through myriad organizations: the Dance Band Directors' Association,[14] the Musicians' Union,[15] the WMA (in which the party now formed a faction),[16] and the hardship organization, the Musicians' Social and Benevolent Council.[17] Communists found impecunious dance band musicians exposed to ruling-class pleasure in West End restaurants and hotels highly receptive to party propaganda ('all of those rich people were beneath contempt,' Phillips recalled).[18] As new party structures, including an Entertainment Industry Bureau, suggested, the backs-to-the-wall discourse was primarily economic and industrial.[19] The key claim was that the capitalist culture industry, whose bottom line was ruined by war, was now effectively locking out cultural workers from their means of production.[20] In this spirit, the work of the government-funded Entertainments National Service Association (ENSA) and the Council for Education in Music and the Arts (CEMA) was affirmed as a bulwark against unemployment for cultural workers – and infiltrated.[21]

Implicit in this productionist paradigm was a broader argument about access to culture. This contrasted an expensive, metropolitan culture dominated by 'a well-to-do minority' with those 'new sources of cultural vitality' inherent in the 'whole people.'[22] It was an emerging discourse about capitalism, crisis, and the need for state redistribution of cultural resources that animated the William Morris Music Society, founded by the party in 1940 to promote Marxist discourse on music, as well as the cultural networks and initiatives of the People's Convention.[23] It was pushed hardest by Thomas Russell, a viola player with the London Philharmonic Orchestra (LPO), who, inspired in 1939 by what he knew of Soviet arrangements, drove the transformation of the cash-strapped LPO into a democratic, self-managing organization that hired conductors, rather than being insecurely employed by them.[24] The party leadership was heartened by the size of the Communist faction in the LPO. Russell, eager to make 'the whole country orchestra conscious,' was focused on retooling the LPO to meet the mass audience for serious music that he was convinced existed beyond 'a small coterie of super-sensitive souls.'[25] Working closely with the like-minded J.B Priestley, for whom cultural elitism was a long-standing bugbear, Russell was instrumental in mounting the 'Musical Manifesto' concert at the soon-to-be-bombed Queen's Hall in the summer of 1940, a sell-out event that sharpened Russell's and the orchestra's commitment to confronting established cultural hierarchies.[26] Assisted by CEMA, the LPO would soon be pioneering wartime cultural diffusion: 20,000 heard the orchestra in a week of Albert Hall concerts in 1941;[27] the musicians would perform in music halls and theatres in over one hundred locations, including in bombed towns, where, as Priestley put it, they arrived 'not very long after the sealed tins of standard soup and the other emergency rations.'[28]

The stubborn contradiction here, however, was that party discourse promoted state intervention in the cultural field (ENSA, CEMA), but opposed the war that occasioned such intervention and for which popular morale apparently needed raising.[29] Release from the party's impasse of accumulating a cultural presence upon which it could not fully capitalize came only with the Nazi invasion of the Soviet Union on 22 June 1941, the subsequent Anglo-Soviet military alliance formalized on 12 July, and the transformation of the war into the 'genuinely antifascist' struggle' that Popular Fronters, including Lindsay, had predicted.[30] Propaganda suddenly seemed to make itself, as Eric Hobsbawm later put it, with British Communism's cultural figures and networks proving especially adept at blending a Popular Front narrative about the nation's long-standing anti-authoritarian traditions with the signature Communist theme: the achievements of the Soviet Union, Britain's new, exotic, and popular ally:[31] in a January 1942 survey, 86 per cent said they wanted to see Britain and the Soviet Union working together after the war; nine out of ten would register a favourable view of the Soviet Union as the Red Army began to push back Hitler's army in the summer of 1943.[32] For individual Communists with strong antifascist feelings recently restrained from joining the war effort by the party line, the sudden prospect of mobilizing cultural activism in the direct service of the Soviet motherland was deeply energizing. Abertillery miner Arthur Cook, for instance, formed the Abertillery Unity Male Choir,[33] and Popular Front party intellectuals including Sylvia Townsend Warner found a new purpose in the causes of Soviet Aid, the Russia Today Society, and the Society for Cultural Relations with the USSR (SCR), tangential spheres of party life whose membership now boomed – that of the notionally independent SCR, for instance, rising to 4,000.[34] Despite the government's determination that that the Communist Party should not benefit from the alliance, the party potently fused its organizational nous at the level of local authorities with its privileged access to all things Soviet, deepening and politicizing enthusiasm for Britain's ally through concerts, Red Army Days, Aid to Russia and Anglo-Soviet Weeks, and Anglo-Soviet Friendship Committees.[35] In promoting such networks, the party was now working with the tide of a Soviet-tinged mainstream in which London mayors commemorated Lenin's former residence in the city, Soviet films enjoyed commercial release, and Hollywood made movies true to Stalin's version of the Show Trials.[36]

'Communists were suddenly so popular,' joked *Daily Worker* journalist Claud Cockburn, 'that it nearly hurt.'[37] Individual Communists with cultural profiles now found themselves disconcertingly acceptable to official institutions committed to promoting the alliance. Alan Bush, blocked from a post in the Army

Education Corps and recently banned from the airwaves as a signatory of the People's Convention, found the BBC suddenly keen to benefit from his detailed knowledge of the SCR's extensive Russian record collection;[38] the recently blacklisted Joan Littlewood (1914–2002) was re-employed by the BBC, although watched carefully while she worked on Home Service programs, including 'Salute to Joseph Stalin.'[39] Other Communists established themselves within the Ministry of Information, where Montagu Slater was promoted to Head of Scripts in the film division and Ivor Montagu was also hired.[40] Although also recently removed from his post at the BBC, A.L. Lloyd worked for the Ministry of Information magazine *Britansky Soyuznik* (The British Ally) to bring news of British culture to the Soviet Union (the Red Army alone absorbed 7,000 copies).[41] Applications to work for ENSA were carefully vetted,[42] but Fred Westacott (1916–2001) became an Army Bureau of Current Affairs (ABCA) instructor, and was surprised by the 'scope allowed.'[43] Jack Lindsay, André van Gyseghem (1906–79), and Ted Willis (1914–92) all secured posts at the ABCA Theatre Unit, bringing their Left theatre backgrounds and People's War political perspectives to thousands of troops.[44] Francis Klingender and Eric Hobsbawm worked with the Army Education Corps, albeit precariously.[45]

Communists were now seeking to bring their perspectives to bear on these state bodies. There was also much work to do through residual Popular Front cultural institutions previously split or weakened by the pact, which rediscovered their purpose under the Soviet ally and People's War rubric. Leeds Unity Theatre wrote and staged *Comrade Enemy*, a play dramatizing popular resistance to the Nazi invasion;[46] in Bristol, Unity created *Landmarks of Liberty*, a play performed for troops that celebrated the alliance and closed with 'The Internationale' segueing into 'God Save the King.'[47] In London, Unity Theatre, which had gained kudos in defying the West End cultural blackout, formed an Outside Show Group that presented material including a Living Newspaper, *Russia's Glory: The Red Army*, in air-raid shelters, barracks, factory canteens, and hostels for munition workers through 1941 and 1942.[48] The AIA found renewed ideological clarity, opening a new centre at 83 Charlotte Street and staging exhibitions, including 'War Pictures' in Charing Cross Underground station, which attracted up to 150,000 visitors, and 'Hogarth and English Caricature,' based on Francis Klingender's book of the same title, which CEMA supported on tour.[49] The WMA became a crucial vector of Soviet culture through its choirs, concerts, work for the BBC, books, sheet music, and recordings, with its previously struggling in-house label, Topic Records, finding a lucrative market for Soviet gramophone discs.[50]

There was no longer friction between celebrating Soviet culture, advocating the principle of state intervention in the arts, and supporting the war for which it was mobilized.[51] Some Communists approved of the disintegration of an established metropolitan highbrow culture symbolized by the transformation of Covent Garden into a dance hall and the wartime closure of the Royal Academy.[52] CEMA was widely celebrated as a medium for cultural democratization, and affirmed for transforming elite cultural institutions over which Communists had little or no direct influence – notably, the Old Vic, now dividing its energies between presenting Konstantin Simonov's *The Russians* to raise funds for the Stalingrad Hospital Fund and touring Welsh mining towns, or Ballet Rambert, bringing ballet to factory canteens.[53] The scale and significance of the 'cultural upsurge' has been debated by historians, but the spike in attendance figures at theatres, concerts, and for serious music on the BBC suggests that, at the very least, as Angus Calder puts it, wartime people 'found it harder to use what spare time they had, and were willing to venture their new earnings on culture, to give it a try.'[54] At many levels, Communists were active in this culture, not least through their own carefully choreographed wartime mass meetings – for Anglo-Soviet Unity, production drives ('Tanks for Russia'), and the opening of a second front – through which such meetings keyed into 'people's craving,' as Malcolm MacEwen put it, 'in the wartime blackout for participation and entertainment.'[55] New Communists were made with disconcerting ease at events such as the 'For Speedy Victory and a Better Britain' mass rally at Wembley Town Hall, with its voluminous choir, musical recitals, and pageant dramatizing 'the struggle of the Communist Parties in all the lands.'[56] Thirty-three thousand new members joined the party in 1942, bringing the total membership to its zenith in December that year.[57]

Reading Matters

As Communists realized, public entertainment mattered more in the war. So too did reading, and Communists were now pushing at the open doors of mainstream publishers eager to commission Soviet-related titles, including Francis Klingender's *Russia: Britain's Ally 1812–1942* (1942), with its introduction by Soviet ambassador Ivan Maisky, which handsomely mediated Soviet art to the British public.[58] Newsprint remained central to British culture: during the war, 77 per cent of the population saw a morning newspaper most days, and 87 per cent saw a Sunday newspaper.[59] The cultural significance of newspapers became more highly charged by the combination of wartime conditions congenial to reading – the blackout, the closure of cinemas, the dead time of life in the armed forces – and paper rationing, introduced in February 1940, whose effect was to bottleneck the expanding market into narrower channels. Over 900 magazines and newspapers were wiped out, creating a sharp imbalance between supply and demand.[60] Cyril Connolly famously joked in 1942 that the nation's desperation for reading material was such that reissuing 1930s railway timetables would have been commercially viable.[61] The written word was always central to the party's internal and outward-facing culture, and it made headway, effectively positioning

Home Front journal, 1942. CP archive, LHASC, Manchester.

Second Front rally, Trafalgar Square, 1942. Planet News Ltd., CP Picture Archive, Box 13.

itself on the side of freedom of speech and accumulating prestige in challenging the ban on the *Daily Worker* (January 1941–September 1942).[62] When the ban was lifted, the new-look paper, with its strategically broadened editorial board and pledge to 'speak for the millions of ordinary folk' whose 'toil and courage and sacrifice will bring victory to the new world of security,' gave the party a disproportionate stake in the world of print that remained its lingua franca.[63] The removal of the wholesalers' ban made the paper attractive to advertisers; this revenue stream, combined with funds raised during the eighteen months the paper failed to appear, meant that it could now afford the unimagined luxuries of a late edition and press agencies.[64] Daily sales, buoyed by the national obsession with the Soviet Union, which it copiously reflected, reached 104,000.[65]

If newspapers mattered in shaping popular consciousness, periodicals mattered in constructing communities of readers, in shaping cultural discourse, and in defining the relationships between cultural levels of high, low, and middle that continued to preoccupy and define British culture and party assumptions alike. Here too the party held its stake when key arbiters of taste were folding (the *Criterion*, the *London Mercury*, *Twentieth Century Verse*, and *New Verse* all disappeared).[66] The party's scientifically prestigious *Modern Quarterly* (1938–39) was gone, but would be revived in 1945, while sales of Dutt's now more culturally focused *Labour Monthly* trebled to reach 20,000 in the early 1940s, becoming the party's in-house alternative to the fragmenting Left Book Club with its small counterculture of *Labour Monthly* pamphlets, conferences, and regional discussion groups.[67] The cultural politics of the Popular Front formation of the Swingler circle were sustained through the journal *Poetry and the People* (1938–40). Most significant, however, was the new cultural journal that superseded it, *Our Time*, launched by the group behind Fore Publications in February 1941 and positioned as an egalitarian corrective to Cyril Connolly's elitist *Horizon* to which 'the ghosts of literary values long defunct' had allegedly retreated.[68] As with the *Daily Worker*, the new journal enjoyed some luck, this time in the form of a cross subsidy from a more lucrative journal acquired by Fore Publications, *Seven: A Magazine of People's Writing*, a publication that expressed People's War populism and was selling as many as 100,000 copies per issue.[69] *Our Time*'s circulation was a fraction as high, but it mattered more as a conscious attempt to occupy vacated cultural ground and to shape a future culture in which the 'people, abandoned to their own resources,' were 'swiftly gaining a new self-confidence.'[70] Standing behind the optimism of *Our Time* was the conviction that extraordinary wartime conditions and state subsidy were drawing the productive class into cultural production, thereby revitalizing a moribund cultural world dangerously polarized between commodified mass culture – created for the masses, not by them – and a high culture whose bloodless introspection measured disconnection from production, social progress, and the rhythms of popular life.[71] For Communists like Lindsay, the function of the journal was to support and develop a cultural upsurge now manifested in the labour movement's staging major cultural events, such as the Malcolm Sargent–conducted LPO premiere of Christian Darnton's *Stalingrad Overture*, organized by the Postal Engineers' Anglo-Soviet Committee at the Albert Hall in the Spring of 1943.[72] Eventually retrieved from the wartime incursions of stiff-necked party functionaries with narrower visions by the CPGB's Popular Front literary circle – Randall Swingler, Jack Lindsay, Montagu Slater, plus actor Beatrix Lehmann – *Our Time* would install Rickword as editor and become a focal point for the 'cultural upsurge,' sales climbing impressively to 18,000, six times the circulation of the better-known *Left Review*.[73]

The Production Paradigm

Increasingly, *Our Time's* framework for its optimistic reading of the apparent reconnection of culture and production was a broader shift in Communist attitudes to party, class, and economic production in the context of the Anglo-Soviet alliance. Gramsci was clear that 'though hegemony is ethical-political … it must also be economic' and 'based on the decisive function exercised by the leading group in the decisive nucleus of economic activity.'[74] The effective class, party, and its intellectuals, in other words, needed to exert influence at the level of the economy and to build the prestige necessary for leadership by prefiguring in the capitalist present outlines of a future social order grounded in an alternative, collective mode of production. This idea of the economy as a site of constructive, rather than oppositional and defensive, interventions was anathema to Third International Communism, which naturally stressed confrontation, dual power, and building the party through resistance under capitalism. The Anglo-Soviet alliance changed that overnight. The economy was transformed in Communist conception from the location of alienation and the extraction of surplus value into a key nexus of antifascist activity, a bulwark supporting both the actually existing Soviet Union and the new civilization understood to be immanent there. The British party was well-placed to take advantage of the moment, finding the national government in alliance with the workers' state and being the only completely legal Western European party in a country at war.[75] A new proto-Gramscian note in Communist discourse stressed that the party, on behalf of the nation's working class, would give 'leadership to the whole people' by 'solving the industrial, military and political problems of organising the nation for the common struggle, side by side with the Soviet Union.'[76]

One important and often overlooked manifestation of this was the 'Women's Parliaments,' proposed and organized by the party initially under the auspices of the People's Convention, which were held four times in London between July 1941 and November 1943 with local offshoots, and which directly involved thousands of women across the social strata.[77] Productionist in orientation (angled at equal pay for women and overcoming 'the inefficiency, corruption and profiteering which is hampering production')[78] and emphatically pro-Soviet ('our great ally and glorious example of working-class freedom'), the parliaments applied some of the pressure that resulted in a Royal Commission on equal pay.[79] And although eschewing feminist discourse in the name of antifascist unity ('we seek the benefit of [men's] experience in winning the war'),[80] the enterprise nonetheless antagonized the patriarchal Trades Union Congress (TUC).[81] Overall, the Women's Parliaments represented a new, canny form of prefigurative political theatre that not only caught national media attention by dramatizing, through contrast, the usual effective exclusion of half of the population from parliamentary politics; it also took a new proto-Gramscian line in seeing the transformation of the means of wartime production here and now (equal pay, workplace-based health, welfare, educational, and social service provision) as potentially prefiguring different social relations ('building a new world').[82]

As this implied, the central location of this unprecedented and fundamental shift – driven by the alliance and handled in an improvised rather than theorized way – was the munitions and aircraft factories, which above all gave Communism its wartime prestige. Between 1936 and 1945, the government spent almost £4 million on the infrastructure of the aircraft industry at 2,800 premises,[83] a rearmament drive that made it possible for the party to establish a presence in factories that had been stronger as a post-Bolshevization principle than in fact.[84] In Coventry, the epicentre of war production, Communist trade unionists in the late 1930s played a typically decisive role in building organizational mass through the Amalgamated Engineering Union (AEU) and the Transport and General Workers Union (TGWU), work that laid the foundations for the party's wartime expansion (Coventry party membership was 70 in November 1940, but 1,500 in September 1942, with members across forty factories).[85] The key unit of shop-floor wartime Communism was the Joint Production Committee (JPC), through which workers could play a role in planning production and challenge impediments to it. Following a campaign driven by the Shop Stewards' National Council, JPCs were officially recognized by the government in February 1942, and would soon be established in 4,500 engineering and allied workplaces representing a total of three and a half million workers.[86] The conjuncture pushed the party outside its usual patterns of thought and activism, and was experienced and sometimes articulated in ways that approximated the Gramscian emphasis on the prefiguration of different social relations driven by working-class leadership at the level of production. The publications produced by Communist women, whose numbers in factories were proportionately swelled ('Come on Women – Man the Factories'), affirmed the work of the JPCs and developed early Women's Parliament interventions in reimagining the factory as a space that could 'give something to people who have never had much' in the form of collectively managed health care provision, vitamin supplements, library facilities, and cultural events.[87] Jack Lindsay's wartime novel, *Hullo Stranger* (1945), celebrated the transformation of an aircraft factory under the JPCs into an anticipation of 'the mystery of a fuller life' in which the working class led society.[88] The degree of shop-floor receptiveness to Communism certainly made it feel like a moment charged with the future: at Austin Aero, there were 15,000 employees and 400 party members; 1,000 copies of the *Daily Worker* were sold, along with over 2,000 of the engineers' shop stewards' paper, *New Propeller*; at Metro Vickers in Manchester, there were 250 party members out of 30,000 employees (before the war, there had been just 10 in a workforce half the size).[89] At Fairey's Aviation Works in Stockport, party membership doubled and the *Daily Worker* sold 250 copies daily;[90] in the Rover Aero works in Birmingham, lunchtime lectures on 'Communist Theory and Policy' were attracting 150 ('our prestige has increased a hundredfold,' noted the Communist shop steward, 'the respect we are given is quite noticeable');[91]

in Coventry, activists felt 'a foretaste' of taking over industry in peacetime.[92] It was an instance, however, of history's throwing up circumstances for which there was no adequate analytical framework and whose promise was never in the moment meaningfully articulated or integrated into the party's strategy or program, despite its fundamental commitment to JPCs during and after the war. As James Hinton has argued, individual Communists were certainly alert to the need to embed and broaden their advances by connecting together the JPCs in and through regional and national planning apparatuses and to create what he calls 'a chain of command linking worker power on the shop-floor into the administration of production as a whole,' an endeavour in which they were blocked by the Engineering Employers' Federation, which was all too clear about what was at stake.[93] In 1944 Harry Pollitt took retrospective satisfaction in the JPCs' having pushed beyond individual factory production to 'tackle the higher organisation of production' by pooling their expertise, notably in the production of the Lancaster bomber, and having created the pressure on the government to form boards to coordinate production.[94] But at the high point of the Anglo-Soviet alliance conjuncture in 1941–2, party discourse stayed predominantly within a workerist and Soviet-facing emergency productionist paradigm, lambasting 'appalling waste, inefficiency, lack of planning' and 'the thousands of non-producers floating around factories.'[95] Before 1943 the party had no economics committee to supply a more clearly articulated strategy around JPCs. Such a strategy might have enabled it to benefit further from a brief but propitious moment in which much was achieved. Time, however, was very limited: munitions production was wound down from 1944 (by the end of the war, there were only around 520 Communists in Coventry, a third of the 1942 membership).[96] Long before then, the key debate had shifted to questions of post-war reconstruction, which Communists, naturally fixed on defence of the Soviet Union, were slow to join.

Popularity Crisis

Debates about post-war reconstruction were brushed aside by the Communist Party between 1941 and 1942 as the 'happy-hunting-ground' of those content to let the Soviet Union do the fighting.[97] Towards the end of 1942, the fact that the party lagged behind the key national discussion was undeniable: former Communist Tom Wintringham was making headway via the new Common Wealth Party, largely by pledging to implement in full the Beveridge Report, which sold over 100,000 copies when published in December 1942.[98] That month the party belatedly issued a memorandum, *Guiding Lines on Questions of Post-War Reconstruction*, pledging 'to give leadership on all questions of the future.'[99] The *Daily Worker* was redefined as a conduit for these discussions, bringing to its 100,000 readers 'post-war policies' equipped to provide 'security to the people' and to 'pave the way to socialism.'[100] The Political Bureau appointed a post-war planning commission, chaired by Dutt, which oversaw the work of a range of new subcommittees tasked with formulating positions and producing documents in the terms of the national reconstruction debate.[101] A coordinating Cultural Groups Committee was simultaneously formed to synchronize the work of wartime bodies and, for the first time, the party created an Economics Committee, whose initial concern was reconstruction.[102]

The moon to this turning tide was the centrifugal momentum in international Communist politics implicit in Stalin's late 1942 rhetoric and explicit in May 1943 when he dissolved the Comintern for the sake of smoothing relations with wartime allies (he had already replaced the provocative 'Internationale' with a solidly patriotic Soviet anthem).[103] Talk of 'mature' national parties independently building national roads to socialism supplanted the older metaphor of parties as 'different divisions in a single army … with a single, directing centre.'[104] The abrupt dissolution of the Comintern was naturally disorienting for many Communists. The CPGB, which was already in a state of flux in struggling to assimilate and socialize the many new members,[105] responded through a renewed phase of the national acclimatization begun during the Popular Front years, anglicizing its own administrative nomenclature and rebadging its top bodies.[106] It was a deeply paradoxical moment in which the possibility of greater autonomy exposed deep contradictions, not all of the party's own making. The party was uncoupled from what Dutt euphemistically called 'formal international obligations,' and in principle enjoyed new freedom to benefit from the prestige of the Soviet Union while also possessing the independence to consolidate itself as a credible, national political force.[107] At the same time, its relative autonomy was still governed by the Soviet Union in the form of the overarching Soviet geopolitical analysis of the so-called Tehran, Crimea, and Yalta perspectives, international colloquy that stressed, and predicted, peace and mutual economic and political cooperation between the antifascist Big Three under the aegis of the United Nations, a collaborationist perspective at some remove from Leninism. Unprecedented tones of togetherness provided the mood music for the period's key policy statement, *Britain for the People: Proposals for Post-war Policy* (issued in May 1944, adopted that October), and for Pollitt's pamphlets *How to Win the Peace* (1944) and *Answers to Questions* (1945). These texts revoked without theoretical explanation both core Leninist positions on the inexorable logic of imperialist rivalry and more recent Dimitrovian analysis that fascism and capitalism differed in degree, not in kind. The new 'epoch-making' era announced by the groundbreaking international conferences, it was claimed, called for collaboration between the labour movement and progressive capitalists at the national level in the creation of a state capitalism that would mirror and reinforce the overarching international alliance between Britain, the United States, and the Soviet Union.[108] That a question like

'Who really believes the scare stories of the coming domination of the rest of Europe by Anglo-American imperialism?' was now rhetorical, or that assertions that the post-war spirit was equivalent to the Russian Revolution as an advance for workers that 'settled the question of future wars' did not seem hostages to fortune, was a measure of the pervasive unreality of the moment. In the United States, the Communist Party, under Earl Browder, considered itself a fly in the ointment of class collaboration, and dissolved itself.[109] And that the party's leadership in Britain accepted the new analysis so easily was not only a problem of unquestioning obedience to the Soviet Union, which Pollitt defensively presented as a virtue – 'the policy of the Soviet Union ... is always in the interests of its people and the working people of every other country in the world' – but of gaping theoretical blind spots around capitalist resilience, the bourgeois state, and civil society in developed economies, questions that had never been meaningfully explored in the inter-war period.[110] In party discourse, there was a new tough-minded analysis of national class composition and the balance of class forces,[111] but accounts of how the capitalist class administered its rule remained stuck in a conspiratorial discourse of 'wire pulling, corruption and the influencing of the key people.'[112] Questions of how oppositional class consciousness might be augmented remained economistic: such consciousness was seen as straightforwardly driven by material conditions or by the membership of trade union and labour movement organizations.[113] The routine catastrophism of inter-war Communist economic analysis left the party ill-equipped to analyse what Gramsci called a 'passive revolution,' in which the ruling class was stabilizing the state through the incorporation of planning.[114] Without a meaningful theory of the bourgeois state and the class dynamics of civil society, the party was unable to negotiate the imposed shift from an essentially insurrectionist vision to one stressing long-haul struggles in a context considered ripe for what Pollitt called 'peaceful transition to socialism.'[115] The clearest guidance available from the international Communist movement was the 'People's Democracy' model, a term which soon became a cover for single-party states in Eastern Europe, but initially designated, in an extension of Popular Front thinking, post-war regimes led by coalition governments in which Communist Parties would share power and whose politics would emphasize nationalization, trade union participation in planning, and a foreign policy sympathetic to the Soviet Union as foundations for further advance.[116] In France, Italy, and Finland, the existence of mass and electorally credible Communist Parties made this a viable course, with parties in all three countries rethinking basic questions of their form and function and joining coalitions with left and centre parties.[117] The much smaller British party, by contrast, repeatedly blocked by the imperviousness of the Labour Party to its attempts at affiliation, was at loss. Behind the scenes, the leadership did not itself sound convinced of the new orientation, and struggled to define the status of *Britain for the*

People: Proposals for Post-war Policy and the chronology of revolution it envisaged: was it describing socialism or rather a staging post to be followed by unspecified and more traditionally expropriative struggles?[118] The party was locked into an analysis of coalition between 'progressive' capital and labour articulated in the pamphlet *The Crimea Conference: Safeguard of the Future* (1945). It then infamously misjudged the national mood, advocating support for a cross-party progressive electoral bloc as late as March 1945, by which time it was obvious to many, especially in the armed forces, that a large Labour majority in the General Election was likely.[119] Having dithered in the lead-up, the party arguably did less well in the election than it might have, struggling to differentiate itself from the Labour Party and converting its political capital into just two MPs and an average of 11 per cent of the vote in the twenty-one constituencies contested.[120] In an unprecedented upsurge across party press, congress floor, and branch and district meetings, many now challenged 'Browderism' and the leadership's opportunism and class collaboration, often in the name of fidelity to Leninism.[121]

Class Composition and Civil Society

The ideological drift of the period in which the CPGB, like some other Communist Parties, struggled to orientate itself in the late war and early post-war world was most manifest in a number of key areas: misjudging the popular mood prior to the General Election of 1945; continuing support for a production drive that seemed to many to exacerbate, rather than confront, the exploitation of workers; the scaling back of the Industrial Department with the downgrading of factory branches to factory committees;, and the transfer of industrial cadres to residential branches. Although substantially driven by the discontinuation of munitions production, the latter shift ran against the grain of Bolshevization, effectively promoting the neighbourhood branch into the primary unit of Communist organization, symbolically shifting Communist identity from the point of production to the electoral ward and constituency, and bringing the party's structure closer to the political mainstream.[122] Although the party conducted no searching, open analysis of whether its structure and strategy were adequate to the challenges it faced, some saw these changes as exceeding what was required by the munitions contraction, instead reflecting a 'changed political attitude' that was never fully articulated or debated.[123] The changes would certainly prove highly significant to the party's broader identity and work.

The factory branches inscribed into party identity by Bolshevization were fundamental to its former revolutionary program, *For Soviet Britain* (1935), as embryonic workers' councils, or soviets. Equally clear were revolution's chronology (first, revolution; then, socialist reconstruction) and the party's pecking order (first, industrial workers; then, 'technical, clerical, administrative and cultural workers').[124] The primary revolutionary agent was the former; after the revolution, the latter group would be active in socialist construction across spheres including housing, health, and education.[125] But although it was never articulated as such, or its strategic implications fully debated, that policy – and the assumption about the chronology of revolution – was now tacitly reversed in the context of support for reconstruction. Reconstruction became a precondition of future advance, or accelerating 'the mass movement in the direction of securing the conquest of power and the establishment of socialism.'[126] In a word order unimaginable a decade before, Dutt spoke of 'the scientists and workers in alliance' building 'the new Britain.'[127] Paradoxically, in other national contexts, notably the Italian, Communist Parties underestimated the need to secure a powerful presence in the sites of national reconstruction, instead mainly establishing cultural authority through the medium of a traditional intellectual elite.[128] Not so in Britain and its scientifically minded party, where Communist scientists, technicians, planners, and administrators potentially implanted Communist visions into key nodes of national reconstruction. Professional workers already accounted for between 10 and 20 per cent of delegates to the party's 1944 Congress, and were addressed with increasing directness in this period, being told to 'make up their minds which political line they mean to follow.'[129] Geneticist J.B.S. Haldane (1892–1964) wrote a recruitment pamphlet pitched at them in 1945,[130] students were targeted through the period,[131] and early in 1946 the party assembled a large meeting of professionals whom Pollitt assured that white-collar comrades were fulfilling their Communist duties in part by being visibly outstanding in their respective professions.[132] Frequently self-flagellating and ingratiating in the past, professional workers enjoyed a new profile as their numbers increased and their role in the Communist project became clearer.[133] These cadres now formed nuclei of Communist prestige and influence in the body politic of demobilizing Britain, and their work often exceeded the guidelines and even the knowledge of the party centre, as their vocational obligations and party priorities reinforced one another in a charmed circle. As one Communist working in adult education put it, 'it was widely assumed that the leftward movement would be maintained ... left-wing intellectuals had an obvious part to play and communists *a fortiori*.'[134]

Science

During the Popular Front years, Communist scientists had established themselves as leading public intellectuals in explaining the frustration of science's emancipatory force by capitalism. During the war, the establishment's initial hesitations about the reliability of these figures had been trumped by a recognition of their obvious value to the war effort, and the risk had proved worth taking.[135] Soon close to Churchill, J.D. Bernal in particular had the most exceptional of wars, progressing from air-raid analysis (correctly predicting the effect of the 1940 bombing of Coventry) to becoming Lord Mountbatten's scientific adviser in Combined Operations, where he was integral to the planning of the Normandy landings.[136] Having exerted influence over many key areas of the war's prosecution, Bernal was officially named the scientist who 'had done the most to win the Second World War.'[137] His reputation as 'the sage of science' was firmly consolidated in the mid-1940s as his central ideas about science as the dynamo of enlightenment in opposition to barbarism seemed confirmed by a war in which planning was indeed seen to have defeated atavism.[138] No British Communist intellectual was more prominent in public debate about reconstruction than the ubiquitous Bernal in this period. He communicated his ideas to a large national audience via channels that included the BBC's peak-time *Brains Trust*, with its 10–12 million listeners, the pages of the *Listener*, with its circulation approaching 150,000, and the day's most prestigious scientific and cultural journals, including *Nature* and Cyril Connolly's *Horizon*.[139]

Always skilled at pitching his ideas to different audiences and media, Bernal now saw world civilization at a dialectical switchpoint between its discredited 'liberal individualistic' phase inaugurated by the Renaissance and the 'consciously directed human society' pioneered by the Soviet Union.[140] For Bernal, the ruling class knew that its anarchic, anachronistic system had been incapable of beating fascism and that Soviet-style national planning had been mobilized as 'a condition of national survival.'[141] The wartime Anglo-Soviet alliance was never, therefore, merely a military alignment but possessed an irresistible historical logic: the future lay in the scientifically informed planning with which the wartime British state had been forced to improvise.[142] The genie, Bernal hoped, would not go back in the bottle, and he and his associates now used the institutions through which they had worked since the 1930s, especially the Association of Scientific Workers (AScW), to promote the refashioning of Britain's economy in these terms. No longer merely a think tank committed to analysing the social relations of science, the association registered as a trade union in 1941, affiliated to the TUC in 1942, and had 11,000 members by 1943 – a tenfold increase on its 1939 membership mainly comprising technicians and industrial scientists – and 8,000 more by 1947, at which point Bernal became president.[143] Through the war, the scientific Left also established a stronger presence in the traditionally conservative British Association for the Advancement of Science; Bernal was elected to its council in 1946.[144] The prestige of Bernallian science within the party was such that its National Science Advisory advised the Industrial Department, rather than the other way round, and the party was naturally keen to associate itself with these culturally prominent scientists and their visions.[145] A regular contributor to the *Daily Worker* since the late 1930s, Haldane had become the chair of the newspaper's editorial board in 1940, joined the party in 1942, was elected to the Executive Committee in 1943, and was visibly deployed to emphasize the link between science and Communism during the 1945 General Election.[146] But the more important question was the scientists' influence over national and international institutions, and debates and policies around reconstruction; here too they were sporadically successful. On the international stage, Bernal was at the fore in the creation of the World Federation of Scientific Workers (WFSW) in July 1946, an influential front organization dominated by British and French Communists and committed to 'the fullest utilisation of science and the greatest degree of cooperation' among scientists globally.[147] With others on the Left, he played a significant part in bringing a scientific dimension to the identity of the newly formed United Nations Educational, Scientific and Cultural Organization, whose work the WFSW supported.[148] The overriding objective was to make nation-states' interventionist planning and organization of science an automatic process, and Bernal's subsequent claim to have played an important role in shifting the discourse is generally justified.[149] At home, addressing the broader Left and strategically working with the upbeat collaborationist rhetoric of the Tehran gathering, Bernal tirelessly pressed the case for a 'new industrial revolution' in which a modern British economy would be undergirded by the levels of scientific research already supported by the other two of the 'Big Three': the United States and the Soviet Union.[150] That the post-war Labour Party's *raison d'être* was to eradicate the 'technical backwardness' of inter-war capitalism made it receptive to Bernal's lessons, as did the conspicuous lack of its own coherent scientific policy.[151] Bernal met minimal resistance, and the new government's vagueness around scientific matters was soon corrected by a distinctly Bernallian rhetoric through the unlikely conduit of Lord President of the Privy Council, Herbert Morrison, who attended a conference organized by the AScW in 1946. Bernal was soon appointed chairman of the Ministry of Works' Scientific Advisory Committee; at the same time, the imperatives of reconstruction also reinvigorated the TUC's moribund Scientific Advisory Committee, in which AScW figures were active.[152] It was a propitious turn for Communists in which Bernallian positions about the form and function of science in modern societies, potently defused through established and new institutions, were coming to seem a political common sense.

Rebuilding Britain

The crisis in working-class housing against which Communists had long campaigned was now irrefutable: few houses had been built during the war, and around half a million homes had been destroyed or made uninhabitable by the Luftwaffe.[153] The population had grown by a million, and three and a half million demobilized service personnel were returning home.[154] It was no longer controversial that what the former minister of food Lord Woolton called the 'machine of government' was responsible for solving the crisis; his private view was that its failure would create 'the tendency and the excuse for revolution.'[155] The Barlow Report (1940) and the Scott and Uthwatt Commissions (1942) were in different ways blueprints for a nationalized, planned solution, and were welcomed by Communists as 'a shattering condemnation of "laissez-faire" economics.'[156] Eager to outflank Labour, even Churchill invoked a Soviet-sounding 'Four Year Plan' as necessary to solve the housing shortage in March 1943, and a White Paper of March 1945 suggested that 3–4 million houses needed to be built by the late 1950s, a turn welcomed by the party's Building Bureau.[157]

In the past the argument was that the 'proletarian order' would be necessary before the building industry could achieve 'important conquests.'[158] Now those conquests were seen as route maps to the latter, and party members and fellow-travellers were actively engaged in the planning and rebuilding of Britain. As the radical edge of a broader consensus, Communists were prominent in the bodies through which the physical reconstruction of Britain was coordinated, and enjoyed profiles and influence within and beyond their respective professions. As well as his role as chair of the Ministry of Works' Scientific Advisory Committee, Bernal was an adviser for the Building Research Station and the Architectural Science Board; across all three, he was assiduous in seeking to bring scientific research to bear on building practice.[159] In this capacity he was also vociferous on the BBC, arguing that the living spaces required by modern civilization were incompatible with private property, monopoly, and class privilege, whose record was rotting slums.[160] Fellow-traveller and future Stalin Peace Prize winner, Dr Monica Felton (1906–70) was another regular BBC contributor active in shaping public discourse on housing questions, and was directly involved in envisaging Britain's post-war built environment, working on the New Towns Committee with Sir John Reith before becoming vice-chair of the development committees for the New Towns of Stevenage (1947) and Peterlee (1948), hiring Berthold Lubetkin to work as an architect on the latter project.[161] Lubetkin envisaged for the miners of the North East a high-rise, modernist Peterlee befitting their 'loyalty, cohesion and courage.' He was dismissive of the suburban atmosphere he associated with most New Towns, and had never lost his materialist conviction that beautiful, functional public buildings could be a premonition of a better world.[162] His plans soon ran into well-documented problems, but his modernist vision found expression in his Spa Green Estate (1943–50), opposite Sadler's Wells, for which the minister of health with responsibility for housing, Nye Bevan, approvingly laid the foundation stone.[163] Communist architects in private practices, notably Lubetkin's Tecton, enjoyed new influence and contracts as the rebuilding began in earnest, with Tecton strengthening its long-standing relationship with Finsbury Council.[164] Communist and fellow-travelling planners trained in the 1930s were now also rising up through their profession in the public sector, including Frederick Gibberd (1908–84), who oversaw the design of Harlow, and Arthur Ling (1913–95), author of *Planning and Building in the USSR* (1943) and an assistant to Britain's most eminent planner, Professor Abercrombie, in the preparation of *The County of London Plan* (1943) and *The Greater London Plan* (1944). Ling went on not only to become in 1945 the chief planning officer at the London County Council, where between fifteen and twenty Communist Party architects were employed, but a key architect of post-war Coventry.[165] More significant still in bringing a Communist accent to the debate on architectural reconstruction was the Association of Architects, Surveyors and Technical Assistants, built up during the Popular Front, all of whose full-time officials were Communists and whose membership was energized by the union's unequivocal support for the war effort from mid-1941: membership rose sharply from 1,568 in November 1941 to 2,883 in October 1943, with branches almost doubling in number in the twelve months from December 1941.[166]

Soviet culture remained a source of professional and cultural prestige for Communists in planning and architecture: the sheer scale of Soviet reconstruction outshone, for now, less edifying prescriptions about socialist realism.[167] At the Architectural Association School, 25 out of 500 students, or 5 per cent, were in the Communist Party by 1950.[168] Another source of cultural authority in architecture was Communist science, especially a distinctly Bernallian discourse that saw in the coordinated combination of science and architecture a break with the competition and specialization that had characterized the epoch of industrial capitalism.[169] This discourse emphasized architects working in comradely, dynamic, mutually enriching collaboration with surveyors, engineers, researchers, technicians, designers, and builders, a tendency reflected in the union's new name, the Association of Building Technicians (ABT). Seeking to extend and deepen wartime collaborative practices, the post-war ABT actively promoted group working in public offices and factory-style Joint Production Committees throughout the building industry, measures conscientiously applied in the construction of the sleek new *Daily Worker* premises in Farringdon Road, designed by ABT member and fellow-traveller Ernö Goldfinger.[170]

Communists naturally attacked the Churchill government for falling short of the recommendations of Barlow, Scott, and Uthwatt, and for pledging to build only 300,000 houses in the first two years of peace, but approvingly pored over Labour's policies on planning through 1943. Expecting to find there a broad framework with which they could engage, they were not disappointed.[171] They welcomed the Attlee government's rash electoral pledge to build five million homes in 'quick time,' having themselves proposed a slightly lower figure, and endorsed Bevan's strategy of prioritizing low-income groups and of tackling the crisis by empowering local authorities to build subsidized houses for rent.[172] Links between party architects in the ABT and Bevan, the incoming, overstretched minister reponsible for housing, were immediately close.[173]

Bevan addressed the ABT conference, 'The Technician's Part in Housing,' in November 1945, and wrote the foreword to the ABT book, *Homes for the People*, edited by party architects Colin Penn and Andrew Boyd.[174] Bernal was tasked by Bevan to research for the government the best options among the 1,300 types of prefabricated houses on offer.[175] Bevan, whose architectural vision was conservative and suburban, viewed such accommodation as 'rabbit hutches,' but Communists like Bernal saw the post-war moment as an opportunity to push forward in the name of technologically driven modernity: for Bernal, the best available prefabs were glimpses of a scientifically planned and mass-assembled future.[176] He kept his counsel when Bevan disregarded his advice and invested in cheap prefabricated models, 125,000 of which were assembled by 1948.[177]

Differences over prefabrication were contained in the name of unity, but it was in the highly combustible sphere of access to housing – voters' most important concern in 1945 – that the challenges of retaining a distinct Communist identity within a broad process of reconstruction came to a head in the squatters' movement of 1946, especially its the lesser-known second phase.[178] Here the party's London District sought to sustain and direct the momentum of that summer's mass squatting in military camps by 46,000 people. Party members led the occupation of five blocks of privately owned luxury flats and a hotel in the capital, most of which had been used by the government during the war.[179] Apparently unauthorized by the party's central leadership, this was a savvy intervention. It was technically an act of support for the Attlee government – the party targeted properties in those Tory-run boroughs reluctant to exercise their right to requisition properties for housing – but one that exceeded their allies in challenging the basic logic of private property through redeploying direct-action street politics that had no place in Labourism and that had served the Communist Party well in the occupation of the Savoy's air-raid facilities during the Blitz.[180] Broad support of the government, however, was evidently more important than confrontation with it, and after nine days the party advised squatters to withdraw from the occupied and besieged buildings, having been taken aback by the uncomradely ferocity of the government's response (heavy policing, the disconnection of power and water supplies, writs against individual squatters, the arrest of four Communist councillors on conspiracy charges). In fact the party had already drawn blood: it was the *Observer* rather than the *Daily Worker* that noted the focusing of local government's minds that followed, commenting that many Local Authorities had done 'more in the last few days than in the last few months.'[181] The lenient sentencing suggested there was no desire by the government for a *cause célèbre* likely to foment further resistance.[182] Party documents were justified in citing here an example of how the party could give 'new hope,' challenge Labour's 'toleration of abuses,' and 'improve conditions for the workers.'[183] They might have put it more strongly, as Jack Lindsay did in his fictional reworking of the squatters' campaign in his novel *Betrayed Spring* (1953).[184] In fact the London District had worked with the grain of popular impulses, and combined characteristic organizational efficiency, the long-earned credibility with London's working-class community on questions of housing that had aided the 1945 election of Communist MP Phil Piratin (1907–95), and its wartime social and moral authority. It had briefly become an effective if hesitant vanguard through direct action, exposing and exceeding the government in enacting a confrontation between human need and the system that thwarted it, dramatizing a solution – families in empty properties – and prefiguring the more radical transformations airily described in party propaganda.[185] But ultimately it was an exception that proved the rule: business as usual was a more tentative approach of 'constructive opposition' towards Labour in which the first word was taken more seriously than the second.

New School Ties

In the past, Communist involvement in debates about school education had been curbed by a dominant reflex – sometimes challenged, never vanquished – that regarded educational structures and practices as an unreformable capitalist superstructure to be confronted after the seizure of the state.[186] Even in the Popular Front period, when 88 per cent of all children and almost all of the working class were consigned to elementary schools in which the mere separation of younger and older children was considered a pedagogical innovation,[187] the party had strategically avoided radical proposals in the name of building antifascist unity among teachers.[188] Now, however, with reconstruction hazily seen as a *sine qua non* of socialism, rather than a consequence of it, Communist teachers moved to the forefront of struggles over the future of education. A recently created National Educational Advisory Committee (NEAC) coordinated activity and formulated policy.[189]

A new emphasis held that valuable reform of the structure of school education was possible, a position that led to Communist support for the Council for Education Advance from its formation in May 1942.[190] This novel position of campaigning for specific legislation now aligned with the more established one of winning union influence.[191] Head of Acton Grammar School and newly elected CP Executive Committee member G.C.T. Giles became vice-president and then president of the NUT while the 1944 Education Act was being prepared, and was consulted in this capacity by the president of the Board of Education and minister for education, R.A. Butler.[192] Giles duly fed in key NEAC positions.[193] These insisted that established hierarchies should be dissolved, and teachers should more actively determine practice through 'consultative committees' modelled on the wartime JPCs; the whole educational system should be brought under national or local control, with no private sector or exemptions for religious schools; local authorities should provide nursery education; the school leaving age should be raised to sixteen; and compulsory full- or part-time provision secured for sixteen-to-eighteen-year-olds.[194]

In order to remain within the discussion's framework, the party held back for now on proposals about curriculum and pedagogy. And despite some divisive misgivings about religion in schools and the existence of the private sector, it supported the broad thrust of the 1944 Education Act, which raised the school leaving age to fifteen, pledged free secondary education for all, and abolished grammar school fees.[195] The central issue, however – the future structure of secondary education – was left open by the Act, which declined to prescribe the future form of secondary education, instead delegating the vexed question to local authorities.[196] Inside the incoming Labour Party, the Left-liberal consensus for radical change that had built across the labour movement through the 1920s and 1930s collapsed now that real change looked possible. Notionally committed to what was then called the non-selecting 'multilateral' or 'common' school, Labour saw few votes in education, and remained attached to grammar schools as engines of working-class social mobility. Increasingly the government's position reproduced, rather than broke with, pre–Butler Act 'common sense' on education, which saw children as either academic (destined for grammar school and white-collar occupations), technically minded ('technical schools,' skilled working-class work), or neither ('modern schools,' unskilled work), and was soon recommending that all three types of corresponding schools – which essentially replicated what had previously existed – should be maintained.[197] Since May 1942, Communists, on the other hand, had been committed to a one-model system of secondary schooling, and were distinct among allies in insisting that all children should be taught the same curriculum until fifteen or sixteen. They took issue with a fudged version of the 'multilateral' school that simply brought the existing models under the same school roof.[198] From 1944 Communists used the word 'comprehensive' to signal the more integrated system they favoured.[199]

The 'three-headed myth' of the Butler Act was attacked as a 'sham' that reproduced existing class divisions. The fundamental principle of an educational democracy was defended against a system that could be manipulated by those with the necessary educational knowledge and cultural capital.[200] Teachers were already the party's biggest professional cohort, and their numbers were swelled year on year by the fast-track Emergency Training Scheme, introduced in May 1944 to create the 70,000 new teachers necessary to staff the new classrooms created by the 1944 Education Act's raising of the leaving age by a year.[201] Relevant educational and cultural experience was now taken into account in lieu of traditional academic qualifications, a policy which opened the profession to applicants from working-class backgrounds, including those shaped by the autodidact traditions of the labour movement. Among the thousand candidates per week putting themselves forward by the end of 1946 were many individual demobilized Communists in search of secure, stimulating work broadly aligned with the party's direction of travel;[202] by 1949, 2,000, or five per cent, of the party's total 40,000 membership were in the profession – around 1 per cent of the national total of teachers.[203] Some of these eagerly anticipated a day when Marxism could be taught openly, and even lapsed prematurely into lessons in elementary class consciousness, imploring working-class seven-year-olds to recognize 'their responsibility as future workers and leaders of the country.'[204] Others argued in the party press that Communists needed to confront more directly a curriculum and pedagogy that was geared to the production of 'efficient wage-slaves'; the official line was that the Butler Act provided 'the structural opportunity for radical and fundamental changes' in the 'purpose, content and methods of education.'[205] For Communists including the recently demobilized Brian Simon, now a teacher in the North West, the form and content of education were indeed powerfully linked: an 'overall reconstruction of educational practice using modern methods and techniques' was needed, he argued, with classroom practices geared to 'defined and desirable ends.'[206]

Over the next few years, Simon and others would begin to inscribe these formulations with more specific content. Education, Communists argued, was necessary for the advance of democracy and the creation of an active and civic-spirited population capable of holding to account 'elected rulers and appointed administrators'; the truly comprehensive school was viewed as a force for democratization and the breaking up of class divisions.[207] Simon went further, arguing that egalitarian comprehensive education potentially could shape and anticipate socialist consciousness, and was therefore a key site of political struggle whose transformation was propitious for Communist advance.[208] An impediment to this was the classics-based grammar school curriculum favoured by many in the Labour Party, which was considered to encourage passive appreciation and intellectual deference and to promote individual attainment over 'self-discipline and co-operation.'[209] The new structures would require new textbooks, which Communists proposed to write.[210] Science was to the fore, and Bernal was often cited in party interventions.[211] In broad support of the government, Communists now functioned effectively as self-styled representatives of Labour's better conscience, staying true to a position from which Attlee's cabinet was backsliding. They strove to formulate and sustain alternative conceptions, working with and through the unions, especially the NUT, local authorities, and the National Association of Labour Teachers to argue the case for more fundamental restructuring. Like Bernal in science and architecture, they communicated effectively on many fronts, challenging compromise formations in the *Times Educational Supplement*, on prime-time national radio, and most extensively in Giles's quasi-official conspectus of post-war education, *The New School Tie* (1946), written for Charles Madge's prestigious Pilot Press series, consignments of which were bought in bulk by the Army Bureau of Current Affairs and used as textbooks.[212] The government capitulated. The new types of schools went unbuilt and the more radical textbooks unwritten: there were only twenty genuine comprehensive schools in England and Wales by the time the Conservative victory in the 1951 election buried the question for over a decade.[213] Communists continued to recruit well in the teaching profession, launching a new journal, *The Educational Bulletin* in 1948 that was selling 3,000 copies per issue by the early 1950s.[214] Despite the well-known Cold War marginalization and victimization that followed, Communist teachers remained principled advocates in the long-haul struggle for comprehensive education, partially achieved in 1965.[215]

The Universities

The loose idea that Communists were champions of processes of economic modernization and reconstruction that would prime the ground for more radical transformations made universities matter more. Communists welcomed the post-war trebling of expenditure on universities between 1939 and 1950, which saw student numbers increasing from 38,000 in 1945 to 50,000, regarding this as a necessary dimension of educational, economic, and cultural modernization.[216] On one level this was a structural question that saw as necessary the expansion and dilution of a sector whose class composition made it traditionally resistant to Communist penetration.[217] The challenge of wartime campus organization had been merely to maintain a 'skeleton party' presence so that party organization could resume 'when conditions returned to normal.'[218] In fact, the unforeseen scale of the abnormality of the late war and immediate post-war period pleased Communists, who welcomed the more hospitable atmosphere on campuses created by the influx of 30,000 demobilized armed forces personnel – many of them working class – and sought to engage this khaki transformation.[219] Projections were upscaled to winning 'the leadership and support of the majority of students' through concerted recruitment drives.[220] Just as professionals had been actively targeted with carefully pitched propaganda, so now were students, the professionals of the future. A glossy leaflet was distributed across campuses that presented the party's support for industrial nationalization, increased productivity, and the extension of social services as means to secure the economic future of graduates. A new form of Communist iconography was deployed, identifying not industrial workers, but middle-class Communist martyrs – Frank Thompson (1920–44), John Cornford (1915–36) – and some of the world's best brains as 'turning to Communism' including Picasso, Joliot-Curie, and Prokofiev.[221] By 1946, the party had around 600 student members, or 1 per cent of the total student body – including the NUS president Tony James, a University College London

(UCL) chemistry graduate student – organized across twenty branches. It was a promising foundation on which to build, but one whose enabling discourse of national cultural reconstruction and modernity would be rapidly undermined by the Cold War beginning in 1948, when the party would revert to a more oppositional position that identified universities as citadels of 'the ideas of the present ruling class.'[222]

A small number of Communist academics secured posts in what one of them, Eric Hobsbawm, called the 'brief relaxation of anti-communism' that followed the war. The influx significantly swelled the party's miniscule University's Teachers' Group, whose stalwarts were Roy Pascal (1904–80) and George Thomson (1903–87) at Birmingham, Maurice Dobb at Cambridge, Haldane at UCL, Bernal at Birkbeck, Hyman Levy at Imperial College, and classicist Benjamin Farrington (1891–1974) at Swansea.[223] Between 1946 and 1948, they were joined by young academics including Hobsbawm at Birkbeck, Medievalist Rodney Hilton (1916–2002) at Birmingham, English lecturer Arnold Kettle (1916–86) at Cambridge, then Leeds, economic historian John Saville and sociologist and art historian Francis Klingender at the University College of Hull, and Victor Kiernan (1913–2009) at Edinburgh. Ron Bellamy (1917–2009) was hired at Christ Church, Oxford, in 1946, moving to Leeds two years later, the same time that E.P. Thompson joined the Extra Mural Department there.[224] These new appointments augmented Communist influence in the academics' union, the Association of University Teachers – Pascal was president in 1944–45 – and created the necessary critical mass for the specialist groups whose formation the party encouraged. The most significant of these was the scientists' Engels Society and the Historians' Group, established in 1946 (analysed in the next chapter), which added critical mass that shaped party publishing initiatives – notably, Benjamin Farrington's 'Past and Present' series, which supplanted his wartime 'Marxism Today' pamphlets with more developed and scholarly titles from academics within and beyond the party, including anthropologist Gordon Childe.[225] With more members in what were now seen as key locations in the struggle for economic and cultural reconstruction, the party's Organising Committee took an unprecedented interest in university affairs, approvingly scrutinizing the rulebook of the newly formed Cambridge Graduate Communist Party, an organization created in 1946 and chaired by Maurice Dobb, which existed to support critically the government's process of national university expansion and democratic restructuring and to confront 'resistance to such change' from 'senior Universities.' Overlapping in personnel with the party's retitled University Staff Committee, the group's remit would include making policy suggestions on higher education, campaigning for university senate elections, and correcting ivory-towerism by reminding Communist academics of their 'special role and responsibilities' to the wider labour movement.[226]

Why STUDENTS should be COMMUNISTS

WITH the destruction of fascism, the most barbarous force in the history of the world, the biggest obstacle to the progress of humanity has been removed.

By electing a Labour Government the people took a long step towards building a free and prosperous country.

But this is only a prelude to what can and must be done. Peace must be made secure. Students need peace if they are to study and follow their professions.

The new Government must push on to nationalise the key industries, to expand production for consumption and trade, and to extend the social services. This will give the student—whether he is to be doctor, teacher, scientist or architect—assurance of constant employment, and will raise science and the arts to a new level. Atomic energy must be put to work to increase the world's wealth and to

FRANK THOMPSON
Formerly of New College, Oxford. Major Thompson fought with the Bulgarian partisans and was murdered by the occupying Gestapo in June, 1944, when he was only 23 years old. His valour and magnificent spirit has been recognised by the Bulgarians, who recently proclaimed him one of Bulgaria's "National Heroes".

Student recruitment leaflet, 1946. CP Archive, LHASC, Manchester.

Adult Education

No such reminders were necessary in the more working-class field of adult education. For Churchill, the Army Bureau of Current Affairs, running education classes in six out of ten military units by 1942, had provided openings for 'the agitator with a glib tongue.'[227] Letters from his MPs urged him to stamp out an organization allegedly turning the British forces 'pansy pink.'[228] For the broader Left, the ABCA was one of a number of cultural phenomena suggesting that the war had released popular creative and intellectual energies blocked by inter-war structural and educational inequalities, and that the 150,000 people who typically participated in formal adult education were a fraction of those who might be reached. The 1944 Education Act further resourced the adult education sector (fourteen members of the Attlee government had been tutors, students, or executives of the Workers' Educational Association, WEA). The expectation was that the incoming government would take the sector seriously.[229]

A report produced by the party's educational committee in August 1945 mapped the terrain, and argued that the conditions were ripe for the spread of Marxist education through the established and burgeoning institutions of adult education.[230] It reported that the Co-operative Education Committees spent £25,000 per year and were not hostile to Communism; the National Council of Labour Colleges boasted eighty-three national affiliated bodies, including forty-three trade unions, ran postal courses for 12,5000 students, and taught classes for a further 11,500; the WEA had 35,8000 individual members, 90,000 students taking courses, and a leading role in the Workers' Education Trade Union Committee, which had provided 4,710 classes for 85,000 students in 1944. The report was also critical of the party's inward and even sectarian tendencies through which it had 'held aloof' and 'not yet played a leading role' in adult education. It had few links with the Co-op, had largely severed ties with the NCLC back in the 1920s, and was generally dismissive of the WEA, having preferred to channel its energy and resources into the training of cadres through party schools and Marx House. But a new stage had now been reached, ran the argument, which called for more constructive engagement. The dissemination of Marxist thought through the educational networks of the working-class movement was 'inevitably the responsibility' of the party. The party must look outwards from Marx House, pressurize the labour movement to make greater use of existing structures, and get its people into existing organizations, where they should work in a non-dogmatic way, eschewing theoretical abstraction in favour of the concrete application of Marxism to pressing matters.

There was evidently no great enthusiasm for the proposals in the upper echelons of the party. The report was never published, Pollitt was deeply attached to Marx House, and the traditionally Leninist education officer, Douglas Garman, continued to focus on cadre training.[231] But the adoption of these new principles at the 1945 Congress nonetheless released considerable energy that gathered its own momentum.[232] This focused on the largest sphere, the complicated institutional networks of the WEA – especially in the university extramural departments that delivered much of the WEA's provision. Every university with the exception of Reading would have such a department by 1947, and Communists already had a toehold in the WEA, where a handful of individual members had been earning a living since the 1930s. The most significant of these was Thomas Hodgkin (1910–82), a Popular Front recruit with a long career in adult education who was appointed as secretary of the Oxford Extra Mural Studies Delegacy and a professorial fellow at Balliol in September 1945.[233] He found himself in the right place: the Oxford Delegacy intermeshed historically and organizationally with the WEA, and provided classes across Berkshire, Buckinghamshire, Kent, Lincoln, North Staffordshire, and Sussex.[234] The sector was growing fast in this period, with the number of staff tutors increasing from 70 in 1939 to 207 in 1953, and Hodgkin's own university trebled funds for adult education under the Attlee government.[235] Hodgkin was in a position to hire, and the expanding sector was an attractive destination for demobilized Communists where the needs of class loyalty, intellectual expression, and a decent salary could be reconciled, and Hodgkin built around him a team of the like-minded with some input from Garman.[236] Under Hodgkin, around ten out of thirty-one of the Oxford Delegacies' full-time tutors were either Communists or fellow-travellers, and the party established an Adult Education Group in which experiences were shared and priorities formulated.[237] The Communist WEA presence began to spread nationally: the pro-Soviet A.T. D'Eye and the Communist J.A. Mclean were in Kent; the now former Communist Raymond Williams was hired by Hodgkin and based in East Sussex; Communist John Saville was at Hull, and Ron Bellamy and E.P. Thompson were at Leeds. There was a particular concentration of the values promoted by Hodgkin in the Delegacy's central initiative of the period, the Wedgewood Memorial College at Barlaston Hall in North Staffordshire. Opened in July 1947, the college was run in collaboration with the WEA and the local authorities; at least four of its full-time tutors, plus the warden, J. Vickers, were Communists.[238]

Charismatic and intellectually articulate, Hodgkin held what Raymond Williams remembered as 'a very strong and principled conception of how to develop a popular working-class education.'[239] Individual tutors working remotely from Oxford enjoyed much freedom in what and how they taught the 4,000 students enrolled through the Delegacy.[240] There was also a strongly shared concern among those close to Hodgkin – by no means all Communists – to constitute adult education as a space for working-class empowerment as opposed to a mode of social mobility or assimilation into the dominant culture.[241] From there, more particular priorities emerged: maintaining, developing, and strengthening links with the trade unions through the Workers' Education Trade Union

Committee; extending the reach of shorter courses, which were not assessed by written work and were therefore more accessible to workers without secondary education or much spare time; and increasing access to the three-year-long university-level Tutorial Courses, which were always in danger of being prioritized by the universities and dominated by more privileged students.[242] The traditional educational and pedagogical ethos of the WEA was 'to cultivate powers and to form intellectual habits which are the necessary basis of good citizenship and social activity.'[243] In that context, Hodgkin promoted engagement with contemporary issues – including the politics of reconstruction – and supported the right of tutors to declare their own political position as long as this was what Williams called 'totally challengeable, naturally subject to opposition and discussion.'[244] The emphasis was not political persuasion or recruitment but the opening of minds through the rigours of a dialectical method. 'One believed,' Hodgkin later commented, 'that if one taught honestly and seriously and raised basic and serious problems in whatever one was teaching, people would find their way to Marxism.'[245] Although almost immediately subsumed in the bitter Cold War ideological divisions that brought an end to warden Vickers's contract in 1949, the breaking up of the radical group, and the onset of defensive struggles for those who remained, Barlaston Hall was briefly a hub for Hodgkin's vision of the theory and practice of adult education.[246]

The Arts

'The revival of culture,' Edgell Rickword wrote in *Our Time* in September 1945, 'now necessitates the intervention of organs of democratic government as a part of the general planning of our material and intellectual resources.'[247] The journal and its key intellectuals had been at the forefront of the 'cultural upsurge.' Debate about the forms that such state intervention should take, however – notably around the key event of national cultural reconstruction, the formation of the Arts Council in mid-1945 – now revealed tensions and some anachronistic limitations in the thinking of the party's cultural wing, which contained the most passionate advocates of wider struggle across civil society. Much later, New Left critics including Francis Mulhern and Alan Sinfield would see the Arts Council as an expression of the cultural logic of post-war Keynesian social democracy, or 'welfare capitalism,' a medium through which an inter-war 'liberal minority culture,' whose most significant groups centred around the Bloomsbury circle and Leavis's *Scrutiny*, 'would be diffused through an ever-widening audience' without any 'fundamental questioning of what counted as cultural value or the proper forms of cultural participation.'[248] There are grounds to put it more strongly and to see the moment's top-down diffusion as the cultural logic of capitalist stabilization, or as a process of 'passive revolution' in Gramsci's terminology, through which the ruling bloc maintained and extended its definition of culture – a body of great works awaiting appropriate appreciation – through the mechanism that otherwise challenged its power, namely state planning.[249] Communists, who advocated a separate 'Ministry of Fine Arts,' asked few fundamental questions about the process.[250] They shared much ground with Leavis's Scrutineers – especially over the lamentable loss of a common culture said to arise organically from agrarian labour – and mostly harboured a begrudging respect for Bloomsbury, a bugaboo viewed with friendly contempt whose imprint on the Labour Party's thinking and the nascent Arts Council in the figure of John Maynard Keynes enhanced rather than reduced the organization's appeal for them.[251] It was apparent from the strong resemblances between the cultural proposals contained in *Britain for the People* (1944) and the Labour Party's 1945 General Election Manifesto that Communist discourse on cultural reconstruction shared more with Labour than it would have ever owned, with the cultural thinking left to party intellectuals who, like Labour's equivalent figures, were middle-class dissidents shaped by and unquestioningly committed to high culture.[252] The formation of both groups was as 'traditional intellectuals' in Gramsci's terms, a cultural aristocracy close to dominant logic around matters of cultural value.[253] The essentially diffusionist discourse of both parties duly assumed culture to be a stable body of great works awaiting dissemination amongst the culturally disenfranchised.[254] What made it worse for the Communists was that a culture of habitually privileging masculine proletarian identity paradoxically narrowed the cultural debate and entrenched divisions by excusing working-class cadres with different perspectives from what were seen as relatively unimportant cultural discussions. Insight into culture was simply not what was expected from industrial cadres – they were too important for cultural matters; inside the party as out, the culture of their communities was not recognized as culture at all. This outlook served to exclude from cultural discussion the perspectives of rank-and-file working-class Communists of both sexes whose perspectives on what counted as cultural participation might have productively unsettled the analytical framework and given the party something distinctive to say. Lacking either a strong regional presence or an alternative cultural discourse committed to popular education and popular culture, the party's cultural wing consequently reproduced rather than challenged the contradictions that the cash-strapped Arts Council itself could not resolve.[255] The party naturally affirmed centrifugal energies, from the wartime Forces Centres in Salisbury – a requisitioned furniture showroom that became an art and educational centre used by a thousand service men and women per week.[256] And it endorsed the Arts Council's *Plans for an Arts Centre* and the White Paper on Community Centres, which proposed the building of prefabricated centres in small towns.[257] That leading cultural Communists struggled to imagine how wartime 'cultural upsurge' might be developed and transformed in the post-war context, however, was apparent even from Jack Lindsay's novel *Time to Live* (1946), which, drawing perhaps surprising inspiration from the White Paper, dramatized a London community's coming together for a street party. Lindsay's notional theme was collective social and cultural empowerment and transformation, but the emphasis instead fell on the individual, a Lindsayian, alienated, young middle-class novelist struggling to find his true subject matter.[258]

These tensions and blind spots around the meaning of the cultural democratization promised in *Britain for the People* came sharply to a head in the world of theatre, where the legacy of Popular Front–period innovations – notably the formation of Unity Theatre – gave the party a strong presence, not least in theatre journalism.[259] A broadened Unity Theatre now incorporated into its General Council key labour movement figures and theatre professionals, including London Trades Council secretary Julius Jacobs, Geoffrey Whitworth, founder and secretary of amateur theatre's national body, the British Drama League, and long-standing fellow-travellers J.B. Priestley and Michael Redgrave. There was a growing recognition that the consolidation of the nascent Arts Council's investment in existing and predominantly metropolitan institutions potentially shored up the status quo, and Unity's March 1946 conference 'Theatre and the People,' which involved Arts Council representatives,[260] duly stressed the importance of amateur theatre aerating the professional centre.[261] Reflecting broader discussions within the party around cultural priorities and strategy, Communists were themselves torn. Some emphasized sustaining wartime participatory and grassroots culture as an antidote to passivity through deepening and developing the cultural upsurge of amateur mass-cultural participation from which its own organizations had benefited (Unity's membership had boomed to 10,000 by May 1947).[262] Others stressed greater professionalization and the accumulation of high cultural prestige in the name of winning state subsidies in a context where the cautious Arts Council increasingly funded only professional theatre. After much acrimony, professional companies were formed inside Unity, which attracted limited Arts Council support but failed – quickly in London, more gradually in Scotland.[263]

Other perspectives were available in these struggles to imagine a progressive culture, however – notably those of former leading lights in the pre-war Manchester theatre scene, Joan Littlewood and Jimmie Miller/Ewan MacColl (1915–89), who saw in post-war Britain a fundamentally new conjuncture open for bolder culturally interventions that would overturn the existing cultural frameworks of high, middle, and low. This was a time, they argued, for a freshly conceived type of popular culture, a theatre 'arising out of the needs of the most important and vital sections of society,' those 'young men and women who have fought for civilization' and who sought – here they echoed the rhetoric of *Britain for the People* – a 'richer, fuller life for themselves and their children.'[264] Young, working-class, largely self-educated Communists attuned to popular culture's pleasures, they were beyond the range of the party's central cultural apparatus and assumptions, and confident in their ability to attract to the theatre those who had rarely, if ever been and to incorporate 'high' and 'low' in forms relevant to what MacColl termed 'the radio and film generation.'[265] Jack Lindsay lamented that, for culturally starved workers, 'drama' meant the *News of the World*.[266] For MacColl and Littlewood, workers' innocence of dominant theatrical conventions made them receptive to genuine innovation.[267] While London's new professional Unity group would court the government with a worthy 1930s-style living newspaper that supported the nationalized coal industry's production drive and Glasgow's would seek to bring vernacular realist theatre to London's theatreland, Theatre Workshop was testing its theories among the people in a gruelling tour of places remote from the country's cultural centres. Most strikingly, the company brought their work to the brave new world of post-war mass leisure, staging MacColl's balletic history of modern science, *Uranium 235*, for the campers during a residency at Billy Butlin's Filey holiday camp in the early summer of 1946 as part of a scheme that saw the former Armed Services camp also play host to the San Carlo Opera and the Old Vic.[268] For J.B. Priestley, who visited Butlin's at the same time, there was 'too much noise and fuss on the surface' of the usual camp entertainment schedule 'and too little going on down in the depths.'[269] For Theatre Workshop, such high-low definitions and assumptions were precisely the problem: there was nothing inherently deep about ballet or fixed and superficial about entertainment at Butlin's: culture was open for reconfiguration. Disregarding high-low opposition, Theatre Workshop deployed a bewildering mix of cinematic-style lighting, film pastiche, radio voiceover, jitterbugging, and popular song all folded into a loose, variety show structure in order to teach the apparently engaged and enthusiastic campers what the company had had to teach themselves in order to write and present the play: the history of science from ancient Greece to atomic physics and the Bomb. They concluded with Bernal's argument that science was a force for liberation perverted by an irrational system and that they – the people – must choose how it was applied in the future.[270] The media who stumbled across the show were perplexed but impressed, sensing a 'theatrical event of the first importance.'[271] The party's metropolitan cultural apparatus, however, was blocked by a combination of structures and assumptions from recognizing the resources available to it. Only dimly aware of the company, even the Swingler circle would appreciate it little more than the Arts Council, with which key assumptions were shared and which likewise conspicuously failed to offer support.[272] (Theatre Workshop would go unfunded; Unity soon lost its limited grant.)[273] Surveying the immediate post-war conjuncture, cultural historians and critics including Raymond Williams have persuasively argued that the absence of more theorized, radical perspectives on culture and popular consciousness prevented the Labour government from sustaining the 'cultural upsurge' by recognizing and resourcing those grassroots wartime educational and cultural currents in the ABCA and CEMA that were 'one of the sources of its hegemony' in 1945, but conspicuously not in 1951.[274] This is also true of the Communist Party in these years. The party was stuck in the same framework of assumptions, and lost some of its wartime momentum by reproducing rather than contesting the defensive reflexes of a cultural elite that sought sanctuary from post-war cultural change in the writings of Matthew Arnold – *Culture and Anarchy* (1869) was reprinted five times between 1935 and 1950 – and the creation of the Third Programme, whose always miniscule share of the national audience fell off to 0.9 per cent within a year.[275] Although they would have blanched at the suggestion, even leading cultural Communists who argued for a wider field of struggle were too traditionally minded and too close to diffusionist assumptions to resist the incorporation of wartime cultural energies into dominant cultural frameworks and to forge what Randall Swingler himself called 'an entirely new and immensely enriching way of life, of thought and action, a philosophy.'[276]

Theory Wars

Pollitt's controversial *Answers to Questions* (1944) asserted that the party needed to 'make the working class conscious of its own strength and what it has won.'[277] His follow-up *Looking Ahead* (1947) asserted that the reconstruction outlined in Labour's 1945 election manifesto would 'change the country in which we live, and change the minds of the people who live in it.'[278] In the first version, the creation of radical consciousness was identified as central to the party's work; in the second, such consciousness was assumed to arise naturally from the improvement in material conditions being delivered by the Labour government. The lack of clarity reflected a party that, despite its greatly increased membership and profile, lacked a theoretical framework for analysing popular consciousness, the components of the national culture, the processes of consent formation, or for appreciating, analysing, and developing its own often-impressive reconstruction-period advances into a long-haul strategy to build leadership across civil society. At the same time, the party was failing to gain traction in the traditional political contexts on which it increasingly focused. Unlike the mass French and Italian parties, the British party was outside government, and the prospects of socialist advance, according to its own analysis, depended on the Labour government's implementing its manifesto. The party's notional strategy was still loosely articulated in the 'People's Democracy' model, seeing itself as a whalebone stiffening Labour's corset. But there was no reason for the majority Labour government to be anything but oblivious to such ideas, while the Communist Party itself struggled to formulate a clear line on its own relationship to the government. Party documents spoke imprecisely of supporting the government on one hand and challenging and correcting it on the other, but there was no clear measure for determining when each approach was appropriate.[279] Overwhelmingly the line taken meant staying within the parameters of Labour discourse and building little or no independent credit or prestige, especially in the industrial field, where its strength lay but where class collaboration in the name of raising production remained the key priority. The problems attendant on critically supporting a process of reconstruction being shaped by another organization would sharpen as the government, confronted with a balance-of-payments crisis and the notorious winter of 1946–7, tacked to the right.[280]

The party leadership's performance was now bumbling. Pollitt seemed at a loss, and Dutt was a diminished figure in a period of great turbulence that had seen, in quick succession, the dilution of membership, the disappearance of the Comintern, changes in party nomenclature, the downgrading of factory branches, and the upgrading of the professional strata in the context of reconstruction.[281] All this weakened traditional deference: archives covering the 1942–7 period are rich in letters and diaries of Communists dissatisfied with their leadership, the narrowness of party strategy, and its inability to think independently about the national road. Criticism was now often informed by unflattering comparison to the work of European parties to which wartime service had exposed many members.[282] Countercurrents challenging the leadership flared up between 1944 and 1946 in four key episodes: a long-running debate in the party weekly, *World News and Views* (1944), the submission of a tranche of highly critical branch resolutions prior to the Eighteenth Congress (November 1945) printed in *World News and Views*,[283] an explosive Writers' Group Aggregate meeting (November 1945), and a suppressed journal article (1946).

The voices of more traditionally minded 'anti-revisionist' Communists decrying 'serious retreats from the basic position of the Leninist Party' have been recovered and documented.[284] Those of others, which reactivated earlier cultural countercurrents and anticipated later ones, raising pressing questions about the identity, purpose, and strategy of the CPGB and Communist Parties more generally in the context of a transforming post-war world in the West, have been lost. One stream of criticism here flowed from the disjunction between the party's stubborn self-image – as Soviet facing, internationally oriented, traditional, proletarian, and industrially grounded – and its broader 'national front' wartime profile, demographic, and work. It came predominantly from an emboldened professional stratum that was centrally involved in the spheres of reconstruction, and committed to enlarging conceptions of the party and to clarifying the question of revolution's chronology – especially the relationship between radical interventions across civil society and the creation of socialism. Opening the first debate in *World News and Views* in the spring of 1944, Alastair Wilson (1913–81), a Communist doctor, councillor, and member of the South Wales District Committee, argued that the party was inward, sectarian, insufficiently grounded in national tradition and culture, and incapable of fulfilling its historic role while its 'conception' of the party and politics was 'too narrow.' Communism should be a 'way of life,' he argued, and needed to anticipate a better future in the present, producing not only disciplined cadres, but 'men and women who will be able to lead the British people' and whose all-round character the party should 'develop.'[285] Wilson and those sympathetic to him presented culture in the broad sense as a crucial site of consent formation, but one neglected by narrowly conceived political party activism. The ensuing debate was pulled between a traditional economism that saw culture as secondary – revolutions were made 'by the masses whom capitalism dooms to be uncultured' – and a new note that identified wartime cultural democratization, which brought to working people 'a taste of what the world can hold for them,' as a radical force in the formation of popular consciousness to which Communists needed better to attend in the future.[286] It was a discourse that anticipated J.B Priestley's in the pages of the *Daily Worker* later in the year.[287]

This line of critique was fleshed out and developed by Jack Lindsay, who circulated a brief document, 'Practice and Theory in Cultural Matters: Notes on a Basis for Discussion,' to key Communist writers and intellectuals early in 1945.[288] This argued that lingering anti-intellectualism and prolet-cult attitudes that regarded culture as an expression of class were anthropologically, historically, and theoretically misguided, as 'culture existed before classes and class war' and could not therefore 'be derived' from them. In reducing culture to a secondary manifestation of class position, he argued, dominant assumptions prevented party intellectuals from engaging convincingly with 'the general intellectual stream,' as their crude positions were easily dismissed. The model was no less damaging in legitimating a wider party logic that saw cultural struggle as secondary to 'real' politics, and blocked it from building prestige for Communism across civil society and constructing alliances for the party of the rising class. A more substantial paper, precirculated and then presented to an open meeting hosted by the party's Writers' Group in central London in November 1945, went further, situating the party's shortcomings in the broader argument that Marxism itself, necessarily geared towards political economy in its nineteenth-century foundational texts, had failed to produce an adequate theory of culture and popular consciousness. Unwittingly echoing the still-untranslated prison writings of Gramsci, Lindsay argued that, in developed societies with their enlarged civil strata, culture broadly defined became proportionately more significant as a medium of class power and consciousness, and that a broader conception of the revolutionary party and its work was therefore required. This was truer than ever, Lindsay argued, in a conjuncture in which the case for a planned, state-run, reconstructed economy had been effectively won by the war and conceded by capital. 'The tasks of our era,' he continued, were 'above all tasks of the cultural levels.'[289] The challenge now was to work at the level of culture, civil society, and popular conceptions to solidify fluid but widely shared enthusiasm for these innovations into an appetite for socialism – ideological work for which Marxism in general and the party in particular were poorly equipped.[290] Undeterred when faced with a humiliating public dressing down by party functionaries that reasserted the base-superstructure model ossified in the *Short Course*, Lindsay went further, submitting an article to the party's theoretical journal, *Communist Review*. Written partly in response to the 'heavy rejection' by the Labour Party of Communist affiliation in 1946, this called for a clearer conception of the Communist Party's relationship with Labour, as 'only by finding the right relationship can we throw our weight effectively into the balance'; what was needed was more energetic commitment to building the cultural and intellectual authority necessary to 'gain a position of leadership' across a wider terrain and a clearer theoretical model of the links between intellectual and 'politico-economic' work.[291] Invoking the broader strategy of the PCI as an alternative model, and again writing in Gramscian tones, he argued that the October Revolution had occurred in a situation without analogy in Western Europe, that the differences between the situations were growing ever wider, and that a strategy which mechanically applied the lessons of one to the other was doomed.[292] For Lindsay, 'the pattern of 1917' exerted 'too powerful a pull on our minds,' impeding the creative development of a flexible Marxism in the true spirit of Lenin. Again unconsciously echoing Gramsci, he argued that to make an advance the party had to 'think nationally – in terms of the whole life of the people.'[293] The theoretical implications of Dimitrovian Popular Frontism – itself, for Lindsay, a creative extension of Lenin's United Front position – needed to be developed, as did the party's understanding of the function of intellectuals in developed societies, whose significance was for Lindsay proportionate to a nation's cultural level.[294] Developing the earlier analysis, he argued that 'the political situation in which find ourselves is more than ever a cultural one' ('there is no problem of reconstruction which is not also a cultural problem').[295] In this conjuncture intellectuals were especially important, not only to raise the party's theoretical and cultural levels, but also to 'affect an increasingly large portion of the public with Marxist ways of work within the various fields, and therefore to assume leadership in those fields.'[296] 'Only by such an approach,' Lindsay argued, 'can we move towards an effective leadership.'[297] Although his analysis remained stuck in an essentially diffusionist model of cultural empowerment, it was a sharp reading of both the post-war conjuncture and those party positions and reflexes that, for Lindsay, had blocked greater advances from being made and prevented the party from recognizing where its strengths now lay. Once again, the party leaders – who fell under Lindsay's criticism for their adhesion to the Crimea perspective – displayed precisely the stiff-necked defensiveness against which he warned.[298] The article was rejected as 'harmful to the Party,' and Lindsay ominously warned of 'considerable danger' in his 'present attitude.'[299] It was an episode that anticipated many of the clashes to come in the decade ahead.

3
The British Road to Socialism, 1947–1956

'I think the time has arrived,' wrote Harry Pollitt to James Klugmann in August 1947, 'when … we need to say something new.' Behind the scenes, those Pollitt called his Soviet 'Instructors' had put pressure on him to make the argument that, as he put it, 'the prerequisites for the peaceful transition towards socialism in a country like Britain now exist.'[1] A chapter charting such a national course, 'The British Road to Socialism,' duly appeared in Pollitt's new pamphlet, *Looking Ahead* (1947), before the road-building metaphor was reused as the title of *The British Road to Socialism* (1951), the party's first formal program since *For Soviet Britain* (1935). The defining paradox of the period was that the unfurling of this new national emphasis coincided with the alienation of Communists from the nation or, more specifically, from the nationally grounded advances of the 1943–6 period. Communists had made most headway when, as in these years, they seemed to embody the future; the future was now American, and Communists were opposed to it. Nineteen forty-seven would be what Donald Sassoon calls the 'annus horrendous' of Communism.[2] Lingering delusions that the anti-fascist rapprochement between 'progressive' capitalist states and the USSR could create a framework for socialist advance were dashed by the division of Europe and the set pieces of the early Cold War. Communists in France, Italy, Norway, Belgium, Austria, and Luxemburg were excluded or withdrew from ruling coalitions that year, and mostly went willingly, recognizing that they were now unable to shape events inside governments and too compromised by their presence there to influence events outside.[3] The creation of the Communist Information Bureau (Cominform) in September 1947 fixed them in direct opposition to the geopolitical 'camp' in which the governments they notionally served belonged, now defined as 'anti-democratic with the basic aim of establishing world domination of American imperialism.'[4] In Britain, within months of the publication of *Looking Ahead*, residual reconstruction-era rhetoric about national advance duly gave way to denunciation of erstwhile Labour allies as imperialists, and developed a militaristic twist in the name of the so-called Battle of Ideas. This saw the world as cleaved into the camps of East and West, considered 'peace' as imperilled only by the West, and sought to defend 'national dignity and independence' against 'cultural invasion from America.'[5] Defending civil rights in the West while saying nothing about their erosion in the East cost Communists the moral prestige accrued during the war, and waves of Cold War persecution of Communists that followed made the going even harder: scientists, writers, civil servants, broadcasters, teachers, adult educators, Anglican priests, and even boy scouts were targeted by the state and its intermediaries.[6]

The period intensified the pattern traced in the previous chapter of a party required to develop – ideally through deep, theoretically informed analysis – a strategy for advance and being ill-equipped to do so. The culture was now changing in ways that seemed inhospitable to the party's traditional mores. Class composition was becoming more differentiated: the working class was shrinking and better off, although still composing 72.19 per cent of the population, or 36 million, in 1951; it had been 78.07 per cent in 1931. The middle class, at 28 per cent of the population, was 6 per cent bigger than it had been in 1931.[7] Class and ethnic geography were being transformed: slum clearance, rehousing, and suburbanization were breaking up traditional Communist strongholds such as the East End, represented by Communist MP Phil Piratin between 1945 and 1950. Moreover, the party's Jewish support in the East End and beyond would be eroded in this period by the party line on Israel as a 'semi-colony' of American imperialism and its denial of Soviet antisemitism.[8] Working its way into the national culture through this period was the phenomenon of mass 'mobile privatization,' a way of life structured around telephones, cars, hire-purchase, and televisions, most pronounced in the new suburbs described by Jack Lindsay, after a visit to Dagenham, as 'hell.'[9] These new communities and cultures to which the party needed to pitch its electoral wares were overlaying its formative terra firma, what Eric Hobsbawm retrospectively called the 'common style of British proletarian life,' formed in the 1880s – a culture structured around the street, trade unionism, co-operative membership, football, and the pub, and embodied by its leader, Harry Pollitt.[10] In later years Hobsbawm's deeply contentious 'The Forward March of Labour Halted' (1978) would identify 1951 as a watershed year after which the working class and its seventy-year-old collectivist proletarian identity would be substantially incorporated into the consumer and credit society.[11] The party was not seriously analysing these trends at the time: had it been doing so, it might have felt heartened by a complicated picture in which the level of working-class self-identification actually rose from 43 per cent to 51 per cent between 1948 and 1956.[12] To make headway now, however, it needed at least a map of the complexities of contemporary capitalism and its superstructures; that Pollitt in 1947 was convinced that the Tories would never again return to office was just one indication of how it conspicuously lacked the intellectual resources to produce such a map.[13] Its commitment to advance through the transformation of the nation's democratic institutions cruelly coincided with the permanent reversal of the 1945 General Election achievements that had brought the party MPs in West Fife (Willie Gallacher) and Mile End (Phil Piratin) and an aggregated vote of 102,780, 31 per cent of the Labour vote in the contested seats.[14] In the 1950 General Election, it stood 100 candidates but counted fewer total votes than in 1945, losing both seats and 97 deposits, a pattern mirrored in local elections.[15] Long welded to Leninist conceptions in principle, if not in practice, the British party lacked a theory of the bourgeois state or a tradition of analysing its composition and procedures. Also, although the party belonged to an international movement committed to an economic account of history, it was almost entirely economically illiterate in terms of analysing capitalism's exponential flexibility and resilience, characteristics now busy laying the foundations for the longest economic boom in history (the UK economy would quadruple in size between 1948 and 1973), a recovery to which the unanalysed passive revolution of the formation of the world's most advanced welfare state was integral.[16] In these years, the Economics Committee brushed aside Keynesian theory as unworthy of differentiation from laissez-faire economics – mere 'camouflage' for 'teamwork between the monopoly capitalists and their friends, the Right-Wing leaders of the labour movement'[17] – insisted on actual and imminent capitalist crisis (contrasted with Soviet economic advance),[18] and puzzled over 'the relation' between Stalin's analysis of 'maximum profit' and that of Marx.[19] By the early 1950s, its analytical edge was further blunted by a conspiratorial, nationalist, anti-American discourse in which Britain was implausibly presented as a colony in some ways equivalent to those it had long oppressed. On the questions of race, empire, and immigration that came to the fore politically in the period of imperial disintegration and mass diaspora – Britain's black population was 7,000 before the war, 40,000 in 1952; net immigration was 2,000 in 1953 and 42,700 in 1955 – the party would struggle.[20] The dominant paradigm for the analysis of race had always been that of imperialism, conceived in Leninist terms.[21] How this could be applied to mid-century complexities of decolonization, diaspora, and immigration was unclear. The party would take its cues from Stalin, keen to appease former allies; when required to think independently, it would lack critical distance from cultural common sense on Britain's changing ethnic composition.[22]

On one hand, then, a consoling 'two camps' narrative distracted the party from serious-minded analysis of the complexities of capital and class in mid-century Britain.[23] On the other, as I argue in this chapter, the 'two camps' line threw the cultural fight, or the 'Battle of Ideas,' onto the domain of popular culture, where the party had always been weak.[24] American mass culture – films, comics, magazines – ran the official analysis, was the superstructural front line of the Marshall Plan, whose function was to 'barbarise and brutalise' the British people, softening them up for consumerism, individualism, and anti-Soviet war.[25] The party's antidote to the gum-chewing, 'Star-Spangled-Banner' future

The British Road to Socialism

Programme adopted by the

Executive Committee of the Communist Party

January, 1951

3d.

The British Road to Socialism (1951). CP Archive, LHASC, Manchester.

that so chilled Harry Pollitt was an elusive authentic national culture that Communists were to embody and constitute at the same time that they were required to fall behind jarring Soviet prescriptions on science, music, and literature.[26] Although the strapline of the period was the 'Battle of Ideas,' its central plot was the desperate quest for an idea of culture and corresponding cultural material with and through which the party could fight.

In short, the marginalized party's repertoire of politico-cultural responses in the Cold War period was constricted, as Jack Lindsay had recently found, not only by geopolitics and 'Stalinism,' but also by deep theoretical aporia and a defensive anti-intellectualism that was especially pronounced in the British party.[27] This permitted little discussion of economics, the state, the composition of the national culture, or fundamental strategic questions; those who raised such matters were defensively sidelined. In the decade after the war, the party was caught between a paralysing geopolitical framework, multiple theoretical blind spots, and a British society undergoing rapid transformation. But to a degree not sufficiently registered to date, muted counterimpulses existed in the CPGB through the period. These would come especially to the fore, signalling different possibilities, between the death of Stalin in 1953 and the beginning of 1956.

The British Road to Socialism

The talismanic text of British Communism in the 1947–56 period was *The British Road to Socialism* (1951), the twenty-two-page official program that supplanted the more provisional *Britain for the People* (1944); it had a print run of 250,000, of which 176,000 copies were sold within three months.[28] Despite the text's new emphasis on the transformation of 'capitalist democracy into a real People's Democracy' and the spiky refutation of the 'slanderous misrepresentation' that the party was committed to 'Soviet Power in Britain,' the process of its composition was profoundly undemocratic. A codification of many of the controversial 'revisionist' conceptions of the immediate post-war period formulated in *Looking Ahead* (1947), it was ghost written by Stalin,[29] and barely discussed by either the membership or, indeed, the leadership[30] (the National Cultural Committee was asked to work out the document's cultural logic only after it was written).[31] The usual explanation for the text's follies is that the party claimed to speak for the national interest while actually functioning as mouthpiece for another nation; as E.P. Thompson would later joke, *The British Road to Socialism* ought really to have been called 'The Russian Road to Socialism, Done into English.'[32] But the problems with the document were manifold, and hinged around the absence, in a movement fundamentally constituted in the model of international revolutionary insurrectionism, of a strong theoretical tradition of thinking about political advance in and through the changing nation and its component classes, regions, and cultures.[33]

For instance, the party had an honourable record of antiracism since Windrush, and potentially a compelling case to make in *The British Road* to the 50,000-strong black British community.[34] But it was at a loss how to integrate new black cadre into its structures – as demonstrated in 1950 by the effective segregation of 150 Nigerian recruits into so-called Robeson branches[35] – and a year later struggled to articulate a clear position on race and empire in *The British Road*.[36] While purporting to break from 'the present abnormal relations' between Britain and its colonies, a fuzzily worded statement in the finished document projected something like their continuation: Britain would, it was naturally but implausibly assumed, achieve socialism before the colonies secured their independence, and former colonies would then provide 'vital food and raw materials' for industrial Britain within an arrangement of 'close, fraternal association,' a set-up that looked to some a lot like the Commonwealth.[37] *The British Road*'s assertion that the Communist Party was not 'aiming at the destruction of the British Empire' clearly reflected Stalin's strategic post-war priorities, but it 'bewildered the faithful' who believed that this was precisely the party's central purpose, as the Comintern had previously insisted.[38] Furthermore, the formulation was unlikely to facilitate the recruitment of potential black cadre with no reason to think favourably of the empire. A number of members resigned, outraged that the party now attached its central strategy for advance to the structures of a British state deeply enmeshed with a history of imperialism, reproduced 'common-sense' imperial assumptions about colonial dependency on the metropole, and made no mention of Britain's new migrant communities in its description of the national demographic from which the projected alliances necessary for advance were to be constructed.[39]

Here, as elsewhere, the text was fundamentally incoherent, pulled between an uneasy commitment to Britain's political structures (Parliament was now 'the product of Britain's historic struggle for democracy') and a more familiar bellicose register ('every effort of the capitalist class to defy the People's Government and Parliament will be resisted and defeated').[40] The structures of the bourgeois state that, until recently, had been regarded as instruments of class rule were seen as available for appropriation, without the case for their transformability being made. Conspicuously absent in the new emphasis on Parliament's capacity to become 'the democratic instrument of the vast majority of the people' was the principle of political pluralism; whether the putative People's Government could be electorally challenged was fudged.[41] There was no acknowledgement of the potentially consciousness-lowering consequences of a parliamentary strategy, a key motif in the 1920s debates; also forgotten was the ideological work performed by Parliament as a symbolic theatre that reconciled the popular masses to the status quo by perpetuating the illusion that they exercised self-determination in the capitalist social order, a lesson so skilfully taught through the Women's Parliaments. The core Marxist argument that bourgeois democracy sanctified economic inequality was not made. The fundamental question of how the bourgeois state, hardwired to defend property relations, might be transformed to facilitate and deepen workers' control of the means of production went unasked.

The document was no less out of focus on the question of revolutionary agency. The central political agent of *The British Road* was not the proletariat or party, but an intra-class 'great broad popular alliance,' although its composition and the motivations and mechanisms that united it barely featured.[42] The working class, said to be two-thirds of the population, and many of those groups through which the party had made headway in the late war period – 'clerical and professional workers, the teachers, technicians and scientists, the working farmers, shopkeepers and small business men' – were potentially a 'mighty political force,' though recognized to be ideologically divided 'by the propaganda of the ruling class' and especially the right-wing Labour government.[43] There was at least here recognition of the ideological work through which 'the capitalist class exercises a disguised dictatorship over the working class,'[44] with the implication that a struggle over culture and popular consciousness was a condition for creating the popular alliance necessary for the electoral breakthrough of the 'People's Government.' But having registered the need for this preparatory politico-ideological work, the text immediately repressed the insight, simply assuming the successful advance of the 'broad coalition or popular alliance' that would form the basis of the People's Government, with the 'united working class as its decisive force.'[45] Cultural struggle and transformation, in other words, were tacitly recognized as preconditions for advance, but then immediately subordinated, in the familiar pattern, to politics. Culture would be transformed *after* the breakthrough election of a People's Government (against the grain of this disguised dictatorship). At that point, newspapers, periodicals, the BBC, and cinemas would be requisitioned and reactionary personnel removed to 'strengthen the determination of the people to carry through the decisive changes in the social order.'[46] The chronology of this revolution sounded a lot like the old dictatorship of the proletariat – first seize the state, then change the culture – and was perhaps intended to do so, as a sop to reassure the membership base. On every page the document revealed the degree to which the party was ill-equipped for the national course on which it was set. It lacked a theoretical model of capital, class, and consciousness, insight into the challenges of socialist democracy, and a coherent strategy for a politics of the long haul.

Losing Ground

The development of the national road strategy required the channelling of increased energy and resources into broader struggle in the period after the war. In a move that signalled a distancing from those Leninist visions, which dimmed but were never revoked, the party's national cultural structures were expanded with a broadly Dimitrovian brief of promoting radical cultural traditions, uncovering and stimulating working-class creativity, promoting the state planning of and access to culture, and defending Soviet positions on cultural and scientific matters.[47] It was, however, a case of investment without a clear politico-cultural strategy. Aside from the writings of Jack Lindsay, there was little in the party's theoretical repertoire from which such a strategy could be fashioned. Lindsay's enthusiasm for developments in the French and Italian parties was not widely shared; Togliatti's innovations of a *partito nuovo* aroused little interest in the CPGB.[48]

The party already had separate subgroups of economists, historians, philosophers, writers, artists, actors, psychologists, musicians, and film writers, plus a scientific advisory committee and commissions on education and higher education.[49] A National Cultural Committee (NCC) answerable to the Executive Committee reflecting these components was planned through late 1946 and running by April 1947, chaired by Emile Burns, and meeting monthly. Its stated purpose for the party and its 38,000 members was to 'plan and guide' work across an 'ideological field' whose importance was seen as newly significant in the context of the national road strategy.[50] That Sam Aaronvitch (1919–98) was designated as full-time secretary coordinating an initial core of ten specialist groups indicated the level of the party's initial investment in it.[51] Embellishments to the NCC would follow, but for eight years (1947–55) it would function as a well-resourced nerve centre of Communist activity in civil society.[52] It would feed to and from the Executive Committee, mediate between the leadership, groups, and cultural activists, instruct, support, and monitor the progress of its constituent groups and individuals, and formulate cultural policy and priorities in terms of the party line. It would also advise the editorial teams of party periodicals, commission publications, including a trilogy of books on national culture collectively written by party intellectuals,[53] and organize regional and national conferences, the biggest being the 1951 national event on 'The American Threat to British Culture,' attended by 2,000 delegates.[54] Never before or since would British Communism commit so heavily to activity in the cultural field.

The composition of the NCC naturally reflected the energies of the respective groups and the party's priorities and areas of strength:[55] its core members were overwhelmingly male, all university educated, mostly in their forties, and working in universities or 'the arts.' The most active groups were the historians, scientists, musicians, and writers – the economists were relatively inactive beyond writing copy for the party press; the philosophers who might have raised fundamental theoretical questions met infrequently and produced little.[56] In terms of prestige and influence on intellectual life, the key shift in the period was away from the scientists – organized into the Engels Society in 1946 – and to the historians. The party's losing its grip on the future while strengthening its influence over the analysis of the past was powerfully paradigmatic of the period's contractions and contradictions.[57]

Aubergines in Moscow

In 1947 it seemed clear that science was the most compelling answer international Communism possessed to the question of where the deep resources of a communist future lay, and science trumped culture in early NCC proposals.[58] The severance of science and culture by bourgeois society, ran the long-established techno-humanist argument popularized by Bernal in the 1940s, would be triumphantly overcome through the emancipatory leadership of a scientifically orientated Soviet Union, modernity's epicentre. Science would then provide not only material abundance, but also society's central purpose and liberating grand narrative, and create the conceptual and perceptual frameworks for the culture of the future in the same way that the great faiths had in the past.[59] British leftist scientists had won intellectual prestige in the 1930s and 1940s precisely by arguing that there was just one true science and that its natural home was now the Soviet Union, where it flourished unimpeded by market distortion and capitalist barbarism.[60] Stalin's ideologically driven elevation of maverick geneticist T.D. Lysenko, a figure whose science had been challenged in the party press,[61] to lead Soviet biology was obviously incompatible with such claims.[62] The suppression of Mendelian genetics that ensued represented the ascension of the 'two camps' idea in science, one being sterile, insular, elitist, and Western, the other practical, egalitarian, and capable of cultivating aubergines even in frosty Moscow.[63] The well-documented controversy that ensued from mid-1948, in which the British media showed an unprecedented interest in scientific affairs, triggered resignations by party scientists, accelerated the decline of the Association of Scientific Workers, fractured alliances with non-Communist progressives, including Julian Huxley and C.H. Waddington, and greatly damaged the public standing of the party's most prestigious intellectual cohort, whether they defended Lysenko (Bernal) or not (Haldane).[64] The Engels Society, which had 250 members at its height, was torn asunder and rapidly petered out.[65] The BBC contracts that had enabled Bernal, Haldane, and Levy to bring their analyses to sizeable national audiences dried up, and a tone of contempt entered mainstream coverage of their writing.[66] That modernity no longer obviously belonged to Communism was evident from the retreat of party scientists into the 'peace' work that became a priority for party intellectuals after the Soviet-inspired Stockholm Peace Congress of March 1950, the unusually contracted range of Bernal's writings, and the convoluted ways in which Communists like Hyman Levy tried to suture science and the arts now that the future-oriented narrative that had recently connected them lay in pieces.[67]

History Wars

The Communist Party Historians' Group's first chair, Christopher Hill, was as unconvincing as anyone else when defending Lysenko.[68] He and his historian colleagues made little headway with the 'Battle of Ideas' in the prescribed sense of guiding the 'honest and sincere patriotic feeling amongst the people into progressive channels,' in opposition to the 'utter decay' of ruling-class culture and 'the ferocious and brutalised culture' of its American 'economic and political masters.'[69] Nor, as we have seen, did they bring what they knew to bear on the contemporary and shifting culture in which the British Road was to be built, being wary of analysing the twentieth century, which required engagement with, and criticism of, the Communist Party's own history – 'notoriously tricky,' as Hobsbawm later put it, with some understatement.[70]

But for all that, the ambitions of British Communist historians as authors of serious historical analysis were long-standing, and flowered in the Cominform period. The party largely saw off a purge of academic historians implored by the *Times Literary Supplement* in a notorious review of Jack Lindsay's *Byzantium in Europe* (1952),[71] and most kept their jobs, protected by their rising reputations and professional discretion.[72] Through a prodigious stream of around 35 books, 120 articles, numerous public lectures, weekend schools, conferences, and broadcasts, the Historians' Group in these years looked to be fulfilling the Popular Front vision of their guiding spirit, Dona Torr (1883–1957), of the party's need to '*breed* new historians – awaken and train them'[73] and to fix 'Marxism as an integral trend within British historiography,' as her protégé John Saville put it.[74] With their one-hundred-plus active members, 'period sections' (Ancient, Medieval, Sixteenth–Seventeenth Century, Nineteenth Century), Teachers' Section, local branches, and periodical (*Local History Bulletin* from 1951, later *Our History*), the historians were the 'jewel in the crown' of the party's intellectual life, according to Aaronovitch.[75] Unlike the creative writers, who were more prone to theoretical deviations and would face repeated King Street intrusions into their work and publications,[76] the historians were entrusted to build a broad, progressive, and soon highly prestigious journal, *Past & Present*, committed to stylistic clarity and scientific rigour.[77] With cornerstone texts such as Maurice Dobb's *Studies in the Development of Capitalism* (1946) and A.L. Morton's *A People's History of England* (1938) – the former a model for explanatory precision, the latter for popularizing brio – they continued to establish themselves as interpreters of the nation's economic and political history, analysis which could plausibly be presented as historical groundwork for building the British Road.[78] Their empirically grounded materialism was mobilized in the 'Battle of Ideas' not only by the writing of new history, but also by critique of historiographic trends and discourses considered to reinforce reactionary and anti-Communist thought, whether Catholic discourse, which led international anti-Communist movements under the banner of Western Christian values,[79] the so-called Clapham-Ashton school, which eschewed the generalization necessary for interpretation, the constitutional approach of the Namier school, or the mysticism-tainted metahistorical discourses associated especially with Herbert Butterfield and Arnold Toynbee.[80] The key forms through which they fought the period's history wars were articles in mainstream academic journals, the documentary anthology – notably the four-volume series that included Christopher Hill and Edmund Dell's English Civil War collection, *The Good Old Cause* (1949) – and the biography. Previously suspected as inclined to produce a non-materialist 'great men' version of history, the latter was now found to be an effective means for popularizing antecedents who might lead the way – notably William Morris, forcefully appropriated as a vital link between British Communism and the radical national romantic tradition of Shelley in E.P. Thompson's *William Morris: Romantic to Revolutionary* (1955).[81] As Hobsbawm later argued, the historians' success in occupying and defining the terrain of serious post-war historiographical enquiry at mid-century was satisfyingly measurable from a book like E.H. Carr's *What Is History?* (1961), a non-Marxist text undergirded by materialist good sense.[82]

Highbrow Communism

As the NCC profile suggested, it was assumed without much discussion that 'the arts' in general and literature in particular would be central to the building of national intellectual and cultural prestige in the years ahead. The party's strongest national cultural resource was considered to be its association with the 'cultural upsurge' of wartime mass participation.[83] Sustaining this wartime process of popular cultural diffusion, or finding proxies for it, was identified as the central 'national road' challenge, even though the relationship between such struggles, class consciousness, and the achievement of the party's ultimate project – a socialist Britain – remained unclear: the investment in top-down cultural diffusion was intuitive, rather than argued, and the ground was now shifting.

The frameworks of high, middle, and low that had structured British culture through the inter-war period and formed the context in which Communist intellectuals' sensibilities had been shaped and the party's cultural politics conducted were being eroded in ways that the party was slow to recognize. The key to its cultural successes of the Popular Front and People's War period, including the Left Book Club, had been working with the grain of a broad, progressive flank of 'middlebrow' culture whose signature commitments were to social reform and cultural democratization, and whose cultural reach was apparent from the one-and-a-quarter-million weekly sales of the culturally uplifting *Picture Post*, launched back in 1938.[84] Communists including A.L. Lloyd had written for *Picture Post*. Party intellectuals bonded powerfully through this period with J.B. Priestley, middlebrow's embodiment, who contributed regularly to the *Daily Worker* during the war.[85] It was, however, a culture now contracting when the party needed it most. The social-reforming cultural current ebbed away with the Attlee government.[86] What cultural historian Christopher Hilliard calls the 'institutional basis of the interwar middlebrow' – circulating libraries and reprint organizations such as the Book Society – was swamped by mass-market paperback sales,[87] and the high culture that the middlebrow mediated was overwhelmed by the volume of general books published every year, proportionately less poetry and drama, making minority culture ever more marginal, as F.R. Leavis recognized.[88] Leavis's *Scrutiny* would cease publication in 1953,[89] the middlebrow journal *Strand* closed in 1950, and *John o'London's Weekly* in 1954.[90]

Now also struggling was the party's strongest stake in this formation: the bright, middlebrow monthly *Our Time*, to which Priestley contributed and whose circulation peaked at 18,000 in the war's final months.[91] Like its rivals, *Our Time* was confronted with the shaking up of a captive wartime readership with demobilization, the gradual removal of the paper rationing that had effectively locked out new titles from the market, competition from restructured BBC radio broadcasting, whose magazine-style programs supplanted actual magazines, and high taxation in a period of economic crisis. In the absence of sustained, lucrative, high-volume sales, it was additionally beleaguered by the anti-Communist sentiments of large wholesalers.[92] By August 1947, *Our Time*'s circulation had halved, and the unseemly internecine behind-the-scenes struggle over the fading publication yields a rare glimpse into Communist cultural unconscious, those usually unrecorded assumptions about culture and political strategy that informed party positions in the period.[93] Seasoned editor Edgell Rickword understood the middlebrow formation on which the journal stood, and argued for a further strategic broadening of the magazine to keep abreast of this culture, shrinking though it was.[94] Others agreed that the publication's reach must widen and embrace 'exciting advances in film and radio.'[95] But the position that won the day combined itchy-footed voluntarist vanguardism – according to which dwindling sales were due not to complex commercial and cultural factors, but to the journal's lack of ideological clarity – with a 'commonsense' confidence in high culture. This was, it was assumed, a cultural oxygen that, diffused appropriately through the working class via the conduits of community intellectuals – 'those who are interested in ideas, and can be moved by works of art' – would re-energize the culture from the bottom up in unidentified ways considered congenial to Communist advance.[96]

The reflex confidence in high-cultural diffusion that had stood behind the journal looked increasingly out of time: the middlebrow contracted as the Cold War effectively exiled Communism from the commercially beleagured high-cultural citadel it valued most. This too seriously damaged its capacity to build the intellectual and cultural prestige upon which its strategy depended. Anti-Soviet, Atlanticist discourses were emanating from Britain's intellectuals even before the Cold War set in: Orwell's *Animal Farm* was written early in 1944 and published in August 1945.[97] The metropolitan high culture through which the party had earned intellectual kudos as critical friends in the inter-war and wartime period now began to pull away from it, and not only because serious writers like Orwell, Grahame Greene, and Arthur Koestler were producing explicit anti-Soviet and anti-Communist discourse.[98] More difficult to counter, because less obviously ideologically driven, was the presentation of Communism as diametrically opposed to the intellectual freedom considered necessary for the creation of the serious art that Communism purported to value. This case was by no means confined to the anti-Communist propaganda bankrolled by the Foreign Office's Information and Research Department, founded in 1948, or to fierce debates within niche periodicals such as *Polemic* and *Horizon,* important though they were.[99] More damagingly, it was conveyed by the mass media, notably in spring 1946 in the prime-time BBC Home Service Talks series, *The Challenge of Our Time*, which brought together eleven major intellectuals, including three Communists, to analyse the relationship between science, culture, and ethics in the age of the atom bomb, and attracted an audience of five million.[100] The damage these broadcasts were seen to have caused was evident from the party's rapid investment in 'The Communist Answer to the Challenge of Our Time,' a counter lecture series and book.[101] Far worse for Communists than the predictable anti-Communist diatribes of former Communist Koestler was a broadcast by novelist E.M. Forster, a figure esteemed by Communists and whose moral authority had been invoked just months earlier *against* the anti-Communist discourse of Koestler and his kind.[102] Forster attacked the planned society promoted by the likes of J.D. Bernal as antithetical to the creative and spiritual values upon which a meaningful culture depended; his concern was that, in such societies, art would have to be justified on the grounds that it was educational, or recreational, or popular.[103] As if on cue, exactly this instrumentalization soon flared up in what became a defining episode in post-war Communism's cultural wars: the 'Soviet Literature Controversy,' unleashed in June 1946, when, in the wake of Churchill's 'Iron Curtain' speech, the Propaganda Department of the Communist Party of the Soviet Union announced the repurposing of literature in the image of the 'historic tasks confronting the Soviet State.'[104] This involved the closing down of eminent literary journals, the appointment of party functionaries on the editorial boards of others, and the expulsion of allegedly 'decadent' writers adrift from the values promoted by the Writer's Union in the so-called *Zhdanovshchina*, a cultural purge that soon spread to children's literature, theatre, film, and eventually music.[105] Though subsequently largely forgotten in Britain, the controversy was widely covered in the national press, and had two enduring effects on national intellectual life that impacted Communists directly.[106] First, self-styled devotees of high-cultural seriousness long disenchanted with Left politics drew the necessary lesson from the subordination of literature to politics in the Soviet Union, and assumed an explicitly anti-Communist position, especially Cyril Connolly, whose *Horizon* was the most prestigious literary journal of the 1940s.[107] Second, the seed of what would much later become an anti-Stalinist New Left seriously committed to the type of analysis of class, culture, and consciousness that the party lacked was sown through the controversy in the form of the new, short-lived journal *Politics & Letters*. Here the coverage was written by the twenty-five-year-old WEA tutor and former Communist Raymond Williams, who had been unmoved after demobilization to rejoin a party he saw as at once opportunistic and theoretically underpowered.[108] His article rejected the choices on offer between the metropolitan minority culture affirmed by Connolly and the prematurely fixed culture of the Soviet Union, where even Priestley, as Williams noted with scorn, was considered a good novelist.[109]

The party leadership damagingly confirmed Williams's point, swinging behind the Soviet line in the relaunched and ideologically tightened intellectual journal, *Modern Quarterly*. Editor and former LBC organizer John Lewis accelerated the self-exile of Communism from high-cultural seriousness by imaginatively importing the *Zhdanovshchina* to Britain, insisting that an equivalent 'scalding steam of criticism' would benefit the 'inward turning, utterly corrupt and anti-social' tendencies at home embodied by the likes of *Horizon* co-editor Stephen Spender, who soon aligned himself as a committed anti-Communist.[110] The effect of such talk was to embolden the workerist anti-intellectualism always latent within British Communism: soon, those who admitted even reading the novels of Grahame Greene would be viewed askance, and those who drank wine or read Edith Sitwell were ridiculed by what one activist decried as the 'pseudo-proletarianism' of the *Daily Worker*'s book page.[111] In an attempt to resist the bifurcating 'two camps' logic and the surrender of the ground of cultural seriousness to the likes of Connolly, Lindsay and Swingler's Fore Publications launched a new journal, *Arena*, which maintained that broader European culture was neither entirely 'decadent' nor 'securely progressive.' Leading editor Lindsay presented as a possible model the cultural currents that had emerged from the French Resistance and been taken forward by Louis Aragon and Paul Éluard; *Arena* published work from these writers, plus Albert Camus, Edith Sitwell, and Sam Selvon, and the journal was flanked by a new Key Poets book series that included titles by Sitwell and George Barker.[112] Ignored by booksellers and literary periodicals in an increasingly hostile Cold War atmosphere, both ventures were attacked by the party for obscurity and rootless cosmopolitanism. *Arena* was soon co-opted, redesigned, and 'given a strong political kick' as counterblast to 'the synthetic imperialist culture of the States.'[113] At the same time, struggles within and around *Our Time* would continue, before its final closure in August 1949 cut the party loose from the diminishing cultural formation through which it had made uneven progress since the mid-1930s. The coda to the recently rich world of Communist literary periodicals would be bleakly regressive,[114] a new journal, *Daylight* (1952–4), holding faith in an inherently pure proletarian soul untouched by educational, cultural, and social disempowerment, and believing that, as Arnold Rattenbury later put it, 'you had but to turn the right tap and a flood of proletarian literature would gush forth.'[115] Its contents, as the recently recruited Doris Lessing (1919–2013) later observed, were almost indistinguishable from parody,[116] including verse obituaries of Stalin ('Can Death bind him, who broke a people's chains?').[117] Despite the party's insistence that the contents contained premonitions of a future culture – two now-long-forgotten party novelists would be 'discovered' and their novels published by Lawrence & Wishart through the venture – off the record even the journal's editor Margot Heinemann found the contents 'incredibly drab.'[118] The sorry enterprise would draw to a close a sporadically distinguished twenty-year history of British Communist literary periodicals.

The function of serious writers in the party was no longer obvious.[119] The ongoing restructuring of the Writers' Group struggled to keep abreast of the haemorrhaging talent: Patrick Hamilton (1904–62), Arthur Calder-Marshall (1908–92), Hubert Nicholson (1908–96), and Pamela Hansford Johnson (1912–81) barely resurfaced after the war;[120] Sylvia Townsend Warner was long inactive; Valentine Ackland would formally withdraw in early 1953;[121] even Rickword and Randall Swingler were now pulling back; and Priestley was publicly 'disowned' after attacking the Soviet Union.[122] The leadership's ongoing marginalization of independent thought was further reinforced by the so-called Caudwell Controversy, in which the reputation was stiffly dealt with of a figure some saw as well placed to give the party a distinct national identity when it sorely needed it.[123] The very recently feted writings of Christopher Caudwell (1907–37),[124] British cultural Communism's biggest intellectual reputation, and those 'temporarily hyponotised by his mistakes' were 'corrected' by leading party figures in a provincial genuflection to the Soviet Literature Controversy.[125] The episode was conceived 'to rid our literary work and our literary criticism of the hangovers of idealism,' as orthodox party philosopher Maurice Cornforth put it,[126] by imposing the Stalinist position that the world was divided into 'two camps' with distinct cultures and that Communists in whom lingering traces of 'bourgeois idealist theory' were detected should be purged – actually in the Soviet bloc, ritualistically and reputationally in the West.[127] Caudwell was charged by Cornforth with obscurity, idealism, Freudianism, misdating the rise of the bourgeoisie, uncritically assimilating bourgeois science, and developing ideas opposed to Marxism.[128] In a context of hardening anti-intellectualism in which Jack Lindsay was almost expelled for the idealistic taints of his *Marxism and Contemporary Science* (1949),[129] the necessary debate about the place of culture in expressing and shaping social and political energies in modern societies receded still further, despite the cowed resistance to Stalinist Marxism that such episodes actually revealed.[130] But *cowed* was the key: as party writer Mervyn Jones later put it, 'the weakness and isolation of the Party, which in hard-headed judgement made it pointless to stay in, also made it difficult to leave.' The escalation of countercurrents into open internal opposition was temporarily suspended in a party now 'held together by the ferocity of the Cold War' from which, for Jones at least, 'it seemed cowardly, even indecent, to withdraw.'[131]

Socialist Realism

Socialist realism was officially the pole around which Communists should gather, but Jones was not alone in being perturbed by the 'banality' of Soviet novels, 'proclaimed as masterpieces by the Zhdonovite propaganda machine.'[132] In other countries, the post-war period had produced *sui generis* realist cultural movements through which the deadening prescriptions of Zhdanov's writings on 'socialist realism,' soon ballasted by Stalin's on linguistics, were dispersed, diluted, quietly resisted, and even found usefully provocative.[133] British Communism's intense investment in international realists such as Renato Guttuso in Italy, Louis Aragon and André Still in France, and the Australian Frank Hardy reflected at some level the lack of equivalent figures at home.[134] Zhdanov's metallic discourse about national in form, socialist in content boomed loudly through the vacuum, eagerly amplified by functionaries such as Cornforth, now promoted to director of Lawrence & Wishart. As the Caudwell Controversy showed, it was a discourse keen to instrumentalize culture and to impress on party intellectuals that loyalty to the working class meant loyalty to the Soviet Union and that it was their place to assimilate, rather than query, Soviet positions.[135] Increasingly in short supply, critical thinking about socialist realism was further weakened by the onset of the Korean War, which sharpened pressure to choose sides, and reduced to shells most of those 'peace' organizations formed in the late 1940s and early 1950s as rallying points for resistance to Atlanticist militarism.[136]

In what remained of the party's literary circles, the search for the holy grail of a socialist realist aesthetic took on an unreal quality; even the prolific Lindsay suffered writer's block when tasked to produce the genre manual that Cornforth commissioned.[137] Some significant critical work was undertaken under the broader rubric of recovering a usable national realist tradition on which to build: a pioneer was found in Robert Tressell (1870?–1911), whose *The Ragged Trousered Philanthropists* (1914) was now belatedly identified as the literary cornerstone of a radical tradition and an 'inspiration' adequate to the challenge of 'Yankee war menaces.'[138] Fred Ball's biographical study of Tressell was published by Lawrence & Wishart in 1951 and an unexpurgated version of the novel – free from 'bourgeois' editorializing – in 1955.[139] Further back, the 'critical realism' of the nineteenth-century realist novel was widely identified as an accessible and vital antecedent to socialist realism awaiting Communist appropriation;[140] the form's radical energies were charted by Jack Lindsay's studies of Charles Dickens and George Meredith, both published by mainstream presses, and by Arnold Kettle's *An Introduction to the English Novel I: To George Eliot* (1952), a popular education textbook and counterstroke to Leavis's *The Great Tradition* (1948), which presented six key novels as textual crystallizations of broad, progressive historical impulses.[141] But, as both Lindsay and Kettle found, the more prominent the intervention into the cultural mainstream, the greater the Cold War backlash: Stephen Spender defended Dickens against Communist appropriation;[142] the *Guardian*, now actively sifting the *Daily Worker* for potential anti-Communist copy, ridiculed Kettle's political readings in a potentially career-damaging attack.[143]

The prevailing orthodoxy locked out new theoretical and critical thought, impeding debate about whether realist traditions might indeed provide a recodeable cultural form relevant to bringing Marxism's insights to bear on the modern world. A potentially useful book in these terms, Hungarian Georg Lukács's *Studies in European Realism* (1950), was by the time it appeared already mediated by knowledge of its author's breach of the 'two camps' logic, dutifully detailed for them by Eric Hobsbawm and Alick West, among others.[144] This work, which might have helped to define a mid-century Communist realist aesthetic, was effectively lost to a movement that badly needed it.[145] Some writers who remained in the party quietly carried on regardless of socialist realist injunctions: debut novels from Alexander Baron (*From the City, from the Plough* [1948]) and Mervyn Jones himself (*No Time to Be Young* [1952]) were relatively untroubled by Zhadanovite prescriptions and more or less ignored by the party press as a result; by the time Lessing trained her gaze on Britain in *The Golden Notebook* (1962), Communism was the subject, rather than the inspiration, to the chagrin of her former comrades.[146] Only Lindsay, an acquaintance of Lukács deeply versed in contemporary Soviet literature and temporarily restored to party orthodoxy after a visit to the 1949 Pushkin celebrations, was sufficiently inspired to grapple seriously in criticism and fiction alike with the problem of forging a nationally grounded socialist realism that aspired to the social reach of Balzac, Dickens, and Zola with a view to re-energizing Communist cultural production. His 'British way' trilogy tracking post-war history began promisingly with *Betrayed Spring* (1953), bringing the nuanced readings of his best historical fiction to the contemporary scene.[147] Written in intellectual isolation and a fast-deteriorating political atmosphere, however, the series quickly buckled beneath the weight of the Cold War and its 'two camps' ways of seeing, lacking the 'imaginative insights and sympathies' he rightly identified as necessary to the realist mode, leaving the project vulnerable to justifiable attack from the cultural mainstream.[148]

In the visual arts, 'socialist realism' and the Soviet controversies irreversibly divided the key residual Popular Front organization, the AIA, through which outward-facing debate might have occurred.[149] Picasso's party membership had added lustre to the Communist movement in general in 1944 and to British Communism in particular when, in November 1950, the artist defied the Labour government and arrived in Sheffield for the aborted World Peace Congress, and was photographed taking tea in a local cafe.[150] Nonetheless he was attacked by Communists for his career-long deviation from socialist realist principles.[151] Intellectuals well versed in the various meanings of realism in art who might have resisted Zhdanovism and raised the pitch of the discussion, like the NCC's art-historian Francis Klingender, were now drifting away, in his case over the expulsion of Yugoslavia from the Cominform. Klingender had already puzzled over the underwhelming socialist realist Soviet art recently on display at the Royal Academy.[152] Given that many Communists of his generation shared the Leavisite assumption that a society's quality could be judged by its cultural level, uninspiring Soviet art was never only an artistic problem.

Communist architects constituted as a group under the NCC in 1948 likewise struggled to see merit in the Soviet Union's wedding-cake designs and cod-classicism that loomed into view once the brick dust of Soviet reconstruction settled.[153] Some echoed Klingender and sought to explain socialist realism away as the passing cultural logic of an industrializing nation equivalent to Victoriana.[154] Others defended it,[155] often while remaining more guided in practice by Scandinavia rather than by Moscow.[156] Some, like Lubetkin, held firm to their modernist instincts and pulled back from the party.[157] The closest the conflicted architects got to an official position was when they denounced the 'cosmopolitan character' of modernism for eroding national tradition and thereby facilitating American imperialism, and scratched around for an indigenous and more palatable socialist realist architectural model in the writings of 'towering genius' William Morris.[158]

The situation in music was little better. At the end of the war, Communist composers seemed ascendant, especially when Bernard Stevens's award-winning *Symphony of Liberation* was performed at the Royal Albert Hall.[159] Victimization now blocked avenues and compounded the insularity: Thomas

Russell's LPO lost its LCC funding in 1949, and Russell, increasingly considered a liability to the orchestra's future security, was removed from his post as managing director three years later, bringing to an end the party's association with the orchestra.[160] The departure from the party of self-styled 'subjective composer' Benjamin Frankel, who was attuned to the significance of modernism and increasingly alert to the anti-Semitism of high Stalinism, left the way clear for the domination of British Communist music by the more conservative trend.[161] The party's leading composer, Alan Bush, could no longer access the prestigious concert platforms open to him in the Sovietphilia and reconstruction years. Although he won an Arts Council Award for his opera, *Wat Tyler* (1951), the BBC declined to broadcast it, now hearing in his music only 'delayed action' Marxism.[162] His marginalization by the cultural intermediaries of the British state did nothing to sharpen his critical faculties where the Soviet Union was concerned, and he proved fluent in the Zhdanovite discourse attacking the 'homeless cosmopolitanism' of 'decadent formalists' and defending the Soviet state's intervention into national musical life as vociferously as the now-ageing Rutland Boughton; both saw in the official line a vindication of their abiding antimodernism.[163] The course of Bush's music epitomized the fate of much Communist culture of the period. There was much boosting in the Soviet bloc: his *Wat Tyler* was broadcast from Berlin and premiered in Leipzig with Dutt in attendance, not at the Festival of Britain or on the BBC, as the WMA hoped.[164] At home the available channels were narrowing to party and SCR events and the contracting networks of the WMA, which lost its Ministry of Education funding awarded in 1946 in 1952, and assumed an increasingly hagiographic attitude to its president, Bush, as Popular Fronters fell away and the party's cultural influence declined.[165] The primary point of 'socialist realism,' as the publications and conferences mounted in its name repeatedly stated, was to provide a framework for cultural production. In these terms it was a dismal failure in Britain, narrowing conceptions away from contemporary popular cultural forms, stimulating at the time little significant, film, theatre, literature, painting, or architecture, and further isolating Communists from the currents of national cultural life that their political strategy required them to lead and transform.

Dreary Decadence

National culture was crucial to the British Road, but socialist realism, the silver bullet of Cominform period cultural politics, was in Britain's case clearly a blank. The middlebrow was in contraction; attitudes to high culture thrashed wildly between veneration and denunciation, while its custodians now spurned Communists. There was, however, no doubt about high culture's opposite in the mid-century culture wars: popular culture, repeatedly identified as a key ideological frontline in the 'Battle of Ideas.' Phobia towards mass culture's 'shards of shit'[166] and 'slick dreary decadence'[167] ran deep in the socially and culturally conservative party. Behind the scenes, Communist intellectuals worried that the culture casually bracketed as 'ordinary cinema, *Daily Mirror*, dog-racing,' now placed sizeable elements of the working class altogether beyond the party's reach.[168] Like the Labour Party, Communists bemoaned without analysis the cultural passivity of a working class that allegedly squandered its money on cinema going and gambling.[169] A combination of default NCC highbrowism, a long-standing anti-Americanism now legitimated by the 'two camps' line, and entrenched gender assumptions incurious about cultural activities popular with women had long blocked the party from engaging seriously with national popular culture. Whether it was a conspiracy or a morbid symptom of Western culture's death spasm remained an open question.[170] Not since the withdrawal from the party of Charles Madge at the end of the 1930s had there been a current serious about analysing the pleasures and meaning of actually existing popular culture.

Beyond the party's cultural range, for instance, was Britain's second-most-important leisure pastime, dancing.[171] The 450 dance halls that attracted three million people per week by 1951 and were more popular than football nationally or than cinema with many young working-class women barely appeared on Communism's radar, with dancing associated since the early 1940s with unwelcome Americanization after the arrival of jitterbugging GIs and their Armed Forces Network on the wireless.[172] Even those Communists who heard in American jazz and blues music authentic working-class cultural expression largely agreed about the pointlessness of dancing, and opposed its introduction into the traditional jazz clubs popular with some Communists more interested in 'chewing seriously' on their pipes and listening to either records or home-grown, proletarian revival bands.[173]

The same assumptions about consciousness-lowering escapism prevailed with regard to cinema, Britain's foremost medium of popular culture. There had been signs, during the late war and immediate post-war period, of a more sophisticated Communist engagement with mainstream cinema, attendance at which peaked in 1946 (a third of the English population attended once a week that year).[174] The documentary propaganda films in which Ivor Montagu and Montagu Slater had been involved at the Ministry of Information had enjoyed mass circulation and critical acclaim; wartime films, especially Frank Launder and Sidney Gilliat's *Millions Like Us* (1943), were celebrated by Communists for integrating a feature format with sharp documentation of working-class life; a new journal, *Film Today*, was mooted by party intellectuals around Fore Publications; even the complex pleasures of Hollywood films such as *Mr Deeds Goes to Town* (1943) were taken seriously and analysed in Jack Lindsay's fiction, where they were considered to identify real social problems before imaginatively resolving them with individual rather than social solutions.[175] Paradoxically, however, the shrill, conspiratorial tenor of the 'Battle of Ideas' analysis, which stressed cinema's crucial ideological work as 'insidious ... propaganda for the capitalist way of life,' sanctioned disengagement from it; the late 1940s saw a falling back from the more nuanced analysis of the late war period: *Film Today* never materialized; popular cinema was not addressed in the party's flagship theoretical journal, *Modern Quarterly*; analysis in the *Daily Worker*, the YCL's journal *Challenge*, and even the film panel of the Communist-dominated front organization the Authors' World Peace Appeal rarely advanced beyond plot summaries or ranking films for their political messages.[176] In the absence of more serious analysis of the type contained in Jack Lindsay's novels, Communist responses to films were driven down predictable channels, such as protesting against the anti-Soviet espionage thriller *Iron Curtain* (1948), or in favour of the unseasonally radical factory film *Chance of a Million* (1950), a late flowering of wartime radical populism that offended the powerful *manqué* American film tycoon Arthur Rank – in control of two in three British cinemas – for its positive vision of worker-management.[177] The limited work of individual Communists including Montagu Slater in feature film production, meanwhile, amply confirmed the sense of a reverse alchemy process in which promising radical content, like Slater's novel *Once a Jolly Swagman* (1944), was transformed into big-screen dross by dominant cinematic conventions. The actual complexities of this ideological recoding, however, went unanalysed.[178]

Inclined towards high culture, the party was weak on the cultural and ideological implications of movies and movie going, though much stronger on the industrial and economic side: the failure of the NCC to oversee the integration of the two seriously weakened the party's interventions when some cultural headway might have been made in the late 1940s. Since the 1930s Communists had built a strong presence in the Association of Cine Technicians' Union – Ralph Bond (1904–89), Sidney Cole (1908–98), and Ivor Montagu were on the executive – and as a result the party's industrial department was adept at analysing the political economy of the vast British cinema industry, one-tenth of the global market, which was structurally dependent on American films.[179] As Communists had long pointed out, American visions suffused Britain's dream palaces: in 1946, for instance, when 1635 million trips were made to the cinema, viewers could see only 83 new British films, but 342 American ones, an imbalance that handed the United States an effective monopoly and drew £20 million from the national economy.[180] The economic if not cultural implications of this troubled the Labour government, which, in August 1947, implemented a policy Communists had long advocated, imposing a heavy duty (75 per cent) on new American films, which in turn provoked a Hollywood boycott and a film drought.[181] This was a 'cultural' crisis that was mainstream news, affecting millions of working-class people and vividly dramatizing fundamental questions about capital, culture, and national autonomy at the core of the national road strategy. It is striking how little the NCC did or said. Montagu and Bond were highly active and vocal, but now had no credible front organizations through which to operate, and disagreed about strategy.[182] They received little guidance or support from leading party intellectuals, who were much more exercised by the aristocratic authoritarianism of the ageing T.S. Eliot, doubly decorated in 1948 with an order of Merit and a Nobel Prize.[183] As Ross McKibbin has rightly argued, the Labour government stumbled into the film boycott, being dominated by 'upper-middle class men for whom the world of cinema, predominantly working-class and female, was unimportant,' and was forced into a humiliating U-turn on Hollywood's terms in March 1948.[184] Much the same was true of the NCC, a body in which film expertise barely figured and which failed to capitalize on the six-month crisis in which a cultural space briefly opened for alternative visions and cultural prestige might have been earned by advocating different models for the British industry and stronger connections with European film-making networks.[185]

From 1948 onwards, the 'two camps' line further weakened the party's critical engagement with the government's film policies.[186] At a time when the most significant story in British cinema was the withdrawing of funding from the documentary film movement in which inter-war Communists had played an important role in projecting a national collectivist ideology, the party was more or less silent.[187] The difficulty of accessing the airwaves during the 1950 General Election and the failed attempts to goad the increasingly anti-Communist TUC into the production of radical feature films strengthened an eastward-turning tendency.[188] The inward-looking New Era Film Club – with 440 members by 1950 – and three small companies were formed.[189] 'See the other half of the world,' invited the most significant, Plato Films, but the material it distributed was no longer culturally prestigious Soviet cinema of the late 1920s, but the often-plodding socialist realist and documentary films of the mid-century Soviet Union and People's Democracies. Even without the Cold War, films such as *Donets Miners* (1950), which boosted coal-mining innovations in the Donbass region in technicolour, had a limited appeal, despite party press claims that it proved the Soviet Union to be the vanguard of world film.[190] Such imports were supplemented by homespun British films and newsreels, some chronicling demonstrations, others the international peregrinations of now-ageing party leaders.[191] Such initiatives shaped a brief and unseasonal resurgence of an early 1930s–style Communist film subculture enjoyed by many at branch meetings, conferences, film club screenings, and, occasionally, prebooked commercial cinemas. Mainly, however, this culture of consolation marked a further retreat from the mainstream in which the party's strategy required it to be making its presence felt.[192]

Opposed to the 'penetration of American culture' into Britain, Communists here have refashioned a billboard advertising *Mighty Joe Young* (1949), a King-Kong spin-off movie pitched at children. CP Picture Archive, Box 73.

A Tabloid Culture

A recognizably modern tabloid print culture anathema to a party deeply committed to autodidacticism and the sanctity of the written word was also taking root in this period. The ten-percentage-point reduction of the middlebrow share of the newspaper market, including the *Daily Herald* and *News Chronicle*, down to 57 per cent of the total occurred largely at the expense of a burgeoning tabloid sector whose market share increased by eight percentage points to 35 per cent. The leaders in the field were the *News of the World*, read by 55 per cent of the working class according to one 1949 survey, the *People* (35.9 per cent) and the pioneering working-class *Daily Mirror* (28.6 per cent), which had trebled its 1930 market share (9 per cent) by 1950 (27 per cent).[193] In particular, the *Mirror*'s narrow vocabulary, simple sentences, and preference for one- or two-syllable words, Communists argued, engendered 'cultural and intellectual infantilism,' a retardation that potentially made it 'impossible for the reader of such material to participate as a thinking adult in modern society.'[194] The party was clearly disinclined to follow this lead in its own publications. The *Daily Worker* symbolically resisted the tabloid world and assumed a broadsheet format in 1948, just as the cultural traffic in working-class newspapers was moving the other way. Its plunging circulation – from a height of 120,000 in 1948 to 63,000 by April 1956 – cannot be explained away by Cold War politics alone, important though they were in emboldening sectarian tendencies that kept the paper's most able and respected journalist, Allen Hutt (1901–73), from the editor's chair.[195] A proletarian, patriarchal superego ever watchful for 'veritable reactionary snake[s]' in the 'bosom' like the 'dress design and fashion section' held the paper at arm's length from the changing textures of working-class life.[196]

This discourse of mass culture's effeminacy and passivity, always deeply enmeshed in ideas about American vulgarity, increasingly came to structure interventions in the cultural field in ways that, although sometimes resonant with broader cultural anxieties, situated the party squarely on the side of social and cultural conservatism. The party's attitude to the coming of mass television was symptomatic of a head-in-the-sand disconnection from these complicated mid-century questions of class and popular consciousness with which any modern socialist party would now have to grapple to make ground. Its most dissident figures were here as conservative as anyone. Jack Lindsay regarded television as a 'terrifying form of abstraction and ossification' inherently incompatible with the activism and collectivism upon which socialism depended; to discuss 'better programmes' was for him to mask over 'something dead inside the room.'[197] Although, as one correspondent for the *Daily Worker* put it, the workers had 'taken to the telly' on a 'massive scale' – 15,000 television licences were sold in 1947, one and a half million in 1952, by mid-1955 26 per cent of working-class households had sets[198] – and the working class clearly preferred commercial ITV to the BBC, it seemed obvious to Communists that commercial television, introduced in September 1955, would bring what Pollitt called 'the vilest forms of pornography and the vilest portrayal of crime, murder and sadism.'[199] There were anguished debates in the *Daily Worker* deep into the 1950s about whether good Communists should boycott the 'one-eyed-monster' or, indeed, whether the paper should indulge readers with a television column.[200] That television was almost never discussed by the Cultural Committee reflected the view that the medium was not culture at all. When Communists did enter the national discussion, it ended badly, as when Dutt, who possessed no television set, joined the controversy created by a notoriously graphic December 1954 television broadcast of Orwell's *Nineteen Eighty-four*.[201] His determination to detect proto-Communist sympathies in the disturbed viewers' 'healthy instincts' was easily ridiculed,[202] with the most vocal objections coming from Tory MPs, socially conservative Christians, the Rothermere Press sensitive about references to 'prole-feed,' and the British Housewives' League, concerned about family values.[203]

More at home in the world of print, Communists naturally had more to say about the pullulating market in imported American children's 'horror comics' that created a moral panic in the early 1950s. Outrage gripped party leaders, teachers, psychologists, women's groups, and those active in the Authors' World Peace Appeal, motivating them to run conferences and exhibitions and to issue press releases and broadsides against an 'insidious medium' that 'deals in brute force and direct sadism, disguised pornography' and promoted 'the unquestioned superiority of the capitalist way of life.'[204] In a climate in which the party was more usually at odds with the cultural mood and former members were busy writing best-selling denunciatory memoirs,[205] Communists were disposed to be carried away by such an unusually resonant campaign, even if it again positioned them against freedom of speech, modernity, and youth, and made political bedfellows of morally censorious Labour MPs and the Tory government, which eventually legislated to control imports of the comics.[206] Others on the Left were now reading the shifting culture with much more measure and intelligence. Former Communist allies at the *Picture Post* were successfully appropriating and ideologically recoding the American comic's format in 1950 with *Eagle*, whose 'right kind of standards, values and attitudes' reached 800,000 children per issue.[207] By the mid-1950s, Priestley was ahead of Communists in grasping that talk of cultural 'Americanization' was a way of evading discussion of deeper global processes and that the emerging social and political fault line was that of the generation.[208] Richard Hoggart was already scrutinizing what he called the 'abuses of literacy,' and trying to gauge the deeper sociological meaning of *Life*.[209] Raymond Williams, deeply frustrated by orthodox party positions on class and culture, was now embarking on the project that would eventually become *Culture and Society 1780–1950* (1958).[210]

A Third Way?

According to the party's own reading, it was now operating in a constricted space between 'a minority culture … shoring up the fragments of the past' and mass culture 'providing opiate and substitute life,' both of which propped up the system[211] – 'T.S. Eliot is the blood-brother of the Chicago writer of sadistic shockers,' as Jack Lindsay put it.[212] Soviet-inspired socialist realism was taking the party nowhere; to a degree easily forgotten, however, alternative politico-cultural models assumed to be more relevant to Communists in the late 1940s and early 1950s were those of the so-called People's Democracies, countries said to be finding their national roads to socialism and pioneering a route that others might emulate.[213] In terms of culture, the key claim was that these countries were paradoxically assisted, rather than disadvantaged, by patterns of underdevelopment that had left intact peasant and folk culture.[214] A third culture endured, it was argued, neither minority or mass, made by the people and not

Communist artist and *Daily Worker* national organizer Barbara Niven (1896–1972) addressing a street meeting, early 1950s. Photography by AV Izod. CP Picture Archive, Box 47.

Activist selling *Arena* at Sadler's Wells, London, 1951. CP Picture Archive, Box 59.

for them, an inherently communal body of works and traditions 'national in content,' close to the textures of everyday lives, and providing what classicist and CPGB Executive Committee member George Thomson (1903–87) called 'a natural reservoir for the new socialist culture.'[215]

The usual assumption, shared by the Leavisites and many Communists in the inter-war years, was that, in Britain, an equivalent popular culture rooted in agricultural life had been destroyed by industrialization. There were now ample reasons for Communists, however, marginalized by high culture and alienated by mass culture, to revisit whatever remained of this culture: seeking intimations of a socialist future in the resources of the past would be a significant and forgotten, if desperate, current in Communist cultural politics of the period.[216] Recovering national 'workers' folk music' had been a mainstay of Communism since the 1920s, which had found ideological ratification during the Popular Front;[217] by the late 1940s, folk culture was being commonly identified as a valuable resource of resistance to the cultural 'Marshallization' said to be eroding national identity and independence.[218] The claim that Morris dancing would enable Britain's youth to 'repudiate' 'without difficulty' the lure of American comics was met with some scepticism, and a fist-fight broke out when folk dancing was imposed on the 1952 YCL Congress dance.[219] But Communist folk music enthusiasts A.L. Lloyd and Ewan MacColl were energized by the 'two camps' line, and developed their arguments that bourgeois folksong antiquarians, traditionally fixated with rural Britain, had missed the continued fermentation of folk creativity into the industrial age.[220] When they were not collecting and chronicling the remaining scraps of this urban folk culture – in Lloyd's case with the assistance of the National Coal Board – they were doing in their own unorthodox way precisely what the NCC was advocating but failing to do, and linking a cultural politics angled at the national past with contemporary creativity and new modes of expression.[221] Since the war, both Lloyd and MacColl had been fusing folksong and theatre.[222] Working now with existing cultural institutions and networks – the World Federation of Democratic Youth's international festivals, Lawrence & Wishart, the WMA, the London Youth Choir, Topic Records – they were soon recording and performing their music separately and together.[223] They found that folk music could possess an uncanny cultural charge – at once exotic and familiar – especially when they reached beyond labour movement bookings and tapped into the latent energies that would find expression in skiffle from 1956. Here was a younger audience bored of crooners, the hit charts published by the *New Musical Express*, cultural standardization, and receptive to their unvarnished music, especially when presented as ancestral voices of jazz and blues.[224] And at a time when, despite the best efforts of Communist BBC producer R.D. Smith (1914–85), Communists including Lloyd were finding it increasingly difficult to access the airwaves, MacColl's discourse of anticommercial authenticity chimed with the traditionally anti-American BBC.[225] He was commissioned to script and present serious-minded programs exploring his central ideas about folk music and its genealogies for the Home Service and Light Programme, notably in the high-profile six-part *Ballads and Blues* (1953), which involved British and American artists, including Lloyd, Humphrey Lyttelton, Alan Lomax, Jean Ritchie, and Big Bill Broonzy.[226] MacColl's later claim that the series had 'triggered' the folksong revival of the late 1950s was an exaggeration, but the series helped to consolidate a popular format – a framing narrative punctuated with songs and music – hitherto conspicuously lacking in and around the Communist Party.[227] He, Lloyd, and their associates were soon presenting spinoff informal concerts that combined the radio programs' material with the formats of the now rapidly declining variety theatre on which Theatre Workshop had also drawn.[228] 'Ballads and Blues' concerts were used to raise funds for Theatre Workshop and the *Daily Worker*, the latter in a flagship jazz, blues, and folk concert at the Royal Festival Hall.[229] The model was soon co-opted by some YCL branches – at

MacColl's suggestion – as an attractive social and cultural event.[230] There were certainly ample grounds for scepticism about the wisdom of staking a claim to the future by structuring party cultural policy around the traces of folk culture and about MacColl's more extravagant claims that folk music provided the key to cultural policy.[231] Nonetheless, NCC mistrust of MacColl and his associates meant that debate within the party did not get even that far, and the ageing and unmusical NCC missed an opportunity in neglecting to support a subcultural movement that fell beyond its cultural range.[232] 'The apparatchiks of the Communist Party didn't understand what we were on about,' explained Communist music journalist Karl Dallas (1931–2016), who worked closely with MacColl and Lloyd in the period, adding that the folk revival would have been 'much more effective' if it had been supported by the party.[233]

Festivals of the People

Dallas's argument that folk music, open to Communist reaccenting, had a role to play in the party's cultural politics was backed up by events in Scotland. Here the 'district' Cultural Committee proved much more adept at reading the cultural scene, outstripping the party centre and becoming a driving force behind the Edinburgh Labour Festival (1951), rebranded as the Edinburgh People's Festival (1952–4), perhaps the most impressive cultural event yet mounted by the party.[234] The festival integrated characteristic Communist organizational efficiency with a sophistication of cultural vision, the latter supplied in no small part by Communist philosopher Martin Milligan (1923–93) and Marxist Scottish nationalist and fellow-traveller Hamish Henderson (1919–2002), a multilingual poet drawn at Cambridge to Leavis's ideas of a lost, organic culture.[235] The party's softening of its long-held opposition to Scottish nationalism as divisive of the British working class, registered in *The British Road to Socialism* (1951), made its cultural fringes more amenable to Henderson,[236] who could legitimately claim the title of Britain's first Gramscian Marxist, having learned of Gramsci from Italian partisans during his wartime service, translated the 'Prison Letters' between 1948 and 1951 (unpublished until 1974), and attended in 1950 the consciously 'Gramscian' mass festivals organised by *L'Unita*, the PCI's newspaper.[237] Henderson's subsequent assertion that the Scottish festivals were 'kicked into being' by Gramsci overstated the directness of the link.[238] Nonetheless the event was unique among Communist cultural interventions of the period in raising, through debates and lectures, the matter of what culture was and for whom, and in formulating questions around cultural values more typically prejudged in defensive events organized under the 'Battle of Ideas' rubric south of the border. Always a conscious 'fringe' alternative to the prestigious 'highbrow' Edinburgh International Festival, which was founded – with the Communist Party's support – by the Labour government in 1947, the dominant discourse of the first People's Festival challenged the official festival on the grounds of ticket prices and 'snootiness,' rather than 'decadence.'[239] It also effectively countered the more prestigious event, frequently upstaging it with the strongest elements of radical culture – notably Theatre Workshop – and international currents, including Italian neorealist cinema.[240] Here, folk culture, like football, was presented as one element among many, and the ceilidhs through which the audience encountered, often for the first time, Scotland's musical 'folk' – including fishermen, crofters, and travelling people singing and performing the music passed down to them – lent credence to Henderson's claim that a movement that preserved and developed this culture in a creative rather than antiquarian spirit might have something distinctive to say.[241] For Henderson, the alien, colonizing culture was England; that the CPGB saw it as the United States and hesitated around the Scottish national question only enriched the festival at first, bringing rambunctious Marxist nationalist currents into the broad, progressive formation that soon encompassed forty-seven organizations, including Labour Party groups, the WMA, and Edinburgh Trades Council.[242] A larger event followed in 1952, which ran for the duration of the official festival and involved Alan Bush, Hugh MacDiarmid, Sorley MacLean, Alexander Trocchi, Norman McCaig, and Naomi Mitchison, before Labour Party anti-Communism cut away the ground on which the festival had been created.[243]

Fallibility, in Fact

Writing to her future husband, the industrial militant Eddie Frow (1906–97), in January 1954, Communist school teacher Ruth Haines (1922–2008) took issue with what she saw as his ideal Communist ('a 'taciturn semi-human machine'). 'If we mechanically accept the fact that we do not matter and the Party is paramount,' she warned, 'then we lose our humanity, our fallibility, in fact.'[244] As the couple's private discussion registered, tensions between individual ethical responsibility and obedience to party discipline came to the fore in the mid-1950s, a period defined for Communists by the death of Stalin, the Soviet suppression of the workers' uprising in East Germany, and the rehabilitation of the 'Titoites,' whose judicial murder the CPGB had recently supported.[245] Not only Soviet infallibility but the structuring clarity of the 'two camps' became blurred as the resurgent discourse of 'peaceful co-existence' – undergirded by the Soviet hydrogen bomb – took the edge off the 'Battle of Ideas' (the Cominform would soon be dissolved).[246] Traditionally the historiography of British Communism has read the mid-1950s period through the prism of 1956, rightly detecting intimations of the convulsions to follow.[247] In terms of the party's analysis of the broader society and strategy, however, and of its intellectual and cultural work in civil society, the brief hiatus between the death of Stalin and the Twentieth Congress possessed a character of its own.

Despite Cold War victimization, Communist teachers had remained principled advocates in the long-haul struggle for comprehensive education. In the mid-1950s, former teacher and now professor of education Brian Simon emerged as a significant public intellectual, attacking the methodology of the 'intelligence tests' that underpinned grammar school selection in books that included *Intelligence Testing and the Comprehensive School* (1953), 'a formidable indictment of the theory and practice of intelligence testing,' according to the pro–grammar school *Times Educational Supplement*.[248] At the same time, franker discussions at the 1954 Soviet Writers Congress seemed to signal an opening up of the vexed question of realism;[249] these were amply mediated by Lindsay, who was also heartened to learn that Marx's 'Economic and Philosophical Manuscripts,' a key source for his humanist deviations, were now finally being translated by Martin Milligan for Lawrence & Wishart.[250] Across the party's cultural world were signs of a gradual awakening from benumbed collective delusion as certitudes were turned into questions. The 'socialist humanism' usually associated with E.P. Thompson and the post-1956 convulsions began to appear in party discourse from around 1954,[251] discussions about humanism, realism, and visual art – hitherto largely a matter of second-guessing gnomic Soviet formulations[252] – being sharpened by articles in the party press from fellow-traveller John Berger (1926–2017).[253] These informed the long-standing work of Artists for Peace (sponsors included Berger, Sir Jacob Epstein, Augustus John, and Stanley Spencer), which had fared better than many of its sister 'peace' organizations, mounting three exhibitions under that name between 1951 and 1953, and, most significantly, bringing Iri Maruki and Toshiko Akamatsu's Hiroshima Panels to Britain for display in 1954.[254] Paul Hogarth's 'Looking at People' exhibition of figurative art, for which Berger wrote the catalogue introduction, was seen by 250,00 in Britain (1955–56) before transferring to Moscow's Pushkin Museum (1957).[255]

As these developments suggest, realism was becoming less an imposed code than the location of an argument, as the thawing of the 'Battle of Ideas' made outmoded the formulation that 'art was a weapon' in the war for socialism and re-energized those who had long argued that socialism was in fact a weapon in the struggle for culture.[256] The recently 'decadent' view that art mattered because it could enrich perception and help humanity to 'realise the whole truth of their world, the potentialities of enjoyment which a divided society could only crucify and distort' was beginning to enjoy some currency by the mid-1950s, when Arnold Kettle defended the inherently valuable consciousness-enriching character of aesthetic experience.[257] More open debates about aesthetics were part of a broader analysis of the idea of culture, a strikingly unscrutinized term through the height of the 'Battle of Ideas.' In a debate led by Kettle, Thomas Russell and others introduced anthropological definitions of culture as a way of life.[258] Here and elsewhere, Communists began to raise some of the key questions about class, culture, and consciousness that would soon find forceful expression in key New Left texts, especially Hoggart's *The Uses of Literacy* (1957) and Williams's *Culture and Society 1780–1950* (1958). Although the glossy realities of modern Britain showcased at the Festival of Britain were still repressed by talk of brass bands and vegetable growing, there was at least progress from positions that bracketed everything unwelcome as 'Americanization,' and in which phobic cultural nationalism short-circuited analysis of capital, class, and cultural life.[259]

Internal party dynamics and hierarchies were also showing some signs of change. Back in 1951 the NCC had been tasked to work out and implement the cultural logic of *The British Road* only after it was written, despite the document's nebulous identification of civil society as a key location of politics.[260] By 1954 the NCC was already assuming some responsibility for *The British Road*'s revision, and a widely circulated document summarizing discussions held by the University Staff Committee explicitly engaged with the chronology of revolution in the West and the relationship between struggles at the level of civil society and the escalation of these struggles into confrontation with the state.[261] At the same time there was some development in the party's analysis of race and class: the essentially liberal discourse of charitably 'welcoming' the growing black community hardened into the argument that the 'colour bar' and other forms of racism were impediments to a 'socialist Britain,' a point made forcefully in the leaflet 'No Colour Bar for Britain' (1955), 100,000 copies of which were circulated.[262] This was in turn one dimension of a long-overdue analysis of Britain's broader demographic and class composition and what it meant for *The British Road*'s hazily conceived 'broad popular alliance.' A 'Commission on the Middle Class' (1954) was convened to develop the passages of *The British Road* dealing with 'the various sections of the people apart from the industrial working class,' with a view to helping 'make the whole Party conscious of the importance of the broad popular alliance and the basis on which it can be built.'[263]

For party intellectuals, then, the more open atmosphere of the mid-1950s briefly ventilated the Cold War bunker, and allowed new insights about culture to begin to mesh with questions of political strategy and revolution's chronology, a process that also re-energized some of its leading figures.[264] John Gollan (1911–77), the ageing Pollitt's heir apparent, produced an unjustly forgotten book, *The British Political System* (1954), which marked an advance in British Marxist analysis of the bourgeois state, even if its concluding chapter, dutifully restating the key positions of *The British Road*, failed to do justice to the many insights that had preceded it.[265] For the more traditionally minded elements in the leadership, however, Moscow still set the limits to thinking, and the blurring of the 'two camps' and the scaling back of the 'Battle of Ideas' merely justified the reallocation of party resources into industrial and political channels, priorities which quickly closed down the spaces where the necessary debates were beginning to ferment. By 1955, *Our Time*, *Arena*, *Daylight*, *Communist Review*, and *Modern Quarterly* had all disappeared in a contraction driven through largely by Cornforth, who would soon regret being a tool of those he called 'political zombies.'[266] Debate was pushed to the small-circulation, cyclostyled publications of the separate groups, which reached at best hundreds of readers, and into the short-lived *Marxist Quarterly* (1954–57).[267] The full-time NCC secretary, Sam Aaronovitch, who had gradually earned the respect of wary party intellectuals with his sincere commitment to the NCC, was redeployed, and the cultural groups were effectively subsumed by the Industrial Committee or the Social Services Committee.[268] They continued to formulate their draft cultural material for the upcoming revision of *The British Road to Socialism*, although, like the 'Commission on the Middle Class' and Gollan's book, this would be lost in the maelstrom that tore through the party from early 1956.[269]

4
The Struggle for Renewal, 1956–1968

'I cannot think of any comparable event in the history of any major ideological or political movement,' wrote Eric Hobsbawm of Khrushchev's February 1956 'secret speech' to the Twentieth Congress of the Communist Party of the Soviet Union and its aftermath. 'To put it in the simplest terms, the October Revolution created a world communist movement, the Twentieth Congress destroyed it.'[1] In Poland the revelations of Stalinist terror unleashed mass strikes, demonstrations, and a new party leadership under the previously purged Władysław Gomulka. In Hungary it catalyzed a revolution quickly crushed by Soviet military intervention. This darker history made what Hobsbawm termed the 'collective nervous breakdown' of British Communists appear minor in comparison, but the cost to the party was clear enough.[2] The psychological structures that ballasted its hierarchies were broken, as the Special Congress reluctantly arranged by the leadership at the Hammersmith Town Hall in Spring 1957 revealed. Hardliners were barracked as 'dirty old swine'; unused to such uncomradely disorder, the stenographer was unsure whether to continue typing.[3] Loyalists brushed aside the haemorrhaging membership as a 'handful,' but the scale of the exodus was reported even in the *Times*.[4] A quarter of the membership (25.5 per cent, per cent or 8,455 resignations) left between February 1956 and February 1958 – around two thousand after Khruschev's revelations, five thousand after Hungary, and two thousand more after the Special Congress failed to deliver change. YCL membership plunged as well, from 3,500 in 1955 to 1,387 in 1958. The *Daily Worker* lost its best staff and fourteen thousand readers.[5]

To fix narrowly on the unprecedented high drama of that *annus mirabilis*, however, is to stress crisis over long-brewing conditions. Feeding into the explicit terms of the crisis – Stalinism, Hungary, democratic centralism, inner party democracy – was a widely shared sense of waking up to find oneself in a party that had not only colluded with and concealed terror, but had been living 'in a world of illusions,' as Christopher Hill put it. The party had long lost the political and cultural plot in Britain, seeking sanctuary from kaleidoscopic social change in its own ossifying narratives and rituals.[6] For some who now left, such as Stepney membership organizer John Gorman (1930–96), what looked and felt like a sudden break was actually a process of a crisis-driven awakening in which semi-repressed disillusionment with a party that seemed out of time was brought traumatically into consciousness.[7] He was not alone in leaving gradually, then suddenly. And among the many well-known intellectuals who left in 1956 and 1957 – including E.P. Thompson, John Saville, Edgell Rickword, Randall Swingler, Paul Hogarth, Doris Lessing, Rodney Hilton, and Bernard Stevens – motivations and feelings were shared with those who had already fallen away or departed in the period since Pollitt's *Looking Ahead* (1947), among them Harry McShane, Douglas Garman, Eric Heffer, Mervyn Jones, F.D. Klingender, Sylvia Townsend Warner, and Valentine Ackland. A key issue now, as then, was the chronology of revolution or, more specifically, the leadership's anti-intellectualism, resistance to theoretical work, ambivalence around cultural work, inability to formulate positions independently from Moscow, or engage in serious analysis of how parties in developed Western democracies could take and hold power. Other historians have for good reason dwelt on the stellar New Left post-party trajectories of those who departed, privileging the cultural, political, and intellectual national significance of key figures, especially E.P. Thompson.[8] As part of the same pattern, the historiography of British Communism itself frequently takes the 1956–7 conjuncture as the party's *terminal ad quem*, a switch point at which the old guard began to depart the stage (the ailing Pollitt retired in 1956), the intriguing complexities of the relationship between the party and the international Communist movement thinned (the Cominform was dissolved in 1956), and an air of historical inevitability weighed against the prospect of the party's renewal in consumer and credit Britain.[9] Although the 1960s is certainly the lost decade in terms of historical analysis of British Communism, however, the gap in analysis cannot be justified by the usual gauge for significance: membership figures. Even at the low point (25,313 members in 1959), the party had 7,500 more members than at any point between the wars (the zenith then was 17,756 in 1939), often considered British Communism's heyday. It had recovered its lost membership by 1963 (33,008, climbing to 34,281 the following year) before entering a period of decline checked only briefly during the militancy of the early 1970s (29,943 in 1973 against 28,803 in 1971).[10] This chapter takes as its analytical frame the long 1960s – the twelve years after 1956 – a period of tentative reconstruction in which, despite some new energies, the traditions of the past weighed like a nightmare on the brains of the living and a benumbed party clung to old habits and conceptions. Deeply symptomatic here was the leadership's notorious solution to the crisis in party finances – because of depleted membership dues and the desertion of wealthy donors – by secretly accepting funds of up to

£100,000 per year from Moscow, via the Soviet Embassy, laundered into apparently anonymous donations. This reveals less the duplicitous fifth-column cunning of journalists' imaginings than the sheer depths of British Communism's dependency on the lost world of its international movement and the leadership's lack of confidence and conviction in the party's political sovereignty and the nationally grounded project as spelled out in *The British Road*. Accepting Soviet funds was only the more sensational part of a pattern of clinging to the wreckage, which extended to maintaining 'iron' party discipline, 'democratic centralism,' and workerism.[11] What had been learned in the mid-1950s about changes in culture and class composition was repressed in the search for stabilization and existential security. Traditional spheres were prioritized at the expense of 'intellectuals' and the struggle across civil society, slackening even productive tension between the advocates of each for almost a decade. The revised version of *The British Road* (1958) no longer directly mentioned the Soviet Union, and tacitly conceded that the party needed to transform culture and popular consciousness in order to shift the country leftwards. However, the party was further than ever from analysing capitalism's boom or the ideological work performed by civil society under developed capitalism, in formulating positions on how to resist and contest it, or in developing models and structures for linking such work with its industrial and political activism. This problem was not new. What was new was that Communism's late 1950s crisis coincided with the sharp intensification of economic, social, and cultural changes – economic boom, immigration, hire-purchase credit culture, youth culture, and sharpening generational division – which made society more mediated and 'culture' matter much more in the processes of hegemony and the formation of identity and consent. 'Stalinism' is necessary but by no means sufficient to explain British Communism's conspicuous failure of renewal, although it continued to block receptiveness to ideas necessary for the process.

One key theme of this chapter is that of a censorious and culturally conservative Communist Party struggling to read an emerging culture whose watchwords were experimentation on the frontiers of 'high' and 'low' and whose key agent was 'youth.' Another theme is how a combination of entrenched hierarchies, outworn perceptions, depleted cultural prestige, and an eroded and demoralized membership base among cultural workers and intellectuals blocked the party from making real ground in those few spheres of civil society in which it retained strength and might have made real advances, especially science, education, and among Britain's new migrant communities. A third theme of the chapter is to challenge the standard history according to which the party's cultural work underwent a post-1962 'revitalization.'[12] Conceptions of 'socialist humanism' long latent in the party, runs that narrative, were amplified in synch with the priorities of a new leadership supplanting retiring veterans (Kerrigan, Campbell, Dutt).[13] While it is certainly the case that, broadly in tandem with equivalent developments in sister European parties, the CPGB's cultural work in the 1960s underwent a gradual, partial working loose from dogmatic, base-superstructure conceptions that had long restricted and marginalized the party, the process was tortuous and strikingly uneven, and occurred mostly in a flurry at the end of the decade as the party adjusted to opportunities already missed. I argue that the 1960s was in fact the nadir of the party's cultural work: never before had its ideas been less distinct or its interventions in civil society more muted.

The Making of the New Left

The far Left in British politics cleaved post-1956. On one side emerged an essentially traditional, industrially focused Communist Party, increasingly adept at working in the unions but less committed to activism across civil society than during the 'Battle of Ideas' period (the NCC was never again resourced to the same degree). On the other was a New Left, fluent about civil society but increasingly remote from the industrial working class and ambivalent about the idea of the party as a necessary vehicle for political transformation. This bifurcation was arguably costly to the British Left in the long term. It was by no means inevitable, and the common procedure of analysing the formation of the New Left as a separate process – and thereby observing its self-styled novelty – conceals the degree to which the remaking of the party and the making of the New Left were deeply intermeshed and mutually constitutive, inhabiting each other.[14] The gap that opened between a culturally focused New Left and an industrially focused CP after 1956 was substantially a matter of what the party did not, or could not, do.

It was never the case, for instance, as the leadership insisted and some critics accepted, that 1956 bisected the party along class lines, with loyal workers remaining while querulous intellectuals migrated to the New Left.[15] Intellectuals who remained in the party knew what was happening, and identified and confronted what they called 'a trend of hostility and condescension towards professional comrades *as a group* ("the intellectuals"),' rightly arguing that a culture of deep-rooted anti-intellectualism was being used to contain and discredit all critics of the leadership.[16] Resignations were spread across the party's social base.[17] Many leading industrial cadres left, including Lawrence Daly (1924–2009), John Horner (1911–97), and Les Cannon (1920–70), initially weakening the party's union strength.[18] In civil society the party potentially still had much to work with after the Special Congress. It retained a national newspaper, a publishing house, a strong influence over Topic Records, and an admittedly much-weakened presence at Unity Theatre, where in November 1956 activists broke rank and vented questions over Hungary that the leadership was keen to suppress.[19] In terms of personnel, it still had many intellectuals with international and national reputations: in science, it retained the prolific J.D. Bernal; leading educationalists including Max Morris (1913–2008), G.C.T Giles, Brian Simon, and Joan Simon stayed; the music group had Alan Bush, Ewan MacColl, and A.L. Lloyd; some major literary figures, among them Alick West, Arnold Kettle, and Jack Lindsay, remained, while Hugh MacDiarmid (1892–1978) rejoined. There were eminent classicists George Thomson, Robert Browning (1914–97), and R.F. Willetts (1915–99). Even among historians, where its intellectual loss had been heavy, it retained Dobb, Morton, George Rudé (1910–93), Lionel Munby, and an admittedly recalcitrant Eric Hobsbawm. That these resources and figures were considered at best peripheral to the party that emerged was determined by a process of defensive anti-intellectual reconstruction along traditional lines in which many intellectuals – especially Ivor Montagu, Arnold Kettle, Alan Bush, and George Thomson – eager to differentiate themselves from what Dutt called 'ivory tower dwellers in fairyland,' actively participated, intent on proving that they were subordinate to 'working-class leadership' and bore no relation to Dutt's characterization of their type.[20] A narrative of 1956 that partitions off those who left from those who stayed also obscures the powerful synergies between figures who ended on different 'sides.' 'Loyalists' Jack Lindsay, Eric Hobsbawm, and Maurice Cornforth and the departing Christopher Hill and Jack Beeching were among those who momentarily entertained the thought of 'toppling' the existing leadership and installing an alternative intellectual or 'long hair' group, a plot quickly recognized as fanciful given the party's traditional identity and mores.[21] Some of the best-known leavers – Saville, Thompson, Malcolm MacEwan, and Brian Pearce (1915–2008) – were initially committed to reforming the party rather than departing from it. Both 'groups' shared the perception that Stalinism had gone native and that no external agent now compelled the continuation in Britain of those defensive and sectarian habits officially renounced but actually alive and well in the Soviet Union.[22] British Stalinism was recognized to be manifested in a repertoire of habits, reflexes, and administrative protocols and set pieces; routinely mobilized at a moment of crisis, this repertoire was integral to the making of the New Left.

The creation of E.P. Thompson and John Saville's incendiary, smudgy, cyclostyled journal the *Reasoner*, around which the polarization initially occurred, was necessary precisely because what its first issue called the 'far-reaching discussion going on' among party members was so effectively blocked by the leadership across all party publications.[23] The saga of the leadership's stiff-necked approach to the journal is well known. At deeper stake in the discussion here and across the many other sites of the struggle – the Society for Cultural Relations, the letters sent by Communists to the *New Statesman* and *News Chronicle*, the modest proposals contained in the Minority Report on Inner Party Democracy blocked by the leadership – was the very idea of 'the party.'[24] Standing behind and sporadically surfacing through these encounters was a cluster of frequently recited preconditions for renewal that had long featured in debates about the form and function of the Communist Party in a changing world. These were communicated with telegrammatic urgency by Jack Beeching in 1956: 'rethinking the theory on the state, freedom, inner party democracy, real democracy …; a clear-cut of the leadership who are compromised and unable to change; an attitude to the Labour Party that responds to reality and Marxism.'[25] '[M]ost of us left the CP in the last analysis because we believed that intellectual dishonesty on the scale practised by King Street was an impossible foundation on which to build a movement,' wrote John Saville in 1958.[26] But initially Thompson and Saville wanted to remain in the party because they always suspected that, to a greater degree than they could prove, the impulses to which they gave expression were part of a better, subterranean countercurrent within the history of British Communism; that is why so much of the struggle in 1956–8 was fought over the party's past.[27] Brian Pearce was a dissident close to Saville and an obsessive archiver. Immersed in the party's past, he was permitted by the leadership to join the commission belatedly and reluctantly established in 1956, as a concession to critics, to oversee the writing of a party history. For him and for Saville the challenge was never merely to establish the true history of crucial moments such as the advent of the Third Period that had brought Pollitt and Dutt to the fore, or the Soviet pact and U-turn, important though they were. It was to recover a usable tradition of dissident Communism with the force to overturn a culture in which cadres were required 'to believe or forget whatever is demanded by the current line.'[28] Impeding this, as Pearce told Saville, were those Orwellian 'memory holes,' smoothed by long use, in which the inconvenient past was incinerated.[29] It was never, as he and Saville knew, going to be a question of simply claiming a coherent buried life or 'cultural opposition' in British Communism that could be appropriated en bloc. It was instead one of reconstructing disconnected episodes that perhaps represented something greater than the sum of their parts. To read back through the copious correspondence between Communists thrown up in the maelstrom of 1956 – and especially that between Pearce and Saville – is to feel the countermovement that soon coalesced as the first 'New Left,' struggling and failing to consolidate a tradition *within* the party. It was blocked by the 'discipline' whose forbidding forms were democratic centralism, and rules against factionalism and against publishing outside party channels, forms that effectively had kept dispersed and tentative the countercurrents from the past I analyse in this study. The monuments of the party's 'victory,' meanwhile, were resoundingly hollow. One was the new journal that appeared in October 1957, without any editorial explanation for the eight-month silence since the abrupt closure of *Marxist Quarterly*, as *Marxism Today*. It was self-evidently what Eric Hobsbawm called 'a sop to critics,'[30] and evaded the necessary discussions about Communist crisis and socialist identity, much as *Marxist Quarterly* had.[31] Its fragmentary form – there was no editorial until July 1960 – reflected the intellectual crisis of a party without a narrative or strategy. The other monument was the official party history, whose preparation was entrusted to James Klugmann, an unsurprising choice given his notorious fluency in the memory-hole genre, as demonstrated in *From Trosky to Tito* (1950), a publication cited by Christopher Hill during the 1957 Congress as an instance of high Stalinism.[32] The decision to suspend the unruly history commission and simply leave the writing to Klugmann would cost the party dearly in the 1960s as it sought to renew its credibility. Klugmann's loyalty would prove incompatible with historical objectivity. Relieved of party duties for a year to write his book, thirteen years passed before he produced two turgid volumes that inched the party's story only as far as 1927. Hobsbawm's assessment of his former mentor's work was cutting but fair: Klugmann, 'paralyzed by the impossibility of being both a good historian and a loyal functionary,' had 'wasted much of his time.'[33] By the time the volumes appeared – as Hobsbawm and his associates had warned[34] – a flourishing and far more readable body of often anti-Communist historiography of Communism was firmly established, including searching volumes by the now Trotsky-oriented Pearce.[35] The irony was that a party whose historians had enriched the terrain of British historiography was denied, by its own lingering Stalinism, a credible counternarrative to defend what was honourable in its own record. This situation was epitomized in early 1960 when the task of confronting Neal Wood's Rockefeller Foundation–subsidized, Cold War–coloured account, *Communism and British Intellectuals* (1959) in the national media fell to none other than E.P. Thompson.[36] Within the party, skirmishes around the memory holes would rumble away between a searching, sceptical tradition increasingly upheld by Monty Johnstone (1928–2007) – a recently rising cadre whose ascent was abruptly terminated after he clashed in 1957 with the leadership over its interference in the affairs of the YCL – and the evasiveness and doctrinaire dishonesty of Dutt and Andrew Rothstein.[37]

The British Road to Socialism (1958)

Much has been written about the rebooted Stalinism that stymied real debate in 1956–7 and consolidated the party's organizational processes and structures at the Special Congress, notably through the commission on 'Inner Party Democracy.'[38] Easily seen off by a commission overwhelmingly composed of reliable loyalists were the modest proposals contained in the 'minority report' – signed by Hill, MacEwen, and Peter Cadogan – that challenged the culture of 'iron discipline' ('essential for the CPU in Lenin's time' but 'inappropriate for our Party'), queried the opacity of the political committee (whose 'very large powers' were 'nowhere defined'), lamented the banning of the *Reasoner* (which revealed 'fear of independent thinking by Party members'), and took issue with the 'recommended list' system (whereby the retiring Executive Committee determined the composition of its successor).[39] Less has been said about the commission that drafted the revisions to the party's outward-facing program, *The British Road to Socialism*, dominated by Burns, Dutt, Gollan, George Matthews, and Arnold Kettle, and which met thirteen times between August and December 1956 and drafted the document discussed by the Executive Committee in December 1956 and at the 1957 Special Congress.[40] Some rich and challenging perspectives in the dissident and broadening spirit were clearly available to the commission. These ranged from the 947 suggested amendments submitted by branches, including insistence that, under socialism, 'creative artists in all fields shall be immune from any form of direction or interference,'[41] the findings of the 'Commission on the Middle Class' discussed in the previous chapter, and an especially detailed mapping of the politico-cultural terrain produced by the Artists' Group conceived to enrich *The British Road*'s coverage of 'the place of culture and cultural advance.'[42] In proto–New Left terms, the latter insisted that the party must clarify its ideas of the popular alliance, 'deal concretely' with the interests of the so-called middle strata, and – speaking with some prescience – take seriously restless teenagers who 'are trying everything once (even us).'[43] John Lewis, a figure much maligned by the New Left and especially by E.P. Thompson – who later characterized him as 'King Street's lay preacher of the most vulgar orthodoxy'[44] – also spoke compellingly. Lewis identified the theoretical chasm at the heart of British Communism and the ever-widening but unacknowledged gap between the party's vague but reassuring idea of itself (working-class, vanguardist, Leninist, revolutionary) and its actual muddled program, rooted in a parliamentarianism that evaded analysis of the bourgeois state.[45] The contradiction was no less glaring to Alick West, who noted the disjunction between what party leaders said at the 1957 Congress about 'smashing the state' and what the document actually contained.[46] 'Reformism' was the term of abuse levelled at those who presumed to query the precise meaning of reassuring mantras about democratic centralism and the dictatorship of the proletariat. The function of the abuse was to drown out discomfiting awareness of the dissonance between such concepts and what *The British Road* actually stressed ('the transition to socialism within the system of western democracy') and the lack of a 'theoretical basis' for such a strategy.[47]

Lewis had much to go at in terms of the revised text's contradictions. The account of class power – more or less unchanged from Pollitt's *Looking Ahead* (1947) – was one of a ruling-class conspiracy in which a 'small group of rich families' and their representatives ran the state and 'kept their hold over the minds of the people' through control of the media.[48] Culture was here identified as a key source of power, and the importance of the party in 'the spread of socialist consciousness through the working class' was repeatedly cited, but the document barely mentioned how the dominant culture was to be resisted, as West pointed out, and the broader strategic vision was no more coherent.[49] In the 1951 version of *The British Road*, hope had hinged around the 'broad popular alliance' that would create the consensus necessary for electoral breakthrough. This time, the capacious phrase nowhere appeared, and the question of alliance with elements of the middle strata was toned down – it had been altogether missing from the first draft – defensively suggesting that this was desirable but not necessary, despite one sentence that insisted otherwise.[50] Women were added to the final version, but barely registered in the draft.[51] Debates on socialist Britain's future relationship with former colonies escalated again during the document's writing as Dutt, licensed to speak his mind by Stalin's death, led a winning vote in favour of new wording that emphasized independence and self-determination, and inserted the adjective 'voluntary' to refine the hitherto mandatory 'fraternal relations.'[52] Although this was a necessary step forward, there was an air of unreality about such agonizing over subjunctive clauses and imagined scenarios in relation to the disintegrating empire while actually existing black Britons, facing oppression, discrimination, and racially motivated violence, were overlooked in the draft version, before being registered in the final version as 'colonial people in Britain' – which implied transience – rather than as British workers.[53]

While the 'middle section,' women and black Britons, remained out of focus, the traditional party, a shadowy presence in the 1951 version, was sharply recentred and commitment to Marxism and 'democratic centralism' affirmed – 'democratic centralism,' absent from the1951 version, now made two appearances.[54] If such language was a sop to the faithful, the imagined breakthrough scenario was unlikely to please them, being strictly parliamentary – unlike its strategically ambiguous predecessor, the 1958 document explicitly committed the party to political pluralism.[55] The key moment would be a General Election held in a propitious moment of 'mounting class struggle,' enabling the election of 'a socialist Labour and Communist majority to establish a Socialist Government.'[56] In other words, the emphasis shifted from the 'broad popular alliance' to the narrower political process of building an alliance with the Labour Party, with which the CP still imagined affiliating or even fusing into 'a single working class party' if and when 'the majority of the movement has been won for the Marxist outlook.'[57] This was, to say the least, deeply unrealistic given the depth of the Labour Party's hostility to Communists and the further diminution of the CP as a credible electoral force – the days of Communist parliamentary representation were now permanently over, with fifteen out of seventeen candidates having finished last in their constituency votes in the 1955 General Election.[58] In short, the worst aspects of the original version of *The British Road* – bellicose rhetoric, vague formulations, giddily optimistic descriptions of the political scene – were magnified in its new, crisis-written version. At a time when the party needed to replenish its ranks, re-establish intellectual credibility, and draw into conversation an incipient New Left, it produced a document more, not less, defensive and anachronistic than its predecessor. It salved the wounds of those who stayed, but was very easily dismissed by others, including former members and now-expanding Trotsky-influenced groups to the party's left.[59]

All Kinds of Silliness

Internal struggles between a greatly depleted intellectual strata and a punch-drunk leadership determined to stabilize the party also focused on the now-underresourced National Cultural Committee, whose very existence, at least, unlike the new edition of *The British Road to Socialism*, identified the cultural sphere as a site of ideological struggle to which the party must respond. Here the process of control and containment deployed by the leadership instrumentalized the base-superstructure model, which saw culture as playing an unspecified but insistently secondary role, further narrowing the party's potential appeal and capacity for self-renewal. A reforming wind blew briefly when the NCC was tasked by the Twenty-fourth Congress (1956) to produce a blueprint for its own reorganization. The NCC proposed a bottom-up model through which membership would be overwhelmingly elected by the main cultural groups, supplemented with just two or three members of the party's Executive Committee.[60] Emile Burns, however, was in no mood for what he called 'all kinds of silliness,' and the familiar model was instead imposed whereby the NCC would remain a subcommittee responsible to the Executive Committee, not to the groups, and the Executive Committee would appoint the majority of membership and approve all of it.[61] To take matters forward was a core membership, initially drawn from the Executive Committee, comprising the hard-line Bill Wainwright (1908–2000) – Gollan's assistant secretary, newly promoted to the Executive Committee in 1957, now doubling as NCC chair (replacing Burns), and tasked to reform the NCC on these terms – flanked by Brian Simon, elected to the Executive Committee in 1957 and a more moderate figure of the type required to lend some credibility to the body, and Arnold Kettle, who had distinguished himself in the eyes of a leadership with his loyalty.[62] A demoralized Alick West was just about respectable enough to be included on the committee selected by these three, and immediately observed that the nomination of the NCC by the Executive Committee meant 'they can keep people off that don't want,' which they did.[63] Eric Hobsbawm, and the far-from-outspoken Margot Heinemann fell into that camp.[64] After much deliberation by the leadership, Jack Lindsay was invited back onto the underpowered and dysfunctional NCC in April 1958, despite being considered 'wonky as hell,' having protested against the expulsion of Hyman Levy.[65]

How New Is the New Left?

The party's relations with the New Left were now clearly a key front line in its struggle for renewal. Here too the dominant mode, for which Executive Committee and NCC member Kettle set the tone and assumed the main responsibility, was inward, defensive, and damaging.[66] As with the revisions to *The British Road*, other perspectives were available, but quashed. Eric Hobsbawm's May 1958 report to the Executive Committee took the New Left seriously, challenging the conspicuous absence of the party's youth and student organizers from the movement's events and demonstrations.[67] For Lindsay, the party was paying the price for its failure since 1945 to analyse properly the 'unprecedentedly devious nature of the class war' in a context of monopoly capitalism, welfarism, and credit;[68] he identified the intellectual power of the New Left as an integral site in the 'gigantic task of reviving Marxism'[69] in this context, and wrote directly to the leadership, challenging 'ostrich tactics' and advocating the more open position towards non-party currents pursued by the Partito Comunista Italiano.[70] Echoing Hobsbawm, he warned that the party was making 'a sad mistake' if it assumed that the New Left's journals, *New Reasoner: A Quarterly Journal of Socialist Humanism* and *Universities & Left Review*, with their combined readership of around ten thousand, and packed meetings, were 'peripheral.'[71]

The approved discourse under Kettle, however, was what Lindsay called a 'steady withdrawing from reality – the kind of thing meant by the proverb that those whom the gods wish to destroy they first send mad.'[72] In this vein early NCC documents concerned with the New Left and 'Winning Intellectuals to the Party' blithely glossed over the fact that those it most needed to win had recently been members.[73] Kettle was unwilling to recognize or accept that, having lost its effective monopoly on Marxism, the party would have to go to others, rather than their coming to it. One stock response was that those who had deserted for the New Left, especially Lessing and Thompson, were overrated in any case.[74] Another was that the New Left, like the cultural wave of the 'Angry Young Men' – anti-establishment playwrights and novelists – was a passing 'petit-bourgeois' fad.[75] The leadership ignored contrary views, including those voiced in response to the *Daily Worker's* brusque dismissal of the 20,000-selling state-of-the-nation essay collection *Declaration*, which brought together key New Left thinkers and 'Angry Young Men' (John Osborne, Kenneth Tynan, Colin Wilson, and the honorary man and former Communist, Doris Lessing).[76] Extending the position taken on the *New Reasoner*, the leadership now forbade members from contributing to the

New Left's two journals on the grounds that such debate legitimated these 'hostile' elements, which implied that the movement needed the imprimatur of the party.[77] Lindsay and Hobsbawm defied the edict and contributed to the *New Reasoner*, launched in summer 1957 and edited by Thompson and Saville with the assistance of an editorial board comprising (with one exception, Ralph Miliband) former Communists.[78] Eric Hobsbawm also wrote for the Oxford-based *Universities & Left Review*, which had been launched a few months earlier and whose twenty-something editors included former Communist Raphael Samuel (1934–96).[79] The leadership recognized the need to retain at least some of its intellectuals, including Lindsay and Hobsbawm, and applied the edict differently according to who broke it. Malcolm MacEwan, whom Gollan now wanted rid of, was expelled for joining the editorial board of the *New Reasoner*.[80] The others were merely chastized, although Lindsay in particular was openly unrepentant.[81] Similar self-isolating tendencies also prevailed in relation to the broad-based and genuinely open initiative that became the Society for the Study of Labour History, dominated by 'enemies of the party,' according to Dutt, who warned Lindsay against having anything to do with the organization.[82]

The more open dialogue to enrich Marxism proposed by Lindsay and Hobsbawm was one thing.[83] Dialogue presupposed, however, that what remained of the party had new things to say. In fact, by definition, the New Left rooted itself in Communism's intellectual blind spots, not least in expanding the reach of Marxism to engage precisely with those more 'cultural' spheres in which, as Lindsay had long argued, the party's thinking had been weak for years. 'Stalinism bred a fear,' argued the editorial of the first issue of *Universities & Left Review* with the British party clearly in mind, 'whose consequence has been that whole areas of contemporary life have fallen beyond the reach of our "political" commitment,' adding, 'when socialist values lose their relevance for the total scale of man's activities, they lose their "political" point as well.'[84] One significant site of struggle in 1956–8 duly concerned the activity of writing and socialist censorship – Zhdanovism being understood by Thompson, the Writers' Group, Lindsay, and others as the cultural logic of Stalinism from which a party serious about renewal should distance itself.[85] Other Communist Parties, as many, including Lindsay and the New Left, noted,[86] were now marking distance from the Soviet Union, in the Italian party's case by overseeing the publication of Boris Pasternak's 'anti-Soviet' historical novel of the revolutionary years, *Doctor Zhivago*, which the Soviet state had refused to publish.[87] Lindsay, like the New Left, challenged the Soviet decision, and regretted the backsliding in Soviet cultural policy between the Second and Third Writers' Congresses of 1955 and 1959.[88] Kettle was in no mood, however, for a cultural *glasnost*,[89] and defended the Soviet decision in the national media.[90] Repeating John Lewis's rhetoric from the

Soviet Literature Controversy a decade earlier, he imagined the application of Zhdanovite measures to Britain, presenting the party as a 'parent' of unassailable wisdom and authority morally obliged to offer 'pressure' and 'influence' over a wilful and infantile British culture.[91]

An overlapping site of conflict centred on the core New Left contention – also a mainstay in Lindsay's turn-of-the-decade novels, which grappled with a changing working class – that post-war affluence was producing a more mediated society (identity came less from work, family, and community and more from culture) and that the proliferation of commercial culture blurred distinctions between 'economy' and 'culture' in ways that called into question existing theoretical paradigms.[92] A key focus for a new socialist analysis was therefore necessarily contemporary British capitalism – a newly variegated economy shored up by credit and welfare and metabolized by 'the magic system' of vast advertising networks – and the much-rumoured 'classlessness' and 'embourgeoisification' of the working class which exercised sociologists, the arts, and the mass media in the second half of the 1950s.[93] In terms of the working class, the New Left contention was that 'glossyism' (Richard Hoggart preferred the phrase 'shiny barbarism') was 'the authentic expressions of certain features of contemporary society,' and that deep changes were being lived 'into the fibres,' as Raymond Williams later put it, of working-class life and culture.[94] The party's monoglot response was one of defensive denial. The annual surveys produced by the Economic Committee maintained that, despite the epiphenomena of sustained growth and full unemployment, capitalism was in long-term decline and recession imminent.[95] Predicting economic bust and a return to crisis as usual – what Thompson called 'frightening the children of the 1950s with the Ogre of the 1930s' – remained a standard response, and the limited recessions recorded in the United States in 1948–9, 1951–4, and 1957–8 were grasped enthusiastically as intimations of looming slumps.[96] There were some tentative discussions about why the crisis failed to materialize, and why Marx's analysis of the long-term tendency of capitalism to depress working-class living standards was apparently not being fulfilled.[97] But with internationally derived Communist identity in a state of convulsion, the party was not inclined to detect significant changes in capitalism as well. It denied that 'class structure' had 'been in any serious sense changed' by ten years of Keynesianism.[98] It repressed not only the idea of changes in working-class culture, but also shifts in the broader contours of class composition and consciousness that it had begun to assimilate through its 1954 'Commission on the Middle Class,' a document effectively buried by the crises of 1956 and 1957 before resurfacing as Andrew Grant's *Socialism and the Middle Classes* (1958), a defensive work far below the pitch of New Left discussion whose central thesis was that rumours of economic change were overstated.[99] *New Reasoner* reviewer Peter Worsley accurately described it as 'comfortable self-delusion.'[100]

One muted plotline running through the history of British Communism from the 1920s had been a struggle – sometimes hidden, sometimes open – to 'humanise and make concrete' what Thompson called 'the abstract schema of Communist orthodoxy' in general, and in particular to develop a more nuanced approach to 'culture' and consciousness in the face of *Short Course* vulgarizations.[101] That countertradition was almost extinguished by now, and some of its key proponents – Swingler, Thompson, Saville, Williams, Lessing, Hilton, Kiernan, and Hill among them – were criticizing from the outside. The force of the New Left's most innovative work, like Raymond Williams's breakthrough *Culture and Society 1780–1950* (1958), which would go on to sell 200,000 copies, came precisely from a critical working with, through, and beyond the positions learned in the party.[102] The problem was not only that the critics knew the party's positions too well, but that these positions still formed the horizon of its thinking, and it had no others. Behind the scenes, Communists were at a theoretical loss how to respond to Williams's books. Hardliners attacked the work on the grounds that the mainstream press found there 'a supposed ideological weapon against our views,' and Kettle vacillated between arguing that Williams should be kept onside for 'tactical' reasons and admitting that the party lacked the theoretical weight to produce compelling counterarguments.[103]

Making it worse was that Communism's 1956–8 crisis, in which culture was relegated further down its list of priorities, coincided with the unprecedented eruption of debates about culture and class across the well-documented 'new wave' in theatre (John Osborne, Shelagh Delaney, Arnold Wesker, John Arden), fiction (Alan Sillitoe, John Braine, Keith Waterhouse, Raymond Williams), 'Free Cinema' (which emphasized working-class leisure and consumerism rather than work as sources of identity), and cultural sociology (Michael Young and Peter Wilmott's *Family and Kinship in East London* (1957), Hoggart's *The Uses of Literacy* (1957), Williams's *Culture & Society*). This new formation brought to the centre of national culture and debate the very questions the party was keen to evade about 'classlessness,' class identity, and social mobility.[104] The party's responses typically appeared after the debate had moved on, and ranged from condescension ('Colin Wilson, a sort of intellectual Elvis Presley'),[105] to indignation that *it* knew the working class best (the consumerist, individualistic, and anarchic mindset of Arthur Seaton in Sillitoe's *Saturday Night and Sunday Morning* (1958) were not representative of the real working class),[106] to a wounded tone that asked why there were so few Communists in these books and plays, and implausibly overvalued those few in which some appeared.[107] The New Left, by contrast, was shaping discussion, arguing that many of the key 'political' challenges were now 'cultural' in the sense that the 'culture' – different ways of life increasingly permeated by a commercial flow of words and images – was assimilating the working class into capitalism's structures and mores.[108] The challenge for the left, argued Thompson in particular, was to formulate analyses, narratives, and movements capable of speaking to core class identities and interests across such socio-cultural transformations.[109] Above all, the New Left's central intervention was an insistence on the theoretical integration of these two frames – the structural and the cultural – into analysis of contemporary society and sensibilities.[110] The cruel irony was that New Left criticism of party doxa and Stalinized Marxism were increasingly enriched by two sources published, after much backroom trouble, by the party press itself: a selection from Gramsci's writings edited and translated by former CP Historians' Group member Louis Marks, *The Modern Prince & Other Writings* (1957), and Martin Milligan's translation of Marx's *Economic and Philosophic Manuscripts of 1844* (1959).[111] Whereas early Marx and Gramsci energized a New Left seeking to emphasize agency over structure and, in the words of Randall Swingler, to 'start from the people again,' the sheer weight of sedimented conceptions and the instinct to defend traditional positions prevented the party from truly recognizing the significance of what was under its nose, or from using it to revitalize its calcified theories.[112] Party readings of Marx remained economistic: the Manuscripts were intriguing juvenilia, according to the party's Marx expert, Maurice Cornforth, but Marx should be read from *Capital* backwards.[113] If discussed at all, Gramsci was presented as a model Communist intellectual who had properly immersed himself in party life.[114] Lindsay and Lewis would offer more suggestive assimilations, arguing that these texts needed to be sources for a revitalised humanist Communism, but the party publishers declined Lindsay's manuscript, 'Man and the Alien Thing,' which applied early Marx to contemporary issues in East and West; *Marxism Today* lagged far behind New Left publications in dealing with the new translations.[115] The more dogmatic Marxism offered by Cornforth's primers, the revised *History of the Communist Party of the Soviet Union* (translated in 1961), and the 800-page Soviet manual of 'the theory and practice of world communism,' *Fundamentals of Marxism-Leninism* (1961) – 'a magnificent gift to the working class,' according to *Marxism Today* – remained dominant.[116]

Sporadically at first and more assuredly towards the end of the 1950s, the party would begin to identify weaknesses in a soon-splintering New Left, raising important questions about its vagueness around revolutionary agency, its lack of internationalism, its 'cultural' remoteness from economic fundamentals, and its increasing detachment from working-class organizations, especially after the New Left's two journals merged into the more academic *New Left Review* at the turn of the decade. Even here, however, when Communists were acute in identifying faultlines that increasingly opened within the New Left itself around central priorities – were they really about publishing, discussion, or the creation of a political movement or party? – the tone was often of a spiky irritability or smug *Schadenfreude* that made their criticisms matter less than they might.[117] 'How New is the New Left?' asked Kettle rhetorically in the title of an often-penetrating article from October 1960 that used the term 'petty-bourgeois' twenty-five times in seven pages, attacked his former colleague and friend E.P. Thompson with particular venom, and took evident satisfaction in the disappearance of the *New Reasoner*.[118] Five years after the crises of 1956, there would be a begrudging post-mortem of the damaging sectarian approaches that had characterized the party's approach to New Left currents, including some very sharp criticisms of Kettle and the Execitive Committee from SOAS academic Ralph Russell (1918–2008), who saw party inwardness as an impediment to renewal.[119] Kettle remained unrepentant about his approach to a movement that allegedly had seduced intellectuals by offering 'communist *élan* minus the discipline of the Party.'[120]

Growing Points

'The New Left is concerned,' wrote Thompson in an early overview of the movement, 'not to wait hopefully for the old disasters,' but 'to discover the new frustrations and potentials within contemporary life, the new growing points.'[121] But when it came to the growing point of Britain's black community, which had increased in size from fewer than two thousand before the war to one hundred times that number by 1959, with over forty thousand migrants arriving between 1955 and 1957, the New Left was little better than the mainstream labour movement, and had nothing to teach the CP, whose own record was at best uneven and contradictory.[122] As some in the party recognized, overcoming these contradictions was clearly one necessary route to renewal as Britain's working class was being transformed. According to the party's own self-criticism in 1957, it had paid insufficient attention to racism in Britain until around 1954, when a latent discourse insisting that the 'colour bar and all forms of racial discrimination' was an obstacle to a 'socialist Britain' was promoted into a key claim, notably in the 100,000 copies of its leaflet, 'No Colour Bar for Britain' (1955), part of a campaign that exerted real influence over the Movement for Colonial Freedom in focusing energies on racism within Britain's borders.[123] Many instances of Communist creative grassroots antiracism would follow,[124] from trade-union-level struggles to the tireless and self-effacing campaigning of John Williamson (1903–79), who initiated and orchestrated the National Paul Robeson Committee, an international campaign for the restoration of Robeson's passport, withdrawn by the US State Department in 1950.[125]

In part, however, that campaign was successful because, in being essentially a Cold War struggle, it sidestepped the tensions that otherwise bedevilled the party's work around questions of 'race.' The agonized revising of *The*

British Road revealed a party stuck in a framework that read the new traumas faced by a settled black community in terms of imperialism and empire, a model implying that the communities were epiphenomena of imperialism and that the oppression they faced would somehow be magically resolved by a clarification of post-imperial arrangements. Paradoxically, therefore, a traditional strength of the party's analysis – insistence on the economic basis of imperialism – played a part in impeding the formulation of new conceptions in a changing world. At a crisis conjuncture when it crucially needed clarity on racism in Britain, the party was pulled between a fixation on relations between Britain and its former colonies and what sounded like a tolerant 'open-door' liberal discourse of 'welcoming the arrival of colonial immigrants,' sublimating structural matters into a question of decency and good manners.[126] As discussed in the previous chapter, these conceptions had structured not only party discourse and documents, but also the modes of organization through which the party engaged with these new communities. The challenge of how to assimilate these groups, and to reorientate and revitalize the party in the process, was not met, and the organizational arrangements created were ineffective, makeshift structures from which recruits drifted. As mentioned in the previous chapter, the so-called Robeson branches into which West African and other 'national' groups had been organized in the early 1950s proved divisive and were dissolved in the mid-1950s, to be replaced by committees including the West Indian Advisory Committee under the aegis of the International Department, while new 'national' branches' (Cypriot, West Indian, and Indian) were formed, to be finally dissolved in 1966 amidst concern about Maoist infiltration.[127] Fundamentally, in agonizing about 'national' provenance or cultural identity of constituent groups, the party missed the key point that new 'black' identities were being created under historical pressure ('I became black in London, not Kingston,' as *New Left Review* editor Stuart Hall later put it).[128] Although new black recruits including Asquith Gibbes (1934–2013), Vishnu Sharma (1921–92), and Winston Pindar contributed to the party press, official discourse and policy statements were typically handed down from the International Department. The party, meanwhile, proved structurally resistant to the rapid assimilation of new talent – especially that which bore little resemblance to the white, skilled, male industrial worker – and remained governed by a paternalistic hierarchy that expected long apprenticeship and appropriate deference.[129]

Perhaps the worst consequence of this was the marginalization of the Trinidad-born Communist Claudia Jones (1915–64), a fellow US deportee of Williamson, a former leading American Communist and *Daily Worker* editor, and perhaps the best leader that the CPGB never had.[130] Disinclined to kowtow, she attacked Emile Burns in her debut speech at the fractious

1957 conference for his reference to 'backward people,' and cautioned that, as far as black Britons were concerned, being Communist offered no automatic absolution from 'infection of imperialist ideology.'[131] Consigned to subcommittees, her activism took on a semi-autonomous character that brought little or no credit to the party, being centred on the monthly newspaper she founded and edited, the *West Indian Gazette* – the first major Caribbean newspaper in Britain – launched in March 1958 and pitched at the 80,000-strong Caribbean population.[132] Jones knew her Lenin, and the newspaper was never conceived as a secondary reflection of an existing community, but as a primary site in its making, whose production and distribution, no less than its contents, were designed to create common identities and sensibilities and foment new ways of feeling and seeing. Linking together local and international news, culture, and sport, it soon functioned as the organizing hub of the first London Caribbean Carnival, the forerunner of the Notting Hill Carnival, held in St Pancras Town Hall on 30 January 1959, a defiantly affirmative festival of West Indian political and cultural identity defined in opposition to the white riots of the previous year. Unwittingly taking forward what was best about the Edinburgh People's Festivals of the early 1950s, the Carnival and newspaper exceeded and sought to correct, rather than break with or displace, the party's own discursively and organizationally bound modes of engagement with Britain's black community. 'Struggle begets more struggle' was Jones' motto, by which she meant that 'community' or 'cultural' struggles susceptible to being dismissed by the party as cultural or superstructural always ultimately came up against the structures of capitalism, and that 'race' and 'class' were deeply implicated and therefore a false dichotomy.[133] She would prove a source of inspiration for fellow-embattled black CP activists like Trevor Carter (1930–2008) – a member of the London branch of the Caribbean Labour Congress and stage manager at the Carnival – who shared her conviction that capitalism was the ultimate horizon of oppression, that a Communist Party was the necessary means of struggle against it, and that what Africa Committee member Peter Seltman called 'the patriarchal relationship that existed between the CPGB leadership and Party members coming from colonial countries' was a reason to transform the party, rather than to leave it.[134] Thinking back over the post-1956 decade in 1986, Carter would rightly see the late 1950s as a missed opportunity for the party's regrowth and self-transformation.[135] He would draw the comparison between the well-documented membership lost during the 1956 crisis and the little analysed consequences of the party's inability to attract and retain black recruits, arguing that 'the stubborn class-before-race position of the party during the fifties and sixties cost the party dearly in terms of its members,' actual and potential.[136] The party's virtually unchanging racial composition and tentative analysis made it easily outflanked by black power

Communists protest against racism in Notting Hill, late 1950s. CP Picture Archive, Box 2, 'Anti Racialism' Sub File; NMLH 2000.10.84.1.

currents in the late 1960s, which could plausibly present it as part of the conservative labourist mainstream movement in matters of race, although that was never the whole story.

Sputnik Socialism

Despite the lost thousands Carter identifies, and the party's inability to transform its own composition in synch with the changing face of Britain, its declining membership was checked and reversed from February 1958, rising steadily through 1959 and 1960 and more sharply through 1963, reaching 34,218 in February 1964 – higher than the 1955 figure – while the YCL membership increased by two-thirds over the same period, reaching 4,666, the highest since 1945.[137] The usual explanations given for the increase are threefold. First, the party clarified its position over the Campaign for Nuclear Disarmament, which it supported from 1960, bringing the official stance in line with the YCL's long-standing instincts and enabling it to provide some organizational backbone and win recruits, despite charges of double standards regarding the Soviet or 'workers' bomb.' Second, it found itself in increasingly congenial conditions on the industrial front (near full employment, economic turbulence, and a government from 1961 inclined to wage-control measures). Third, it was able to recruit in the new campaigns opposing Apartheid and supporting decolonization and national liberation movements (Algeria, the Congo, Cuba).[138] Assisting recruitment in all these spheres and others, however, was something more difficult to pinpoint: a shift in broader social perceptions about Communism and modernity closely related to the Soviet Union's launch of the first satellite in September 1957.[139] After Sputnik, Gallup reported that 36 per cent of Britons felt an increased respect for the Russians, 27 per cent could not comprehend why the Americans were lagging behind, but only 14 per cent felt more anxious about the Soviet Union as a consequence.[140] While the Soviet Union forged ahead, late-imperial Britain, humiliated through Suez, seemed to be spent: Sputnik coincided with a fire at a nuclear reactor at Windscale (later Sellafield) and the ignominious pumping of thousands of gallons of contaminated milk into the ocean. The impression that, as the *New Statesman* put it, 'over a wide sector of scientific knowledge the Russians are advancing further and faster than the West' was shared across the political spectrum from Nye Bevan to Churchill.[141]

The party was clearly a beneficiary of the link between Communism and Soviet science, but not merely a passive one. Bernal had played a modest role in the liberalization of Soviet science from around the time of Stalin's death.[142] He and his associates' long-standing analysis of the social relations of science and the importance of state planning had been integral in helping to create in Britain an intellectual framework and medium of perception through which the discrepancy between Soviet sputniks and Britain's woeful backwardness was apprehended and discussed.[143] Nowhere was this influence more apparent than in the high-profile public dissemination of a recognizably Bernallian analysis by Bernal's old friend, the novelist and scientific advisor to the Civil Service Commission, C.P. Snow, whose 1959 Rede lecture at Cambridge was rapidly published as *The Two Cultures and the Scientific Revolution* (1959) and whose arguments dominated national intellectual discussion about science, the state, and the economy as the decade turned.[144] Snow's swingeing analysis of a damagingly influential British elite that prided itself on scientific ignorance had been standard fare on the Communist-led scientific Left for a quarter of a century.[145] Communists naturally protected and developed a thesis that integrated their deeply ingrained positions about the dangers of an antiscientific, reified intellectual world cut off from historical progress and that affirmed the Soviet Union for possessing 'a deeper insight into the scientific revolution.'[146] The grounds for such positive references to the Soviet Union became firmer in

1961 when in April telegenic cosmonaut Yuri Gagarin entered orbit.[147] (Communists were doubtlessly relieved that the live television transmission of his return to Moscow eclipsed reports of the start of the trial into the rigging of ballots by Communists in the Electrical Trades Union, also in the news that week.)[148] Within the Labour Party meanwhile – the organization central to *The British Road to Socialism*'s strategy – this recognizably Bernallian discourse now framed discussion around the retention of Clause 4: as Richard Crossman argued in his Fabian pamphlet, 'Labour and the Affluent Society' (1960), renouncing the principle of the public ownership that undergirded Soviet modernity would consign the country to permanent second place.[149] The Bernallian analysis of driving economic modernization through science soon also gained traction in the Labour Party thanks in part to a ginger group attended by Snow, Crossman, James Callaghan, Harold Wilson, and others through whom it would morph into the talk of white heat and technological revolution that framed the 1964 General Election, and which the party naturally supported.[150]

In this respect, Communist science was at the vanguard of the party, in that the party's broader strategy was now dedicated to enriching the Labour Party's 'socialist consciousness' exactly as its Bernallian scientific discourse had done.[151] In no other sphere did it have an equivalent intellectual influence, and it was natural that the revised *The British Road* (1958) began with a Bernallian flourish about 'great scientific advances' having 'opened up entirely new perspectives for mankind.'[152] The trouble was that this vanguard position actually reflected the delayed-action working through of long-held ideas into the mainstream culture in the 1930s and 1940s, rather than contemporary realities. Lysenko had devastated the Engels Society and Communist science organization; 1956 had completed the exodus of its scientific strata.[153] Post 1956 the party lacked even a functioning science group to take forward Bernal's work, and in 1958 struggled to find scientists willing to staff the reformed NCC.[154] Despite the best efforts of the second NCC secretary, Francis Aprahamian – Bernal's Birkbeck research assistant and effective co-writer of *Science in History* – the high point of Communist science had long passed.[155] Bernal, British Communism's most influential public intellectual, on whom so much of its scientific work had rested, would suffer his first stroke in June 1963 and never fully recover.

Educational Wars

Debates about elites, science, and modernity interlocked with those about education in the late 1950s, and school education in particular was widely considered a potential site of Communist revival.[156] Communist teachers' membership – buttressed by their established and sometimes quasi-autonomous organizational

Communists in Ilford basking in the reflected glory of the Soviet Sputnik launch, 1957. CP Picture Archive, Box 8, NMLH 2000.10.327.3.

Communists with membership cards, 1958. CP Picture Archive, Box 13; NMLH 2000.10.526.

structures (NEAC), networks (Teachers for Peace), and lively publications (*Education Today and Tomorrow*) – held up disproportionately through the crisis; as already mentioned, key trade unionists and intellectuals in education remained in the party, notably Max Morris, G.C.T. Giles, Joan Simon, and Brian Simon.[157] As the crisis receded and the Cold War eased, Communist teacher numbers swelled further, doubling between 1956 and 1963, reaching 2,520, or about 7 per cent of total party membership, in that year; only engineers (8,280) and builders (3,000) were better represented.[158]

The increase owed much to tireless staffroom trade union work, but also crucial was Communists' profile and position in debates around systemic educational reform. 'It seemed to many,' education academic, Executive Committee member, and future NCC chair Brian Simon noted, 'that the mortar holding together the fractured and divisive education system lay in the theory and practice of intelligence testing' that 'dominated, but above all legitimated school selection at eleven and inner school differentiation from the age of seven and sometimes five.'[159] As I argued in the previous chapter, few if any did more to demonstrate that these tests measured cultural capital rather than 'innate' ability than Simon, whose untiring and wide-ranging campaign commanded the respect of many in the teaching profession and beyond. *Intelligence Testing and the Comprehensive School* (1953) had sold 8,000 copies across two editions, and was followed by *The Common Secondary School* (1955).[160] Professor Philip Vernon's widely cited report *Secondary School Selection* (1957) – which irreversibly undermined the logic of testing at eleven – substantially drew upon Simon's work and corroborated his central claims.[161] Like the journal Simon co-founded in 1958, *Forum for the Discussion of New Trends in Education*, the edited symposium *New Trends in English Education* (1957) was at the forefront in further undermining 'common sense' about inherited intelligence, in communicating new developments, and in constructing an effective alliance for educational transformation, an objective partially realized from the mid-1960s through a Labour government broadly committed to the single secondary school.[162] In 1963 Simon would present evidence to the Plowden Committee, appointed by Conservative education minister Edward Boyle to analyse the impact of junior school streaming; when published four years later, the report endorsed the position of Simon and his associates and came out against streaming.[163]

The irony, however, was that, while Simon's profile as a leading figure in the struggle against the educational marginalization of working-class children added lustre to British Communism and showed what could be done at the level of building intellectual and moral prestige, Simon found himself up against narrower conceptions within the party, despite his seniority (on the Executive Committee since 1957, he would become NCC chair in 1962). Simon's intuitively Gramscian line was that the NEAC, the central body in formulating educational policy, should be integral to the party's long-term strategy and cultural work, not 'a purely teacher's affair,' but a broader body 'concerned with thinking about and developing policy over the whole field of education,' assimilating and developing broader struggles over provision, curriculum, pedagogy, and, ultimately, the creation of intellectuals.[164] As Simon knew all too well, such ideas were anathema to dominant conceptions: having left the teaching profession to become an academic in 1950, he had been pressured to withdraw from the NEAC, a body dominated by teachers, primarily focused on trade union struggle, and increasingly centred around prominent NUT activist Max Morris, the leading figure on the left of the union after G.C.T. Giles's retirement in 1956.[165] Simon's alternative visions were stoutly resisted by the more trade-union minded when the question of the NEAC's status flared up again in the early 1960s, a propitious moment for teacher militancy when the NUT Executive broke precedent by rejecting the pay scales approved by the Burnham Committee.[166] As so often before, the more traditional industrial view prevailed – supported by the leadership – as Simon's wife Joan found when the mistrustful and monopolizing NEAC blocked the publication of her manuscript entitled 'Marxism and Education.'[167] That even Arnold Kettle was concerned about the teachers' doctrinaire and anti-intellectual tendencies indicated the bitterness of a internal struggle that drove a demoralized Joan Simon from the party.[168] The unpleasant episode – a late spasm of Zhdanovism – was most significant, however, not only as a symptom of long-standing party anti-intellectualism deeply internalized by its teachers, but of a deeply embedded binary logic that opposed hard industrial work to soft cultural work. As such, it spoke of the party's inability to conceive a strategy or organizational forms capable of integrating these different modes – the industrial, the cultural – into a coherent strategy. The struggles here anticipated the opening out of such oppositions into explicit ideological differences in the decade ahead.

Cultural Policies

Rubbing salt in the Communist wound were former members who now brought recognizable but mutated versions of Communist cultural politics to spheres of national cultural life in which the party itself lacked a significant presence. As he acknowledged, former YCLer Lionel Bart's (1930–99) feel-good music-hall-style songs that created pop hits and international fame with the proletarian pastoral *Oliver!* (1960) owed much to the aesthetic of Unity Theatre.[169] Lapsed Communist and former Unity stalwart, screenwriter Ted (later Baron) Willis (1914–92) and future speechwriter for Harold Wilson, was another coming man as the decade turned, producing work for both the small and big screen that bore a Unity imprint.[170] Centre 42, the liveliest cultural initiative of the early 1960s, was devised and driven by another former YCLer, Arnold Wesker (1932–2016), assisted by two more former Communists, Theatre Workshop actor and future Theatre Studies academic Clive Barker (1931–2005) and Doris Lessing. The problem Centre 42 sought to remedy was straight out of the 'Battle of Ideas' period: an 'American derived but anonymously cosmopolitan culture' that had 'debased classical and folk art in the name of entertainment.'[171] The solution was the Popular Front imperative to reconnect artists and popular life.[172] The route to it was that of the cultural upsurge: a national cultural infrastructure along the lines prefigured in ENSA and CEMA but never realized by the Arts Council, to be substantially supported in a period of Conservative government by the trade unions.[173] It was a Communist, Association of Cinematograph, Television and Allied Technicians (ACTT) general secretary Ralph Bond, who had driven forward the idea by bringing a resolution – number 42 – before the TUC Isle of Man Congress in September 1960, arguing that the 'spiritual heritage' of 'culture' was being 'distorted and vulgarized by the purveyors of mass-production entertainment' and that the TUC needed to step in.[174] Despite exerting its influence in all of these ways, no less than in Bond's presence on the Centre 42 management committee, patterns of depleted personnel, demoralization, disorganization, and anti-intellectualism stunted the party's capacity to renew its cultural work through this initiative. There were local exceptions through the festivals run in six towns and cities in 1962, Centre 42's strongest initiative.[175] In Birmingham, the only provincial city that ran a Centre 42 festival in which the party had a regional cultural committee, CP activists including Katharine Thomson (1906–2006) and the Ian Campbell Folk Group were to the fore, organizationally and musically.[176] In Hayes, Frank Stanley, a Communist shop steward at the town's biggest factory, EMI, effectively mediated between Centre 42 and the Trades Council, enabling poet Christopher Logue to give a reading in the works canteen heard by over a thousand workers.[177] In Teesside, which had no festival in 1962, Communists were active in the 'Friends of Centre 42,' which ran one-night shows in local social clubs including Middlesbrough's British Legion, where bemused bingo players 'listened hard' to a recital of a Brecht poem.[178] Elsewhere the inward party, wary of New Left disorderly elements, remained suspicious of an initiative it could not directly control. Some favoured staging a rival initiative.[179] Across much of the country, the party lacked the culturally inclined activists capable of influencing events. 'Our members should take far more interest in future festivals,' lamented one dispirited activist, 'as such festivals could become a practical demonstration of our beliefs in the cultural field.'[180]

As Centre 42 suggested, the cultural implications of 'having it so good' – especially in terms of state support for arts and leisure – was highly topical before and after the 1959 General Election.[181] A tranche of proposals, pamphlets, and policy statements was produced by major charitable bodies and by both main political parties.[182] New Left intellectuals, especially Raymond Williams, intervened decisively in these debates.[183] The Labour left also made

Facing the challenge of renewal: right to left, Communist literary critic Arnold Kettle (1916–86) and Communist composer Alan Bush (1900–95) share a platform with film director Lindsay Anderson (1923–94) and art critic John Berger (1926–2017), 1960s. CP Picture Archive, Box 36.

headway, with MP Arthur Blenkinshop working to the advantages of the North East a new devolutionary impulse in patterns of arts funding.[184] The NCC needed a distinct line, and commissioned a 'cultural programme for the whole people' 'and a special contribution towards *The British Road to Socialism*,'[185] a tacit recognition that the party's key document lacked a compelling account of the cultural field.[186] Almost immediately, however, it was struggling to produce a coherent analysis. 'There are a great many gasps in our information and in proposals for particular aspects of culture,' the committee frankly admitted in 1960.[187] 'What is our way of life?' asked the title of another draft, a tissue of questions with few answers.[188] A further draft produced after two and a half years was indistinguishable from the Labour Party's position with the exception of condemning bingo and advocating more support for pigeon fancying, carpentry, and amateur archaeology.[189] Another version, 'Policy for Leisure' (1963), was circulated to cultural workers who considered it flimsy, and referred it back to the NCC;[190] left behind by the incoming Labour government's shake-up of the Arts Council after the 1964 General Election, the document was never published.[191] Amidst four years of intense national debate about the state, culture, and national life, the NCC contributed little more than an article by Barbara Niven in *Marxism Today* that summarized the policies of others.[192]

The Challenge of Revival

The unenviable challenge of reviving the party's torpid cultural work through the NCC fell to the long-suffering Brian Simon, who took up the chair in the summer of 1962.[193] The NCC had been so undervalued and underresourced through the tumultuous 1956–8 period and subsequently (it had already lost its full-time secretary in 1955) that records were at best patchy. To discover what was left of the party's scattered cultural resources, Simon combed through back issues of *Marxism Today*, counting articles and noting down often-unfamiliar names.[194] The picture was mixed: a party without a functioning science committee still had thirty-two scientists among its seventy university employees.[195] The traditionally well-run Historians' Group was still active and its membership was rising (thirty-seven in 1958, fifty-six by 1964).[196] The Music Group was meeting regularly, and its cyclostyled journal, *Music & Life*, was selling five hundred copies per issue.[197] But the Writers' Group was moribund, the Artists' Group was doing just a little better, and the 'sections' that existed among the doctors, scientists, actors, psychologists, philosophers, architects, lawyers, and film workers were barely functioning.[198]

Working in Simon's favour, however, was a new 'interest in Marxism and Communism, especially among youth and students' in New Left environs, a growth that coincided with an apparent thawing of the deeply 'inhibitory' Zhdanovism in the Soviet Union.[199] General Secretary John Gollan proved open to Simon's argument that association with Zhdanovite censorship was at odds with rejuvenation or electoral credibility in the age of the Lady Chatterley trial, and made a statement to the Twenty-eighth National Congress (1963) spelling out that the Political Committee did not intend to 'issue any directive' or 'exercise any control' over the work of party members in the fields of culture or science.[200] This was an important first step in distancing the party from the positions forcefully restated recently by Kettle, and there was a parallel opening of party channels to facilitate the necessary discussions. Matters including abstract art and the base/superstructure model were debated in the more open NCC meetings, symposia, and especially the pages of *Marxism Today*, ably edited by Klugmann from 1962, for whom 'openness' now became a form of expiation for former dogmatism, and on the book page of the *Daily Worker*, reinvigorated by literary editor Bob Leeson.[201] The renewed wave of cultural debate was energized by the publications of John Berger, who remained close to the party, and by the translations of major works of Marxist aesthetics, notably Lukács's *The Historical Novel* (1962) and *The Meaning of Contemporary Realism* (1963) and Austrian communist Ernst Fischer's *The Necessity of Art* (1963), all analysed in the periodical.[202]

Although this looked promising, Simon's attempts to reconnect the party with broader currents, in the form of an open week of CP-hosted Marxist lectures and discussions in London in November 1963, cruelly measured the scale of the task in hand. Asa Briggs, John Berger, E.H. Carr, Alan Sillitoe, and Arnold Wesker were all invited, and all declined.[203] The alternative was to 'rely on our own people,'[204] which meant Communists talking mainly to themselves in a flat event, 'The Challenge of Marxism,' whose proceedings formed the substance of another ill-fated relaunch initiative, a tie-in book edited by Simon and published in 1963 with the same title.[205] Four years in the making,[206] *The Challenge of Marxism* (1963) was written by a combination of middle-aged male party leaders (Gollan, Campbell) and trusted intellectuals (Simon, Morton, Kettle; E. Rowsell stood in for Bernal and summarized his ideas).[207] Sporadically deploying a discourse of 'humanism' calculated to steal New Left thunder, the core text actually revealed the shallowness of the thaw among the leading intellectuals, and why the CP was so unattractive to young readers of Marx outside its ranks.[208] Kettle's chapter, republished as a party pamphlet entitled 'Communism and the Intellectuals' (1963), stood by his forbidding, earlier positions and told those intellectuals that there was no Marxism outside the Communist Party.[209] Despite the recent shifts in the Soviet Union and the party's support for the unbanning of *Lady Chatterley's Lover*, the censorship of artists in the socialist bloc was tacitly supported ('society must always have the last word.)'[210] Familiar CP hostility to artistic experiment was restated in A.L. Morton's chapter – also republished as a stand-alone pamphlet – at a time when, as he disapprovingly noted, experimentation was becoming the cultural watchword.[211] *The Challenge of Marxism* had been conceived to 'put Marxism and the CP back on the map among intellectuals in the country,' to demonstrate that 'Marxism has something important to say in all fields of human thought' and to show 'that there are a body of Communist intellectuals in this country prepared to say it.'[212] It came close to proving the opposite. The structuring assumption about what culture was – the fine arts – was now anachronistically narrow, the book wearily glossing over 'cinema, television, "popular" music, pulp fiction, comics,' and 'the rest.'[213] Planned chapters on music and the visual arts were abandoned.

Film, Television

That film and television were never considered as topics accurately reflected that the party was outside the media, lacking the industry personnel to sustain a functioning television and film group.[214] The party was predictably exercised by the mainstream success of the anti-Communist films *I'm All Right Jack* (1959) and *The Angry Silence* (1959), and was conflicted around British new wave films' depiction of an individualistic, consumerist, and sexually adventurous working class, but had little influence at the level of film production.[215] Two exceptions, the 1961 adaptation of Wesker's 1956 play, *The Kitchen*, by the ACTT's in-house film unit, led by Bond, and *Live Now, Pay Later* (1962), an adaptation of Jack Lindsay's *All on the Never Never* (1961), reinforced the abiding sense of a medium impervious to Communist recoding.[216] The first tried to foreground the experience of work, typically sidelined in new wave cinema's principal focus on escape from working-class life;[217] failing to combine political purpose with engaging narrative, it flopped.[218] The latter sensationally extracted Lindsay's novel's central plotline of a working-class woman who turns to prostitution to meet mounting hire purchase debt from the broader, serious analysis of the quality of life in Britain's New Towns – another pressing early 1960s issue on which party analysis lagged.[219] (For Lindsay, the film's only merit was the £1,000 in royalties that subsidized his fiction writing.)[220] Much more representative of Communism in the film industry was the work of Plato Films, still dominated by the party[221] and whose main lines in the 1960s, like the best chapters of *The Challenge of Marxism*, were now emphatically backward looking.[222] Grainy footage of inter-war Britain was sold to television companies; colourful coverage of eminent Communists' funerals was exported to the Soviet bloc (*Harry Pollitt's Funeral* (1960), *Gallacher's Funeral* (1965)).[223]

Despite its absence from *The Challenge of Marxism*, no one could accuse the Communist Party of being uninterested in television. It had been obsessed with it since 10 September 1957, when, amidst the party's crisis, incoming general secretary John Gollan had appeared on a BBC discussion program series. Accustomed, as the TV writers noted, to far 'stormier meetings,' he had performed surprisingly well.[224] The scores of letters that arrived at King Street alerted even ageing Communists without television sets to the power of the medium: some Communists felt their faith restored;[225] others noted how the broadcast had stimulated workplace discussion;[226] new recruits were won;[227] and party activists and the leadership were convinced that television was integral to the process of reversing the party's fortunes.[228] In this respect, at least, it was keeping abreast of the culture: by the early 1960s, Britons owned 12 million TV sets, with 40 million out of a population of 53 million tuning in.[229] The *way* in which the party was interested, however, reflected the limited range of its thinking around politics, civil society, and the chronology of revolution. A party without a coherent position on how to influence the broader shifts in culture and consciousness that *The British Road* required fixated on its exclusion from party political broadcasts, a focus that displaced more nuanced analysis of the medium's potential and sometimes obscured myriad other reasons for the party's flagging fortunes, electoral and otherwise.[230] The tunnel vision over television was apparent in the party's remoteness from the impassioned early 1960s debates on broadcasting's three-channel future that culminated with the Pilkington Report published in June 1962. Richard Hoggart sat on the committee; Williams responded to it in *Communications* (1962). The NCC had no such profile, although it submitted evidence and analysed the Pilkington Report in *Marxism Today*,[231] affirming the BBC's commitment to anti-Americanism and cultural uplift[232] while denouncing its anti-Communist bias.[233]

As in film, the party was almost entirely absent from the television industry. Outside the party, a rising generation of New Left and Trotskyite writers and producers including Ken Loach, David Mercer, Alun Owen, Tony Garnett, Jeremy Sandbrook, and Jim Allen were entering the industry and finding spaces to bring radical inflections to a mass medium that could reach, as David Mercer noted, 'more people in one transmission than a stage play running to packed houses for years.'[234] Too few rising Communist cadres had entered a world seen as inherently consciousness lowering, and the best of those who had were among the 1956 exodus.[235] Dominant party discourse still typically saw television in terms of ruling-class conspiracy, rather than socialist opportunity, attitudes apparent in its censorious response to *That Was The Week That Was*, with its twelve million viewers on Saturday nights in 1963, which smarted at jokes about Castro and Khruschev.[236] In 1964 the pitch of party discussion of the medium improved when television writers including Mercer and the Communist Stuart Douglass analysed the blocks to and possibilities for radical television interventions in a *Marxism Today* debate eclipsed by the nine-month-long parallel debate on classical music that exercised party intellectuals far more.[237] Only Mary Whitehouse and her watchdog organization, the National Viewers and Listeners Association, however, believed that Communists had 'infiltrated broadcasting.'[238] Where television was concerned, Communist debate constantly returned to party political broadcasts: a campaign in 1964 sought to expose the unwritten rules that determined the number of candidates standing for election before broadcasts were permitted;[239] the party had fallen foul of these rules in 1955 and 1959, and did so again in 1964, when it stood thirty-six candidates and wasted resources on a never-broadcast election film.[240] In terms of television production or meaningful analysis of a medium now central to national culture, the party was absent.[241]

Youth Culture?

As its omission from *The Challenge of Marxism* indicated, the popular music that proved so influential over youth sensibility in the decade after 1956 was also, at best, peripheral to the party's cultural work. Branch meetings in the mid-1950s had considered 'how young people spend their leisure time,' but 'youth culture' was for most Communists oxymoronic.[242] Forms such as rock and roll,

Young Communist League activists in Openshaw, Manchester, during the December 1963 by-election. Eddie Marsden was the Communist candidate, and received 4.9 per cent of the vote. CP Picture Archive, Box 73.

if considered at all in the late 1950s, were regarded as low cultural dope, 'the corruption of youth by pop music' being one possible campaigning opportunity considered by the regrouping NCC in 1958.[243] Letters calling for the *Daily Worker* to stand firm against 'juke-box deterioration of our working-class culture' were uncontroversial and troubled few, young or old.[244] The regrowth of the YCL in the late 1950s and early 1960s occurred mainly in the Campaign for Nuclear Disarmament and on the shop floor, and despite disengagement from new cultural trends.[245] Judging by the pages of late 1950s issues of *Challenge*, part of the YCL's appeal was precisely that its orderly world of branch discussions, paper sales, and socials, whose soundtrack was jazz or folk music, provided a sanctuary from the social and cultural discord associated with rock and roll's early years, a conservative social impulse from which the early New Left also benefited.[246]

From the early 1960s, however, a new focus fell upon the cultural world of the teenager, partly in response to Colin MacInnes's *zeitgeist* novel *Absolute*

Beginners (1959), which dramatized the possibility of new forms of identity derived from consumerism and musical subcultures (in his case, modern jazz) and in which generation (being an 'absolute beginner' or 'teenager') trumped class as a social identity.[247] Troubled NCC documents by turns registered the teenager as a social phenomenon, remarked on the exoticism of youth ('strange and uncongenial ways'), or assimilated the new phenomena – teenage 'pride' 'enjoyment,' 'buoyancy' – into familiar frameworks by reading them as healthy 'class consciousness' in chrysalis form.[248]

What soon emerged as the key question for Communists in terms of class, youth, culture, and consciousness was whether the products of the culture industry so valued by absolute beginners were open for political reinscription, or whether rejection was the only resistance available. A dissonant text here was Eric Hobsbawm's *The Jazz Scene* (1959), written under his *New Statesman* jazz critic alias Francis Newton.[249] Hobsbawm read early jazz as a folk music rooted in popular life – a standard position in party analysis – but more controversially argued that the commercial assimilation of this music was not merely a story of degradation.[250] This incorporation, he argued, had challenged and expanded the parameters of the commercial, feeding and creating popular tastes that in turn created openings for new initiatives, including small independent companies.[251] Formerly Communist analysis had assumed that commercial mass culture was inherently consciousness lowering, and that its apparatus could be requisitioned and transformed only when power was taken. According to Hobsbawm's account, written in the context of the do-it-yourself skiffle craze whose vital energy he registered, the culture industry was available for limited modification.[252] Such arguments implied that a party serious about changing popular consciousness could no longer merely throw a *cordon sanitaire* around what A.L. Lloyd called 'the brain-softening commercial culture that the masters think fit for the masses.'[253] Rather, the terrain of the popular must be somehow territorialized and made to carry different values.

This proposition remained an abstraction in terms of Hobsbawm's preferred jazz, where the party now had negligible influence.[254] It flared up, however, in relation to the folk music scene that consolidated itself in the wake of skiffle and where the party, which otherwise lacked meaningful youth cultural presence, had a real stake and an opportunity to engage new audiences. As bemused NCC documents noted, here was a booming, serious-minded youth subculture with a rapidly expanding network of one hundred folk clubs with 25,000 members where the party had leading figures,[255] was winning young recruits,[256] ran high-profile concerts,[257] dominated journalism,[258] and commanded significant positions in the folk music world's various projects and institutions,[259] including the BBC.[260] What was to be done? For leading figures such as Ewan MacColl, and for rising party cultural figures including Stephen Sedley and David Craig, the answer to the party's cultural marginality was here in plain sight.[261] Folk culture was, as MacColl had long argued, a distinct class culture of which the working class had been robbed;[262] the CP should therefore make folk traditions the core of Communist cultural strategy and production.[263] Folk activists MacColl, Lloyd, and Communist *Melody Maker* journalist Karl Dallas once again made the case for more support for folk music to the NCC at a series of divisive meetings held in the early 1960s.[264] Hobsbawm's earlier analysis now set the tone, however, in warning that the 'third' space harboured by Communist folk revivalists since the mid-1950s was a fantasy in the context of 1960s mass society, and would by definition lead to marginality and amateurism.[265] The 'Canutes of folk' like MacColl who attacked a 'bobby-socks vogue,' 'selling out,'[266] and Bob Dylan – praised by the new party weekly *Comment*[267] as 'the perfect symbol of the anti-artist in our society'[268] – were berated for sectarianism.[269] 'We have to break down barriers everywhere,' wrote the incoming NCC secretary Betty Reid (1915–2004), who was more attuned to early 1960s youth cultural shifts than many; 'we have to stop crying about commercialism' and to 'discriminate, to single out and foster and welcome what is positive and helps us.'[270] Such cultural revisionism was too much for MacColl and others: the party lost *en bloc* much of the folk scene to Maoism[271] in a series of departures that effectively brought to an end the 'third way' vision of Communist Party cultural politics against which Hobsbawm had warned.[272]

Within the YCL, rising cadres were now intuitively in step with Betty Reid's position on youth culture, including from 1964 the incoming YCL national secretary, Barney Davies. YCLers were beginning to work the grain of the popular culture they enjoyed, notably in Wembley, where a YCL band, The Bow Street Runners, hosted a rhythm and blues club. Audiences reached three hundred, YCL membership grew from a handful to around a hundred, and one of the acts booked was the band that later became The Who, whose creative force, Pete Townshend, was briefly a YCLer.[273] Even so, popular music remained a divisive issue, rather than a source of re-energization and renewal in a movement that historically had viewed it as feminized, Americanized, and consciousness lowering. Scepticism and resistance was not confined to folk-oriented Maoists,[274] and party overtures to the new culture – read by some historians as an instance of an emerging cohort confidently embracing youth cultural energy[275] – were often mawkish, whether in *Challenge*'s 'Yeah, Yeah, Yeah' cover story of The Beatles in December 1963[276] or the YCL's 'The Trend' recruitment drive of 1966–7 that culminated in a concert by The Kinks.[277] The awkwardness was perhaps unsurprising given that those who advocated more flexible positions were on the outside – the party had no more presence in the new music industry than in film or television – and, beyond Hobsbawm's preliminary provocations and Betty Reid's urges to do better, had no theoretical tradition of analysing questions of popular culture and consciousness. No clearly argued position appeared on these pressing questions in the 1960s, despite the founding in 1968

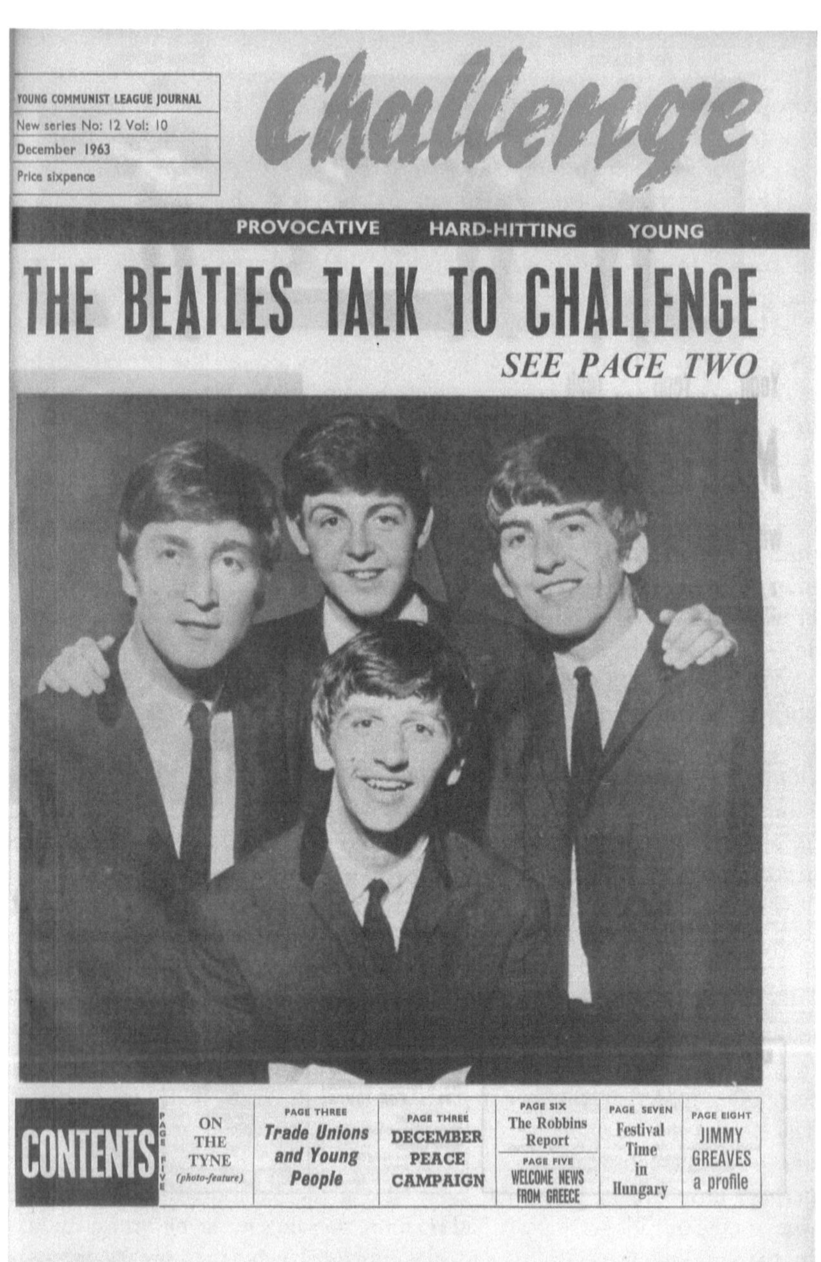

YOUNG COMMUNIST LEAGUE JOURNAL
New series No: 12 Vol: 10
December 1963
Price sixpence

Challenge

PROVOCATIVE HARD-HITTING YOUNG

THE BEATLES TALK TO CHALLENGE

SEE PAGE TWO

CONTENTS

PAGE FIVE ON THE TYNE (*photo-feature*)

PAGE THREE *Trade Unions and Young People*

PAGE THREE DECEMBER PEACE CAMPAIGN

PAGE SIX The Robbins Report

PAGE FIVE WELCOME NEWS FROM GREECE

PAGE SEVEN Festival Time in Hungary

PAGE EIGHT JIMMY GREAVES a profile

The Beatles in *Challenge*, December 1963. CP Archive, LHASC, Manchester.

Handbill for *The Trend* Young Communist League recruitment drive, 1967. CP Archive, LHASC, Manchester.

of a new theoretical publication, *Cogito,* potentially well suited to developing such work. Far from engendering rapid renewal as some have argued, patterns of untheorized, tentative accommodation with this culture played its part in sowing division and driving major cultural figures out of the party in the second half of the 1960s.[278] Where questions of youth, popular culture, and resistance were concerned, the decisive shift that converted hesitations into clearly articulated positions would come at the beginning of the 1970s.

Permeated with Liberalism?

The misshapen party was in flux in the mid- to late 1960s. CP membership was shrinking by around a thousand a year; student work was in the doldrums;[279] only the YCL was bucking the trend and growing (1,400 joined in 1965, with numbers peaking at around 6,000 in 1967, half of the membership of the Labour Party's Young Socialists).[280] Leadership personnel was changing with the retirement of guiding spirits (Dutt, Campbell, Kerrigan).[281] From early 1965, industrial work was in transition from the clandestine approaches ingrained by the Cold War to the so-called Broad Left strategy associated with incoming industrial organizer Bert Ramelson (1910–94).[282] And at a time when increasing industrial militancy was reinforcing traditional ideas of where the focus should be, core ideas were beginning to be openly challenged.[283] Party intellectuals including Bill Warren (1935–78) were beginning to suspect a link between wage-claim militancy and inflation, a debate that opened in the Economics Committee in 1966 and would prove explosive in the decade ahead.[284] Gollan too was drawn to uncommunist ruminations, admitting that implanting visions of social transformation in a working class enjoying improving living standards raised new challenges.[285] His controversial commitment to modernizing the *Daily Worker* in 1965–6 was motivated by engaging with those changes in class composition that the party had been keen to deny a decade earlier, especially the 46 per cent of the population who were not manual workers.[286] The eclipse of the traditional class identity emblematized by the replacement of the title of the *Daily Worker* with the *Morning Star* angered many, provoking agonized debate and jokes about the liquidation of proletarian character by the 'Daily Professional Man.'[287] At the same time, the nuanced positions put forward to defend changes in the newspaper – which stressed the significance of youth, popular culture, and the need to build alliances and learn from the successes of the Italian and French parties – were not reflected in party strategy, a mismatch cruelly revealed in the General Election of March 1966, which coincided with the launch of the *Morning Star.*[288] Despite the party's stretching resources to field fifty-seven candidates – enough to secure a much-coveted TV broadcast[289] – the vote slipped back on the dismal 1964 performance, with a 38 per cent drop in the 'heartland' fourteen seats contested consistently in elections since 1955.[290] With only total 62,112 votes cast for the party – barely double the party's membership – and the Labour Party's share of the vote increasing from 44.1 per cent in 1964 to almost 48 per cent in 1966, delivering a majority of ninety-eight seats, the core strategy of exerting real influence on Labour on account of Communist MPs looked as delusional as the idea of television as a means to rejuvenation.[291]

Communists who wanted a more traditional line and modernizers who wanted distance from the socialist countries now agreed about one thing, at least: the need for debate about fundamental questions.[292] The crucial moment for a possible reorientation was less the second revision of *The British Road* (1968) – inevitably restrained by the parameters of the existing text – but *Questions of Ideology and Culture* (1967), a document that emerged from the ferment of long-brewing international discussions dominated by the French and Italian parties.[293] Although nominally concerned with 'aesthetics,' these debates confronted the challenges faced by Communism in the developed West, addressing many of the core questions tracked by this study (the chronology of revolution, communist 'leadership' over cultural life, socialist censorship, the relevance or obsolescence of the dictatorship of the proletariat, the relationship between state and civil society in terms of class power and resistance). The text that emerged in 1966 from the French party's three-day discussion on 'ideological and cultural issues,' soon published and adopted as a party resolution,[294] fed the momentum for an equivalent statement in Britain, elements of which could be incorporated into the forthcoming revision of *The British Road*.[295] A document was drafted by Simon in the autumn of 1966 and circulated to the NCC and party intellectuals in October.[296] A revised version was adopted by the Executive Committee in March 1967, published as *Questions of Ideology and Culture* the following month (3,000 copies were printed for sale as a pamphlet) and again in the May 1967 issue of *Marxism Today*. It was launched at a high-profile press conference that attracted international newspaper and BBC coverage.[297]

Although the preparation of the document was far from democratic – members' comments were invited only after it was published in *Marxism Today* – 'Communists call for a wider democracy' was the heading over an abbreviated version of the statement published in the *Morning Star*, strongly signalling that the document was broader than its title and conceived as a stage in the party's strategic reorientation.[298] An opening section on science echoed the long-standing Bernallian argument about the incompatibility between true science and the profit motive, anticipating the similar beginning of the soon-revised *The British Road*.[299] The errors of Lysenko were frankly admitted. The positions on censorship and artistic experimentation that had effectively locked the party out of 'the sixties' were revoked.[300] A section on religion renounced 'sectarian approaches' and affirmed the importance of the extensive 'Dialogue between Christianity and Marxism' that Klugmann and *Marxism Today* had fostered.[301] But on the more contentious questions about class, party, state, and civil society, the document was out of focus, reflecting the broader crises in the party's identity and thought. 'Revolutionary change' and 'the transition from one social system to another, from capitalism to socialism,' were discussed as though straightforwardly synonymous.[302] The party's role in that undifferentiated transformation was now unclear even to it, and the scattered verbs seeking to pinpoint the party's true function in the process ran from 'speed up' and 'help' to 'lead' and 'bringing about.'[303] The document registered that the day's fundamental struggles were 'reflected in the realm of ideology' – a formulation that implied the real fight took place in a space free of ideology – but there was no mapping of the changing terrain of this struggle nor of any strategy for confronting this ideology through struggle across civil society capable of resisting 'the degrading commercialism of capitalist society.'[304] A document that was at least frank in identifying 'a lack of theory and perspective' as the central weakness of the British working-class movement – and by implication the party – was itself a striking instance of it.[305] 'The Party line is that there is no line,' scoffed the BBC,[306] rightly detecting that what John Lewis called the expression of 'penitence for past errors,' rather than the formulation of new positions, was the key driver, a point that Simon did not refute.[307] The document claimed to look outwards, but was most revealing as a final chapter in a decade-long story around the deep and ongoing internal struggle to exorcise Stalinism and the party's inability to develop from the currents available to it the clear theory of civil society and consciousness that *The British Road* strategy required. Under pressure to prove what it was not, the party retreated to what Lewis called 'neutrality and impartiality' – inoffensive and essentially liberal notions of openness, eclecticism, and tolerance – that effectively converted ideology and culture into a neutral space. 'Never objecting to anything,' commented Maurice Cornforth caustically, 'is as stupid as objecting to everything.'[308] For these critics within the party, *Questions of Ideology and Culture* was a missed opportunity at a crucial moment and a text that, despite its protestations, failed to take culture seriously as a location of political struggle. As so often, better perspectives were now available. The section on art, experimentation, and consciousness might have assimilated the recent debate on Marxist aesthetics that drew heavily on Berger's recent writing and argued for forms of analysis angled not at 'content' or the supposed ideological orientations of artists, but at the ways in which works challenged, enriched, or expanded existing modes of perception; modernism was, according to this position, a revolution in consciousness – regardless of the reactionary political views of some of its key figures, whose energies Marxism should welcome and attempt to shape.[309] As Lindsay argued, the section on 'humanism' might have integrated the early Marx on alienation – ably discussed in the party press by him and Lewis – to inscribe the nebulous 'broad popular alliance' central to party strategy with real content by making the necessary link between cultural and industrial workers in stressing capitalism's impediment to productive creativity.[310] Instead, the humanism here offered a bland vision of humanity's potential, a version watered down still further in the revised *The British Road*, which spoke vaguely of how capitalist crisis 'affects adversely every aspect of life.'[311] 'Feeble-minded,' summarized Cornforth.[312] 'Permeated with liberalism,' 'lame, limp and superficial,' was the verdict of Katharine Thomson, now inclined to Maoism.[313] 'In every other field than the economic we are nowhere,' was Lewis's verdict;[314] 'one does not strengthen Marxism by opting out of the ideological struggle.'[315]

As Lewis warned, opting out of struggle by roping off culture as a separate, sensitive sphere was the document's paradoxical effect: the fervid debates about culture and Communism of the mid- to late 1960s – driven in a period of cultural ferment by a deep sense of unease with those prescriptive modes of thought reasserted by the leadership in the wake of 1956 – melted away with the document's production. It was as though, now that Zhdanov's ghost was exorcised, liberal good sense restored, and positions on culture as above politics realigned with mainstream common sense, Communists could forget about culture and get back to real politics. *Marxism Today*, which was beginning to make real ground under Klugmann as a necessary reference point in cultural debates for the broader Left, fell almost entirely silent on cultural matters at the end of decade. The revised *The British Road* reflected the retreat in having nothing meaningful to say about culture and civil society as locations of class power or possible resistance. The *problem*, according to the newly revised program, remained one of conspiratorial capitalist control of 'everything that influences the minds and attitudes of the people.'[316] The same chronology of taking the state and *then* transforming society that had always structured Communist strategy prevailed, even though the political course mapped – 'broad popular alliance,' the election of a socialist majority of Labour and Communist MPs, the transformation of 'traditional institutions' into 'a socialist state machine' – was no longer insurrectionary but gradualist, and fundamentally the same as in 1958.[317] According to the new program, the only culture or cultural work required to create the consciousness necessary for the breakthrough was the *Morning Star* – 'a platform for every section of the anti-monopoly struggle' – sales of which stood at 60,000.[318] After taking the state, ran the projection, civil society could be transformed through various administrative measures: the creation of a national body to review publicly owned broadcasting, the ownership of all newspapers by political parties and social groups, the support of 'popular organisations' to promote the arts and youth organisations.[319] At the heart of the Communist project in Britain remained the theoretical contradiction that simultaneously acknowledged the ideological work of culture and civil society in the reproduction of capitalist social relations and saw it as either secondary to politics or beyond it. In the absence of a strategy that dialectically connected economy and culture, and what Gramsci called wars of position and wars of manoeuvre, binary thinking was perpetuated and culture sidelined. The development of alternative perspectives on these questions would soon emerge, however, and irreversibly divide the party in the decade ahead.

5
The Spectre of Eurocommunism, 1968–1979

The Prague Spring of 1968 and its suppression by the Warsaw Pact invasion of 21 August marked a watershed in the history of British Communism. 'Tankie' would soon emerge in the Communist lexicon to describe those for whom unquestioning loyalty to the Soviet Union remained a basic condition of Communist identity.[1] Clashes between such Communists and a leadership that criticized the 'tragic error' of Soviet 'intervention' in the spirit of comradeship rather than renunciation[2] would be played out in a series of stand-offs in the decade ahead, culminating in the highly contested rewriting of *The British Road to Socialism* in 1977.[3] The new document was 'too short on coercion and too free with liberalism,' according to hard-line figurehead Sid French (1920–88), Surrey District Secretary, for whom the leadership's tentative independent-mindedness over Prague represented a grave 'weakening in our internationalism,' party code for distance from the Soviet Union.[4] Increasingly he saw 'no way forward' in the revised text, and left to form the New Communist Party, taking seven hundred followers with him.[5] Such drama was sufficiently compelling to attract the attention of even commercial television, which produced a prime-time, three-hour fly-on-the-wall documentary, *Decision: British Communism*, transmitted in the summer of 1978 chronicling a party at war with itself and providing the type of exposure about which the party had often fantasized. Despite the program's inevitable fixation with it, however, division around the Soviet Union is not sufficient to explain the party's loss of ten thousand members in the 1970s (30,607 in 1969, 20,599 in 1979) or its failure to renew itself in a decade of capitalist crisis and explosive industrial militancy.[6] The more subtle but lingering significance of Prague 1968 for the British CP lay less in Soviet tanks than in the ideas codified in the Czech Action Programme, deeply welcomed by some, including the recently rehabilitated Monty Johnstone, which stressed consent over coercion and spelled out the need for Communist Parties in power to support a pluralistic political model in which oppositional parties were free to organize.[7] That what Johnstone, who witnessed the Czech invasion first hand, called 'the first glimpse of a democratic, just and human form of socialism in an advanced industrial country' was overwhelmed not by Western imperialism, but by the world Communist Movement with which many wanted tighter affiliation, greatly raised the stakes in the ideological struggle.[8] The Czech experience also focused minds on thinking seriously about whether *The British Road to Socialism*, which remained for many something of a cover story concealing more traditional visions, currently represented anything like a dependable map. It took a few years for critical impulses to develop into sustained debate. But the failure of the party to advance amidst the industrial and political crisis of the early to mid-1970s underscored for many the urgency of addressing fundamental questions about revolutionary strategy in the West and the need to think seriously about structures and concepts that had long been evoked in *The British Road*, notably Parliament and democracy, strikingly underanalysed in Communist discourse. Momentum was added for a strategy that broke with the dictatorship of the proletariat model and its visions of socialist transformation being effected *after* the seizure of the state. A new emphasis increasingly identified as key those spheres of civil society where successes might be achieved *before* socialism and that in turn might prefigure or help to prepare the way for broader transformations. In short, 1968 mattered because the new emphasis on consent and pluralism opened a space for alternative visions whose key site would be civil society, identified as politically significant in proportion to a nation's levels of economic development and political stability. The question of breaking out of the 'before' and 'after' mindset regarding the chronology of revolution and identifying as sites of potentially transformative struggle here and now locations more traditionally seen as problems that would be taken care of by the new state in a process of post-revolutionary socialist construction – the culture, the family, the economy, and education, among them – would be a recurrent preoccupation of 1970s, although little that happened in the 1970s was entirely new. Rather, for a complicated range of economic, historical, demographic, political, and theoretical reasons, the decade saw the release into open and explicit clashes in Western Communism issues latent as far back as the Comintern debates with which this study began around the chronology of revolution. These had now existed in the British party for fifty years. Communism's uneven and diminishing interventions in British civil society and its struggle to respond to new cultural phenomena are necessarily a central concern of this chapter, as they were of the last. So too are the party's inhibited engagement with emerging social movements, especially feminism, and its inability to reinvigorate itself in their image. The chapter also reflects its subject in turning inwards, focusing upon the internal debates about the party's form and function that absorbed much of British Communism's energies in the 1970s. A degree of eleventh-hour diminuendo to this study is therefore unavoidable: in terms of national political, social, and cultural profile, the party mattered less than it did, although even now there was much unevenness in its national presence, notably in its centrality to early 1970s industrial struggle and its unseasonal intellectual and cultural renaissance in the mid-1970s, culminating in the People's Jubilee in 1977. These are not only historical matters, however. As I argued in the Introduction, the positions formulated but not adopted in the struggle and failure of the Communist Party to renew itself under great historical pressure remain politically resonant when so much of its world has passed into history.

Intellectuals

Those most focused on the question of the chronology of revolution were an emerging intellectual stratum that, in keeping with the period's broader social and generational anti-authoritarian trends, was less and less inclined to observe party protocol in which questions of theory and strategy were typically left to ageing full-time officials. What, though, enabled young intellectuals now to emerge as a vocal and influential force in a political party that had traditionally marginalized their type so effectively? One answer lay in broader demographics. As the previous chapter showed, the political significance of the long-term expansion of the so-called middle strata of Britain's class structure, long evaded by Communist analysis, was firmly recognized by the end of the 1960s.[9] In terms of Communism's internal culture, this recognition eroded the ground for the ritualistic invocation of the male industrial worker as the authentic Communist subject and curtailed the marginalization of other groups, especially intellectuals, whom such workerism traditionally had often held in check. Furthermore, in the past, class structure had determined that party intellectuals were typically public school and university educated and made to feel the antithesis of true Communists.[10] The rising intellectual stratum was, by contrast, typically grammar-school-educated baby boomers, rather than upper-middle-class public schoolboys, many of whom had followed their working-class parents into the party and could not easily be dismissed on the basis of class background. The party's growing anxiety about its own ageing membership and disconnection from youth drove the uneven incorporation of young rising cadre into more senior positions – notably Martin Jacques, who was elected to the Executive Committee at the age of twenty-two in 1967, having graduated from Manchester University, en route to graduate study at Cambridge.[11] Although Jacques would later present himself as 'an intellectual, a revisionist and a free spirit' whose generationally specific cultural outlook – the informal way he dressed and communicated – set him irreversibly at variance with the starched, be-suited formality of the 'old men' who led the party, he was co-opted onto the committee precisely because some in the leadership recognized there was a generation gap to bridge; being at variance, within approved limits, was Jacques's role, and he largely played it.[12] The leadership opened up because it knew that it was losing intellectual and theoretical ground to new developments. Key among these was so-called revolutionary romanticism, represented by student power, black power, and theorists of Third World liberation struggles – currents drawn together by the writings of Herbert Marcuse that saw developed capitalism as inherently totalitarian and now identified revolutionary agents outside the incorporated industrial proletariat.[13] Another threat was the *New Left Review*'s version of a selected tradition of 'Western Marxism' from which Communists were conspicuously absent.[14] A third was the Trotskyite Left, whose advances in the late 1960s and early 1970s preoccupied the party in general and Betty Reid and Monty Johnstone in particular, much as the New Left had exercised it a decade earlier.[15] The rising party intellectual stratum, alongside the rehabilitated and perennially young-at-heart dissident Johnstone, to whom many younger Communists now looked for leadership, was recognized as indispensable in the necessary ideological counteroffensive. There was also a vague sense among the leadership that the party was not making enough of the continental Communist currents now energising the movement, especially in France through the writings of Étienne Balibar and Louis Althusser. As so often, however, change was driven by the coming together of external social, cultural, and intellectual shifts and particular coincidences and circumstances within the organization. A restructuring of the National Cultural Committee was set in train by the death of its long-standing secretary, Ted Ainley (1903–68) in March 1968,[16] and pushed by the committee's chair, the intuitive Gramscian Brian Simon, assisted by Betty Reid, Ainley's replacement as NCC secretary. Reid was especially frustrated by the inactivity of the old guard around the 'important youth scene':[17] 'additions to the Cultural Committee should now be made mainly on the basis of younger comrades,' she insisted, a view Simon shared.[18] Simon, who had stoically endured prejudice and marginalization within the party on account of his own class background and academic career, and who had been frustrated in the past in his visions of using the NCC as a hub for broader cultural interventions, wanted to see coordinated struggle across national intellectual life, with younger Communists 'working in the various fields of the social sciences and humanities (and science) who have themselves achieved a definite level of Marxist thinking in their own field' prominently involved.[19] He pressed for and addressed the first Communist University of London (CUL) in July 1969, the student forum created by the party to 'combine academic, political and mass activity' in the battle against 'reactionary ideas'; the forum would grow in significance in the 1970s, but began modestly as a party school, attracting 159 delegates, 63 of them university students.[20] Amidst these changes, and as part of the broader analysis of class composition, by the end of the 1960s the party was more inclined not only to listen to intellectuals, but to think about their formation and role in society. This was most strongly signalled by the hosting of an

NCC sponsored event, 'Intellectuals and Their Role Today' in April 1969, with papers from Brian Simon's brother, Roger Simon (1913–2002), who had long lobbied Lawrence & Wishart to undertake the translation and publication of more of Gramsci's writing, and younger academics – the traditionally minded Phil Goodwin and the self-styled revisionist Jacques. The event was frank in appraising the intellectual and theoretical ground that the party had lost. It also represented a regrouping and determination to recover, as Monty Johnstone put it, 'a position we were in in the 1930s, then seen as the main Marxist force in the intellectual sphere,' and to underpin and develop *The British Road* with 'basic theoretical material' assumed to be lacking.[21]

'Ideology' and 'intellectual' were becoming charged words in the party, the former associated with Althusser,[22] who graced the pages of *Marxism Today* in a high-profile debate with Reid's husband and party philosopher, John Lewis, and which ran from 1969 for five years.[23] The rising stratum in particular was drawn to Althusser, who had a strong and enthusiastic following among Jacques and his fellow Cambridge graduate students, including Grahame Lock, writing his doctorate at Trinity, and the PCF's Jean-Jacques Lecercle, studying at Trinity en route to a post at Nanterre.[24] Althusser relieved such young Communists from the sensation that the liveliest intellectual developments on the Left were now occurring outside their movement; Jacques would go too far for Betty Reid by calling a meeting at Cambridge entitled 'From Leninism to Althusser,' which implied not only equivalence but ascension.[25] Most striking about Althusser for these young intellectuals was his analysis of ideology and the complexity of the modes through which 'subjects' were constituted ('interpellated') by the structures and ideological apparatuses – education, family, communications, culture, the political and legal system – of capitalist society.[26] The clear implication was that the operations of contemporary capitalist ideology were deeper, more subtle, and complicated than party discourse typically assumed (Althusser deployed the terms of psychoanalysis to analyse it). It followed that a sharp upgrading of intellectual and theoretical enquiry was necessary to grasp the dynamics of contemporary capitalism and class power and to underpin Communist cultural and intellectual interventions.

The word 'intellectual,' on the other hand, swelled in significance through the spreading influence of Gramsci, the other and initially less divisive figure to enhance Communism's intellectual reputation at this juncture. Gramsci's *Modern Prince* collection was republished in 1968, followed, belatedly, by *Selections from the Prison Notebooks* in 1971, for which Roger Simon had long petitioned (his commitment to the publication extended to contributing £2,000 of his own money; his own influential Gramsci primer would appear eleven years later).[27] The English version of the Notebooks conspicuously brought intellectuals to the front, editorially presenting them as the key to what followed. The book prompted Communists to think not only about such figures in relation to society, but also in terms of their own movement, as older Communist intellectual Bill Carritt (1908–99) had insisted they should.[28] The effect was naturally emboldening to party intellectuals. Jacques, who read Italian and had already been working with Gramsci in the original Italian, now became the key figure in mediating Gramsci's ideas about the role of intellectuals to the broader party. Intellectuals were for Jacques the missing link necessary to impart 'wider theoretical understanding of the nature of capitalist society' and 'socialist consciousness' to a working class that would not acquire it by 'economic class struggle' alone.[29] He was duly critical of the party's long-standing tendency to 'over emphasise "activism," to underestimate the importance of theoretical discussions, and to consider reading and writing a "lesser form" of political activity.'[30] Like Johnstone, Jacques drew on Gramsci to corroborate rather than refute the core arguments of *The British Road to Socialism*, especially through the claim that the intellectuals modern capitalism needed to stabilize its system were themselves vulnerable to economic insecurity and thus susceptible to falling under the leadership of the working class and the labour movement in the context of monopoly capitalism's recurrent crises.[31] For other intellectuals, however, who shared this sense that the events of 1968 had created ideological convulsions inside the party and out, the program and the fundamental assumptions that undergirded it were less a framework for renewal than the source of the problem.

Voices Off

Key here was SOAS academic Bill Warren (1935–78), a development economist and critic of the CP's position on inflation and wage militancy, whose disaffection was all too apparent at the 1969 meeting on intellectuals. Here he criticized the party's theoretical failure through the 1960s and the ground consequently lost to *New Left Review* and *Black Dwarf*, its the lack of openness apparent in its unwillingness to publish minutes of key meetings, its disabling quietism over the Soviet bloc and Sino-Soviet dispute, and its general failure seriously to debate socialist strategy.[32] He was already active in a group committed to reversing these trends, the so-called Smith Group (soon renamed the Party Group), a gathering of like-minded party intellectuals in the wake of 1968 and whose other core figures included Mike Prior, Derek Boothman, Antonio Bronda (London correspondent for the PCI daily *L'Unita*), and Beatrix Campbell. Most active between 1971 and 1974, the London-based group variously involved up to forty members, and held discussion meetings, circulated documents, engaged in debates about strategy in the party press, and submitted critical resolutions to Congress.[33]

According to the group's swingeing analysis, sharply reinforced by some direct experience of the party's dispiriting electoral work[34] – nationally, the

Communist vote was 43 per cent lower in the 1970 General Election than in 1966[35] – the CP was ageing, shrinking, remote from the political ferment of the young, and held back by a bumbling leadership.[36] The group estimated that half the party's 28,000 members were inactive; the effort of keeping them as paper members was an unacknowledged drain on dwindling party resources.[37] Warren traced the party's ills to its basic strategy through a detailed critique of the 1968 edition of *The British Road* – the latter 'nothing more than a badly written rationalisation of an electoral shopping list'[38] – which was declined by *Marxism Today* but publicly aired outside party channels in *New Left Review* in 1970 as 'The Programme of the CPGB – A Critique.'[39] The party's lodestar document was, he argued, characterized by 'grave theoretical ambiguities and unresearched but crucial formulations,' and he identified and dismantled what he saw as its three interlocking central propositions.[40] First, Warren argued, the text's assumption that capitalist monopolistic tendencies created common ground across classes on which alliances could be built was unsupported by evidence, and the equivalence between fascism and monopoly capitalism the document implied – as perils likely to galvanize cross-class unity – was a distraction predicated on confusing economic and political phenomena. Second, the idea that the future CP, its prestige somehow enhanced by the electoral success that had spectacularly eluded it since 1950, could drive forward socialism in union with the Labour Left was clearly delusional: the working class would and did support dependable Communist candidates in trade union positions, but self-evidently not in local or parliamentary elections. Third, the parliamentary strategy was itself predicated on a never theoretically justified confidence in the availability of Parliament for transformation. Warren preferred the more classical Marxist position of Parliament as the wolf of the dictatorship of the bourgeoisie in the sheep's clothing of democracy, whose true function was to stabilize class power by identifying and implementing the minimal concessions necessary to sustain bourgeois rule. Electoral strategies had an inherently depoliticizing effect, he argued, defusing rather than escalating class tension, and short-circuiting the building of grassroots support and organs of popular power that would be necessary to defend a program of socialist development in the unlikely event that elections breached capitalist power in the first place. 'No attempt is made to present an alternative strategy,' Warren wrote in the draft, somewhat disingenuously, 'since the writer doesn't have one.'[41]

In fact, despite its recourse to classical Leninist positions on the state and dual power, the critique contained new ideas that would prove crucial in the coming decade in terms of pushing analysis about democracy beyond that found in party discourse or *The British Road*. 'The most general political-economic contradiction in modern capitalism,' Warren argued, 'is that between the increasing role of the state in the economy and social and political life generally' and 'the structures of formal democracy [. . .] – a contradiction which puts the question of democracy on the order of the day.'[42] The deeper penetration of the post-war state into hitherto private spheres of economic and popular life, in other words – Warren was presumably thinking of nationalized industry, the National Health Service, council housing, welfare provision, mass education, child care – enabled a broader concept of democracy, and democratic struggle, than *The British Road*'s consciousness-lowering fixation with 'the transformation of Parliament into an instrument of the people's will.' For Warren, what was really necessary was struggle around 'a new kind of democracy' in these spheres that might be capable of '*prefiguring in practice* the socialist vision and thus of supplying the integrating link which transforms the struggle from contestations against capitalism to efforts to achieve socialism.'[43] Though at this crucial point Warren's analysis faltered, his associate in the group, Mike Prior, would soon push further, arguing in *Marxism Today* that the party's fixation with transforming the Labour Party, through alliance with its left, 'into a revolutionary force' distracted it from the more promising sites of militancy in groups 'often considered the most quiescent,' many of them active in spheres of the state's penetration into popular life to which Warren had alluded: the newly restive 'women, students, immigrants, sections of organised and unorganised labour' (council workers, postal workers, teachers) and the squatters and environmentalists now showing 'how much force can be generated from a community that is threatened.'[44] According to this reading, the concept of the broad popular alliance was on the right track – revolutions were made by class alliances, Prior argued – but theoretically underpowered and too narrowly conceived. Casting a critical eye over the CP leadership, Prior and his associates conceded that what they called the 'social democratic' faction was in control in part because it did at least have the outline of a strategy, however imprecise in *The British Road to Socialism*, and that 'it does clutch on to one shred of reality – that British society has changed and that new forces of opposition to capitalism do exist.'[45] The problem was that the leadership did not know what to do with this insight. The challenge was to depart from reassuring certitudes about monopoly capitalism galvanizing the 'broad popular alliance' and to 'plunge into the confusion of present day militancy and try to bring some common purpose and direction to it.'[46]

Arthur Scargill on Page Three

Increasingly central to the Party Group's intellectual energy and vision of renewal was the Women's Liberation Movement (WLM) in which, among other Communists, *Morning Star* journalist Beatrix Campbell was highly active from 1970.[47] In Britain the WLM was always enmeshed in the politics of the Left, emerging from the 'consciousness-raising' groups of young women whose central provocation was that the counterculture's emancipatory promise left untouched, and indeed depended upon, traditional divisions of sexual labour. 'I ended up having all these crazy boyfriends,' recalled feminist journal *Spare Rib* co-founder, Marsha Rowe, 'and I would be doing all the boring jobs to pay for their creativity.'[48] Much stronger in Britain, therefore, than the separatist feminist currents that prevailed in the United States[49] was that in which 'the formative influences of feminism and socialism were encountered more or less simultaneously and inseparably' in the late 1960s and early 1970s, and which was increasingly committed to thinking through their relationship and, potentially, mutual reinforcement.[50] In this milieu the CP had some presence, and not only because of its association with a key text over which feminist-socialists pored, Engels' *The Origin of The Family, Private Property and the State* (1884). Some, like Campbell, were from party families, and encountered Second Wave feminism as Communists, finding in it a critique of patriarchal structures and assumptions disconcertingly applicable to the party (Campbell had joined the party in 1967, and initially had resisted a feminism traditionally seen as divisive).[51] Other activists, like feminist and Gay Liberation Movement campaigner Elizabeth Wilson, were impressed by Communists with whom they worked in local campaigns, finding the party's intellectual seriousness and high levels of organization a welcome contrast to the chaotic impossibilism of the far Left or Labour's downbeat electoralism. In particular, they were inspired by older feminist Communist activists such as Florence Keyworth (1919–2010), Gladys Brooks, and Marie Betteridge (1922–2010).[52] Some moved towards the party precisely because, unlike Maoist and Trotskyite groups, it appeared open to the real challenges of changing from what Joanna de Groot called a 'traditional male dominated gender-blind left party.'[53] The presence of Communists in the WLM should not be overstated, but by the WLM national conference held in Manchester in 1975, it could summon around fifty delegates, 5 per cent of the total.[54]

From 1971 Communists, including those in the Party Group, were convinced that the full assimilation of the positions and practices of the WLM was now a crucial condition of the party's revival, and committed themselves to transforming the CP into what Campbell later called a 'feminist Communist Party.'[55] Documents drafted by Campbell that year and circulated among the Party Group were deeply critical of the line offered by the party's National Women's Advisory subcommittee; the critique was worked up into an amendment to the official draft resolution presented to the 1971 Congress for ratification, 'Women and Society,' prepared by National Women's Organiser, Rosemary Small (1927–81). Whereas the official statement stressed the centrality of class unity and remained lukewarm about the WLM, the various versions of the alternative proposal took an altogether bolder tone.[56] The party's economistic fixation with equal pay, the amendment argued, marginalized the 'social aspects of women's oppression' and evaded 'the complex of social, psychological and sexual oppressions,' notably, the ways in which institutions, practices, and culture normalized and reinforced the sexual division of labour and assumptions about socially constructed gender characteristics being 'natural' and inborn.[57] The leadership's unwillingness to debate 'private life' was challenged, a criticism justified in light of the repeated thwarting of the efforts of some, including Monty Johnstone, to open a debate through the NCC and a party conference about sex and society.[58] Campbell and her associates directly confronted the 'dangerous chauvinistic attitudes' of the 'top leadership'; these, they argued, legitimated a pervasive culture of sexism that normalized the lack of creche facilities for party meetings and the relegation of women to administrative roles and of questions affecting women to 'any other business' on meeting agendas. The 'struggle for the liberation of women is not a luxury for Communists,' insisted the document, which received just four votes at Congress, 'it is a necessity.'[59]

Myriad factors prevented the party from the deep transformation that might, indeed, have altered its course at the height of the WLM. As the feminist critique that culminated in Campbell's powerful *Wigan Pier Revisited: Poverty and Politics in the 80s* (1984) emphasized, the labour movement, including the CP, mirrored rather than challenged patriarchal common sense and the sexual division of labour that prevailed in its heartlands. The enduring iconography of 'militant masculinity' in which miners were proletarians *par excellence* was part of what Campbell called the 'sexual apartheid' all too apparent to those feminists gathered for the 1971 WLM Skegness conference who disrupted the striptease laid on for delegates at the National Union of Mineworkers (NUM) conference next door.[60] Feminists at the May Day rally in Birmingham a few years later would dramatize the labour movement's collusion with the objectification of women by carrying effigies of male nudes with Arthur Scargill's head superimposed.[61] This everyday sexism of the dominant culture was not only shared by the labour movement and the party, but was screened off from real scrutiny by core Communist assumptions about gender, class, and the chronology of revolutionary transformation. To call the traditional position a 'theoretical' one is perhaps to overstate the case; it was by now an embedded body of assumptions and habits beyond analysis that justified not engaging too seriously with those forms of politics which assumed that social relations could be meaningfully transformed this side of the state's seizure.

These assumptions came sharply into view around the question of the family that unfolded in *Marxism Today* between 1972 and 1974; the fact that the family had been so little discussed by Communists over the previous fifty years was a striking instance of both the party's embeddeness in dominant assumptions about the 'natural' sexual division of labour and its own common sense about the chronology of socialist transformation. Marriage – the institution upon which much Communist male activism relied – was vaguely thought of, if at all, as something that would somehow wither away or undergo reconfiguration under Communism.[62] As others have argued, that 'prominent women cadres in Britain either did not have children' or had only one child had seldom, if ever, been formulated as a phenomenon requiring analysis or self-criticism.[63] Discussion of the family, such as it was, tended to regard it as either a core unit of working-class society and solidarity or, less often, as a proto-Communist formation whose collectivist ethos bucked the individualistic competitiveness of capitalist society.[64] The WLM, however, now pushed the family's function in the reproduction of class society to the fore. The divergence and mutual incomprehension between the old and new positions was striking.

Speaking squarely within the terms of party common sense, Rosemary Small opened the debate by arguing that, while distorted and commodified by capitalism, the 'molecular' family unit had an essential and transhistorical legitimacy and represented 'even under capitalism … some sort of bulwark to cling to … a source of support and security, warmth and happiness.'[65] Following Engels, she argued that, while the family's function as 'the economic unit of society' should 'be abolished,' this did not imply that 'the individual family be abolished.' She argued that current CP women's groups' activism – the defence of nursery provision, campaigning around education, housing, and equal pay – was in fact productively attacking the family as an economic unit because it 'challenges the structure of society,' a conviction seen to be backed up by the existing socialist states that apparently were leading the way in advancing from 'formal equality for women' to 'true equality.'[66] For the WLM feminists, this sounded like leaving everything the same. Lacking from Small's analysis, ran the multivoiced critique (sixteen contributed to the discussion), was any real sense of what WLM feminist Maria Loftus called the complicated and interpenetrating relationship between 'the economic aspect of existence' and 'social institutions and ideologies,' or how the latter naturalized the former.[67] If it was true, ran her argument, that gender equality followed inevitably from economic equalization, then why was more rapid progress not being made in the Soviet Union? Failure there allegedly revealed that patriarchy did not wither with capitalism and that progressive forms did not 'simply develop spontaneously under socialism' but had to be thought through.[68] Small, it was charged, also overlooked the family's structural significance as a site of the reproduction of the labour force – in terms of the economics of consumption and as a site of dangerous power imbalances – not only between men and women, but also between adults and children. Her account missed the family's role in producing and containing female sexuality ('to maintain the production of the labour force, women's sexuality is defined in terms of her future capacity for motherhood and men's pleasure').[69] Small was accused of reproducing bourgeois ideology in arguing that the family was an oasis of collectivity. Rather, others insisted, it produced 'people suited to capitalist relations of production'; far from promoting solidarity, it encouraged social divisions that 'serve the maintenance of class rule.'[70]

Poster for Communist Women's Struggle event, London, 1975. CP Archive, LHASC, Manchester.

Campbell would later push this further, arguing that the idea of the home as a 'safe place' was itself an ideological construct and that domestic violence and rape were on a continuum of everyday patriarchy, 'an expression of *ordinary* domestic conflict between unequals.'[71] According to such logic, the dissolution, rather than the defence, of the family was the correct line, since the family was, if anything not a prefiguration of communism but a miniature version of 'the power structure outside.'[72] Workerist attempts to distinguish between idealized notions of warm proletarian hearths and cold, bourgeois drawing rooms was sentimental self-consolation as 'the family is not the creation of a single class … there is not a form of it under capitalism that does not serve an ideological function.'[73] Communists should therefore also advance beyond Small's 'idealised view of bourgeois monogamy' and support experiments in countercultural communal living usually dismissed as 'petty bourgeois deviation.'[74] They should be thinking through possible alternative social structures inherent in the notion of comradeship with a view to the dissolution of the family, 'one of the chief parts of the apparatus which allow the state machine to function,' and reaching for different arrangements that would 'allow for the liberation of all its members, but specifically women and children from oppression.'[75] Small's quasi-official summing up of a discussion that greatly animated the party and revealed the breadth of views within it was less an opening out than an act of containment.[76]

Red Rags

It is worth recalling this debate at some length, as it not only brought to the surface commonsense assumptions about class, gender, and the family, but was another articulation of the broader theoretical positions now dividing the party around *when* transformation of the social and cultural life shaped by capitalism was possible. 'We are in no mood,' ran the inflammatory editorial of *Red Rag*, the 'Marxist journal of Women's Liberation' set up without prior Executive Committee approval by communist feminists in alliance with non-communists in 1972, 'to wait for socialism to bring us liberation. We are interested in liberation now and in wrenching from capitalist society every advance we can get.'[77] The point was that the feminist struggle could not be deferred, but was at once inherently necessary for social justice, and would energize, prefigure, and illuminate broader socialist transformations. The journal clearly challenged the binaries of class/gender and party/social movement within which the party operated, although *Red Rag* editorial board member and feminist Communist Gladys Brooks clearly saw it as a means of revitalizing the party, and wrote to the Executive Committee to make the case, albeit after, rather than before, the first issue appeared.[78] She presented the journal as an exercise in creating the broad popular alliance to which the party was committed: in particular, it was to be a site of resistance to separatist feminist currents with the potential to 'divert' the WLM away from 'alliance with the working class.' To be in these vital feminists currents, she argued, and to shape and benefit from the 'enormous new interest in Marxism and especially the writings of Engels, Marx and Lenin on women's place in society' among young women, some freeing up of party protocols was necessary, as the young preferred 'a minimum of formality, "rules of debate" and committee work and a maximum of "total democracy."'[79] Much to Brooks's chagrin, the nervously watchful Exective Committee had already imposed Gerry Cohen, a male full-time functionary, onto the party's National Women's Advisory Committee, and for the leadership these words were a red rag, indeed: 'There is no guarantee with "Total Democracy,"' ran the committee's anguished report on the affair, 'that the people concerned ... will have any responsibility to anyone.'[80] The committee's deep unease was expressed not only by compiling names of non-party contributors and their alarming affiliations – 'Sheila Rowbottom [*sic*] IS' [International Socialist]; Selma James 'a known Trot ... opposed to our views' and 'waiting to clobber Party' – but procedurally by the application of the well-known party rule, deployed inconsistently but with deep origins in the conditions of Comintern membership and the principles of democratic centralism, which stipulated that party members could not 'produce journals without prior consultation' and the clearance of the Exective Committee.[81] Letters received amidst the brewing controversy cautioned the committee from employing disciplinary measures, emphasizing the need for a journal to facilitate discussion within the WLM left.'[82] One Southend activist pointed out that association with the journal was in fact enhancing the party's reputation in women's groups and creating demand for party speakers;[83] the conservative cautioned that, 'if the party says no to *Red Rag*,' then at least 'it must not come out' as being associated with such illiberal censoriousness.[84] In fact the moment of optimum synergy between the party and the journal was already passing. As Brooks had suggested, the journal's first editorial had been close to the party line in stating that the 'organised labour movement' was the 'decisive force in this country for social progress and socialism,' despite the suggestion that, where questions of women were concerned, the movement was more part of 'capitalist society' than it would have conceded.[85] By the second issue, *Red Rag* was already pulling away from the party's core assumptions, querying rather than assuming the idea that the WLM needed the labour movement's imprimatur, and reflecting a much broader range of feminist perspectives in which Communist voices were audible but by no means dominant. The party's solution was emblematically inward looking: fearing a damaging breach, it eschewed disciplinary processes, but created an in-house 'women's journal,' *Link*, launched in the spring of 1973 and edited by Small.[86] A throwback to party women's publications of the 1940s and 1950s, its earnest articles on 'Women and the trade union' and 'news about women in Party Districts' ensured that it never became even so much as a footnote in the history of the WLM.[87]

As far as Communist feminists were concerned, the lesson was that, for a range of reasons – pervasive patriarchy, party tradition, weak theory around the chronology of revolution, economism – class trumped gender, or indeed any other 'social movement,' and there was no positive political identity yet available for feminist Communists in the party. Rather, there was a series of tensions between identities that felt sharply distinct, if not mutually exclusive. Such tensions were experienced, for instance, by the Communist women who resented the unspoken expectation that they should distribute party literature at WLM events, and who believed that such proselytizing was contrary to the spirit of a political culture that stressed the importance of non-didactic communication in which everyone was learning.[88] Some feminists aligned with the WLM – Campbell, Sally Hibbin, and Sue Slipmann – would establish themselves on the National Women's Advisory in the course of the mid-1970s and fight internal struggles from there. Nonetheless, the formulation of radical policy that might have aligned the party meaningfully with the WLM was effectively resisted by more conservative positions – defended by incoming Women's Officer, Jean Styles – which made the committee a site of often acrimonious conflict rather than transformation. Lesbianism was marginalized as a topic for discussion, and the WLM position of 'abortion on demand' was considered a step too far (the party policy described abortion as a 'regrettable final stage in birth control and family planning').[89] Despite the prominent activism of significant Communist feminists in the WLM and broader society, a new debate in 1976 on the party's official position on 'Women and Society' revealed how impervious the party had remained to new thinking over the past five years, during the height of Second Wave feminism.[90] With some weariness, Elizabeth Wilson complained of a party that persisted in reducing the subordination of women to 'one facet of capitalist oppression' and clung to the belief that 'the achievement of socialism will itself lead to the solution to women's problems.' 'The party,' she concluded, 'has to decide what it really believes in.'[91] Campbell put it more strongly, arguing that the real, practical political advances of the WLM – around abortion, the defence of battered women, child care, discrimination, and rape law – were brushed aside by the leadership, as were complaints of sexism among party members. For Campbell, the party had singularly missed the opportunity to transform itself in the light of the WLM, and was now 'stuck in a narrow, economist conception of class struggle.'[92]

Less than Zilch?

It was a revealing paradox of these years that, while feminists including Campbell felt at a loss around the party's resistance to women's liberation, she and her associates made more rapid headway around the oppression of homosexuals;

where women were concerned, the party believed its existing structures and policies were essentially sound, but it was more open on homosexuality, where it lacked a line and knew it needed one. Taking a position against 'the oppression of homosexuals' – a persecuted minority – was less unsettling to the party's usual class-centred modus vivendi than feminism, the main problem with women being that there were so many of them, and the problem with feminism being that its critique challenged fundamental assumptions, as the debate on the family had revealed. As with women, so with homosexuality: the party historically had mirrored the common sense of the culture in a low-level homophobia occasionally deployed to marginalize 'public school' or 'long-haired' intellectuals.[93] Propelled by advances of the Gay Liberation Movement at a time when the Campaign for Homosexual Equality had a respectable and growing 5,000 members in 130 branches and *Gay News* had a circulation of 20,000, the party debated gay liberation in the *Morning Star* in 1973, formally endorsed gay liberation in 1975, and adopted a statement at the Executive Committee meeting in September 1976 that was praised by the lesbian Left and was greeted by *Gay Times* as 'the fullest and most far reaching such policy ever adopted by a non gay organisation.'[94] This was certainly to its credit, as Campbell spelled out in an interview with the journal *Gay Left*.'[95] The misgivings of more traditional Communists who voiced their homophobia through the familiar wait-for-the-revolution logic used to contain the WLM – 'gay liberation' was a 'secondary issue to the main direction of the class struggle,' and an 'unstable platform' that should not be 'elevated' into 'the overall arena of the working class' – proved misplaced, as no such elevation was forthcoming nor likely to be.[96] Despite the best efforts of party activists including Campbell and Sarah Benton (chair of the National Gay Rights Committee), the party did not advance beyond the essentially liberal discourse of its statement (the Liberal Party, indeed, soon followed suit with a similar statement), and supported the 'rights' of a minority without substantially analysing its own work or transforming its own culture in the light of the struggle against homophobia. The newly formed Gay Liberation Advisory Committee was a mere 'isolated pressure group,' according to Glasgow-based activist Bob Deacon, 'without clear backing from the Party as a whole.'[97] Deacon noted that, once the eye-catching radical statement has been issued, the knot of traditional structures, hierarchies, and habits (economism, class centrism) combined to impede the development of an active gay Communist politics as it had a feminist politics; gay men and lesbians were left sceptical about the depth of the party's commitment, and Communists about the relevance of gay liberation to their work.[98] 'The trouble with the Communist Party,' continued Deacon, looking back over a decade of trying to integrate the identities of Communist and gay activist, 'has been that whilst its policy on gay and lesbian rights is sound, its commitment is less than zilch.'[99]

Red Bases in the Universities?

Another key constituency for visions of party renewal was students. Although students were barely mentioned and undifferentiated from 'youth' in the 1968 version of *The British Road to Socialism*, their numerousness in late 1960s Britain was, in one sense, a rare instance of Communists having got what they wished for.[100] A much-muted version of the post-war Bernallian vision of an expanded educational sector as a dynamo of scientific modernity had become reality by the end of the decade with the restructuring and expansion of higher education: four new universities were founded in 1961 and six more pledged with the acceptance of the Robbins Report two years later.[101] In inter-war Britain there had been 70,000 university students; there were 216,000 in 1962, 310,000 by 1965, and 418,000 by 1968, around 10 per cent of those in their late teens and twenties, a demographic itself rising with the population (there were 579,000 eighteen-year-olds in 1959, 881,000 six years later).[102]

The late 1960s surge in YCL membership, however, had not been matched by campus recruitment, and the new level of scrutiny brought to students in party publications by leading Communists like Jack Woddis (1914–80) was at some level a defensive response against political and intellectual currents in student politics often indifferent and sometimes openly hostile to Communism. The party had minimal presence in the student disturbances at the London School of Economics (early 1967), the University of Hull (May 1968), and the Hornsea College of Art (June–July 1968). One problem was the uninspiring student organization registered in the previous chapter, with its censorious mores, culture, and publications at some distance from countercultural horizontalism, a gap revealed rather than bridged by earnest attempts to overcome it. Senior Communists agonized over why young people took drugs ('disgust with features of capitalist society';[103] 'no thanks, I'm a Communist' was one young comrade's standard reply when offered marijuana).[104] Communism's already distinctly unfashionable, illiberal, Cold War aura among students only got worse after Paris in 1968, due to the common perception that the PCF had reneged on the Sorbonne soviet.[105] It got worse still after the crushing of the Prague Spring, and it naturally meant nothing to students born around 1950 that the CP had done better in 1968 than in 1956 in distancing itself from the Soviet regime; what mattered was that it was tainted by association with such a regime at all. The 'typical left wing student today,' explained *Comment*, with some understatement, 'has been brought up with as many fears and reservations about Communist parties and socialist practice as his predecessors.'[106] 'Being a communist was just about on the edge of left-wing respectability,' explained Mike Prior, a CP activist at the new University of Essex before becoming a Party Group critic in the 1970s.[107] 'In 1968,' added Digby Jacks, soon to become the first Communist NUS president since the onset of the Cold War, 'it suddenly became harder to be a communist in student politics. I had a feeling that things were passing the party by.'[108]

As so often with the CP, the problem of British Communism's lack of appeal to students was not only a matter of cultural habits and history beyond its control, but also of its own *sui generis* inwardness and theoretical limitations. While official party discourse assumed it knew students' place in society, and was constitutionally disinclined to see them supplant the proletariat as principal revolutionary agents, bigger sister Communist Parties were offering more positive readings and building student support proportionately. Spanish Communist Party leader Santiago Carillo argued that the cultural and technical expertise brought by students to the party and the working class would ease the future process of socialist construction;[109] Gianfranco Borghini, student organizer of the PCI, told students that they had the power to disrupt 'the development of new productive forces practised by the ruling class' through campus activism.[110] Outside the Communist movement in Britain and beyond, influential New Left intellectuals, journals, and groups were now speaking more positively, if sometimes feverishly, about students' social status and potential political significance. In their pamphlet on May 1968, Tom Nairn and Angelo Quattrocchi identified universities as the 'higher nervous system' of developed capitalist society and students as 'harbingers of the real revolution'; Trotskyite Ernest Mandel argued that social and intellectual privilege equipped students to see through bourgeois ideology more easily than workers, and should and could 'play the role of the detonator.'[111] More substantially, Herbert Marcuse argued that students, like peasants and disaffected minorities, represented a potential vanguard with little to lose in a context where the old revolutionary subject of the traditional working class had been incorporated by collective bargaining, hire-purchase, and mass culture into the enveloping, pacifying structures of modern capitalism. The party, including younger activists, produced the predictable critique of ultra-leftist voluntarist vanguardism, recentring the working class and cautioning against sectionalism.[112] They were outside the 'ferment among the students,' looking in, and knew it.[113]

A combination of core assumptions, organizational structures, and outside perceptions, rather than individuals, was the problem, but Communist student work at the turn of the decade was certainly not assisted by the personnel leading it. Hardline National Student Officer Fergus Nicholson was best remembered by some for pulling the plug on the pop music at a lively YCL branch social in the summer of 1968 to deliver a speech defending the Soviet invasion of Czechoslovakia.'[114] Nicholson's associate Phil Goodwin, who viewed the student scene through the prism of quotations from Harry Pollitt, saw only quantitative, rather than qualitative, shifts in the form and function of higher education since the war.[115] Together they dismissed the potential political significance of a demographically swelling social group inclined to radical visions.

Students were evaluated squarely on the basis of what they would become, rather than what they were, and seen as 'apprentices' of a future expanded 'middle strata' central to the visions of the electoral strategy and *The British Road*.[116] Committed to traditional party hierarchies, Nicholson and Goodwin created an atmosphere more likely to repel than recruit, complaining about the difficulty of organizing a group that refused to behave like workers, stressing the importance of bringing students 'towards the labour movement,' and warning ominously that no special licence would be granted to newly recruited students in terms of 'attitudes and breaches of rule that nobody else would get away with.'[117]

The party's perspectives on students were, however, broader than Nicholson's, and new struggles were soon in motion. Some Communist students, including future academics and modernizers Martin Jacques and Alan Hunt, were more at home than Nicholson and Goodwin in the milieu of the late 1960s campuses, and had been prominent in the October 1966 formation of the Radical Student Alliance, a broad left body whose purpose was to challenge the now-entrenched quietism of a NUS leadership still mired in the 'no politics' ethos that had prevailed since the start of the Cold War.[118] In line with the party, Jacques in particular supplied a critique of the ultra-leftism unleashed by events in 1968, arguing that the point of economic production was a necessarily privileged site in socialist politics. He also drew the historical lesson that revolutionaries should always take seriously organizations with mass memberships, like the NUS, however compromised they had become.[119] This initially won few friends among more radical currents, who denounced the NUS as unreformably bourgeois, created an alternative organization to the Radical Student Alliance, the Revolutionary Socialist Student Federation, in June 1968 that attracted the support of the majority of Trotskyite and Maoist organizations, and theorized in the *New Left Review* and bespoke publications about campus 'red bases' as nodes of the coming British revolution.[120] Once the tear gas cleared, however – campus occupations fell off after renewed militancy at the London School of Economics in the first half of 1969 – the qualities of level-headed persistence that had formerly marginalized the party now put it in a position to build support. Relatively sober positions were taken on the contentious topic of how students should be selected by institutions and assessed once there – the latter was an issue that would spark unrest in the Economics Faculty at Cambridge in 1972 and 1973 – the party arguing that 'no selection' was unrealistic and that the removal of all assessment, which the more radical favoured, would reduce education to 'a rather purposeless activity or mere amusement.'[121] Substantially, however, the party focused on the NUS, where a mounting groundswell of leftist resistance to a top-down NUS bureaucracy had been building from the mid-1960s and the president, Geoff Martin (1966–68), who had failed to provide leadership over the 1968 campaign about grants and had condemned the Vietnam demonstration of October 1968, was unseated by left Labour candidate Jack Straw in 1969 with Communist support. Communist Digby Jacks was elected to the executive as part of a new left majority around Straw. Jacks was the first Communist to serve since the 1950s, and would be joined on the NUS executive by two more Communists in 1971, before succeeding Straw in 1971–3, giving the party its first NUS president since Tony James.[122]

That the party leadership reduced the full-time national student organizer post to part time at a moment (May 1970) when the density of student branches was increasing (twenty-eight in 1969, thirty-six by 1972) and it was reaching the point where it could 'give a degree of leadership to the NUS' through the elections of a CP NUS president (Jacks), vice president (Dave Wynne), seven full-time NUS officials nationally, and three out of fifteen of the central NUS executive was a measure of both stretched resources and traditional under-valuing of student work.[123] After a bitter, behind-the-scenes struggle, however, Dave Cook (1941–93) was appointed as Nicholson's full-time replacement, and became prominently associated with the implementation in student work of a broad left strategy of the kind outlined in *The British Road to Socialism*.[124] He and like-minded comrades had previously been in sympathy with the objectives of the RSA, which had retained a presence at NUS conferences, and they now supported the formation of a Broad Left group of student activists comprising Communists, Labour students, and non-aligned supporters at a conference in Leeds in 1972.[125] A loose organisation, the Broad Left would soon establish the *Broad Left Journal*, and commit itself to the domination of the NUS, which it rapidly achieved: by October 1974, thirteen of the seventeen-person NUS Executive were elected with Broad Left support.[126] Defined by its organizational suppleness and oriented towards the mobilization of the maximum number of students to 'collective action' on both student issues and 'in solidarity with other progressive forces in society,' the Broad Left became a visible and often cohering presence in numerous campaigns.[127] It had a revitalizing effect on the party's student section, soon its fastest-growing sphere, with membership peaking at almost a thousand in February 1973, up from 619 six months earlier.[128] Cook, a libertarian Communist and keen reader of Gramsci, emerged as an activist committed to developing a strategy for party renewal and long-haul Communist advance that integrated different social movements, attended to the relationships between the different levels of struggle, and eschewed sectarianism and economism by recognizing that participation in particular sectional struggles made people receptive to 'deep political lessons.' Necessary to press such lessons home, he argued, was 'propaganda, argumentation and education that *links* the politicising experience through which people pass, to the need for revolutionary change in society.'[129] Meetings, teach-ins, articles, pamphlets, and the *Broad Left Journal* were instances of that process, but for Cook and other Communists the crucial forum would now become the annual Communist University of London, which, as we have seen, had been established in 1969,

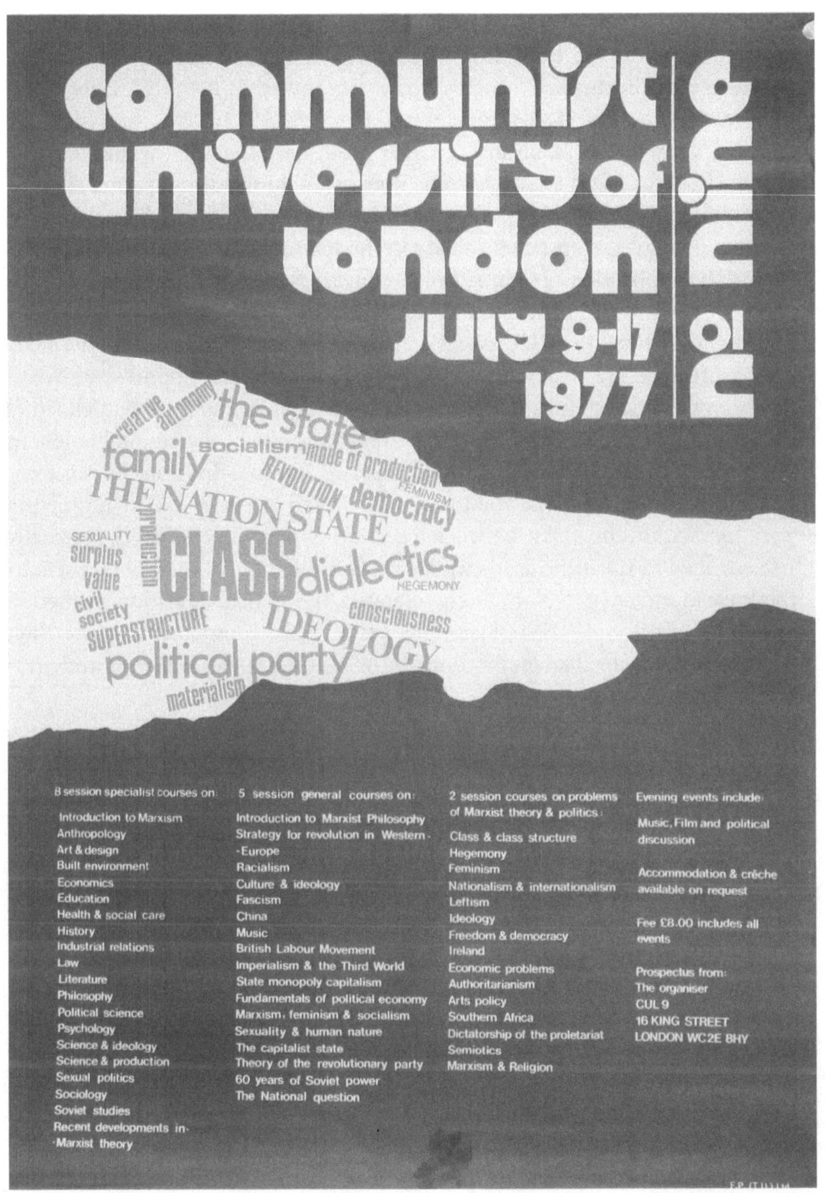

Poster for Communist University of London, 1977. CP Archive, LHASC, Manchester.

but which, in the Nicholson years, had remained essentially a slightly broadened version of the old Education Department schools dominated by leading Communist intellectuals.[130] Much energy was invested in the CUL by Cook and his associates, and it was transformed from the 1972 event, for which 632 registered, only half of them in the CP.[131] From here the CUL would become infused with Broad Left logic, welcome non-party thinkers, and formulate new theoretical perspectives and strategic emphasis, especially through stressing the importance of culture and civil society in the formation of popular consciousness and the application of Gramscian perspectives to contemporary problems. Run by the student committee, rather than the NCC, whose input would diminish further over time, the CUL would quickly become as significant for the challenges it presented to received party thinking as to the development of Broad Left student politics. A forum that became an annual fixture for the intellectual and cultural Left and enabled the party to regain some of the credibility lost in the aftermath of 1956, the CULs also sharpened internal divisions by reinforcing the 'disturbing trend' of what one disgruntled attendee called 'a growing separation' within the party 'between a section of party intellectuals, primarily those engaged in full-time academic work, and the mass of members, particularly those in industry.'[132] Not merely tolerated, theoretical deviation seemed to some almost *de rigeur*.[133] 'People holding party cards,' complained another, 'felt able to deny the dialectical method' and 'proclaim the Soviet Union as undemocratic,' asking 'What is the world coming to?'[134]

Advanced Capitalism, Backward Socialism

Far beyond the field of student politics, the party and its press were naturally eager to cite instances of the successful application of a 'Broad Left' or 'broad popular alliance' strategy in the late 1960s and early 1970s as evidence that *The British Road* was charting the right course. The Lampeter University's Socialist Society hosted a visit from young workers at the radiator factory in Llanelli;[135] Bristol activists worked with a local vicar and others to secure access to playing fields for local children;[136] in Cambridge, Communists were highly active in the Left Forum, which held weekly meetings regularly attended by three hundred, and campaigned on international, national, and local issues;[137] as Left Forum stalwart Raymond Williams later noted, Communists subsequently made a positive and comradely input into the National Convention called to promote the *May Day Manifesto* (1968).[138] In Harlow there were small triumphs over free school milk.[139] For many, including those newly recruited in the early 1970s, such grassroots work was the essence of modern Communist identity, and about 'starting from where people are,' consolidating small gains and taking 'people with you and having them be part of the success.'[140]

The hub of the Broad Left strategy, however, was considered the trade union movement, in line with *The British Road*'s emphasis on the labour movement as the core of the 'broad popular alliance.' A period of low unemployment and high union density – in which employers increasingly struggled to defend their profit margins against wage demands and the government sought to curb the unions – generated industrial militancy unprecedented since the General Strike. More days were lost to strikes in 1972 than at any point since 1926 – 6.5 million in a single quarter of 1974.[141] As mentioned in the previous chapter, the late 1960s upturn in the party's trade union fortunes was substantially driven by the forceful Bert Ramelson, the CP Industrial Organiser from 1965, whose considerable personal dynamism – a combination of pugnacity, shrewdness, and disarming charm – worked a promising moment to the maximum. The line was firmly away from the clandestine operations that had brought discredit to the party during the early 1960s Electrical Trades Union ballot-rigging scandal. With Ramelson coordinating operations from the Industrial Department, the CP accumulated an unprecedented degree of industrial influence, beginning with the seamen's strike of mid-1966, which was supported through the union's executive council by Communists including Ramelson, clearly the lynchpin figure among that 'tightly knit group of politically motivated men' controversially condemned by Harold Wilson in the House of Commons (Ramelson's picture appeared on the front page of the *Daily Mirror*).[142] The party's pleasure in such notoriety was palpable; its press release did not deny that the CP was out to 'torpedo' Wilson's income policies, and in 1967 General Secretary John Gollan spoke proudly of the 'dozens' of Communists who had led recent strikes.[143] In terms of direct struggle, the party pushed the wage militancy that always promised to escalate into conflict with the state (employers believed that high wages were damaging national competitiveness and driving inflation upwards). It had a strong presence in the familiar flashpoints of the period: the dockers' strike of October 1967, which set in train the run on the pound that culminated in the sterling devaluation that November;[144] the Upper Clyde Shipbuilders (UCS) work-in of 1971–2, through which Communist Jimmy Airlee (1936–97) and CP Executive Committee member Jimmy Reid (1932–2010) were successful in politicizing the threatened yard closure by campaigning for the 'right to work';[145] the strike provoked over the imprisonment of the Shrewsbury Pickets (1972), which included Communist Des Warren (1937–2004);[146] the campaign around the Pentonville Five, three of whom were Communists;[147] and the miners' strikes of 1972 and 1974, in which a long-haul strategy of shifting the NUM leftward had clearly produced results, notably when the 1974 strike provoked the Conservative government unwisely to call a General Election on the question, 'who governs?' – which it lost.[148] The party also became a self-styled tribune of trade union rights, building its prestige in the labour movement through leading resistance to restrictions on trade union activity through the Liaison Committee for the Defence of Trade Unions, integral to the defeat of Barbara Castle's *In Place of Strife* in June 1969 and resistance to the Industrial Relations Bill and Act.[149] The overarching strategy of Ramelson, whose reference point was naturally *The British Road*, lay in entrenching the party in key unions affiliated to the Labour Party and using block votes to dominate the party conference and its decision-making bodies.[150] By the onset of the new militancy of the late 1960s, the party already occupied prominent positions in key unions: the NUM, the Union of Construction, Allied Trades and Technicians (UCATT), the NUT, the Amalgamated Union of Engineering Workers (AUEW), and the AEU.[151] From here followed the election into top positions of a new generation of leading trade union leaders including Ken Gill (AUEW, Technical, Administrative and Supervisory Section [TASS]), elected as a national official in 1968 before becoming general secretary in 1974.[152] By 1974, 10 per cent of union full-time officials were estimated to be in the CP, and the party had its cadre on the executives of key unions: the NUM, the National Union of Railwaymen, the Union of Post Office Workers, UCATT, TGWU, the AEUW, NUT, TASS, and the Associated Society of Locomotive Engineers and Firemen.[153] More significantly in terms of evolving a flexible Broad Left strategy, the Industrial Department under Ramelson subordinated narrow party interests and supported likely Left winners at the expense of worthy but electorally risky CP candidates. 'Broad Left' trade unionists who clearly answered Ramelson's calls included two former Communists, Lawrence Daly (NUM) and Hugh Scanlon, the latter elected to the presidency of the AEU in 1967, and Jack Jones, elected as leader of the TGWU two years later, whose union had approaching two million members by the mid-1970s, one in six of national trade union membership.[154] The new influence secured through a combination of upfront militancy, mass campaigns to defend union rights, and patient Broad Left manoeuvring created an unseasonal rejuvenation in British Communism, enhancing the party's reputation for strategy and seriousness and compelling the TUC in 1972 to rescind its long-standing ban on party members attending trades councils as elected delegates from their branches.[155] 'We have more influence now in the labour movement than at any time in the life of our party,' claimed Ramelson without overstatement in 1974.[156]

The influence achieved by the Broad Left strategy in the industrial field was considerable. It enabled the party to play an active role in the formulation and ongoing revision of the so-called Alternative Economic Strategy, the program of economic reforms pushed by the Labour Left, especially Tony Benn and Stuart Holland, from the early 1970s, which called for wealth redistribution, more nationalization, more planning and public spending, opposition to the Common Market, and advocated import controls and price freezes.[157] It also gave it some indirect traction within the Labour Party, as *The British Road* projected: Labour's more radical policies between 1971 and 1973 and its decisively more radical 1974 manifesto owed something to the discourses and atmosphere that Communists had created on the Left. Combined with union influence and the profile of the Liaison Committee for the Defence of Trade Unions, these successes confirmed for many the central thrust of *The British Road* and provided a welcome distraction from the party's ever-deteriorating 1970s electoral performance, dampening down the internal divisions about fundamental strategy that had rumbled through the Smith and Party Groups in the very early 1970s.

Central to the projections of *The British Road*, however, was always a growing party membership and a small number of Communist MPs, envisaged as a principled presence stiffening the Labour Party's socialist resolve and pushing the government leftwards. The return in 1974 of a Labour government that, despite the manifesto, proved welded to crisis management and moved rapidly to the right raised matters of fundamental strategy with a new sharpness, exposing the asymmetry between the party's industrial presence and its political weakness. Despite the upbeat tones of Jack Woddis's *Time to Change Course* (1973), party membership continued to fall, from 30,607 members in 1969 to 28,513 six years later. The remaining membership was becoming less active, and the sale of party publications plunged (*Comment* sold 6,429 copies in the first quarter of 1968 and 5,121 in the first quarter of 1972, which meant that, at best, one in five members was buying the key weekly publication).[158] Factory branches – still considered the 'key points' of the class struggle, according to the party chair in 1966 – were fast disappearing as party strategy focused on top-end trade union structures.[159] Militancy within different sections of the economy self-evidently was not translating into an upsurge in either party membership or radical political consciousness; workers were voting for Communists in trade union elections, but not in local or General Elections, a pattern that not even the charismatic Jimmy Reid could break – despite being elected as a councillor in Clydebank, he only just saved his deposit when he contested the parliamentary seat.[160] And the social contract, embryonic from 1972 and instituted in 1974, through which the government ceded some policies the unions wanted – the repeal of the Industrial Relations Act, increased welfare spending, price controls – in return for wage restraint fundamentally imperilled the Broad Left strategy.[161] The idea of pushing Labour leftwards through backroom union influence made little sense given the new monthly meetings at Transport House, while the escalation of wage militancy instinctively favoured by Ramelson was now antagonistic to the governing Labour Party, the political force considered to be crucial for the broad popular alliance and advance on the British Road to Socialism.

What was to be done? The party's position in relation to what Ramelson dismissed as 'the social contrick' now became a key site of contention in the party's Economics Committee, in the party press, and in Congress. This was notionally a debate about immediate tactics, but what now unfolded reactivated and made explicit fundamental questions about class, power, and strategy that had rumbled through the party's history and loomed up in different guises at different moments. The key issue concerned revolutionary strategy in the advanced West, and more particularly the significance of the economy and economic production as a location of politics and the political interventions that were possible and necessary there. Despite Ramelson's tactical suppleness around the unions, there was no movement on the core issue: the economy was a site of mutually exclusive class interests, the front line of conflict between capital and labour. The inflation that the social contract in part existed to control was, for him, simply a capitalist problem, caused by factors including arms expenditure, an expanding 'non-productive' tier of workers, monopolization, and post-war deflationary budgets.[162] Derided was any suggestion of a significant link between wage increases, inflation, and Britain's international competitiveness.[163] The unsettling implication that Bill Warren had long entertained – that wage militancy might actually be counterproductive in that it drove up inflation and indirectly eroded living standards for the working class – was for Ramelson unthinkable.[164] Ramelson also gave short shrift to those who saw production as a potential site of political working-class advance through greater workers' control over industry, notably the Institute for Workers' Control, established in 1968; such ideas, for Ramelson, were likely to 'spread confusion and weaken the struggle' and were best left to' fringe extremist groups.'[165] His main line on the chronology of revolution, the same in 1966, 1968, and 1974, was defiantly traditional: a sharp distinction needed to be drawn between what was possible 'before the working class take power and after.' The true strategy was the old one: increased trade union militancy and arching over it 'political action guided by a revolutionary party' committed to securing 'political power for achieving the transformation of society'; 'industrial democracy' could be an effect of the transformation, but was not a route to it.[166]

Ramelson's instincts were as out of tune with the realities of 1974 as they had been fitting in the late 1960s. The 1974 crisis, and the debates about inflation, wage militancy, and the social contract it generated, now opened space for alternative projections. By their own admission, the Party Group in the early 1970s had been stronger on critique than on alternative strategy. One key source for fresh thinking was debates on workers' control, whose dismissal by Ramelson was now challenged by Bill Warren and Mike Prior, notably in their pamphlet 'Advanced Capitalism and Backward Socialism,' published in a series associated with the Institute for Workers' Control. In particular, Warren and Prior were drawn to the UCS work-in of 1971–2, which for them demonstrated the potential efficacy of workers' seeking to occupy the means of production. Here was a different mode of industrial action, they argued, a prefigurative and partially symbolic strategy in which workers occupied and continued to work, dramatizing in their industry not only the old adage that the bosses' brains were really under the workers' caps, but also forming an embryonic version of what the party used to call 'Britain without capitalists,' organized not by the ruling class and its state, but by themselves and their elected representatives, including the highly telegenic and eloquent Jimmy Reid. The work-in captured the popular imagination in ways the white noise of unending sectional wage disputes did not. Its compelling drama – workers working to save their industry – was difficult for a hostile media to discredit, and mobilized wide solidarity (John Lennon sent red roses, then £1,000 for the Fighting Fund).[167] For Warren and Prior, party 'petty denigrations' of the UCS struggle, 'which complain that it was only a partial victory,' missed the mark. It had 'opened up areas of struggle hardly considered by the working class movement in previous years,' and suggested that strategies other than wage militancy might now be necessary to generate real momentum for advance towards socialism.[168]

The potential significance of Institute for Workers' Control currents and the UCS work-in were now amplified by a theoretical source, Gramsci's *Selections from the Prison Notebooks* (1971), which exerted a direct influence on inner party debates about what was to be done.[169] In terms of Gramsci's thought, what mattered in 1974–5 was less the ideas about intellectuals and culture that galvanized the party's cultural spheres, and more his fundamental thinking about class, power, and the chronology of revolution in developed societies. Viewed through a Gramscian lens, Ramelson's before-and-after position looked like a bullish manifestation of the deeper paradox that, while the party had long possessed a parliamentary strategy, it had, as Warren had formerly argued, no coherent theory of the nature of capitalist power in developed societies. Gramsci mattered now in offering a corrective model of class power and revolutionary chronology that emphasized not only coercion and the state, but also the need to win and build consent, and that, as Warren glossed it, 'the working class must become, culturally, the leading class before it could conquer the state.'[170] The location of this 'cultural' process was 'civil society,' a sphere deeply entwined with the productive forces, relations of production, and 'the mode of economic behaviour' ('hegemony begins in the factory,' Gramsci had written of American Fordism).[171] The process of 'intellectual and moral reform' that, for Gramsci, a rising class needed to effect in order to make the transition from its 'corporate phase' and become hegemonic thus 'has to be linked with a programme of economic reform – indeed the programme for economic reform is precisely the concrete form in which every intellectual and moral reform presents itself.'[172] As Warren put it, 'if the working class is to develop as the leading class within society, as a hegemonic class, it must itself become a leading class within capitalism before it conquers state power.'[173]

These arguments now possessed great force, their implication being that the working class would never be in a position to build hegemony and take power if it remained, as Ramelson advocated, oppositional in a merely defensive sense – 'saying "no" every time the representatives of the bourgeoisie say "yes", playing Tweedledum to the ruling class's Tweedledee,' as Warren and Prior's associate, the young University of Manchester economics lecturer David Purdy put it with the social contract in mind.[174] The Ramelsonian denial that wage increases were linked with inflation was by this reckoning a self-reassuring delusion undergirded by an old logic that refused to think about the complex ways in which labour was enmeshed in the system's reproduction. In turn, Purdy argued, the 'irrational desire to exempt the working class from any involvement in the processes at work in modern capitalist economies actually impedes the mobilisation of broadly based struggle for a fundamental redirection of economic policy.'[175] So recoiling from meaningful engagement in discussions about the running of the economy in the context of high inflation and the social contract was a measure of defeatism. The party's positions, ran the critique of wage militancy and free collective bargaining, put the working class in a position where it was 'doomed always to defend, never to lead or control.'[176]

It was much better, argued Warren, Prior, and Purdy – in an Economics Committee increasingly polarized between the official, Ramelson line (wage increases played little or no part in inflation) and their 'conflict theory' (inflation was substantially caused by struggle between capital and labour) – to acknowledge the embeddedness of labour in the system and to work the contradictions through decisive leadership, especially at a moment when the party needed to confront the discrepancy between union presence and political absence. That capital clearly could not solve its crisis provided just such an opportunity.[177] Wage militancy would not lead to advance, Purdy argued, for 'inflation can be brought under control only in a collectivised and rationally planned economy for whose management the mass of people are responsible because they collectively own and control it.'[178] More Gramsci informed the analysis at this point. The working class was not confronted with wall-to-wall market forces from which it must create such a collectivized and rationally planned economy, but, as Warren had previously argued, mixed and contradictory economic structures that had long absorbed elements of state planning. To a limited degree, the working class had already 'been able to impose its own social priorities upon capitalist society, through its growing economic and political strength,' notably through, in Gramscian terms, the 'passive revolution' of welfare-ism and consensus by which post-war capitalism had stabilized itself.[179] A great many workers were already in spheres that were determined by social need, rather than directly by the market (health, education).[180] At the same time, as Warren had also argued, the state was already substantially in the market economy: half of British investment passed through public hands, largely because the market could not handle the investment and planning requirements of modern large-scale industries – 'computers, shipbuilding, aircraft, atomic energy'

– 'the development of the forces of production is now beginning to outstrip the capacity of the market economy.'[181] This tension, and the struggles it produced around the allocation of resources – what Warren and Prior called the 'inchaote movement towards democratic control of economic and social life' – suggested that 'capitalism has fully set the stage for socialism.'[182] As a hegemonic class-in-waiting, the working class needed to direct this process, cutting with the grain of systemic contradictions and shaping production structures and systems that would undergird and shape socialist social relations. In other words, 'the working class should, as Gramsci argued, develop its own political and cultural hegemony over society, prior to the achievement of state power.'[183] In Britain, Warren and Prior argued, with the failures of the CP clearly in mind, there existed a 'profound disparity between the immense actual social and economic power of the working class and its defensive and primitive economistic psychology and politics – essentially those of a subordinate class.'[184] The necessary advance was substantially a matter of unlocking new modes of class consciousness and confidence whose development the party was actually impeding rather than encouraging. The working class needed not to be hoodwinked by the party's simplifications, but made to understand the complexities of modern capitalism and its own decisive role in it (actual and potential) and to develop a politics that could at once both advance its economic interests and 'permit its economic and social weight to exercise an increasingly hegemonic control within society.'[185] The Ramelsonian position of 'incessant escalation of industrial struggle orientated to the increase of money wages, gathered under the title of free collective bargaining' was bad economics, as it was shaped by and reinforced the mistaken assumption that those struggles would lead to higher living standards. It was bad politics in that it drew too sharp a line between base and superstructure, economy and politics, present and future – Gramsci by contrast emphasized the need for hegemonic strategies that 'weld the present to the future' – and locked the working class into 'the ghetto of merciless economism.'[186]

The alternative was initially sketchy, but becoming less so. The party should grasp the real complexity of modern capitalist economies and shape debates about wage restraint and working-class incomes policies on the basis of securing more control over production and distribution.[187] It should advance 'those demands which are simultaneously within the scope of capitalism to grant and will raise most clearly the issues of exploitation within capitalism and the necessity of socialism.'[188] The significance of this would clearly exceed the economy, it was argued, as 'modifying the decaying market economy in a positive direction towards the democratic satisfying of social needs' had the capacity to galvanize disparate social movements currently chipping away at social contradictions or, as Purdy put it in a high Gramscian register, of 'cementing together the bloc of social forces which over the difficult years that lie ahead for us in Britain can transform our programme from a gleam of the eye into a living reality.'[189] The strategy's potential strengths were multiple. It built on the idea of democracy as a key concept in unifying disparate social forces and, as such, especially in Purdy's writing, elaborated upon rather than erased the formulations of *The British Road* by proposing new ways of building the alliances central to its visions. In fixing on areas where the party had reason to think itself strongest – the economy, industry – and in addressing the day's pressing issues – inflation, wages policies, the social contract – the strategy could not be as easily sidelined by workerism or reference to ivory tower intellectuals as had those theoretical countercurrents that came in the past from culturally minded intellectuals like Jack Lindsay.[190] Those proposing an alternative route were not on the margins, but already represented on the Economics Committee, naturally chaired by Ramelson (Bill Warren, Pat Devine, Dave Purdy, Mike Prior).[191] The obvious weakness was that the strategy was unduly optimistic in 'expecting the workers,' as one not unsympathetic sceptic put it, 'to jump to record levels in consciousness and sophistication in coordinating an alternative policy which has the transition to socialism as a concrete practical objective.'[192] More particularly, the mechanisms through which the party would transmit to the working class lessons around what Warren and Prior called 'the actual economic realities of its role in British capitalism' were by no means clear given the diminution of strikes that the policy implied, not to mention the general depletion of the party's educational networks, the falling circulation of its publications, its lack of access to the airwaves, and the shift of the always student-dominated CULs into the vector of high theory that many rank-and-file industrial activists found alienating.[193] It is possible that, initially at least, those advocating the position missed an opportunity to persuade more traditional elements of its case by failing to spell out that something like the envisaged strategy had already been used, and had succeeded, in the party's own past: as I argued in Chapter Two, the party had fought nimble 'wars of position' across the economy around Joint Production Committees and workers' control in the context of the Anglo-Soviet alliance and post-war reconstruction, a history of prefigurative struggle soon buried beneath the Cold War. The inevitable charges of 'class collaboration' and 'total surrender' might have been better countered with instructive history lessons into moments when the party had made real advances, rather than with Gramscian terminology.[194] Ultimately, however, the party was not ready for a change that ran contrary to its core identities and assumptions, and never would be. A combination of lingering pride in the party's role in the high militancy of 1966–74, a deep-seated sense that the escalation of industrial struggle was in Communist DNA, and the considerable force of Ramelson's character and rhetoric was enough to contain the position. A version of the alternative strategy was debated and overpowered at the 1975 Congress, a pivotal moment before the bail-out by the International Monetary Fund (IMF), when a different course might have been most effective. Despite the defeat, however, the level of support these positions attracted in the ensuing debate in *Comment* was a measure of an escalating sense of crisis in which many were open to a new direction. 'We are calling for a wages offensive because that is what we always do,' wrote one disillusioned activist.[195] 'The line on inflation put forward in our propaganda,' wrote another, 'is pathetic considering that it is one of the major characteristics of the postwar capitalist world.'[196] 'We have isolated ourselves politically,' wrote a third, 'at that moment when economic crisis is generating ideas about the whole way in which the economy is managed.'[197]

A Cultural Front?

Central to the critique produced by Warren, Purdy, and their associates was the notion that an economistic confidence in industrial militancy as the dynamo of socialist consciousness had long legitimated the party's neglect of those everyday social and cultural practices in which subordinate working-class consciousness was formed and reproduced. As economists, this was not their primary concern, although the weakest point of their analysis was around the processes and structures through which hegemonic ambition might be transmitted through the party to the working class. For more culturally minded activists, the party's cultural weakness was obvious ground on which to challenge core assumptions and practices in an attempt to reinvigorate the party in the 1970s in a project that would parallel, but too infrequently mesh with, that of the Gramscian economists.

Why the party was losing rather than gaining ground amidst industrial tumult was a key question across the board. The traditional Communist view of the workplace as the key site of working-class consciousness – the location where the contradiction between private ownership and socialized labour was experienced most acutely – was now under pressure from social change, it was argued, and especially among the young. As Martin Jacques pointed out, with the coming of mass education the workplace mattered proportionately less to the young: in 1961, he noted, 14 per cent of the 15–24 age group were full-time students as against 20 per cent in 1970–1, which meant that, of the eight million young people in that group, three-quarters of a million were in higher and further education and more than one million 15–18-year-olds were still at school.[198] The family – a structure integral to the reproduction of new Communists all too apparent to the modernizers themselves (Jacques, Campbell, and Devine were from CP families) – was also changing, while opportunities for social mobility complicated the relationship with working-class community. In this context it was clear that, in terms of the formation of social and political identity and popular consciousness, the proliferating networks of the culture industry – advertising, television, radio, mass market publishing, music, fashion, and cinema, much of it targeted at youth – played an increasingly important role alongside work and education in socialization, especially among the young.

One basic problem the party faced in terms of grappling with this situation – and perhaps bringing to this changing cultural field something like the prestige it had once enjoyed – was clearly generational. As Jacques, Reid, and others pointed out, there was a hole in the party's cultural and intellectual strata roughly the size of the generation that had left in the aftermath of 1956, or that never joined during the Cold War.[199] Its leading intellectuals had been formed either in the 1920s (Maurice Dobb, A.L. Morton) or the 1930s and early 1940s (Alan Bush, Barbara Niven, Brian Simon, James Klugmann, Jack Lindsay, Maurice Cornforth, John Lewis). These figures still dominated the CP culturally, and shaped the NCC's mode of organization and priorities. As I argued in the previous chapter, the party lost ground culturally through the 1960s and early 1970s because this group was often looking in the wrong place for 'culture.' Its reflex assumption was that culture meant 'the arts,' a sphere for them above, critical of, and incompatible with the values of the commercial world. The party now needed cultural rejuvenation, but these figures were busily anxious about the border between 'high' and 'low' when the overturning of such constructs was a dominant cultural motif, from the eclectic musical pastiche of The Beatles' *Sergeant Pepper's Lonely Hearts Club Band* (1967) to genre-blurring postmodern novels such as John Fowles's *The French Lieutenant's Woman* (1969) – a problem encapsulated by former artist and NCC stalwart Barbara Niven's perturbed and dismissive response to American pop art in general and that of Roy Lichtenstein in particular.[200] Lichtenstein's discovery of artistic possibility and even beauty in the tawdry world of American comics was beyond the range of her comprehension: pop art could only be either a morbid symptom of late capitalism or a conspiracy of the ruling class to rob art of its critical power.[201]

Redefining culture and reconceptualizing the role it played in shaping and reinforcing experience of the world was therefore one task to which culturally minded modernizers like Jacques naturally applied themselves. They made significant headway here, pushing beyond the more tentative advances made by the YCL in the mid- to late 1960s, bringing in fresh perspectives, notably through Althusser on ideology and Gramsci on hegemony, and entering into dialogue with a wide range of non-party thinkers, including Raymond Williams and especially Birmingham University's Centre for Contemporary Cultural Studies, at which Stuart Hall – who was on good terms with the party, though never a member – succeeded Richard Hoggart as director in 1968. The central breakthrough was in widening the field of party cultural discussion by working with essentially anthropological rather than traditional definitions of culture: 'culture' was not 'only or even mainly High culture,' wrote Jacques in a key article, but 'an integral part of every person's life'; not 'a neutral island within class society,' but 'an important, indeed an increasingly important area of class conflict.'[202] Jacques in particular deconstructed the opposition between high and low that had rendered party analysis anachronistic and blocked the formulation of radical analysis likely to engage the young, notably in his presentation on 'Youth Culture' given to the NCC in February 1973, a version of which was then published as an extended article in *Marxism Today* in September 1973, provoking a debate that ran for eighteen months. Here new ground was being prepared. Jacques decisively rejected the more conspiratorial theories of popular culture as a medium of either distraction or false consciousness. Making the case for youth as an increasingly important group to which popular culture was especially significant in the formation of identity and consciousness, he focused on popular music, a sphere in which the party lacked not only cultural presence but coherent analysis. Nudged by the young-at-heart Betty Reid, who was all too aware of this deficit, he presented popular music as a site of tension and therefore possibility. In order to satisfy the market, he argued, echoing Hobsbawm on jazz and Charles Madge on inter-war tabloid newspapers, the music industry needed to sell products, and 'hence in some measure respond to, express, meet the needs and tastes of young people.' The 'balance between these contradictory influences within pop music is in a constant state of flux,' he argued, the creative element being to the fore in musical breakthroughs of the highly fertile 1963–7 period between The Beatles' first album and the seemingly emulation-defying *Sergeant Pepper*.[203] He saw the dissident, countercultural energies that had enlivened the flowering of that period as likewise contradictory, and pulled between individualistic and even anarchic tendencies that made the counterculture a funhouse mirror image of the commodity culture it sought to disavow, and more progressive, collectivist, internationalist, and emancipatory impulses expressed most forcibly in the 1968 national demonstrations against the war in Vietnam. For Jacques, the future direction of these cultural energies was politically crucial if the Left was to advance in the mid-1970s, but always open to incorporation and contestation. They might be 'absorbed and integrated by the bourgeoisie'[204] – he saw the post-1967 falling off in the power of popular music, whose manifestation was the celebrity of Donny Osmond, as symptomatic of that very real possibility[205] – or they might 'move in the direction of a more generalised consciousness which saw the causes of that dissatisfaction and disaffection in terms of the nature of class society.'[206] This struggle over the meaning of the popular, and the possible development of countercultural dissonance into structural critique and socialist perspective, was therefore for Jacques to be a crucial one of the 1970s. There were grounds for cautious optimism, he argued, in that expressions of disillusionment with Harold Wilson, including the radicalisation of the NUS, and especially the rising tide of industrial militancy involving young and old workers, had opened up new possibilities. Organized labour had now been brought into conflict with the state, underscoring 'by example the nature and significance of class conflict,' and revealing that 'the fundamental divisions in society are essentially class rather than generational' – putting paid to the lingering *Absolute Beginners* idea that youth was a 'highly autonomous and even independent social group' that somehow transcended class division.'[207] Jacques was keen to detect in the cultural scene arising from the remains of the counterculture this new collectivist spirit open to structural questions, citing as examples the resurgence in street and community theatre aligned with the working class and the pop concerts staged to raise funds for the UCS Fighting Fund. The party's potential role in this was clear, and his analysis here paralleled that of Purdy et al., who emphasized the imperative of heightening class consciousness. The party needed to support the positive elements in resisting incorporation, to steer social movements angled at specific sites of oppression towards 'a more generalised opposition based on a more universal understanding of their causes,'[208] and to find ways to transform itself in synch with this 'highly variegated' picture.[209] In part, Jacques argued, there was a precedent for what was necessary in the recent past, the 'cultural awakening' driven by early 1960s initiatives to shape cultural events and practices around the infrastructure of the labour movement, notably Centre 42. This energy, he argued, had soon lost ground to more individualistic countercultural patterns as, through the 1960s, youth increasingly had come to regard the institutions of organized labour, the Labour Party and the TUC, with their right-wing leaderships, as part of the one-dimensional society, deeply incorporated into the capitalist system – a pattern that could now be challenged in the spirit of the new militancy.[210] Crucial on all counts was the party's involvement in these spheres and struggles, where it must both teach and learn.[211]

Regrouping

The emerging analysis of class, culture, and consciousness driven by Jacques created a new framework for engaging with the contemporary cultural scene that both fed into and was reinforced by a revitalization of the cultural groups that in turn reinvigorated the party's cultural life. At the end of the 1960s, the only dependably active group had been History (Science had become an Advisory Committee; Music, still dominated by Alan Bush and his devoted loyal followers, was regarded by the NCC as a law unto itself and frustratingly uninterested in popular music).[212] This situation was reversed in a context shaped by the translation of Gramsci – which provided a rallying point for those inclined to emphasize the importance of cultural work – and the general elevation of intellectuals in party life already discussed, a process pushed by Betty Reid and Brian Simon, who wanted to see 'our specialists overcome hesitations, and announce an assault' across a wide front.[213] A National Cultural Conference, the first in nineteen years, entitled 'Arts and the Fight for Socialism in Britain,' was held at Conway Hall in October 1972. Attended by around two hundred activists, the event was inspired by the perception that time was 'ripe for a great expansion of our work.'[214] The initially small annual CULs formed an increasingly important hub. Incoming National Student Coördinator Cook drove various initiatives to bring together academics and students in their fields to discuss how Communists could best 'contest the ideological assertions of the bourgeoisie at every level of their subject.'[215] It was a process readily facilitated by the CUL structure, where subcourses aligned with academic disciplines ran across the eight-day event; the new-look 1973 CUL, for instance, held at Imperial College, had courses on art, economics, education, history, law, literature, philosophy, science, and sociology, which fitted around a nine-session core course on Marxism.[216] Groups were duly formed. A Sociology group was established that year (Ron Frankenburg at Keele and Alan Hunt at Middlesex were key figures);[217] by the late 1970s, its events would be addressed by thinkers including Nicos Poulantzas, Barry Hindess, and Stuart Hall, and it would produce an edited collection, *Marxism and Democracy* (1980).[218] A new Built Environment Group was formed the same year, which produced a bulletin and ran meetings attended by around forty architects, town planners, and housing managers.[219] Ideology was recognized to inhere in the built environment, and the controversial development of Birmingham city centre, with its capital investment, £5 million shopping centre, and erasure of civil amenities, was challenged for implanting individualistic and consumerist subjectivities anathema to socialist advance.[220] The History Group was reorganized and would enjoy a 1970s revival thanks to the input of younger intellectuals including Willie Thompson, Hywel Francis, Mary Davis, Jude Bloomfield, Joanna de Groot, Stuart MacIntryre, Robbie Gray, and John Foster.[221] With an energetic young new secretary, John Attfield, it would launch a newsletter, *Our History*, and organize significant gatherings, including a weekend conference on 'Problems of Marxist History' and a bigger event in October 1975 on pre-capitalist societies, run in conjunction with the Sociology Group and attended by over 250.[222] A Philosophy group met only sporadically (Cornforth was still a key figure), but nonetheless had sixty members by 1975, many of them post-graduates, and was part of a left turn in the subject that also led to the formation of the journal *Radical Philosophy*.[223] A Literature group was embryonic by 1972, with Jeremy Hawthorn, who taught at Lampeter and then Sheffield Polytechnic, as a leading figure. It would be formally constituted by 1976, establish its own journal, *Red Letters*, with an eventual circulation of 1,500, and hold conferences, including one on Brecht in March 1976 addressed by John Willett and attended by 150, and another on 'Culture and Commitment in the Thirties' in October 1976, from which an edited essay collection, published by Lawrence & Wishart, would emerge.[224] A Psychology and Psychiatry Group was formed in 1972, and ran meetings attended by a small group of doctors, psychiatrists, psychologists, and academics, some of whom were attempting to apply Althusserian insights to their practice.[225] A Visual Arts group was formed in 1973, and provided decorations for the party Congress that year and organized a festival for the Chilean Resistance in October 1974 at the Royal College of Art.[226] A new Theatre group was formed at the NCC conference in 1972, and involved Buzz Goodbody, a director at the Royal Shakespeare Company, and Val Lester from the Belgrade in Coventry.[227] Although it had minimal impact in terms of its own productions, it enthusiastically supported the early 1970s revival of 1930s-style agit-prop and street theatre groups,[228] with events including a conference on 'Marxism and Theatre,' addressed by non-party member Caryl Churchill,[229] and by backing the activities of the umbrella organization comprising forty recently formed independent grassroots theatre groups, many of them on the Left, which lobbied the Arts Council for more support.[230]

The *NCC Newsletter* distributed through party branches – moribund since the mid-1960s – was relaunched to report on cultural activities, but the energy now came less from the NCC than from the CULs and individual groups.[231] These drove a new breadth of semi-autonomous Communist cultural activity – part of a broader culture affirming working-class life and struggle that enjoyed an unseasonal and widespread resurgence in ways Jacques had noted. This new cultural tone sanctioned long-standing Communist impulses for the promotion of proletarian culture. Some argued for more party support for cultural ventures emerging 'directly out of the class struggle'; activists enjoyed party backing in working with the grain of this proletarian cultural turn.[232] Communist schoolteacher Ben Ainley, for instance, was a founding member and president of the Unity of Arts Society, formed in Salford back in November 1969 in an effort to revive the dimming energies of Centre 42.[233] The party now supported his Manchester-based classes on literature, Marxism, and the working class, which in turn led to the creation of the magazine *Voices* (1972–84); printed at the city's CP party offices, the magazine would publish new writing, including poems by future editorial board member John Cooper Clarke, the son of a party member.[234] Another significant initiative was the pugnaciously proletarian Cinema Action, in which young Communist film-makers John Green and Georgia Kalla were active. A revival of early 1930s–style initiatives, backed by veteran Communist film activist Stanley Forman of Plato Films, Cinema Action was formed in 1970, and committed itself to making 'authentic films of contemporary class struggle,' chronicling key disputes – the 1969 Vauxhall Strike, resistance to the anti-union Bill, UCS – and screening its films to workers and the labour movement as a means to focus strategy and spread solidarity.[235] Like some of the theatre groups, Cinema Action, which drew upon CP artist Ken Sprague in its *Fighting the Bill* (1971), attracted funding from trade unions.[236]

One emerging but surprisingly overlooked problem for the party, however, was that its intellectual stratum was overwhelmingly university based. CUL attendance, especially strong among students, doubled from around 500 to 1,000 between 1974 and 1975;[237] and, like Jacques, now a lecturer in economics at Bristol University, a number of the rising cohort had found their way from graduate studies to academic posts at the end of the 1960s and 1970s: there were at least ninety Communist academics by the mid-1970s, to the consternation of those alarmed by the 'radical penetration' of Britain's universities.[238] Articles on academic freedom and the centrality of universities to 'bourgeois ideological hegemony' were a staple of *Marxism Today* in the early and mid-1970s.[239] The party, however, had few rising figures on the front line of cultural production equivalent to Alan Bush, Ewan MacColl, Hugh MacDiarmid, Beatrix Lehmann, Joan Littlewood, or Jack Lindsay, and from here on would become better at analysing culture than at producing it.[240] A related problem was that, although the party could maintain a presence in regional and community-based cultural projects, working with its preferred cultural forms (theatre, agit-prop film, creative writing), some of which effectively tapped into the decentralizing and regionalist emphasis of the 1970s Arts Council, it remained remote from the levers of the modern culture industry – popular music, television, film – that Jacques and the Gramscians saw as central to modern subject formation. The party retained a presence in the folk music scene and its residual networks of clubs, festivals, independent labels, and magazines, especially in the form of the Ian Campbell Folk Group, and it would find a new enthusiastic member in the subculture's rising star, Dick Gaughan, committed to claiming for his class the resources of folk culture. Overall, however, that scene was now withering, and despite Jacques's theorizing about youth culture as a crucial site of Left and party renewal, the post-1960s decline of the YCL estranged the party still further from youth culture (YCL membership would plummet from 2,576 to 1,021 between 1974 and 1979).[241] Where punk was concerned, some efforts were made: *Challenge* editor Paul Bradshaw was an enthusiast, and the YCL issued an opportunistic open letter to The Sex Pistols in the summer of 1977 urging them to work with Communists;[242] punk groups including Sham 69 played at YCL 'red festivals' in 1977 and 1978.[243] Towards the end of the decade, YCLer Green Gartside, the driving force behind the Gramsci-inspired Scritti Politti, would write songs about hegemony and Red Bologna, and serve on the editorial board of *Challenge*; in the 1980s, party member Dave Laing would produce an enduring retrospective analysis of the punk phenomenon.[244] Even so, the party had no organic presence in the punk scene when it mattered most, in the explosive 1976–7 period, when punk swept aside the remnants of the counterculture; the party was conspicuously absent from the Trotskyite-dominated Rock Against Racism, whose first carnival, held in April 1978 in Victoria Park, attracted 80,000 (the 'inadequacy of the party's involvement' was a concern for Jacques; others thought the party should create its own 'folk against racism').[245] In film things were little better: caught between its own high cultural predilections and Cold War exclusion, the party had never commanded much of a presence in British film production,[246] which, as now former ACTT president Sidney Cole pointed out, was itself in crisis (eighty-six British feature films were made in 1972, only fifty-four in 1975), with cinema attendance plummeting and picture houses closing.[247] The situation was no better in broadcast media, where the party's presence was never strong after the BBC blacklisting of the early 1950s.[248] The party struggled to sustain its own media or television group, its most significant figure being the young film-maker Jeff Perks, who quickly drew the attention of MI5 while at college by making a film about the Shrewsbury Three, a clip from which caused controversy after being broadcast on Thames Television's *This Week*.[249] Despite the best efforts of Paul Olive (1944–2011), who as incoming editor of *Comment* introduced a television column, the party lacked even a coherent language with which to analyse the medium: debate of the nation's key mass cultural form remained either self-righteously denunciatory or so steeped in the language of contemporary semiotics that *Comment*'s readers complained of 'indigestible jargon' whose mere reading 'was a feat of intellectual stamina.'[250] The party still often overlooked analysis of television altogether in its cultural events – the medium being an afterthought, for instance, at the 1972 NCC conference – while others on the Left were now doing better: the International Marxist Group, for instance, organized a high-profile Sunday night seminar series entitled 'Marxism and the Mass Media,' addressed by speakers including Raymond Williams, who attracted an audience of two hundred.[251] In terms of Britain's larger broadcasting structures, the party failed to develop a position distinct from that of the Labour Left, the TUC, or the Institute of Workers' Control, or to move far beyond its fixation with securing election broadcasts, still seen by the leadership as a panacea that would lead to electoral breakthrough, or at least staunch the haemorrhaging Communist vote.[252]

Despite the uneveness of its cultural presence, however, the combination of Gramsci, the non-sectarian CULs, a new generation of Communist academics, and the often highly active rejuvenated groups gave the party an intellectual presence and credibility it had lacked since the 1940s. It could now mobilize broad support across the cultural sector, often with the backing of the Executive Committee. When, in 1976, for instance, the NCC targeted theatre groups, rock bands, and folk groups for help with party fundraising, around thirty were willing to assist, including major theatre outfits (Banner, 7:84, Monstrous Regiment) and musicians including leftist experimenters Henry Cow and former Elvis impersonator and future pop star Shakin' Stevens. Indeed, fellow-travellers now proved more eager to help than long-suffering members, notably the Ian Campbell Folk Group, 'sick of playing for nothing to 12 people at a branch social.'[253] Exactly this type of good will and credibility enabled the party to stretch in the mid-1970s to stage small-scale imitations of Communist festivals – the Fête de l'Humanité in France and the Festa de l'Unità in Italy – that were necessary summer pilgrimages for Britain's European-oriented young Communists in the 1970s.[254] The Moving Left Show (five hundred attended), the NCC's 'Marxism – Politics – Ideology – Culture' week of discussion, and the Festivals of Marxism in Manchester and Scotland, all in 1975, and a Gramsci conference two years later, were, in different ways, prequels to the highly ambitious People's Jubilee at Alexandra Palace on 19 June 1977, a CP-hosted event that marked the zenith of the party's 1970s cultural upturn.[255] Derived from the European models, the People's Jubilee also looked back to the mass pageants of the Popular Front years in seeking to inscribe a potentially conservative cultural form – this time, the jubilee street party – with radical content (CPGB General Secretary Gordon McLennan, who had replaced the retiring Gollan in 1975, envisaged the event as 'a one day festival of revolutionary politics and culture').[256] Gramscian to the core in its emphasis on the preservation and development of progressive impulses in the national culture ('the national popular') and on the 'recapture' of 'lost political ground for the left,' at a time when the right was on the move in the Conservative Party and on the streets alike, the event raised over £2,000 for the party, an additional £1,800 for districts and branches, attracted mainstream media coverage, and was attended by 11,000 people, 3,000 of them non-party members, and 880 students.[257] But as well as placing considerable organizational strain on party structures – full-timer Nigel Tanburn planned the event, alongside fulfilling other duties – it more strongly resembled a last spasm than a fresh start. A quarter of the adults present were Old Age Pensioners (they outnumbered students by a thousand) and, according to the party's own classifications and calculations, there were fewer members of 'ethnic minorities' present than people who had travelled from Yorkshire or the Midlands.[258] Despite the rhetoric of the program notes ('a continuous battle is being fought within the popular music industry for real expression'), punk was not represented, the three headline acts being reggae band Aswad, Shakin' Stevens, and countercultural experimental outfit Soft Machine, whose drummer, Robert Wyatt, would soon join the CP.[259] Overall, the event's political breadth, which encompassed a wide range of organizations and new social movements, was substantially wider than its culture, dominated by theatre, folk music, jazz, and chess displays the week that The Sex Pistols' 'God Save the Queen' caused a moral panic by coming uncomfortably close to topping the pop charts.[260] Old tensions resurfaced when feminists objected to the sexist content of folk singer Bob Davenport's act; he defended himself on the ground that he, unlike them, was true to actually existing working-class culture.[261] Overall, despite the protestations of the party's cultural wing, the People's Jubilee was instantly identified by the Executive Committee as too ambitious for the shrinking party and as placing too great a strain on diminishing resources to become an annual event in anything like its current form.[262] A scaled-down version the following year confirmed that, despite its foray into what was now being called 'cultural politics' work, the party was a more competent curator than a creative force.[263]

The Road to Nowhere

Naturally, the party's cultural stratum – which saw in the People's Jubilee a new mode of political communication and a 'clear rebuff' of those who viewed the party 'only in terms of declining membership and potential splits' – was actively engaged in the rewriting of *The British Road to Socialism* through 1977.[264] Jacques and his culturally minded associates were not alone in thinking that a new version of the party program potentially 'laid the basis for the urgently needed regeneration.'[265] All ideological tendencies within the party were fixated on centring their priorities in the party's most important document, and this time the process engaged the length and breadth of the organization. The revision was overseen by a party commission slightly balanced in favour of modernizing tendencies; the writing was done by the unlikely pair of Martin Jacques and George Matthews (1917–2005), who had served on the party's leading committees since 1943 and had edited the *Daily Worker/Morning Star* since 1959. Adopted by the Executive Committee in November 1976, the draft text was published in February 1977, extensively debated in *Comment* and the *Morning Star*, revised at the 1977 (Thirty-fifth) Congress that November by the acceptance of 780 of the 2,600 amendments submitted by branches and district committees, and formally published as the new program early in 1978.[266] The *Guardian* accurately called it 'the first major revision' of the party's 'political programme for 26 years;'[267] ITV, which filmed the process of the rewriting, clearly wondered whether the overhaul might herald the beginning of an Anglo version of the Eurocommunism that was now making electoral gains in Italy and Spain – developments that modernizers enthusiastically tracked from 1976 in the party press, especially in a new 'Eurocommunist' party journal, *Eurored*.[268]

Historians of British Communism have naturally been drawn to the divisive process of the document's composition, tracing the struggles between competing tendencies over key phrases and formulations.[269] But although necessary to catch the very tensions that the rewriting hoped to shore up, this inward focus on a party-wide, year-long process also risks reproducing rather than gauging the party's own obsession, which was fast becoming a form of displacement or even of self-consolation. As demonstrated by a minor institutional change when, after hundreds of hours of discussion over eight years, the NCC was finally split into two – an Arts and Leisure Committee and a Theory and Ideology Committee, bodies that still overlapped in remits and personnel – the bureaucratic and administrative committee work that had always framed Communist political interventions was now becoming, at a moment of existential crisis, a substitute for them.[270]

The deep tensions between Gramscian and industrially based identities and strategies became especially acute during the period of the document's revision,

Granada Television filming the 1977 Congress for *Decision: British Communism*. CP Picture Archive, Box 27.

a process of polarization that manifested itself in different tendencies aligning with particular journals such as *Red Letters*, *Eurored*, and *Socialist Europe: Communist Party Journal of Soviet and East European Studies*, long before the *Morning Star* and *Marxism Today* became gravitational poles for more traditional and modernizing groups, respectively.[271] The deterioration of conditions congenial to Ramelsonian, full-blooded industrial militancy seemed only to intensify the convictions of those committed to it. Gone were full unemployment and the long boom. Britain now faced a capital accumulation crisis, racing inflation (26 per cent), falling working-class living standards, rising unemployment (over one million by 1975), and the breaking up of the post-war consensus: incoming Prime Minister Callaghan's rhetoric of 'fundamental changes in our society and in our economy' and the punitive terms of the IMF 1976 bailout softened up the British economy for the incipient neoliberal order already being envisaged by the Institute of Economic Affairs, the newly formed and increasingly influential Centre for Policy Studies (created in 1974), and the Adam Smith Institute (1976).[272] One costly and paradoxical consequence of the top-down, Broad Left industrial strategy driven so effectively by Ramelson had been the neglect of rank-and-file militancy and even workplace organization. Powerless to pull strings or escalate militancy during the effective lockdown of the social contract, his Industrial Department now faced the worst of both worlds: diminished leverage in a trade union hierarchy predominantly committed to the social contract, and the absence of grassroots agitation in CP factory branches, just twenty-six of which existed by 1978 (the far Left now easily outflanked the CP on the shop floor).[273] There were bruising public resignations by four of the CP's leading industrial militants in 1976: Jimmy Reid ('our Georgie Best,' according to the *Morning Star*), engineering union stalwarts and former Executive Committee members Bernard Panter and Cyril Morton, engineer and former party chair John Tocher, and NUT veteran Max Morris, all departing disillusioned, Reid acrimoniously.[274] 'The whole strategy of the *British Road to Socialism*,' pointed out one despondent activist, 'depends on such resignations NOT happening.'[275]

The unseasonal flaring up of divisions around the party's relationship with the Soviet world was a sign of an organization now clutching for an identity in the face of a present threatening to obliterate it. Hardliner Sid French's calls for the ballast of 'international links' were usually coupled with statistics about declining industrial influence, as though closer affiliation with the Soviet Union could improve the latter; opponents to such tendencies were by no means above caricaturing opponents, linking 'workerist economism' with 'Stalinism,' as if the two were synonymous (by no means all who stressed the primacy of industrial struggle were uncritically pro-Soviet).[276] The correspondence between the unlikeliness of the scenarios debated and the strength of feeling they aroused was another morbid symptom, notably during the retrospective analysis of 1956 to mark the two-decade anniversary of that *annus mirabilis*.[277] Most incendiary here was outgoing General Secretary Gollan's proposition, aired in fiery follow-up meetings to his *Marxism Today* article on the topic, that a socialist regime of the type envisaged in the 1968 version of *The British Road to Socialism* would not only permit a plurality of oppositional parties to exist, but would leave office if electorally defeated.[278] Its abstractness aside – the party had been without MPs since 1950 and was not likely to acquire any soon – this was a calculated provocation from the tentatively modernizing leadership designed to force the party to shed questionable baggage of the type cherished by French.[279] Standing down or not was code for 'dictatorship of the proletariat,' a shibboleth that for fifty years had effectively blocked serious discussion of class power and revolution's chronology in insisting that the transformation of civil society would occur after, rather than before, the levers of power had been seized. The matter had already been fudged in relation to the aborted revision of *Questions of Ideology and Culture* in 1973.[280]

No fudge was possible during the redrafting of *The British Road*, shadowed not only by the Eurocommunist electoral breakthroughs that gave succour to modernizers, but also by the US-backed crushing of Allende's democratically elected socialist government in Chile, evidence to more traditional minds that a dictatorship of the proletariat remained crucial to defend socialist advance. 'Dictatorship of the proletariat' was jettisoned after a unanimous vote at the November 1976 Executive Committee as the new draft of *The British Road* was adopted, the concept being 'completely inappropriate as a description of the socialist society we want to build,' according to the official statement, in implying that socialism would be reached by 'armed insurrection.'[281] Its abandonment caused much theoretical discussion and division in sister parties with more prominent intellectuals, especially in France, where Étienne Balibar argued that the concept was too sketchy theoretically even to be available for deletion.[282] In Britain the main function of the symbolic revocation was to create an atmosphere charged with modernizing intent in which the redrafting of *The British Road* would occur. The leadership knew that the concept, deeply imbued with associations of Leninist purity for the likes of French, would form a key area of the coming struggle.

In search of a strong plotline to give shape to interminable footage of smoke-filled King Street committee meetings, the ITV television documentary dealing with *The British Road* revision and party Congress foregrounded the sensationally exotic question of the party's association with the Soviet Union, which indeed loomed large at the event. Predictably, perhaps, the broadcast did nothing to enhance the CP's dimming reputation, constructing for viewers not the master class in democratic process that Ramelson had envisaged, but a party torn between unrepentant Stalinism and paralysing indecision:[283] the *Daily Mail* wondered if the party intended to 'bore their way to power'; the *TV Times* was distracted by the career of Irene Brennan, 'the novice nun who changed her habit for a red flag'; the *Financial Times* reported that the party could not organize a 'knees up in a brewery.'[284] The real crisis of British Communism, however, was not in the intense discussions about the party's relationship with the Soviet Union upon which the documentary fixed; it was in plain sight in the various iterations of the text itself. On one level, the text was a fantasy space in which the crises faced by the entire Left were sublimated into boldly plotted projections and frictionless subjunctive sentences. There was little sense of a nation in which political discourse was moving sharply to the right. Still envisaged was a society 'without classes in which the need for the state as an instrument of class rule will have disappeared.'[285] More substantially, the approved document staked out political problems and struggled to position the Communist Party as their solution.

In terms of the problems, little had changed in the party's diagnosis since the late 1960s: there was no sense of an embryonic neoliberal order, although

Communist schoolteachers had already clashed with Margaret Thatcher in her former role as an education minister deeply hostile to local authorities and the comprehensive principle alike – 'we know all about Brian Simon,' she muttered darkly during one ill-tempered exchange with teachers.[286] Monopoly capitalism, a system owned and controlled by 'a tiny minority of the people,' was still the 'main enemy in the way of democratic, economic and social progress,' dragging the country in a direction at odds with 'the interests of the great majority.'[287] The solution was to be found in monopoly capitalism's gravediggers, markedly more diverse than they had been in 1968, and included trade unionists (listed first), ethnic minorities fighting racism, national movements in Scotland and Wales, women's liberation, and the various struggles of young people, environmentalists, peace activists, and those opposing the Common Market. The 'common thread' running through all the struggles was said to be the extension of democracy.[288] The collective agent of socialist transformation was therefore to be the 'broad democratic alliance,' a bitterly contested construct that infuriated many with its overtones of class collaborationism and 'removing the party from its proletarian foundation,' but that now supplanted the 'broad popular alliance.'[289] What was soon being called the 'BDA' would, according to the final document's highly contentious seventh page, evolve from a force that strategically worked common ground to one assimilating 'all the political, social and economic demands of these forces.'[290] As Martin Jacques had previously argued, a pedagogic process was key to raising the sights of the new social movements from single-issue struggles to structural analysis and transformative political visions.[291]

Theoretically, however, the document lacked clarity at a moment when a clear, compelling and dynamic account of the relationship between capital, class, and the new social movements might indeed have generated interest; certainly no one else was providing one, and the eagerness with which, two years later, Hilary Wainwright, Lynne Segal, and Sheila Rowbotham's *Beyond the Fragments: Feminism and the Making of Socialism* (1979) was received implied that many were indeed seeking answers to these very questions.[292] *The British Road*, inevitably a compromise between striking out in a new direction and keeping the disoriented aligned, failed to provide it. Contradictions abounded across the text. Fulsome rhetoric emphasized the significance of the new social movements, but these remained ultimately secondary, derivative epiphenomena of the economic base in a base-superstructure theoretical model that accorded an automatic but unscrutinized priority to the industrial working class and labour movement. A new Gramscian passage partially finessed cruder formulations by emphasizing that the ruling class, although 'prepared to use coercion and violence,' mainly achieved 'a social consensus and class collaboration through its ideological control and influence' (Jacques had wanted a stronger, italicized formulation stressing that class struggle 'takes place in *all* areas of society. It concerns *every aspect* of people's lives').[293] Having at least signalled here the need for a mode of politics that resisted in and through 'ideology and culture,' the document retreated to familiar notions of 'politics,' or the importance of constructing essentially political alliances capable of escalating struggle to the 'achievement of state power by the working class and its allies' and the subsequent resolution of the various problems with which the social movements concerned themselves.[294]

On one hand, then, the document identified as crucial the pedagogic work of explaining to the social movements how the injustices against which they campaigned were structural – features of capitalism and its reproduction – and how their ultimate objective needed to be socialism. On the other, it conspicuously failed to offer such an explanation, or even to be coherent on the central matters – a poor beginning to a process widely seen as crucial for the party's rejuvenation.[295] What made it worse was that, as so often in the past, richer perspectives that worked beyond the debilitating state/civil society and coercion/consent binaries were in circulation but muted in the spirit of compromise.[296] Far in advance of anything in *The British Road*, for instance, was the contribution of Gramscian feminist Jude Bloomfield, who had called for a model grasping 'the unity of the working class both as a class in its relations of production and a class which is reproduced – i.e. lives its existence to go to work again the next day, in society, in communities, in families, in social, cultural and political institutions.' From here she pushed for a correspondingly non-economistic conception of politics that saw economic production and the reproduction of the social formation not as primary and secondary, but as indissolubly linked, a formulation which made the work of social movements integral rather than peripheral to the process of political change.[297]

The most fully articulated perspective in this vein drew on and developed insights from the analysis that had emerged from the Smith Group in the early 1970s. It had been sharpened through the 1974–5 crisis, and would soon find more detailed elaboration in Mike Prior and Dave Purdy's incendiary book, *Out of the Ghetto: A Path to Socialist Rewards* (1979). Developing the harder-edged, more economically savvy version of Gramsci than that soon associated with Martin Jacques and *Marxism Today*, this analysis marked a high point in the countercurrents of British Communism. Prior and Purdy's critique insisted that hegemony was neither a top-down conspiracy, nor a 'purely a cultural relationship,' nor a matter of ideas potently diffused through society by intellectuals.[298] Rather, it was effected by a set of institutions and practices, and the precondition of working-class hegemony lay in the class possessing the moral, ideological, and cultural authority and vision – what Gramsci called 'intellectual and moral leadership' – to advance beyond the defence of its own immediate economic interests to reconfigure and determine the totality of social relations in alliance with others.[299] Key passages from the Prison Notebooks were clearly perceptible behind the analysis. 'A social group,' wrote Gramsci, 'can, and indeed must, already must, exercise "leadership" before winning government power (this is indeed one of the principal conditions for the winning of such power).'[300] Purdy's contribution to *The British Road* revision duly refuted the idea that 'the development of socialism cannot get off the ground until *after* the revolutionary government has amassed all the levers of power in its hands in a single moment of supreme initiative.'[301] 'The value and significance of socialism,' he went on, 'needs to be demonstrated in practical, constructive and intelligible ways here and now.'[302]

Detecting opportunities for socialist advance in the context of an economic crisis that capitalism self-evidently could not solve, and seeking a strategy to weld together present and future, as Gramsci outlined, the critique reactivated the older Bernallian position that socialism needed to embody modernity. It did so by developing the earlier argument that the economy was not merely a site of resistance and party building, but of a war of position over the future.[303] Purdy and his associates now sharpened the earlier criticisms of Ramelson-style economism and sectionalism: the militant labourism that dominated socialist thought, they argued, was a consciousness-lowering blind alley concerned with 'short term gain and not long term control';[304] the 'free collective bargaining' that remained a central demand of *The British Road* represented 'no more than a stage of working class incorporation which itself causes the problem of inflation' and fed the machine.[305]

The critique they produced during and especially after *The British Road* discussions drew out what was at once implicit and unsayable in the Communist Party program: 'that social developments and the strategic requirements for achieving socialism have outrun the capacity of the existing organisations of the left.'[306] For Purdy, socialism was 'a developing set of social practices, organizing principles, and modes of thought and action,' not merely the 'expropriation of capital and the collectivisation of the economy.'[307] The shocking conclusion followed that 'the nature of modern capitalism requires a view of socialist change which lies substantially outside the concept of revolution developed by the Bolshevik Party.'[308] The logic behind this was clear enough. If one stuck with a traditional model of an inherently unstable capitalism that governed through the combination of false consciousness and coercion, then traditional visions of the party as consciousness-raising class vanguard and agent of socialist transformation in the Bolshevik vein were at least internally coherent, regardless of whether or not they matched late twentieth-century social reality. If one accepted the newer, nuanced description of a variegated social formation, in which processes of passive revolution had already incorporated elements of the political economy of the working class, in which reproduction and production both mattered, in which class power was diffused, in which consent was crucial and democracy a site of ongoing contestation rather than a mere ideological illusion, then other conclusions were necessary, not least that civil society and the economy were key locations of the struggle for hegemony. Cultural and ideological struggle were, by implication, upgraded, as the party had partially conceded. The components of the projected 'broad democratic alliance' – the 'socialising movements' that 'challenge some of the most important supports of capitalist society' such as the family and the sexual division of labour (the women's movement), property rights (the squatting movement), and capital's profit-driven arrogation of the natural world (environmentalism) – became crucial agents in the project of socialist transformation.[309] Once this was conceded, the form and function of the party needed to be fundamentally rethought.

As so often in the past, the countercurrents that caused the most disquiet were those that hooked contradictions whose denial was necessary for a stable, coherent Communist identity. At some level the party *knew* what the critique of Purdy et al. stated: in the cobbled and compromised *British Road*, which would remain the party's program for another twelve years, there was a jarring disjunction between insights that conceded new problems and conclusions that sought to contain them in old frameworks. Purdy and Prior's critique rattled cages because it made the latent blatant – it had been distributed in draft form at both the Thirty-fifth Congress and the 1977 CUL, to the chagrin of the leadership.[310] The entire logic of *The British Road* registered that traditional assumptions and modes of organization were inadequate, and decentred the party – no longer assigned the exclusive leading role it had, just about, still occupied in the 1968 version.[311] As a document also compelled to shore up and unify the party, however, it was unable to concede directly that this decentring raised fundamental questions about the shape, work, and perhaps obsolescence of a party that had no claims to be even a weak presence in the new social movements. The Warren-Purdy-Prior-Devine critique did not know all the answers, and did not pretend to, but it was asking the penetrating questions. 'Somehow,' Pat Devine wrote in his contribution to *The British Road* discussions, 'the different interests and levels of development of all the sectional or issue-based movements have to be integrated into an overall programme of advance behind which the various movements, which constitute the broad democratic alliance, can unite.'[312] In *The British Road*, however, the gaping hole signalled by that 'somehow' was covered with a threadbare algebra which stitched together the key indices: working class, labour movement, Communist Party, Labour Party, new social movements, Broad Democratic Alliance.[313] The knottiest section seemed almost to concede what could not be openly stated: 'The vital need is for an organisation of socialists, guided by the principles of scientific socialism, active everywhere among the people, in all the struggles, in all the unions, in all the progressive movements, and able to give leadership to them – in other words, an organised party, as distinct from the left groups in the Labour Party, the separate unions and the other social forces and movements. It was to fulfil this role that the Communist Party was founded in 1920 by Marxists in the Labour movement.'[314]

Was this a proud historical summary of the party's achievements, a stringent self-criticism of its shortcomings, or the admission that, in terms of embodying what was now needed, the party did not yet exist? There was just about enough in such ambiguous sentences to enable different tendencies to see themselves in *The British Road*, and therefore in the party; in that sense, the revision was a success. But the document, and all the discussion that surrounded it, also marked an end point. It was felt at the time to be a make-or-break moment for the CP, and it was widely discussed on the political Left, including in *Socialist Register* (Ralph Miliband privately thought the new text essentially 'a rehash' of the 1968 version, 'with some of the more absurd formulations left out, but many left in').[315] In terms of the party's history, it would be the last moment when significant fresh positions aerated the CPGB and created openings for meaningful renewal. Seen in the long view, the substance of that 'new' content represented essentially the fuller and more systematic articulation of impulses long latent in the party around class, culture, civil society, and the chronology of revolution in developed societies. In the preliminary *British Road* discussions, Prior and Purdy stayed within the terms of the debate – Labour Party, CP, new social movements, Broad Democratic Alliance – and added modest proposals. The unfolding logic of their argument, however, now exceeded what could be achieved within the party and its defining traditions, and pointed in another direction. They were now struggling to envisage a very different type of organization capable of turning 'hegemonic politics from an idea into a material force,' and reconciling 'that divorce between Marxism and practical politics which has characterised the British Left for over fifty years.'[316] The ageing, shrinking Communist Party was not available for such radical refashioning, even had Purdy et al. found themselves in a position to respond to that 'somehow' and to describe what was needed more fully. But there was little help here from the tradition in which they worked. As their associate Monty Johnstone had long argued, Marxism surprisingly lacked a tradition in terms of developed theories of 'the party' in general, while Jack Lindsay had long been alert to its deficiencies in terms of theories of culture and struggle in and through civil society. Despite the translation of more of his writings, Gramsci remained silent at the crucial moment, leaving blurred the outline of the modern Prince, the refashioned party form adequate to the challenges of simultaneous struggle against consent and coercion at the levels of civil society and state and of integrating wars of position and wars of manoeuvre in the developed West.[317] 'We may conclude,' noted Roger Simon, Prior and Purdy's like-minded associate, who continued to finance translations of Gramsci's work considered indispensable to the party's renewal, 'Gramsci does not advance the theory of a revolutionary party beyond the stage it reached under Lenin. His thinking on the party, as on parliamentary democracy, was not brought into line with his concepts of hegemony, civil society and war of position.'[318]

The moment for renewal was passing. Eurocommunism, recently a source of potential revitalization, now offered fewer answers, with the stalling of electoral advance, the defeat of the PCI's 'historic compromise,' and divisions within the Spanish Communist Party (*Eurored*, which existed to chronicle encouraging continental developments, was deprived by history of its core content and folded after just ten issues). Warren, a significant but largely forgotten figure, had died prematurely in 1976. Purdy soon succumbed to 'deep despair' at the party's structural resistance to being 'won for the cause of enlightenment'; he, Prior, and Devine were among the intellectual exodus that followed a failed attempt to transform inner party structures in the projected image of looser organization in 1979.[319] The end of the decade saw the reassertion of more traditional positions by the jittery party leadership: the formerly rehabilitated Monty Johnstone was considered unsuitable to give the keynote at the 1979 CUL; Jacques was unseated from the Political Committee.[320] 'The decline of the party's work in every measurable aspect has if anything been accelerated since 1977,' wrote demoralized party activist and its future historian, Willie Thompson, in October 1979. 'The extinction of the Party as a significant force is likely to be unavoidable,' he added. 'But that is the certain fate of organisations which ignore the plain verdict of history and refuse to accept such opportunities as exist.'[321]

The Communist Party of Great Britain would limp on for another thirteen years, its membership falling by a further 5,000 between 1979 and 1983 (to 15,691) and another 5,000 between 1983 and 1987 (to 10,350).[322] YCL membership dropped from 1,663 to 699 between 1977 and 1979,[323] student membership was down to 585 by 1978, a quarter of the 1973 figure, and the CUL effectively collapsed in 1979, with attendance falling to half the 1978 registration.[324] Broad brushes, however, miss significant patterns: a striking paradox of disintegration would be sharply contrasting regional experience. Some young recruits, including the poet Andy Croft, for instance, had in 1980 an experience common to many in the preceding sixty years: being struck on first encountering Communists by their seriousness and 'political, intellectual and international reach.' Croft would go on to find in the energetic activism of the well-run Middlesbrough branch a welcome contrast to the 'one-more-push electoralism of the Labour Party that had no presence in the life of the town between elections.'[325] Elsewhere, too, the rhythms of activism remained intact: Communists selling newspapers outside underground stations were attacked by fascists, as they had been in the 1930s.[326] There were also initiatives that found new ways to integrate the politics of the social movements with the labour movement in the mutually reinforcing ways that *The British Road* could not fully describe – as in the campaign driven by CP shop stewards

The Communist Party stall at the Glastonbury Festival, 1984. CP Picture Archive, Box 8, NMLH 2000.10.323.

to persuade building workers to remove degrading pictures of women from the worksite; they successfully pressured recalcitrant managers to remove such material from their own offices and to return sexist promotional calendars to suppliers.[327] More substantial still in demonstrating what could be achieved when Communists were genuinely active in the social movements was the work of gay rights activist and mid-1980s YCL General Secretary Mark Ashton (1961–87), who, with fellow Communist Mike Jackson, formed Lesbians and Gays Support the Miners (LGSM) in the summer of 1984. The organization would develop deep links with the Neath, Dulais and Swansea Valleys Miners Support Group, chaired by Communist Party member and future Labour MP Hywel Francis, and raise over £22,000 for the communities in the course of the strike.[328] Air-brushed from the feature film about LGSM, *Pride* (2014), the party cemented the unlikely alliance even though the youthful LGSM was far more successful than the party ever was in drawing into struggle the energies of popular culture, notably via the fundraiser concert 'Pits and Perverts,' headlined by Bronski Beat.[329]

From here on, 'Communist' struggles would mainly be of the internal kind, while those currents that looked outward to civil society and the broader culture would function despite the party, rather than being coordinated by it or geared towards its rejuvenation, as with *Marxism Today*. Under Jacques's editorship from 1977, the 'magazine,' as Jacques preferred to call it, was a rare good news story amidst a party in now-irreversible decline, which is why the leadership more or less left it to its frequently disturbing devices. Circulation almost doubled to 10,255 by 1981, assisted by a new format and national WH Smith distribution, and reached over 14,000 in 1987, making *Marxism Today* the most significant party periodical since *Our Time*.[330] But though very briefly seen by the dispirited but still integrated Jacques in 1977 as a project to revitalize the party, it soon became an alternative to that dead horse, with 52 per cent of the contributors in 1983 left-wing academics, ten times the number of party officials who now graced its pages.[331] Jacques would retrospectively admit that it 'may have come from the CP' but 'was never of it.'[332] It certainly made the greatest impact by moving beyond inward party identity and problems, and committing itself instead to a year-long debate working through the provocations contained in Hobsbawm's essay, 'The Forward March of Labour Halted,' published in September 1978.[333] Ably assisted by Stuart Hall, the magazine would also commit itself to grappling with the 'great moving right show' of an insurgent Thatcherism with a version of powerfully descriptive Gramscian analysis that largely dispensed with the problem of summoning into being what Hall termed the 'absent ghost' of the modern Prince.[334] The bitter and increasingly internal CP struggles through which, in worsening political circumstances, and with mounting rounds of recrimination and expulsions, the party's energies would be consumed from here on were peripheral to the concerns of *Marxism Today*, despite the backlash provoked by its intemperate attack on allegedly corrupt shop stewards in September 1982.[335] In that inner party world, feverish and unreal scenes would play out with mounting intensity, especially after further international shocks to Communist identity – the Soviet invasion of Afghanistan, Solidarity in Poland – and the class climacteric of the miners' strike in Britain four year later. Faced with two Conservative electoral victories and the emergence of the SDP-Liberal Alliance, benumbed Communists would comb the writings of Lenin for consolation or guidance ('it is undialectical, unscientific and theoretically wrong,' wrote Monty Johnstone, 'to regard the course of world history as smooth').[336] Veteran Communists like Eddie and Ruth Frow, co-founders of Salford's enduring Working Class Movement Library, would be driven by modernizing factions from the party they had spent their lives building.[337] Anti-Stalinist New Left historian Raphael Samuel, who had left the party thirty years before, would re-enter the fray to defend more traditional elements against the sectarianism of self-styled modernizers, mourning, in an atmospheric work of memoir-cum-cultural anthropology, the 'lost world of British Communism' now passing into history.[338]

Tragedy was replayed as farce as a mood of historical re-enactment came to define the positions of those clinging to lost certitudes. Appalled that those he regarded as modernizing elements effectively had won control of the dysfunctional party, seasoned industrial militant Kevin Halpin visited Moscow in 1987 to seek support in the Kremlin for a more traditional breakaway Communist Party, sincerely presenting his case as analogous to the Bolshevik/Menshevik split. 'This was met with hand throwing,' he recalled with undimmed indignation a quarter of a century later. 'I remained firm.'[339] Halpin wanted civil society and culture subordinate to state and politics by the traditional vanguard party; the modernizers' last word, the optimistically titled *Manifesto for New Times*, issued in June 1989, struck away from politics – the party, vanguardism, taking the state, and structuring the totality of social relations[340] – in favour of an organization rooted in debates within civil society.[341] Theirs was an emphasis that anticipated the course soon taken by the party's successor organization, the Democratic Left, a short-lived ginger group that stepped aside from political ambition and derived its initial credibility primarily from its association with *Marxism Today*.[342] Deep at work beneath the scenes of vituperative delusion of those years were fundamental and unresolved tensions that had always existed in twentieth-century Communism around the chronology of revolution and how to conceive relationships between capitalism and class power, coercion and consent, state and civil society, and how to formulate appropriate revolutionary strategies in response. As the party disintegrated, these tensions were expressed in splintering, sharp, mutually exclusive terms that reprised and reduced rather than advanced beyond the richer but fast-fading perspectives developed during the 1970s.

Conclusion

'Does capitalism have a future?' asked leading social scientists in a 2013 symposium. Perhaps not, they concluded.[1] Even before the coronovirus pandemic – whose full economic devastation remains unclear at the time of writing[2] – the flagging system proved unable to jump-start a new Kondratieff wave post 2008.[3] Keynesian measures gained minimal traction against the scale of structural inequality and accumulated debt.[4] In the United Kingdom wages fell by 10 per cent between 2007 and 2014, making the 2010s the weakest decade of pay growth since the Napoleonic Wars;[5] the economies of Hungary, Austria, Portugal, and Latvia were no bigger in 2019 than in 2008.[6] Unemployment remained endemic – 25 per cent in Greece and Spain, and youth unemployment at 50 per cent – and looks set to rise exponentially.[7] According to the Bank of England's 2015 projection, technological change will cost fifteen million jobs in Britain over the decades ahead, 40 per cent of the labour market; the Millennium Project predicts global unemployment rising to 16 per cent by 2030 and to 24 per cent by mid-century;[8] others project 50–70 per cent unemployment by 2040, at which point the system will face what Randall Collins calls a crisis 'from under-consumption and political agitation – that it cannot survive.'[9] Irreversible environmental catastrophe is ten years away, according to the UN report of October 2018.[10]

There is debate about what will break the system first, but little doubt that we live in the protracted endtimes of the neoliberal regime.[11] Morbid symptoms are breaking out: in Britain a disoriented political elite called for and lost the 2016 Brexit referendum, with 52 per cent of the electorate disregarding the advice of Labour, Liberal Democrat, and Conservative politicians, Barack Obama, Hillary Clinton, the IMF, the OECD, and the Bank of England.[12] Incumbents are unseated by nationalist populist regimes across Europe and North and South America that variously combine political corruption, misogyny, homophobia, racism, and the strategically mobilized phobia of the destitute 'other' – including the 3,770 people who died in the Mediterranean trying to reach

Europe in 2015 alone[13] – migrant populations created by structural adjustment programs, uneven development, regional destabilization, and war.[14] No faction of the ruling elite shows signs of facing what Immanuel Wallerstein and his co-authors call 'their systemic costs and responsibilities' or of developing strategies for renewing the depleted hegemony of neoliberalism, whose legitimating narratives, like the system's spent economic dynamism, look, for now at least, beyond repair.[15]

The doxa that markets self-regulate for the common good rings hollow: even before the 2008 financial crisis, the wealth ratio between the top one hundred households in the United States and the bottom 90 per cent was 108: 765 to 1, roughly the difference between a senator and a slave during the Roman Empire.[16] In 2017, Oxfam reported that the world's richest eight individuals owned the same amount of global wealth as the bottom 3.7 billion, or 50 per cent of the world's population;[17] in 2018, 82 per cent of new global wealth went to the top 1 per cent.[18] The system's regressive brutality has seldom been more apparent: the 'austerity measures' imposed in the United Kingdom since 2010 to pay for the 2008 crisis not only failed to reinvigorate the economy, but caused 130,000 preventable deaths, according to the Institute for Public Policy Research;[19] between 2014 and 2016, life expectancy in England and Wales decreased for the first time in over a century.[20] The notion of a charmed circle encompassing hard work and social mobility is discredited: in 2016, 60 per cent of those below the poverty line in Britain lived in a household with a wage earner; food banks and stamps are rare growth areas in the UK and US.[21] An ideology buttressed by private home ownership – the strategic linking of the interests of large sectors of the electorate with those of the financial sector – has been fundamentally weakened: in Britain home ownership is at the lowest level since 1985; Americans are less likely to own a home than at any time since 1965; 20 per cent of 20–34-year-olds lived with their parents in 2008, 25 per cent did so in 2015; levels of home ownership among young British adults have halved in the past two decades.[22]

Contradictions sharpen. Digital technology undermines the logic of ownership – 'the natural price of digital property tending towards zero,' as Keir Milburn argues[23] – defying paradigms of economic analysis and outstripping capitalism's 'capacity to adapt.'[24] New technologies exist with the potential to lay the foundations, as Aaron Bastani argues, 'for a society beyond scarcity and work' if 'allied to a project of collective solidarity and individual happiness.'[25] Political dissent spreads: new environmental movements stress 'system change';[26] state racism gives rise to new social movements in the United States, and hegemonic misogyny to a revitalized feminism in Europe and North America.[27] Precarity creates common ground between precarious salaried intellectual labourers, the old manual working class, and the 'outcast' or unemployed.[28] Crisis entrenches generational division: millennials faced with escalating property prices, falling wages, rising debt, and diminished career prospects are disproportionately inclined to socialism.[29] Since 2014 the energies of the diverse social movements of 2011 – the Arab Spring, the 'Indignados' in Spain, Occupy in Zuccotti Park, UK Uncut, and the wave of protests in Britain against the threefold increase in university tuition fees – have found expression in electoral party politics: the brief Syriza breakthrough in Greece; the fluctuating fortunes of Podemos in Spain and Left Bloc in Portugal; the rise of 'class struggle social democrats' in the United States supported by the networks of the Democratic Socialists of America (60,000 members, chapters in forty-nine states in 2019);[30] and Jeremy Corbyn's leadership of the UK Labour Party (2015–20), which grew to become the largest in Europe during this period (500,000 members) and came close to breakthrough in the 2017 General Election, securing the highest popular vote for Labour – 12.9 million votes – since Blairism's heyday.[31]

Struggles and setbacks, however, measure the scale of the challenges faced. What is so far lacking across recent analysis of capital and class is confrontation with history's lesson – recently reinforced by the reversals of Syriza, Sanders, and Corbyn – that the party form, as socialists habitually understand it, has proved too narrow in its field of operations to deal with the forces mobilized against it.[32] These post-2014 formations and parties, like their antecedents, have so far been unable to stimulate, coordinate, and sustain the breadth and depth of economic, social, and cultural work necessary to begin to break capital. Crises, Gramsci reminds us in his analysis of the rise and fall of modes of production, can last for decades, and mark 'incurable structural contradictions' within a historically obsolete system, generating a struggle between those attempting to conserve the system and those convinced that 'the necessary and sufficient conditions already exist' to change it.[33] The key stage comes when the ascendant force realizes that its own 'interests in their present and future development' contain in outline the future society.[34] Here, 'previously germinated ideologies become "party,"' 'the first cell in which there come together germs of a collective will tending to become universal and total.'[35] This process has the potential to bring about 'not only a unison of economic and political aims, but also intellectual and moral unity' that encompasses economy and civil society, whose emphasis is leadership over different classes and class fractions, and whose ultimate aim is 'founding a new type of State.'[36] Neither 'class,' nor 'social movement,' nor 'party,' as traditionally imagined, this 'party' is the organizational form of an economically and ethically justifiable vision of the future that operates simultaneously in the spheres of politics, the economy, and civil society, and is also the necessary agent to bring that future into being. For this futuristically oriented 'modern Prince,' the contestation of political power through democratic processes is necessary but not sufficient – merely one manifestation of leadership over a broader project of economic, political, and cultural modernization.

Now, as in the twentieth-century, a reconceived form of 'the party' able to coordinate a full spectrum of struggle along the lines intimated by Gramsci awaits invention. It is a forbidding process that needs to draw on the widest possible range of sources. I have asserted in this study that analysis of twentieth-century Communism has at least a small part to play. I have argued that the narrow conceptions of the 'political' that shaped the work of the twentieth-century Communist Parties, and the rigid assumptions about the chronology of revolution that governed them (build the party, seize the state, reconfigure social relations), mattered more in their failure than historians have realized, and remain live issues in our very different times. In that spirit, the book has staged a critical dialogue between Gramsci's fragmentary writings on the nature of the party that he considered necessary to organize and orchestrate the transition to socialism in developed industrial societies and the struggles of a small party that, while blighted by Stalinism and falling very far short of its revolutionary objectives, also represents the most serious failure of the nationally grounded revolutionary party available for historical analysis in modern Britain. In the preceding chapters, I detailed the manifold failures of that organization: its narrow construction of the party as a 'Bolshevik machine,' which brought clarity and energy at the cost of suppressing many of the strengths of preceding socialist traditions; the intellectual dependency on the Soviet experiment that inspired the party's formation; the pulverizing cycles of Stalinism, which blunted its work and drove out outstanding cadre; its theoretically underpowered struggles to read the complex operations of the capitalist state; its failure to grasp the dynamics of long-boom Keynesian welfare capitalism; its 'cultural unconscious' and inability to analyse the shifting class composition of twentieth-century Britain or to distance itself from dominant 'commonsense' assumptions, especially around race, gender, and the sexual division of labour. What remains is to extract from the failure key positions and principles that might be of some use in the ongoing process of socialist realignment and the reinvention of the Left.

The twentieth-century Communist movement was shadowed by a semi-repressed awareness of the inadequacy of dominant 'Leninist' conceptions of the chronology of revolution. Confronted with developed mass societies resistant to the logic of this chronology, the party in Britain, as elsewhere, sporadically produced initiatives, countercurrents, and conceptions that faintly gestured towards alternative models that have yet to be created. The party's cultural networks, committees, and specialist groups were woefully inadequate, underresourced, often theoretically underpowered, and frequently discredited in succumbing to pressure to endorse Soviet models. Nonetheless, they have no equivalent in mainstream social democratic parties, then or now, parties which historically have not known how to draw upon or fully mobilize the particular specialisms, skills, or expertise of their activists in coordinated work. These Communist initiatives spoke to a conviction, however conflicted, that culture was a place where new ways of seeing could be created, that civil society mattered in terms of class power, and that, as Raymond Williams put it, 'the systems and meanings and values which a capitalist society has generated have to be defeated in general and in detail by the most sustained kinds of intellectual and educational work.'[37] As Wolfgang Streeck argues, forty years of neoliberal regimes have effectively hollowed out democratic structures and collective bargaining processes, shifting the ideological 'burden of organizing everyday life' from 'macro' to 'micro,' from institutions to 'culture,' 'the thin thread of an accompanying repertoire of individual action filling the widening gaps in the society's systemic architecture.'[38] 'Structuralist critique of *false institutions*,' he concludes, 'have to be complemented by a new culturalist critique of *false consciousness*.'[39] In short, cultural struggle matters more than ever. At its best, the work of the national Communist Parties in the 'Battle of Ideas' is a legacy worth revisiting in the process of analysing what it might mean to organize struggle across civil society. This history demonstrates that significant interventions and cultural presence can be built by small numbers of determined activists. Highpoints in the CPGB experience include: the creation of significant and sometimes enduring cultural events, networks, and communities (the Left Book Club, the WMA, Topic Records, the Edinburgh People's Festivals, the Notting Hill Carnival, the People's Jubilee); the inscription of radical agendas into powerful cultural organizations, including the BBC; the production of historians and historiography able to contest hegemonic narratives of nation (the Historians' Group); the creation of new cultural works that cut with the grain of popular traditions and detected the outlines of a better future in the resources of the radical past (mass pageants); the leading of long-haul campaigns for mass educational democracy and empowerment (Brian Simon); and the implanting into popular consciousness, through wide-ranging programs of education and communication, of the association of socialism with rational, scientific modernity (J.D. Bernal). Informed by these currents, some of the party's most forceful interventions called into question and dissolved the distinctions between 'culture' and 'politics' as usually understood, by symbolically loaded acts of resistance that prefigured different possibilities, whether in wartime factories, the Women's Parliaments, or the UCS work-in.

Also recoverable from these countercurrents is a more nuanced conception of political power in capitalist society than that which dominates either social democratic labourism – whose electoral focus narrows the very conception of the political – or the base-superstructure reductionism and economism that dominated much twentieth-century Communism, a model that dictated the bracketing of 'culture' from 'political' work, and was often used, as I have argued, to discredit and contain creativity, 'idealism,' and intellectualism. This is no narrowly 'theoretical' matter. A different modelling of the social world produces a different concept of the 'political' and of the hierarchies and relationships between its components, summoning and affirming new ways of struggle. As the 1970s Gramscians Mike Prior and Dave Purdy argued, models that conceived 'the three levels of the social structure which Marxists normally distinguish – the economic, the political and the ideological – as resting on top of one another like storeys of a building' simplify the reality in which 'all are jointly necessary to the constitution of a mode of production,' and damagingly restrict what counts as 'politics.'[40] Now, as then, effective radical politics requires an appropriately full sense of the social formation and the complicated interconnectedness of its parts. As Gramscian feminists including Jude Bloomfield and Beatrix Campbell argued in the 1970s, the alternative model has the potential to confront and overturn logics that have bedevilled the Left, including the assumption that the sexual division of labour is secondary to the economic or political and that its injustices can therefore be resolved after the seizure of the state. The reproduction of human beings, in other words, and the structures and arrangements through which this occurs, is integral to the reproduction of the capitalist social formation itself, and therefore to socialist struggles for alternatives to it. In this model, alternative arrangements that resist dominant logic are significant not only as sites of resistance, but also as anticipations of alternative futures.

More generally, these countercurrents were often animated by a different Marxism than that congealed in primers such as *The Short Course*, especially the current most strongly upheld by Jack Lindsay, which saw in Marx's early writings, especially the *Economic and Philosophical Manuscripts,* the source of a powerful radical humanism. According to this Marx, private property is an impediment to a human 'species being' forever open to further evolution, and to which creativity and communication are integral. As John Lewis wrote, this theory provides socialism with 'an ethic' the significance of which 'has been too often obscured by the emphasis which has been laid on economic analysis and political strategy.'[41] This lost tradition speaks to two mutually reinforcing currents on the contemporary Left. One foregrounds the ideological function of private property in the creation of conservative political sensibility, and the paradoxical political promise, therefore, of the propertyless-ness enforced on so many, especially the young, by the neoliberal system's crisis – dispossession affording here an 'epistemological vantage point that those inside the system lack' in terms of 'a remodelling of adulthood around the attributes of the commons.'[42] The other current stresses the philosophical and ethical grounding of a revitalized socialism in a radical humanism.[43] The contention that 'the biologically given purpose of human beings is to set themselves free, using technology to change both their environment and themselves'[44] forms the core of this new current geared towards, as Nick Srnicek and Alex Williams put it, 'liberating ourselves from the decrepit economic image of humanity that capitalist modernity has installed, and inventing a new humanity.'[45]

Notes

Introduction

1 Leon Trotsky, 'Where Is Britain Going?' (1925), reprinted in *Leon Trotsky on Britain*, ed. George Novack (New York: Pathfinder, 1973), 148.

2 Alastair J. Reid and Henry Pelling, *A Short History of the Labour Party*, 12th ed. (1961; Basingstoke, UK: Palgrave, 2005), 207; Stephen Gundle, *Between Hollywood and Moscow: The Italian Communists and the Challenge of Mass Culture 1943–91* (Durham, NC: Duke University Press, 2000), 25; CPGB party membership figures in Andrew Thorpe, 'The Membership of the Communist Party of Great Britain, 1920–45,' *Historical Journal* 43, no. 3 (2000), 781, table 1; the French CP figure is for 1936. Donald Sassoon, *One Hundred Years of Socialism: The West European Left in the Twentieth Century* (1996; London: I.B. Tauris, 2014), 40.

3 Noreen Branson, *History of the Communist Party of Great Britain, 1941–51* (London: Lawrence & Wishart, 1997), 157; John Callaghan, *Cold War, Crisis and Conflict: The CPGB 1951–68* (London: Lawrence & Wishart, 2003), 77–8.

4 The electoral height of Eurocommunism came in 1976 when the Italian party took 34 per cent of the national vote. Eurocommunism fell into sharp decline after 1979, with the 'historic compromise' of the PCI, splits in the Spanish party, and the challenge to the French party by Mitterand's Socialists. Geoff Andrews, *Endgames and New Times: The Final Year of British Communism 1964–91* (London: Lawrence & Wishart, 2004), 194; CPGB membership was 15,691 in July 1983, 10,350 by 1987, and down to 7,615 by July 1989. Figures from CPGB Exec Minutes for 1987 in Labour History Archive and Study Centre, Manchester [hereafter LHASC], CP IND JOHN 4/1/24; membership figure list for April 1985 in LHASC CP IND OLIVE. See Andrew Pearmain, 'Whatever Happened to the CPGB?' *Socialist History* 38 (2011): 58.

5 Susan Watkins, 'Left Oppositions,' *New Left Review* 98 (March-April 2016): 5–31; Pablo Iglesias, 'Understanding Podemos,' *New Left Review* 93 (May-June 2015):

7–22; Iglesias, *Politics in a Time of Crisis: Podemos and the Future of Democratic Europe* (London: Verso, 2015), especially 176–96; Bécquer Seguín, 'Podemos and Its Critics,' *Radical Philosophy* 193 (September-October 2015): 20–33; Paul Mason, *Postcapitalism: A Guide to Our Future* (2015; London: Penguin, 2016); Naomi Klein, *No Is Not Enough: Defeating the New Shock Politics* (London: Allen Lane, 2017); Mike Makin-Waite, *Communism and Democracy: History, Debates and Potentials* (London: Lawrence & Wishart, 2017); Nick Srnicek and Alex Williams, *Inventing the Future: Postcapitalism and a World Without Work*, rev. ed. (2015; London: Verso, 2016); Paul Mason, *Clear Bright Future: A Radical Defence of the Human Being* (London: Allen Lane, 2019); Leo Panitch and Sam Gindin, *The Socialist Challenge Today: Syriza, Sanders, Corbyn* (London: Merlin, 2018); Bhaskar Sunkara, *The Socialist Manifesto: The Case for Radical Politics in an Era of Extreme Inequality* (London: Verso, 2019).

6 Here the party is to be rejected along with other allegedly outmoded organizational forms and practices of the twentieth century – Alain Badiou's long list includes 'Marxism, the workers' movement, mass democracy, Leninism'; Alain Badiou, 'The Communist Hypothesis,' *New Left Review* 49 (January-February 2008), and Badiou, 'The Communist Hypothesis,' *New Left Review* 49 (January-February 2008). These ideas are developed in Alain Badiou, *The Communist Hypothesis*, trans. David Macey and Steve Corcoran (London: Verso, 2010), and Badiou, 'The Idea of Communism,' in *The Idea of Communism*, ed. Costas Douzinas and Slavoj Žižek (London: Verso, 2010), 1–15.

7 Raymond Williams, *Modern Tragedy* (1966; London: Hogarth, 1992), 76.

8 Chantal Mouffe, *For a Left Populism* (London: Verso, 2018), 56.

9 Here I reflect the terms used in inter-war Communist discourse, however problematic, in which West meant primarily Western Europe. Sassoon, *One Hundred Years*, xxvii–xxvix.

10 International studies include Jessica Wardhaugh, *In Pursuit of the People: Political Culture in France 1934–39* (New York: Palgrave Macmillan, 2009); José Gotovitch, *Du communisme et des communistes en Belgique: approaches critiques* (Brussels: Aden, 2011).

11 E.P Thompson, 'Socialist Humanism,' *New Reasoner* (Summer 1957): 107.

12 Eric Hobsbawm, *Age of Extremes: The Short Twentieth Century* (London: Abacus, 1997), 5.

13 Sassoon, *One Hundred Years*, 32.

14 Ibid., 83.

15 Mason, *Postcapitalism*, 79.

16 Ibid., 48.

17 Ibid., 32.

18 Vladimir Lenin, *Imperialism: The Highest Stage of Capitalism* (1916), in *Selected Works* (London: Lawrence & Wishart, 1968), 261.

19 Allen Hutt, *This Final Crisis* (London: Gollancz, 1935); the earliest Economics Committee minutes are archived in CP CENT ECON 6/15.

20 There was and could not be, as the party's leading theorist wrote in 1934, a 'third alternative' – 'capitalist "democracy," "planned capitalism," etc'; such a compromise formation was unimaginable before the war and bewilderingly indecipherable once it materialized. Rajani Palme Dutt, *Fascism and Social Revolution* (London: Martin and Lawrence, 1934), ix; Wolfgang Streeck, *How Will Capitalism End?* (London: Verso, 2016), 4.

21 Aporia described in Perry Anderson, *Considerations on Western Marxism* (1976; London: New Left Books, 1977), 11, 114, 117.

22 Vladimir Lenin, *The State and Revolution*, in *Selected Works* (London: Lawrence & Wishart, 1968), 328. Perry Anderson concludes that the price paid for this 'theoretical blockage' was the failure of the Third International to make meaningful headway, especially in Britain and the United States, and that a 'another type of party and another type of strategy were needed in these societies and were not invented'; Anderson, *Considerations*, 117.

23 Leon Trotsky, address to the First All-Union Congress of Soviet Librarians, published as 'Leninism and Library Work,' in *Problems of Everyday Life and Other Writings on Culture and Science* (New York: Pathfinder, 1973), 146–7. Trotsky here elaborated on points made two years earlier at the Fourth Congress of the Comintern.

24 'Culture' not in the bourgeois sense of 'eternal verities,' but in the Marxist-Leninist meaning of the 'sum total of all knowledge and skills amassed by mankind'; Trotsky, 'Leninism,' 142–3.

25 In *Where is Britain Going?* (1925), reprinted in *Leon Trotsky on Britain*, ed. George Novack (New York: Pathfinder, 1973), 48.

26 Ibid.

27 Trotsky, 'Leninism,' 144.

28 Ibid., 147.

29 Ibid., 148.

30 Written between 1929 and 1935, the Notebooks occupied simultaneously multiple time frames of Communist thought: they challenged their present moment of Third Period delusional sectarianism, anticipated much of Popular Front logic with their emphasis on 'the national' as necessarily 'the point of departure' of working-class political advance, and did so, in part, by reviving and developing those now jettisoned United Front positions of the early 1920s that many, including Gramsci, had opposed the first time round. Quintin Hoare and Geoffrey Nowell-Smith, eds. and trans., *Selections from the Prison Notebooks of Antonio Gramsci* (London: Lawrence & Wishart, 1971), 240. This case for reading the Prison Notebooks in the light of earlier debates is made by Perry Anderson, 'The Antinomies of Antonio Gramsci,' *New Left Review* 1/100 (November-December 1976). See also Anderson, 'After Gramsci,' *New Left Review* 100

(July-August 2016): 71–99; and Peter D. Thomas, *The Gramscian Moment: Philosophy, Hegemony and Marxism* (Leiden: Brill, 2009), 29–40.

31 Hoare and Nowell-Smith, *Selections from the Prison Notebooks*, 236. Lenin quotation from 'Report on War and Peace,' 99. Gramsci alludes to Lenin's position, in Hoare and Nowell-Smith, *Selections from the Prison Notebooks*, 56. Due largely to the endeavours of PCI leader Palmiro Togliatti, selections from Gramsci's letters were published in some of the 'people's democracies' before the death of Stalin and long before they appeared in English; a three-volume selection of his work was published in the USSR in 1957–9; the first Congress of Gramsci Studies was held in Rome in January 1958 and the second in 1967. See Eric Hobsbawm, 'Introduction,' in *The Antonio Gramsci Reader*, ed. David Forgacs (London: Lawrence & Wishart, 1999), 10–11; Thomas, *Gramscian Moment*, 199.

32 'Civil society' is a term with a long and complicated history in Marxism and beyond, and Gramsci's own use of it is by no means stable, as commentators have argued. Thomas (*Gramscian Moment*, especially 173–95). Hegel used it interchangeably with 'bürgeliche Gesellschaft' (bourgeois society) to designate a new social formation enabled by the modern market economy that made possible the preservation of both individual freedom and the 'universality' of the state. Marx overturned the distinction, insisting that the state expressed class relations. See Ellen Meiksins Wood, 'The Uses and Abuses of Civil Society,' *Socialist Register* 1990, 60–84.

33 Meiksins Wood, 'Uses and Abuses,' 62.

34 A key formulation here comes in Gramsci's letter to Tatiana Schucht, 7 September 1931. Antonio Gramsci, *Prison Letters*, trans. Hamish Henderson (London: Pluto, 1996), 161.

35 Hoare and Nowell-Smith, *Selections from the Prison Notebooks*, 238, 243. Following Gramsci's central emphasis, 'civil society' here refers to the system of 'private' superstructural institutions and practices that interpose between 'the economic structure and the state' (208).

36 *Trotsky on Britain*, 48; Hoare and Nowell-Smith, *Selections from the Prison Notebooks*, 57, 133.

37 What Trotsky called 'culture' could not be left until after the seizure of power, as power could not be seized and held without it. Nor could culture simply be collapsed into 'Leninism' in Trotsky's sense of political strategy, although, for Gramsci, Leninist tenets remained crucial, especially the ultimate need for what Gramsci termed 'wars of manoeuvre,' or frontal assault on the state.

38 Hoare and Nowell-Smith, *Selections from the Prison Notebooks*, 56.

39 As Timothy Brennan argues, his ideas became 'Gramscian' only when 'he found himself in prison,' and so was able to explore 'more fully and shrewdly' issues that had concerned the movement in which he was formed. Brennan, *Wars of Position: The Cultural Politics of Right and Left* (New York: Columbia University Press, 2006), 255.

40 Jodi Dean, *Communist Horizon* (London: Verso, 2012), 239; Dean's *Crowds and the Party* (London: Verso, 2015) continues this line of argument.

41 In line with Gramsci's emphasis, the book is necessarily centrally concerned here with 'organic' intellectuals, crucial figures for disseminating and renewing the hegemony of the ruling classes via the organizations and structures of civil society, but also for resisting and countering it on behalf of subordinate and rising classes and their alternative conceptions of how the world is and should be (Hoare and Nowell-Smith, *Selections from the Prison Notebooks*, 5–24).

42 The best mapping is provided in Andy Croft, ed., *A Weapon in the Struggle: The Cultural History of the Communist Party in Britain* (London: Pluto, 1997), which deals mainly with the 1930s through the 1950s. Other works on culture and communism include Philip Bounds, *British Communism and the Politics of Literature, 1928–39* (Pontypool, UK: Merlin, 2012); Edwin A Roberts, *The Anglo Marxists: A Study in Ideology and Culture* (Lanham, MD: Rowman & Littlefield, 1997); and John Green, *Britain's Communists: The Untold Story* (London: Artery, 2014).

43 Throughout the text, I give, where possible, the dates of the study's most significant figures in brackets the first time they are mentioned, and only for those who are no longer alive. In some cases, it was not possible to find dates, which leads to some unavoidable inconsistency. See Nick Srnicek and Alex Williams, *Inventing the Future: Postcapitalism and a World Without Work* (2016; London: Verso, 2015), 70, 71. The Afterword to the revised edition responds to criticism of the work, 185–201.

44 Ibid., 131, 132–4.

45 Mike Makin-Waite, *Communism and Democracy*, 1–13.

46 Hoare and Nowell-Smith, *Selections from the Prison Notebooks*, 150.

47 Anderson, 'Antinomies.'

48 Fredric Jameson, *The Political Unconscious: Narrative as a Socially Symbolic Act* (1981: London: Routledge, 1989), 20.

49 See, for instance, Andrew Thorpe, *The British Communist Party and Moscow, 1920–43* (Manchester: Manchester University Press, 2000); Callaghan, *Cold War*; Matthew Worley, *Class Against Class: The Communist Party in Britain Between the Wars* (London: I.B. Tauris, 2002); James Hinton and Richard Hyman, *Trade Unions and Revolution: The Industrial Politics of the Early British Communist Party* (London: Pluto, 1975); Nina Fishman, *The British Communist Party and the Trade Unions 1933–1945* (Aldershot, UK: Scolar Press, 1995). A different mode of analysis, geared to the expectations and experiences of party members, can be found in Kevin Morgan, Gidon Cohen, and Andrew Flinn, *Communists and British Society 1920–1991* (London: Rivers Oram, 2007); and Thomas Linehan, *Communism in Britain 1920–1939* (Manchester: Manchester University Press, 2007).

50 Srnicek and Williams, *Inventing the Future*, 51–69; Mouffe, *Left Populism*, 25–39; Mark Perryman, 'The Great Moving Left Show' and Hilary Wainwright, 'Mind

the Gap,' in *The Corbyn Effect*, ed. Mark Perryman (London: Lawrence & Wishart, 2017), 5–35, 112–125; Panitch and Gindin, *Socialist Challenge Today*; Makin-Waite, *Communism and Democracy.*

51 Eric Hobsbawm, 'The Forward March of Labour Halted?' *Marxism Today* (September 1978): 279–86.

52 Stuart Hall, 'The Battle for Socialist Ideas in the 1980s' (1981), reprinted in *Thatcherism and the Crisis of the Left: The Hard Road to Renewal* (London: Verso, 1988), 180.

1. The Chronology of Revolution, 1920–1940

1 Vladimir Lenin, '"Left Wing" Communism – An Infantile Disorder,' in *Selected Works* (London: Lawrence & Wishart, 1968), 581.

2 Ibid., 560; Lenin, 'Message to the First Congress of the Communist Party of Great Britain,' 8 July 1920, reprinted in *Lenin on Britain* (1934; London: Lawrence & Wishart, 1941), 261.

3 Andrew Thorpe, 'Comintern "Control" of the Communist Party of Great Britain, 1920–43,' *English Historical Review* 113, no. 452 (1998): 648.

4 Harry Pollitt, *Serving My Time* (1940; London: Lawrence & Wishart, 1941), 123.

5 These were spelled out in the circular calling the National Convention issued by the joint provisional committee. See Monty Johnstone, 'Early Communist Strategy: An Assessment,' *Marxism Today* (September 1978): 287.

6 They should 'support' social democratic parties, as Lenin memorably put it, 'as the rope supports the hanged man' (Lenin, 'Left Wing,' 569). Many, like Pollitt, were persuaded by Lenin's insistence – peremptorily relayed to the first Convention by wire – that the new party should work strategically through the structures of the organized labour movements. Suffragist Sylvia Pankhurst of the Workers' Socialist Federation argued that alignment with such reformist movements would only discredit the party in the eyes of the workers. See Mary Davis, *Sylvia Pankhurst: A Life in Radical Politics* (London: Pluto, 1996), 83.

7 In Moscow there was agreement across the Communist movement that the proletarian revolution would have fared better had its vanguard been in the West, with its developed productive and cultural capacities. There was concern that, as Trotsky put it, world revolution was 'winding her skein' from the wrong end, with the underdeveloped East unspooling most easily. See Isaac Deutscher, *The Prophet Unarmed: Trotsky 1921–29* (1959; Oxford: Oxford University Press, 1987), 6. Paul made similar points, arguing that, in undeveloped Russia, the destructive work of smashing the old regime's political apparatus was less of a challenge than the creative work of socialist construction; in developed Britain, by contrast, the difficulties were reversed: ruling-class power was more firmly established and entrenched through an elaborate network of mediating institutions and traditions; here revolutionary destruction would be more

difficult than the building of socialism with and through the already developed economy. Paul, *Communism and Society* (London: CPGB, 1922), 185–9.

8 Ibid., 171.

9 Ibid., 65–96. Paul's book naturally registers the force of this model, at once making the case for a broader struggle encompassing civil society before presenting 'industrial organisation' as 'the true constructive agency for the creation of the new social system' (ibid., 135).

10 Rajani Palme Dutt, 'Communism,' *Encyclopaedia Britannica*, 12th ed., 732. Dutt Papers, British Library [hereafter cited as BL] BL CUP 1262/K1. Communism meant a party 'based on the strictest internal discipline,' each national party 'different divisions in a single army' (733).

11 The third commission member was Happy Inkpin, brother of the party's first general secretary, Albert. 'Draft Theses on the Organizational Structure of the Communist Parties' had been presented to the Third Congress of the Comintern in July 1921. See John Callaghan, *Rajani Palme Dutt: A Study in British Stalinism* (London: Lawrence & Wishart, 1993), 48; *Report on Organization Presented by the Party Commission to the Annual Conference of the CPGB* (London: CPGB, 1922), 10. Prompted by the Comintern's Third Congress's theses on 'The Organizational Structure of the Communist Parties,' the *Report* comprised a blueprint for the 'efficient machine of the class struggle' required by the Comintern.

12 Vladimir Lenin, *State and Revolution*, in *Selected Works* (London: Lawrence & Wishart, 1968), 273; *Report on Organization*, 15.

13 James Klugmann, *History of the Communist Party of Great Britain*, vol. 1, *Formation and Early Years, 1919–1924* (London: Lawrence & Wishart, 1968), 207; Vladimir Lenin, 'The Dual Power,' *Pravda*, 9 April 1917, reprinted in Lenin's *Collected Works*, vol. 24 (Moscow: Progress Publishers, 1964), 38–41; Lenin, 'The Tasks of the Proletariat in Our Revolution,' 'Draft Platform of the Proletarian Party' (1917), in *Collected Works*, vol. 24, 60–2.

14 'The Revolutionary Education of the Workers' [1923], Dutt Papers, Working Class Movement Library, Salford [hereafter WCML].

15 *Report on Organization*, 61.

16 J.T. Murphy challenged the uncritical implementation of the *Report* – for many a 'Holy Bible' – and the top-heavy structures it introduced. Tommy Jackson amplified Murphy's criticisms, and argued that discussion was rendered all but impossible. Murphy, 'The Party Conference,' *Communist Review* (January 1924); the discussion continued in the February and April issues. See also *Report on Organization*, 72.

17 Klugmann, *History*, 205–7; Albert Inkpin of Organising Bureau, circular to all districts and locals, 5 October 1923. Pollard Papers, Bodleian Library, Box 8.

18 *Report on Organization*, 15.

19 Thomas Linehan, *Communism in Britain 1920–39* (Manchester: Manchester University Press, 2007), 30–1, 33; YCL, 'Outline of Work in the Children's Section'

[1923], Pollard Papers, Box 8; 'A Short History of the Working Class Children's Movement,' Pollard Papers, Box 5.

20 Linehan, *Communism in Britain*, 51.

21 William Rust, *What the Young Communist League Stands For* (London; CPGB, 1925), 11–12. I am grateful to Thomas Linehan's work or bringing this source to my attention; see also Mick Jenkins, 'Early Days in the YCL,' *Marxism Today* (February 1972): 48–54.

22 Donald Sassoon, *One Hundred Years of Socialism: The West European Left in the Twentieth Century* (1996; London: I.B Tauris, 2014), 78.

23 With its impressive range of contributors (Siegfrid Sassoon, Claude McKay, John Maclean, John Reed, Lenin) and breadth of political and cultural concerns (Marxism, socialism, feminism, anticolonial struggle, working-class education) the young party could have done with it. *Workers' Dreadnought,* 17 September 1921; Davis gives a useful summary of the paper's range, *Sylvia Pankhurst*, 55–7; Lenin, 'Conditions for Joining the Comintern,' in *Lenin on Britain*, 218.

24 *Workers' Dreadnought*, 17 September 1921; Pankhurst shared a stage with Communists subsequently, including in Poplar in January 1924, but incensed activists by 'advertising the *Workers Dreadnought* and herself to the detriment of the Soviet Government'; Minutes of St Pancras LPC meeting, 28 January 1924, Pollard Papers, Box 4.

25 Jack Jones, *Unfinished Journey* (London: Hamish Hamilton, 1937), 194. Jones gives a vivid account of the party's early meetings.

26 A key article here was by Dutch communist S.J. Rutgers, 'The Intellectuals and the Russian Revolution,' *Communist Review* (December 1921): 106–24.

27 Apart from work on the party's refashioned paper or theoretical journals, the in-house *Communist Review* (launched in May 1921), and Dutt's *Labour Monthly* (launched July 1921, notionally independent of the party but almost certainly funded from Moscow), the only legitimate outlet for the university training of this cohort was the Labour Research Department, whose function was to investigate for affiliated trade union and labour movement bodies the industrial terrain. For the formation of *Labour Monthly*, see Callaghan, *Rajani Palme Dutt*, 42–4; the Labour Research Department's concern was those 'actual objective conditions under which workers' struggle proceeds … facts which bourgeois researchers do not or are not allowed to reveal.' See Maurice Dobb, 'Labour Research,' *Labour Monthly* (December 1925): 747–54, 751. Founded in 1912 as the Fabian Research Department, the Labour Research Department was co-opted by Guild Socialists six years later. Some of the party's core intellectuals (Burns, Dutt, Robin Page Arnot) had met there prior to the party's formation. The party controlled the department from 1921. That it showed no interest in co-opting its subsidiary publishing house, the Labour Publishing Company and its educational list ranging across politics, poetry, fiction and drama, was an indication of where its priorities lay. Pat Francis, 'The Labour Publishing Company 1920–9,'

History Workshop 18 (Autumn 1984): 115–23; Dutt was certainly baffled when prospective authors assumed he or the party might have any editorial influence. Dutt to Ness Edwards, 11 April 1924, CP IND DUTT 5/8.

28 William Paul, *The Path to Power: The Communist Party on Trial* (1924; London: CPGB, 1925), 18; Michael Hurd, *Rutland Boughton and the Glastonbury Festivals* (Oxford: Clarendon Press, 1993), 173; Heslop to Dutt, 19 July 1929, CP IND DUTT 5/10.

29 Rutgers, 'Intellectuals and the Russian Revolution,' 123.

30 Kevin Morgan, Gidon Cohen, and Andrew Flinn, *Communists and British Society 1920–1991* (London: Rivers Oram, 2007), 76.

31 By March 1928 the party's 5,556 members still included only 277, or 5 per cent, of members of the professional classes, the largest percentage of which were schoolteachers. See Andrew Thorpe, 'The Membership of the Communist Party of Great Britain, 1920–45,' *Historical Journal* 43, no. 3 (2000): 786; Stephen H. Parsons, 'Communism in the Professions: The Organisation of the British Communist Party among Professional Workers 1933–56' (PhD diss., University of Warwick, 1990), 475, 477–8, 504. The number of schoolteachers in the party's early period is difficult to determine, although a number of founder members were teachers; there were 103 CP teachers by 1930; schools, universities, and education were, for instance, a central concern of debates in the Italian party. See David Forgacs, ed., *The Antonio Gramsci Reader: Selected Writings* (London: Lawrence & Wishart, 1999), 53–75.

32 John Callaghan and Ben Harker, eds., *British Communism: A Documentary History* (Manchester: Manchester University Press, 2011), 106.

33 In order to establish 'mutual consciousness of the political aims of the task in hand.' *Communist* (December 1928): 136; John McIlroy, 'The Establishment of Intellectual Orthodoxy and the Stalinization of British Communism, 1928–35,' *Past & Present* 192 (August 2006): 187–226.

34 Rajani Palme Dutt, 'Intellectuals and Communism,' *Communist Review* (September 1932): 428.

35 Betty Cooper, 'Disreputable?' letter, *Discussion* (December 1936): 10; HB, 'The Position of Intellectuals,' *Discussion* (April 1936): 25.

36 Geoff Eley, *Forging Democracy: The History of the Left in Europe, 1850–2000* (Oxford: Oxford University Press, 2002), 260. Also cited in McIlroy, 'Establishment of Intellectual Orthodoxy,' 192.

37 For Alick West (1895–1972), who was formed as a Communist in the Third Period, the Popular Front line had always been muddled in requiring Communists to shore up the institutions of a capitalism correctly identified as proto-fascistic. The reorientation now brought a welcome return to Leninist clarity, the Comintern's new injunction that the working class should end the war 'after their own fashion' being read as an imperative to escalate war into civil war through revolution. Lenin's article, 'Defeat of One's Own Government in

the Imperialist War' (1915), became a touchstone text in party education classes, branch meetings, and literature sales. See Alick West, *One Man in His Time: A Personal Story of the Revolutionary Century* (London: Allen & Unwin, 1969), 170, 175; Kevin Morgan, *Against Fascism and War: Ruptures and Continuities in British Communist Politics, 1935–1941* (Manchester: Manchester University Press, 1989), 164; Douglas Hyde, *I Believed* (1950: London: Reprint Society), 70–2.

38 Karen Hunt and Matthew Worley, 'Rethinking British Communist Party Women in the 1920s,' *Twentieth Century British History* 15, no. 1 (2004): 2.

39 Helen Crawfurd, Untitled and unpublished autobiography, 232. CP IND MISC 10/1/A. The key document was the Comintern's 'Theses on the Communist Women's Movement' (1921), which spoke of liberating women 'not only on paper, but in reality.' Feminists found even paper guidelines in short supply in the early 1920s; see Hunt and Worley, 'Rethinking,' 8. It was a conviction increasingly bolstered by upbeat descriptions of women's lives in the Soviet Union, which became a standard feature in the party press, including local women's journals such as the *Islington Woman Worker* (July 1927), the *St Pancras Woman Worker* (December 1925), and the *Hackney Woman Worker* (6 September 1927). For a more extended exercise in the genre, see Rose Smith, 'The Proletarian Revolution and the Emancipation of Women,' *Communist Review* (November 1930): 11–16.

40 Crawfurd autobiography, 233; G. and E. Breensdon to the St Pancras LPC, 25 June 1923, Pollard Papers, Box 8.

41 For Browne, birth control – women's ownership of the means of reproduction – was not secondary to social ownership of the means of production. Abortion, the social construction of gender, and the liberation of women through radical transformations in the structures of social child care were crucial sites of opposition to capitalism. See Hunt and Worley, 'Rethinking,' 15; Linehan, *Communism in Britain*, 16–19. Only 11 per cent (550 members) of the party's members were women in 1922, a figure which did not improve substantially before the influx of miners' wives during the General Strike; see Thorpe, 'Membership,' 784. The poor recruitment patterns were registered at the Congresses of 1924 and 1925 (Hunt and Worley, 'Rethinking,' 8). Brown's pioneering positions of the early 1920s are succinctly outlined in Linehan, *Communism in Britain*, 16–18.

42 As the party soon discovered when it found itself lacking the organizational structures necessary to connect meaningfully with the militant women at the forefront of the industrial disputes in the Lancashire and Yorkshire textile industry in the early 1930s. There was no mention of women, for instance, at the party's Tenth Congress in 1929; the monthly *Working Woman* established in 1926 had folded by the following year. Sue Bruley, 'Women Against War and Fascism,' in *Britain, Fascism and the Popular Front*, ed. Jim Fyrth (London: Lawrence & Wishart, 1985), 133.

43 Claude McKay, for instance, remembered them as 'that very brilliant and talented writing couple'; see *A Long Way from Home: An Autobiography* (1970: London: Pluto, 1985), 87. Pollitt also recalled them with affection (*Serving*, 93).
44 Paul, *Communism*, 65; Eden Paul and Cedar Paul, *Creative Revolution: A Study of Ergotocracy* (London: George Allen and Unwin, 1920), 193.
45 These debates were sporadically relayed to the British Left via the pages of the *Communist*, *Plebs*, and Dutt's *Labour Monthly*. 'Art and Revolution: The "Prolet-cult" in Russia,' *Communist*, 7 October 1920; A. Lunarcharsky, 'Working-Class Culture, *Plebs* (12 October 1920): 157–62, and (12 November 1920): 189–92; Valerian Poliansky, 'The Banner of Prolet-cult,' *Plebs* (13 January 1921): 3–6.
46 Paul and Paul, *Creative Revolution*, 176, 22; Paul and Paul, *Proletcult (Proletarian Culture)* (London: Leonard Parsons, 1921), 101.
47 The movement had previously broken with Ruskin College and pitched its independent working-class education against the Arnoldian cultural diffusion of the university dominated WEA. It was subsidized by the South Wales Miners' Federation and the National Union of Railwaymen, and twenty-four trade unions were affiliated. See Linehan, *Communism in Britain*, 167; Andy Miles, 'Workers' Education: The Communist Party and the Plebs League in the 1920s,' *History Workshop* 18 (Autumn 1984): 102–14.
48 Paul and Paul, *Proletcult*, 21.
49 A psychologist by profession, Eden Paul was a leading figure in the running of the Children's Section of the St Pancras LPC in 1923–4; Minutes of LPC meetings, 12 November 1923, 26 November 1923, 28 December 1923, 24 January 1924, Pollard Papers, Box 4.
50 Eden Paul and Cedar Paul, 'Revolutionary Education in Britain,' *Plebs* (15 July 1923): 307.
51 Ibid., 307.
52 Andrew Rothstein, 'The Workers' Culture,' *Plebs* (14 February 1922): 41; Rothstein's article is in part a review of the Pauls' *Proletcult*.
53 J.T. Murphy, 'Still Wanted, the Marxism of Marx,' *Plebs* (August 1923): 337. Murphy cites Trotsky's address to the 1922 Congress to justify the line that culture could wait.
54 J.H. Burns, 'Independent Working Class Education,' *Communist*, 9 September 1920; unsigned review of new Plebs series, *Communist*, 23 September 1920; Mark Starr, 'Working-Class Education,' *Labour Monthly* (January 1922): 53–6; Rajani Palme Dutt, 'A Prejudice for Truth,' *Plebs* (July 1921): 201–3.
55 Rajani Palme Dutt, 'The British School of Marxism,' *Labour Monthly* (June 1922), 429–31; Dutt, 'British Marxism,' *Labour Monthly* (February 1923), 124–8; Murphy, 'Wanted: the Marxism of Marx,' *Plebs* (April 1923): 152–6; the decisive meeting between the Party Training Committee and the Plebs Executive was held on 27 February 1923, Minutes in Dutt Papers, Box 1, WCML. After failing to capture the independently minded network, the party bullishly went it alone,

taking in-house the education of its members through Training Groups and a Party Training Department that it consistently lacked the personnel or resources to support. Judging by the picture in London, from where the most detailed records have survived, the party's training arrangements were in a more or less permanent state of crisis through the mid-1920s, with too few tutors, poor attendance, poor levels of engagement from members, and LPCs that allegedly failed to take training seriously. The St Pancras LPC, for instance, had 49 members out of around 200 not in a training group in the spring of 1926 (LPC Minutes, 21 April 1926, Pollard Papers, Box 1); only 3 out of 21 passed the end-of-course test, according to the Report on Training in the LPC Annual Report of 1926–7 (Pollard Papers, Box 3); all London Party Committees were chastized by a circular of 25 November 1925 for a 'falling off in activity in Party Training' (Box 10); in October 1924 the designated Training Department in the London District had been abandoned through lack of support; a tranche of scripts and reports had also been mislaid (Report on Training Department for District Congress, 8 October 1924, Pollard Papers Box 10).

56 The Pauls stayed, but journalist and former *Communist* editor Raymond Postgate (1896–1971) went, and would suffer sustained abuse for years to come. Pollitt, *Serving*, 150. Winifred Horrabin (1887–1971) and Frank Horrabin (1884–1962) – distinguished educationalists and historians of the adult education movement to which they were central – would also depart from 'a stupid, vain-glorious and disagreeable set of folk,' taking with them the future Labour MP and education secretary, Ellen Wilkinson (1891–1947) – a mere chancer and 'big-wig' for Pollitt, in pursuit of a 'brighter limelight,' and Morgan Phillips Price (1885–1973), an astute reader of political economy in the pages of the NCLC's journal *Plebs* and beyond. J.T. Walton Newbold (1888–1943), already a member of the CPGB's most senior body, the Political Bureau, and briefly one of its three 1920s MPs, would also leave, as would Mark Starr (1894–1985), the autodidact collier, committed Esperantist and educationalist. Mark Starr, 'Communism and the International Language,' *Communist Review* (February 1922): 246–67; 'ABC of the International,' *Communist Review* (July 1924): 152–4. They were also attacked subsequently in the *Labour Monthly* by W.N. Ewer; Postgate and J.F. Horrabin responded in 'Trotsky's "Comrades,"' *Plebs* (July 1925): 286; Harold Heslop, 'Raymond W. Postgate: A Memoir,' *Communist* (April 1928): 228–31; Pollitt, *Serving*, 125; Winifred Horrabin, review of P. Braun, *Problems of the Labour Movement*, *Plebs* (July 1925): 278–80.

57 Raymond W. Postgate and J.F. Horrabin, 'Trotsky's "Comrades,"' *Plebs* (July 1925): 286; Winifred Horrabin also wrote to Dutt personally, taking him to task for having 'insulted in the bitterest way a group of fellow communists.' Horrabin to Dutt, 15 March 1923, CP IND DUTT 5/10.

58 R. Louzon, 'How Shall We Prepare for Revolution?' *Plebs* (July 1925): 271. The article was translated by the Pauls. Horrabin's reported comments in the next

issue made it clear that he had a hand in its publication. 'The Cober Hill School: A Diary of the Week,' *Plebs* (August 1925): 306.

59 Horrabin, quoted in 'Cober Hill School,' 306.

60 See, for instance, Gramsci's, unsigned article in *Avanti!*, 14 June 1920, reprinted in *Selections from the Cultural Writings*, ed. David Forgacs and Geoffrey Nowell-Smith (London: Lawrence & Wishart, 1985), 41.

61 Louzon, 'How Shall We Prepare?' 271.

62 Proletcult debates were reprinted, but seldom debated, in the party press, appearing mainly in Dutt's *Labour Monthly*. A. Bogdanov, 'Proletarian Poetry 1' (May 1923): 276–85; 'Proletarian Poetry 2' (June 1923): 357–62; 'The Criticism of Proletarian Art' (December 1923): 344–55; 'Religion, Art and Marxism' (August 1924): 489–97; 'The Workers' Artistic Inheritance' (September 1924): 549–56.

63 W.T. Colyer. Colyer's words were reported in 'Cober Hill School' (306), and a disciplinary hearing swiftly ensued; the matter was eventually dropped after Colyer was cautioned. Secretary of St Pancras LPC to Colyer, 25 September 1925, and John Mahon of London District to St Pancras LPC, 10 October 1925, Pollard Papers, Box 4.

64 In Dutt's *Workers' Weekly*. Iris Kingsley was treated more stiffly. Minutes of St Pancras Local, 20 May 1925, Pollard Papers, Box 4; Minutes of Group B, 23 December [1925?], Pollard Papers, Box 1; undated letter from St Pancras LPC to London District; letter from John Mahon, 22 March 1926 confirming the expulsion, Pollard Papers, Box 10. This case is mentioned in Raphael Samuel, *The Lost World of British Communism* (London: Verso, 2006), 90–1, although Samuel mistakenly refers to Kingsley as Kingston.

65 W. Gallacher, 'How Not to Prepare for Revolution,' *Plebs* (August 1925): 316.

66 Klugmann, *History*, 206.

67 Meynell's commitment to reinvigorating in Communism's image traditions of radical cartooning had led to a prosecution for libel. The action was brought by Labour MP and National Union of Railwaymen leader J.H. Thomas in response to a cartoon published on 16 April 1921 that depicted him as having killed a miner, an allusion to his union's betrayal of the miners on 'Black Friday.' For the trial and the *Communist* under Meynell, see Samuel S. Hyde, '"Please, Sir, he called me Jimmy!" Political Cartooning before the Law: "Black Friday," J.H. Thomas and the Communist Libel Trial of 1921,' *Contemporary British History* 25, no. 4 (2011): 521–55.

68 Meynell's former *Daily Herald* colleague Raymond Postgate became editor between July 1921 and May 1922, at which point Jackson took over. Klugmann, *History*, 215; Dutt, 'Report on Workers' Weekly and Party Publications to the Control Committee,' CP IND DUTT 26/2, and Dutt, 'Memorandum on "The Workers' Weekly,"' Dutt Papers, BL, CUP 1262 K4; also quoted in Hyde, '"Please, Sir, he called me Jimmy!"' 542.

69 Eric Verney, 'The Workers' Press,' *Communist Review* (August 1924): 196; similar articles appeared by C.M. Roebuck (alias Andrew Rothstein) in the *Communist*

Review (April 1923) and *Labour Monthly* (April 1923). Sales of the *Communist* were in decline by the time it was withdrawn; sales of *Workers' Weekly* peaked in the year of the General Strike. L.J. Macfarlane, *The British Communist Party: Its Origin and Development until 1929* (London: MacGibbon and Kee, 1966), appendix D, 302.

70 Verney, 'Workers' Press,' 198; the Bodleian Library has rich holdings of these, including, from the mid-1920s, *The Spark: Organ of the Bishopgate and Broad Street Railway Workers, The Bus: A Paper of the London Bus Fleet Workers, Juice: Organ of the Underground Workers* (Communist Papers Box File); the WCML in Salford has regional equivalents such as the *Salford Docker* and *The Ward and Goldstone Spark*.

71 The pursuit of the United Front tactic became imperative from 1923 when the Labour Party stepped up its opposition to Communist Party affiliation and proscribed Communists from individual membership. In political terms, the United Front initiative re-energized in response found multiple positive expressions, including the National Minority Movement, formed in August 1924 to consolidate rank-and-file currents in the trade union movement and soon claiming to represent almost a million workers. The ban on individual CP members was ratified at the Labour Party's 1925 conference, but was defied by some local Labour parties. Matthew Worley, *Class Against Class: The Communist Party in Britain Between the Wars* (London: I.B. Tauris, 2002), 6–7.

72 Edited by founder Communist Party member, and NCLC activist William Paul, the *Sunday Worker* was bankrolled by Moscow, but numbered shareholders among miners' lodges, ILP branches, and trade councils, and would soon become the de facto organ of the United Front National Left Wing Movement it helped to shape.

73 R.G. Graham, letter, *Sunday Worker*, 3 October 1926.

74 Paul, *Communism and Society*, 71.

75 Sassoon, *One Hundred Years*, 81; Hoare and Nowell-Smith, *Selections from the Prison Notebooks*, 148–9.

76 There was little of the national culture reflected in its journal, *Communist Review*. Prior to the launch of the *Sunday Worker*, cultural coverage in the *Communist Review* was limited to a defence of the crudest proletcult positions by W. McLaine (June 1921); the anti-intellectualism of Dutch communist S.J. Rutgers ('The Intellectuals and the Russian Revolution,' December 1921); an article by Boughton on 'Revolution and the Arts' (June 1923); and Mark Starr on Esperanto (February 1922, July 1924). In the same period, Dutt's *Labour Monthly* ran articles on proletcult, adult education, and drama, plus hostile reviews of H.R. Barbor's revolutionary novel, *Against the Red Sky* (October 1922) and Sinclair Lewis's *Babbitt* (February 1924).

77 *Sunday Worker*, 22 March 1925, 19 April 1925, 10 May 1925. Bruley, 'Women Against War,' 132; Lily Domb of Bethnal Green challenged what she saw as inertia

after taking over the Women's Department at the local level in 1927; a Women's Department circular tried to reinvigorate activism through bespoke party training for women in May 1927; a Women's Department circular of 21 January 1926 called for more active women's sections. Pollard Papers, Box 11.

78 William Paul, review of Margaret T. Hodgen, *Workers' Education in England and the US*, *Sunday Worker*, 9 August 1925; Paul also provided reading recommendations for the expanding NCLC movement's 30,000 students on 29 August 1926.

79 'Clydebank riveter's hammer at work,' *Sunday Worker*, 26 September 1926. Even Ralph Fox was immediately cowed into appeasing Ferguson – a self-styled super ego of proletarian rectitude – and the arts page became less assured in the months that followed. Fox would face ongoing goading from Ferguson through the rest of the paper's four-year life.

80 Dutt, 'A Prejudice for Truth,' *Plebs* (July 1921): 201–3; Lenin, 'The Task of the Youth Leagues' (1920), in *Selected Works*, 610.

81 W. McLaine, 'Art and the Worker,' *Communist Review* (June 1921): 20; William Paul, 'Stage and propaganda,' *Sunday Worker*, 29 November 1925.

82 These debates ran in *Communist Review* in January, February, and April 1924, and are summarized in Brian Pearce and Michael Woodhouse, *A History of Communism in Britain* (1969; London: Bookmarks, 1995), 163.

83 Review by Charles Ashleigh, *Sunday Worker*, 1 November 1925, and received sympathetically despite rapidly hardening party attitudes to Trotsky. The *Sunday Worker* also debated Upton Sinclair's *Mammonart* (1925), an early and now forgotten attempt at a materialist history of culture that was a touchstone text of the 1920s intellectual Left; *Sunday Worker*, 22 March 1925, 12 April 1925; 'Peacham,' 'The Books They Write,' 7 June 1925. Fox and Jackson guided readers through contemporary international writing – Henri Barbusse, Sinclair Lewis, Theodore Dreiser – and the English novel from Defoe to Conrad, Hardy, and Robert Tressell in a series that would later feed into Fox's survey, *The Novel and the People* (1937).

84 Also cited in Andy Croft, *Red Letter Days: British Fiction in the 1930s* (London: Lawrence & Wishart, 1990), 37; *Sunday Worker*, 26 February 1928.

85 The membership was announced in a lengthy article by Boughton for *Workers' Weekly*, 12 February 1926.

86 Boughton, *Sunday Worker*, 15 March 1925, 1 November 1925; 'authentic' folksong anthologies and performances from the likes of Cedar Paul, William Paul, and the tenor John Goss were promoted (12 April 1925, 24 January 1926); 'high cultural' appropriations of this birthright, as in the 'anti-Labour' antiquarianism of the English Folk Dance and Song Society, were scorned (29 August 1926).

87 *Sunday Worker*, 22 March 1925; 6 December 1925; Hurd, *Rutland Boughton*, 170–1; Boughton broke with Morrisson and the choir in the summer of 1929.

88 Worley, *Class Against Class*, 204; *Sunday Worker*, 27 June 1926, 11 July 1926, 8 August 1926. These included the Workers Theatre of the Woolwich Trades Council and the Hackney Dramatic Group. The initial committee included Eden and Cedar Paul, William Paul, Rutland Boughton, Christina Walshe, who co-organized the Glastonbury Music Festival with Boughton, and the *Sunday Worker* theatre and film critic Huntley Carter.

89 As at the 1925 International Women's Day Concert held at the St Pancras LPC's premises on 6 March 1925; Cedar Paul sang songs and the Workers' Theatre Group performed a sketch entitled 'Baldwin's Pipe Dream,' program in Pollard Papers, Box 1.

90 What soon became the 'Workers' Theatre Movement' staged productions in 1926 and early 1927 of Upton Sinclair's *Singing Jailbirds* and collier playwright Joe Corrie's miners' lock-out drama *In Time of Strife*, marking the beginning of Communism's long engagement with drama. The movement's formation is described in Raphael Samuel's Introduction to Raphael Samuel, Ewan MacColl, and Stuart Cosgrove, eds., *Theatres of the Left 1889–1935* (London: Routledge, 1985), 33–64.

91 Unsigned, 'The Last of the sheik,' *Sunday Worker*, 29 June 1926; Lockitt, 'The films they screen,' *Sunday Worker*, 27 September 1925, 3 January 1926.

92 Letter from 'A Common Man' to Mr A.R. Burrows, Assistant Controller of the British Broadcasting Company, 31 May 1925; Huntley Carter, 'Radio, Arm of Mass Attack,' 27 March 1927; Debates on the Left about Esperanto as a potential lingua franca to unite the international working class were also widely reported by Mark Starr, chair of the British League of Esperantist Socialists, e.g. 13 December 1925.

93 Bert Hogenkamp, *Deadly Parallels: Film and the Left in Britain 1929–1939* (London: Lawrence & Wishart, 1986), 21; Jackson prepared the Lenin memorial issue of 1924. Jackson, 'Interim Report,' 203–4.

94 'Camera notes,' *Sunday Worker*, 15 March 1925.

95 Hogenkamp, *Deadly Parallels*, 28n34; 'The camera,' *Sunday Worker*, 29 March 1925.

96 Launched in 1912, the *Daily Herald* was the first concerted attempt by the labour movement to challenge the 'capitalist' press. Its circulation was around 60,000 before the war and over 300,000 in 1920. Once bought out by the Odham's group at the end of the 1920s, its circulation reached 2,000,000. Hyde, 'Political Cartooning,' 529; Arthur Calder-Marshall, *The Changing Scene* (London: Chapman & Hall, 1937), 124, table on 136.

97 Dutt to Political Bureau, 26 November 1929; cited in Callaghan, *Rajani Palme Dutt*, 132; Dutt, 'Bourgeois Journalism and Our Press,' *Communist Review* (July 1932): 325–32.

98 *Daily Worker*, 25 January 1930; Dutt, 'Intellectuals and Communism,' 429.

99 Dutt's diatribe against 'Capitalist Sport' (*Daily Worker*, 25 January 1930); 'HF' objected to the lack of wireless listings (*Daily Worker*, 18 January 1930), G.W.

Newport wanted to see more *Sunday Worker*–style cultural coverage (*Daily Worker*, 21 January 1930), and W.H. Dareen wanted betting tips (*Daily Worker*, 11 February 1930). A victimized textile worker lamented that even though the 'overwhelming majority of workers declare for the inclusion of capitalist sport … the Editorial Board decide to exclude it (*Daily Worker*, 6 February 1930). Linehan summarizes these debates in *Communism in Britain*, 135.

100 Kevin Morgan, 'The Communist Party and the *Daily Worker*, 1930–1956,' in *Opening the Books: Essays on the Social and Cultural History of the British Communist Party*, ed. Geoff Andrews, Nina Fishman, and Kevin Morgan (London: Pluto, 1995), 144.

101 For Ewer, see McIlroy, 'Establishment of Intellectual Orthodoxy,' 187–8; McIlroy also analyses the case of Utley (201–2). See also Freda Utley, *Lost Illusion* (Philadelphia: Fireside, 1948), 20.

102 Freda Utley, 'Raising the Theoretical Level of Our Party as a Party of Mass Work,' *Communist Review* (October 1930): 436.

103 Freda Utley, 'Economism Today: The "Iskra Period" and Ourselves,' *Communist Review* (May 1930): 207.

104 Utley, 'Raising,' 432–41.

105 W. Tapsell, 'The Opportunism of Comrade Utley,' *Communist Review* (December 1930): 82–3; Allen Hutt, 'Fundamental Questions for Our Party,' *Communist Review* (September 1930): 393–400; 'The Theoretician of "Left" Sectarianism and Spontaneity: The Political Bureau's Reply to Freda Utley,' *Communist Review* (January 1931): 11–19. The treatment of Utley is summarized in McIlroy, "Establishment of Intellectual Orthodoxy,' 202. The tightening orthodoxy to which Utley was subjected was further sanctioned from the autumn of 1931 with the translation and active promotion across the party press of Stalin's notorious 'letter,' a key text in the subordination of Soviet intellectuals that dealt with the 'errors' of Russian historian A.G. Slutsky and further castigated Trotsky and marginalized Rose Luxemburg in order to present Stalin as Lenin's embodiment. Only Tommy Jackson criticized this time. McIlroy, 'Establishment of Intellectual Orthodoxy,' 210–17.

106 Among a group that comprised the historian, poet, and critic A.L. Morton (1903–87), film critic and producer Ivor Montagu (1904–84), structural crystallographer, J.D. Bernal (1901–71), and future party functionaries Allen Hutt (1901–73) and Philip Spratt (1902–71). Ivor Montagu, *The Youngest Son* (London: Lawrence & Wishart, 1970), 196–7.

107 Dobb, 'The Webbs, the State and the Workers,' *Plebs* (April 1923): 171; Dobb, 'Labour Research,' *Labour Monthly* (December 1925): 750.

108 Parsons, 'Communism in the Professions,' 87.

109 John Lehmann, *The Whispering Gallery: Autobiography I* (London: Harcourt, Brace, 1954), 178. Dobb contributed to the list of the quintessential Bloomsbury publisher, Leonard and Virginia Woolf's Hogarth Press, suddenly dominated

by books about the Soviet Union, working-class life, and the plight of the unemployed. The Hogarth Press list for spring 1931 included John Hampson's novel about a struggling pub, *Saturday Night at the Greyhound*, Margate Llewelyn Davies, ed., *Life as We Have Known It by Co-operative Working Women*, R. Trouton's *Unemployment*, C.E.M. Joad's *The Horror of the Countryside*, and two pamphlets about the Soviet Union, including a reprint of Dobb's *Russia Today and Tomorrow*. Advertisement in *Times Literary Supplement*, 2 March 1931, 192.

110 Notably G.D.H. Cole's Socialist League, to which former educationalists had now migrated (the Horrabins, Mellor, Postgate), and the new journal, *Twentieth Century*, launched in March 1931 by the young radicals of the Promethean Society, to which he contributed. Cole set up the Society for Socialist Inquiry and Propaganda in the early 1930s, soon incorporated into the Socialist League. Pat Francis, 'The Labour Publishing Company 1920–29,' *History Workshop* 18 (Autumn 1984): 122; Samuel Hynes, *The Auden Generation: Literature and Politics in the 1930s* (Princeton, NJ: Princeton University Press, 1972), 83–4; Murry's brand of 'ILP' Marxism was attacked by 'RP' [Robin Page Arnot?] in 'Marxism and Middleton Murry,' *Communist Review* (January 1933): 38–43. Dobb's article, 'Marxism and the Crisis,' appeared in the June 1932 issue of *Twentieth Century*; the pamphlets were 'Russia To-day and Tomorrow' (1931) and 'On Marxism Today' (1932). Dobb had argued in 1927 that Marxist theory was insufficiently creative and poorly developed and that 'the knowledge of Marxism even among "Marxists" is elemental in the extreme'; Dobb, 'New Light on Karl Marx,' *Labour Monthly* (November 1927): 704.

111 Most were unemployed workers – between 50 per cent and 60 per cent of the party's total membership was unemployed in 1932. Thorpe, 'Membership,' 781.

112 'They're cropping up all over the place now,' wrote Wintringham to Dutt, eagerly chronicling an influx into the party of professionals, including four London doctors, two barristers, and a group of aeronautical engineers who had been recruited on the boat home from a tour of the Soviet Union. Wintringham to Dutt, 3 August 1932, CP IND DUTT 6/3.

113 Dobb had retained his links with the NCLC, and contributed to *Plebs* until 1932; he was on the executive of the LRD; he argued the case for the Soviet Union on the BBC National Programme in March 1931 ('Looking at Russia') and for Communism on the BBC in March 1933; these talks were published in the BBC's in-house journal, The *Listener* (4 March 1931, 356; 29 March 1933, 484); his letters appeared sporadically in the *Manchester Guardian*, as on 26 September 1933. MI5 file, KV 2/21758.

114 Key recruits in Cambridge included David Guest (1911–38), who helped to establish a University CPGB branch and became its first secretary, his Trinity contemporary Maurice Cornforth (1909–80), who set up a Cambridge City branch, poet and future Mass Observation co-founder Charles Madge (1912–96), and James Klugmann (1912–77), whose Communist sister Kitty (1908–65),

a Girton student, Cornforth married. Neal Wood, *Communism and British Intellectuals* (London: Gollancz, 1959), 84–7. Other sources for this sentence include the KV2 files.

115 Collaborating with medical practitioner Alex Tudor Hart, who had joined the party in 1929, and Dmitri Mirsky, a future critical chronicler of the British intellectual scene who lectured in Russian at London University. D.S. Mirsky, *The Intelligentsia of Great Britain* (London: Gollancz, 1935).

116 The proposed journal was to be open to sympathetic non-members, including Dutt's Oxford contemporary and friend, archaeologist V. Gordon Childe, scientists J.B.S. Haldane and Lancelot Hogben, and party figures including Utley, Dutt, Fox, and Pascal. Undated memo, Theodore and Andrew Rothstein MI5 File, KV 2/1579. Also quoted in McIlroy, 'Establishment of Intellectual Orthodoxy,' 218.

117 Dobb was discussed by the Political Bureau, attacked in the *Daily Worker* (10 June 1932) and by hardliner Hugh Rathbone in *Communist Review* under the heading 'Marxism Vulgarised' (July 1932): 343. He was forced into a reluctant recantation, published as 'Maurice Dobb's Distortions of Marxism – A Reply which Confirms Our Criticism' in the *Daily Worker* (26 July 1932), which in fact gave little ground and reasserted the importance of communicating with the intellectual strata. The disciplining of Dobb is detailed in McIlroy, 'Establishment of Intellectual Orthodoxy,' 217–23.

118 The Comintern almost certainly advised the formation of student cells; Geoff Andrews, *The Shadow Man at the Heart of the Cambridge Spy Circle* (London: I.B. Tauris, 2015), 37. Wintringham informed Dutt of both the literature magazine *Storm* and *Cambridge Left* in a letter of 3 August 1932. The first issue of *Storm* appeared in February 1933, and the journal lasted less than a year, running to just four issues; the journal's course, which evolved from belated, nativist proletcultism to an emphasis on international antifascist writing, is mapped by James Smith, 'The Radical Literary Magazine of the 1930s and British Government Surveillance: The Case of *Storm* Magazine,' *Literature & History* 19, no. 2 (2010): 69–86; MI5 kept a watchful eye on its flamboyant leading light, Douglas Jeffries, KV 2/2806. Scott McCracken gives an overview of *Cambridge Left* in Peter Brooker and Andrew Thacker, eds., *The Oxford Critical History of Modernist Magazines*, vol. 1, *Britain and Ireland 1880–1955* (Oxford: Oxford University Press, 2009), 599–623. Madge's input is described in Hubble, *Mass Observation*, 44.

119 The latest provocation was Fox's biography of Lenin. The official accusation was that the book was too 'narrowly subjective, personal,' and suffused by a 'romantic literary tone'; the underlying problem was that Trotsky was insufficiently airbrushed from the narrative. Dutt's 'report' was the most lenient of the three produced by senior party figures. (Dutt to Pollitt, 4 October 1933, CP IND DUTT 10/4). A new policy ensued, stating that 'no party member shall write a book until

it has been approved by the Secretariat, and the line approved by the Agit-Prop [department].' Dossier on Ralph Fox, KV 2/1377.

120 A member from the mid-1920s, in the United Front period Bernal was active in the Holborn Labour Party, and seems to have allowed his membership to lapse on returning to Cambridge to take up a post in the Cavendish laboratory in 1927. His first book, *The World, the Flesh & the Devil* (1929), identified society's fundamental fault line as between a scientific elite and a traditionally minded population, rather than social classes. Andrew Brown, *J.D. Bernal: The Sage of Science* (Oxford: Oxford University Press, 2005), 55–77.

121 J.D. Bernal, 'The Scientist and the World Today,' appeared in the second issue of *Cambridge Left* (Winter 1933); it is reprinted in J.D. Bernal, *The Freedom of Necessity* (London: Routledge & Kegan Paul, 1949), 334–49.

122 An event analysed many times, never better than in Gary Werskey, *The Visible College: A Collective Biography of British Scientists and Socialists of the 1930s* (London: Allen Lane, 1978), 138–49. Bernal reviewed the event for the *Spectator* in July 1931, and considered it 'the most important meeting of ideas' since the Russian Revolution. The review is reprinted in *Freedom of Necessity*, 335.

123 Brown, *J.D. Bernal*, 107ff; Werskey, *Visible College*, 139–49.

124 Marxism as science was standard fare in the period; see, for instance, Dutt's 'Intellectuals and Communism,' 421.

125 Bernal, 'Scientist and the World Today,' 340.

126 *For Soviet Britain: The Programme of the Communist Party Adopted at the XIII Congress, February 2 1935* (London: Marston, 1935), 9, 11, 12, online at www.marxists.org; page numbers refer to transcript.

127 Ibid., 11, 16.

128 Tom Wintringham, 'Allies are needed for the revolution,' *Daily Worker*, 30 August 1932. The article was roundly criticized in subsequent issues (2 September 1932, 7 September 1932, 8 September 1932, 9 September 1932); Wintringham's responses, sent to both the *Daily Worker* and the *Communist Review*, went unpublished. Hugh Purcell, *The Last English Revolutionary: Tom Wintringham, 1898–1949* (Stroud, UK: Sutton, 2004), 80–1.

129 G. Dimitrov, *The Working Class Against Fascism* (London: Martin Lawrence, 1935), 122.

130 Ibid., 11.

131 Ibid., 11, 39.

132 Ibid., 75, 33.

133 Ibid., 99.

134 Ibid., 98.

135 Ibid., 33, 80, 29.

136 Dimitrov cited the earlier debates on the question of Communist and established political structures. Back then, he argued, the debate had polarised into simple binaries: the reformist right had forgotten core Marxist lessons about class

and state, opportunistically supporting the formation of so-called workers' governments under capitalism; the left had proved inflexible, dogmatically arguing that true workers' governments could only be formed by 'armed insurrection *after* the overthrow of the bourgeoisie.' Ibid., 65.

137 Ibid.

138 Ibid., 67.

139 Ibid., 71, 23, 83.

140 Ibid., 72.

141 Ibid., 119, 116.

142 Ibid., 66, 34–5.

143 Eric Hobsbawm, 'Fifty Years of People's Fronts,' in *Britain, Fascism and the Popular Front*, ed. Jim Fyrth (London: Lawrence & Wishart, 1985), 240.

144 Dimitrov, *Working Class Against Fascism*; Ralph Fox, 'The Fight of Communism on the Front of Culture,' *Daily Worker*, 11 September 1935; Harry Pollitt, 'One year ago today,' *Daily Worker*, 24 August 1936; Ralph Fox, *The Novel and the People* (London: Lawrence & Wishart, 1937), 124–38.

145 It licensed committed intellectuals like Wintringham to explore the same questions around the chronology of revolution and the role of civil society in class rule that now became the focus for many communists internationally in the 1930s, questions that underpinned Gramsci's 'Prison Notebooks' and the various international gatherings of Popular Front intellectuals, notably the Congress for the Defence of Culture held in Paris in June 1935, attended by three of *Left Review*'s founder editors and reported extensively in the journal's August 1935 issue.

146 Editorial Statement, *Discussion* (January 1936): 1.

147 Linehan, *Communism in Britain*, 140; Morgan, 'Communist Party and the *Daily Worker*,' 147; Claud Cockburn, *In Time of Trouble* (London: Rupert Hart-Davis, 1956), 247.

148 Morgan, 'Communist Party and the *Daily Worker*,' 149; Andy Croft, *Comrade Heart: A Life of Randall Swingler* (Manchester: Manchester University Press, 2003), 89.

149 Thorpe, 'Membership,' 781. Ted Bramley, 'London's historical pageant: Thousands march behind CP banners to Hyde Park,' *Imprecorr* 26 September 1938, 1201.

150 The moneyed Eva Collett Reckitt (1890–1976), formerly a stalwart of the Labour Research Department and long-standing supporter of Burns and Communist cultural networks, was nudged by Burns and Pollitt to take over the notorious 'Bomb Shop' of revolutionary books in Charing Cross Road, which became Collett's. Sister stores opened in central Glasgow (1934), Manchester (1935), and Cardiff (1936). Aligned with the party without technically belonging to it, they would be run with a zest often lacking in the party's own often uninviting 'Workers Bookshops,' whose shelf contents were determined by the party's Literature Commission.

151 The party's rather dour press, 'ML' or Martin Lawrence, code for the Marx and Lenin who dominated the list, was refashioned in quintessential Popular Front style through a carefully controlled merger with the leftward-turning liberal publisher Wishart Books, managed by its hard-nosed, wealthy proprietor, Ernest Wishart (1902–87). Wishart's stock-market dealings would often be needed to underwrite the venture. Lawrence & Wishart was run editorially by Wishart's former circle of distinguished literary editors. These brought with them the considerable cultural cachet of the flagship *Calendar of Modern Letters* (1925–7), notably his brother-in-law and future party education organizer, Douglas Garman (1903–69), and the poet and editor Edgell Rickword (1898–1982). They would enhance the party's cultural profile in integrating its two companies' strengths, Marxist and Soviet titles from the former, and fiction and more general leftist titles from the latter, publishing key novels of the period such as John Sommerfield's *May Day* (1936) and Lewis Jones's *Cwmardy* (1937) and *We Live* (1939) and John Lehmann's impressively cosmopolitan conspectus of the decade's emerging writers, *New Writing*.

152 Don Melville, '2, 000,000 Left books sold: Rally a huge success,' *Daily Worker*, 26 April 1939. That the LBC could not *technically* be described as a Communist affair – its selection triumvirate was socialist publisher Victor Gollancz, fellow-traveller John Strachey, and LSE academic, political theorist, and Labour Party NEC member Harold Laski – was a measure of the party's success of diffusing its politico-cultural priorities through the intellectual Left in the Popular Front period. The project would thrive as long as the indefatigable Gollancz's idea of a Popular Front aligned with that of the party. As intended, the set-up effectively communicated the impression of the party as a leading and rising cultural and intellectual force, projecting books by Communist intellectuals – whose manuscripts were still assiduously screened by both Moscow and the party leadership – to a ready-made and expanding reading community that greatly exceeded either the party membership or the typical sales achieved by Lawrence & Wishart. As a Book of the Month purchased by all members, for instance, Dutt's own *World Politics 1918–36*, sold around ten times as many copies as a typical Lawrence & Wishart title. John Strachey's *Why You Should Be a Socialist* sold half a million copies.

153 Left scientists around Bernal collaborated with Front populaire French equivalents to establish a Science Commission within the International Peace Campaign (Werskey, *Visible College*, 234), while Bernal's friendship with French communist scientists Paul Langevin and Frédéric Joliot-Curie led to the formation of the front organization For Intellectual Liberty, modelled on their Comité de vigilence des intellectuels antifascistes (Brown, *J.D. Bernal*, 125). Richard Overy, *The Morbid Age: Britain and the Crisis of Civilization 1919–1939* (London: Penguin, 2009), 302.

154 Established at Whitechapel Art Gallery in London in February 1936, it initially comprised eight organizations, including the London Labour Choral Union, and took inspiration from the Front populaire's Fédération musicale populaire. It developed the earlier work of Boughton in a more congenial political climate, staging events and running courses. Ben Short, 'Music: Building a People's League,' *Daily Worker*, 30 March 1936; Short, 'Songs for the People,' *Daily Worker*, 21 July 1937.

155 Handbill, 'New Review 1937'; Handbill, 'Help Spain by Showing Kino Films'; Handbill, 'It's Simple to Run a Film Show: All You Need Is Electricity'; *Kino News* 3, n.d., CP ORG MISC 4/4. Formed in 1933 as a section of the Workers' Theatre Movement, Kino was incorporated as a non-profit company in March 1935. It established stronger regional representation during the height of the Popular Front, and worked with Labour Party branches, trade unions, and through the Left Book Club. Hogenkamp, *Deadly Parallels*, 136–9; James Smith, 'Soviet Films and British Intelligence in the 1930s: The Case of Kino Films and MI5,' in *Russia in Britain 1880–1940: From Modernism to Melodrama*, ed. Rebecca Beasley and Philip Ross Bullock (Oxford: Oxford University Press, 2013), 247.

156 Now emphasizing not socialism or the Soviet Union but antifascism and the defence of culture. Its *Artists Against Fascism and War* exhibition in November 1935, organized by a committee including Eric Gill, Laura Knight, Augustus John, Duncan Grant, and Henry Moore, attracted six thousand visitors. Montagu Slater, 'Artists' International Exhibition,' *Left Review* (January 1936): 160–2; Lydia Morris and Robert Radford, *The AIA, 1933–1953* (Oxford: Museum of Modern Art, 1983).

157 Nationally theatrical Communists were encouraged to work with the existing amateur networks of the British Drama League, with its two thousand affiliated amateur dramatic societies. Actor, 'A Real Workers' Theatre Movement,' *Discussion* (March 1938): 42–3. Its name synonymous with Popular Front priorities, Unity Theatre in London now fulfilled a long-standing ambition of the Left to establish a permanent base in central London, and significantly moved out of the WTM's East End heartlands to establish itself in Britannia Street, King's Cross (1936–7) and then nearby Goldington Street (1937–75), where its General Council comprised a who's who of Popular Front intellectuals from within the Communist Party (Alan Bush) and beyond (Sean O'Casey, Paul Robeson, Stafford Cripps, Harold Laski, Victor Gollancz). It had three hundred active members, two thousand subscribers, and represented scores of affiliated organisations – Labour Party organizations, trade union bodies, co-ops, and Communist and YCL branches. Colin Chambers, *The Story of Unity Theatre* (London: Lawrence & Wishart, 1989), 107, 122 note 22.

158 The Marx House School in Clerkenwell had been opened in 1933 to educate party cadre in political economy. It was now expanded into a Popular Front–style 'intellectual centre' that proposed to irrigate the 'present arid wastes' of national

intellectual life with weekly classes on science, literature, art, and film taught by party intellectuals. Alick West, 'Marx House,' *Left Review* (September 1935): 499; S. Bodington, 'Marxism and Education,' *Labour Monthly* (September 1935): 558–61.

159 Dimitrov, *Working Class*, 60.

160 The party now reversed the Third Period contraction of its internal structures to maximize contact with these spheres, reviving its Women's Department as a central coordinating committee and instituting regional and branch committees. Sue Bruley, 'Women Against War and Fascism,' in *Britain, Fascism and the Popular Front*, ed. Jim Fyrth (London: Lawrence & Wishart, 1985), 148–9. Not all women drawn towards Communism as a consequence were as quiescent on the sexual division of labour as the official line or the new *Daily Worker* sewing groups. Women's World Committee secretary Hilda Vernon in particular brought back into the party long-exiled currents, gently questioning whether party structures, logic, and unscrutinized reflexes reproduced rather than challenged bourgeois conceptions. The current she reintroduced would develop into more confrontational challenges much later. Morgan, Cohen, and Flinn, *Communists and British Society*, 170.

161 *Daily Worker* articles advocating a 'League of the Godless' were replaced by those arguing that religious belief was no impediment to party membership, a shift reinforced by the grassroots experience of Communists' working closely with church groups through tenants' committees, the British Youth Peace Assembly, and the Peace Pledge Union. Tommy Jackson, 'League of Godless,' *Daily Worker*, 8 August 1932; Margot Heinemann, 'The People's Front and the Intellectuals,' in Fyrth, *Britain, Fascism*, 176–7; Kevin Morgan, *Against Fascism and War*, 38. These synergies created a space in which Hewlett Johnson (1874–1966), the 'Red Dean' of Canterbury Cathedral between 1931 and 1963, could become a de facto Communist, speaking out on the Spanish Civil War and in favour of the Soviet Union, and enhancing the party's moral prestige by association. John Butler, *The Red Dean of Canterbury: The Public and Private Faces of Hewlett Johnson* (London: Scala, 2011).

162 In the wake of Dimitrov's emphasis on taking the masses as they were, Communist poet and *Daily Mirror* reporter Charles Madge focused on actually existing popular media and culture in his 'Press, Radio and Social Consciousness,' in *The Mind in Chains: Socialism and the Cultural Revolution*, ed. Cecil Day Lewis (London: Muller, 1937), 145–65. The process of knowing where the working class really was culturally, politically, and intellectually was for him a priority and precondition of political advance, and would become the central concern of Mass Observation, which he co-founded in 1937. Expressing his frustration with the nostalgic, elitist, and undialectical discourse on the Left around mass culture, Madge argued that the vicarious pleasures afforded by mass journalism, which delivered experience unavailable in the real capitalist world, should not

necessarily be seen as reconciling subjects to the system, but rather as churning up frustration – 'formidable psychological reserves of dissatisfaction' (150) – with a radical potential that the Left should recognize and channel. There were new notes here that outstripped dominant party conceptions and anticipated not only Gramsci but the post-war study of popular culture and consciousness in the form of Cultural Studies. Madge's commitment to Mass Observation ultimately would exceed that of a party only marginally interested in the questions around class, mass culture, and popular consciousness that absorbed him; much would be lost with his withdrawal from the party at the end of the decade.

163 Ben Harker, '"The Trumpet of the Night": Interwar Communists on BBC Radio,' *History Workshop* 75 (Spring 2013): 81–101.

164 Parsons, 'Communism in the Professions'; Eric Hobsbawm, *Interesting Times: A Twentieth Century Life* (2002; London: Abacus, 2003), 115. Recruits in 1934 included future translator and educationalist Brian Pearce (1915–2008), future novelist and literary critic Margot Heinemann (1913–92), educational theorist and historian Brian Simon (1915–2002), and historian Christopher Hill (1912–2003).

165 Andrews, *Shadow Man*, 51.

166 One of the three political student organizations, the others being those of the Liberals and the Conservatives. John Saville, *Memoirs from the Left* (London: Merlin, 2003), 12; Brian Simon, *A Life in Education* (London: Lawrence & Wishart, 1998), 240; *CUSC Bulletin* (23 November 1937).

167 'Draft Statement on the Present Situation and Our Tasks in the Universities,' 15 September 1938, Eric Hobsbawm Papers, 937/6/1/2, Modern Records Centre [hereafter MRC], University of Warwick.

168 Hobsbawm, *Interesting Times*, 115.

169 Simon, *Life*, 29.

170 Key NUS activists in this period were the communists Ram Nahum, Freddie Vickers, Margot Gale (later Margot Kettle), Arnold Kettle, James Klugmann, George Matthews, and Betty Matthews. Ibid., 33.

171 James Klugmann, 'Introduction,' in *Culture and Crisis in Britain in the 30s*, ed. Jon Clark, Margot Heinemann, David Margolies, and Carole Snee (London: Lawrence & Wishart, 1979), 32; an injunction that apparently led to a spike in communist Firsts at Cambridge, up from single figures to 60 per cent, according to Klugmann (34). See also Andrews, *Shadow Man*, 43.

172 Including Arthur Ling, Erno Goldfinger, Frederick Skinner, and fellow-traveller Berthold Lubetkin (1901–90). Parsons, 'Communism in the Professions,' 416n2; John Allan, *Berthold Lubetkin: Architecture and the Tradition of Progress* (London: RIBA, 1992), 314.

173 Parsons, 'Communism in the Professions,' 420; Allan, *Berthold Lubetkin*, 325.

174 Allan, *Berthold Lubetkin*, 353.

175 Werskey, *Visible College*, 236.

176 Noreen Branson, *History of the Communist Party of Great Britain*, vol. 3, *1927–1941* (London: Lawrence & Wishart, 1985), 211; Matthew Kavanagh, 'Against Fascism, War and Economies: The Communist Party of Great Britain's Schoolteachers during the Popular Front, 1935–39,' *History of Education* 43, no. 2 (2014): 208–31.

177 A party pamphlet, 'School at the Cross Roads' (1935), analysed international fascism's incursion into educational provision. Identifying British schools as a potential vector for fascism, the emphasis fell upon defending existing national forms and structures. Liberal traditions rather than Soviet models were foregrounded as the bulwark against fascist advance. Party educationalists also addressed the practical, everyday matters they had formerly tended to deal with, at best, cursorily, such as class sizes and milk and meals for the children of the unemployed. This newly 'constructive' tone in educational debate was soon amplified in the writing of Communist teacher Max Morris – a future NUT president – notably in his LBC title, *The People's Schools* (1939), which again privileged progressive, gradualist proposals over more radical injunctions in the name of situating Communism at the centre of debate on matters such as the school leaving age and maintenance allowances for poor children.

178 Kavanagh, 'Against Fascism,' 13.

179 Robin Heath, 'Our Children, Our Schools,' *Discussion* (September 1937): 11–12.

180 F. French, 'Do We Need a Reorientation in Education?' *Discussion* (October 1937): 15; Amabel Williams Ellis and F.J. Fisher, *A History of English Life*, reviewed in Edward Upward's lively CP-fronted journal, *Ploughshare: Organ of the Teachers' Anti-War Movement* (April-May 1936): 15; Parsons, 'Communism in the Professions,' 485.

181 Matthew Kavanagh, 'British Communism and the Politics of Education' (PhD diss., University of Manchester, 2015); Brown, *J.D. Bernal*; John Green, *Britain's Communists: The Untold Story* (London: Artery, 2014); Steve Parsons, 'British Communist Party School Teachers in the 1940s and 1950s,' *Science & Society* 61, no. 1 (1997): 46–67.

182 Dimitrov, *Working Class*, 122. A core-periphery model which imagines that authorized ideas were simply imposed from the centre via dependable conduits is inadequate to deal with the complexity involved, a case well argued by Elinor Taylor, *The Popular Front Novel in Britain* (Leiden: Brill, 2018), 17.

183 Hobsbawm, 'Fifty Years of People's Fronts,' 244.

184 Ben Harker, '"Communism is English": Edgell Rickword, Jack Lindsay and the Cultural Politics of the Popular Front,' *Literature & History* 20, no. 2 (2011): 18–19.

185 I use formation in the sense that Raymond Williams means it: 'those effective movements and tendencies, in intellectual and artistic life, which have significant and sometimes decisive influence on the active development of a culture.' Formations, Williams notes, often comprise a group of the same generation with

common ways of seeing shaped by shared social, cultural, and political impulses and experiences. They embody 'a social experience which is still *in process*' with its 'emergent, connecting and dominant characteristics' that are often most visible later, 'when they have been (as often happens) formalized, classified, and in many cases built into institutions,' although formations have 'a variable and often oblique relation to formal institutions' and their significance cannot be captured by analysis of institutions alone. Raymond Williams, *Marxism and Literature* (Oxford: Oxford University Press, 1977), 117, 132.

186 Edgell Rickword, Interview with John Lucas, *The New 1930s: A Challenge to Orthodoxy* (Brighton: Harvester, 1978), 7; THW, 'The Test,' *Labour Monthly* (March 1934): 144; Tom Wintringham, 'Who Is for Liberty?' *Left Review* (September 1935): 482–7.

187 Wintringham, 'Who Is for Liberty?' 484.

188 Jack Lindsay, *Life Rarely Tells* (Harmondsworth, UK: Penguin, 1982), 762.

189 Dutt effectively ghost-wrote the review of the first five issues for literary critic Alick West, published as 'A Critical Appraisal of *Left Review*,' *Labour Monthly* (March 1935): 185–7. Dutt produced an outline of what was required; West reported to Dutt on the inner workings of *Left Review*, and would join the editorial collective in July 1935. Dutt, 'Suggested Lines of Critique of Left Review'; West-Dutt Correspondence, 1934–35, CP IND DUTT 6/2 and 6/3.

190 Rickword was a director at Lawrence & Wishart and editor of *Left Review* in 1936–7; Edgell Rickword, *War and Culture: The Decline of Culture under Capitalism* (London: CPGB, 1936).

191 An ambitious conspectus of the cultural field that spanned Communism's intellectual and cultural range in the period, and brought together specially commissioned themed essays from party members and Popular Front fellow-travellers. Much of the book was largely continuous with traditional Communist priorities in seeing culture as a secondary superstructure whose deformations would be corrected by politics, but Rickword's proto-Gramscian chapter extended the range of existing positions in giving voice to a political project to which civil society and culture were central. Edgell Rickword, 'Culture, Progress, and English Tradition,' in *The Mind in Chains: Socialism and the Cultural Revolution*, ed. Cecil Day Lewis (London: Frederick Muller, 1937), 235–56.

192 Ibid., 253.

193 Ibid., 254, 256.

194 Ibid., 251.

195 Ibid., 246.

196 Ibid. That culture had been weakened by its capitalist-driven disconnection from labour and by becoming the effluvia of a leisure class was apparent, for Rickword, from the fashion for seeking answers to unhappiness in Freud, the hollow virtuosity of modernist literature, or indeed 'the briefest visit to Mayfair' (250).

197 Ibid., 247.

198 Ibid., 255.

199 Antonio Gramsci, 'Questions of Culture' (1920), reprinted in *Antonio Gramsci: Selections from the Cultural Writings*, ed. David Forgacs and Geoffrey Nowell-Smith (London: Lawrence & Wishart, 1985), 41.

200 Rickword, 'Culture,' 255; Edgell Rickword, *War and Culture: The Decline of Culture under Capitalism* (London: CPGB, 1936), 14.

201 The report appeared in February 1936; Purcell, *Last English Revolutionary*, 94.

202 Jack Lindsay, 'The Problem of Liberty,' *Discussion* (July 1936): 27–8; Lindsay, 'Non-dialectical,' *Discussion* (December 1936): 31; Lewis Day [*sic*], 'England Expects,' *Discussion* (November 1936): 26; Lewis Way, letter, *Discussion* (January 1937): 32–3.

203 Valentine Ackland, 'Intellectuals,' *Discussion* (March 1936): 2.

204 The quotation about cliques is from Rachel Kay, 'Intellectuals,' *Discussion* (April 1936): 24; the others are from 'HB,' 'A Reply to Valentine Ackland,' *Discussion* (April 1936): 25.

205 Betty Cooper, letter, *Discussion* (December 1936): 31. The Comintern's watchfulness over national parties, and national parties' suspicion of their cultural fringes, increased once more. The broad Comintern journal the *Eye* was withdrawn, and the long-mistrusted *Daily Worker* was attacked by Moscow as a toxic cocktail of 'alien ideology' and 'literary cafe crawlers' jokes'; ideologically wayward journalists were removed. Morgan, 'Communist Party and the *Daily Worker*,' 149. The party leadership and its mediating figures now tightened up the cultural apparatus: public lectures on Leninism were promoted by Burns over more inclusive events. *Discussion* was narrowed into a party organ in which Communists spoke only to themselves. The list of the impecunious Lawrence & Wishart was cut back to the Marxist canon and books such as *Trotskyism in the Service of Franco* (1938) and *Traitors on Trial* (1938). Rickword, who remained an advocate of a broader Popular Front list either resigned or was sacked in the process, also withdrawing in July 1937 from *Left Review*, where he had spent eighteen months as sole editor.

206 E.P. Thompson, 'Edgell Rickword,' *PN Review Supplement* 6, no. 1 (1979): xxvii.

207 The party press owned the copyright but in 1938 refused to grant serialization rights to the *News Chronicle*, a decision justified by J.R. Campbell in the *Daily Worker* (11 April 1938). A controversy blew up around the issue in the pages of *Tribune* in February and March 1962. Dutt flatly denied the history when it was recounted by *Tribune* reviewer Daniel Bair. Many, including Brian Pearce, Maurice Cornforth, Tamara Deutscher, and Jock Haston, accused him of falsifying the past. Cuttings archived in Monty Johnstone Papers, CP IND JOHN 1/1/3.

208 Ben Harker, 'Jack Lindsay's Alienation,' *History Workshop* 82, no. 1 (2016): 87; 'History of the CPSU,' *Party Organiser* (April 1939); 'History of the CPSU,' *Party Organiser* (May 1939); 'Studying the History of the CPSU,' *Party Organiser*

(June 1939); Dave Cope, *Central Books: A Brief History* (London: Central Books, 1999), 16.

209 Especially Jack Lindsay and Edgell Rickword's *A Handbook of English Freedom: A Record of English Democracy through Twelve Centuries* (London: Lawrence & Wishart, 1939), a collective 'essay towards an understanding of the strategy of socialist advance' (vii) that took forward the insights of *The Mind in Chains* and rearticulated Rickword's Popular Frontism at an unseasonal moment. While Stalin's book compacted quotations from Marx and Lenin into an orthodox and mechanistic 'reflection' model of economic base and cultural superstructure that effectively exiled intellectual agency and culture from politics, Lindsay and Rickword insisted that ideas and intellectuals were necessarily shaped by their moment but were also able to 'stimulate and instruct the future'(viii). And whereas the very structure of the *Short Course* folded theoretical Marxism squarely into the irrefutable story of the advancing 'Leninist' party and the Soviet Union, Lindsay and Rickword's selections emphasized the role of culture in struggle and ideas in prefiguring and shaping history, and constructed a chronicle of class struggle in which William Morris, rather than Stalin or Lenin, received the last word, and from which, as Rickword later noted, mention of the Soviet Union was conspicuously absent. See Charles Hobday, *Edgell Rickword: A Poet at War* (Manchester: Carcanet, 1989), 214. None of this was lost on the party leadership. Emile Burns heard in the book's very title a disrespectful riposte to his own earlier thousand-page reader of Marx, Engels, Lenin, and Stalin *A Handbook of Marxism* (1935), authorized by Moscow and reprinted by the Left Book Club in 1937. Burns's suspicion that the assembled radical readings represented a critical or corrective attitude to contracting party Marxism epitomized by books like his and the *Short Course* – consolidations of the Stalinization of Marxism to which the theoretically wayward including Jack Lindsay would be referred in future – would be borne out. *The Handbook*, like the dissonant writings of Christopher Caudwell, would enjoy a long afterlife, representing a late flowering of Popular Front Communism that always exceeded in its reach, richness, and dialectical conceptions of structure and agency the narrowly tactical visions of the official line. E.P. Thompson, in particular, would claim not only *Left Review* but also Lindsay and Rickword's work as 'socialist humanist' antecedents, finding here a model that conjoined 'an international socialist theory and a vigorous national historical practice' and whose true value would flare up only much later 'at a time when they were needed once again.' Thompson, 'Edgell Rickword,' xxviii.

210 Thompson, 'Edgell Rickword,' xxvii; Hobday, *Edgell Rickword*, 186; Edgell Rickword, 'Stalin on the National Question,' *Left Review* (November 1936): 746–62.

211 He took over the paper's book page in May 1939 (*Daily Worker*, 3 May 1939). Croft, *Comrade Heart*, 94–100.

212 Letter, 18 March 1938; Pearce and Woodhouse, *History of Communism in Britain*, 244.

213 Thompson, 'Edgell Rickword,' xxvii.

214 Purcell, *Wintringham*, 162; Madge's unpublished autobiography makes little mention of the CP, although his letters indicate that he was active until autumn 1938; Charles Madge Papers, 2.1, University of Sussex SXMS 71/1/3/1; Correspondence Madge Papers 8.3, SXMS 71/2/4/1. Day Lewis drifted away at around the same time, according to Burns 'because he felt the Party was taking an anti-cultural line' (8 January 1943; KV 2/1385). Accounts of these trajectories are given in Nick Hubble, *Mass Observation and Everyday Life: Culture, History, Theory* (Basingstoke, UK: Macmillan, 2006), 160–1; and James Smith, *British Writers and MI5 Surveillance* 1930–1960 (Cambridge: Cambridge University Press, 2013), 48–52.

215 Jack Lindsay, *1649: A Novel of the Year* (London: Methuen, 1938); Sylvia Townsend Warner, *Summer Will Show* (1936; New York: New York Review Books, 2006).

216 John Mulgan, ed., *Poems of Freedom* (London: Gollancz, 1938); Lindsay and Rickword, *Handbook of Freedom*.

217 Ralph Fox, *The Novel and the People* (London: Lawrence & Wishart, 1937); Jack Lindsay, *A Short History of Culture* (London: Gollancz, 1939).

218 Described by John Strachey as inaugurating 'something very like a new historical school; Strachey, Review of H. Fagan's *Nine Days That Shook England*, *Left News* (June 1938): 845.

219 Composers including Rutland Boughton and Ralph Vaughan Williams contributed music. The ten thousand figure is for the three-day festival, of which the pageant was the centrepiece. Alan Bush, 'Festival of Music for the People,' *Left News* (February 1938): 1162; 'Why all this painful class consciousness?' asked the *Sunday Times*, 12 March 1939; Croft, *Comrade Heart*, 95.

220 Attuned to national tradition; corrective of party insularity (eschewing what was diplomatically termed the party's 'present scientific and informative style'); non-party (asking 'nothing from the Secretariat but sanction and advice'); 'educational rather than agitational'; and shrewd about the contemporary cultural technology (the paperback) and distribution networks (the newsagent rather than the overtaxed branch Literature Secretary). Memo on Publishing Scheme, n.d., Lawrence & Wishart Records, GEM MSS 703, Box 5, Beinecke Rare Books and Manuscript Library, Yale University. Underwritten by Swingler's inherited wealth, and including Swingler, Rickword, and Lindsay as shareholders, they produced tupenny bimonthly 'Key Books' in print runs of 50,000 that bypassed the party's internal networks in favour of direct distribution to newsagents. Croft, *Comrade Heart*, 75; Andy Croft, 'The Boys Round the Corner: The Story of Fore Publications,' in *A Weapon in the Struggle: The Cultural History of the Communist Party in Britain*, ed. Andy Croft (London: Pluto, 1998), 142–63.

221 Lindsay, *Life Rarely Tells*, 786. Published the same year were J.B.S. Haldane's *Science and You* (1939), Salme Dutt's *When England Arose* (1939) and children's author Geoffrey Trease's *North Sea Spy* (1939).

222 George Orwell, 'Inside the Whale' (1940) in *Collected Essays, Journalism and Letters of George Orwell*, vol. 1, *1920–1940*, ed. Sonia Orwell and Ian Angus (1968; Harmondsworth, UK: Penguin, 1970), 562.

223 J.B. Priestley, 'March of the People' (review of *A Handbook of Freedom*), *Daily Worker*, 24 May 1939; Dutt had written to Priestley in 1934 enclosing a copy of *Labour Monthly* and asking him to contribute (1 September 1934). Priestley declined, considering the journal 'too Marxist for me' (7 September 1934). 'We are simply plain people trying to face realities,' Dutt replied (12 September 1934). CP IND DUTT 6/1.

224 This cultural work was driven back into the networks of the Workers' Music Association and the journal *Poetry and the People*. Harker, 'Communism is English,' 27.

2. Constructive Communists, 1940–1947

1 Harry Pollitt, *How to Win the Peace* (London: CPGB, 1944), 77.

2 The Labour Party's individual membership fell to 219,000 in 1942, meaning that there were four members of the Labour Party for one of the Communist Party; the ratio had been 22:1 in 1939. James Hinton, 'Coventry Communism: Study of Factory Politics in the Second World War,' *History Workshop* 10 (Autumn 1980): 90–1.

3 Andy Croft, 'Writers, the Communist Party and the Battle of Ideas,' *Socialist History* 5 (1994): 2.

4 Paul Addison, *Now the War Is Over* (London: Jonathan Cape, 1985); Peter Hennessy, *Never Again: Britain 1945–51* (London: Random House, 1992), K.O. Morgan, *Labour in Power 1945–51* (Oxford: Oxford University Press, 1985).

5 Pollitt, *How to Win*, 96.

6 Kevin Morgan, *Harry Pollitt* (Manchester: Manchester University Press, 1993), 147; Lawrence Parker, *The Kick Inside: Revolutionary Opposition in the CPGB, 1945–1991* (London: November Publications, 2012), 14–30.

7 '[A]mid all the heavy and disintegrative strains of war,' wrote Jack Lindsay, 'we have laid a basis of a vital people's culture … a cultural revolution has been initiated'; Jack Lindsay, *British Achievement in Art and Music* (London: Pilot, 1945), 2, 36. The book appeared in the series Britain's Wartime Achievement, which sold over 300,000 copies.

8 Douglas Hyde, *I Believed* (1950; London: Reprint Society, 1952), 71; Ernie Trory, *Imperialist War* (Brighton: Crabtree, 1977), 51.

9 40.5 per cent in June 1939; Andrew Thorpe, 'The Membership of the Communist Party of Great Britain, 1920–45,' *Historical Journal* 43, no. 3 (2000): 790, table 2.

10 ‘The People’s Convention,’ *Labour Monthly* (November 1940): 601–2.
11 ‘Memorandum: To the Ministry of Labour from the Musicians’ Union,’ n.d. [1940–1], KV 3/375.
12 The party’s work in the Musicians’ Union and the WMA was monitored intensively by Special Branch, which had an informant (Norman Himsworth) known as Ian MacKay, codename ‘Conquest,’ working undercover in these networks. The scrutiny was not unrelated to the fact that the headquarters of the WMA in Newport Street was also used by the party to collate information about Communists in the armed forces. The surveillance reports gathered run across five large files; KV 3/375–KV 3/380, with additional material in KV 2/382. Conquest Report, 9 October 1941; report from Inspector G. Holmes, 19 October 1942, KV 3/376.
13 This milieu is described by Kevin Morgan, ‘King Street Blues,’ in *A Weapon in the Struggle: The Cultural History of the Communist Party of Great Britain*, ed. Andy Croft (London: Pluto, 1998), 125–9.
14 Ibid., 129
15 Especially its militant Voluntary Organising Committee and Stewards’ Section; ibid., 128.
16 ‘General Introduction on WMA Fraction,’ n.d. [1942?], KV 3/377; just 88 members in June 1942 (‘Membership Report on WMA, June 1942), but 362 in September 1942 (Special Branch Report on WMA, 19 November 1943, KV 3/377).
17 ‘Further Detail about Anti-Communist Activity in the Musicians’ Union,’ 15 April 1941, KV 3/376; Morgan, ‘King Street Blues,’ 129.
18 Much of the above is drawn from this source, including Handbill, ‘Actors! Musicians! Technicians! The Policy of Munich Resulted in the War’ [meeting held 18 July 1940]; ‘Memorandum: To the Ministry of Labour from the Musicians’ Union,’ n.d. [1940–1], KV 3/375. See also Christopher Andrew, *The Defence of the Realm: The Authorized History of MI5* (London: Allen Lane, 2009), 273–4.
19 A party Cultural Committee was in place by the end of 1939, with Central Committee member Emile Burns as the leading figure. An Entertainment Industry Bureau, a London Arts Committee, and a Committee of Art and Entertainment Professions were added; Joanna Bullivant, *Alan Bush, Modern Music and the Cold War* (Cambridge: Cambridge University Press, 2017), 102–3. The Party’s Cultural Groups Committee was formed at the end of 1942; Andy Croft, ‘The Boys Round the Corner: The Story of Fore Publications,’ in Croft, *Weapon in the Struggle*, 149.
20 ‘To All Actors, Artists, Musicians, Film Technicians and Writers,’ n.d., CP ORG MISC 1/9; ‘Memorandum: To the Ministry of Labour from the Musicians’ Union,’ n.d. [1940–1], KV 3/375.
21 ENSA was formed shortly before the outbreak of war and principally focused on entertaining the forces; CEMA was formed in January 1940 and subsidized to

protect the arts; see Angus Calder, *The People's War: Britain 1939–1945* (1969; London: Pimlico, 2000), 372. Special Branch monitored Communist presence (reports, 19 February 1941, 9 October 1941, 9 January 1942); Martin Lawrence was convinced that his ENSA touring was blocked on account of his politics (9 October 1941). Special Branch reported on a Communist faction in ENSA (24 November 1942); the same report noted that Van Phillips was on the ENSA Advisory Council; Thomas Russell was secretary of the Musical Advisory Council of ENSA (9 January 1942); 'Strong efforts are being made by the CP to influence the policy of CEMA' (report, 5 December 1942), KV 3/376 and KV 3/377.

22 'To All Actors, Artists, Musicians, Film Technicians and Writers,' n.d., CP ORG MISC 1/9.

23 The William Morris Music Association was also concerned with overcoming the amateur professional divide in music making. Alan Bush was the chair before his Armed Forces call up. Activities included producing a bulletin and staging debates. The People's Convention had a Committee of Art and Entertainment Professions that issued publicity material and resolutions; its activities are archived in CP ORG MISC 1/4 and 1/9. Another forum for this cultural analysis was the short-lived YCL journal *Alive*, which published issues in February and March 1940; CP YCL 21/4.

24 Thomas Russell, *Philharmonic* (London: Hutchinson, 1942), 38–9.

25 Special Branch reports, 25 February 1943, 15 February 1944, 7 November 1944, KV 3/378; Thomas Russell, *Philharmonic Decade* (London: Hutchinson, 1944), 110, 91.

26 Concert on 18 July 1940 (Russell, *Philharmonic Decade*, 86); the defence of traditions of people's music making against antiquarians, Americans, and big business is the central plotline of Priestley's *Let the People Sing* (1939). The novel's title was reused as the ENSA theme tune.

27 Russell, *Philharmonic*, 67.

28 Priestley, Introduction to Russell, *Philharmonic*, 11; H.G. Sear, 'Music for all,' *Daily Worker*, 24 April 1945); Russell, *Philharmonic Decade*, 109.

29 Culture that promoted the party's actual line of insurrectionist opposition to the war was quickly dealt with by the authorities. See Ben Harker, 'Mediating the 1930s: Documentary and Politics in Theatre Union's *Last Edition*,' in *Get Real: Documentary Theatre Past and Present*, ed. Alison Forsyth and Chris Megson (Basingstoke, UK: Palgrave, 2009), 4–38; Harker, *Class Act: The Cultural and Political Life of Ewan MacColl* (London: Pluto, 2007), 58–60.

30 Jack Lindsay, *Life Rarely Tells* (Harmondsworth, UK: Penguin, 1982), 790.

31 Eric Hobsbawm, *Interesting Times: A Twentieth-Century Life* (London: Abacus, 2002), 164.

32 Calder, *People's War*, 349; John Callaghan, *Rajani Palme Dutt: A Study in British Stalinism* (London: Lawrence & Wishart, 1993), 209.

33 Arthur Cook, 'Message in Music,' *Daily Worker*, 12 August 1943.

34 Warner had recently contrasted the Spanish Civil, where there 'was room for one,' and this one, where there was 'none.' Claire Harman ed., *The Diaries of Sylvia Townsend Warner* (London: Virago, 1995), 106; Emily Lygo, 'Promoting Soviet Culture in Britain: The History of the Society for Cultural Relations between the Peoples of the British Commonwealth and the USSR, 1924–45,' *Modern Language Review* 108, no. 2 (2013): 594, 593.

35 Lygo, 'Promoting Soviet Culture in Britain,' 595; Hyde, *I Believed*, 119.

36 W.F. Drake, Mayor of Finsbury, was active in the campaign to build a memorial to Lenin in Holford Square, where the Bolshevik leader had lived in 1902–3; this was unveiled on 22 April 1942 but subsequently defaced by fascist sympathizers ('Perish Judah!'). Drake, circular letter, 14 April 1942, CP LON EVT 1; *Daily Worker*, 18 February 1943). The vandalism continued; the memorial was subsequently planned as a feature in the Holford Square Housing Scheme designed by Lubetkin and envisaged as 'Lenin's Court' (1946–54); the scheme was subsequently retitled Bevin's Court, after the notoriously anti-Communist foreign secretary Ernest Bevin. The empty shell that formerly contained the bust of Lenin's head was buried in the foundations as a gesture of protest by an incensed Lubetkin. John Allan, *Berthold Lubetkin: Architecture and the Tradition of Progress* (London: RIBA, 1992), 415–18. Soviet films were shown, notably, at the Tatler Theatre, Charing Cross Road. Randall Swingler, 'The Sense of History in Soviet Films,' *Labour Monthly* (February 1943): 62–3; film column, *Daily Worker*, 18 January 1943, 22 March 1943. *Mission to Moscow*, on general release in the summer of 1943, was praised for being 'genuinely objective' by fellow-travelling KC and MP D.N. Pritt; 'Mission to Moscow,' *Daily Worker*, 22 July 1943.

37 Claud Cockburn, *Crossing the Line* (London: MacGibbon and Kee, 1958), 103.

38 Stephen Parsons, 'Communism in the Professions: The Organisation of the British Communist Party among Professional Workers, 1933–56,' (PhD diss., University of Warwick, 1990), 217. Bush's music was banned in March 1941 on the grounds of his alignment with the People's Convention; the ban was lifted later that year. Nancy Bush, *Alan Bush: Music, Politics and Life* (London: Thames Publishing, 2000), 40. Bush had made a card index of the library of Soviet records at the SCR. His expertise was sought in September 1941. K.A. Wright to Bush (2 September 1941), Bush to Wright (17 September 1941). BBC WAC R Cont 1, Composer, Alan Bush File, 1A.

39 Joan Littlewood's MI5 File, KV2/2757; broadcast on the BBC Home Service, 20 December 1942, BBC WAC, Joan Littlewood, Artist File.

40 Montague [*sic*] Slater, 'Documentary,' *Poetry and the People* (July 1940); JB, 'Montagu Slater,' *World News*, 19 January 1957); Montagu to Hewlitt Johnson, 11 April 1944, CP IND MONT 7/7.

41 This is discussed in Ben Harker, '"The Trumpet of the Night": Interwar Communists on BBC Radio,' *History Workshop* 75 (Spring 2013): 81–101; Vladimir O. Pechatnov, 'The Rise and Fall of *Britansky Soyuznik*: A Case Study in Soviet Response to British

Propaganda in the mid 1940s,' *Historical Journal* 41, no. 1 (1998): 293–301; Dave Arthur, *Bert: The Life and Times of A.L. Lloyd* (London: Pluto, 2012), p140–43.

42 Extracted letter in Littlewood's MI5 File, KV 2/2757; Joan Littlewood, *Joan's Book* (London: Methuen, 1994), 124–5; Special Branch reports, 9 January 1942, 9 October 1942, KV 3/375.

43 Fred Westacott, *Shaking the Chains* (Chesterfield, UK: Joe Clark, 2002), 197.

44 Jack Lindsay, 'Dramatic Experiment: The Story of the ABCA Play Unit and Documentary Theatre [1946],' unpublished typescript, Lindsay Papers, National Library of Australia [hereafter NLA], File 284; Lindsay, *Life Rarely Tells*, 798–9.

45 Hobsbawm's line on current affairs soon aroused suspicion, and he was confined to teaching basic German. KV 2/3980; Hobsbawm, *Interesting Times*, 164–6; Klingender's work was sporadic, and a permanent appointment was blocked. Grant Pooke, *Francis Klingender 1907–1955: A Marxist Art Historian of Our Time* (London: Marx Memorial Library, 2008), 158; KV 2/2155.

46 Script and correspondence in File A5, Alec Baron Papers, Brotherton Library, Leeds University; I am grateful to Claire Warden for bringing this collection to my attention.

47 Script and Correspondence in Bristol Unity Players Collection, MRC, MSS 212/L/1/2.

48 Colin Chambers, *The Story of Unity Theatre* (London: Lawrence & Wishart, 1990), 201.

49 Lynda Morris and Robert Radford, *The AIA 1933–1953* (Oxford: Museum of Modern Art, 1983), 89, 3; the SCR exhibition of Soviet Life held at the Suffolk Galleries in September 1941 attracted 12,000 visitors. Lygo, 'Promoting Soviet Culture in Britain,' 594, 593; F.D. Klingender, ed, *Hogarth and English Caricature* (London: Pilot, 1944); Parsons, 'Communism in the Professions,' 215.

50 The WMA had just 88 members in June 1942 ('Membership Report on WMA, June 1942), but 362 in September 1942. Special Branch report, 19 November 1943, KV 3/377. Rena Moisenco, *Twenty Soviet Composers* (London: WMA, 1942); Alan Bush, *Music in the Soviet Union* (London: WMA, 1944); early Topic Records included balalaika renditions of Soviet songs, *The Topic Record* (Monthly Bulletin, July 1940); 'You will no doubt know of the tremendous amount of Russian music which is being performed in London by Communist and pseudo Communist organisations,' wrote Conquest in his report of 6 October 1941, KV 3/376; the WMA's *Popular Soviet Songs* sold 7,000 copies; the BBC and cinemas were supplied with Soviet music by the WMA. WMA circular, n.d. [1942], KV 3/377.

51 Bush framed the free, open-air Hyde Park performances of the WMA Choir in these terms, using the occasions 'to ventilate his views on the blessings of a Communist state,' according to Special Branch officers who kept a close eye on proceedings; Report on Evening in Hyde Park, 17 July 1941; Bush, *Music in the Soviet Union*, 26.

52 Lindsay, 'Dramatic Experiment,' 183; Jack Knife, 'Peoples' war – peoples' culture [*sic*],' *World News and Views*, 29 May 1943; Sheila Lynd, 'Arts are no longer the British Cinderella,' *Daily Worker*, 20 July 1945; Honor Arundel, 'Music and the workers,' *Daily Worker*, 9 April 1943; Beatrix Lehmann, 'Profits come first in London theatre,' *Daily Worker*, 24 July 1944; Ted Willis, 'Theatre,' *Daily Worker*, 31 July 1944.

53 'The Russians at the Old Vic,' *Daily Worker*, 8 June 1943); CEMA was 'splendidly successful … doing all it could to meet the demand for art, music and drama.' Lindsay, 'Dramatic Experiment,' 183; Knife, 'Peoples' war,' 176; Beatrix Lehmann, 'Learning to be an actor,' *Daily Worker*, 10 June 1943; Ted Willis, 'Theatre,' *Daily Worker*, 31 July 1944.

54 Calder, *People's War*, 373. Ross McKibbin is justly sceptical about whether the assumptions of the BBC and CEMA that, 'in the right circumstances, the democratic public could be brought to an understanding of "serious" music' were fulfilled; Ross McKibbin, *Classes and Cultures in England 1918–1951* (Oxford: Oxford University Press, 1998), 387.

55 Malcolm MacEwen, *The Greening of a Red* (London: Pluto, 1991), 94.

56 Musicians Group circular, 21 March 1942. Seasoned Communists were taken aback by the popularity of meetings and the willingness of those who attended to join and donate. 'We are still slow in estimating the interest now awakening on all sides in the policy and work of the party. We fail to grasp the extraordinarily favourable conditions for recruiting at this time,' KV 3/377; handbill in CP LOND EVENT 1/3.

57 Thorpe, 'Membership,' 781.

58 Francis Klingender, *Russia: Britain's Ally 1812–1942* (London: Harrap,1942). Faber commissioned Andre van Gyseghem to write *Theatre in Soviet Russia*, reviewed in the *Daily Worker*, 13 October 1943; Herbert Marshall and Ivor Montagu edited *Soviet Short Stories 1942–3*, *Daily Worker*, 15 December 1943.

59 McKibbin, *Classes and Cultures*, 503.

60 Christopher Hilliard, *To Exercise Our Talents: The Democratization of Writing in Britain* (Cambridge, MA: Harvard University Press, 2006), 166; Croft, 'Boys Round the Corner,' 148.

61 Hilliard, *To Exercise*, 171.

62 Lewis Young, 'The Communist Party of Great Britain, the *Daily Worker*, and the Battle to Lift the Ban, 1941–42.' *Socialist History* 53 (Summer 2018): 32–47.

63 'How to win the war,' *Daily Worker*, 7 September 1942); the editorial board included Sean O'Casey, Haldane, the Dean of Canterbury, Arthur Horner, and Beatrix Lehmann; *Daily Worker*, 18 August 1943).

64 Kevin Morgan, 'The Communist Party and the *Daily Worker* 1930–1956,' in *Opening the Books: Essays on the Social and Cultural History of the British Communist Party*, ed. Geoff Andrews, Nina Fishman, and Kevin Morgan (London: Pluto,1995), 151.

65 Ibid. The party's Central Books reported that twenty of its bestselling titles in 1943 were Soviet related; Allen Hutt, 'Books bought in 1943,' *Daily Worker*, 22 December 1943. Coverage of such works includes reviews of Faber's *Russian Stories* and Cape's *Soviet Anthology* (*Daily Worker*, 7 April 1943): *The New Soviet Theatre* (*Daily Worker*, 21 April 1943), *Pictorial History of Russia from Rurik to Stalin* (*Daily Worker*, 8 September 1943), *Russian Music* (*Daily Worker*, 23 September 1943), *Our Soviet Ally* (*Daily Worker*, 6 October 1943), *The Crocodile Album of Soviet Humour* (*Daily Worker*, 20 October 1943), *Eight Soviet Composers* (*Daily Worker*, 4 November 1943), and Vassili Grossman's novel *The People Immortal* (*Daily Worker*, 8 December 1943).

66 Hilliard, *To Exercise*, 166.

67 Morgan, *Against Fascism and War*, 274–5.

68 *Our Time* was published by 'Newport Publications' (a subsidiary of Fore Publications), initiated and financed by Swingler, and always conceived, at some level, as a second phase of *Left Review*. It took over the paper ration of *Poetry and the People*, which Swingler had attempted unsuccessfully to broaden by involving former Popular Front allies Day Lewis and Wintringham. Randall Swingler, 'The English Twilight,' *Our Time* (April 1941): 8.

69 The publication mattered more for its lucrative sales than for the ideological line, which was kept strategically broad after Swingler bought the journal from the wayward Communist Philip O' Connor in late 1941. Hilliard, *To Exercise*, 169, 164; Croft, 'Boys Round the Corner,' 148–9; Andy Croft, *Comrade Heart: A Life of Randall Swingler* (Manchester: Manchester University Press, 2003), 122–4.

70 Swingler, 'English Twilight,' 8; Croft, *Comrade Heart*, 122–4.

71 The core theoretical argument of the Popular Front cultural formation was that labour was the 'basis of culture' and that modern culture, produced by a privileged rentier class 'which merely owns, and does not operate the means of production,' was by turns etiolated and inward (high culture) or devitalized and passivity-inducing (low culture). Edgell Rickword, 'Culture, Progress, and English Tradition,' in *The Mind in Chains: Socialism and the Cultural Revolution*, ed. Cecil Day Lewis (London: Muller, 1937), 245, 248.

72 Honor Arundel, 'Music and the Workers,' *Daily Worker*, 9 April 1943); not only an 'enlargement of demand,' but working-class cultural participation and production that brought with it what Lindsay called the 'continual penetration from below into the upper levels of activity'; Jack Lindsay, 'A Fuller Life,' *World News and Views*, 9 December 1944, 400.

73 The struggles between Burns and other hardliners and Swingler's circle over the purpose and identity of *Our Time* are recounted in Croft, 'Boys Round the Corner,' 149–50.

74 Quintin Hoare and Geoffrey Nowell-Smith, eds. and trans., *Selections from the Prison Notebooks of Antonio Gramsci* (London: Lawrence & Wishart, 1971), 161.

75 Donald Sassoon, *One Hundred Years of Socialism: The West European Left in the Twentieth Century* (1996; London: I.B. Tauris, 2014), 86.
76 Marx House Correspondence Course, 'The Soviet Union, Socialism and War,' n.d. [late 1941–early 1942], CP CENT ED 1/6.
77 The core material is archived in CP ORG MISC 1/3.
78 *Parliament of Women: Report on the First Session of London's Women's Parliament*; the quotation is from Beatrix Lehmann's Introductory Address, 4. CP ORG MISC 1/3.
79 *West Riding Women's Parliament Report on First Session, Bradford, September 1942*. CP ORG MISC 1/3; Noreen Branson, *History of the Communist Party of Great Britain, 1941–51* (London: Lawrence & Wishart, 1997), 47.
80 *West Riding Women's Parliament*, 13.
81 Branson, *History of the Communist Party of Great Britain, 1941–51*, 46; two pamphlets, 'Health and Housing Report' and 'You Can Get a Wartime Nursery in Your District'; CP ORG MISC 1/3. This line of the prefigurative modern factory was developed in the wartime party journal *Home Front*, which first appeared in March 1942. Five women were elected onto the CP's Executive Committee in August 1943, and a National Women's Advisory Council was established, signalling a small but significant shift in the party's attention to gender matters. Branson, *History of the Communist Party of Great Britain, 1941–51*, 48.
82 The *Daily Mail* praised speeches that 'in brevity and sincerity were models for any politician,' the Ministry of Information filmed the final session. Branson, *History of the Communist Party of Great Britain, 1941–51*, 47; *Parliament of Women*, 2.
83 In 1936 car manufacturers were brought into the field of aircraft production by the 'shadow factory' scheme; by 1938 over a quarter of the nation's budget was allocated to defence. Calder, *People's War*, 31.
84 The idea of the factory cell as 'the basic unit of the party' had been integral to Communist strategy since Bolshevization, but historically its factory presence had been patchy. It was reaffirmed in documents such as *The Communist Party and the National Front: Syllabus for Four School Sessions* (London: CP, 1942, 9). In 1925 only around ten per cent of the overwhelmingly proletarian membership was in factory groups, a percentage which decreased after the General Strike and did not improve until the rearmament drive of the late 1930s. Hinton, 'Coventry Communism,' 93.
85 Hinton, 'Coventry Communism,' 93, 95.
86 Calder, *People's War*, 397–8.
87 Advertisement in Coventry newspaper, cited in Hinton, 'Coventry Communism,' 99; the proportion of women in the party increased to almost a third. Parsons, 'Communism in the Professions,' 207; Mary Ackroyd, 'A New Outlook,' *Home Front* (May 1943): 6–7.
88 Jack Lindsay, *Hullo Stranger* (London: Andrew Dakers, 1945), 104. Narrated from the perspective of a politically awakening working-class young woman engineer,

it subtly criticizes blinkered and self-righteous Communist factory cadres for off-putting jargon ('What's the use of being right if you can't make others see it?') and aloofness ('You'd be more convincing if you showed a bit more of that world in your own lives' (137, 161).

89 John Callaghan, *Cold War, Crisis and Conflict, The CPGB 1951–68* (London: Lawrence & Wishart, 2003, 228.

90 Mick Jenkins, 'Prelude to Better Days,' unpublished autobiography, WCML; Jenkins worked at Faireys Aviation Works in Heaton Chapel, Stockport; combined membership of this factory and the adjacent Errwood Park Works increased from 140 in October 1942 to 280 by 1944 (228).

91 Harry Poole, 'Factory Gate School,' article circulated by CP Central Education Department, 18 June 1943, CP CENT ED 2/6.

92 Parsons, 'Communism in the Professions,' 208.

93 James Hinton, 'The Communist Party, Production and Britain's Post-War Settlement,' in Andrews, Fishman and Morgan, *Opening the Books*, 165–6. Though retrospectively it seems that, as Hinton argues, 'the class struggle' had become 'a war of position within the emerging structures of "state capitalism," designed to open up practices of democratic participation through which working people could gain the awareness, confidence and ambition to make the transition to socialism,' where the CP is concerned 'designed' implies a consciously articulated strategy that was at best implicit (163).

94 Pollitt, *How to Win*, 39–40.

95 Harry Pollitt, 'The Way to Victory,' *Labour Monthly* (October 1941): 418.

96 Hinton, 'Coventry Communism,' 107; The Economics Committee was formed in 1943. Minutes of the early meetings are archived in CP CENT ECON 6/15, and focus on full employment and the writing of documents, including 'Planning for Plenty,' which informed *Britain for the People*.

97 *Guiding Lines on Questions of Post-war Reconstruction: Central Committee Memorandum* (December 1942).

98 It became familiar to nineteen out of twenty Britons, almost all of whom thought its proposals for social security should be implemented. Calder, *People's War*, 528; Juliet Gardiner, *Wartime Britain 1939–1945* (London: Review, 2004), 582. Wintringham attacked the CP in 'Marxism and Acrobatics,' *New Statesman and Nation*, 5 July 1941; Dutt clipped and filed the article (Dutt Papers, BL, CUP 1262/K6); for the CP's response to the Commonwealth, see Kevin Morgan, 'Away from the Party and into "the Party,"' *Socialist History 37* (2010): 80, n48.

99 *Guiding Lines.*

100 William Rust, 'A job has been done,' *Daily Worker*, 7 September 1943.

101 Published policy statements included: *A National Health Service*; *Housing*; *Transport for the People*; *The Beveridge Report*; *and British Agriculture*; many of these were accompanied by press statements (CP CENT STAT 1/3); a list of the published titles appears on the back of *How to Win the Peace* (1944).

102 Croft, 'Boys Round the Corner,' 149; Special Branch report on the Workers' Music Association, 19 November 1943, National Archives, KV 3/377.

103 Stalin's speech of 6 November 1942, which emphasized matters of national self-determination, was noted in *Guiding Lines*; for 'The Internationale,' see Callaghan, *Rajani Palme Dutt*, 209.

104 Rajani Palme Dutt, 'Communism,' *Encyclopaedia Britannia*, 12th ed. (1922), Dutt Papers, BL CUP 1262/K1.

105 The question of the assimilation of new members was recurrent in the discussion in *World News and Views*.

106 The shadowy-sounding 'secretariat' was replaced by named secretarial posts, the Political Bureau became the Political Committee and the Central Committee the Executive Committee. The 'Great' was also dropped from Great Britain. MacEwen, *Greening of a Red*, 97–8; Branson, *History of the Communist Party of Great Britain, 1941–51*, 24.

107 'The Communist Party and the Comintern' circular of 26 May 1943 noted that 'The Communist Parties now develop as independent national parties of the working class within each country ... not tied to any formal international obligations'; Dutt Papers, BL, CP 1262/K3. The metaphor of roads to and towards socialism loomed large, for instance, in the opening section of Harry Pollitt's *Answers to Questions* (London: CPGB, n.d. [1945]).

108 Pollitt, *How to Win*, 57.

109 Ibid., 16; Pollitt, *Answers to Questions*, 40.

110 Pollitt, *Looking Ahead* (London: CPGB, 1947), 42.

111 Pollitt, *How to Win*, 32–6.

112 Ibid., 32.

113 Ibid., 34.

114 Hoare and Nowell-Smith, *Selections from the Prison Notebooks*, 108; Anne Showstack Sassoon, *Gramsci's Politics* (London: Croom Helm, 1980), 204–18.

115 Pollitt, *Answers to Questions*, 39.

116 Sassoon, *One Hundred Years of Socialism*, 99.

117 Ibid., 102.

118 'Main Points from R.P. Dutt's Statement, 16 June 1944, Britain for the people' (published by the CP, 17 June 1944); a subsequent statement clarified that 'the proposals did not represent the ultimate aim of the CP, which is socialism, but a broad, common programme'; Dutt Papers, BL, CUP 1262/3; 'For the Information of the Executive Committee,' 13 March 1945, CP CENT EC 1/31.

119 Westacott, *Shaking the Chains*, 203.

120 Kenneth Newton, *The Sociology of British Communism* (London: Allen Lane, 1969), 166, appendix 4, General Election Table.

121 Unusually critical submissions from branches appeared in *Communist Party 18th Congress, November 1945: Resolutions and Agenda* (London: CPGB, 1945) and in the weekly *World News and Views* in October and November; some of these

are reprinted in John Callaghan and Ben Harker, eds., *British Communism: A Documentary History* (Manchester: Manchester University Press, 2011), 160–2. See also Parker, *Kick Inside*, 15–32.

122 Branson, *History of the Communist Party of Great Britain, 1941–51*, 110–11; Morgan, 'Away from the Party,' 37–8; Parker, *Kick Inside*, 20–1; Joan Ford, 'Redundancy in the Factory,' *Home Front* (May 1944): 8. There were over 1,500 Communists in the factory stronghold of Coventry in 1942, 520 in the summer of 1945 and only around 250 by 1946. Hinton, 'Coventry Communism,' 106; James Hinton, 'Self-help and Socialism: The Squatters' Movement of 1946,' *History Workshop Journal* 25, no. 1 (1988), 103.

123 Westacott, *Shaking the Chains*, 247.

124 *For Soviet Britain: The Programme of the Communist Party adopted at the XIII Congress, February 2nd 1935* (London: CPGB, 1935), 2.

125 Ibid., 21–4.

126 'Socialism,' Britain for the People Policy Leaflet 8 (London: CPGB, 1944). The quotation is from Pollitt's address to the Seventeenth Congress in October 1944.

127 Dutt's Report to the Sixteenth Congress, 1943, *Unity and Victory: Report of the 16th Congress of the Communist Party, 1943* (London: CPB, 1943), 31.

128 Stephen Gundle, *Between Moscow and Hollywood: The Italian Communists and the Challenge of Mass Culture, 1943–1991* (Durham, NC: Duke University Press, 2000), 13.

129 79 out of 754 (Branson, *History of the Communist Party of Great Britain, 1941–51*, 84); 10 per cent were professional and technical workers and a further 7 per cent clerical and administrative; Newton, *Sociology*, appendix 2, 162–6; Pollitt, *How to Win*, 41.

130 J.B.S. Haldane, *Why Professional Workers Should be Communists* (London: CPB, 1945).

131 The colour leaflet 'Why Students Should Be Communists' [1946] was central to a new recruitment drive.

132 Harry Pollitt, *Professional Workers* (London: CPB, March 1946); this paragraph draws on Stephen R. Parsons' excellent thesis, 'Communism in the Professions: The Organisation of the British Communist Party among Professional Workers, 1933–56 (PhD diss., University of Warwick, 1990), 237.

133 'I never knew a cultural comrade who had the nerve to give a union comrade advice,' recalled national Industrial Policy Committee member Bob Darke; on the committee, 'professional workers' were 'more or less a decoration'; Bob Darke, *The Communist Technique in Britain* (London: Penguin, 1952), 60.

134 Jim Fyrth to Roger Fieldhouse, cited in Fieldhouse, *Adult Education and the Cold War: Liberal Values under Siege, 1946–51* (Leeds: Leeds Studies in Adult and Continuing Education, 1985), 11.

135 'The fact that the Communists' first loyalty may be to Moscow,' stated a secret report on Bernal, 'cannot constitute an argument in the pleasant circumstances

[of Anglo-Soviet alliance] for not employing him. It might perhaps constitute an argument for locking up Communists in the event of there being a patched up peace'; KV 2/181, item 73a.

136 Andrew Brown, *J.D Bernal: The Sage of Science* (Oxford: Oxford University Press, 2005), 228–30.

137 Gary Werskey, *The Visible College: A Collective Biography of British Scientists and Socialists of the 1930s* (London: Allen Lane, 1978), 266.

138 As Werskey spells out, this assessment was given in the official history; see J. Crowther and R. Whiddington, *Science at War* (London, 1947), 119–20. Crowther was the *Guardian*'s science correspondent and close to the CP.

139 The listening figure is from Calder, *People's War*; the circulation of the *Listener* is from Hennessy, *Never Again*, 313. For Bernal on the Brains' Trust, see Brown, *J.D. Bernal*, 205–6, and for his relationship with Connolly, see 171–2. Bernal was a regular BBC contributor from 1940, and made occasional broadcasts during the war. He was an adviser and contributor for the flagship post-war conspectus of the intellectual and cultural scene, *The Challenge of Our Time*; Bernal's talk was transmitted on 31 March 1946; BBC Written Archives, Caversham, J.D.Bernal, R Cont 1 Talks 1940–61. His talks published in the *Listener* include 'Science and Human Affairs' (1 February 1945) and 'The Social Responsibility of Science' (4 April 1946).

140 J.D. Bernal, 'Belief and Action,' first published in the first issue of CP's relaunched intellectual journal, *Modern Quarterly*, at the end of 1945. Reprinted in J.D. Bernal, *The Freedom of Necessity* (London: Routledge and Kegan Paul, 1949), quotations from this version, 82, 77.

141 Bernal, 'Freedom of Necessity,' first published in Connolly's *Horizon* in 1942, and republished in *Freedom of Necessity*, 5.

142 Central ideas in both essays, and also to 'The Challenge of Our Time' (1946) in *Freedom of Necessity*, 85–90.

143 Werskey, *Visible College*, 268.

144 Brown, *J.D. Bernal*, especially 274–97; Werskey, *Visible College*, 270, 276.

145 Parsons, 'Communism in the Professions,' 239, 242.

146 For Haldane's trajectory, see Werskey, *Visible College*, 158–61.

147 J.D. Bernal, 'International Scientific Organisation,' *Pilot Papers* (July 1946), reprinted in *Freedom of Necessity*, 234–53, 250; Werskey, *Visible College*, 276.

148 Brown, *J.D. Bernal*, 288.

149 In 1949 Bernal claimed with some justification that 'many of the suggestions' he had made in his reports, essays, and broadcasts had been accepted (*Freedom of Necessity*, 214). Three key essays were 'Organised Research for Peace' (1945), 'Information Service as an Essential in the Progress of Science' (1945), and 'International Scientific Organization' (1946). Reprinted in *Freedom of Necessity*, 215–53.

150 The key essay here is 'British Industry and Science' published in *New Statesman and Nation*, 2 June 1945 and 16 June 1945; reprinted in *Freedom of Necessity*, 262–72.

151 Werskey, *Visible College*, 275.

152 Ibid., 276.

153 Addison, *Now the War Is Over*, 56.

154 Paul Burnham, 'The Squatters of 1946,' *Socialist History* 25 (2004): 21.

155 Cited in Hennessy, *Never Again*, 163.

156 CP CENT SEC 1/5, Papers of the Building Bureau, 'Memo on the Barlow, Scott and Uthwatt Reports' (1943).

157 Nicklaus Thomas-Symonds, *Nye: The Political Life of Aneurin Bevan* (London: I.B. Tauris, 2015), 114; Addison, *Now the War Is Over*, 56; 'Memo on the Barlow, Scott and Uthwatt Reports.'

158 Anon ['A Group of Economists, Scientists and Technicians'], *Britain Without Capitalists: A Study of What Industry in Soviet Britain Could Achieve* (London: Lawrence & Wishart, 1936), 181.

159 Brown, *J.D. Bernal*; Werskey, *Visible College*, 276; Bernal's key essay is 'Science in Architecture,' based on a paper read at the Royal Institute of British Architects (12 February 1946) and subsequently published in *Journal of R.I.B.A* (March 1946); reprinted in Bernal, *Freedom of Necessity*, 201–13.

160 Positions familiar from 1930s essays including 'Architecture and Science' (1937) and restated in broadcasts, including his contribution to 'The Challenge of Our Time' (BBC Home Service, 31 March 1946; published in the *Listener*, 4 April 1946, as 'The Social Responsibility of Science'), 'Should we call a halt to science? A discussion between C.E.M. Joad and J.D. Bernal' (BBC Home Service, published in the *Listener*, 8 March 1945, 'Science and Human Affairs' (BBC Pacific Service, published in the *Listener*, 1 February 1945). Brown also cites 'Science in Building' (BBC Home Service, 1946), 'The Housewife' (1945), and an article, 'The Organization of Building,' *Builder* 169: 400–2. Brown, *J.D. Bernal*, 286, 589, n36–8.

161 Felton's obituary in the *Times*, 5 March 1970; her BBC broadcasting career began during the war when she worked in forces' education and contributed regularly to 'Your Questions Answered' on Forces' Radio on political and economic questions. She broadcast regularly on housing in 1946 (Monica Felton, BBC Written Archives File); her 'Where do you live?' for instance, was broadcast on the Home Service and published in the *Listener*, 24 January 1946.

162 John Allan, *Berthold Lubetkin: Architecture and the Tradition of Progress* (London: RIBA, 1992), 452.

163 Ibid., 405; the speech Lubetkin gave at the ceremony for laying the foundation stone – attended by Bevan – is quoted on 385; for Lubetkin's thoughts on New Towns, see 450–2.

164 Ibid., 375ff; another leftist partnership with CP leanings, the Architects' Co-operative Partnership developed links with Hertfordshire County Council, which commissioned from it the building of schools. Parsons, 'Communism in the Professions,' 445.

165 Addison, *Now the War Is Over*, 74–5, Parsons, 'Communism in the Professions,' 443, 447; Owen Hatherley, 'Strange, Angry Objects,' *London Review of Books*, 17 November 2016, 11–17.

166 Parsons, 'Communism in the Professions,' 435–6.

167 Ling and Lubetkin actively communicated Soviet developments to British audiences through journals and the events of the newly formed Architecture and Planning Group of the SCR; ibid., 447–50.

168 Ibid., 446, 449.

169 A recurrent motif in Bernal's writing; see, for instance, *Freedom of Necessity*, 204, 191, 125.

170 Morgan, 'Communist Party and the *Daily Worker*,' 151

171 CP CENT SEC 1/5, Building Bureau documents 'Labour Party Policy on Housing and Planning after the War' (July 1943); 'Memo on the Barlow, Scott and Uthwatt Reports (1943).

172 Hennessy, *Never Again*, 171; *Memorandum on Housing* (London: CPGB, 1944); *Britain for the People: Proposals for Post-war Policy* (London: CPB, 1944), 10.

173 Addison, *Now the War Is Over*, 56; Parsons, Communism in the Professions,' 439; Building Bureau documents 'Labour Party Policy on Housing and Planning after the War' (July 1943); 'Memo on the Barlow, Scott and Uthwatt Reports (1943).

174 Parsons, 'Communism in the Professions,' 441.

175 Brown, *J.D. Bernal*, 286.

176 Bernal, 'Science in Architecture,' 212. The party reassured building workers anxious about redundancy that they would be upskilled by working with prefabrication; party speakers' notes in this period advocated the mass building of permanent prefabs from the abundant stocks of aluminum left over from the war. CP, 'Information for speakers,' 22 February 1945, 8 March 1945, 25 July 1945, CP CENT SPN 1/3.

177 Brown, *J.D. Bernal*, 287; Addison, *Now the War Is Over*, 57.

178 Hinton, 'Self-help and Socialism,' 103.

179 Burnham, 'Squatters of 1946,' 20–46.

180 Hinton, 'Self-help and Socialism,' 110, 119; Branson, *History of the Communist Party of Great Britain, 1941–51*, 120–1.

181 *Observer*, 25 September 1946; CP, 'Information for speakers,' 25 September 1946, CP CENT SN 1/5.

182 Hinton, 'Self-help and Socialism,' 116.

183 CP, 'Information for speakers,' 25 September 1946, CP CENT SN 1/5.

184 Jack Lindsay, whose fictional reworking of the squatters campaign in his later novel *Betrayed Spring* (1953), would draw different conclusions from the party's

own, and conspicuously insist that 'defeat was no defeat' and that the collectivism and shared cultural life engendered in the squatting of a Bloomsbury hotel was an intimation of a better future. Lindsay, *Betrayed Spring* (London: Bodley Head, 1953), 14.

185 As in the penultimate paragraph of Pollitt, *Looking Ahead*, 128.

186 This logic had been very pronounced in the inter-war period, when teachers had been called 'educational workers' and 'industrial' trade union work prioritized. In the late 1920s and early 1930s, Communist teachers had been conspicuously absent from debates on the 'Hadow Report' (1926), which had advocated a secondary education for all and the raising of the school leaving age. They had remained strategically silent during the Popular Front years, when contentious issues were avoided in the name of building antifascist unity across the profession.

187 Addison, *Now the War Is Over*, 142–3; only a tiny percentage of working-class children were among the 11 per cent of children nationally who entered the grammar sector dominated by fee-paying, middle-class children.

188 Matthew Kavanagh, 'Against Fascism, War and Economies: The Communist Party of Great Britain's Schoolteachers during the Popular Front, 1935–39,' *History of Education* 43, no. 2 (2014): 217.

189 This replaced the Teachers Bureau, established during the war; quoted in G.C.T. Giles, *The New School Tie* (London: Pluto, 1946), 44; Steve Parsons, 'British Communist Party School Teachers in the 1940s and 1950s,' *Science & Society* 61 no. 1 (1997): 52.

190 The CEA was formed by the TUC, the Co-operative Education Committee, the NUT, and the WEA to lobby for a new education bill. It was supported by the party's *Britain's Schools: A Memorandum Issued by the Communist Party of Great Britain* (1942) and the *Daily Worker*, 23 November 1942. See Matthew Kavanagh, 'British Communism and the Politics of Education, 1926–1968' (PhD diss., University of Manchester, 2015), 122–3.

191 In 1944 Pearl Tibbles was London president of the NUWT and Nan MacMillan was on its Central Council; in the NUT, Dave Capper was London president and Ben Ainley was on the General Committee in Manchester. Kavanagh, 'British Communism,' 132–3.

192 Ibid., 140; Giles, *New School Tie*, vii.

193 Nan MacMillan was also invited by the London chief education officer to address a conference of London head teachers in December 1944; Parsons, 'Communist Party School Teachers,' 55.

194 As spelled out in *Britain's Schools* (1942), a party memorandum produced late in 1942 in response to an invitation for proposals issued by the Board of Education.

195 Kavanagh, 'British Communism,' 124–8.

196 Addison, *Now the War Is Over*, 148; McKibbin, *Classes and Cultures*, 233.

197 McKibbin maps the earlier emergence of the consensus for change, which included the Assistant Masters' Association, the *Times Educational Supplement*, the National Association of Labour Teachers, the Labour Party, and the TUC. By 1947 the NUT and the *Times Educational Supplement* had declined to support multilaterals; McKibbin, *Classes and Cultures*, 231–4.

198 The National Association of Labour Teachers also advocated the one-model approach, but proposed that the curriculum be differentiated according to children's ability from age thirteen; Kavanagh, 'British Communism,' 129.

199 National Educational Advisory Committee, *The Multilateral (or Common) School; A Memorandum issued by the Educational Advisory Committee of the Communist Party, October 1944* (London: CPGB, 1944).

200 'Syllabus on Youth,' CP CENT YOUTH 1/2; Joan Whittenbury, *A New Chance in Life for the Children: The Fight for the Carrying Through of the 1944 Education Act in Lancashire and Cheshire* (CPB: Manchester, 1946). Thanks to Matthew Kavanagh for bringing this publication to my attention.

201 Addison, *Now the War Is Over*, 151–3; Parsons, 'British Communist Party School Teachers,' 51–2.

202 Addison, *Now the War Is Over*, 153; Parsons quotes letters from individual Communists written to G.C.T. Giles in 1944 seeking advice about entering the profession ('British Communist Party Schoolteachers,' 52); Ruth Frow, who would go on to co-found the Working-Class Movement Library in Salford, was among the intake.

203 '2000 Teachers in the Communist Party,' *Times*, 29 November 1949; Kavanagh, 'British Communism,' 156; Parsons, 'Communist Party School Teachers,' 47.

204 Ruth Frow to Eddie Frow, 12 February 1954, Frow Papers, WCML. I am grateful to Kevin Morgan for bringing these letters to my attention.

205 Joan Thompson, letter, *World News and Views*, 10 June 1944; reply from Pearl Tibbles, 17 June 1944; cited in Kavanagh, 'British Communism,' 132–3.

206 Brian Simon, *A Life in Education* (London: Lawrence & Wishart, 1998), 54.

207 Giles, *New School Tie*, 73, 77.

208 Kavanagh, 'British Communism,' 149–56. The key document, unearthed by Kavanagh, is an unpublished manuscript, probably written by Brian Simon, entitled 'The Content of Education' and dated January 1947. Quotation from 9, Brian Simon papers, DC SIM 4/6/39; Simon's wife, Joan Simon, was also in the CP, and contributed regularly to the *Times Educational Supplement*, as well as staking out similar positions in the party press. Joan Simon, 'Educational Theory and Practice,' *Modern Quarterly* (Autumn 1948): 35–52; Joan Simon, 'Educational Policies and Programmes,' *Modern Quarterly* (Spring 1949): 154–69.

209 Giles, *New School Tie*, 76, 66.

210 Addressing a conference of the recently formed Communist Party Historians' Group in late September 1946, CP teacher Max Morris shared a detailed report explaining that comprehensive education potentially put 'all syllabuses in the

melting pot,' and identified the types of alternative textbooks that might be written: 'the fault of the existing books,' he noted, 'is that they are cluttered up with useless facts and don't *explain* anything, least of all change.' Another CP teacher, Joan Browne, provided an equivalent outline of new openings in primary education, noting 'considerable freedom in the junior forms to experiment'; Morris, 'Note on School-Text Books,' Lindsay Papers, NLA, Folder 420.

211 Giles showed Teheran-spirited nimbleness in making the case, arguing that both the United States and the USSR – both 'great democratic and industrial communities' – provided models for non-selective comprehensive schools conceived in the image of technological modernity, and that Britain should do the same; Giles, *New School Tie*, 77, 96–7. Simon participated in debates and conferences about alternative educational content through the New Education Fellowship; Giles, *New School Tie*, 96–7; Kavanagh, 'British Communism,' 144.

212 G.C.T. Giles, 'Secondary Education for All,' *Times Educational Supplement*, 26 May 1945; Giles appeared as an expert in 'Parents in the Witness Box,' a Home Service broadcast featured in the *Radio Times*, 25 November 1946, and *Daily Worker*, 26 November 1946. One of the 'parents' also interviewed was the CP EC member and industrial organizer, Peter Kerrigan. Giles's MI5 File, KV 2/17851/1; Charles Madge, Untitled Autobiography, SXMS 71/1/3/1, Madge Papers, Box 2.1, University of Sussex Archives (155, 161).

213 Addison, *Now the War Is Over*, 150

214 The journal's circulation reached 3,000 by the early 1950s; Parsons, 'Communism in the Professions,' 500.

215 Conservative peer Lord Vansittart's red-baiting rhetoric in 1949 and 1950, the virtual elimination of communists from the NUT executive (1949–50), the formation of a Conservative and Unionist Teachers' Association (1948), and the notorious Middlesex 'ban,' which sought to exclude Communists and their associates from the profession (1950–8). See Steve Parsons, 'British "McCarthyism" and the Intellectuals,' in *Labour's Promised Land? Culture and Society in Labour Britain, 1945–51*, ed. Jim Fyrth (London: Lawrence & Wishart, 1995), 231–3.

216 McKibbin, *Classes and Cultures*, 258–9. Bernal estimated that Britain needed a sevenfold increase in science graduates; cited in Giles, *New School Tie*, 97.

217 The universities presented 'a less favourable class composition' than adult education according to one post-war report on students; 'Report on Students,' n.d. [1946?], CP CENT YOUTH 1/1.

218 Peter Kerrigan, Organisation Department Report, 23 October 1945, CP CENT YOUTH 1/1.

219 'Report on Students.'

220 Ibid.

221 Handbill, 'Why Students Should Be Communists' (1946), CP CENT YOUTH 2/12.

222 'Report on Students'; Handbill, 'Why Students Should Be Communists' (1946); 'The Situation in Universities,' n.d. [1949], CP CENT YOUTH 1/3.

223 The group's meeting on 6 January 1945 was attended by just fourteen, including the more peripheral figures Norman Wilson at Liverpool and Beryl Smalley at St Hilda's; Levy's MI5 File, KV 2/3211/2; Hobsbawm, *Interesting Times*, 177, 182.

224 John Saville, *Memoirs from the Left* (London: Merlin 2003), 78; Grant Pooke, *Francis Klingender, 1907–1955: A Marxist Art Historian of Our Time* (London: Marx Memorial Library, 2008), 169–70; Parsons, 'Communism in the Professions,' 233.

225 Announced in the *Daily Worker*, 11 May 1945; titles included Gordon Childe's *History* and Pascal's *The Growth of Modern Germany*; see Hobsbawm, 'The Historians' Group of the Communist Party,' in *Rebels and their Causes: Essays in Honour of A.L. Morton*, ed. Maurice Cornforth (London: Lawrence & Wishart, 1978), 33, 46n10.

226 George Owen was the Group's chair; Owen to Allen Hutt, 19 December 1946; Owen, circular to members, n.d. [1946]; David Holbrook to Hutt, 28 October 1946), CP IND HUTT 1/3.

227 Cited in Paul Addison, *The Road to 1945: British Politics and the Second World War* (1975; London: Pimlico, 1994), 148.

228 Maurice Petherick, MP for Penryn and Falmouth, to Churchill's parliamentary private secretary, cited in Addison, *Now the War Is Over*, 13.

229 Roger Fieldhouse, 'Adults Learning for Leisure, Recreation and Democracy,' in Fyrth, *Labour's Promised Land?*, 267–9.

230 'Report of Education to Political Committee, August 1945,' CP CENT ED 2/6.

231 The proposed publication of the document never occurred, and the traditionally minded Leninist educational organizer Douglas Garman took a distinctly backseat role, preferring to concentrate on running party schools for demobilized cadres; Garman, circular to District Secretaries and Propaganda departments, 6 December 1945; 'Education Report, 1946'; 'Communist Party Education Plan, January–June 1946,' CP CENT ED 2/6. Overwork might well have been a factor in his lack of engagement; CP CENT ED 2/6; Garman Papers, University of Nottingham, DG3. Pollitt resisted the proposed diminution of Marx House, fearing that such scaling back would play into the hands of those in the Labour Party who advocated the liquidation of the CP; Harry Pollitt, 'Comments on Report of Education Commission,' 26 August 1945.

232 Little effort seems to have been made with the Co-op, and the mutual hostilities between the CP and the NCLC were evidently difficult to overcome, although some limited collaboration occurred in London, according to 'Education Report, 1946,' CP CENT ED 2/6.

233 Hodgkin had gone from Balliol to the British Civil Service in Palestine before turning to Communism, school teaching, and adult education, working first for the Friends Service Council teaching unemployed miners in Cumberland, then

becoming a staff tutor for the Oxford Extra Mural Studies Delegacy, based in North Staffordshire. A former *Left Review* contributor, he had joined the CP in 1938. See Christopher Allen and R.W. Johnson, eds., *African Perspective: Papers in the History, Politics and Economics of Africa Presented to Thomas Hodgkin* (Cambridge: Cambridge University Press, 1970), xi; Michael Woolfers, *Thomas Hodgkin: Wandering Scholar* (London: Merlin, 2007).

234 John McIlroy, 'Retrospect and Prospect,' in *Border Country: Raymond Williams in Adult Education*, ed. John McIlroy and Sallie Westwood (Leicester: NIACE, 1993), 271.

235 Fieldhouse, 'Adults Learning for Leisure,' 267–9; McIlroy, 'Retrospect and Prospect,' 271–4; Lawrence Goldman, *Dons and Workers: Oxford and Adult Education Since 1850* (Oxford: Clarendon, 1995), 251.

236 Fieldhouse, *Adult Education*, 11.

237 McIlroy, 'Retrospect and Prospect,' 277–8; Goldman, *Dons*, 270; Fieldhouse, *Adult Education*, 35; 'Education Report, 1946'CP CENT ED 2/6.

238 Fieldhouse, *Adult Education*, 33–6.

239 Raymond Williams, *Politics & Letters: Interviews with New Left Review* (London: Verso, 1979), 80.

240 Ibid., 81; Goldman, *Dons*, 250.

241 Raymond Williams was keen to work for Hodgkin, but was unpersuaded by the party's post-war direction and was not inclined to rejoin on demobilization; McIlroy, 'Retrospect and Prospect,' 273, 277; Williams, *Politics & Letters*, 65.

242 McIlroy, 'Retrospect and Prospect,' 272–4.

243 In the words of WEA pioneer and president, R.W. Tawney; Tawney, Introduction to *The Future in Adult Education: A Programme Adopted by the Annual Conference of the WEA, 1947* (WEA, 1947), 5.

244 Williams, *Politics & Letters*, 80.

245 Fieldhouse, *Adult Education*, 36.

246 Struggles recounted in ibid., 28–55. It also drew in the work of an older generation of Communist intellectuals, including Randall Swingler; see Croft, *Comrade Heart*, 186.

247 Writing as 'JE,' review of Jack Lindsay's *British Achievement in Art and Music*, *Our Time* (September 1945): 39.

248 Francis Mulhern, *Culture/Metaculture* (London: Routledge, 200), 50. Alan Sinfield takes a similar line in *Literature, Politics and Culture in Postwar Britain* (Oxford: Blackwell, 1989), 50–5.

249 Showtack Sassoon, *Gramsci's Politics*, 204–17.

250 'Proposal for a Ministry of Fine Arts,' n.d. [early 1947], Lindsay Papers, NLA, Folder 413; the CP was slow to criticize the Arts Council's metropolitan and high cultural emphasis, and was defending the levels of spending on Covent Garden as late as January 1952 in the NCC's 'Draft Statement on the Arts Council,' CP CENT CULT 3/6.

251 The Arts Council's Bloomsbury founder and chair, John Maynard Keynes, spoke the Communists' language on planning, on the Soviet Union, and on robust national tradition as a wall of resistance to American cultural invasion ('Death to Hollywood!' he thundered on a BBC broadcast the day the Arts Council's formation was announced). The St Pancras party branch – which encompassed Bloomsbury – was always one of the party's intellectually liveliest; John Collier, 'Civic culture,' *World News and Views*, 6 July 1946. On his death, John Maynard Keynes was warmly lauded for his wartime work as chairman of CEMA, and was presented as 'living proof that the Planner is not the unimaginative kill-joy'; unsigned 'Notes and Comments,' *Our Time* (June 1946): 23. The broadcast is cited in Andrew Sinclair, *Arts and Cultures: The History of the 50 Years of the Arts Council of Great Britain* (London: Sinclair-Stevenson, 1995), 46–7.

252 David Kynaston, *Austerity Britain 1945–51* (London: Bloomsbury, 2007), 175–7. 'We want the widest access to culture for the people,' stated the CP's *Britain for the People* (1944). 'Public encouragement of art, music and the drama should help to bring enjoyment within reach of everybody' (5). The equivalent passage in Labour's 1945 manifesto ran: 'By the provision of concert halls, modern libraries, theatres and suitable civic centres, we desire to assure our people full access to the great heritage of culture in this nation.' Neither document sounded fully convinced that the people would want what was offered or would find it enjoyable ('should help to bring,' 'we desire to assure'). The Communists gestured towards participation as well as consumption ('public encouragement'), but were no more explicit than Labour about why culture mattered and what its benefits might be, either for political movements that widened access to the arts or to the individuals newly exposed to it.

253 This stratum represented 'historical continuity uninterrupted even by the most complicated and radical changes in political forms'; Hoare and Nowell-Smith, *Selections from the Prison Notebooks*, 7.

254 As Alan Sinfield has argued, the party was dominated by 'middle-class dissidents, brought up in the old-middle class manner'; its attitude to culture represented a largely unscrutinized paternalistic desire to uplift others to appreciate their own cultural preferences; Sinfield, *Literature, Politics and Culture*, 50.

255 The strongest countervision was presented by S.J. Coulsen, 'Culture: Boom or Slump,' *Our Time* (August 1946), and saw the Salisbury Centre as a model of what was possible. More often, like the early Arts Council itself, the party vacillated between the positions of 'the best and the most,' metropolitan distillation and nationwide diffusion, wanting both in principle but struggling to envisage fully what the latter might mean. Nor did it point out that the early Arts Council's principle of 'compete with none and collaborate with all' was inherently contradictory given that very limited budgets were available to the Council and that investment in one sphere unavoidably meant denying another.

256 'Notes and Comments,' *Our Time* (November 1945): 63; (December 1945): 87.

257 Coulsen, 'Culture,' 4–5.

258 Lindsay, *Time to Live* (London; Andrew Dakers, 1946). Wartime high-cultural uplift – 'Midday concerts at the national Gallery' (265) – is stressed above what the novel actually records: the creation of a space for the community's own cultural self-expression; this is important only to the novel's more marginalized voices (266).

259 In 1946 Montagu Slater was theatre critic at *Reynold's News* and co-editing a new Fore magazine, *Theatre Today*, which was quickly selling 20,000 copies; Unity's own *New Theatre* was selling 15,000 copies per issue, and could be bought in the foyers of West End theatres. Croft, 'Boys Round the Corner,' 151; Chambers, *Story of Unity Theatre*, 280.

260 The conference was in March 1946; Unity then exerted significant influence over the bigger follow-up event, the 'British Theatre Conference' in February 1948, chaired by Priestley. Chambers, *Story of Unity Theatre*, 279; Ted Willis, 'The Theatre Means Business,' *Our Time* (November 1947): 58–9; John W. Collier, 'The Theatre Conference.' *Our Time* (March 1948): 135–7.

261 Chambers, *Story of Unity Theatre*, 279

262 Those who had long called for the creation of a professional company at Unity now argued that the Left faced an unprecedented opportunity to influence dominant theatre in reconstructed Britain, but was marginalized by its own inward deference for the amateur-professional divide; ibid., 268, 280.

263 A professional Unity Repertory Company was launched in London in February 1946 and in Glasgow three months later with the tacit support of the Arts Council's future drama director, and limited funding followed. The venture south of the border survived just fourteen months, quickly laying bare the odds stacked against a parlous and rough-and-ready Left theatre of finding contexts and theatrical forms through which to engage audiences beyond its existing networks. Chambers, *Story of Unity Theatre*, 270–5, 282; Scottish Unity fared better, and limped on until 1951, thanks largely to an exceptionally resonant play, a slice of Glaswegian social realism, Robert McLeish's *The Gorbals Story*, which gave expression to widespread support for the Communist-led squatters' movement and proved a minor theatrical sensation, running to full houses for five weeks in Glasgow before transferring to London's West End Garrick for six weeks. Chambers, *Story of Unity Theatre*, 282; John Hill, 'Towards a Scottish People's Theatre: The Rise and Fall of Glasgow's Unity,' *Theatre Quarterly* 27 (Autumn 1977): 61–70.

264 Theatre Workshop 'Manifesto' (1945), Box 8.1, Merseyside Left/Unity Theatre Archive, Liverpool; Theatre Workshop handbill, Theatre Workshop Archive, Theatre Royal, Stratford East, London ('Pre 1953' Box). The phrase 'a fuller life' was common currency in reconstruction-era CP discourse. *Britain for the People* (London: CP, 1944), 5; Lindsay, 'Fuller Life.'

265 Barely thirty at the end of the war, they were fifteen years younger than Jack Lindsay or Bernal. Outsiders culturally, they were more or less innocent

of metropolitan culture and formal education (MacColl was self-educated, Littlewood had dropped out of RADA). See Ewan MacColl, *Journeyman: An Autobiography* (London: Sidgwick and Jackson, 1990), 252.

266 Jack Lindsay reported on the experience of giving a talk to army groups about theatre in 1943; Lindsay, 'Dramatic Experiment.'

267 MacColl, *Journeyman*, 252.

268 Addison, *Now the War Is Over*, 117.

269 Priestley, 'Tables in the sun,' *Listener*, 4 July 1947.

270 Ewan MacColl, *Uranium 235* (Glasgow: MacLellan, n.d.); Howard Goorney, *Theatre Workshop Story* (London: Methuen, 1981), 52–3; Goorney, interview with author, Bath, 9 April 2003.

271 Ian McKay, 'Red bearded playwright's drama of the atom,' *News Chronicle*, 23 May 1946.

272 The company imagined securing Arts Council support on its own terms, and eventually establishing a base within the provinces, ideally at Manchester's Library Theatre or in the new town of East Kilbride, as opposed to Shaftesbury Avenue and 'the roaring boys who run the racket'; MacColl to Hamish Henderson, 19 February 1950, Hamish Henderson File, Ewan MacColl/Peggy Seeger Archive, Ruskin College, Oxford; Harker, *Class Act*, 84, 92.

273 Glasgow Unity lost the Arts Council's favour and funding for insisting that it would stage a fringe event to the first International Edinburgh Festival in 1947, from which it had been formally excluded. Hill, Towards a Scottish People's Theatre,' 68. Montagu Slater was aware of the company, and singled them out in his 'Theatre in 1946' retrospective, *Our Time* (January 1947): 134–5; Theatre Workshop's own W. Davidson wrote about the company, 'Theatre with a Method,' *Our Time* (July 1946): 258–9; the company is conspicuously absent from the *Daily Worker* and NCC discussions in the late 1940s; Lindsay evidently only learned about it from newspaper coverage; Lindsay, 'Dramatic Experiment.'

274 Andy Croft, 'Betrayed Spring: The Labour Government and British Literary Culture,' in Fyrth, *Labour's Promised Land?*, 211. 'I still believe that the failure to fund the working-class movement culturally when the channels of popular education and popular culture were there in the forties became a key factor in the very quick disintegration of Labour's position in the fifties'; Williams, *Politics & Letters*, 73.

275 Broadcasting began on 29 September 1946; the listening share was 2.22 per cent in the months that followed, but 0.9 per cent by the July–September 1947 quarter; Kynaston, *Austerity Britain*, 177.

276 Echoing Arnold himself to affirm the Third Programme for offering 'the best of the world's art and thought'; 'Notes and Comments,' *Our Time* (October 1946): 51; Randall to Geraldine Swingler, 8 November 1945, cited in Croft, *Comrade Heart*, 172.

277 Pollitt, *Answers to Questions*, 36.

278 Pollitt, *Looking Ahead*, 87.

279 'Socialism,' 9; 'Why Students Should Be Communists.'

280 The increasing strain of holding a clear line is abundantly evident in Pollitt's *Looking Ahead* of August 1947 and especially in the disconnection between its tone – querulous bluster against Labour's shortcomings – and the argument, which unconvincingly reasserts faith in the Labour Party's forming a united front with Communists against American imperialism, the Tories, and its own right-wing leadership.

281 'All the isms, Pollitt's pamphlets seemed to confirm,' writes Pollitt's biographer Kevin Morgan, 'were wasms.' The diminution of Dutt is also described by Morgan, *Harry Pollitt*, 143, 145.

282 Stationed on the Italian-Yugoslav border, Randall Swingler witnessed the Communist Parties of both countries close at hand; while they looked set to flourish under the devolutionary movement of the Communist movement, the British CP, he feared, seemed hesitant in the absence of Soviet guidance, 'fumbling about on a superficial level' of political tactics and programs, instead of offering 'an entirely new and immensely enriching way of life, of thought, of action, a philosophy'; Randall to Geraldine Swingler, 8 November 1945, cited in Croft, *Comrade Heart*, 172. See also Swingler to Jack Lindsay, 16 May [1946], Lindsay Papers, NLA, Folder 413; Miles Carpenter to Jack Lindsay, 17 September 1944, 26 August 1945, Lindsay Papers, NLA, Folder 191. Letters exchanged between Arnold Rattenbury, Edgell Rickword, and E.P. Thompson dwell on similar themes; Arnold Rattenbury Papers (MS556), Box 11, University of Birmingham Special Collections.

283 One new and significant note was struck by the Nottingham University Branch, which called for the party to scrutinize its previous mistakes and to commission an open history of the party along the lines of that recently produced by the Australian party; Joan D. Smith (Nottingham University Branch) and H.F.W. Taylor (Beeston Branch), *World News and Views*, 27 October 1945).

284 Bob McIhone, *World News and Views*, 10 November 1945; notably in Parker, *Kick Inside*, 15–32.

285 Alastair Wilson, *World News and Views*, 8 April 1944.

286 R. Page, *World News and Views*, 20 May 1944; M. Knowles, *World News and Views*, 27 May 1944.

287 Priestley saw in Harry Pollitt's *How to Win the Peace* (1944) a deadly blueprint for a 'Public-Control-and Social Security State in which there will be no genuine breaking down of class distinctions, no release of the people's creative energies, no real new spirit, no fresh inspiring incentives'; J.B. Priestley, *Daily Worker*, 20 November 1944.

288 Jack Lindsay, 'Practice and Theory in Cultural Matters,' undated, but circulated in February 1945, Lindsay Papers, NLA, Folder 595.

289 Jack Lindsay, 'Marxist Theory of Culture,' 16. Lindsay Papers, NLA, Folder 595; also contained in CP CENT CULT 4/11.
290 Ibid. I have written about this paper in detail; see Ben Harker, 'Jack Lindsay's Alienation,' *History Workshop* 82, no. 1 (2016): 83–107.
291 Lindsay, 'Fundamental Reconsiderations,' 9a, 15, Lindsay Papers, Folder 209.
292 Ibid., 2–3.
293 Ibid., 7–8.
294 Ibid., 3.
295 Ibid., 9a.
296 Ibid.
297 Ibid.
298 Ibid., 15.
299 Emile Burns to Lindsay, 15 July 1946, Lindsay Papers, NLA, Folder 209.

3. The British Road to Socialism, 1947–1956

1 Harry Pollitt to James Klugmann, 4 August 1947, CP IND KLUG 12/2.
2 Donald Sassoon, *One Hundred Years of Socialism: The West European Left in the Twentieth Century* (1996; London: I.B. Tauris, 2017), 97. The year 1947 saw the Truman Doctrine, the Marshall Plan, Stalin's creation of the Cominform, and the party's denunciation of erstwhile Labour Party allies as belonging to the imperialist camp; Sam Aaronovitch, circular letter, 2 April 1947, Lindsay Papers, NLA, Folder 413.
3 Danish Communists left the government in 1945, the Finns would depart in 1948; Sassoon, *One Hundred Years of Socialism*, 111.
4 *World News and Views*, 11 October 1947; cited in Noreen Branson, *History of the Communist Party of Great Britain, 1941–51* (London: Lawrence & Wishart, 1997), 156.
5 The NCC's first national conference, held in April 1948 (600 attended), was entitled the 'Battle of Ideas.' It was followed a month later by a spin-off event in Merseyside (78 attended). A.L. Morton's claim, from the first event, that America had 'a Marshall Plan in the field of ideas' was widely cited in the late 1940s and early 1950s. Jack Woddis, 'Another American export for Britain,' *World News and Views*, 5 June 1948, 235; Denis Ellwand, 'Battle of Ideas conference on Merseyside,' *World News and Views*, 19 June 1948. The tone of these events anticipated that of the Wroclaw Congress for Peace, held in late August 1948.
6 Steve Parsons, 'British "McCarthyism,"' in Jim Fyrth ed, *Labour's Promised Land? Culture and Society in Labour Britain 1945–51*, ed. Jim Fyrth (London: Lawrence & Wishart, 1995), 224–46. Anti-Communism in schools reached its height in 1950 when Middlesex County Council excluded Communist teachers from its schools (231–3); the Cold War struggles were especially fierce in and around Wedgewood Memorial College, Barlaston. These are

recounted in Roger Fieldhouse, *Adult Education and the Cold War: Liberal Values under Siege, 1946–51* (Leeds: Leeds Studies in Adult and Continuing Education, 1985), 28–55. In a discussion that mirrored that in the *Times Literary Supplement* about university lecturers, Communists in adult education were compelled to justify their pedagogy, not least through a year-long debate in the WEA's journal *Highway* that began with Thomas Hodgkin, 'Objectivity and Ideology and the Present Situation,' *Highway* (January 1951): 79–81. Anglican priest Alan Ecclestone formally joined the CP in 1948, was chair of the Sheffield Committee of the World Peace Council, whose initiatives led to the proposal that Sheffield should host the Second World Peace Congress in 1950. The event moved to Warsaw after the government blocked visits from many international delegates, excluding Picasso, who famously spoke at an event in Sheffield chaired by Ecclestone. See Tim Gorringe, *Alan Ecclestone: Priest as Revolutionary* (Sheffield: Cairns, 1994), 123ff; and Edward Poole, 'Troublesome Priests; Christianity and Marxism in the Church of England, 1906–1969' (MPhil thesis, University of Manchester, 2014), 126–59. The even fiercer hostility of the press, church, and state to 'Red Dean' Hewlett Johnson is described in Dianne Kirby, 'Ecclesiastical McCarthyism: Cold War Repression in the Church of England,' *Contemporary British History* 19, no. 2 (2005): 176–203; Kirby also deals with the 'blacklisting' of clergy associated with the Society of Socialist Clergy and Ministers and those who signed the 1950 Stockholm Peace Petition, especially fellow-traveller and occasional *Daily Worker* correspondent Stanley Evans, who was increasingly marginalized at the height of the Cold War. Nineteen-year-old Communist scout Paul Garland, who was also secretary of the west of England YCL, was expelled from the Boy Scout Association early in 1954 on the grounds that his Communist beliefs were incompatible with the movement's defining loyalty to God and Queen. A media and political storm followed, including debate in the House of Lords and questions in the House of Common from Garland's MP, Anthony Wedgewood Benn; CP CENT YOUTH 4/10. The episode is recounted in Sarah Mills, 'Be Prepared: Communism and the Politics of Scouting in 1950s Britain,' *Contemporary British History* 25, no. 2 (2011): 429–50.

7 Peter Hennessy, *Having It So Good* (London: Penguin, 2006), 65. In 1936 Seebohm Rowntree had estimated that 31.1 per cent of York's working class was living in poverty; in 1950 he estimated 2.8 per cent. Paul Addison, *Now the War Is Over* (London: BBC, 1985), 199; David Kynaston, *Family Britain 1951–57* (London: Bloomsbury, 2010), 144.

8 The population of party stronghold Bethnal Green, for instance, halved from 108,000 in 1931 to 53,860 in 1955. Michael Young and Peter Willmott, *Family and Kinship in East London* (1957; London: Penguin, 2007), 123–4; John Callaghan, *Cold War, Crisis and Conflict: The CPGB 1951–68* (London: Lawrence & Wishart, 2003), 186.

9 Young and Willmott report that between 1953 and 1955 the number of TV sets per 100 households went up from 21 to 32 in Bethnal Green but from 39 to 65 in the new suburban estate they call 'Greenleigh' (*Family,* 143). Lindsay visited Dagenham to address a meeting in the mid-1950s and found there 'a sort of Van Dieman's Land to which the worst housed of Stepney, Poplar etc were transported.' It was a place where the population 'have no way whatever of expressing themselves socially or politically except the ballot box and booing Churchill at the local cinema. The only social grouping seems in Carnation or Rose Clubs.' Lindsay to Alick West, n.d. [mid-1950s], Lindsay Papers, NLA, Folder 191.

10 Eric Hobsbawm, 'The Forward March of Labour Halted?' *Marxism Today* (September 1978): 281.

11 Ibid., 279–86.

12 Ben Jones, *The Working-Class in Mid Twentieth Century England: Community, Identity and Social Memory* (Manchester: Manchester University Press, 2012), table 2.1, 31.

13 'The people ... will never again return a Tory government'; Harry Pollitt, *Looking Ahead* (1947), 117.

14 Callaghan, *Cold War,* 184.

15 Ibid.

16 Paul Mason, *Postcapitalism: A Guide to Our Future* (London: Penguin, 2015), 79; Sassoon, *One Hundred Years,* 141.

17 'The Crisis: Marx Versus Keynes' (December 1949), CP CENT ECON 1/1.

18 'The Economic Situation and Prospects for Britain in the First Half of 1948,' CP CENT ECON 4/7; 'The Economic Crisis of 1952,' CP CENT ECON 4/8.

19 Syllabus for National School, 'What Is Meant by Maximum Profit?' [1954?], CP CENT ECON 6/15.

20 For good historical reasons, from their inaugural affiliation to the Comintern, national Communist Parties were focused on bourgeois imperialism, and committed to exposing and confronting what the foundational documents of the Comintern called 'the tricks and dodges of "its" imperialists in the colonies.' 'Conditions of Admission to the Communist international' (1920), in *The Communist International 1919–1943, Documents,* vol. 1, *1919–22,* ed. Jane Degras (London: Frank Cass, 1971), 170.

21 The tensions between this insurrectionist model and Stalin's still-frequently cited writings on nations and national cultures were neither acknowledged nor confronted until the late 1950s; George Thomson, 'Notes for Discussion on the National Question,' n.d. [1959–60], CP CENT CULT 1/4. Thomson was responding in part to a long discussion on the 'Jewish Question' in *Marxism Today* in 1959, provoked by Bert Ramelson's article on Jewishness, Zionism, Israel, and Yiddish culture, 'An Old Problem Re-Discussed,' *Marxism Today* (January 1959): 21–7.

22 Home Office figures cited in Kynaston, *Family Britain*, 449; see also 367.

23 *The British Road to Socialism* (London: CP, 1951), 9–12; Rajani Palme Dutt, 'The national independence of Britain,' *World News*, 3 July 1954.

24 'We cannot allow afford our cultural life to become dominated by the uncouth tycoons of Wall Street any more than we can allow them to dominate our economic life,' stressed party analyst Jack Woddis, 'Another American export for Britain,' *World News and Views*, 5 June 1948.

25 George Thomson, 'Our Cultural Work in the Light of Our Party Programme,' *Communist Review* (September 1951): 272.

26 Pollitt, *Looking Ahead*, 11. The key statement is by Sam Aaronovitch, Introduction to *Arena* 2, no. 8 (1951): 3–23. They were also widely circulated in the party press; see, for instance, Aaronovitch's articles in *World News and Views*, 17 March 1951, 2 February 1952, 16 August 1952, 3 January 1953, 24 October 1953.

27 Stalin's *Foundations of Leninism* was republished by the party press in 1949.

28 *British Road*; sales figure from Callaghan, *Cold War*, 25; *Communist Party Weekly Letter*, no. 20, 18 May 1951, CP IND JOHN 4/1/1.

29 *British Road*, 14.

30 Kevin Morgan, *Harry Pollitt* (Manchester: Manchester University Press, 1993), 168–70; Executive Committee member George Thomson voted against the draft version of the document and was shocked by the lack of discussion; transcript of taped interview with Thomson, n.d., Douglas Garman Papers, University of Nottingham, DG6/11. Even Dutt later conceded that the program 'might have reasonably been considered to merit a full prior discussion and a special congress'; Dutt to Allen Hutt, 12 April 1966, CP IND JOHN 4/1/1.

31 A new resolution on the cultural work of the party was adopted by the Executive in January 1952 and a further motion calling for closer integration of ideological and 'mass political work' at the 1952 Congress. The key documents behind the former were Thomson's 'Draft Outline Report on Our National Cultural Heritage,' CP CENT CULT 3/6; and Thomson, 'Our Cultural Work,' 272–7.

32 Cited in Morgan, *Pollitt*, 169.

33 The central contention was that 'social transformation can only come through internal changes in accordance with the actual conditions' in Britain and by 'transforming' Parliament 'into the democratic instrument of the will of the vast majority of the people'; *British Road*, 8, 14.

34 Figure from Kynaston, *Family Britain*, 264. Unlike the 11 Labour MPs who had scare-mongered about Britain's becoming 'an open reception centre,' Communists had welcomed those 493 Jamaicans who disembarked from the *Empire Windrush* in 1948, promptly inviting those domiciled in Clapham South's wartime shelter to a party social ('Jamaicans thrill communists,' ran the headline in the local paper). David Kynaston, *Austerity Britain 1945–51* (London: Bloomsbury, 2007), 276.

35 Hakim Adi, 'West Africans and the Communist Party in the 1950s,' in *Opening the Books: Essays on the Social and Cultural History of the British Communist Party*, ed. Geoff Andrews, Nina Fishman, and Kevin Morgan (London: Pluto,1995), 181–3.

36 The Third World advisory committee forcefully objected to a passage in the draft that argued that, after the 'transition' to socialism, former British colonies should be federally linked with Britain, the model being the relationship between the Soviet Union and Armenia and Uzbekistan. Those who had advocated a stronger statement standing on the side of complete independence were overruled by Dutt, who seems to have known that the contentious passage was written by Stalin, keen not to provoke erstwhile allies. Mervyn Jones, *Chances: An Autobiography* (London: Verso, 1987), 118.

37 *British Road*, 12; Morgan, *Pollitt*, 169; Evan Smith, '"Class Before Race": British Communism and the Place of Empire in Postwar Race Relations,' *Science & Society* 72, no. 4 (2008): 465. Many were unsettled and some resigned over the question.

38 *British Road*, 11; Alison MacLeod, *The Death of Uncle Joe* (Woodbridge, UK: Merlin, 1997), 29. Emile Burns was deployed to reassure activists troubled by the 'new empire line' at a Cultural Workers Aggregate Meeting at Holborn Hall on 28 March 1951. NA, KV 2/1762; 'Conditions of Admission to the Communist International,' 170.

39 Jones, *Chances*, 117–18; Trevor Carter, *Shattering Illusions: West Indians in British Politics*, with Jess Coussins (London: Lawrence & Wishart, 1986), 59.

40 *British Road*, 14, 17.

41 Ibid., 14.

42 Ibid., 17.

43 Ibid., 13.

44 Ibid., 14; the BBC is mentioned four times (10, 14, 15, 17).

45 Ibid., 15.

46 Ibid., 14, 17.

47 Initially the task of guiding the work of the cultural groups formed in the war passed to the cultural committee of the London District, which was very active in 1946, especially in and around St Pancras; John Collier, 'Civic culture,' *World News and Views*, 6 July 1946. This was soon overstretched, and a provisional committee was formed with contributions from the London District, the Party Centre, and the *Daily Worker*; London District circular, 18 January 1946, Lindsay Papers, NLA, Folder 413. Noreen Branson's claim that the NCC was set up in response to resolutions passed at the 19th Congress in February 1947 'to support and encourage the great cultural awakening of the people at this time' is misleading, although the Congress certainly intensified the efforts already afoot. Branson, *History of the Communist Party of Great Britain, 1941–51*, 170.

48 Lindsay was vociferous in early NCC meetings, proposing a body along the lines of the French Union of Intellectuals; the proposal was rejected as too ambitious; NCC Minutes, 15 May 1947, CP CENT CULT 1/3.

49 'Proposals for Work of Cultural Committee,' n.d., but circulated 2 April 1947, Lindsay Papers, NLA, Folder 413.

50 The narrower responsibility of guiding and discussing the activities of the cultural groups – 'writers, actors, film-workers and musicians' – passed initially to the London District Committee; the Propaganda Department at first retained responsibility for 'directing work on a national scale'; the NCC gradually seems to have expanded to assume both roles, and personnel in any case overlapped. Sam Aaronovitch, circular announcing NCC formation, 2 April 1947, 'Proposals for Work of Cultural Committee.' The first NCC meeting was held on 19 April 1947; meetings were subsequently monthly, and held at either King Street or Marx House; minutes of meetings in CP CENT CULT 1/1. Membership was 38,579 in June 1947; Branson, *History of the Communist Party of Great Britain, 1941–51*, appendix 1, 252. Aaronovitch, circular letter, 2 April 1947, Lindsay Papers, NLA, Folder 413.

51 Meetings in the first year were also sporadically attended by representatives from Unity Theatre, the Artists' Group, the National Student Committee, the Cambridge Graduates Group and the Architects' Group, Lindsay Papers, NLA, Folder 413; NCC Minutes in CP CENT CULT 1/1.

52 By 1949 the NCC would evolve two additional committees, one concerned with theoretical matters and the other with the more practical organization of cultural workers; by the early 1950s a substrata of district-level cultural committees would be established that would prove especially active in the Midlands, London, Middlesex, and Scotland; 'Discussion of the Work of District Cultural Committees / Cultural Committee B, 6 July 1954,' CP CENT CULT 1/2.

53 *The USA Threat to British Culture* (London: Arena, 1951), *Britain's Cultural Heritage* (London: Arena, 1952), *Essays on Socialist Realism and the British Cultural Tradition* (London: Arena,1953).

54 Such as the 'Battle of Ideas' Conference in Merseyside in spring 1948, attended by 78. Ellwand, 'Battle of Ideas conference on Merseyside'; Callaghan, *Cold War*, 87; Sam Aaronovitch, 'Britain's cultural heritage,' *World News and Views*, 16 August 1952; Aaronovitch, 'The American threat to British culture,' *World News and Views*, 12 May 1951.

55 Apart from a token trade unionist (Jack Grahl of the Fire Brigades' Union), three party leaders, and functionaries (John Gollan, John Lewis, Douglas Garman), the remainder comprised five academics (George Thomson, F.D. Klingender, Maurice Dobb, Christopher Hill, Hyman Levy), two teachers (G.C.T. Giles, George Rudé), two novelists (John Sommerfield, Jack Lindsay), two actors/theatre professionals (Beatrix Lehmann, Ted Willis), an artist (James Boswell), and a composer (Alan Bush). A BBC producer (Peggy McIver), an academic/literary

critic (Alick West), a film worker (Ivor Montagu), and an orchestra manager (Thomas Russell) would join in the months ahead.

56 'Information Report on Groups,' n.d., circulated to delegates to the 1948 Battle of Ideas Conference, Lindsay Papers, NLA, Folder 413.

57 Five of them were very active: historians (140 members at the beginning of 1948), scientists (whose invitation-only Engels Society was formed in 1946), writers (60 members, regular open meetings), musicians (89 members plus 35 in an amateur musicians' group). Three were reasonably active: film workers and actors (65 members), doctors (25 members, quarterly meetings), and psychologists (23 members). Two were less active: philosophers (seldom met) and economists (mainly London based and primarily involved in writing copy for the party press). Figures from Information Report on Groups, 8 April 1948, Lindsay Papers, NLA, Folder 412.

58 'Proposals for Work of Cultural Committee.'

59 Bernal's most extended version of this argument was the lead article in the newly relaunched *Modern Quarterly* (Winter 1945–6). See J.D. Bernal, 'Belief and Action,' reprinted in J.D. Bernal, *The Freedom of Necessity* (London: Routledge & Kegan Paul, 1949), 69–85; these arguments formed the core of his contribution to *The Challenge of Our Time* broadcast, 'The Social Responsibility of Science,' 31 March 1946, also reprinted in *Freedom of Necessity*, 85–91.

60 Gary Werskey, *The Visible College: A Collective Biography of British Scientists and Socialists of the 1930s* (London: Allen Lane, 1978), 294, 300.

61 Three articles criticizing Lysenko appeared in *Modern Quarterly* in the autumn and winter of 1947–8: R.G. Davies, 'Genetics in the USSR,' *Modern Quarterly* (Autumn 1947): 336–46; J.L. Fyfe, 'The Soviet Genetics Controversy,' *Modern Quarterly* (Autumn 1947): 347–51; F. Le Gros Clark and Harold Thomas, 'On Soviet Genetics,' *Modern Quarterly* Winter (1947–48): 93–5. J.L. Fyfe described Lysenko's theories as 'perverse' and coloured by 'fanaticism' (93). He would go on to produce the notorious *Lysenko Is Right* (London: Lawrence & Wishart, 1950).

62 Werskey, *Visible College*, 293–303; Brown, *J.D. Bernal*, 304–17.

63 AGM [Alan Morton], 'The Position in Biology,' unpublished report, 31 January 1949), CP CENT CULT 5/9.

64 The BBC broadcast a symposium on Soviet genetics in November 1948, contributions to which were published in the *Listener*, 8 December 48; Association of Scientific Workers membership fell from 15,600 in December 1945 to 11,318 by 1954. See Stephen R. Parsons, 'Communism in the Professions' (PhD diss., University of Warwick, 1990), 325; Haldane's especially difficult course, which involved a 'phased withdrawal' from the party begun in 1949, is charted by Callaghan, *Cold War*, 94.

65 The Society was formed in 1946, and was open to qualified scientists who were CP members; at its height around one hundred attended its conferences, such as the weekend conference held in October 1948; it began publishing a bulletin in

July 1948, the last of which seems to have appeared in 1952, by which point the society was moribund. CP CENT CULT 5/9; 'The Communist Science Group, November 1949, Lindsay Papers, NLA, Folder 413.

66 BBC WAS R Cont 1 JBS Haldane, File 2; BBC WAC R Cont 1 J. D. Bernal, 1940–61; BBC WAC Hyman Levy. R Cont 1, Talks 1931–62. 'Many will regard some of Bernal's views as doctrinaire,' ran the *Times Literary Supplement* review of *The Social Function of Science*, 'but it will not be easy to challenge his main thesis' (22 April 1939). *Freedom of Necessity*, a collection of his pre–Cold War writings, was dismissed in the same journal as 'facile optimism' and 'troubled verbiage'; 'Science and society,' unsigned review of *Freedom of Necessity*, *Times Literary Supplement*, 17 June 1949).

67 Assuming a more defensive position, Bernal in the early 1950s was arguing that 'we must prepare actively for the day when science will serve the people'; see J.D. Bernal, 'Britain's Heritage of Science,' in *Britain's Cultural Heritage* (London: Arena [1952]), 28; Science for Peace was formed in January 1952 and was dominated by Bernal. Werskey, *Visible College*, 307–9; Hyman Levy and Helen Spalding, *Literature for an Age of Science* (London: Methuen, 1952); reviewed in *World News and Views,* 17 January 1953, and negatively in 'Materialist aesthetics,' *Times Literary Supplement*, 13 February 1953.

68 Christopher Hill, review of Benjamin Farrington, *Francis Bacon, Philosopher of Industrial Science*, *Modern Quarterly* (Winter 1951–2): 58.

69 Rodney Hilton, 'The Historians' Group and the British Tradition,' CP CENT CULT 8/2.

70 Eric Hobsbawm, 'The Historians' Group of the Communist Party,' in *Rebels and Their Causes: Essays in Honour of A.L. Morton*, ed. Maurice Cornforth (London: Lawrence & Wishart, 1978), 29. Not coincidentally, the party's foremost historians were not specialists in the post-1880 period, and its twentieth-century section was only ever an addendum to the nineteenth-century one. The group was almost always referred to as the Nineteenth-Century Section (the others were Ancient, Medieval, Sixteenth-Seventeenth centuries, and the Teachers' Section); documents from 1950–1 refer to the group as the Nineteenth and Twentieth Section, CP CENT CULT 8/2.

71 The range and tone of the period's history wars was signalled by the notorious skirmish provoked by honorary historian Jack Lindsay's pugnacious *Byzantium in Europe* (1952), a book which foregrounded not Byzantium's decline but its forgotten modernity, and challenged a tendency Lindsay associated with Toynbee: to view Byzantium through a modern East-West optic. This for Lindsay reflected and reinforced contemporary ideology by underplaying Byzantine influence on Western culture in favour of reading its later despotism as an antecedent of the Soviet Union. Christopher Hill, review of *Byzantium in Europe*, *Modern Quarterly* (Summer 1953): 186–9. An unsigned *Times Literary Supplement* review, supported by a leader, attempted to use the book's openly polemical thrust to

query the suitability of Marxists to teach in universities; unsigned review, *Times Literary Supplement*, 12 December 1952; Christopher Hill took issue with the review in a letter (19 December 1952); Lindsay responded, describing the article as 'gutterpress' journalism 'in the service of the witch-hunt' (26 December 1952). Two longer articles responded in the party press: Andrew Rothstein, 'Marxism and the *Times Literary Supplement*,' *Modern Quarterly* (Spring 1953): 69–74; Hill's review of *Byzantium in Europe*, *Modern Quarterly* (Summer 1953): 186–9.

72 Communist academic historians were largely locked out of new academic posts from 1948, and met a glass ceiling when it came to promotion. Most clung on, the exception being Andrew Rothstein, who was removed from his post at London University's School of Slavonic Studies; Eric Hobsbawm, *Interesting Times: A Twentieth-Century Life* (London; Abacus, 2002), 182. Rothstein had been working at the school for four years, and was charged with 'inadequate scholarship.' The AUT union declined to defend him. Parsons, 'British "McCarthyism,"' 234.

73 Dona Torr to Salme Dutt, 22 April 1936, CP IND DUTT 6/3.

74 John Saville to Joan Simon, 3 December 1954, Saville Papers, U DJS 10, Hull History Centre.

75 Raphael Samuel persuasively argues that a 'common moral formation' grounded in 'orderliness, craftsmanship, dedication' united the 'ex-engineers turned full-time organisers and many of the party's historians'; Samuel, 'British Marxist Historians 1880–1980,' *New Left Review* 120 (1980): 52; Sam Aaronovitch, quoted in Parsons, 'Communism in the Professions,' 327.

76 They were less inclined to theoretical deviations than were the literary intellectuals: for historians the base-superstructure model proved a productive metaphor, rather than a model that relegated culture to a secondary reflection of economic processes. As David Parker argues, Stalin's own theoretical inconsistencies left plentiful scope for creative analysis within the parameters of orthodoxy; David Parker, Introduction, in *Ideology and Absolutism and the English Revolution: Debates of the British Communist Historians 1940–56*, ed. David Parker (London: Lawrence & Wishart, 2008), 24–5. Disagreements tended to be dealt with *sotto voce* by the leadership rather than flushed out into open debate, the key exception being when, behind the scenes, the leadership took issue with A.L. Morton's *English Utopia* (London; Lawrence & Wishart, 1952) and its controversially 'idealist' emphasis that utopian thought and cultural production 'entered and made a noble contribution to the great river of the movement for socialism' (275). The leadership was also troubled by Morton's discussion of Orwell and Morris within the same chapter. A critical review was written by R. Page Arnot for *Labour Monthly*, but went unpublished, seemingly at the request of Lawrence & Wishart director, Maurice Cornforth. Dutt agreed that a critical review of a book published by the party press called the party's judgment into question. Morton was incensed with a decision that was 'thoroughly feeble and uncommunist, an abandonment of critical principles merely to avoid trouble,'

but observed party discipline and communicated his frustrations only in private correspondence. Morton to Arnot, 26 November 1953; Morton to Dutt, 5 December 1953; Dutt to Morton, 10 December 1953, CP IND DUTT 5/11.

77 'Introduction,' *Past & Present* 1, no. 1 (1952): iii. Paradoxically, as Eric Hobsbawm later pointed out, the not entirely unfounded Cold War perceptions of Communists as insular, dogmatic, reductionist, and prone to jargon forced them to be the opposite. This was especially apparent in *Past & Present*, subtitled 'a journal of scientific history,' devised to bring together Marxists and non-Marxists, and whose rapidly established intellectual prestige rubbed off. Hobsbawm, 'Historians' Group,' 32–3.

78 The key debates are presented in Parker, *Ideology and Absolutism*; Dennis Dworkin, *Cultural Marxism in Postwar Britain: History, the New Left and the Origins of Cultural Studies* (Durham, NC: Duke University Press. 1997), 10–45, provides an authoritative overview of the group's work.

79 They also confronted Catholic discourse, which led international anti-Communist movements under the banner of Western Christian values; George Thomson, *An Essay on Religion* (London: Lawrence & Wishart, 1949). Party Speakers' Notes ('Notes on the Communist Attitude to Religion,' circulated 6 March 1951) noted that, while Communists respected freedom of religious worship, 'the church as an institution has always been closely connected with the land-owning nobility,' CP CENT SPEAKERS NOTES 1/10. The historians' self-styled 'progressive rationalist tradition' is analysed in Samuel, 'British Marxist Historians,' 72–5.

80 The consciousness of these ideological struggles is apparent from NCC documents such as 'Main trends on the ideological front' (19 November 1947) and Lindsay's 'Some anti-Marxist trends,' n.d., but commissioned by the NCC and written in late 1947, Lindsay Papers, NLA, Folder 413. Hobsbawm later identified as a 'major task' the criticism of non-Marxist history and its reactionary implications'; Hobsbawm, 'Historians' Group,' 32; he also identified their opposition to '"old-fashioned" politico-constitutional or narrative history' (38). One key figure was Herbert Butterfield, and his anti-Communist *The Englishman and His History* (1944), with its Whiggish emphasis on the idea of national continuity as a unifying force against political rupture. This was strongly criticized in the *Daily Worker* book page on its original publication (*Daily Worker*, 9 August 1944); Butterfield's broadcasts, which later fed into *Christianity and History* (London: Bell, 1949), were attacked by Rodney Hilton, 'Jehovah's Witnesses,' *Communist Review* (July 1949): 583–9. Hobsbawm later accused Butterfield of turning history into 'a sub-department of Providence'; Eric Hobsbawm, 'Progress in British Historiography,' *Marxism Today* (February 1962): 44. More significant still was the prolific Arnold Toynbee, whose theories of historical cycles were identified as a key adversary by the 'Battle of Ideas' internationally. See J.D. Bernal, 'Wroclaw and After,' *Modern Quarterly* (Winter

1948–9): 5–28; Roy Pascal, 'Synopsis of the Contributions of Professor Georg Lukács and Ernst Fischer to the Wroclaw Conference,' *Modern Quarterly* (Summer 1949): 235–59.

81 A.L. Morton, 'Light on the English Revolution,' *World News and Views*, 28 January 1950); 'EPT' [E.P. Thompson], 'William Morris,' *World News and Views*, 29 September 1951); William Morris's 'cult of the Middle Ages' had previously caused some concern; see A.L. Morton, 'William Morris,' *Our Time* (February 1944): 8; Samuel, 'British Marxist Historians,' 53–4. These struggles are plotted by Bill Schwarz, '"The People in History: The Communist Party Historians,' in *Making Histories: Studies in History-writing and Politics*, ed. Richard Johnson et al. (London: Hutchinson, 1982), 77–9.

82 Hobsbawm, 'Progress in British Historiography,' 37.

83 A process of cultural uplift described by one activist as 'the new London Philharmonic audiences, the new CEMA, Penguin readers, factory people ..., choirs, musical societies, dramatic societies'; Maurice Carpenter to Jack Lindsay, 17 September 1944, Lindsay Papers, NLA, Folder 191.

84 A figure reached within four months of the journal's launch in October 1938, and sustained until the early 1950s. A typical feature of *Picture Post* was the early pull-out-and-keep guide to the 'Great British Masters' in painting, which ran through 1938–9. Circulation and sales figures from Tom Hopkinson, ed., *Picture Post 1938–50* (Harmondsworth, UK: Penguin, 1970), 10, 18.

85 The party's most striking cultural successes of the 1940s were in a distinctly middlebrow Priestleyan vein, from the LPO (championed by Priestley), to Jack Lindsay's novels (which Priestley admired), to the 1948 British Theatre conference (brokered in alliance with him). Priestley preferred to call himself 'broadbrow' ('About myself,' *Listener*, 21 June 1933). His cultural ubiquity in print and on air indicated the vitality of this culture through the war, culminating in 1945–7, when his plays, including the Moscow-premiered *An Inspector Calls* (1945), were widely lauded for articulating post-war possibilities, his novel *Three Men in New Suits* (1946) sold 250,000 copies, and his views on cultural reconstruction, expressed in texts such as the Fabian Society pamphlet 'The Arts Under Socialism: What the Government Should Do for the Arts Here and Now' (1947), carried great weight. Priestley's MI5 file reveals just how close he was to the party and its cultural networks across many contexts in the mid- to late 1940s, the key nodes being Unity Theatre, the Writers' Group of the Society for Cultural Relations, and the *Daily Worker*. NA, KV 2/3774. Lindsay recalled Priestley's telling him that 'he no longer knew what a chap said when picking up a girl; so he looked to me to carry on his work'; Priestley especially admired *Time to Live* (1946), a novel whose street-party theme clearly resembled his own plotlines about community cultural self-expression. Jack Lindsay, 'The Fullness of Life' [unpublished autobiography], Lindsay Papers, NLA, Folder 473. Priestley wrote a glowing preface to Thomas Russell's *Philharmonic* (London: Hutchinson, 1942),

a book reprinted as a Pelican paperback in 1953, recalling their wartime work together to save the orchestra.

86 The central driver of the most memorable middlebrow inter-war literature – serious but accessible novels including Walter Greenwood's *Love on the Dole* (1933), Winifred Holtby's *South Riding* (1936), A.J. Cronin's *The Citadel* (1937), Lettice Cooper's *National Provincial* (1938), and Priestley's *Let the People Sing* (1939) – was an urge for a benevolent state to correct the structural inequalities of inter-war capitalism and the miseries it caused. This afflatus naturally ebbed away with the Attlee government, in which the prosaic reality of blackouts, ration queues, and incremental reform failed to inspire advocates of social democracy in the way the conditions that called for it had, a point made persuasively by Ross McKibbin, *Classes and Cultures: England 1918–1951* (Oxford: Oxford University Press, 1998), 516.

87 The reduced period between hardback and paperback publication of titles, down from around six years to two, made newly published books more affordable. Christopher Hilliard, *To Exercise Our Talents: The Democratization of Writing in Britain* (Cambridge, MA: Harvard University Press, 2006), 275.

88 18,066 titles in 1951; 18,741 in 52; 18,527 in 1953; fiction rose from 3,871 in 1951 to 4,301 in 1953; poetry and drama fell from 628 to 638 to 578 in the 1951–3 period. Figures from the *Bookseller*, cited in the Writers' Group Report for the Commission on the Middle Class (1954), CP CENT CULT 1/3.

89 Francis Mulhern, *Culture/Metaculture* (London: Routledge, 2000), 51.

90 Hilliard, *To Exercise*, 275–6.

91 By comparison, the party's *Communist Review* sold at best 4,500. Andy Croft, 'The Boys Round the Corner: The Story of Fore Publications,' in *A Weapon in the Struggle: The Cultural History of the Communist Party of Great Britain*, ed. Andy Croft (London: Pluto, 1998), 151; Callaghan, *Cold War*, 25

92 Arnold Rattenbury to 'Ted' [E.P. Thompson], n.d. [1948], Rattenbury Papers, Box 11.

93 Sales were down to 15,682 by July 1946, 12,553 by December 1946, and 9,178 by August 1947; appendix to 'Report on *Our Time* [November 1947], CP CENT CULT 1/1.

94 Charles Hobday, *Edgell Rickword: A Poet at War (*Manchester: Carcanet, 1989), 241.

95 John St John to Jack Lindsay, 18 September 1947, Lindsay Papers, NLA, Folder 420.

96 Report on *Our Time* [November 1947], CP CENT CULT 1/1. The framing vision proposed by the younger university-educated graduate Communists (Arnold Rattenbury, E.P. Thompson, and David Holbrook) was standard post-war fare; 'to encourage all activities that will help the development of a fuller national culture' and to 'stimulate the production of new creative work.' But the privileged term was a high culture seen here as inherently resistant to the market, and offering

critical insight into society's deeper movement. This, for Rattenbury, was the obvious counterforce to the 'shards of shit' published daily, and this strain of highbrow vanguardism chimed with the priorities of leadership – Burns and Garman – who blamed Rickword and to a lesser extent Swingler and Lindsay for the falling circulation and wanted an overhaul. Rattenbury to 'Ted.'

97 George Thomson, 'On the Work of Party Intellectuals,' *Communist Review* (August 1946): 11–15; Emile Burns, circular to London Cultural Committee, 17 January 1947, Lindsay Papers, NLA, Folder 413.

98 Such direct assaults could be countered personally with denunciation of the 'mental sickness' and 'screaming defeatism' of apostates, or statistically via the abundant pro-Soviet propaganda produced by the SCR and the publications of *Russia Today*. An early example is John Lewis and Reginald Bishop, *The Philosophy of Betrayal: An Analysis of the Anti Soviet Propaganda of Arthur Koestler and Others* (London: Russia Today, 1945), 2. The relaunched *Modern Quarterly* was quickly repurposed to 'lead the strongest possible ideological struggle against all forms of reactionary ideology' (Editorial Board Minutes, 18 July 1946); when first mooted fifteen months earlier, the journal had seen itself as a much broader publication including non-Communist editorial board members (Minutes, 4 February 1945), CP IND MONT 5/3. The bitter acrimony that ensued about the purpose and implied readership of the journal was always at some level a response to swelling anti-Communist feeling.

99 Orwell was closely associated with *Polemic*, and retaliated to a criticism of that journal from Bernal in the first issue of *Modern Quarterly* with an extended essay. See J.D. Bernal, 'Belief and Action,' *Modern Quarterly* 1, no. 1 (1945), reprinted in *Freedom of Necessity*, 69–85; Orwell's unsigned editorial essay appeared in *Polemic* 3 (May 1946), reprinted in *Collected Essays, Journalism and Letters of George Orwell IV (1945–50)*, ed. Sonia Orwell and Ian Angus (Harmondsworth, UK: Penguin, 1968), 185–92.

100 The audience figure is given in Werskey, *Visible College*, 288; the talks were published in the *Listener* and then in a tie-in volume of the same title edited by G. Wyndham-Goldie (1948). Bernal was the science advisor, and pushed for the inclusion of other CPers (Bernal, Haldane, and classicist Benjamin Farrington all gave talks); Bernal also suggested Thomson, Pascal, and Hill. 'Summary of Meeting with Bernal, 8 March 1946,. BBC WAC 551/71 Talks. T.S. Eliot was also consulted by the producer (9 November 1945) and suggested Orwell and Michael Polanyi.

101 The well-attended Sunday evening lectures were held at Beaver Hall in London in the winter of 1946–7, and published as *The Communist Answer to the Challenge of Our Time* (London: Thames, 1947). Classicist and newly elected NEC member Professor George Thomson wrote the preface.

102 Forster was approvingly quoted by Lewis and Bishop, *Philosophy of Betrayal*, 6

103 Forster's talk was transmitted on 7 April 1946, original script in BBC WAC. Forster's critique was difficult to deal with. He had always enjoyed a special place in the affections of cultural communism, as a former Popular Front ally who had momentarily considered joining the party and a novelist whose anti-imperialism and critique of the snobbery of bourgeois society had been praised. That Communists were initially wrong-footed by a critique from a figure whose work they affirmed and from whose association they had benefited was apparent in their divided responses: Randall Swingler reassured Forster that planning could be better handled and that personal experience was the 'proper field of the writer's research' in the past, present, and future; Randall Swingler, 'Personality and the Planned Society,' *Modern Quarterly* (Summer 1946): 89–94. The Educational Organiser, Douglas Garman, had no truck with Forster's liberalism, with which Swingler was also charged. Forster was 'one of the most tragic spiritual casualties of capitalist society in decline,' a 'great creative writer of the past' who had degenerated into 'an apologist for reaction'; Douglas Garman, 'Communications,' *Modern Quarterly* (Winter 1946–7): 89.

104 For more detail, see Ben Harker, 'Politics and Letters: The "Soviet Literary Controversy" in Britain,' *Literature & History* 24, no. 1 (2015): 41–57. Editorial, *Culture and Life*, 28 June 1946. Text reproduced in *Horizon* (October 1946): 207.

105 On 29 August 1946, *Pravda* took issue with children's magazines; theatres were criticized on 2 September 1946; clauses were subsequently added to the Central Committee's Resolution addressing theatre on 26 August 1946 and film on 4 September 1946. The assault on music came a little later, beginning in December 1947.

106 The *Manchester Guardian* covered the story most extensively, with articles on 22 August 1946 ('Russian writers denounced'), 26 August 1946 ('The artist's freedom'), 27 August 1946 ('The intelligentsia'); the story resurfaced in September around Zhdanov's address, and was covered on 23 September 1946 ('A period of rest after the war'), 24 September 1946 ('The Soviet writer's task'), 27 September 1946 ('Miscellany'), and 30 September 1946 ('The artist's freedom'). The *Sunday Times* ran the story on 25 August 1946 ('Communist drive in Russia').

107 Connolly's responses were always as much about state interference in culture in Britain as about the Soviet Union. His wartime writings about the former anticipate the later position: 'State socialism in politics is bound to lead to social realism in the arts, until the position is reached that whatever the common man does not understand is treason … Art which is directly produced for the Community can never have the same withdrawn quality as that which is made out of the artist's solitude'; Cyril Connolly, *The Unquiet Grave* (1944; Harmondsworth, UK: Penguin, 1984), 78–9.

108 Raymond Williams, *Politics and Letters: Interviews with New Left Review* (London: New Left Books, 1979), 65–70.

109 'For Continuity and Change,' editorial, *Politics & Letters* 1, no. 1 (1947): 3; Raymond Williams, 'The Soviet Literary Controversy in Retrospect,' *Politics & Letters* 1, no. 1 (1947): 21–31.

110 John Lewis, editorial, *Modern Quarterly* (Winter 1946–7): 11.

111 Alick West to Douglas Garman, 3 November 1951, Garman Papers, DG2; Maurice Carpenter complained of these trends in a letter to the *Daily Worker*, 18 March 1948; the unrepentant editor William Rust replied (2 April 1948), 'If you mean that we do not prostrate ourselves before the obscurities of a writer so utterly alien to us as Edith Sitwell then I must say that there is a wide gulf between us as to what constitutes good literature'; Lindsay Papers, NLA, Folder 191.

112 Jack Lindsay, editorial, *Arena* 1, no. 1 (1949); Lindsay, editorial, *Arena* 1, no. 4 (1950): 3.

113 *Arena* (new series) 2, no. 8 (1951): 2. *Daily Worker*, 12 May 1949; a furious Lindsay wrote to Burns at the time accusing the leadership of 'phoney simplifications' and failing to understand the need for a journal 'concerned with good writing and literary values, which is genuinely left in tone,' and of abandoning the ground to Connolly et al.; Burns replied, threateningly, 'All this flows from your posing your innerlight against the Party … No engineer can do it. No miner can do it. And at least you might have learnt from the Soviet discussions that no writer can do it.' Both letters n.d. [mid-1949], Lindsay Papers, NLA, Folder 413; 'Writers' Group: A Report to the NCC' [n.d.] proposed the co-option of Fore and *Arena*, Arnold Rattenbury Papers, Box 12. Lindsay gives a frank account in *Meeting with Poets* (London: Muller, 1968), 128–31; the reception of the Key Poets series in the *Daily Worker* is summarized by Andy Croft, *Comrade Heart: A Life of Randall Swingler* (Manchester: Manchester University Press, 2003), 205.

114 Beeching summarizes these position in an undated letter to Lindsay, Lindsay Papers, NLA, Folder 9.

115 Rattenbury to Amabel Williams-Ellis, 7 August 1981), Box 11, Rattenbury Papers (MS 556), University of Birmingham; Macleod, *Death of Uncle Joe*, 40; Kynaston, *Austerity Britain*, 337.

116 *Daylight* 1, no. 1 (Autumn 1952); Doris Lessing, *The Golden Notebook* (1962; London: Granada, 1980), 301–4.

117 H. Horsfall, 'A Poem for Stalin,' *Daylight* 1, no. 3 ([n.d.]): 4.

118 Making the journal a 'Supplement' of the weekly *World News & Views* – mandatory reading for party members – masked the publication's limited appeal; the various editorials, meetings, and discussions about the journal's contents vacillated between despair at the poor quality of the material received and serene confidence in its significance. 'Competition for Writers,' *World News and Views*, 26 July 1952; 'Daylight,' *World News and Views*, 13 September 1952; 'Daylight,' *World News and Views*, 17 January 1953; 'Daylight No 3,' *World News and Views*, 9 May 1953; 'Daylight No 4,' *World News and Views*, 5 September 1953; 'Circular re

Daylight meeting on 13 May 1954,' Lindsay Papers, NLA, Folder 6; complete run of journal in WCML. Len Doherty, *A Miner's Son* (London: Lawrence & Wishart, 1955) and *The Man Beneath* (London: Lawrence & Wishart, 1957); Herbert Smith, *A Field of Folk* (London: Lawrence & Wishart, 1957) and *A Morning to Remember* (London: Lawrence & Wishart, 1962). Transcript of Heinemann phone call to Sam Aaronovitch, 9 July 1954, KV 2/2531.

119 The efforts of party writers and literary critics (Lindsay, Jack Beeching, Montagu Slater, Arnold Kettle, Alick West, John Sommerfield), meanwhile, to produce a book criticizing on their own terms the so-called Literature of Decay, variously revealing its authoritarian instincts – Huxley, Greene, Eliot, Waugh, Koestler, and Orwell – were rejected by the party publishers. The proposed book, the publishers said, was contaminated with decadence, and Klugmann, who read the manuscript, sternly told its contributors that they lacked the perspective to 'criticise the literature of the graveyard,' being 'half buried in it'; Report on 'Literature of the Graveyard,' 8 August 1951, Lindsay Papers, NLA, Folder 216.

120 The Group established subdivisions of Professional Creative Writers, Younger Writers, and those in Trades Allied to Writing at the end of 1947; 'Professional Writers' Group of the Communist Party, 2 December 1947, Lindsay Papers, NLA, Folder 419. A new Literature Group arose in 1951, which ran alongside a much-diminished Writers' Group that had been relaunched in 1950.

121 Warner had been inactive for some time; Ackland endorsed Mervyn Jones's critique published in the *New Statesman*, 20 December 1952, and sent Pollitt notice of her withdrawal, 6 March 1953, KV 2/2337.

122 Doris Lessing, Sommerfield, and Jack Beeching were prominent in the early 1950s. Lessing conveys her sense of the atmosphere of the meetings in the 'Red Notebook' sections of *The Golden Notebook* (1962; London: Granada, 1980), 299–301. Priestley had refused to sign the Stockholm Peace Petition, having criticized the Soviet Union in *Collier's* magazine; George Thomson consigned him –with Eliot, Koestler, and Bertrand Russell – to 'the literature of the graveyard; George Thomson, 'Our National Cultural Heritage,' in *Britain's Cultural Heritage*, 9; 'Priestley disowned by Unity,' *Daily Worker*, 24 February 1954.

123 In particular, George Thomson; according to Charles Hobday's recollections, Thomson 'wanted a new slogan: "Marx, Engels, Lenin, Stalin, Caudwell."' Andy Croft, 'Notes on the Writers' Group,' Charles Hobday Papers, MS208, Birmingham University Special Collections, Box 13.

124 Caudwell had begun to feature in party training material in the late 1940s; syllabus on 'The Origins and Characteristics of Poetry Based on Christopher Caudwell's *Illusion and Reality*,' a five-lesson course that ran from 14 January 1949, CP CENT ED 2/8; he was the subject of a London Cultural Committee conference in October 1947; Lindsay Papers, London District circular, NLA, Folder 413. Tributes included Hyman Frankel, 'Christopher Caudwell,' *World News and Views*, 15 February 1947, and Alick West, 'Illusion and Reality,'

Communist Review (January 1948): 7–13. *Further Studies in a Dying Culture* was published in 1949.

125 Maurice Cornforth, 'The Caudwell Discussion,' *Modern Quarterly* (Autumn 1951): 355.

126 Cornforth, summarizing remarks, *Modern Quarterly* (Autumn 1951): 357–8. Cornforth was the party's leading proponent of Cold War–period 'materialist' thought, and also wrote *Science Versus Idealism: An Examination of 'Pure Empiricism' and Modern Logic* (London; Lawrence & Wishart, 1946), the pamphlet 'Dialectical Materialism and Science' (London: Lawrence & Wishart, 1949) and *In Defence of Philosophy: Against Positivism and Pragmatism* (London; Lawrence & Wishart, 1950).

127 AGM [A.G. Morton], 'The Position in Biology,' 31 January 1949), CP CENT 5/9.

128 The so-called Caudwell controversy played out in the pages of *Modern Quarterly* in 1949–51. The genesis of the controversy was an essay in the Spring 1949 issue by WEA Lecturer at the University of London, Oscar Thomson, which had drawn liberally on Caudwell. This was followed by an unsigned article, 'Poetic Instant,' which summarized critical correspondence received in response to Thomson's piece. Accused of 'idealism,' Oscar Thomson answered his critics in the same issue by identifying Caudwell's influence on his essay; this, according to the editorial essay, made it necessary that 'Caudwell's contribution to Marxism should be mastered and used as a weapon,' and 'at least two' articles were promised. Unsigned, 'Poetic Instant,' *Modern Quarterly* (Summer 1949): 287–8. Over a year later, a denunciation of Caudwell as un-Marxist was published by Cornforth, 'Caudwell and Marxism,' *Modern Quarterly* (Winter 1950–1): 16–34. Oscar's brother – NCC member, *Modern Quarterly* editorial board member, and classics Professor George Thomson – seems to have submitted another essay to be run alongside Cornforth's that was not published and has never come to light. Why it was not published alongside Cornforth's piece is not apparent from the *Modern Quarterly* minutes, although the chair, Dutt, suggested it should be; Parsons, 'Communism in the Professions,' 311. George Thomson's piece, 'In Defence of Poetry,' however, appeared in *Modern Quarterly* (Spring 1951): 107–34, and responded to Cornforth mainly by linking Caudwell's work with quotations from the Marxist canon to establish his bona fides; it was followed by an editorial statement claiming that, due to 'regrettable oversight,' it was not made clear that Cornforth's article was 'the first contribution to a discussion on the work of Caudwell' (134).

129 Discussed in Ben Harker, 'Jack Lindsay's Alienation,' *History Workshop* 82, no. 1 (2016): 83–107. Lindsay's disciplining for theoretical deviation was a prequel to the Caudwell controversy, from which the cowed Lindsay was conspicuously absent. The exceptions that prove the rule were Derek Kartun's hectoring essays, 'The creative artist and the party,' *World News and Views*, 5 June 1950 and 12 June 1950.

130 Only Bernal and Margot Heinemann came out behind Cornforth; Montagu Slater sat on the fence; the other ten whose views were published variously defended Caudwell, and some questioned Cornforth's integrity. Commissioned articles by Alan Bush, Montagu Slater, and Alick West appeared in *Modern Quarterly* (Summer 1951): 259–66; Slater took a mediating role, and called for a further conference to explore the issues in greater depth; West and Bush defended Caudwell; unsolicited contributions from G.M. Matthews, Jack Beeching, and Peter Cronin followed (266–75), and from Margot Heinemann, Edward York, Werner Thierry, O. Robb, Bernal, and Edwin S. Smith in the next issue, *Modern Quarterly* (Autumn 1951): 340–53; Cornforth then wrapped up the debate (353–8). Although the episode has become synonymous with the party's disciplining of its intellectuals, E.P. Thompson's claim that it was 'editorially controlled throughout and directed to a foregone conclusion' (273) sits uneasily with the levels of dissent expressed, and is not supported from either the NCC records or those of the *Modern Quarterly* editorial committee. Despite the leadership's objectives, what is most striking is the amount of airtime given to those sympathetic to Caudwell. E.P. Thompson, 'Caudwell,' *Socialist Register* 1977: 273n12; Cornforth, summarizing remarks, *Modern Quarterly* (Autumn 1951): 357–8.

131 Jones, *Chances*, 117.

132 Ibid., 116.

133 On the Italian context, see Stephen Gundle, *Between Hollywood and Moscow: The Italian Communist and the Challenge of Mass Culture, 1943–1991* (Durham, NC: Duke University Press, 2000), 20, 49–53. A.A. Zhdanov, *On Literature, Music and Philosophy* (London: Lawrence & Wishart, 1950); reviewed by RPA in *Communist Review* (March 1951): 93–4, and Alan Bush, *Labour Monthly* (June 1951): 284–6; J.V. Stalin, *Concerning Marxism in Linguistics* (London: Soviet News, n.d. [1951]), reviewed by George Thomson, *Labour Monthly* (June 1951): 284.

134 Italian Communists also had neorealist cinema; the French had artist André Fougeron; the small Australian party had an established Realist Writers' Group with roots in Popular Front cultural politics and a model in Frank Hardy's explosively libellous *roman à clef*, *Power without Glory*. Guttuso loomed large in the discussions of the CP Artists' Group, whose bulletin was developed into the journal *Realism* from June 1955. Guttuso's work was exhibited at the Leicester Gallery in early 1955. 'Renato Guttuso, an Interview with Ray Watkinson,' *Realism* 1 (January 1955): 408; John Berger, 'On Guttuso's "The Beach,"' *Realism* 6 (November–December 1956): 4–5. On Fougeron, see Barbara Niven, 'Painting the miners' struggle,' *World News and Views*, 10 March 1951; Margot Heinemann, 'André Still and the Novel of Socialist Realism,' *Marxist Quarterly* (April 1954): 11–27. Hardy's novel was reviewed glowingly by Dutt in the Cominform journal, *For a Lasting Peace, For a People's Democracy*, but criticized in the *Daily Worker* by Patrick Goldring; the negative review was picked up by the *Melbourne Herald*,

which ran an article 'Hardy's book a bore, say Reds'; Dutt then challenged the *Daily Worker* via letter for doing the job of the 'Australian capitalist press' (12 June 1952; a fortnight-long debate ensued in the letters pages, with some supporting the paper's criticism (16 June 1952) and others echoing Dutt (12 June 1952); CP IND DUTT 8/13.

135 Emile Burns, concluding remarks to Engels Society Conference, 19–20 February 1949, *Transactions of Engels Society 1* (April 1949): 12–13.

136 These groups were set up in the wake of the world peace movement, which was launched in 1948 and by 1950 took the form of the World Peace Council. Groups included Artists for Peace, Musicians for Peace, Teachers for Peace, Architects for Peace, and Scientists for Peace; slightly broader based were the Authors' World Peace Appeal, the National Assembly of Women, and the British Youth Committee. Neal Wood, *Communism and British Intellectuals* (London: Gollancz, 1950), 165–6. The central body, the front organization British Peace Committee, was described in mid-1951 by Dutt as 'a head without a body' for which 'there is practically no non-Party mass support'; Rajani Palme Dutt, 'Notes on Peace Movements, 22 June 1951,' quoted in Parsons, 'Communism and the Professions,' 266.

137 Prompted by Lawrence & Wishart's director Maurice Cornforth, Lindsay struggled to produced a book about socialist realist literature in the early 1950s. His papers contain two unpublished manuscripts, 'The Nature of Socialist Realism' and 'Socialist Realism' (Lindsay Papers, NLA, Folder 320); his mainly undated early to mid-1950s correspondence with Beeching in particular shows exasperation with comrades for refusing to engage seriously with the discussion (Folder 9). A version of the earlier manuscripts appeared, belatedly, under the title of *After the Thirties: The Novel in Britain and Its Future* (London: Lawrence & Wishart, 1956).

138 Sam Aaronovitch, 'Capitalist Reaction against Socialist Realism,' in *Essays on Socialist Realism and the British Cultural Tradition* (London: Arena, n.d. [1952]), 43–60.

138 Jack Lindsay, *Charles Dickens: A Biographical and Critical Study* (London: Andrew Dakers, 1950), 420.

139 Frank Jackson, review of Fred Ball's *Tressell of Mugsborough*, *Labour Monthly* (January 1952): 44. The republication of the Tressell novel, the complete manuscript of which had been bought by CP member Fred Ball in 1946, was a protracted affair. Lawrence & Wishart had declined the opportunity to publish it in 1948. After publishing Ball's biographical study, *Tressell of Mugsborough*, they continued to hesitate, although the emerging emphasis on the need to establish national cultural antecedents clearly enhanced the prospects of republication. The decision was taken in December 1953; the 'Complete Text' was published on 6 October 1955 in a print run of 1,500 copies alongside a 'Special Trade Union Edition,' cross-subsidized by the National Federation of Building Trade

Operatives in a print run of 3,500 (both sold out in three months). Maurice Conforth and Jack Beeching wrote the unsigned forward. Beeching then published an essay, 'The Uncensoring of *The Ragged Trousered Philanthropists*,' *Marxist Quarterly* (October 1955): 217–30. The book was widely reviewed, and the CP clearly benefited from association with its republication. Dave Harker, *Tressell: The Real Story of the Ragged Trousered Philanthropists* (London: Zed, 2003), 153, 165–76; Fred Ball, *One of the Damned* (London: Weidenfeld and Nicolson, 1973), 202–4. For Tressell as the cornerstone of a new literature, see Aaronovitch, 'Capitalist Reaction.'

140 George Thomson, 'Draft Outline Report on Our National Cultural Heritage,' CP CENT CULT 3/6.

141 Lindsay, *Charles Dickens*; Jack Lindsay, *George Meredith: His Life and Work* (London: John Lane, 1956).

142 Lindsay, 'Fullness of Life,' 189; Lindsay, *Meeting with Poets*, 104.

143 Arnold Kettle, *An Introduction to the English Novel*, vol. 1, *To George Eliot* (London: Hutchinson, 1951); volume 2 appeared in 1953. Kettle's debt to Leavis was acknowledged in the Preface to vol. 1, 9. No review of the book appeared in the *Guardian*, but on 23 January 1952 a leader in the paper summarized a recent 'Brains Trust'-type article from the *Daily Worker* in which Kettle had been invited to identify 'the six best novels ever written'; the piece was deeply ironic about Kettle's statements, including his claim that *Wuthering Heights* was 'the greatest emotional protest of the Victorian novel against the tyranny of class society' and that Cervantes' *Don Quixote* 'helped to destroy feudal society.' Kettle defended himself, accusing the *Guardian* of a witch hunt in which his professional competence had been called into question (26 January 1952). Correspondence followed, including supportive responses from Kettle's students and from his Leeds University colleague E.P. Thompson (29 January 1952). The party responded to both book and controversy in the form of Margot Heinemann, 'Class and the classics,' *World News and Views*, 9 February 1952; Alick West, review of *Introduction to the English Novel*, *Modern Quarterly* (Autumn 1952): 244–7.

144 Lukács by now had been denounced for recent libertarian ideas about Hungarian culture and civil society rendered obsolete by the imposition of the Stalinist dictatorship in 1948. The offending texts have only recently been translated into English; see Georg Lukács, *The Culture of People's Democracy: Hungarian Essays on Literature, Art and Democratic Transition, 1945*, trans. and ed. Tyrus Miller (Leiden: Brill, 2013). Jozsef Révai, *Lukacs* [*sic*] *and Socialist Realism* (London: Fore, 1950). Hobsbawm's dutiful mediation of a controversy he clearly had not read was a career low point. Recalling the tone of John Lewis's presentation of the Soviet Literarature Controversy four years earlier, Hobsbawm wrote: 'He [Lukács] has been criticised without landing in labour camps, or being "silenced." Révai's statement is no doubt authoritative' (no page number). Lukács's self-criticism

was considered to be inadequate. Martin Horvath, 'A Note on the Self-criticism of Lucacz [*sic*],' *Communist Review* (May 1950): 154–60. Alick West criticized Lukács for leaving the 'class basis' of realism unclear and for being insufficiently prescriptive about socialist realism; Alick West, review in *Labour Monthly* (February 1951): 92–3). He then emphatically endorsed Révai for exposing in Lukács's aesthetics 'hiding places for the enemy'; *Labour Monthly* (February 1952): 288.

145 Here was a work that potentially encouraged its writers to do what Lenin had said they should: to appropriate, assimilate, and refashion the best of 'bourgeois' culture. Lukács presented the novel form as developed by Balzac and Tolstoy as an epistemology angled at the social totality, extractable from which was a usable methodology – the creation of character types that crystallized historical patterns – which Marxist writers should actively develop in their fictional analyses of contemporary history. Finding fault with Lukács's richly suggestive model became *de rigeur*. Arnold Kettle, review of Georg Lukács, *Studies in Contemporary* Realism, *Modern Quarterly* (Winter 1950–1): 72–8. Beyond one decorative quotation (87), Kettle made no use of the book in his *Introduction to the English Novel 1* (1951); Margot Heinemann, 'Lukacs [*sic*] on Realism,' *World News and Views*, 22 April 1950); Heinemann's review is appended with an editorial note referring readers to Horvath's critique in *Communist Review*.

146 Lindsay recalled that Lessing considered the modern world too 'extended and entangled' for realism in the tradition of Balzac; Lindsay, 'Fullness of Life,' 196; West to Lindsay, 15 September 1962, Lindsay Papers, NLA, Folder 191.

147 In this period Lindsay was sending drafts of his novels to Burns, to whom *Betrayed Spring* was dedicated, for comment (NA KV 2/3254); Lindsay was commended for immersing himself in the working-class movement through his research fieldwork. Gallacher reviewed *The Rising Tide* in *World News and Views*, 28 November 1953, and John Mahon reviewed *Betrayed Spring* in *Labour Monthly* (May 1953): 236.

148 Lindsay, 'Fullness of Life,' 196. An unsigned leader in the *Times Literary Supplement* attacked the series for pushing round its characters in a spirit of 'Marxist Sergeant-Majordom,' 29 April 1955.

149 The AIA split in 1951 and faded away after dropping its contentious political clause in 1953; Lynda Morris and Robert Radford, *The Story of the Artists' International Association, 1933–53* (Oxford: Oxford Museum of Modern Art), 3.

150 Bill Moore, *Cold War in Sheffield: The Story of the Second World Peace Conference, November 1950* (Sheffield: Sheffield Trades Council Peace Sub-Committee, 1990).

151 Pablo Picasso, 'Why I became a communist,' *World News and Views*, 16 December 1944; Derek Kartun, 'Picasso,' *Modern Quarterly* (March 1946): 69–72.

152 Grant Pooke, *Francis Klingender 1907–1955: A Marxist Art Historian of Our Time* (London: Marx Memorial Library, 2008). Klingender's *Marxism and Modern Art* (London: Lawrence & Wishart, 1943) offers a useful genealogy of debates on

realist aesthetics; his *Art and the Industrial Revolution* (London: Noel Carrington, 1947) remains a standard work; both were reprinted in the 1970s.

153 Malcolm MacEwan, interview with Steve Parsons, cited in Parsons, 'Communism in the Professions,' 450.

154 My summary of these debates draws on Parsons' exemplary and detailed analysis. Klingender, 'Russian Art at the Academy,' *Modern Quarterly* (Winter 1945–6): 89–95; R. Rosner, 'Socialist Realism in Soviet Architecture,' *Keystone* (November 1945); Parsons, 'Communism in the Professions,' 448; *Soviet Reconstruction Series* (July 1948); Gerald Marks's letter to *Realism* (4 June 1956) reports back on the trend of apologia for Soviet art by way of asserting a more critical line.

155 Andrew Boyd, 'Marxism and Modern Architecture,' *Communist Review* (April 1949): 122–6, and *Communist Review* (May 1949): 152–5. These articles formed the basis of a symposium hosted by the party's Architects and Allied Technicians' Group, 25 November 1949; proceedings were published in the Group's *Bulletin* 1 (March 1950), CP CENT CULT 5/1.

156 As Owen Hatherley argues, the architectural practice of Harlow designer Frederick Gibbard (close to the CP but not a member) and Arthur Ling (CPer who designed much of post-war Coventry) and many CPers in the LCC Architects' Department was always 'a friendly, rather cutesy amalgam of Scandinavian design and the English picturesque tradition'; Owen Hatherley, 'The brutalist decades,' *London Review of Books*, 17 November 2016.

157 John Allan, *Berthold Lubetkin: Architecture and the Tradition of Progress* (London: RIBA, 1992).

158 David Gregory Jones, 'Some Early Works of the LCC Architects Department,' *Architectural Association Journal* (November 1954); Architect's Group [*sic*], 'British Tradition in Architecture,' in *Britain's Cultural Heritage*, 28–33.

159 The piece won a national *Daily Express* competition for a victory symphony; Joanna Bullivant, *Alan Bush, Modern Music and the Cold War* (Oxford: Oxford University Press, 2017), 114.

160 Parsons, 'British "McCarthyism,"' 238; he took a job as general manager at Collett's bookshop. Thomas Russell to Jack Lindsay, 7 April 1953, Lindsay Papers, NLA, Folder 3.

161 Benjamin Frankel, 'The Composer Speaks,' *Our Time* (January 1949): 12; Frankel's letter to *Modern Quarterly* (Winter 1948–9): 93, took issue with the 'sweeping over-simplifications' made by Burns in his justifications for the controversies; Frankel clashed with Bush at the CP Musicians' Branch meeting called to discuss the controversy on 7 July 1949, arguing that new music should be allowed to be performed for fifty years before it was rejected; composer Bernard Stevens more gently queried the Soviet line, especially the appropriateness of transposing Soviet edicts about 'national' music to developed countries where folk culture had been destroyed by industrialization. Report of Meeting, Lindsay Papers, NLA, Folder 413. Frankel publicly left the CP in 1952. Three years later he would be embroiled

in a notorious court case around the workings of the International Society for Contemporary Music, in which he would accuse CP composers Stevens and Christian Darnton of lying to discredit him; Richard Hanlon and Mike Waite, 'Notes from the Left: Communism and British Classical Music,' in Croft, *Weapon in the Struggle*, 80–1.

162 Overseas Music Director to Bush, 4 December 1941; John Lowe to H. Grisewood, 28 January 1948), BBC WAC R Cont 1, Composer, Alan Bush, File 1A, File 2; *WMA Bulletin* (July 1950).

163 Alan Bush, 'Problems of Soviet Musical Theory,' *Modern Quarterly* (Winter 1949–50): 38–47; Bush, 'Tasks of Cultural Workers,' *Communist Review* (February 1951): 53; Bush, *Marxism and the Battle of Ideas with Special Reference to the World of Music* (London: WMA, n.d.); Boughton's article, 'The Science and Art of Music,' *Modern Quarterly* (Summer 1948): 20–41, slightly predated the controversy but anticipated it with its stout antimodernism; he then eagerly defended the Zhdanov line in his review of journalist Alex Werth's mainstream account, *Musical Uproar in Moscow*, 'Mr Werth's Brain-storm,' *Communist Review* (August 1949): 636–8.

164 The WMA's expectation was that, as a winning entry in the Arts Council (opera commissioning scheme), *Wat Tyler* would be followed by a Festival staging and BBC broadcast (*WMA Bulletin* [July 1950]). A BBC producer listened to the Berlin broadcast with a view to repeating it, only to find it 'melodically uninteresting' and akin to 'works one can hear with such boredom in the company of "Friends of the Soviet" [*sic*] in Kensington Square.' Frank Wade, Confidential Report on Wat Tyler, 7 April 1951, BBC WAC R Cont 1 Composer, Alan Bush, File 1A; '*Wat Tyler* premiere in Leipzig,' *Daily Worker*, 5 September 1953.

165 Bush's plans for invigorating these networks are outlined in 'Music in the Fight for Peace and Socialism,' an article promoting a CP conference, 'Amateur Musicians in the Fight for Socialism' in October 1950, *World News and Views*, 23 September 1950. Nineteen fifty-two was a low point. The WMA grant was cut (it had been secured in 1946 at £400 and had increased to £600 in 1948); individual WMA membership was down to 492 from 557 in 1951; no education classes were held; and the WMA singers had just twenty-three engagements. Secretary's Report for 1952 AGM, NA KV 5/132; 'Ministry to stop subsidy for Red propaganda songs,' *Daily Mail*, 24 June 1952; Bush's fiftieth birthday was prominently celebrated, *WMA Bulletin* (October 1950); his status in the WMA is discussed by Hanlon and Waite, 'Notes from the Left,' 82–3.

166 Rattenbury to 'Ted' [E. Thomson], n.d. [1948], Rattenbury Papers, Box 11.

167 'Report on *Our Time*,' [November 1947], CP CENT CULT 1/1.

168 Ibid.

169 Labour Party memos on 'Socialist Policy for Leisure' (1946–7), summarized in Kynaston, *Austerity Britain*, 175.

170 The conspiracy analysis would come increasingly to the fore with the 'Battle of Ideas' in 1948, but slightly earlier readings saw mass culture as a morbid symptom. Bernal wrote of 'the social vices of capitalism' having 'penetrated' the working class; see Bernal, 'Belief and Action,' 78.

171 The cultural assumptions that siphoned a seventh of the Arts Council's first-year budget into transforming Covent Garden, a former *palais de danse* run by Mecca, into the new home for Sadler's Wells and the future Opera Company was now welcomed, rather than challenged, by Communist intellectuals, who were relieved – even before Cold War anti-Americanism bit deep – that the building would now be saved for high culture and spared the 'the graceless spontaneity of the jitterbug' and the 'cacophony of swing music.' Sinclair, *Arts and Cultures*, 44, 54–5; Elizabeth Frank, 'The Re-opening of Covent Garden Opera House,' *Our Time* (February 1946): 142.

172 Claire Langhammer, *Women's Leisure in England 1920–1960* (Manchester: Manchester University Press, 2000), 66; Addison, *Now the War Is Over*, 129–31; one wartime YCL report from South Wales bemoaned the 'tremendous number of American soldiers billeted in the area' and the fact that 'girls spend all their time with them.' South Wales YCL Report, 1944, CP CENT YOUTH 1/1.

173 The incendiary moment here was in 1947, when Graeme Bell's Australian Jazz Band established the Leicester Square Jazz Club, which emphasized 'Jazz for Dancing.' The ensuing ructions between those for and against jazz dancing are described in Kevin Morgan, 'King Street Blues,' in Croft, *Weapon in the Struggle*, 137–8; the quotation, from Bell's autobiography, is from Morgan, 137.

174 McKibbon, *Classes and Cultures*, 419.

175 Unsigned film column, *Daily Worker*, 9 October 1943; *Film Today* was intended to complement *Theatre Today*, which was launched in March 1946; Jack Lindsay's *Hullo Stranger* (London: Andrew Dakers, 1945), 137–40, agreed.

176 L. Gollhard, 'Politics and the cinema,' *World News and Views*, 18 October 1947; Bert Hogenkamp, *Film, Television and the Left in Britain, 1950–1970* (London: Lawrence & Wishart, 2000), 4; the Film Panel, for instance, held a conference on 11 January 1953 analysing the racism and militarism of mainstream films; *AWPA Bulletin 8*. CP ORG MISC 3/9.

177 The Rank chain eventually buckled when pressured to distribute the film by Harold Wilson, then president of the Board of Trade. Peter Hennessy, *Never Again: Britain 1945–51* (London: Vintage, 1993), 326; the director was Bernard Miles, a fellow-traveller close to Lindsay; *Daily Worker*, 11 May 1950, 27 May 1950.

178 Montagu Slater's popular speedway novel *Once a Jolly Swagman* (1944), which at once detailed the exploitation of mainly working-class riders and the possibility of collective resistance, was filmed in 1948. Directed by Jack Lee, it involved some personnel close to Unity and the CP (Bill Owen acted, Bernard Stevens wrote the score). Slater advised about the script, but did not write the screenplay. The

film capitulates to dominant convention, reworking the novel as a *Bildungsroman* in which Left politics, like speedway, are discarded by an older and wiser hero. Slater's *Our Time* piece, 'The Film Is a Kind of Novel,' conspicuously does not mention the film, although the magazine's editors used his association with it, and stills from it, as an eye-catching device to frame the article. *Our Time* (January 1949): 5–7.

179 The party challenged Rank's effective monopoly stranglehold by proposing fundamental measures at the level of production (studio nationalization and joint production committees, improved preshooting planning to increase efficiencies), and distribution (state and municipal intervention in the running of cinemas. John Ross, 'From Hollywood and Rank – preserve us!' *Daily Worker*, 24 November 1946; *The Film Industry: A Memorandum Issued by the Communist Party* (London: CP, 1947); A Group of Communist Filmmakers, *The Great Film Lock-Out* (London: CP, 1948). Communists also had a strong record in challenging the loophole in the inter-war film quotas through which American companies like MGM simply relocated production to Britain and undermined the national industry through films that distilled American ideas of Englishness, and fetishized its upper classes. See Ivor Montagu, 'British films after the war,' *World News and Views*, 9 December 1944; Ralph Bond, 'British Film Crisis,' *Our Time* (October 1945): 44–5; typical of the genre of what McKibbin (*Classes and Cultures*, 429) calls the Hollywood-idea-of England-film were *A Yank at Oxford* (1938), *Goodbye Mr Chips* (1939), and *Mrs Miniver* (1942).

180 Figures from McKibbin, *Classes and Cultures*, 419; Bond, 'British Film Crisis.'

181 Addison, *Now the War Is Over*, 133; Gollhard, 'Politics and the Cinema.'

182 Bond was committed to defending the existing industry, while Montagu was in favour of a more militant position, calling for all-out nationalization. Bond was running ACT Films Limited, a production company formed by the union in part to provide work for its members; Montagu wanted 'an inspiring vision of what a national film industry could be – drawing on the Soviet Union and the People's Democracies.' Hogenkamp, *Film*, 2–3.

183 The key provocation was *Notes Towards the Definition of Culture* (London; Faber and Faber, 1948). Alick West, 'T.S. Eliot – an enemy of the people,' *World News and Views*, 5 March 1949; Brian Simon, 'The Defence of Culture,' *Communist Review* (December 1949): 762–8; R.S. Hinton, 'Culture and T.S. Eliot,' *Modern Quarterly* (Spring 1951): 147–62; four of the eight chapters of the proposed 'Literature of the Graveyard' book were about Eliot; Lindsay Papers, NLA, Folder 216.

184 McKibbin, *Classes and Cultures*, 430

185 Montagu attended some NCC meetings, but film was never a central item for discussion, even during the crisis; CP CENT CULT 1/1. As McKibbin notes (*Classes and Cultures*, 430), the Board of Trade did not consider importing European films, and rebuffed approaches from the Italian film industry, keen to

bring its films to Britain during the boycott. The party seems to have made no proposals along these lines, although it would successfully align itself with Italian cinema a few years later, during the Edinburgh People's Festivals.

186 Such as the Film Quota (fulfilling this would have required the production of 150 British films per year), the 1948 Film Act, which compelled cinemas to screen British films, and the 1949 National Film Finance Corporation, created to assist the British film industry; McKibbin, *Classes and Cultures*, 430.

187 Sinclair, *Arts and Cultures*, 73–4; Montagu Slater remained associated with the movement until the early 1950s, writing the script for *The Brave Don't Cry* (1952), a film about a Scottish mining disaster, commissioned by John Grierson. The CP documentary film maker Kay Mander increasingly struggled to find work from the end of the 1940s, and moved to Hollywood. John Green, *Britain's Communists: The Untold Story* (London: Artery, 2014), 107–8. Priestley had invested great hope in the movement in the immediate post-war period; his novel *Bright Day* (1946) shows a British scriptwriter, artistically and morally corrupted by his work in Hollywood, undergoing a rejuvenation through association with the movement. The nascent New Left around Raymond Williams was also alert to the consequences of the British Film Institute's not being resourced to support the last state-funded documentary group, the Crown Film Unit. Williams, *Politics and Letters*, 73–4.

188 Bond argued that trade union and co-op–financed films dealing with themes such as the Tolpuddle Martyrs and the Peasants' Revolts could 'break the commercial stranglehold of the monopolies'; Ralph Bond, 'Film,' *Arena* 2, no. 8 (1951): 48. Targeted by an anti-Communist campaign ('Pictures before Politics!'), Bond was temporarily unseated from the ACT General Council in 1954. Hogenkamp, *Film*, 23–4.

189 The New Era Film Club began life in March 1950. The production companies formed in the early 1950s were Plato Films Limited, Contemporary Films, and Bond Films; Hogenkamp, *Film*, 7–9. These developments are detailed in Peter Sutton, 'Reflections of a Cultural Worker,' *Communist Review* (April 1950): 126–8; Sutton, 'The New Era Film Club,' *World News and Views*, 1 April 1950; 'Films and the labour movement,' *World News and Views*, 25 April 1953.

190 Cited in Hogenkamp, *Film*, 10.

191 Examples include *May Day 1950* (1950), *Festival in Berlin* (1951), and *Harry Pollitt in China* (1956); ibid., 7, 16, 25.

192 Bert Hogenkamp, 'The Sunshine of Socialism: the CPGB and Film in the 1950s,' in Croft, *Weapon in the Struggle*, 192–206.

193 Colin Seymour-Ure, *The British Press and Broadcasting since 1945* (1991; Oxford: Blackwell, 1996), 28–9; Hennessy, *Having It So Good*, 105; Kynaston, *Family Britain*, 169.

194 'The Social Significance of Comic-strips,' 13 September 1950, CP CENT Speakers' Notes 9/1.

195 Kevin Morgan, 'The Communist Party and the *Daily Worker*, 1930–56,' in Andrews, Fishman, and Morgan, *Opening the Books*, 152; Hutt was twice passed over for the job, in 1942 and in 1949; on the latter occasion he considered resigning. 'Statement by Allen Hutt,' 14 February 1949, CP IND HUTT 2/1.

196 Report on Daily Worker from D. Bourne, Nottingham, 12 September 1948, CP IND HUTT 2/1.

197 'The three forms of imperialist culture – cinema, radio, and TV – seem to me progressively worse. They are the first three cultural forms which are totally cut off from the audience, destroying all potentiality of actions and interaction'; Jack Lindsay to Alick West, n.d. [1960]. Lindsay Papers, NLA, Folder 191.

198 The 1953 coronation was watched by 40 per cent of the population on two and a half million sets; Hennessy, *Having It So Good*, 112, 244–5, 520; Kynaston, *Family Britain*, 464.

199 'Statement on Commercial Television,' 2 February 1954, CP IND POLL 3/12.

200 Kynaston, *Modernity Britain*, 535; Hogenkamp, *Film*, 91; Macleod, *Death of Uncle Joe*, 40.

201 The broadcast took place on 21 December 1954. 'Hitherto,' wrote Dutt to the *Manchester Guardian* (22 December 1954), welcoming public disquiet, 'Orwell has been the exotic delicacy of the minority of corrupted intellectuals and upper-class reactionaries. Now authority has tried to foist him on the mass of the people, and their immediate revulsion has evidently taken authority by surprise'; CP IND DUTT 8/4.

202 The *Manchester Guardian* (18 February 1955) defended the broadcast; Dutt had objected in a letter to the newspaper (22 December 1954); its line was defended against him in letters published on 29 December 54; he wrote again on 5 January 1955; he was mocked in the *News Chronicle* in an article showing a picture of his eyes, entitled 'Little Brother is watching, too' (7 January 1955).

203 C.A. Smith to Dutt, 5 January 1955, CP IND DUTT 8/4.

204 P.G.M., 'Children in the Battle of Ideas,' *World News and Views*, 21 January 1949; Patrick Goldring, 'The menace of the comic strip,' *World News and Views*, 14 April 1951; Bill Carritt, 'The Battle of Ideas in Middlesex: Protect our children's minds,' *World News and Views*, 15 February 1953. The AWPA had a Children's Panel dedicated to analysing this material (*Authors World Peace Appeal*, Bulletin 6, [n.d.]). The International Women's Day Commitee printed and circulated a glossy 3d pamphlet, 'The Lure of the Comics' (1952), CP ORG MISC 8/6; Speakers' Notes, 'The Social Significance of the Comic Strips,' 13 September 1950, CP CENT SN 1/9.

205 The flourishing genre of ex-communist memoir included Fred Copeman, *Reason in Revolt* (London: Blandford, 1948); Freda Utley, *Lost Illusion* (Philadelphia: Fireside, 1948); Douglas Hyde, *I Believed* (1950: London: Reprint Society, 1952); and Bob Darke's paperback Penguin Special, *The Communist Technique in Britain* (London: Penguin, 1952).

206 The party's line was close to that of Labour MPs including Skeffington Lodge, who attacked American magazines as a 'roaring carnival of quick drinks, adolescent sex, bright lights and dimmed thinking.' Lodge, in Parliament, November 1947, cited in Woddis, 'Another American export for Britain.' Churchill's cabinet scrutinized a sample of comics in 1954 and subsequently banned them. Hennessy, *Having It So Good*, 85, 656n98; Kynaston, *Family Britain*, 437.

207 Hulton Press soon added *Girl* in 1951 and *Swift* in 1953. Kynaston, *Austerity Britain*, 505.

208 J.B. Priestley, 'Our new society,' *New Statesman*, 16 July 1955), reprinted in *Thoughts in the Wilderness* (London: Heinemann, 1957), 125. In 1954 Priestley took a trip to the United States and coined the term 'Admass' to describe the modern culture he encountered there. He saw it, however, not as nationally aberrant but as a continuum of patterns, as John Baxendale argues, described twenty years before in *English Journey* (1934). John Baxendale, *Priestley's England: J.B. Priestley and English Culture* (Manchester: Manchester University Press, 2007), 178.

209 Hoggart's essays for the WEA's *Highway*, notably 'Reflections on *Life* Magazine,' *Highway* (June 1948): 176–7, anticipated *The Uses of Literacy* by almost a decade. 'How far is it true to say,' he asked of the 'colour and sound womb' society invoked in the magazine's glossy pages, 'there, but for the grace of present poverty, go we?' (177). The Abuses of Literacy was the working title of what became *The Uses of Literacy* (1957); Mulhern, *Culture/Metaculture*, 56.

210 Williams would later identify the party's defensive early 1950s discourse of a working class heroically resistant to modern sensibility and the 'glossy futurism' on offer at the Festival of Britain as a catalyst for the book. He was especially irritated by Barbara Niven's 'People and the Artists at the Festival,' *Modern Quarterly* (Autumn 1951): 313–18, which insisted that 'the people' saw beyond and through the emerging consumerism showcased at the Festival. Raymond Williams, 'Notes on British Marxism since 1945,' in *Problems in Materialism and Culture* (1976; London: Verso, 1980), 240–1. The conceptual core of *Culture and Society* was unveiled in Williams's 'The Idea of Culture,' *Essays in Criticism* 3, no. 3 (1953): 240–66.

211 E.P. Thompson, untitled contribution, *Highway* (April 1949): 137.

212 Jack Lindsay, 'Summarising Glance,' conclusion to the unpublished 'Literature of Decay,' Lindsay Papers, NLA, Folder 216.

213 Harry Pollitt, *Looking Ahead* (London: CP, 1947), 14, 90; *British Road*, 14. Friendship Societies, delegations, working parties, travel books, meetings, and articles supporting and detailing these countries' physical and cultural reconstruction were widespread. E.P. Thompson, ed., *The Railway: An Adventure in Construction* (London: British-Yugoslav Association, 1948). In his autobiography, CP artist Paul Hogarth describes his visits to Yugoslavia (1947),

Poland (1948, 1953), and Czechoslovakia (1953); the proposed book based on the last trip – for which Hogarth's travel companion Randal Swingler wrote the text – was considered insufficiently upbeat in party circles, and never published. Paul Hogarth, *Drawing on Life* (London: Royal Academy of Art, 1997), 20–5, 29–34; Jack Lindsay and Maurice Cornforth, *Rumanian Summer: A View of the Rumanian People's Republic* (London: Lawrence & Wishart, 1953); Alan Bush, 'A Musical Journey through the Balkans,' *Changing Epoch* 1 (1947): 11–22; 'Busy building for peace: 250,000 youngster queue to help Bulgaria,' *Daily Worker*, 27 February 1950.

214 E.P. Thompson, 'Comments on a People's Culture,' *Our Time* (October 1947): 34–8.

215 Thomson, 'On the Work of Party Intellectuals,' 14.

216 George Thomson, 'Our Cultural Work in the Light of Our Party Programme,' *Communist Review* (September 1951): 272–7; Alan Bush, 'Tasks of Cultural Workers,' *Communist Review* (February 1951): 49–55; Roy Sear, 'Youth and Heritage,' in *Britain's Cultural Heritage*, 59–63; Sear, 'Bucharest: Britain's cultural contribution,' *World News and Views*, 11 July 1953.

217 Ben Harker, '"Workers' Music": Communism and the British Folk Revival, 1945–55,' in *Red Strains: Music and Communism outside the Communist Bloc*, ed. Robert Adlington (Oxford: Oxford University Press, 2013), 184–205.

218 Thomas Hardy's novels – formerly considered unduly pessimistic – were now praised for their sensitive affirmations of peasant culture that struggled valiantly to anticipate the creation of the industrial proletariat and the socialist revolution. George Thomson, 'Thomas Hardy and the Peasantry,' *Communist Review* (August 1949): 631–5; Thomson was challenging T.A. Jackson's assessment that Hardy's 'jaundiced' view of life need not be taken seriously (*Daily Worker*, 21 May 1949).

219 Sear, 'Youth and Heritage,' 59–63. In a later article, Sear chastized sceptics, arguing that those who maintained that 'our folk tradition is dead must shoulder the responsibility for its further extinction'; Sear, 'Bucharest; Morgan, 'King Street Blues,' 138

220 Ewan MacColl, ed., *The Shuttle and the Cage: Industrial Folk-Ballads* (London: WMA, 1954); A.L. Lloyd, ed., *Come All Ye Bold Miners: Ballads and Songs of the Coalfields* (London: Lawrence & Wishart, 1952).

221 Lloyd's *Come All Ye Bold Miners* was part of the industry's contribution to the Festival of Britain. As Lloyd explains in the Preface, many of the songs included were among the one hundred sent to Lloyd, who had issued an appeal to miners to send in songs in *Coal*, the industry's journal, and *Mining Review*, its newsreel.

222 MacColl's *Johnny Noble* (1946) is discussed in Ben Harker, *Class Act: The Cultural and Political Life of Ewan MacColl* (London: Pluto, 2007), 71–5; it was broadcast on the North of England Home Service, 5, August 1947; Lloyd's song collecting provided the material for the WMA Opera Group's production of *Johnny Miner*. Written by D.G. Bridson, the ballad opera was broadcast on the BBC Home

Service in December 1947, repeated in February 1948, and staged in London in April 1948. Unsigned, 'Johnny Miner,, *Our Time* (April 1948): 185. Lloyd also scripted 'Coaldust Minstrel: The Life and Hard Times of Tommy Armstrong, the Miner Poet,' broadcast on the North of England Home Service, 20 May 1953.

223 The events of the World Federation of Democratic Youth sought to promote music and cultural exchange across East and West; the Workers' Music Association, with its groups, publishing arm, and in-house label, Topic Records, had boomed during wartime Russophilia, but struggled to find a strong identity subsequently; these organizations now provided an outlet for the folk-based recordings and publications of Lloyd and MacColl, among others.

224 *Sing* was a Communist-dominated publication launched in January 1954 by members of the London Youth Choir, and was committed to stimulating and supporting a radical song movement; MacColl published nine songs there in the first year. Harker, *Class Act*, 92–114; Dave Arthur, *Bert: The Life and Times of A.L. Lloyd* (London: Pluto, 2012), 198–218; A.L. Lloyd, 'Folk Song for Our Time?' *Marxist Quarterly* (January 1954): 47–57; Ewan MacColl's late-night performance at the Brighton Jazz Club, for instance, presented the music in these terms. Derrick Stewart-Baxter, 'Preachin' the Blues,' *Jazz Journal* 5, no. 8 (1952): 4–5.

225 File on Reginald Donald Smith, NA KV 2/2533.

226 Lomax's name was listed in the notorious *Red Channels: The Report of Communist Influence in Radio and Television* (New York: Counterattack, 1950), 9. MacColl's broadcasts included *Come All Ye Bold People: A Programme about Ballads,* broadcast on BBC Third Programme, 28 December 1952, and *St Cecelia and the Shovel*, BBC Third Programme, 31 December 1952; both programs were produced by the Communist R.D. Smith; MacColl, 'Ballads and Blues,' *Radio Times*, 6 March 1953); *Ballads and Blues* was broadcast on the Home Service in weekly programs beginning on 10 March 1953; the series was produced by Denis Mitchell and repeated on the Light Programme in June 1953. These programs are discussed in Harker, *Class Act*, 106–8. Despite the support of R.D. Smith, who rated Lloyd more highly than he did MacColl, Lloyd struggled to get his scripts accepted, especially on the Third Programme; BBC WAC R Cont 1, Scriptwriter File, 1939–56, Albert Lancaster Lloyd; Arthur, *Bert*, 219–39.

227 Unpublished statement by MacColl (1968), reprinted in Peggy Seeger, ed., *The Essential Ewan MacColl Songbook* (New York: Oak, 2001), 386.

228 An earlier precedent was Lloyd's 'Singing Englishmen,' a concert version of his 1944 folksong history of the same name, republished by the WMA to mark the Festival of Britain. A performance of *The Singing Englishman* by the WMA Opera Group was premiered in St Pancras Town Hall on 1 June 1951, and repeated in Aylesbury with an introduction by Ralph Vaughan Williams the following month; a choral version, conducted by Alan Bush, was staged in November 1951 and again in June 1952. The production's fortunes are traced in the *WMA Bulletin* over this period.

229 The Royal Festival Hall event was a sell-out and critically acclaimed; Harker, *Class Act*, 111–12.

230 Spin-off concerts from MacColl's broadcast became fundraisers for the impecunious Theatre Workshop, held initially in London, and were developed through a national touring ensemble. A Scottish tour in February 1954 was a commercial flop; MacColl, 'On the trail of a song,' *Challenge* 3 July 1954.

231 When the history of the early post-war folk music revival eventually came to be written, researchers would deduce from the well-known Communism of Lloyd and MacColl and the obvious synergies between their project and *The British Road* that the movement was driven by King Street. These positions are summarized in Harker, 'Workers' Music,' 184–205; Raymond Williams would warn against the self-isolating and delusory temptation to oppose against mainstream culture a 'dissident' but 'fragmentary and meagre' 'working-class culture,' including industrial ballads. Raymond Williams, 'Working Class Culture,' *Universities & New Left Review* 1, no. 2 (1957): 29; Williams, *Culture and Society 1780–1950* (1958; London: Pelican, 1963), 307; Ben Harker, 'Class Composition: *The Ballad of John Axon*, Cultural Debate and the Late 1950s British Left,' *Science & Society* 73 no. 3 (2009): 340–56.

232 Coverage of the emerging folk revival was sparse in official NCC documents, and was discussed only once, according to party records, by a NCC reluctant to make the types of commitments urged by MacColl. Folk music was only fleetingly registered in the three *Arena* symposia dedicated to the new cultural line. 'Draft Plan of National Committee and Sub-Committee Work, 1953–54'; on 19 November 1953, the NCC discussed 'a policy on folk music,' Lindsay Papers, NLA, Folder 10.

233 Karl Dallas, interview with the author, 22 October 2003, Bradford. The relationship between the leftist flank of the folk music revival guided by MacColl and Lloyd and the CP would remain a fraught one well into the 1960s.

234 'Final Draft Constitution, Edinburgh Labour Festival Committee,' Buchan Archive, Gallacher Memorial Library, Glasgow Caledonian University.

235 Henderson's own commitment to folk music had been galvanized by his wartime experiences and what he saw as a lingering folk impulse among allied soldiers who, bored by the inanities of Forces' radio, fashioned new songs from borrowed tunes. Seumas Mór Maceanruig [Henderson], ed., *Ballads of World War II* (Glasgow: Lili Marleen Club, nd), iii.

236 *British Road*, 11.

237 Timothy Neat, *Hamish Henderson: A Biography*, vol. 1 (Edinburgh: Polygon, 2007), 242, 301; he was also well connected in the cultural circles of the PCI, hosting a delegation of Italian writers from the literary Risorgimento in 1948.

238 Ibid., 301; Henderson, 'The Edinburgh People's Festival, 1951–1945,' in Croft, *Weapon in the Struggle*, 163–71.

239 Martin Milligan, 'The Edinburgh People's Festival,' *Communist Review* (March 1952): 86.

240 Osmond Robb, *Daily Worker*, 22 August 1951, 31 August 1951.

241 Honor Arundel, *Daily Worker*, 3 September 1951; recorded by Alan Lomax and issued on CD, *1951 Edinburgh People's Festival Ceilidh* (compact disc, 1161–178–2, Rounder, 2005).

242 Henderson claimed that the national question had now been settled by Stalin's own writings on linguistics; Neat, *Hamish Henderson*, 266; Martin Milligan to Sam Aaronovitch, 4 November 1952, Buchan Archive.

243 Minutes of Scottish Cultural Committee, 13 October 1952, Buchan Archive. Even before the more ambitious second event, the Edinburgh Trades Council was detecting 'a considerable amount of Communist propaganda,' *Reynolds News*, 16 March 1952, cited in Neat, *Hamish Henderson*, 304; suspicions were confirmed at the second festival, not least by Theatre Workshop's production of MacColl's virulently anti-American play, *The Travellers* (1952), which echoed Korean War–era party discourse that equated America's ruling class with fascism. The British Labour Party and the Scottish TUC placed the festival on a list of proscribed organizations, a list that, by 1955, was being prepared with the assistance of MI5. A.E. Davidson to Haldane Porter, 10 November 1955, WMA MI5 File, KV 5/132. The festival contracted in 1953 and faded out the following year.

244 Ruth Haines to Eddie Frow, 30 January 1954, Frow Papers, WCML.

245 Callaghan, *Cold War*, 54, 62; Malcolm MacEwen later dated the 'grovelling' Soviet apology to the Yugolsav government as his turning point from Stalinism. Malcolm MacEwen, *The Greening of a Red* (London: Pluto, 1991), 179; James Klugmann, *From Trotsky to Tito* (London: Lawrence & Wishart, 1951).

246 Callaghan, *Cold War*, 61; George Matthews, 'Towards Peaceful Co-existence,' *Marxist Quarterly* (October 1954): 195–207.

247 Callaghan, *Cold War*, 104.

248 It was followed by *The Common Secondary School* (1955). McKibbin, *Classes and Culture*, 226–31; Kynaston, *Family Britain*, 325–6; Brian Simon, *A Life in Education* (London: Lawrence & Wishart, 1998), 76; Simon quotes the *Times Educational Supplement* reviews, as does Kynaston.

249 Jack Lindsay, 'The Problems of Soviet Writers,' *Marxist Quarterly* (April 1955): 111–23.

250 Cornforth to Lindsay, 29 May 1952, Lindsay Papers, NLA, Folder 11.

251 Undated letters between Lindsay and Beeching about an article, drafted by Beeching, on 'Humanism and Socialist Realism'; undated letter from Arnold Kettle to Lindsay, Lindsay Papers, NLA, Folder 17; Lindsay to West, 6 November 1955, Lindsay Papers, NLA, Folder 191. Berger's debut novel, *A Painter of Our Time* (1958), reprised elements of these earlier debates about socialist realist painting. The first of the award-winning radio ballads written by Ewan MacColl

(1957–64), *The Ballad of John Axon* (1958), brought a version of it to the mass media; Harker, 'Class Composition,' 340–56.

252 The Artists' Group in particular struggled to formulate any workable definitions, as discussions in their optimistically titled journal, *Realism*, registered. 'In our pursuit of Socialist Realism,' noted one article, 'we have never yet found it possible to issue any cut-and-dried manifesto or categorical account of our aesthetic theories'; Ray Watkinson, 'Three Men in Search of Realism,' *Realism* 1 (January 1955).

253 Berger was active in Artists for Peace, attended CP Artists' Group meetings, wrote for its *Artists Group Bulletin* in 1954 and its journal *Realism* in 1955 and 1956. He also contributed to broader debates in the party press, notably 'The Communist Party and the arts,' *World News and Views*, 31 December 1955.

254 Artists for Peace handbills and letters, CP IND ORG MISC 2/9.

255 Paul Hogarth, 'Humanism versus Despair in British Art Today,' *Marxist Quarterly* (January 1955): Hogarth, *Drawing on Life*, 50–1

256 In this spirit Alick West had long insisted that 'the fundamental relation between culture and communism' had still gone unanalysed; West to Garman, 9 December 1950, Garman Papers, DG 2 file; West, *One Man in His Time* (London: Allen and Unwin, 1969), 190.

257 Lindsay, 'Fullness of Life,' 192.

258 The debate, initiated by the NCC, opened and closed with Arnold Kettle, 'Politics and Culture,' *World News and Views*, 26 June 1954, *World News and Views*, 9 October 1954; Thomas Russell, 'Bring me my bow,' *World News and Views*, 14 August 1954; Jack Lindsay, 'The Political Aspect of Culture,' *World News and Views*, 24 July 1954. Brian Behan (*World News and Views*, 7 August 1954) and Derek Kartun (*World News and Views*, 21 August 1954) also contributed.

259 Russell's montage of working-class life – allotments, brass bands, vegetable competitions – is reminiscent of T.S. Eliot's – 'the dog races, the pin table, the dart board, Wensleydale cheese, boiled cabbages cut into sections, nineteenth-century Gothic churches and the music of Elgar' – in *Notes Towards the Definition of Culture* (London Faber, 1948), 31.

260 Thomson, 'Draft Outline Report'; Thomson, 'Our Cultural Work,' 272–7.

261 Broad fields of operation were mapped and more sceptical readings of Soviet discussions advocated. Communists, the document insisted, must learn as well as teach, while recognizing that 'the winning of state power must be our strategic aim' and without it 'our ideological struggle would be diffuse and lack point.' 'Notes on the Battle of Ideas,' a six-page cyclostyled document based on a University Staffs Committee meeting and introduced by Sam Aaronovitch, CP CENT Speakers' Notes, 1/11; also in Lindsay Papers, NLA, Folder 18.

262 Part of a campaign that exerted real influence over the Movement for Colonial Freedom in focusing its considerable energies on racism within Britain's borders.

'West Indians in Britain,' March 1957, CP CENT INT 73/1, cited in Callaghan, *Cold War*, 106; Michael Herbert, *Never Counted Out! The Story of Len Johnson, Manchester's Black Boxing Hero and Communist* (Manchester: Dropped Aitches Press,1992), 90; Callaghan, *Cold War*, 107.

263 NCC circular, July [1954], CP CENT CULT 1/3. By collating bespoke reports from its core professional and cultural groups, the unprecedented Commission integrated empirical analysis of mid-century Britain's class structure with the strategic question of alliance between the working class and 'the middle sections of the population' – identified as one-sixth of the population disproportionately significant in 'creating the climate of opinion on the social and ethical questions of our time.' Commission on the Middle Class (1954), 4, unnumbered introduction, CP CENT CULT 1/3. The document was never published, but elements of it would be integrated into Andrew Grant's *Socialism and the Middle Class* (1958).

264 'Discussion of the work of district cultural committees,' 6 July 1954; NCC, 'Improving Our Ideological Work,' n.d. [spring 1954], CP CENT CULT 1/2.

265 John Gollan, *The British Political System* (London: Lawrence & Wishart, 1954), 167–88.

266 Cornforth to Lindsay, 27 June 1956, Lindsay Papers, NLA, Folder 34.

267 Including the CP Music Group's journal, *Music & Life*, which first appeared in April 1956.

268 Aaranovitch to Lindsay, 31 March [1955], Lindsay Papers, NLA, Folder 13; NCC circular, 19 July 1955, CP CENT CULT 1/2.

269 Artists' Group, 'The Place of Culture and Cultural Advance in the New Draft of 'The British Road to Socialism,' written for NCC meeting, 9 November 1956, CP CENT CULT 1/2.

4. The Struggle for Renewal, 1956–1968

1 Eric Hobsbawm, *Interesting Times: A Twentieth-Century Life* (London: Abacus, 2002), 201.

2 Ibid., 206.

3 Special Congress transcript, CP CENT CONG 10/9.

4 Mick Bennett, quoted by Christopher Hill, Special Congress transcript, CP CENT 10/9; *Times*, 17 February 1958.

5 Figures from John Callaghan, *Cold War, Crisis and Conflict: The CPGB 1951–68* (London: Lawrence & Wishart, 2003), 76–7; Kenneth Newton, *The Sociology of British Communism* (London: Allen Lane, 1969), appendix 1A and 1B, 160–1.

6 Special Congress transcript, CP CENT CONG 10/9.

7 Having left the East End in the mid-1950s for home ownership in Chadwell Heath suburbia, where comrades were few and party work dispiriting, Gorman found Communism at odds with his new pattern of life and the party's identity

and strategy remote from the world it sought to transform. John Gorman, *Knocking Down Ginger* (London: Caliban, 1995), 242.

8 Scott Hamilton, *The Crisis of Theory: E.P. Thompson, the New Left and Post-war British Politics* (Manchester: Manchester University Press, 2012); Paul Flewers and John McIlroy, eds., *1956: John Saville, E.P. Thompson and The Reasoner* (London: Merlin, 2016); Keith Flett, ed., *1956 and All That* (Newcastle: Cambridge Scholars Press, 2007). Madeleine Davis analyses the recent work in 'Edward Thompson, MI5 and the *Reasoner* Controversy: Negotiating "Communist Principle" in the Crisis of 1956,' *Key Words* 16 (2018): 41–62.

9 For instance, the titles of two very significant books in the field – Andy Croft, ed., *A Weapon in the Struggle: The Cultural History of the Communist Party of Great Britain* (London: Pluto, 1998), and Kevin Morgan, Gidon Cohen, and Andrew Flinn, *Communists and British Society 1920–1991* (London: Rivers Oram, 2007) – suggest longer coverage, although in both cases the analysis falls mainly on the 1920–56 period.

10 Willie Thompson, *The Good Old Cause: British Communism 1920–1991* (London: Pluto, 1992), appendix, 218.

11 Although the funding ended in 1979, it was only revealed in November 1991 through KGB documents newly declassified in Moscow. The *Sunday Times* broke the story; ibid., 12, 234n33.

12 Geoff Andrews, *Endgames and New Times: The Final Years of British Communism 1964–1991* (London: Lawrence & Wishart, 2004), 75.

13 Ibid., 75, 95.

14 For the emergence of the New Left, see Michael Kenny, *The First New Left* (London: Lawrence & Wishart, 1995); and Lin Chun, *The British New Left* (Edinburgh: Edinburgh University Press, 1993).

15 'On the whole the Party's working-class membership, drawn mainly from the skilled trade unions, stood by the Party during the crisis, but its middle-class and intellectual members deserted in thousands'; Malcolm MacEwen, *The Greening of a Red* (London: Pluto, 1991), 198.

16 'Statement on the Current Campaign Against Intellectuals in the Party,' n.d. [1957], CP IND KLUG 12/7. In 1955 MacEwen had challenged Pollitt's dismissive equation of intellectuals with public school boys (often a euphemistic code for homosexuals in party discourse) and Pollitt's boast that none was among the party's seventeen General Election candidates. 'If we are to advance among the middle classes,' MacEwen wrote, 'and not deny the Party some good talent … we had better not stick to the line you put forward'; MacEwen to Pollitt, 20 May 1955, NA, KV 2/2987.

17 Steve Parsons, '1956 and the Communist Party of Great Britain,' *Bulletin of the Society for the Study of Labour History* 47 (Autumn 1983): 9–10.

18 Other leading industrial cadres in the NUM (Alex Moffat), the Fire Brigades Union (John Grahl, T. Haston), and the Electrical Trades Union (Frank Chapple)

also left the party, some to emerge as dedicated anti-Communists; Callaghan, *Cold War*, 78.

19 Through the Living Newspaper, *World on Edge*, November 1956. Colin Chambers, *The Story of Unity Theatre* (London: Lawrence & Wishart, 1989), 344. In the wake of 1956, the organization struggled to survive without its block bookings, despite the endeavours of individual Communists who remained committed to the theatre and its work (347).

20 Rajani Palme Dutt, 'The Great Debate,' *Labour Monthly* (May 1956): 194. Ivor Montagu brushed aside Levy's Special Congress critique as 'emotional strain' (Special Congress transcript, CP CENT CONG 10/9). Despite having voted against supporting the Soviet action in Hungary, Arnold Kettle railed at the Special Congress against 'immodest parading of conscience and moral superiority' (Special Congress transcript, CP CENT CONG 10/6). Alan Bush warned against a 'path to counter revolution … paved with good intentions' (*World News*, Discussion Supplement, 26 January 1957). George Thomson argued that nowhere had workers taken power without a disciplined party governed by 'the principles of democratic centralism' ('Strengthen democratic centralism,' *World News*, Discussion Supplement 2, 23 February 1957).

21 Lindsay wrote to Beeching: 'We must consider next steps. I feel we really have the [Executive Committee] on the defensive and near toppling. But they will use every chance to falsify and muscle in. I have written to [Arnold] Kettle to nerve him to a firm stand'; Lindsay to Beeching, n.d. [October 1956?], Lindsay Papers, NLA, Folder 26. 'On the leadership, what is to be done? It may almost be said that the rot has gone so deep that we cannot see who the new leadership consists of: it's got to be primarily a working-class leadership, it's an illusion that you [Jack Lindsay], Eric Hobsbawm and Christopher Hill could lead the working class movement'; Maurice Cornforth to Lindsay, 15 November 1956, Lindsay Papers, NLA, Folder 191.

22 'All the seeds of degeneration which had been brought about by the Stalin terror,' noted the soon-to-be-expelled Malcolm MacEwen, 'were to be seen in our own party'; MacEwen, *Greening of a Red*, 186

23 'Why We Are publishing,' *Reasoner 1* (July 1956). For the emergence of the *Reasoner*, see Madeleine Davis, 'The *New Reasoner* and the Early New Left,' *John Saville: Commitment and History*, ed. David Howell, Dianne Kirby, and Kevin Morgan (London: Lawrence & Wishart, 2011), 30–51. The case of the correspondence suppressed by the editors at the *Daily Worker* and *World News* is covered in the existing literature. See, for instance, John Callaghan and Ben Harker, eds., *British Communism: A Documentary History* (Manchester: Manchester University Press, 2011), 198–206. Lawrence & Wishart director Maurice Cornforth wanted to see the publisher made available for the 'most colossal inquest on theory and practice, and self-criticism.' It was emphatically not available for that purpose, and a proposed book-length symposium, to be

edited by MacEwen, was blocked. Cornforth to Jack Lindsay, 27 March 1956, Lindsay Papers, NLA, Folder 22; MacEwan to George Matthews, 10 December 1956, Lindsay Papers, NLA, Folder 26. Monty Johnstone, the editor of the YCL journal *Challenge*, faced what he called 'strong moral pressure' to bring the publication in line at the time of Hungary; Monty Johnstone, 'Relations between the Communist Party and the Young Communist League,' 1957, CP IND JOHN 3/1. It was this outspoken document that abruptly terminated Johnstone's upward trajectory towards the party leadership.

24 The SCR split was between non-Communists and party figures – especially Andrew Rothstein, who edited the *Anglo-Soviet* journal. The story broke in the *Times* in February 1957; Saville Papers, DJS 107.

25 Jack Beeching to Jack Lindsay, n.d. [early 1956], Lindsay Papers, NLA, Folder 21. Thompson's letter to John Saville, written on 4 April 1956 – immediately after the Twenty-fourth National Congress and in many ways the primal scene of what followed – covers the same ground. He railed against the 'old gang' that had led the party since the late 1920s, enumerating its many failures to value sufficiently intellectual and ideological work, to undertake fundamental revaluation of Marxist theory or the party's own structures, or to form a discussion journal in which pressing questions could be openly debated. Quoted in John Saville, *Memoirs from the Left* (London: Merlin, 2003), 104.

26 John Saville to Ted Bramley, 10 April 1958, Saville Papers, DSJ 109.

27 As Hill and Rodney Hilton recognized, the party leadership's reflex support for the Soviet Union was precisely a crisis in historical knowledge, 'the undesirable culmination of years of distortion of facts and the failure of British Communists to think political problems for themselves'; letter from Hilton and Hill to Victor Kiernan, 15 November 1956, Saville Papers, DJS 111.

28 Quotation, letter from Pearce to John Saville, 7 October 1956, Saville Papers, DJS 110. Pearce recognized as the enemy the official style of party history whose master text was the *Short Course*, which enabled leaders to 'either suppress or distort episodes' and which robbed Communists of the means of drawing on the past when 'formulating present and future policy'; Pearce to Saville, 23 June 1956, Saville Papers, DJS 110. History Commission, Minutes of first meeting, 10 December 1956, CP IND Pollitt 2/10; the rest of the minutes are in CP CENT COMM 10/1.

29 Pearce to Saville, 7 October 1956, Saville Papers, DJS 110. Always a hoarder, Pearce rummaged through years of back copies of party publications to rebut the authorized versions of events. He saw the *Reasoner* as a revival of the short-lived tradition embodied by the party's non-sectarian Popular Front–period journal, *Discussion*; Pearce to Saville, 6 August 1956, Saville Papers, DJS 110. He sent a letter to this effect to *World News*, which went unpublished; Pearce to Saville, 18 November 1956, Saville Papers, DJS 110.

30 Hobsbawm, *Interesting Times,* 209.

31 *Marxist Quarterly* had been highly evasive through 1956, with only oblique criticisms of Stalinist cultural practices, before being closed down all together during the crucial run-up to the Special Congress, 'a blunder of the first magnitude,' according to the usually on-message John Lewis; Lewis, 'Questions of Theory,' *World News* Discussion Supplement 1, 26 January 1957.

32 Pollitt and Dutt wanted, in essence, a British version of the *Short Course*; Pollitt was mainly concerned with the party's reputation, Dutt with that of the long-defunct Comintern. A.L Morton wanted a more 'self-critical account' to 'bring out our mistakes.' Pearce wanted analysis of contested episodes. History Commission, Minutes of first meeting. Pearce had an embattled relationship with the History Committee from the outset, and clashed with the leadership figures repeatedly (History Commission, Minutes, 24 January 1957, 4 March 1957). Having failed to get E.P. Thompson appointed to the commission or to get letters published about murkier aspects of the party history published in the *Daily Worker*, and finding the Stalinist practices and memory holes still operational – the official minutes of meetings he had attended bore little resemblance to the actual discussions he had witnessed (Minutes, 4 March 1957) – he was soon convinced of the futility of his efforts and left the party. Klugmann was tasked to do the writing at the meeting on 26 February 1958, and the commission effectively, though not officially, dissolved. In contrast to Pearce's, Hobsbawm's criticisms were muted; CP CENT COMM 10/1. Hill's contribution is transcribed at CP CENT CONG 10/9.

33 Eric Hobsbawm, 'Problems of Communist History,' in Hobsbawm, *Revolutionaries* (1969; London: Weidenfeld and Nicholson, 1973), 10.

34 Hobsbawm, *Interesting Times*, 209.

35 Brian Pearce and Michael Woodhouse, *Early History of the Communist Party of Great Britain* (1966) was based on Pearce's extended articles in *Labour Review*. Pearce also wrote a 'Reasoner' Pamphlet 1 (April 1957) on 'The Communist Party and the Labour Left 1925–29.' These and other writings on the party's early years were assembled as Brian Pearce and Michael Woodhouse's *A History of Communism in Britain* (1969; London: Bookmarks, 1995).

36 The book was reviewed by Alasdair MacIntyre on the BBC Third Programme, and the talk published in the *Listener*, 7 January 1960. Thompson's letters defending the party's record – especially its cultural interventions of the 1930s and 1940s and the reputations of Ralph Fox, Dona Torr, and Montagu Slater – appeared on 4 January 1960 and 3 March 1960.

37 For example, Rothstein's shrill review of Henry Pelling's *The British Communist Party: A Historical Profile* presented a book – whose limitations were obvious – as a 'try on' on behalf of 'the imperialist powers' to 'take advantage of public correction of serious errors in the USSR' by attacking Communist Parties; Andrew Rothstein, 'Mr Pelling on the Communist Party,' *Marxism Today* (November 1958): 327. Johnstone challenged Rothstein's upbeat *Daily Worker*

review of the revised *Short Course* (Russian edition) in a spate of correspondence with Rothstein in July 1959. In spring 1959 Johnstone wrote to Pollitt seeking clarification over the latter's comments in a 1956 television interview about the party line during the war; Johnstone to Pollitt, 16 March 1959 and 24 March 1959. Another row, tracked by Johnstone, broke out in 1962 amidst claims made – accurately – in *Tribune* that in 1938 the party had refused the *News Chronicle* permission to serialize John Reed's *Ten Days That Shook the World* (Trotsky looms large in the book; Lawrence & Wishart owned the copyright). Dutt flatly refuted the claims in a letter sent to *Tribune* (23 February 1962). Further controversy arose in *Tribune* in 1965 around the publication of Dutt's highly tendentious history of the Comintern; cuttings and letters, Monty Johnstone Papers, CP IND JOHN 1/1

38 Callaghan, *Cold War*, 72–3; Thompson, *Good Old Cause*, 106–10.

39 *The Report of the Commission on Inner Party Democracy, 25th Special Congress* (CPGB, 1957); the minority report was printed at the back, 45–60; David Michaelson Papers, Modern Records Centre, MSS 2333/3/4/4. Callaghan, *Cold War*, 75; MacEwen, *Greening of a Red*, 184–99; Thompson, *Good Old Cause*, 109–10.

40 *Revised Draft Text of the British Road to Socialism for the 25th (Special Congress)* (London: CPGB, 1957), David Michaelson Papers, MSS 2333/3/4/4.

41 Amendment to draft submitted by Golders Green and Childs Hill Branch, 20 April 1957, David Michaelson Papers, MRC, MS233/3/4/4.

42 'Amendments to *The British Road to Socialism*,' CP CENT CONG 10/5.

43 Untitled Artists' Group Document, 2 November 1956, CP CENT CULT 1/2.

44 E.P. Thompson, 'Caudwell,' *Socialist Register* 1977 (London: Merlin, 1977), 273n15.

45 As Callaghan puts it, 'the Party was caught in transition, but the contradictions of the position had not yet entered the consciousness of most of its members'; *Cold War*, 73.

46 West to Garman, 24 April 1957, Garman Papers, University of Nottingham, DG2.

47 As a philosopher, Lewis presented his case (in 'Questions of Theory') in the spirit of one impartially exposing contradictory logic, rather than backing either current, but he was lampooned nonetheless, for example by Lucien Amaral, 'Foundations in the air,' *World News* Discussion Supplement 2, 23 February 1957; Lewis responded in the third issue, 23 March 1957.

48 *The British Road to Socialism: The Programme of the Communist Party* (London: CPGB, 1958), 23.

49 Ibid., 28. West's contribution, Congress Transcript, CP CENT CONG 10/7; West sent the full text of his statement to Douglas Garman for comments, Garman Papers, DG2. The party's richer mid-1950s analysis of culture and class composition was lost in a crisis-driven search for certitude, as was the more

developed analysis of the state contained in John Gollan, *The British Political System* (London: Lawrence & Wishart, 1954).

50 *British Road* (1958), 10.

51 'Revised Draft of *British Road to Socialism*' [circulated pre–Twenty-fifth Congress version], David Michaelson Papers, MSS 233/3/4/4; these omissions were corrected at the suggestion of Pollitt and Gollan.

52 The same line of critique was soon developed by a group centred around the Nigerian party activist Frank Oruwari, who found that, in the words of Muriel Seltman, 'only a little study revealed how deeply party thinking was permeated by imperialist and chauvinist assumptions.' Muriel Seltman, *What's Left? What's Right? A Political Journey via North Korea and the Chinese Cultural Revolution* (Kibworth, UK: Matador, 2014), 70; *British Road* (1958), 25.

53 *British Road* (1958), 16; Pollitt and Gollan, as chair and secretary, respectively, of the commission, had suggested that the first 1956 draft should address the 'coloured community'; note in front of *British Road to Socialism Revised Draft Text for 25th Congress*, David Michaelson Papers, MS 233/3/4/4.

54 *British Road* (1958), 10, 22.

55 Ibid., 23.

56 Ibid., 10.

57 Ibid., 10, 29.

58 Callaghan, *Cold War*, 187.

59 'Revised Draft of *British Road to Socialism*'; *British Road* (1958); for a Trotskyite critique, see *Workers' International Review* 2, no. 2 (1957), which included Ian Wooding's detailed analysis of the 'British Road' document, 16–22.

60 NCC circular, 9 May 1956, Lindsay Papers, NLA, Folder 25

61 Emile Burns to Jack Lindsay, 7 May 1956, Lindsay Papers, NLA, Folder 25.

62 'NCC notes,' Meeting, 12 July 1957, CP CENT CULT 3/7; 'What shocks me about your attitude,' MacEwan had written to him, alluding to the fact that Kettle had voted against the leadership's support of the Soviet invasion of Hungary, 'is that you parade the fact that you have got no conscience'; MacEwen to Kettle, 16 February 1957, NA KV 2/2988.

63 West to Lindsay, 16 July 1957, Lindsay's MI5 File, KV 2/3256.

64 Hobsbawm's perceived unreliability is registered in various tapped phone calls and conversations picked up by Special Branch's King Street bug in spring 1958; transcripts in KV 2/3257. For Heinemann, see Callaghan, *Cold War*, 77.

65 CP Executive to Lindsay, 24, April 1958, Lindsay Papers, NLA, Folder 31. There was much agonizing among the leadership about whether to involve Lindsay; King Street transcripts, 10 July 1957, 27 February 1958, 3 March 1958, 13 March 1958, 16 April 1958, KV 2/3257.

66 Arnold Kettle, 'Rebels and Causes: Some Thoughts on the Angry Young Men,' *Marxism Today* (March 1958): 71.

67 Hobsbawm pointed out that the swelling movement could count among its achievements two journals (one with a circulation of 8,000) and a network of well-attended and youthful clubs and educational series (600 attended some meetings); he persisted in fraternizing with the New Left, and became a director of their Partisan Cafe. 'Information for the NEC, 10–11 November 1958': Some Notes on the Universities & Left Review from Comrade Eric Hobsbaum [*sic*], CP CENT EC 5/8.

68 Lindsay to Kettle, n.d. [early 1957], KV 2/3256.

69 Lindsay to Kettle, n.d., Lindsay Papers, NLA, Folder 29.

70 Lindsay, 'Some Notes on the Cultural Problems at the Moment,' 29 August 1958, KV 2/3257.

71 Lindsay to West, n.d., Lindsay Papers, NLA, Folder 27; Lindsay to Wainwright, n.d. [July 1958], KV 2/3257; Hobsbawm's report revealed that *Universities & Left Review* was claiming a circulation of 8,000; the *Times* gave the *New Reasoner* figure as 3,000 (17 February 1958).

72 Lindsay to Burns, 12 November 1956, KV 2/3256

73 'First Draft Outline Report on Winning Intellectuals to the Party,' CP CENT CULT 1/4.

74 Betty Reid in transcript of King Street Meeting, 13 October 1958, KV 2/3258

75 Kettle, 'Rebels and Causes,' 68, 72.

76 Tom Maschler, ed., *Declaration* (London: MacGibbon and Kee, 1957); 'Our sectarianism blinds us to the depth of the revolt among [these] people against life in Britain,' ran a counterdocument, probably written by West, optimistically entitled 'Opening of Discussion on *Declaration*,' 13 December 1957, CP CENT CULT 1/2.

77 Cornforth also supported the line, despite private misgivings that the party was 'wantonly keeping itself isolated from a large slice of real life, particularly among the youth.' Cornforth to Lindsay, 27 June 1958, Lindsay Papers, NLA, Folder 191. For Kettle, the *New Reasoner*'s aim was 'getting people away from the party'; Kettle to Lindsay, 29 April [1958], Lindsay Papers, NLA, Folder 28.

78 *New Reasoner* 1 (Summer 1957); Lindsay contributed an article on 'Socialist Humanism' to the third issue, Hobsbawm wrote about 'Marx's Victorian Critics' in the first. Former Communist editors included Mervyn Jones, Doris Lessing, Randall Swingler, and economists Ronald Meek and Michael Barratt-Brown.

79 *Universities & Left Review* 1, no. 1 (1957); the other editors were Stuart Hall, Gabriel Pearson, and Charles Taylor. Hobsbawm wrote for the first issue.

80 'We are going to have nothing but trouble from this fellow,' said Gollan in a phone call about MacEwen bugged by Special Branch. 'The best thing is to get him out'; he was expelled. KV 2/2988

81 'We shut ourselves off in righteousness or we accept all bona fide progressive forms'; 'If I had refused it would have been the last straw for Paul [Hogarth, who had asked Lindsay to write] as a proof that the party was hollow in all talk of a

united front.' Lindsay to Bill Wainwright, n.d. [July 1958], KV 2/3257. Lindsay had been discouraged from writing for the journal in correspondence with party leaders and Cornforth; he was also strongly discouraged by the latter from writing a play about Hungary; Cornforth to Lindsay 28 December 1956, Lindsay Papers, NLA, Folder 28. But having already argued that the line was incorrect in forbidding Communists to write for New Left journals, there was little surprise when he did so, and the same was true of Hobsbawm. CP CENT PERSONAL AND DISCIPLINARY FILE/LINDSAY.

82 For Gollan the very invitation was 'an insult' to the party; King Street surveillance transcript, 21 January 1959, KV 2/3258; Lindsay was invited to participate by Ian MacDougall of the 'Organising Committee for the Labour Magazine Project' on 31 December 1958; MacDougall to Lindsay, Lindsay Papers, NLA, Folder 35.

83 Those who attacked the party for sapping intellectuals' energies with bureaucratic processes and hedging real thinking with what Thompson called 'dogmatic anathemas' and 'disciplinary measures' knew the situation from the inside, and could not easily be brushed aside. Thompson, 'Socialism and the Intellectual,' *Universities & Left Review* 1, no. 1 (1957): 34.

84 Editorial, *Universities & Left Review* 1, no. 1 (1957): 1.

85 Writers' Group Statement, n.d. [mid-1956?]. 'The EC or leading members of it are prepared to resist in all ways the uprooting of the last vestiges of those distortions and errors which have come to be known as Stalinism and Zhdanovism in our thinking' Lindsay Papers, NLA, Folder 26. Writing with Soviet censorship in mind, one party critic – probably Alick West – identified 'the relationship between the individual and the collective' as 'the deepest problem of the socialist revolution,' and accused the British party of having 'skirted round it'; 'Opening of Discussion on "Declaration,"' 13 December 1957. The document is unsigned, but contains a number of Alick West's recurrent concerns and preferred phrases such as 'it is not culture that must serve the Party; it is the Party that must serve culture'; CP CENT CULT 1/2.

86 Lindsay, 'Some Notes on the Cultural Problems'; Jack Lindsay, 'On the Artist and Politics,' *Marxism Today* (September 1959): 287.

87 The matter in Britain now became a litmus test of attitudes to renewal, amidst a *Dr Zhivago* brouhaha fuelled in the cultural mainstream by Cold War sentiments rather than by literary convictions (the *Daily Express*, not known for its commitment to serious literature, serialized the book).

88 Lindsay, 'On the Artist and Politics,' 285, Jack Lindsay, 'Dr Zhivago,' *Anglo-Soviet Journal* (Winter 1958): 20–3; Michael Kullmann, 'A Piece of Revelation: *Zhivago*,' *Universities & Left Review* 5 (Autumn 1958): 80–2; '*Dr Zhivago*: A Discussion,' *Universities & Left Review* (Spring 1959): 24–7.

89 Arnold Kettle, 'Reply to Discussion: On the Artist and Politics,' *Marxism Today* (February 1960): 63.

90 Arnold Kettle, 'Pasternak's Offence to Russia: The Novel and the Prize,' *Manchester Guardian*, 5 December 1958.
91 Arnold Kettle, 'The Artist and Politics,' *Marxism Today* (May 1959): 143.
92 E.P. Thompson, 'The New Left,' *New Reasoner* 9 (Summer 1959): 1–18.
93 Raymond Williams, 'Advertising: The Magic System,' in *Problems in Materialism and Culture* (1980; London: Verso, 1997), 170–96; this essay was originally intended as a chapter of *The Long Revolution* (1960), and a shorter version of it was published in *New Left Review* 4 (July-August 1960); John Saville, 'The Welfare State Historical Approaches,' *New Reasoner* 3 (Winter 1957–8): 5–25; Stephen Hatch and Dorothy Thompson, 'The Welfare State: Discussion,' *New Reasoner* 4 (Spring 1958): 124–31; Peter Smith, 'The Welfare State,' *New Reasoner* 5 (Summer 1958): 39–53; Ralph Miliband, 'The Politics of Contemporary Capitalism,' *New Reasoner* 5 (Summer 1958): 39–53; G.D.H. Cole, 'What Is Happening to Capitalism?' *Universities & Left Review* 1, no. 1 (1957): 24–7; David Marquand, 'Lucky Jim and the Labour Party,' *Universities & Left Review* 1, no. 1 (1957): 57–60; Henry Collins, 'What Is Happening to Capitalism?' *Universities & Left Review* 1, no. 2 (Summer1957) : 66–7; Raymond Williams, 'Working-Class Culture,' *Universities & Left Review* 1, no. 2 (1957): 29–32; Stuart Hall, 'A Sense of Classlessness,' *Universities & Left Review* 5 (Autumn 1958): 26–32; Ralph Samuel, 'Class and Classlessness,' *Universities & Left Review* 6 (Spring 1959): 44–50.
94 Raymond Williams, 'Notes on British Marxism since 1945,' in *Problems in Materialism and Culture*, 242; E.P. Thompson, 'The New Left,' *New Reasoner* 9 (Summer 1959): 12; Richard Hoggart, *The Uses of Literacy* (1957; London: Pelican, 1958), 193.
95 As Callaghan explains, the Soviet doxa of the general theory of capitalist crisis that undergirded such conclusions was impervious to contrary evidence; *Cold War*, 157.
96 Thompson, 'New Left,' 13; Callaghan, *Cold War*, 158.
97 'Report of the Economics Sub-Committee: The Trade Cycle in Post-war Britain,' CP CENT ECON 4/12; Economics Sub-Committee for National School, 'What is Meant by Maximum Profit?' CP CENT ECON 6/5; Henry Collins, 'Marxism and the Impoverishment of the Working Class,' *Economics Bulletin* 5, no. 2 (1956), CP CENT ECON 7/5.
98 'What the "Welfare State" has done,' wrote Kettle, 'is to retain all the fundamental contradictions of capitalism'; Kettle, 'Rebels and Causes,' 67. Emblematic in this regard was the operatic workerism of Ewan MacColl's groundbreaking BBC documentary radio program, *The Ballad of John Axon* (1958), which converted an actual modern Stockport railwayman, who enjoyed watching television, eating cream cakes, and reading the *New Musical Express* into a cut-out 1930s-style socialist realist proletarian icon. See Ben Harker, ''Class Composition: *The Ballad of John Axon*, Cultural Debate and the late 1950s British Left,' *Science & Society* 73, no. 3 (2009): 340–56.

99 Andrew Grant, *Socialism and the Middle Classes* (London: Lawrence & Wishart, 158); Grant, 'Capitalism, Socialism and the Middle Classes,' *Marxism Today* (March 1958): 73–9.

100 Peter Worsley, 'The Middle Classes,' review of Grant, *Socialism and the Middle Classes* (1958), *New Reasoner* 7 (Winter 1958–9): 137.

101 [E.P.] Thompson, 'Where Are We Now?' unpublished typescript, Saville Papers, DSJ 109.

102 Sales figure is to 2005; David Kynaston, *Modernity Britain 1957–62* (London: Bloomsbury, 2015), 186; I analyse this working through in Ben Harker, 'Williams' Commitment,' *Key Words* 16 (2018): 5–18.

103 Kettle and the NCC took exception to the dismissive review of the *Long Revolution* (1961), entitled 'Brand X Reformism,' written by Dutt's brother, Clemens, and published in *Labour Monthly* (July 1961): 336–9; Dutt to Kettle, 12 July 1961, 21 July 1961; Kettle to Dutt, 15 July 1961. A letter from Kettle objecting to the 'grossly sectarian' review was published in the September issue of *Labour Monthly* (447–8), although the text was toned down and that phrase removed, with Kettle's agreement. The problem for the party, as Kettle privately admitted, 'was to get a more satisfactory body of work expressing our own standpoint so that we can use that as a basis for discussion with these people … we are often hamstrung by not having authoritative statements of our own position'; Kettle to Dutt, 15 July 1961, CP IND DUTT 5/11 and 5/12. Kettle clearly thought that the earlier, belated debate on Williams's *Culture and Society* in *Marxism Today* had not achieved this; Michael A. Cohen, 'Culture and Socialism,' *Marxism Today* (June 1960): 174–8. His own article, 'Culture and Revolution: A Consideration of the Ideas of Raymond Williams and Others,' *Marxism Today* (October 1961): 301–7, although intended to set the record straight, struggled to formulate responses to Williams's key arguments about base and superstructure.

104 It is rather ironical,' noted the *Times Literary Supplement*, 'that, at a time when the British working class seems to be growing conservative in their political views and growingly middle-class in their tastes we should be enjoying for the first time in many years something like a renaissance in working-class literature'; *Times Literary Supplement*, 26 February 1960, cited in Kynaston, *Modernity Britain*, 387. Classlessness: A process through which, as Francis Mulhern later argued, 'the inherited signs of English social caste were reworked as commodities, turned into styles and spectacles to enliven the mock-democratic world of mass commerce'; Francis Mulhern, *Culture/Metaculture* (London: Routledge, 2000), 55.

105 *Declaration* was a 'rather dim symposium of the more or less angry'; Kettle, 'Artist and Politics,' 141; Kettle, 'Rebels and Causes,' 65.

106 In comparison with 'the political and social consciousness of today,' wrote Margot Heinemann, 'the ideas and discussions actually going on among factory workers … this literature is not so much *avant-garde* as rearguard'; Margot Heinemann, 'Workers

and Writers: Some Modern Novels about the Working Class,' *Marxism Today* (April 1962): 114.

107 Alan Bush considered Sillitoe's *Key to the Door* (1961) the best working-class novel since Tressell, preferring it to *Saturday Night and Sunday Morning* in that it charted the protagonist's developing political consciousness; Alan Bush, 'Workers and Writers,' *Marxism Today* (July 1962): 221. Heinemann unpersuasively argued that the Communist writer Len Doherty – published by Lawrence & Wishart – was 'the most gifted of all the working-class writers'; Bush, 'Workers and Writers,' 117. Kettle considered Arnold Wesker a better playwright than the 'pretentious' Pinter, who spoke mainly to 'life denying highbrows who find the world Absurd'; Arnold Kettle, 'Our Theatre in the Sixties,' *Marxism Today* (September 1962): 276–81.

108 There was a symposium on Hoggart's *Uses of Literacy*, *Universities & Left Review* 1, no. 2 (1957), whose centrepiece was Raymond Williams's review (Summer 1957): 29–32. *Universities & Left Review* debated 'classlessness': Stuart Hall, 'A Sense of Classlessness,' *Universities & Left Review* 5 (Autumn 1958): 26–32; Ralph Samuel, 'Class and Classlessness,' *Universities & Left Review* 6 (Spring 1959); Hall, 'Absolute Beginnings,' *Universities & Left Review* 7 (Autumn 1959): 17–25. 'Commitment' was debated in *Universities & Left Review* 4 (Summer 1958) in articles beginning with Hall's 'Commitment: Inside the Whale Again,' 14–15; key cultural works were analysed by Hall, including Arnold Wesker's *Roots*, *Universities & Left Review* 7 (Autumn 1959): 52–3, and Colin MacInnes's *Absolute Beginners*, *Universities & Left Review* 7 (Autumn 1959): 17–25.

109 E.P. Thompson, 'Socialist Humanism: An Epistle to the Philistines,' *New Reasoner* 1, no. 1 (1957): 105–43.

110 Differences between the key New Left thinkers notwithstanding, they were broadly for a viable 'socialist humanism' capable of repurposing production towards the creation of a non-alienating mode of social organization that enabled and encouraged the fullest expression of human creativity; Thompson, 'New Left,' 1–17.

111 Christopher Hill, 'Antonio Gramsci,' *New Reasoner* 4 (Spring 1958): 107–13. Saville was in touch with Marks and actively seeking Gramsci material for the *New Reasoner*; Saville to Louis Marks, 28 October 1957, Saville Papers, DSJ 109. The journal ran annotated extracts from Hamish Henderson's still-unpublished translations of the Prison Letters; 'Gramsci on the Jews,' *New Reasoner* 9 (Summer 1959): 140–4; 'Document,' *New Reasoner* 10 (Autumn 1959): 123–7.

112 Randall Swingler, 'What about the People?' undated typescript mailed to Saville, n.d. [1956–7], Saville Papers, DSJ 109.

113 Cornforth to Lindsay, 23 January 1961, Lindsay Papers, NLA, Folder 32.

114 The central lesson drawn for readers of *Marxism Today* from Gramsci by George Thomson was the old Duttian adage about the importance of intellectuals integrating themselves into party life, an unsurprising gloss in that the principle

of intellectuals accepting 'the leadership of the working class' – which meant the party – was now the overriding criterion for official and direct involvement in the party's cultural work following 1956, as Kettle had reminded the NCC at its first meeting in July 1957. West to Lindsay, 16 July 1957, Lindsay Papers, NLA, Folder 191; George Thomson, 'Gramsci: The First Italian Marxist,' *Marxism Today* (November 1957): 61–2.

115 Lindsay wrote about early Marx and Gramsci in 'Socialist Humanism,' *New Reasoner* 3 (Winter 1957–8): 94–102. His offer to write an article on alienation and pre-class society drawing on the Manuscripts for *Marxism Today* was declined; Burns to Lindsay, 3 December 1958, Lindsay Papers, NLA, Folder 31. The party press was slow to take up discussion of these texts, but did so, sporadically, in the early 1960s. 'In Marx's theory of *alienation* we have the ethic, the importance which has been too often obscured by the emphasis which has been laid on economic analysis and political strategy'; 'Marxism would gain immensely if it could be restated as a complete philosophy of life for the modern world'; John Lewis, 'The Basis of Marxism,' *Marxism Today* (February 1960): 60. See also Lewis, 'What Is Humanism?' *Marxism Today* (July 1962): 203–4; Lewis, 'Marx's View of Alienation,' *Marxism Today* (January 1964): 17–22; Jack Lindsay, 'Alienation under Socialism,' *Marxism Today* (November 1964): 353–6. In the 1960s Lindsay wrote two manuscripts of a book on Marx's theory of alienation; both remain unpublished.

116 James Klugmann, 'The Challenge of Marxism,' *Marxism Today* (April 1961): 102.

117 Among a plethora of positions, Williams emphasized the former, Thompson the latter; Raymond Williams, *Politics and Letters: Interviews with New Left Review* (1979; London: Verso, 1981), 363.

118 Arnold Kettle, 'How New Is the New Left?' *Marxism Today* (October 1960): 301–9.

119 Thomas Russell, 'On How New Is the New Left?' *Marxism Today* (January 1961): 29–32; Joan Simon defended Kettle and the party's conduct; Simon, 'On How New Is the New Left?' *Marxism Today* (March 1961): 94–6.

120 And 'socialism without tears or embarrassment for hearts at peace under an English heaven.' The problem, as he saw it, was that too few Communists had been willing to take his lead and fight such 'revisionist Marxism'; Kettle, 'On the "New Left": Reply to Discussion,' *Marxism Today* (June 1961): 191–2.

121 Thompson, 'New Left,' 13.

122 Kynaston, *Modernity Britain*, 175. The TUC General Council had recommended as late as 1956 that West Indians should be discouraged from leaving their islands, and barely registered racism in Britain prior to the attacks on the black community in Notting Hill in 1958. The Labour Party soon capitulated to the obvious racism of the Commonwealth Immigration Bill of November 1961; Callaghan, *Cold War*, 105–10.

123 'West Indians in Britain,' March 1957, CP CENT INT 73/1, cited in Callaghan, *Cold War*, 106. See also Michael Herbert, *Never Counted Out! The Story of Len Johnson, Manchester's Black Boxing Hero and Communist* (Manchester: Dropped Aitches Press,1992), 90; and Callaghan, *Cold War*, 107.

124 For instance, Ken Gill's work late 1950s work on Willesden Trades Council and Camden-based railwayman Tony Gilbert's activism in confronting racism and the colour bar in the National Union of Railwaymen; Callaghan, *Cold War*, 110, 120.

125 A Scot who grew up in the United States, rose to the leadership of the CPUSA, was imprisoned under the Smith Act, and finally deported back to Britain in 1955, Williamson functioned as the catalyst of a front organization soon supported by seven MPS and prominent cultural figures (Benjamin Britten, Ralph Vaughan Williams, Sean O'Casey, John Berger, the Lord Bishop of Birmingham, Leonard Woolf, John Betjeman). He activated the party's traditions of organizing large public gatherings and staging events, including a concert at St Pancras Town Hall at which Robeson 'appeared' via transatlantic phone circuit. He drew on the party's influence in the labour movement (eleven trade union general secretaries signed up, and the 1955 TUC sent a telegram to US president Dwight Eisenhower). Via link with the Musicians' Unity and Equity, Williamson pressured promoters, TV shows, and prestigious cultural institutions (the Shakespeare Memorial Theatre at Stratford, the Royal Festival Hall, the Palladium) to invite Robeson to perform. In the assessment of Robeson's biographer, the campaign emboldened American promoters and venues to defy McCarthyism, and themselves to approach Robeson, further isolating the US State Department, whose ban even the conservative *Catholic Herald* saw as an illiberal embarrassment to the anti-Communist crusade. When his passport was restored, Robeson himself was in little doubt about where credit was due, and came to Britain in the summer of 1958 to seek out those who had worked hardest to challenge his effective eight-year house arrest; Martin Duberman, *Paul Robeson* (New York: New Press, 1989), 453.

126 Phil Bolsover, *No Colour Bar for Britain* (London: CP, 1955), 11; Evan Smith gives a tightly argued account of these contradictions, '"Class before Race": British Communism and the Place of Empire in Postwar Race Relations,' *Science & Society* 72, no. 4 (2008): 455–81; unsigned, "Talking points on … colonial workers in Britain,' *World News*, 19 March 1955.

127 Smith, '"Class before Race,"' 466; Morgan, Cohen, and Flinn, *Communists and British Society*, 202–5.

128 Cited in Bill Schwarz, 'Claudia Jones and the *West Indian Gazette:* Reflections on the Emergence of Post-colonial Britain,' *Twentieth Century British History* 14, no. 3 (2003): 282.

129 Smith, '"Class before Race,"' 264.

130 The party actively lobbied the British Consul and passport office on her behalf. Pollitt wrote to the Colonial Office protesting about Jones's case on 19 December 1955; 'Claudia Jones,' CP CENT ORG 1/10.
131 Jones's contribution, Special Congress Transcript, CP CENT CONG 10/8.
132 Later the *West Indian Gazette and Afro-Asian Caribbean News*; Carole Boyce Davies, *Left of Karl Marx: The Political Life of Black Communist Activist Claudia Jones* (Durham, NC: Duke University Press, 2007), 168, 172.
133 Trevor Carter, *Shattering Illusions: West Indians in British Politics*, with Jean Cousins (London: Lawrence & Wishart, 1986), 61.
134 Seltman, *What's Left?* 70.
135 Carter found it 'frustrating and sad' that the party 'lost the allegiance of so many black socialists by not listening to them when it had a chance'; Carter, *Shattering Illusions*, 150.
136 Ibid., 63.
137 Membership had plunged to a third of that in February 1958; figures from Newton, *Sociology of British Communism*, 160; Thompson, *Good Old Cause*, 121, 218; Callaghan, *Cold War*, 22.
138 Thompson, *Good Old Cause*, 114.
139 Attitudes to the Soviet Union had been so negative in 1956 that South Wales miners' leader Will Paynter stopped going to his local pub 'because this hostility threatened to become violent.' He was glad of his 'good hefty friends.' Will Paynter, *My Generation* (London: Allen and Unwin, 1972), 155.
140 Kynaston, *Modernity Britain*, 76.
141 Ibid.
142 Bernal worked through the World Federation of Scientific Workers and Science for Peace. His *Science in History* (1954) was translated into Russian in 1956, and was the subject of a Moscow symposium in November 1957. The book's central claim – that science was a force of production best understood by scientists – was eagerly endorsed by the Soviet scientists with whom he was in regular contact. Support for Lysenko was dropped in the second edition of 1958; Lysenko's resignation had been accepted in 1956. Gary Werskey, *The Visible College: A Collective Biography of British Scientists and Socialists of the 1930s* (London: Allen Lane, 1978), 319, 313.
143 Argued persuasively by Werskey, *Visible College*, 324.
144 Bernal had formerly enjoyed a cameo role in one of Snow's novels and his new book, *World Without War* (1958), and was compared favourably by Snow to the gloomier projections of Orwell's *Nineteen Eighty-Four* (1949). C.P. Snow, *The Two Cultures* (1959; Cambridge: Cambridge University Press, 1969), 155; Andrew Brown, *J.D. Bernal: The Sage of Science* (Oxford: Oxford University Press, 2005), 475.
145 *Marxism Today* now featured essays affirming Snow's claims: Max Morris, 'Two Cultures and Scientific Revolution,' *Marxism Today* (December 1959):

374–80; Ron Willetts, 'A World Without a Hero,' *Marxism Today* (March 1961): 80–5. Communists including Bernal and Heinemann defended Snow from his detractors, especially Cambridge literary critic F.R. Leavis. For Leavis, Snow was 'portentously ignorant' and possessed an 'utter lack of intellectual distinction and an embarrassing vulgarity of style.' Bernal and Margot Heinemann wrote letters to the *Spectator* defending Snow. Leavis's lecture was published in the *Spectator* on 9 March 1962; Kynaston, *Modernity Britain*, 743; Brown, *J.D. Bernal*, 475.

146 'The gap between the cultures' in the Soviet Union, Snow asserted, 'doesn't seem to be anything like so wide as with us'; Snow, *Two Cultures*, 36; Snow's *Science and Government* (1961), based on his 1960 Godkin Lectures at Harvard, was also welcomed and defended by Communists, especially its argument for the involvement of trained scientists at all levels of government and that more scientists 'at the top of Soviet society had led to plenty of better choices being taken.' John Moss, 'Science and Government,' *Marxism Today* (June 1961): 187.

147 Kynaston, *Modernity Britain*, 77, 92. E.H.S. Burhop, 'The Soviet Man in Space,' *Marxism Today* (May 1961): 134–6.

148 Kynaston, *Modernity Britain*, 621.

149 Richard Crossman, *Labour and the Affluent Society* (London: Fabian Society, 1960), 9.

150 Werskey, *Visible College*, 320; a document, 'The Communist Party and Science' (February 1964), which formed the basis of the party's General Election policy for science, approved by the Executive Committee on 20 February 1964, embraced 'scientific-technological revolution,' warning that Britain's current situation – in which science was subordinated to monopoly capitalism – would cost it dear; CP CENT CULT 1/7.

151 *British Road* (1958), 12.

152 Ibid., 5.

153 Levy had berated himself from the Congress floor in 1957 for being 'led up the garden all these years'; Special Congress transcript, CP CENT CONG 10/8.

154 King Street surveillance transcript, 16 April 1958, KV 2/3257.

155 Brown, *J.D. Bernal*, 364.

156 Morris, 'Two Cultures,' 378.

157 Giving the lie to the leadership's myth of white-collar dissidence contrasting with working-class fidelity; analysed in Matthew Kavanagh, 'British Communism and the Politics of Education, 1926–1968' (PhD diss., University of Manchester, 2015), 171–86.

158 Figures from ibid., 172, and Newton, *Sociology of British Communism*, p162–3.

159 Brian Simon, *A Life in Education* (London: Lawrence & Wishart, 1998), 75.

160 Ibid., 79.

161 Ibid., 78; Kynaston, *Modernity Britain*, 229.

162 A detailed conspectus of an educational field in transition that drew substantially but not exclusively on the experiences and reflections of Communist school teachers. In 1954 Simon and the non-Communist Robin Pedley visited every existing comprehensive school in England and Wales (thirteen in total), gathering analysis that informed key publications. Pedley produced *Comprehensive Education: A New Approach* (London: Gollancz, 1956). Simon's edited book included contributions from George Freeland, Communist headmaster of the recently unstreamed Mowacre Junior School in Leicester, Communist teacher George Rudé, who analysed the common history syllabus in the light of his experience at the new Holloway Comprehensive School, and Communist teachers Dean Levin and Marie Philbert, who stressed the educability of all children in maths and science, drawing on their experiences in Walworth Interim Comprehensive and Great Barr Comprehensive, respectively. Kavanagh, 'British Communism,' 193–5.

163 Simon, *Life*, 103, 94.

164 Brian Simon, 'Communist Party Educational Organisation – Note by Brian Simon,' September 1963, Brian Simon Papers, DC SIM 5/7, cited in Kavanagh, 'British Communism,' 207.

165 Kavanagh, 'British Communism,' 203.

166 Ibid.

167 Ibid., 197.

168 Kettle to Bill Alexander, 6 April 1964, CP IND MATTHEWS 7/3; the episode is reconstructed in Kavanagh, 'British Communism,' 197–204.

169 'What did Lionel learn at Unity?' rhetorically ask Bart's biographers. 'Everything.' Bart had also written chart hits for Tommy Steele, Marty Wilde, Frankie Vaughan, and Cliff Richard, including the latter's 'Living Doll' (1959). *Oliver!* appeared in the West End (1960), on Broadway (1963), and on the big screen (1968). David and Caroline Stafford, *Fings ain't wot they used to be: The Lionel Bart Story* (London: Omnibus, 2011). 37.

170 Dominic Sandbrook, *White Heat: A History of Britain in the Swinging Sixties* (London: Abacus, 2006), 33. In Willis's case, social realism's concern for the quotidian – what he called 'the marvellous work of the ordinary' – now carried a more acquiescent political vision in film and television. Willis's feature films included the grammar school rebellion musical, *It's Great to Be Young* (1956), *Woman in a Dressing Gown* (1957), the post–Notting Hill *Flame in the Streets* (1961), and, for television, *Dixon of Dock Green*. John Hill, *Sex, Class and Realism: British Cinema 1956–63* (London: British Film Institute, 1986), 97.

171 *Centre 42: First Stage in a Cultural Revolution* (London: 1961); Clive Barker, 'Report and Recommendations on the Policy of Centre 42,' 26 August 1961, Charles Parker Archive, Birmingham Public Library, CPA 1/8/7/1. Wesker, too, now at the height of his celebrity as his recently finished trilogy played at the Royal Court, railed against ideologically driven mass culture and encroaching

passivity in recognizably party tones, lamenting that '200,000 go to the theatre each night, as compared with two million who go to the cinema and four million who watch TV.' Kynaston, *Modernity Britain*, 453; Arnold Wesker, 'The Modern Playwright' (Oxford, 1960), 3; the arguments were developed by Wesker in a follow-up pamphlet containing more concrete proposals, 'Labour and the Arts : II or What, Then, Is to Be Done?' (Oxford, 1960).

172 David Craig, 'Centre 42 and 'the Movement,' *Marxism Today* (June 1963): 186.

173 The latter argument in particular was a mainstay of the communist-dominated ACTT, the only union mentioned in Wesker's pamphlet, Labour & the Arts: II, or What, Then, Is to Be Done? (1960), the document in which discontent was codified into proposals.

174 Kynaston, *Modernity Britain*, 46. Carried, with the support of the *Daily Herald* but not the TUC's General Council, Resolution 42 created a notional obligation among the trade union movement to support the arts, emboldening Wesker to set up Centre 42 – largely paid for from his own royalties – and to begin the protracted and ultimately divisive and unsuccessful task of establishing a permanent Centre 42 in London.

175 Wellingborough, Nottingham, Leicester, Birmingham, Bristol, Hayes/Harlington.

176 The other two cities with regional NCCs in the early 1960s were Sheffield and Glasgow. The Ian Campbell Folk Group concert in the city's Town Hall attracted 1,500; 'Information for the Discussion of Cultural Work of the Labour movement,' n.d. [1963], CP CENT CULT 1/6. 'A large amount of the success of the festival was due to the activities of Party comrades,' Thomson accurately reported to the NCC; 'the weaknesses were mainly because of the organisation of Centre 42'; Katharine Thomson, undated report on the Birmingham event, CP CENT CULT 3/8.

177 Barbara Ruehl, 'Centre 42,' *Marxism Today* (April 1963): 124–6.

178 Craig, 'Centre 42,' 187.

179 NCC Minutes, 11 February 1963, CP CENT CULT 1/6.

180 John Miller, in a review of the Hayes and Harlington event in the CP Music group's journal; 'Centre 42 in Action,' *Music & Life* 1 (1963): 16.

181 Especially after J.E.S. Simon, Financial Secretary to the Treasury, announced supplementary grants to national museums, galleries, and the Arts Council. Andrew Sinclair, *Arts and Cultures: The History of the 50 Years of the Arts Council of Great Britain* (London: Sinclair-Stevenson, 1995), 130.

182 The Gulbenkian Foundation's *Help for the Arts* and the Bow Group's *Patronage for the Arts*, the Arts Council, *Housing the Arts* (1959) and *The Needs of the English Provinces* (1961); the Conservatives' *The Challenge of Leisure* (1959), Labour's *Leisure for Living* (1959).

183 Arguing that culture was 'ordinary,' Raymond Williams confronted the fundamental high-low paradigm upon which the Arts Council cultural funding was predicated and where party thinking remained (these ideas of cultural

value would be revisited in the Council's 1967 charter) in the *zeitgeist* essay collection *Conviction* (1958), edited by Norman MacKenzie, to which no Communists were asked to contribute. Williams's essay was 'Culture Is Ordinary' (Sinclair, *Arts and Cultures*, 150). His Penguin Special, *Communications* (1962), combined immediate, transitional, and long-term objectives for the reshaping of national cultural structures – education, the press, broadcasting, the arts – and he would go on to serve an embattled three-year term on the Council from 1975 to 1978. Raymond Williams, 'The Arts Council' (1979), in *Resources of Hope*, ed. Robin Gale (London: Verso, 1989), 41–55.

184 Sinclair, *Arts and Cultures*, 112; CP actor Alex McCrindle was working in Sunderland and greatly impressed by the cultural energies released in the North East by Blenkinshop's work. 'What role, if any, has the CP played in this?' he asked rhetorically. McCrindle, 'A new venture in the arts in the North East,' *World News*, 8 December 1962.

185 Barbara Niven, 'Proposals for the Arts,' *Marxism Today* (April 1960): 122.

186 The 1958 version was even worse in this respect than the 1951 original, in Alick West's view; West to Lindsay, 23 March 1957, Lindsay Papers, NLA, Folder 191.

187 NCC circular, 3 March 1960, CP CENT CULT 1/4.

188 'What Is Our Way of Life?' 3 June 1960, CP CENT CULT 1/4.

189 'Time to Spare,' NCC circular, 6 December 1962, CP CENT CULT 1/5.

190 NCC Minutes, 13 September 1963, show this was sent out to sixty comrades for responses, CP CENT CULT 1/5, document in CP CENT CULT 3/9.

191 30 October 1963, CP CENT CULT 1/6; Sinclair, *Arts and Cultures*, 130.

192 Niven, 'Proposals for the Arts,' 117–22.

193 *Cultural Work* (February 1964), CP CENT CULT 3/1.

194 Simon to Nora Jeffrey, 28 April 1962, CP CENT CULT 3/8.

195 Simon to Ainley, 19 June 1962; Simon to Jeffrey, 19 June 1962, CP CENT CULT 3/8; a higher figure of forty-three is given in a typed list of scientists in the same file.

196 The Historians' Group became the History Group in the early 1960s; document on Historians' Group, 11 July 1958, CP CENT CULT 3/7; NCC Minutes, 10 June 1964, CP CENT CULT 1/7.

197 NCC Minutes, 12 January 1961, CP CENT CULT 3/8.

198 Ainley to Simon, 24 October 1962; NCC Minutes, 15 June 1962, CP CENT CULT 3/8; Simon's report, 'The CP and the Ideological Struggle,' September 1962, CP CENT CULT 1/5.

199 Simon, 'CP and the Ideological Struggle.' A reference to the fact that Alexander Tvardovsky, editor of the Soviet cultural journal *Novy Mir*, had recently spoken of a period of 'constraint and restriction' in the Soviet Union coming to an end, and had addressed the shortcomings of socialist realism. Honor Arundel, *The Freedom of Art* (London: Lawrence & Wishart, 1965), 38. The analysis would prove unduly optimistic in the Soviet context, where the repression of writers

returned apace in 1966 with the persecution of Yuli Daniel and Andrei Sinyavsky – treatment publicly condemned by the CPGB – but the shift unblocked more open discussions around censorship and culture elsewhere, including in Britain. George Bridges, 'Freedom!' *Challenge* (April 1966): 5. Monty Johnstone was rehabilitated at this moment, and licensed by the leadership to criticize the imprisonment of the writers on British television in November 1967. Johnstone, interview with Richard Cross, 23 March 2000, CP IND JOHN 2/1/32; Betty Reid to Johnstone, 20 November 1967, CP IND JOHN 1/1.

200 Gollan to Simon, 18 January 1963, CP CENT CULT 3/8. Historian Lionel Munby forcefully argued that the British party should distance itself from bureaucratic and administrative attitudes to culture in socialist countries; Munby, 'For Discussion at Cultural Committee, 8 January 1965,' CP CENT CULT 1/8.

201 A long debate was initiated by Ray Watkinson, 'Abstract Art,' *Marxism Today* (March 1963): 81–9, which included contributions from Barbara Niven (April 1963): 122–4, and Jack Lindsay (June 1963): 189–92.

202 Barbara Niven, 'John Berger: The Success and Failure of Picasso,' *Marxism Today* (January 1966): 10–15; Stanley Mitchell, 'Georg Lukács and the Historical Novel,' *Marxism Today* (December 1963): 374–82; Arnold Kettle, 'A Most Stimulating Book' (review of Lukács's *The Meaning of Contemporary Realism*), *Comment*, 30 March 1963; R.F. Willetts, 'The Necessity of Art,' *Marxism Today* (January 1964): 23–7; Ernst Fischer, 'Art and Ideological Superstructure,' *Marxism Today* (February 1964): 46–51. Fischer's work opened a discussion on art and superstructure that included contributions from David Craig, *Marxism Today* (June 1964): 187–9; Margot Heinemann, *Marxism Today* (October 1964): 322–4; and Honor Arundel, *Marxism Today* (August 1964): 256–7. Arundel's *The Freedom of Art* (London: Lawrence & Wishart, 1965) in turn provoked a debate that involved Bill Carritt, *Marxism Today* (December 1965): 376–7; Hugh MacDiarmid, *Marxism Today* (January 1966): 21–4; and Betty Reid, *Marxism Today* (March 1966): 92–3.

203 Minutes of Challenge of Marxism sub-Committee, 8 March 1963, CP CENT CULT 1/6.

204 Ibid. A determinedly upbeat account of proceedings was given by Simon, 'The Challenge of Marxism,' *Marxism Today* (January 1964): 6–8.

205 The only non-communist of any note to appear to appear was Professor J.R. Sargent of the new University of Warwick, whose interlocutor on the subject of socialist and capitalist economies, Maurice Dobb, found the whole affair dispiriting. 'We are so delighted when someone accepts to debate with us,' Dobb remarked, 'we necessarily fall over backwards not to stress differences. What results is therefore neither stimulating nor particularly useful'; Report on Challenge of Marxism, November 1963, CP CENT CULT 3/9.

206 The book was first mooted in June 1959; Brian Simon, proposal for 'The Challenge of Marxism,' CP CENT CULT 1/4.

207 The book's precedent was *The Mind in Chains: Socialism and the Cultural Revolution* (1937), which had inspired Communist students of Simon's generation. The earlier book had caught the party at the apex of its Popular Front intellectual confidence, and had drawn on a range of major and emerging intellectuals – not all of them Communists – in its analysis of the arts, education, the media, film, psychology, religion, science, and history. The contrast measured the party's intellectual and cultural shrinkage.

208 Brian Simon, ed., *The Challenge of Marxism* (London: Lawrence & Wishart, 1963), notably in Arnold Kettle, 'Communism and the Intellectuals,' 180–92, and A.L. Morton, 'The Arts and the People,' 127–8.

209 Kettle, 'Communism and the Intellectuals,' 204–5.

210 Arnold Kettle, 'Our Morals and Lady C,' *Marxism Today* (April 1961): 123–5; Morton, 'Arts and the People,' 129.

211 Morton, 'Arts and the People,' 129.

212 'Challenge of Marxism,' document, n.d., CP CENT CULT 1/4.

213 Morton, 'Arts and the People,' 130.

214 Brian Simon, proposal for 'The Challenge of Marxism,' CP CENT CULT 1/4.

215 Morton, 'Arts and the People,' 126. The party hesitated around how to respond to British films that gave a new visibility to a changing working class, notably *A Taste of Honey* (1961), whose protagonists bore little resemblance to the ideal proletarian type (male industrial workers). One line affirmed its critique of Victorian morality (Marshall Harris, 'A Taste of Honey,' *Marxism Today* [February 1962]: 63); another found the film 'empty' (Cadmus, 'A Taste of Honey,' *Marxism Today* [March 1962]: 96–7); a third was troubled by the 'fecklessness and rootlessness of the characters,' but argued that, though 'not a class film,' *A Taste of Honey* should be welcomed as part of a broader 'movement' whose key traits were realism and a desire that life should be different (Nina Hibbin, 'A Taste of Honey,' *Marxism Today* [April 1962], 127–80). Party intellectuals also tied themselves in knots to detect more direct modes of class consciousness than the films contained. The generational tensions explored through Tony Richardson's *The Loneliness of the Long Distance Runner* (1962), for instance, were straightforwardly reduced to the class feeling that was by no means the film's whole story. Nina Hibbin, 'Shoestring Film "Great" of 1962,' *Challenge* (December 1962): 2. Hibbin also argued that *Saturday Night and Sunday Morning* (1960) charted Arthur Seaton's progress from 'aggressive individualism' to 'the dawnings of social consciousness.' This sits uneasily with the film's ending, which stresses a hedonistic rebellion incorporated into matrimony, quietism, and suburban working-class consumerism; Hibbin, 'Taste of Honey,' 128.

216 Part of Lindsay's ongoing novelistic analysis of modern British society. Although published with mainstream presses and sometimes in mass paperback formats, the work was little more registered, to his chagrin, in the party press than in the mainstream media. James Klugmann to Lindsay, 24 September 1962, Lindsay

Papers, NLA, Folder 40; diary entry, 4 March 1963, Lindsay Papers, NLA, Box 11 (no separate folder numbers). The series grappled with social phenomena including motorcycle gangs, generational conflict, compulsive television watching, and hire-purchase debt. Novels included *Revolt of the Sons* (1960), *All on the Never-Never* (1961). *The Way the Ball Bounces* (1962) deals with interracial relationship; *Masks & Faces* (1963) is a modern-day *King Lear* with its Committee of 100 supporting teenagers; and the elegiac *Choice of Times* (1964) contrasted working-class Oldham past and present.

217 Bert Hogenkamp, *Film, Television and the Left in Britain, 1950–1970* (London: Lawrence & Wishart, 200), 117; Hill, *Sex, Class and Realism*, 139–40, 207

218 David Robinson, *Financial Times*, 14 July 1961, cited in Hill, *Sex, Class and Realism*, 207.

219 According to the *Marxism Today* analysis, post-war prospects of more egalitarian urban spaces had given way to towns with too many shopping precincts, too few civil amenities, and where 'the national trend towards a more home centred life' of 'working overtime, decorating the house, looking after the car and the garden and watching telly' was quickened rather than resisted. Document on sport by Stan Levenson, 14 November 1960, CP CENT CULT 1/4; Nora Jeffrey, 'Further Work on Town Planning,' n.d., CP CENT CULT 1/4; unsigned, 'Sport in Crisis,' CP CENT CULT 1/4. The party ran a day conference, 'Room to Live and Breathe,' about urban planning, 25 February 1961; documents in CP CENT CULT 3/3. John Tarver, 'The Future of British Sport,' *Marxism Today* (September 1961): 275–81; David Grove, 'Lessons of the New Towns,' *Marxism Today* (March 1962): 91.

220 It was scripted by Trevor Story, Lindsay being phobic of the medium. It was produced by Regal, and premiered on 25 October 1962 at the Carlton Theatre in Haymarket. A resounding flop, it is today forgotten, and goes unmentioned in the standard cinema histories. Correspondence between Lindsay and J. Vegoda of Regal, 18 July 1962, 10 August 1962; contractual details, Muller to Lindsay, 30 March 1961, Lindsay Papers, NLA, Folders 40, 41.

221 Post-1956 work had centred on the distribution of a chilling Hungarian film, *How It Happened* (1957), which justified the Soviet invasion through multiple fabrications, and films from East Germany, notably *The German Story* (1956), premiered at the National Film Theatre in July 1957; Hogenkamp, *Film, Television*, 74.

222 Predictably, the book's strongest passages drew on long-standing traditions of analysis and offered materialist accounts of the national past, whose culture was presented as locations of resistance to the 'cultural Americanisation of the world,' an emphasis soon writ large in the party's celebrations of the 1964 Shakespeare centenary, a more successful venture than *The Challenge of Marxism*, which sensibly resisted the temptation to 'present Shakespeare as some kind of "unconscious Marxist" or to "use" his work to make contemporary

political points.' Morton, 'Arts and the People,' 130; NCC circular, May 1964, CP CENT CULT 1/7. In a well-attended public event (210 people) held at Mahatma Gandhi Hall on 1 November 1964, which featured period music and a lecture from Kettle, the party celebrated the centenary of Shakespeare's birth in general, and especially his progressive 'humanism.' Kettle also edited *Shakespeare in a Changing World* (London: Lawrence & Wishart, 1964), a richly non-partisan collection that brought together non-communist Shakespeare scholars (Kenneth Muir, Charles Barber), former members (Victor Kiernan), and emerging (David Craig) and established (West, Kettle, Matthews) party intellectuals. NCC Minutes, 10 July 1964; Shakespeare 400th Anniversary Programme,' CP CENT CULT 1/7.

223 Hogenkamp, *Film, Television*, 88–9.

224 He was grilled by Peter Calvocoressi of the Royal Institute of International Affairs, Labour MP and former Communist Dennis Healey, and doctor-turned-pundit Edna Romney. Gareth Bowen, 'Mr Gollan Hits Back,' n.d., unlabelled cutting; 'Telecrit,' undated cutting, CP CENT SEC 17/3.

225 The transmission of Gollan's 'coolness and determination' on the national airwaves played a forgotten role in restoring deeply shaken identities; Harry Kennedy to John Gollan, 12 September 1957, CP CENT SEC 17/3. 'We have gone, and are going through a difficult time,' wrote a wavering Communist couple, 'but the principles of Communism have never changed. Last night gave us a lead which made us proud'; George Beard and Molly Beard to Gollan, 11 September 1957, CP CENT SEC 17/3.

226 Jack Ashton to Gollan, n.d., CP CENT SEC 17/3.

227 'Until recently,' ran one letter from Chepstow that must have been music to Gollan's ears, 'I have been a Labour Party enthusiast but now realise that their policy is one of false socialism … your party is the only one that holds out a friendly hand to workers of the country'; R. Lindsay to Gollan, 16 September 1957, CP CENT SEC 17/3.

228 'If only one of our comrades could be given a place once a month on one of other of the TV discussion programmes,' wrote a Manchester full timer, 'it would transform the position'; Pat Devine to Gollan, 11 August 1957, CP CENT SEC 17/3.

229 Bert Baker, 'What Is Television?' *Marxism Today* (January 1964): 28.

230 Even though its own best analysis argued that '[p]olitical inclinations remained almost entirely unaffected by televisual aspects of political campaigning'; ibid., 31; Hogenkamp, *Film, Television*, 91.

231 The party verdict was that, although ITV was in some ways preferable to the BBC – less openly hostile to Communism, more accommodating to unions, including the ACTT – the BBC should be backed on the basis of its greater accountability and availability for reform. 'The Future of Broadcasting: Evidence Submitted by the Communist Party to the Committee on Broadcasting,' *Marxism Today* (March

1961): 90. Additional responses were expressed in an unpublished document, 'Television's Third Channel,' 14 January 1960, CP CENT CULT 1/3.

232 Many of the party's recommendations reflected its long-standing synergies with the Left-Leavisite discourse, itself prominent in the Pilkington Report, which denounced commercialism and Americanism and affirmed the BBC's cultural diffusionism. Communists especially approved of the BBC's 'raising of public taste for classical music' and 'popularising, without vulgarising' the classics of literature through adaptations; 'Future of Broadcasting,' 90.

233 Notably the BBC's failure to cover the World Conference of Communist Parties, its refusal to offer more than a few minutes of air time to Communists in a three-hour Third Programme series on 'Marxism and Communism,' and the Independent Television Authority's ban on small-screen advertising for the *Daily Worker* on the grounds that it was a 'political' newspaper; ibid., 87–8.

234 David Mercer, 'What Is Television?' *Marxism Today* (April 1964): 126.

235 The most promising was Gordon Cruikshank. Also the *Daily Worker*'s Polish reporter, Cruikshank was one of the few BBC Communists who made the transition from radio to television; his BBC file runs to nine volumes. BBC WAC, Gordon Cruikshank.

236 *Marxism Today* griped about the 'neo-anarchism' of privileged Oxbridge graduates whose satire – not as good as Jonathan Swift's – was directed 'within, rather than against, the framework of contemporary capitalism.' Others on the Left, including former CP member and *Tribune* journalist Mervyn Jones, detected here a potential shift in popular consciousness in the weakening of deference for political and cultural elites; Jones, cited in Mike Downs, 'Satire – The New Revolt?' *Marxism Today* (July 1963): 223.

237 Mercer stressed agency over structure, arguing that the fragmented and mutilayered complexity of television production, 'a bewildering hierarchy in which any coherent sense of direction tends to get lost,' could paradoxically create space for radical vision; Mercer, 'What Is television?' 124. 'Television will only be saved from its own clichés,' he emphasised, 'by the responsible stubbornness of individuals whose artistic and political convictions are mature enough not only to resist, but to oppose the idea that "what the audience wants" is a monster demanding endless placation' (125). The medium's subordination to the mediating elites of 'expert' critics was also less than in other cultural spheres, he argued, in that television reviews, unlike those of theatre or exhibitions, were read only after the audience had watched a program and had made up their own minds (125). Douglass also signalled spaces for intervention, arguing that documentary writers often enjoyed considerable scope within the theme chosen by the producer, and that even the 'formula' writing required for soap operas was the location of struggle between unimaginative producers who assumed they knew what audiences wanted, writers whose craft compelled them to push back against these conventions, and audiences who bored more quickly

of conventional plotlines than producers assumed. Stuart Douglass, 'What Is Television?' *Marxism Today* (March 1964): 93–5. Initiated by Alan Bush's 'What Does Music Express?' *Marxism Today* (July 1963): 204–8, the debate ran for almost a year in the journal's pages.

238 Cited in Sandbrook, *White Heat*, 579.

239 Bert Baker's pamphlets 'The TV Tie Up' (1961) and 'The Communists and TV' (1965) had almost nothing to say about the medium beyond chronicling patterns of the party's exclusion. The campaign material is gathered in CP CENT PUB 1/2.

240 *Our Life in Our Hands*. Communists screened their film at meetings and via a cinema van in some streets in the contested constituencies, and duly made access to the airwaves a campaign keynote in the 1964 General Election. One candidate, poet Hugh MacDiarmid, who appeared in the film, subsequently brought an unsuccessful lawsuit against the elected MP and Conservative leader, Sir Alec Douglas-Home, on the grounds that the disproportionate airtime granted to Douglas-Home's campaign amounted to BBC and ITA support of his campaign. Hogenkamp, *Film, Television*, 94.

241 That they lacked the cadres working in television to take forward the ideas was reflected in its own surprised coverage of the career of Douglass, a Unity dramatist who had scripted eight pieces for television by 1965. He was presented in the party press as an exotic novelty from an otherwise impenetrable televisual world; Frank Clearly, 'One of the New Men of Drama,' *Comment*, 9 October 1965, 654–5.

242 Marylebone Branch Agenda, June 1955. CP CENT CULT 1/2. The Executive Committee never discussed youth questions between 1952 and 1958, the years of James Dean, Teddy Boys tearing out cinema seats at screenings of *Blackboard Jungle* (1955), Elvis Presley, Bill Haley, and rioting at *Rock Around the Clock* (1956).

243 They envisaged a campaign along the lines of that waged against 'horror-comics,' although admitted that 'the evil is less easy to pinpoint'; 'Cultural Sub-Committee' circular for meeting, 18 April 1958, CP CENT CULT 3/7.

244 L. Ely to *Daily Worker*, 7 June 1957; Kynaston, *Modernity Britain*, 40.

245 Up from 1,387 in 1958 to 4,019 in 1962; Newton, *Sociology of British Communism*, appendix 1B, 161.

246 A 1958 BBC television documentary suggested that the earnest youngsters who flocked to the New Left's Partisan Cafe were seeking sanctuary not just from Stalinism, but juke boxes; *Panorama* featuring Partisan cafe, broadcast 10 November 1958, DVD in Eric Hobsbawm Papers, MSS 937/5/1/1, MRC, University of Warwick.

247 Alick West thought the novel's satire of Communist cultural positions was disconcertingly accurate; West to Lindsay, 9 June 1960, Lindsay Papers, NLA, Folder 191. Margot Heinemann's starchy comments regretted the protagonist's morality – 'drug taking,' 'taking and peddling obscene photographs' – and found

unconvincing 'his sudden leap into anti-fascist consciousness'; Heinemann, 'Workers and Writers: Some Modern Novels about the Working Class,' *Marxism Today* (April 1962): 113. The New Left, by contrast, immediately grasped the novel's significance; Hall, 'Absolute Beginnings,' 17–25.

248 Music Group to Ted Ainley, 9 January 1963, CP CENT CULT 3/8; NCC document, 2 March 1960, CP CENT CULT 1/4.

249 The theoretically underpowered Labour Party had nothing to say on such matters; the continental 'Western Marxism' promulgated by the 'second' New Left shed little light on it (Theodore Adorno saw the 'culture industry' as broadly synonymous with 'mass deception'); the early New Left in Britain had little interest in the analysis of music before the period in which Stuart Hall became director of the Centre for Contemporary Cultural Studies, an early key work being Stuart Hall and Paddy Whannel, *The Popular Arts* (Boston: Beacon 1967).

250 Laurie Green, 'What Is Jazz?' *Marxism Today* (January 1963): 32; Bruce Turner, 'Jazz Is "Unpopular" Entertainment,' *Music & Life*, n.d. [late 1950s], CP CENT CULT 16/5.

251 The position was soon echoed in the debates on how the British New Wave had ideologically recoded British film discussed above. Nina Hibbin, 'A Taste of Honey,' *Marxism Today* (April 1962): 127–8; Hibbin, 'New Trends in British Film-Making,' *Marxism Today* (June 1964): 151–7.

252 Francis Newton, *The Jazz Scene* (1959; New York: Monthly Review Press, 1975), 177–201. More negatively, Hobsbawm saw the emergence of be-bop and other experimental jazz styles – the types affirmed in MacInnes's novel – as a reaction against cultural dilution and commercialization that drove the music towards high culture and away from its popular origins.

253 A.L. Lloyd, 'The Folk Song Revival and the Communist Party,' *Music & Life* 18, no. 4 (1962): 18.

254 Its ageing and classically dominated music group agonized over whether jazz – now half a century old – was 'merely a fashion' well into the age of rock and roll, of which it seemed serenely oblivious. The party's Music Group, which established a quarterly journal in April 1956, was dominated by figures from classical music (Alan Bush, Tom Russell, Alfred Corum). 'A Plan for Music in Britain: Being a Supplement to the British Road,' CP CENT CULT 16/5; Alfred Corum, 'What Is Jazz?' *Marxism Today* (July 1963): 223–4.

255 Leading folk artists (Ewan MacColl, A.L. Lloyd, Ian Campbell) and up-and-coming musicians and singers (John Faulkner, Sandra Kerr, Luke Kelly) and promoters (Bruce Dunnett, Malcolm Nixon) were Communists. 'We were keen,' stated Singers' Club organizer Bruce Dunnett, 'to develop among young people an understanding of the [folk] musical tradition that is equal to and better than many other musical traditions.' Ann Nolan, 'The Singers' Club,' *Challenge* (July/August 1963): 2; Ben Harker, '"Workers' Music": Communism and the British

Folk Revival,' in *Red Strains: Music and Communism outside the Communist Bloc*, ed. Robert Adlington (Oxford: Oxford University Press, 2103), 89–104.

256 Derek Hepinstall, 'A Devotion to Folk,' *Challenge* (November 1962): 2; 'Information for the Discussion of the Cultural Work of the Labour Movement,' n.d. [1963], CP CENT CULT 1/6.

257 Folk music concerts were the only spheres of Centre 42's activities in which the party made a discernible imprint; Frank Stanley, 'Centre 42,' *Marxism Today* (March 1963): 78; NCC discussion on Centre 42, 11 January 1963, CP CENT CULT 3/8.

258 *Sing* originated from the London Youth Choir; *Folk Music* was established and edited by Dallas, also folk columnist for *Melody Maker*. Dallas reported on the folk scene in *Challenge*. Karl Dallas, 'Entertainment in Pubs,' *Challenge* (March 1963): 3.

259 Lloyd was a vice-president of the WMA, a director at Topic Records, and exerted influence at the more traditional English Folk Dance Society, serving on the editorial board of its journal and co-editing with Ralph Vaughan Williams *The Penguin Book of English Book of Folk Songs* (1959). Dave Arthur, *Bert: The Life and Times of A.L Lloyd* (London: Pluto, 2012), 178–98; Georgina Boyes, *The Imagined Village: Culture, Ideology and the English Folk Revival* (Manchester: Manchester University Press, 1993), 216.

260 Among Communists, MacColl and Lloyd alone retained profiles at the BBC, re-establishing themselves at the corporation after the easing of Cold War blacklisting and increasingly driving and dominating the network's folk-related broadcasts, notably the Prix Italia–winning radio ballads (1958–64). MacColl was effectively kept from the airwaves between 1953 and 1957, but worked his way back with the first radio ballad. Ben Harker, *Class Act: The Cultural and Political Life of Ewan MacColl* (London: Pluto, 2007), 129.

261 Stephen Sedley, 'Art and Superstructure,' *Marxism Today* (December 1964): 385–7.

262 'Here are the foundations of the culture of the future,' Craig wrote, 'where the expropriators have been expropriated and we again control our way of life'; David Craig, 'The People's Songs,' *Comment*, 8 February 1964, 85.

263 David Craig, 'Art and Superstructure,' *Marxism Today* (June 1964): 187–9; Lloyd, 'Folk Song Revival,' 18–19.

264 Lloyd, 'Notes for Conference on Workers' Songs,' event organized by the Music and History Groups of the CP, 8 October 1961, CP CENT CULT 3/6. The traditional high-low mindset made the NCC wary: NCC stalwart and artist Barbara Niven was among those who had worked with MacColl in theatre and now thought he was wasting his time on folk music, a view shared by Hugh MacDiarmid. A debate about culture and commodification soon played out in public in party debates around the 'commercialisation' of folk. For the folk music hardliners, artists like Peter, Paul and Mary, who had a minor hit with Bob

Dylan's 'Blowing in the Wind' in October 1963 and toured Britain in spring 1964, represented the unacceptable adulteration of the people's music, 'one foot in folk,' as MacColl acidly put it, 'and one in pop.' Karl Dallas, 'Focus on MacColl,' *Melody Maker*, 18 September 1965; Harker, *Class Act*, 181–3.

265 Though praising MacColl's work, he drew the lessons from jazz and argued that the Left in the scene needed to jump one way or the other: knowing integration into 'commercialism' as a way to reach a mass audience with the compromises this involved, or constituting folk as a narrow niche feeding highbrow artistic experiment, a trend he detected in the radio ballads. Francis Newton, 'Two cheers for folk-song,' *New Statesman*, 26 July 1963; Karl Dallas, 'Don't Let Tin Pan Alley Spoil It,' *Music & Life* 21, no. 3 (1963): 18–19. According to Hobsbawm's logic, the likes of Peter, Paul and Mary were making the necessary adjustments and bringing their broadly progressive music to a mainstream audience, a line of argument that prevailed in the NCC. 'A few years ago this type of song could only be heard around a YCL campfire or social,' noted the party press. 'Today millions of records have been purchased'; Barney Davies, 'British Youth – Progressive, Reactionary or Indifferent?' *Marxism Today* (March 1966): 78.

266 Lloyd, 'Folk Song Revival'; under his alias Jack Speedwell, MacColl attacked Dylan in the pages of Dallas's *Folk Music* magazine. Harker, *Class Act*, 182–4.

267 Unsigned, 'Bob Dylan,' *Comment*, 8 June 1965.

268 Dallas, 'Focus on MacColl.'

269 Betty Reid, letter, *Daily Worker*, 26 September 1965, CP CENT CULT 1/8.

270 Betty Reid, 'The Freedom of Art,' *Marxism Today* (March 1966): 93. Progressives, ran the argument, should welcome the fact that 'thousands of teenagers are listening to … songs which come down solidly on the side of life and progress'; Reid, letter, *Daily Worker*, 26 September 1965.

271 Grievances around the party's capitulation to 'imperialist' popular culture were a recurrent theme in the Maoism that tore a sizeable hole in British communism's cultural world: George Thomson, Alick West, Claudia Jones, Douglas Garman, and many at Unity were among those drawn to 'anti-revisionist' Maoist groupings at odds with the allegedly diluted Marxism-Leninism of the CPGB. Maoist critique now appeared legitimated by the largest communist party in the world. Thomson, who had spent a sabbatical in China in 1955, backed Chinese currents and found himself on a collision course with the leadership: Thomson, *Marxism in China Today* (London: China Policy Study Group, n.d.); Thomson pushed Dutt and *Labour Monthly* to address the Sino-Soviet difference in *Labour Monthly* in February 1963 (a letter he sent went unpublished); he was cautioned in December 1964 after *Broadsheet*, the publication of the China Policy Study Group with which he was closely associated, openly criticized the *Daily Worker*. Correspondence with Dutt, CP IND DUTT 6/3; 'Transcript of conversation between West and Thomson,' Garman Papers, University of Nottingham, DG 6/11. These currents are traced in Lawrence Parker, *The Kick Inside:*

Revolutionary Opposition in the CPGB, 1945–91 (London: November, 2012), 44–62; and Seltman, *What's Left?*, 94.

272 The most notable cohort was the St Pancras YCL, some of whom were close to MacColl. This Maoist-turning faction organized a fringe meeting at the Skegness Congress/Trend events and attracted national media attention; undated clipping, *Sunday Telegraph*, CP YCL 10/1. West addressed their meetings; West to Garman, 15 January 1967, Garman Papers, DG2. For MacColl and his circle's turn to Maoism, see Harker, *Class Act*, 202–5.

273 Andrews, *Endgames*, 34; Mike Waite, 'Sex 'n' Drugs 'n' Rock 'n' Roll (and Communism),' in *Opening the Books: Essays on the Social and Cultural History of the British Communist Party*, ed. Geoff Andrews, Nina Fishman, and Kevin Morgan (London: Pluto, 1995), 115; Mike Power, 'Asking the Questions,' in *Children of the Revolution: Communist Childhood in Cold War Britain*, ed. Phil Cohen (London: Lawrence & Wishart, 1997), 175.

274 Objections to cultural 'opportunism' were cited in widespread branch-level YCL dissidence of the mid- to late 1960s in which cadres and even entire branches challenged and were expelled, in some cases preferring a purer form of party vanguardism, including that offered by Trotskyism. Elizabeth Brown of Lambeth YCL, soon expelled for Trotskyism, objected to *Challenge*'s 'concentration on music and sport,' which has 'decreased the political content to a pathetically low level'; Terry Monaghan of Paddington YCL saw the magazine's function as to fight 'the decaying system of capitalism and not try to revive it'; letters, 13 June 1964 and 11 April, 1964, respectively, CP YCL 10/1. Some YCLers refused to sell a follow-up issue featuring Ringo Starr, thinking 'this was not the way to boost sales' (the issue sold an additional 7,000 copies); John Evans, letter, *Music & Life* 26, no. 1 (1965): 3. The deeper story of The Trend campaign was contained not in the 250 new membership applications, but in the campaign's outmoded iconography of a young woman in a mid-1960s mini-skirt and a middle-aged jazz trumpeter; as one activist later put it, Communists 'were on the outside looking in' and never 'really integrated with young people'; Power, 'Asking the Questions,' 176; the recruitment figure is from George Bridges, 'London District YCL,' document, 1 November 1966, CP YCL 10/1.

275 Andrews, *Endgames*, 34.

276 The eye-catching appearance of The Beatles on the cover of *Challenge* in December 1963 was strikingly aberrant in terms of *Challenge*'s usual cultural coverage. Rolf Harris was more likely to appear than The Rolling Stones in the 1960s, and pop and rock and roll musicians only tended to feature in 'political' stories, such as Dusty Springfield's deportation from South Africa after refusing to sing to segregated audiences. Gina Young, 'A Didgeridoo Comes to Central Hall,' *Challenge* (February 1963): 2; unsigned, 'Protest against Apartheid,' *Challenge* (January 1965): 1. *Challenge* grasped that The Beatles were significant and worthy of respect, but could not fully articulate why, and affirmed them

through a familiar discourse that presented the group as a regionally grounded British antidote to Americanization; 'Yeah, Yeah, Yeah,' *Challenge* (December 1963): 2.

277 Through which 10,000 copies of a poster-leaflet were circulated; *Challenge* (September 1966): 7; *Challenge* (November 1966): 5. The campaign culminated in an international youth festival in Skegness in 1967 to coincide with the YCL's Twenty-sixth Congress. The event's promotional material was an unstable mixture of psychedelic imagery, faux-naive prose, and old-fashioned party paternalism. Delegates were initially promised roller skating, and drawing and writing competitions; the headline act, The Kinks, were invited at the eleventh hour.

278 That a rising cadre 'sought to develop a new politics derived from shifts in popular culture' that 'deeply challenged the party's own ethos and cultural outlook' implies a systematic project; this perhaps overstates the case for the mid- to late 1960s, although that would indeed come later. Waite, 'Sex 'n' Drugs,' 215; Andrews, *Endgames*, 33–4.

279 Led by unenticingly orthodox National Student Organiser Fergus Nicholson in a period of rapid university expansion. The party closed down its loss-making student magazine, *Mainstream*, with its 5,000 print run, just as the tempo of student politics was picking up in 1965. Andrews, *Endgames*, 52–3; Dave Cope, *Bibliography of the Communist Party of Great Britain* (London; Lawrence & Wishart, 2016), 190; a sense of deep frustration colours 'The Development of Communist Work among Students,' n.d. [1965], CP CENT CULT 18/1.

280 Having lost 1,300 members between 1956 and 1958, it counted 4,000 in 1962–3. Newton, *Sociology of British Communism*, 161; Andrews, *Endgames*, 34. The Young Conservatives had twenty times more members than the CPGB; Barney Davies, 'British Youth – Progressive, Reactionary or Indifferent?' *Marxism Today* (March 1966): 77.

281 Andrews, *Endgames*, 75

282 The new position was thrashed out at King Street discussions on industrial work held in late 1964 and early 1965; Callaghan, *Cold War*, 246–8.

283 Substantially in response to Harold Wilson's provocative July 1966 wage freeze. Although Harold Wilson famously, if inaccurately, flattered the party's industrial strength in attributing the 1966 seamen's strike to Communists – 'a tightly knit group of politically motivated men' – Communists were indeed to the fore in the creation of the Liaison Committee for the Defence of Trade Unions, which would prove effective in the late 1960s and early 1970s. Wilson in House of Commons, 20 June 1966; industrial disputes rose from 1966, with 4.7 million days lost to strikes in 1968. Sandbrook, *White Heat*, 281, 707; Thompson, *Good Old Cause*, 137–9.

284 These debates first broke to the surface at a conference organized by the Economic Committee in October 1965. The key shift in the discourse was driven

by Warren – writing as William McCallum – 'The Economic Policies of Post-war Tory and Labour Governments till November 1964,' *Economic Bulletin* (April 1966): 1–7, CP CENT ECON 7/9; Callaghan, *Cold War*, 164.

285 John Gollan, 'Labour in Power – What Next?' *Comment*, 28 November 1964, 761.

286 John Gollan, 'A New Name for the Six Page *Daily Worker*,' CP CENT STAT 2/3. Thanks to John Callaghan for bringing this document to my attention.

287 The debate ran from February 1966. The Maoist *Marxist Forum* was not alone in detecting unpalatable revisionism; James Cameron, the war correspondent, joked whether 'the *Daily Professional Man*' might be a better title, given the leadership's obsession with a group seen as central to the 'broad popular alliance' (letter to Allen Hutt, 4 February 1966); John Berger was among those who opposed the rebranding. Deeply disillusioned by the name change and the 'behind-your-back' processes that had driven it through, the distinguished journalist and typographer Hutt now retired from the paper. Hutt, 'Allen Hutt and the *Daily Worker*,' cuttings and correspondence in CP IND HUTT 2/7.

288 Key documents grew more rhetorically 'Marxist,' as if to mask the narrowing of the party's work to industrial and especially electoral strategies. The party existed to 'provide the organisation for the vanguard of the working class'; *The Role of the Communist Party* (London: CPGB, 1965), 7.

289 'Television tames even the terrible Communists,' noted the *Times*, 24 March 1966; Hogenkamp, *Film, Television*, 95.

290 Thompson, *Good Old Cause*, 143.

291 Callaghan, *Cold War*, 192.

292 Traditional groupings whose preference was a more direct and prescriptive cultural line wanted a frank debate on the cultural implications of 'peaceful co-existence,' the dictatorship of the proletariat, and the peaceful transition to socialism. Birmingham Cultural Committee to NCC, 4 January 1963, CP CENT CULT 3/8; 'The Writer's Responsibility,' *Comment*, 17 October 1964, 667–9. Lionel Munby rhetorically asked what could be concluded from the fact that theoretical Marxism was at a higher pitch in capitalist democracies than in socialist states where it was the official ideology; 'For Discussion at Cultural Committee,' 8 January 1965, CP CENT CULT 1/8.

293 National variations of these debates occurred across Communist Parties in the 1960s; they had rumbled away on the British party's fringes since the Twentieth Congress and Khruschev's distinctly mixed messages around a more capacious conception of socialist realism. Lindsay attended the Second and Third Congresses in 1955 and 1959, respectively, and noted that the position actually stiffened between them; Lindsay, 'On the Artist and Politics,' 284–8.

294 The resolution appeared in the May–June issue of *Les Cahiers du communisme*; extracts are reprinted in David Craig, ed., *Marxists on Literature: An Anthology* (Harmondsworth, UK: Penguin, 1975), 527–8.

295 Simon to Gollan, 5 September 1966, CP CENT CULT 3/11.

296 'Ideology and Culture,' document, n.d., CP CENT CULT 1/8
297 NCC Minutes, 12 May 1967, CP CENT CULT 1/10; 'Questions of Ideology and Culture,' *Marxism Today* (May 1967): 134–9.
298 *Morning Star*, 28 April 1967.
299 'Questions of Ideology and Culture: Statement from the Executive Committee of the Communist Party of Great Britain,' *Marxism Today* (May 1967): 134; *The British Road to Socialism* (London: CPGB, 1968), 5.
300 'Questions of Ideology and Culture,' 135.
301 In line with European models, this asserted the principles of working with Christians around shared objectives and the right of freedom of religious worship under socialism (ibid., 136–7); the genesis of the dialogue was initiated by Pope John XXIII and the PCI, involved international and national symposia, some of them including significant religious figures and party members, notably Klugmann and John Lewis. A dozen contributions on the topic published in *Marxism Today* between March 1966 and October 1967 furnished the material for a book edited by James Klugmann, *Dialogue of Christianity and Marxism* (London: Lawrence & Wishart, 1968). Analysed in Geoff Andrews, *The Shadow Man at the Heart of the Cambridge Spy Circle* (London: I.B. Tauris, 2015), 213–19.
302 'Questions of Ideology and Culture,' 134.
303 Ibid.
304 Ibid.
305 Ibid., 138.
306 General News Talk, BBC European Service, 28 April 1967, CP CENT PUB 1/3.
307 Lewis to Gollan, 27 February 1967, CP CENT CULT 3/11. The document was clearly driven by a deep-rooted desire to be rid of the obligation to equivocate around or justify the prescriptive and dogmatic cultural attitudes evident in the Soviet bloc, which Communist intellectuals were weary of defending, and to state views, as Gollan put it, 'we have held for some time'; Gollan to Simon, 1 November 1966, CP CENT CULT 3/11; Brian Simon, 'Questions on Ideology and Culture: A Reply to Discussion,' *Marxism Today* (May 1968): 156.
308 Lewis to Gollan, 22 February 1967; Cornforth to Ted Ainley, 8 February 1967, CP CENT CULT 3/11. West thought the document cast the party as 'an indulgent and enlightened parent letting the children play creatively'; West to Garman, 4 June 1967, Garman Papers, DG2.
309 Michael Long, 'Marxism and Criticism,' *Marxism Today* (November 1966): 341–50; Terry Eagleton, 'Marxism and Criticism,' *Marxism Today* (March 1967): 94–6; Margot Heinemann, 'Marxism and Criticism,' *Marxism Today* (April 1967): 123–8.
310 John Lewis, 'Marx's View of Alienation,' *Marxism Today* (January 1964): 18–22; Jack Lindsay, 'Alienation under Socialism,' *Marxism Today* (November 1964): 353–6; Lindsay to Ainley, 2 December 1966, CP CENT CULT 3/11; Lindsay to Ainley, 29 November 1966, Lindsay Papers, NLA, Folder 52. Lindsay's two

unpublished work on alienation, the first version of which was entitled 'The Crack across the World's Face' and the second ''The Whole Man and the Alien Thing,' were from this period; Lindsay Papers, NLA, Folders 63, 328. Lindsay was impressed by István Mészáros's enduring *Marx's Theory of Alienation* (1969), and abandoned attempts to revise and publish his own manuscript after reading it. Mészáros to Lindsay, 16 May 1971; Lindsay to Mészáros, n.d. [1971], Lindsay Papers, NLA, Folder 70.

311 *British Road* (1968), 5.

312 Cornforth to Ainley, 8 February 1967, CP CENT CULT 3/11

313 Birmingham Cultural Committee, response to 'Questions of Ideology and Culture,' 19 November 1968, CP CENT CULT 3/11.

314 'We are an absolutely negligible force in the ideological discussions of our time … Zhdanov killed our intellectuality stone dead in 1948; and we have never recovered'; Lewis to Ainley, 5 December 1966, CP CENT CULT 3/11.

315 Lewis to Gollan, 27 February 1967, CP CENT CULT 3/11.

316 *British Road* (1968), 11.

317 Ibid., 2, 49, 53.

318 Ibid., 25; Gollan, 'New Name.'

319 *British Road* (1968), 39, 56, 67.

5. The Spectre of Eurocommunism, 1968–1979

1 Jude Bloomfield, in Phil Cohen, *Children of the Revolution: Communist Childhood in Cold War Britain* (London: Lawrence & Wishart, 1997), 73

2 Gladys Brooks, 'Czechoslovakia,' *Comment*, 31 August 1968.

3 The multiple sites included the bitter controversy about the expulsion of Solzhenitsyn from the Soviet Writers' Union in late 1969 – correspondence archived in CP CENT CULT 18/3 – the retrospective row about the meaning of 1956 conducted on the twentieth anniversary set in train by John Gollan's article in *Marxism Today*, the Political Committee's revocation of an invitation for Soviet dissident Zhores Medvedev to speak at the 1977 Communist University of London, and the question of how the party should mark the 60th anniversary of the Russian Revolution in 1977. Geoff Andrews, *Endgames and New Times: The Final Years of British Communism, 1964–1991* (London: Lawrence & Wishart, 2004), 167.

4 Surrey District to *Comment*, 6 September 1969.

5 Surrey District to *Comment*, 30 April 1977.

6 Strike days reached a level not seen in Britain since the inter-war period – 6.5 million days lost in one quarter of 1974. Andy Beckett, *When the Lights Went Out: What Really Happened to Britain in the Seventies* (London: Faber & Faber, 2009), 404; Willie Thompson, *The Good Old Cause: British Communism 1920–1991* (London: Pluto, 1992), 218.

7 A 'document of major importance in the development of twentieth century Marxism;' Monty Johnstone, *Czechoslovakia's Struggle for Socialist Democracy* [publication of the YCL theoretical journal *Cogito*], n.d., 8; similar texts were soon produced by the Italian, Austrian, Swedish, and Spanish parties.

8 Ibid., 32.

9 It had stood behind the 1960s quest for electoral credibility, with the controversial transformation of the *Daily Worker* into the *Morning Star* and the centrality of the 'broad popular alliance' of classes and class fractions said to share interests in the overcoming of post-war capitalism's monopolistic tendencies. The growth of the middle strata, which had increased from 23 per cent of the employed population in 1921 to 35.9 per cent at the beginning of the 1960s, was a common theme in party debate. Alan Hunt, 'Class Structure in Britain Today,' *Marxism Today* (June 1970): 168.

10 As previously mentioned, Pollitt, for instance, had boasted in 1955 that none of the party's election candidates was 'old school tie,' a phrase that carried associations of homosexuality as well as ivory tower other-worldliness. Malcolm MacEwan to Pollitt, 20 May 1955, KV2/2987; Alison Macleod, *The Death of Uncle Joe* (London: Merlin, 1997), 28.

11 Francis Beckett, *Enemy Within: The Rise and Fall of the British Communist Party* (1995; London: Merlin, 1998), 163; Geoff Andrews, 'Young Turks and the Old Guard: Intellectuals and the Communist Party Leadership in the 1970s,' in *Opening the Books: Essays on the Social and Cultural History of the British Communist Party*, ed. Geoff Andrews, Nina Fishman, and Kevin Morgan (London: Pluto, 1995), 228.

12 Beckett, *Enemy Within*, 67; Martin Jacques, 'The Last Word,' *Marxism Today* (December 1991): 28.

13 Mediated by Willie Thompson, 'The "New Left" Ideas of Marcuse,' *Comment*, 22 June 1968; 'Revolutionary Romanticism,' *Marxism Today* (May 1970): 153–60.

14 A deeply felt, retrospective critique of this trend came in Alan Hunt's review of New Left Book's *Western Marxism: A Critical Reader* in 1977. 'There is a consistent tendency,' wrote Hunt of the book in particular and the *New Left Review* in general, 'to present the phenomenon of Western Marxism as taking place "outside" or unconnected with the Communist movement (despite the presence of Lukács, Gramsci or Althusser)'; Hunt, review, *Eurored* 6 (n.d.): 24.

15 Johnstone's extended critique of Trotskyism appeared in *Cogito* in 1969; a second part was added in 1975 and reprinted in 1976; Lawrence & Wishart planned a book based on the essays, which never appeared. Betty Reid, 'Respectable Man' (critique of *Black Dwarf*), *Comment*, 19 April 1969; Reid, *Ultra Leftism in Britain* (London: CPGB, 1969); currents recently described in John Kelly, *Contemporary Trotskyism: Parties, Sects and Social Movements in Britain* (London: Routledge, 2018), 36–59.

16 Brian Simon, 'Cultural Committee Memo,' 1 January 1971, CP CENT CULT 2/1.

17 'It is impossible,' she wrote, 'for the party to be close to the important youth scene without understanding some of the current trends and evaluating them'; Betty Reid, circular to NCC, 18 May 1971, CP CENT CULT 2/1.

18 She courted leftist music writer Dave Laing, who had produced the first serious account of 1960s British pop music and pushed his work at the *Morning Star* (Laing would join the party); Betty Reid, circular to NCC, 29 August 1972, CP CENT CULT 2/2.

19 Simon, 'Cultural Committee Memo.'

20 Phil Goodwin, 'Communist University,' *Comment*, 14 July 1969; Brian Durrans, 'Communist University,' *Comment*, 26 July 1969.

21 Reid's typed notes of meeting, 18 April 1969, CP CENT CULT 1/12.

22 The key essay, Louis Althusser, 'Ideology and the Ideological State Apparatuses,' was written in 1969, published in 1970, and translated the following year. Ben Brewster, trans., *Lenin and Philosophy and Other Essays* (London: New Left Books, 1971), 121–77.

23 The debate was brokered by the journal's still-well-connected editor, James Klugmann. Louis Althusser, 'How to Read Marx's "Capital,"' *Marxism Today* (October 1969): 302–5; John Lewis, 'The Althusser Case, Part One,' *Marxism Today* (January 1972): 23–8; Lewis, 'The Althusser Case, Part Two,' *Marxism Today* (February 1972): 43–8; Althusser, 'Reply to John Lewis (Self Criticism),' *Marxism Today* (October 1972): 310–72, (November 1972): 343–9. Additional reflections were provided by Graeme Lock (June 1972): 180–7, who translated Althusser's response; Gordon Gray (July 1973): 220–1; Maurice Cornforth (May 1973): 139–47; and concluded by Lewis, 'On the Althusser Discussion,' (June 1974): 168–75.

24 Reid NCC circular, 16 July 1970; Jacques to Simon, 23 April 1970, CP CENT CULT 1/13.

25 'He obviously thought me a pernickity old shell,' she wrote to Simon, 'but I told him I didn't want him to call a meeting with a title like this'; Reid to Simon, 25 April 1970, CP CENT CULT 3/12.

26 Althusser, 'Ideology,' 162, 136–7.

27 Roger Simon, review of *The Modern Prince*, *Comment*, 16 March 1968; Andrews, *Endgames*, 142; David Forgacs, 'Gramsci and Marxism in Britain,' *New Left Review* (July–August 1989): 83; Simon, *Gramsci's Political Thought: An Introduction* (London: Lawrence & Wishart, 1982).

28 Carrit wrote to Simon of the 'need to develop a clearer approach to the role of intellectuals in the party'; Carritt to Simon, 24 June 1969, CP CENT CULT 1/12.

29 Martin Jacques, Contribution to Congress discussion, *Comment*, 8 November 1969.

30 Developing the point, he argued that, in a context where a shrinking party faced the challenge of imparting radical socialist consciousness to a working class more inclined to industrial than political militancy, the party should 'especially

encourage and appreciate those who, by their position in capitalist society, are closely involved with the production of ideas'; Martin Jacques, 'Congress Discussion,' *Comment*, 8 November 1969.

31 Martin Jacques, 'Notes on the Concept of Intellectuals,' *Marxism Today* (October 1971): 307–16; the article was based on Jacques's brief paper on intellectuals from April 1969, but was augmented by reference to the now-translated Prison Notebooks; Quintin Hoare and Geoffrey Nowell-Smith, eds. and trans., *Selections from the Prison Notebooks of Antonio Gramsci* (London: Lawrence & Wishart, 1971).

32 Writing as William McCallum, Warren produced 'The Economic Policies of Post-war Tory and Labour Governments till 1964,' which argued that excessive wage demands damaged national competiveness. It went unpublished in the party press; CP CENT ECON 6. Reprinted in John Callaghan and Ben Harker, eds., *British Communism: A Documentary History* (Manchester: Manchester University Press, 2011), 213–14; Reid's notes on the 1969 meeting, 18 April 1969, CP CULT 1/12.

33 Andrews, 'Young Turks,' 229; the most detailed analysis available of the group's work is Andrew Pearmain, 'Dissent from Dissent: The "Smith/Party" Group in the 1970s CPGB,' in *Against the Grain: The British Far Left from 1956*, ed. Evan Smith and Matthew Worley (Manchester: Manchester University Press, 2014), 115–33.

34 That its electoral strategy was in ruins was soon confirmed during their involvement in the May 1971 Municipal Elections in Tower Hamlets. The neighbourhood was once a CP stronghold of the Jewish East End: in 1947 the party had a thousand members in Stepney alone (1 per cent of residents), two London councillors, eleven borough councillors, twenty branches, fourteen factory branches, and an MP, Phil Piratin. Twenty-four years later, it was reduced to eight skeletal branches, and its best hope was holding its two remaining council seats. In the course of the campaign, the party was shown to be out of touch with the now predominantly Pakistani community, and embarrassed itself by lacking a coherent position on the Bangladesh question, which mattered greatly to the local electorate. Apparently unmindful of its role in the 'broad popular alliance' described in *The British Road*, the Labour Party, in its determination to unseat the two CP councillors, bussed in activists to the key wards and campaigned on a '100 per cent Labour Council' ticket. A fight almost broke out at the count when a Communist activist called the incoming Labour councillor a 'hypocritical bastard' and told him to 'fuck off.' For this group of intellectuals – Beatrix Campbell and her husband Bob had been pushed by the leadership to stand as candidates in Shadwell and Wapping wards – such events cruelly illustrated the mismatch between the self-deluding abstractions of *The British Road* and the reality on the ground. The party in Tower Hamlets had reached 'rock bottom and is politically bankrupt,' reported its grim post-mortem. 'Only when the Party is

seen to be part of the people's day-to-day political struggles will they be able to gain support in any form. The days of sticking up token candidates is over.' 'Local Elections in Tower Hamlets,' [1971], CP ORG MISC 6/8.

35 In the five constituencies contested in every election since 1950, it was polling a mere 13 per cent of the 1950 vote, as pointed out in a letter from Surrey District, *Comment*, 22 August 1970; letter from Willie Thompson, *Comment*, 19 September 1970.

36 Smith/Party Group documents are archived in CP ORG MISC 6/8.

37 'The Crisis in Capitalism and the Crisis in the Communist Party,' n.d., CP ORG MISC 6/8.

38 Bill Warren, 'Strategy of Socialist Revolution in Britain,' *Marxism Today* (August 1972): 253.

39 Bill Warren, 'The Programme of the CPGB – A Critique,' *New Left Review* 63 (September–October 1970): 27–41.

40 Ibid., 27. The draft document is in the CP archive as Warren, 'The British Road to Socialism and the Strategy for Revolution,' [January 1970], CP ORG MISC 6/8.

41 The published version softened this to 'the elaboration of an alternative strategy is not the aim of this paper but such an elaboration can usefully begin from a critique of the most clearly worked out existing strategy'; Warren, 'Programme,' 27.

42 Ibid., 40; Warren, 'British Road,' 18.

43 Warren, 'Programme,' 41, emphasis in original; the defence of Parliament was strategically necessary in order to safeguard 'the most propitious conditions for the struggle,' but not sufficient; Warren, 'British Road,' 9, 18.

44 Mike Prior, 'The Strategy of Socialist Revolution in Britain,' *Marxism Today* (May 1974): 157.

45 'Crisis in Capitalism,' 22.

46 Prior, 'Strategy of Socialist Revolution,' 157.

47 Their broader context was a growing body of international feminist writing abroad and closer to home sharpening contrast between positive social change – increased participation of women in higher education and paid work (36 per cent of women between ages twenty and sixty four were working in 1951, 42 per cent in 1961, and 52 per cent by 1971) – and a stubborn and actually widening pay gap.

48 Beckett, *When the Lights Went Out*, 223. For Rowe and scores of others, the non-hierarchical discussion sessions revealed a shared experience of exclusion, oppression, and violence for which there was little language; in Rowe it inspired the eventual formation of the feminist magazine *Spare Rib* in July 1972, the demand for which took its editors by surprise – 20,000 copies were sold (226).

49 Some took a 'radical feminist' and ultimately separatist direction, a trend galvanized by the second WLM conference at Skegness in October 1971, at which Maoist men, some dressed in drag, attacked the WLM as a diversion and

lesbianism as symptomatic of bourgeois decadence. Elizabeth Wilson, *Mirror Writing: An Autobiography* (London: Virago, 1982), 129.

50 Kevin Morgan, Gidon Cohen, and Andrew Flinn, *Communists and British Society 1920–1991* (London: Rivers Oram, 2007), 180.

51 Ibid.; biographical note in Beatrix Campbell, *Wigan Pier Revisited: Poverty and Politics in the 80s* (London: Virago, 1984).

52 Morgan, Cohen, and Flinn, *Communists and British Society*, 180.

53 Cited in Andrews, *Endgames*, 62.

54 Judith Hunt, 'Women and Liberation,' *Marxism Today* (November 1975): 328; Judith Gray, 'Where Next for the Women's Movement?' *Comment*, 12 June 1976.

55 Beatrix Campbell, *British Road* Discussion, *Comment*, 3 September 1977.

56 One version was the Party Group document, 'Alternative Motion to Women in Society'; this is missing from the CP Archive, but is discussed at length by Andrews, *Endgames*, 64–5. The version proposed to replace the deleted official statement seems to have been a strategically toned-down rewrite, and appears in *Comment* as Branch Amendment 847, 25 September 1971.

57 Cited in Andrews, *Endgames*, 65.

58 Brian Simon, 'Cultural Committee,' 11 October 1972, CP CENT CULT 1/13; NCC Minutes, 12 January 1973, CP CENT CULT 2/3; NCC Minutes, 9 February 1973; 'Pornography – Censorship – Sex and Society,' CP CENT CULT 2/3.

59 The alternative motion advocated eleven concrete policies, including the four key demands of the WLM (equal pay, equal education and opportunity; twenty-four-hour nurseries; free contraception; abortion on demand); Andrews, *Endgames*, 64–5; Branch Amendment 847, *Comment* (25 September 1971.

60 Campbell, *British Road*, 110, 111; Beckett, *When the Lights Went Out*, 225.

61 'The Great Male Cover-Up,' *Comment*, 27 October 1979.

62 Morgan, Cohen, and Flinn, *Communists and British Society*, 174.

63 Ibid., 178.

64 Jack Lindsay, 'Marxist Theory of Culture,' (1945), CP CENT CULT 4/11.

65 Rosemary Small, 'Marxism and the Family,' *Marxism Today* (December 1972): 363.

66 Ibid., 364; Small, 'Reply to Discussion,' *Marxism Today* (April 1974): 103.

67 Maria Loftus, 'Marxism and the Family,' *Marxism Today* (April 1973): 124.

68 Sue Slipmann, 'Marxism and the Family,' *Marxism Today* (March 1973): 96.

69 Loftus, 'Marxism and the Family,' 126.

70 Ibid., 127.

71 Campbell, *British Road*, 93, emphasis in original.

72 Slipmann, 'Marxism and the Family,' 95.

73 Ibid., 96.

74 Judith Hunt and Alan Hunt, 'Marxism and the Family,' *Marxism Today* (February 1974): 60.

75 Slipmann, 'Marxism and the Family,' 95.

76 The radical analysis was courteously described, minor points conceded and the original position re-stated without acknowledgement of the pressure to which it had been subjected. Small, 'Reply to Discussion,' 103.
77 'Declaration of Intent,' Editorial, *Red Rag* 1 [1972]: 2.
78 Gladys Brooks, '*Red Rag*,' n.d., CP CENT WOM 5/8.
79 Ibid.
80 EC Report, 'Red Rag,' CP WOM 5/8
81 Ibid.; Minutes of EC Meeting, 8–9 July 1972, CP CENT EC 13/8.
82 Sue Beardon to EC, 19 August 1972; Irene Brennan to EC, 3 September 1972, CP CENT EC 13/20.
83 Margaret Heartfield to EC, n.d. [summer 1972], CP CENT EC 13/20.
84 EC Report, 'Red Rag.'
85 Brooks, '*Red Rag*'; 'Declaration of Intent,' Editorial, *Red Rag* 1 [1972]: 2.
86 Minutes of EC Meeting, 9–10 September 1972, CP IND JOHN 4/14 and CP CENT EC 13/20.
87 *Link* 1 (Spring 1973); the journal ran for forty-four issues, closing in 1984.
88 'Whereas we do not see the need to submerge our policies under false concept of sisterhood we do not think that giving out such leaflets was necessarily the best way to put our idea forward'; Gray, 'Where Next for the Women's Movement?' 183.
89 Andrews, *Endgames*, 156; NWA Minutes, CP CENT WOM 3.
90 Jean Styles, Report to the EC, 'Women in Society Today,' *Comment*, 7 August 1976.
91 Elizabeth Wilson, letter, *Comment*, 4 September 1976.
92 Beatrix Campbell, letter, *Comment*, 2 October 1976.
93 Heterosexual industrial workers, whose militancy was supported by traditional sexual divisions in family structures, were conceived as the primary agents of class struggle. Intellectuals, tainted by association with public schools, were easily differentiated from such cadre and sometimes seen as querulous, effeminate, 'long-haired' elements likely to corrupt them.
94 Andrews, *Endgames*, 158; Dave Cook, 'Against the Oppression of Homosexuals,' *Comment*, 16 October 1976; the statement was printed as part of the *Comment* article; letter from Lesbian Left to *Comment*, 27 November 1976.
95 'Organisations don't commit themselves to unpopular uncomfortable issues just because they're going to recruit a few people from gay lib'; Nigel Young, 'Communist Comment: Interview with Bea Campbell and Sarah Benton,' *Gay Left* 4 (1976), cited in Lucy Robinson, *Gay Men and the Left in Post-War Britain* (Manchester: Manchester University Press, 2007), 97.
96 Eric W Edwards, letter, *Comment*, 16 October 1976.
97 Andrews, *Endgames*, 158; Bob Deacon, letter, *Focus* (November 1984). LHASC LGSM 4/1.
98 Deacon, letter, *Focus* (November 1984).

99 Ibid.

100 *The British Road to Socialism* (London: CPGB, 1968), 26.

101 Alan Sked and Chris Cook, *Post-War Britain: A Political History* (1979: London: Penguin, 1993), 198. New universities included University of East Anglia (1963), Essex (1965), Kent (1965), Lancaster (1964), Sussex (1961), Warwick (1965), and York (1963).

102 Dominic Sandbrook, *White Heat: A History of Britain in the Swinging Sixties* (London: Abacus, 2006), 537; Digby Jacks, *Student Politics and Higher Education* (London: Lawrence & Wishart, 1975), 15.

103 Betty Reid, 'The Drug Scene Today,' *Comment*, 7 February 1970.

104 Beckett, *Rise and Fall*, 167

105 Jack Woddis, '"Red Bases" in the Universities,' *Comment*, 15 February 1968; Martin Jacques, 'A Look at the Tactic of Violent Protest,' *Comment*, 22 March 1969.

106 Fergus Nicholson, 'Students and the Labour Movement,' *Comment*, 16 January 1971.

107 Mike Prior, quoted in Andrews, *Endgames*, 54.

108 Jacks, quoted in Beckett, *Enemy Within*, 167.

109 Santiago Carillo, 'Workers, Intellectuals, Youth and Revolution,' *Comment*, 28 September 1968.

110 Gianfranco Borghini, 'Italy: Students and the Working-Class Movement,' *Comment*, 8 February 1969.

111 Quoted in Digby Jacks, *Student Politics & Higher Education* (London: Lawrence & Wishart, 1975), 111.

112 Woddis analyses not only Marcuse but also Fanon and Debray in *New Theories of Revolution* (London: Lawrence & Wishart, 1972); Willie Thompson, 'Student Power,' *Comment*, 18 January 1969.

113 Fergus Nicholson, 'Ferment among Students,' *Comment*, 16 January 1971.

114 Young activist and future party leader Nina Temple recalls that those close to him 'got rid of the branch secretary by saying he was a poofter'; Nina Temple, in Cohen, *Children of the Revolution*, 95.

115 Phil Goodwin, 'Higher Education in Capitalist Society,' *Marxism Today* (September 1970): 263–77, especially 276–7.

116 Nicholson, 'Students and the Labour Movement.'

117 Ibid.; Goodwin, 'Higher Education,' 275.

118 Dave Cook, 'The Student Movement, Left Unity and the Communist Party,' *Marxism Today* (October 1974): 292–302.

119 Jacques, 'Look at the Tactic.'

120 Jacks, *Student Politics*, 88, 113; *New Left Review* (January–February 1969) included three articles on the subject by David Trieseman, who would later join the CP, David Fernbach, and Anthony Barnett.

121 Jacks, *Student Politics*, 124.

122 Ibid., 95; the other two were Dave Wynne and Jeff Staniforth, 'Report to PC,' 9 June 1971, CP IND JOHN 4/1/3.
123 'Draft Report on 'Communist Work among Students,' 11–12 November 1972, CP IND JOHN 4/1/4; 'Report to PC.'
124 Reuban Falber to National Student Commitee, 17 May 1972, CP IND JOHN 4/1/4. That Cook, who had not been a student for many years, was imposed by the leadership on the divided National Student Committee was a concession that the version of Communism projected by Nicholson would lead to further marginalization. Cook was controversially appointed without the consultation of the committee. These internal struggles are described in Andrews, *Endgames*, 56–7.
125 Cook, 'Student Movement,' 292–302; Andrews, *Endgames*, 57.
126 Cook, 'Student Movement,' 292–302.
127 Ibid., 296.
128 Andrews, *Endgames*, 57.
129 Cook, 'Student Movement,' 301, emphasis in original.
130 One hundred and forty (sixty-three of them students) had attended the first CUL, in June 1969, to hear Brian Simon, Maurice Dobb, James Klugmann, Maurice Cornforth, and others; Durrans, 'Communist University.'
131 Cook, 'Student Movement,' 300.
132 Julian Cooper, letter, *Comment*, 18 September 1976.
133 'Members holding more orthodox views on basic questions of Marxist theory (and even on the current policy of the party) often found themselves on the defensive, stigmatised as "dogmatists"' (ibid.). The event became more Gramsci focused as the years went by. 'The value of the course on Gramsci,' complained one member who attended, 'was much reduced by the failure of a number of speakers to make a distinction between Gramsci's views and their own'; Bill Tait, 'Culling Gramsci,' *Comment*, 1 September 1979.
134 Nick Wright, letter, *Comment*, 16 October 1976.
135 Bob Hitchon, 'Workers and Students,' *Comment*, 4 January 1969.
136 Neville Carey, 'Left Unity in Bristol,' *Comment*, 30 November 1968.
137 Lionel Munby and John Foster, 'Working for Left Unity,' *Comment*, 6 July 1968.
138 'The only people who observed all the rules that had been set up at the beginning were the Communist Party,' he noted, who 'as so often had been contributing more than its share to the donkey work'; Raymond Williams, *Politics and Letters: Interviews with New Left Review* (London: Verso, 1979), 374–5.
139 Alan Booth, 'SUCCESS! Free School Milk for Harlow Children,' *Comment*, 20 November 1971.
140 Lorna Reith, 'We Will Rebuild Our Country Ten Times More Beautiful,' in *After the Party: Reflections on Life since the CPGB*, ed. Andy Croft (London: Lawrence & Wishart, 2012), 93.
141 Andrews, *Endgames*, 114; Beckett, *When the Lights Went Out*, 404.

142 Roger Seifert and Tom Sibley, *Revolutionary Communist at Work: A Political Biography of Bert Ramelson* (London: Lawrence & Wishart, 2012), 144.
143 Callaghan and Harker, *British Communism*, 225, 207.
144 Seifert and Sibley, *Bert Ramelson*, 149.
145 Callaghan and Harker, *British Communism*, 207.
146 Andrews, *Endgames*, 114
147 Ibid.
148 Seifert and Sibley, *Bert Ramelson*, 207.
149 Half a million workers participated in the strike called by the Liaison Committee for the Defence of Trade Unions in December 1970, three million in the strike of March 1971; Thompson, *Good Old Cause*, 158.
150 Callaghan and Harker, *British Communism*, 206; Seifert and Sibley, *Bert Ramelson*, 114.
151 Callaghan and Harker, *British Communism*, 207.
152 Andrews, *Endgames*, 109, 119.
153 Seifert and Sibley, *Bert Ramelson*, 198.
154 It also counted as Broad Left allies Ray Buckton (Associated Society of Locomotive Engineers and Firemen), Alan Sapper (UCATT), and Ken Cameron (FBU). Callaghan and Harker, *British Communism*, 207. 'Vote Jack Jones, Cut Out the Middle Man' was written on walls during the 1974 election; Britons in the mid-1970s commonly regarded him as more powerful than the prime minister. Beckett, *When the Lights Went Out*, 292; 301.
155 Seifert and Sibley, *Bert Ramelson*, 198.
156 Cited in Andrews, *Endgames*, 117.
157 Ibid., 126–32.
158 Thompson, *Good Old Cause*, 218; *Comment* sales figures in Political Committee Report, 12 April 1972, CP IND JOHN 4/1/3.
159 Frank Stanley's address to CP Factory Branch Conference, 11–12 June 1966, CP CENT ORG 2/1, reprinted in Callaghan and Harker, *British Communism*, 221.
160 Thompson, *Good Old Cause*, 160.
161 Beckett, *When the Lights Went Out*, 291.
162 Bert Ramelson, *Incomes Policy: The Great Wage Freeze Trick* (London: CPGB, 1966).
163 'Wage increases play a very minor, if any, part in the inflation process,' 'Inflation and the Economics Committee,' n.d. [1974], CP CENT ECON 4/2.
164 William McCallum, alias Bill Warren, 'The Economic Policies of Post-war Tory and Labour Governments till November 1964,' unpublished typescript, CP CENT ECON/6, reprinted in Callaghan and Harker, *British Communism*, 213–14.
165 Although Ramelson would cautiously countenance the idea of workers being elected to the board of nationalized industries, he saw ideas of 'consultation' and 'participation' as ruses to legitimate class power; Bert Ramelson, 'Workers' Control? Possibilities and Limitations,' *Marxism Today* (October 1968): 296–303.

166 Ibid., 296.
167 Robin Denselow, *When the Music's Over: The Story of Political Pop* (London: Faber, 1989), 107.
168 Bill Warren and Mike Prior, *Advanced Capitalism and Backward Socialism* (Nottingham: Spokesman, n.d.), 21.
169 Roger Simon, a director at Lawrence & Wishart who drove through and underwrote the publications of four Gramsci volumes between 1971 and 1985, was never in any doubt about the relevance of Gramsci to 'working out the way to advance towards socialism in Britain'; Roger Simon, 'Gramsci's Concept of Hegemony,' *Marxism Today* (March 1977): 86.
170 Bill Warren and Ernst Mandel, 'Recession and Its Consequences,' *New Left Review* 1/87–8 (September–December 1974): 118.
171 Alluding to the control of the outlook and behaviour of workers recognized by Ford as inseparable from purely 'economic' relationships; Hoare and Nowell-Smith, *Selections from the Prison Notebooks*, 285, 208.
172 Ibid., 133.
173 Warren and Mandel, 'Recession and Its Consequences,' 118.
174 Dave Purdy, 'Viewpoint,' *Comment*, 26 June 1976.
175 Ibid.
176 Warren and Prior, *Advanced Capitalism*, 3.
177 'Inflation and the Economics Committee,' n.d. [1974], CP CENT ECON 4/2.
178 David Purdy, 'Some Thoughts on the Party's Policy towards Prices, Wages and Incomes,' *Marxism Today* (August 1974): 251.
179 Warren and Mandel, 'Recession and Its Consequences,' 120.
180 Ibid.
181 Ibid., 118.
182 Warren and Prior, *Advanced Capitalism*, 26.
183 Ibid.
184 Ibid.
185 Ibid.
186 Ibid.
187 In short, what was needed was 'a policy of workers' control combined with a working class incomes policy'; ibid., 27.
188 Mike Prior, 'Inflation and Marxist Theory,' *Marxism Today* (April 1975): 125.
189 Purdy, 'Viewpoint.'
190 This position lingered in the minds of some. One member dismissed Purdy's ideas on the grounds that 'university lecturers are particularly susceptible to capitalist ideology'; Max Aldreth, *Comment*, 7 August 1976; Gideon Ben-Tovin countered in *Comment*, 2 October 1976.
191 Andrews, *Endgames*, 127–8.
192 Andrew Dade, letter, *Comment*, 18 September 1976.
193 Warren and Prior, *Advanced Capitalism*, 26.

194 Bill Ward, *Comment*, 10 July 1976; Purdy would make a version of this case later, in his contribution to the discussion on *The British Road to Socialism*, arguing that the war showed 'how far the political economy of the working class can be imposed on the functioning of capitalism'; David Purdy, *Comment*, 9 July 1977.

195 Andrew Dade, *Comment*, 18 September 1976.

196 Michael Bleaney, *Comment,* 10 July 1976.

197 David Parker, *Comment*, 7 August 1976.

198 Martin Jacques, 'Culture, Class Struggle and the Communist Party,' *Comment*, 29 May 1976); Jacques, 'Trends in Youth Culture: Some Aspects,' *Marxism Today* (September 1973): 269.

199 'There was almost a wall between the generations,' Jacques later observed. 'People used to talk about the missing generation that left the party in the 'Fifties'; cited in Beckett, *Enemy Within*, 163.

200 The work could, she argued, be read in one of two ways. It was 'either the last word in pathetic alienation,' a reading that revived the older argument which saw fragmented modern art as a morbid symptom of capitalist disease. Or it was part of a ruling-class conspiracy whose ideological function was 'a deliberate head-shrink at a time when young people in America are becoming more conscious of the life process and those who oppose it'; Barbara Niven, 'Why I Dislike Pop Art,' *Comment*, 9 March 1968.

201 Bob Dawson, 'Roy Lichtenstein: A Reply to Barbara Niven,' *Comment*, 4 May 1968.

202 Jacques, 'Culture, Class Struggle,' 163.

203 Jacques, 'Trends in Youth Culture.'

204 Martin Jacques, 'Trends in Youth Culture: Reply to the Discussion,' *Marxism Today* (April 1975): 112.

205 Jacques, 'Trends in Youth Culture,' 278.

206 Jacques, 'Trends in Youth Culture: Reply,' 113

207 Jacques, 'Trends in Youth Culture,' 279.

208 Jacques, 'Trends in Youth Culture: Reply,' 113.

209 Jacques, 'Trends in Youth Culture,' 280.

210 As young art and design students who came together through the 1971 CUL put it in a sharp exchange with the NCC, this energy was either 'standing still, rubbing its bleary eyes, or has gone back to sleep, without a murmur of protests from either the Labour Movement or the party'; 'For Cultural Committee,' from the editorial board of the newly formed journal *Artery*, 7 July 1972, CP CENT CULT 3/5, also in CP CENT CULT 2/1; Jacques, 'Trends in Youth Culture,' 275.

211 Jacques, "Trends in Youth Culture: Reply,' 113.

212 Betty Reid, 'For the Cultural Committee (August 1972),' CP CENT CULT 2/1.

213 'National Cultural Committee,' n.d. [1971], CP CENT CULT 2/1

214 There was a 'wealth of evidence up and down the country that there are groups of individual comrades with special interests keen to exchange ideas'; handbill

for 'Arts and the Fight for Socialism in Britain,' held on 7 October 1972; unsigned document, 'Welcome to Our Conference'; Simon's Report, 11 October 1972; Martin Jacques, 'The Party and the Arts,' CP CENT CULT 2/2.

215 Dave Cook, 'Ideological Work within Disciplines and Departments in Universities and Colleges,' *NCC Newsletter* (August 1973); Cook, circular to NCC, 14 August 1973, CP CENT CULT 2/3.

216 *NCC Newsletter* (April 1973), CP CENT CULT 3/2.

217 *NCC Newsletter* 2 (April 1973).

218 Alan Hunt, ed., *Marxism and Democracy* (London: Lawrence & Wishart, 1980), the collection was based on a conference held in December 1978.

219 New Towns remained a key focus, not only because their young populations offered a 'terrific field of work for our Party,' but also because an appropriate emphasis on community life and civic amenities at the blueprint stage was seen to promise communities whose lived experience would make them more open to socialist ideas. *NCC Newsletter 5* (September 1974); Eddie Jones, 'The New Towns,' *Comment*, 31 October 1971).

220 Ted Baker, 'Exploitation, Culture and Birmingham,' *Comment*, 3 January 1970.

221 'Report on History Group' for AGM, 18 July 1976, CP CENT CULT 18/4.

222 *NCC Newsletter* 5 (September 1974); NCC Minutes, 5 December 1975, CP CENT CULT 18/04; 'Report on History Group AGM'; John Attfield, report, NCC Minutes, 10 May 1974, CP CENT CULT 2/4.

223 *NCC Newsletter* 1 (February 1973); Philosophy Group List sent by the NCC to Irene Brennan, 31 December 1975, CP CENT CULT 2/5.

224 *Red Letters* contributors included Kettle, who had become head of arts at the Open University, emerging literary academics (Colin Mercer, Graham Holderness, Antony Easthope, David Margolies, Francis Barker, Ben Brewster), and the young poet Jackie Kaye. It would carry translations from significant international thinkers, notably Pierre Macherey. NCC Minutes, 7 May 1976, CP CENT CULT 18/4; Carole Snee, report on Literature Group, Theory and Ideology Committee Minutes, 1 January 1977, CP CENT CULT 2/8; the LHASC has a complete run of the journal; Jon Clark, Margot Heinemann, David Margolies, and Carole Snee eds., *Culture and Crisis in Britain in the Thirties* (London: Lawrence & Wishart, 1979).

225 *NCC Newsletter* 4 (January 1974).

226 *NCC Newsletter* 5 (September 1974).

227 *NCC Newsletter* 3 (August 1973); *NCC Newsletter* 4 (January 1974); Buzz Goodbody, 'Street Theatre,' *Comment*, 15 January 1972).

228 Including Red Ladder, whose production 'A Woman's Work Is Never Done' was filmed by the BBC to form a resource for the TUC's education facilities; Belt and Braces, who were commissioned by shop stewards at Vickers to produce a play about their dispute; and Foco Novo, who collaborated with the South Wales NUM on a production marking the fiftieth anniversary of the General Strike.

Graham Jones, 'Independent Theatre's Financial Crisis,' *Comment*, 15 November 1975.

229 Caryl Churchill, 'Marxism and Theatre,' *Comment*, 15 October 1977.

230 Jones, 'Independent Theatre,' 381; the Arts Council's broadened definitions of fundable culture created limited openings that were worked by these groups, especially via the Experimental Drama program.

231 Runs of both the 1960s and 1970s version are in CP CENT CULT 3/1 and 3/2; Reid, 'For the Cultural Committee.'

232 'Draft Statement on the Role of the Specialist Groups and Journals,' n.d. [1973?], CP CENT CULT 2/3.

233 Unity of Arts program and documents, CP CENT CULT 18/3; *NCC Newsletter* 3 (August 1973).

234 'Notes on the Arts in the Regions,' *NCC Newsletter* 4 (January 1974); Antony Rowland, '*Voices* Magazine: A Cultural History,' *North West Labour History* 34 (2009–10): 25–31.

235 John Green, 'The Function of Film in the Working Class Struggle,' *Marxism Today* (February 1973): 54–7.

236 *NCC Newsletter* 4 (January 1974). Despite its emphasis on propagandistic directness, it made films of artistic merit, and won a prize at the Leipzig Film Festival for *Arise ye Workers* (1973), about the Pentonville five; John Green, *Britain's Communists: The Untold Story* (London: Artery, 2014), 110.

237 278 registered in 1973, around 400 in 1974, 1,034 by 1977, 1,023 in 1978. 'Communist University of London,' CP CENT CULT 18/5. Additional figures from *NCC Newsletter* 3 (August 1973), CP CENT CULT 3/2.

238 'Index of University Comrades,' n.d. [mid-1970s], CP CENT CULT 18/4. Notably, Julius Gould of Nottingham University and the Social Affairs Unit, author of the widely debated 'Gould Report,' *The Attack on Higher Education: Marxist and Radical Penetration*. Green, *Britain's Communists*, 222.

239 Pat Devine, 'A Note on Academic Freedom and Democracy,' *Marxism Today* (May 1971): 145; Martin Jacques, 'Universities and Capitalism – The Present Crisis,' *Marxism Today* (July 1975): 196–206.

240 Jon Bloomfield, 'Notes on the Development of the Work of the Specialist Groups,' n.d. [early 1976]. The report sidestepped the question of cultural production, concentrating instead on the 'ideological-technical orbit,' or the relationship between the groups, the CULs and particular academic disciplines, CP CENT CULT 2/5.

241 Matthew Worley, 'Marx-Lenin-Rotten-Strummer: British Marxism and Youth Culture in the 1970s,' *Contemporary British History* 30, no. 4 (2016): 513.

242 'Open Letter to the Sex Pistols,' *Challenge* (August/September 1977).

243 Matthew Worley, 'Shot by Both Sides: Punk, Politics and the End of Consensus,' *Contemporary British History* 26, no. 3 (2012): 333–54; Paul Bradshaw, 'Trends in Youth Culture in the 1970s,' *Cogito* 3 (1976): 3–13; *Challenge* (February–March

1977): 14; *Challenge* (November–October 1977): 3; and *Challenge* (April 1978): 8; Antony Wall enthused about the Sex Pistols and The Clash, *Comment*, 7 March 1977.

244 Worley, 'Shot by Both Sides,' 350n35; Scritti Politti, *Skank Bloc Bologna*, extended play [EP] (St Pancras, 1978); 'Hegemony,' on *4 A-Sides*, EP (Rough Trade, 1979), collected on *Early*, compact disc (Rough Trade, 2004); Dave Laing, 'Interpreting Punk Rock,' *Marxism Today* (April 1978): 123–8; Laing, *One Chord Wonders: Power and Meaning in Punk Rock* (Milton Keynes: Open University Press, 1985).

245 Evan Smith, 'Are the Kids United? The Communist Party of Great Britain, Rock Against Racism, and the Politics of Youth Culture,' *Journal for the Study of Radicalism* 5, no. 2 (2011): 90; Arts and Leisure Committee Minutes, 5 May 1978, CP CENT CULT 2/7. Proposal from Karl Dallas, *Melody Maker* folk correspondent who rejoined the CP in the 1970s; Arts and Leisure Committee Minutes, 30 June 1978, CP CENT CULT 2/7.

246 A rare crumb of comfort here was the shoestring-budget English Civil War feature *Winstanley* (1976), for which former member Christopher Hill had been a consultant. That this was considered a success was a marker of the party's marginality. Phil Cohen, 'Winstanley: A Film on Yesterday … And Today,' *Comment*, 6 March 1976.

247 Sidney Cole, 'The Future of the British Film Industry,' *Comment*, 7 February 1976.

248 As some pointed out, the CP was now paying the price for having 'failed to recognise in the late 1960s and early 1970s the impact of the new sections moving into the entertainment professions,' and had thus 'left a vacuum which has been open to leftist and Trotskyist groups to fill'; Jon Chadwick and Sue Beardon, 'Notes and Proposals arising out of the Arts and Leisure Committee Meeting on Theatre,' n.d. [1976], CP CENT 2/8. 'Our forces are very thin' in 'TV and radio,' conceded one document produced in consultation with Jacques that sought to identify areas for future work; Arts and Leisure Committee circular, 9 December 1976, CP CENT CULT 2/8.

249 Perks would go on to make a critically acclaimed BBC Omnibus documentary, *Posterman* (1976), about fellow-Communist Ken Sprague, but a line was quickly drawn under a projected follow-up series, almost certainly after an objection from MI5, and the Sprague film remained an isolated instance of the type of cultural visibility the party clearly needed. Perks left the party in 1977, and would make follow-up films with Sprague for Channel 4 a decade later. Green, *Britain's Communists*, 108–9.

250 John Salway, letter, *Comment*, 10 January 1976.

251 The IMG Series ran through the early months of 1977 and was held at the London Film Makers Co-op premises in Chalk Farm; handbill in CP CENT 2/7. Television was absent from the original conception as formulated in the NCC circular of 17 August 1972, but added by the NCC at a meeting of 8 September 1972, a month before the event; CP CENT CULT 2/2.

252 One was formed in 1973, but made little impression on the party's cultural work. *NCC Newsletter* (February 1973); Arts and Leisure Committee Minutes, 15 April 1977, CP CENT CULT 2/7. Party activists attended an event, the 'National Conference of Democratic Accountability,' arranged by the latter in spring 1979, CP CENT CUL 2/8. Ian Connell, 'Television at the Crossroads,' *Marxism Today* (December 1978): 380–6.

253 'Report on Artists, Entertainers Etc for National Fund Appeal, 1977,' 29 November 1976, CP CENT CULT 2/8.

254 Temple, in Cohen, *Children of the Revolution*, 96.

255 Material relating to these events in CP CENT CULT 2/5; Jacques, 'Culture, Class Struggle,'165; the Gramsci conference was sponsored by Lawrence & Wishart and held at the Polytechnic of Central London, 5–6 March 1977, and involved CPI members; folder in CP CENT CULT 2/8

256 Document for Political Committee, 2 December 1976, CP CENT CULT 2/8.

257 Antonio Gramsci, 'Concept of National Popular,' in *Selections from the Cultural Writings*, ed. David Forgacs and Geoffrey Nowell-Smith (London: Lawrence & Wishart, 1985), 206–16. 'The ruling class,' explained the organizer, Nigel Tanburn, 'has been able to link something socially progressive (street parties) with something reactionary (the monarchy) hence strengthening its position. An important aim of the People's Jubilee was to help break this link and to recapture some of the lost political ground for the left.' Nigel Tanburn, 'After the Show,' *Comment*, 23 July 1977; 'Document for Political Committee,' (2 December 1976); Tanburn, 'EC Report on the People's Jubilee,' 8 July 1977, CP CENT CULT 2/8.

258 Tanburn, 'EC Report on the People's Jubilee.'

259 Program cited in Robinson, *Gay Men and the Left*, 109.

260 Political groups represented included international Communist Parties, Spare Rib, Abortion Law Reform, Friends of the Earth; Tanburn, 'EC Report on the People's Jubilee.'

261 Robinson, *Gay Men and the Left*, 109.

262 EC Minutes, 9–10 July 1977, CP IND JOHN 4/1/5.

263 Held on 11 June 1978 at Alexandra Palace; jazz was provided by Quaternity, reggae from The Cimarons, folk music from Leon Rosselson; Adrian Mitchell appeared, and matches from the 1978 World Cup were screened; handbill in CP CENT CULT 2/7.

264 Tanburn, 'After the Show'; Alan Bush to Arts and Leisure Committee, 21 October 1977; Colin Chambers, Report to Arts and Leisure Committee on Thirty-fifth Congress, CP CENT CULT 2/8.

265 Martin Jacques, Contribution to BRS discussion, *Comment*, 29 October 1979; the party had lost 5,000 members between 1969 and 1977, and would shed as many between then and 1979; Thompson, *Good Old Cause*, 218.

266 The process was formally inaugurated with a retrospective article in the party fortnightly journal; James Klugmann, 'The British Road to Socialism: A Brief History since 1945,' *Comment*, 5 February 1977.

267 *Guardian*, 2 February 1977, quoted in Brian Davies, letter, *Comment*, 5 March 1977.

268 *Eurored* was formed in 1976 by the West Europe subcommittee of the party's International Department; the initial editors were Jon Bloomfield, George Bridges, and Gerry Pocock; complete run in LHASC. Derek Bootham, 'Italy's Elections: A Reader's Guide,' *Comment*, 12 June 1976; Jon Bloomfield and Jane Woddis, 'Spain Builds It Tomorrow and Today,' *Comment*, 2 October 1976. A key work was PCE General Secretary Santiago Carrillo, *'Eurocommunism' and the State* (London: Lawrence & Wishart, 1977); Sam Aaronovitch, 'Eurocommunism: A Discussion of Carrillo's "*Eurocommunism" and the State*,' *Marxism Today* (July 1978): 222–7.

269 Thompson, *Good Old Cause*, 171–5; Andrews, *Endgames*, 163–8.

270 Announced to the party in Jacques, 'Culture, Class Struggle'; Betty Reid, NCC circular, 14 July 1976, CP CENT CULT 2/5.

271 '*Red Letters* seems to me to be written not only by, but for, university lecturers,' complained one more traditionally minded reader unimpressed by the high structuralist theory on offer. 'If I had not read *Wuthering Heights* the article would have put me off for good'; Jean Feldmer, letter, *Red Letters* (Spring 1977): 13; 'a separation of specialists from the rest of us is something I dislike,' added Ian McLeod, letter, *Red Letters* 2 (Summer 1976): 8. The new journal, *Socialist Europe: Communist Party Journal of Soviet and East European Studies*, was formed by those including Monty Johnstone eager to break decisively with one-party models of the actually existing socialist states, and incensed more traditional sensibilities. 'You will not learn there of the Soviet Union's achievements in this 60th anniversary year,' complained one reader, 'you will read articles on Solzhenitsyn, "Stalinism" and the Soviet superstructure which rival the *Guardian* or Robert Conquest'; Pat Thurnball, letter, *Comment*, 9 July 1977.

272 David Harvey, *A Brief History of Neoliberalism* (Oxford: Oxford University Press, 2005), 57, figure 1.1, 14; Beckett, *When the Lights Went Out*, 335.

273 Andews, *Endgames*, 191.

274 Geoff Brown, 'John Tocher and the Limits of Commitment,, *North West Labour History Journal* 42 (2017–18): 47–53.

275 John Tarver, letter, *Comment*, 25 December 1976.

276 Surrey District pre-Congress contributions, *Comment*, 25 September 1971; 6 October 1973; 18 October 1975; 30 April 1977; Alan Hunt, 'Stalinism,' 3 March 1977.

277 John Gollan, 'Socialist Democracy – Some Problems: The 20th Congress of the Communist Party and the Soviet Union in Retrospect,' *Marxism Today* (January 1976): 4–30; responses were gathered and printed in a supplement to the December issue.

278 Thompson, *Good Old Cause*, 170.

279 These matters had always tended to arise most strongly among cultural strata keen to identify the status accorded to cultural work in the process of socialist transformation. They had recently been back on the agenda amidst hesitation around whether the bland and out-of-print *Questions of Ideology and Culture* (1967) document should be formally updated to reflect cultural changes (the issue was fudged, almost certainly to avoid division). Brian Simon and Martin Jacques thought it should, and the publication of Raymond Williams's seminal, Gramsci-inspired revisiting of the base-superstructure model was seen as an obvious source for the process. Martin Jacques, 'The Party and the Arts,' [late 1972], CP CENT CULT 2/1; *NCC Newsletter* (January 1974); Brian Simon, 'Cultural Committee,' 11 October 1972, CP CENT 1/1/13. The contentious question in that context was whether or not the Communist Party would provide 'leadership in cultural matters' in the event of coming to power in the West, and precisely what that might mean in terms of censorship, surveillance, and the state. The NCC had got round the problem by tasking English Literature academic Jeremy Hawthorn to facilitate an NCC discussion addressing 'contemporary developments in postwar British culture' in September 1973, which in turn formed the substance of an article for *Marxism Today*: Jeremy Hawthorn, 'The Communist Party and Developments in British Culture,' *Marxism Today* (December 1973): 366.

280 There had been nervousness about actually rewriting the document, and the sense that doing so would clearly incense a vocal contingent that preferred more prescriptive lines on culture and that saw Solzhenitsyn, recently expelled from the Soviet Writers' Union, as 'guilty of propagating anti-Soviet ideas' and the *Morning Star* as impertinent for presuming to criticize his punishment. Bob Selkirk, letter, *Morning Star*, 23 December 1969; J Adams, letter, *Morning Star*, 15 December 1969; controversy archived in CP CENT CULT 18/3.

281 Statement on the Dictatorship of the Proletariat,' 14 December 1976, cited in Andrews, *Endgames*, 163.

282 Étienne Balibar, 'The Dictatorship of the Proletariat,, *Marxism Today* (May 1977): 144–53; Balibar, *On the Dictatorship of the Proletariat* (London: NLB, 1977); Bob Jessop, 'Democracy and Dictatorship: Eurocommunism and the State,' *Eurored* 6 (n.d.): 18–24.

283 Bert Ramelson considered the producer Graef and executive producer Gus McDonald 'very progressive and friendly to the party,' and believed that the program could usefully show the party's commitment to 'the democratic process'; Ramelson to George Matthews, 1 June 1976, CP CENT COMM 4/5.

284 *Decision British Communism*, produced by Roger Graef for Granada Television, broadcast 25 July 1978, 1 August 1978, and 9 August 1978; *Daily Mail*, 29 July 1978, 2 August 1978; *TV Times*, 28 July 1978; *Financial Times*, 26 July 1978; cuttings archived at CP CENT COMM 4/5 and CP CENT MAT 6/8. I am grateful to Sheryl Buckley for bringing this material to my attention; Buckley, 'Division

British Communism? Televising the Decline of the Communist Party of Great Britain,' *British Politics* 14 (2014): 1–10.

285 *The British Road to Socialism: Programme of the Communist Party* (London: CPGB, 1978), 61.

286 Former member Joan Simon wrote the pamphlet 'Indictment of Margaret Thatcher, Secretary of State 1970–73'; Brian Simon, *A Life in Education* (London: Lawrence & Wishart, 1998), 123.

287 *British Road* (1978), 17.

288 Ibid.

289 Ibid.; Kevin Halpin, *Memoirs of a Militant: Sharp and to the Point* (London: Praxis, 2012), 158.

290 *British Road* (1978), 17.

291 It was necessary 'to show that these struggles can be linked with each other' and that 'the social forces and movements' can be 'won to an awareness' of common interest; ibid.

292 The 3,000-copy print run sold out almost instantly, surprising all concerned. A central focus was on the fixation of the Labour Party and far Left parties with 'organizing for power before organizing to change consciousness,' overlooking 'the necessary preliminaries of raising and extending socialist consciousness and grass-roots organization among the majority of working people'; Hilary Wainwright, 'Introduction,' in Sheila Rowbotham, Lynne Segal, and Hilary Wainwright, *Beyond the Fragments: Feminism and the Making of Socialism* (1979: Pontypool: Merlin, 2013), 109, 108; Caroline Rowan, '*Beyond the Fragments*: What Does It Offer the Left?' *Marxism Today* (September 1979): 282–7; the book was widely debated within the CP; Monty Johnstone to Dave Cook, 24 July 1980, CP IND MONT 1/2/6. What impressed young activist Mark Perryman about the book was the emphasis on building coalitions and 'a feminist critique of a left framed by masculine values and ways of working'; Perryman, in Croft, *After the Party*, 12.

293 *British Road* (1978), 10, cited in David Forgacs, 'Gramsci and Marxism in Britain,' *New Left Review* 176 (July-August 1989), 81; Jacques's draft here reworks material from his 'Culture, Class Struggle.'

294 *British Road* (1978), 37.

295 Theoretically this artificial division of production from reproduction, which falsely narrowed the political field into the primary economic and secondary social layers, was a residue of a crude base-superstructure model that, as Mike Prior and Dave Purdy argued, privileged 'mode of production' over 'social formation' as an analytical frame, and persisted with the illusion that 'the three levels of the social structure which Marxists normally distinguish – the economic, the political and the ideological' could be found 'resting on top of each other like the storeys of a building with the implication that the upper tiers could somehow be removed to leave an intact economic base in full working order.' Mike Prior

and Dave Purdy, *Out of the Ghetto: A Path to Socialist Rewards* (Nottingham: Spokesman, 1979), 21.

296 The problem was not only, as is often argued, of the Philistine advocates of traditional strategies sidelining culture. Rather, the deep tensions between more Gramscian emphasis on strategies angled at the prefigurative transformation of 'civil society' and those fixed on the point of production, dual power, and the state that had always pulled through twentieth-century Communism in the West were sedimenting, for overdetermined reasons, into the crude binary to which they were always susceptible. An equally reductive framework governed the perceptions of many of the more culturally minded, whose analysis tended to sideline economic questions and reduced counter hegemonic work to a cultural process.

297 Jude Bloomfield, 'Viewpoint,' *Comment*, 19 March 1977.

298 Prior and Purdy, *Out of the Ghetto*, 32

299 Ibid.; Hoare and Nowell-Smith, *Selections from the Prison Notebooks*, 57.

300 Hoare and Nowell-Smith, *Selections from the Prison Notebooks*, 57.

301 Dave Purdy, *British Road to Socialism* Discussion, *Comment*, 9 July 1977; the phrase was repeated in the book: 'The strategic task facing socialists is not that or preparing for a seizure of state power in some moment of supreme initiative and then proceeding to construct socialism from scratch'; Prior and Purdy, *Out of the Ghetto*, 56.

302 Purdy, '*British Road to Socialism* Discussion.'

303 Antonio Gramsci, 'Workers' Democracy' (1919), in *Selections from Political Writings 1910–1920*, ed. Quintin Hoare (London: Lawrence & Wishart, 1977), 65.

304 Prior and Purdy, *Out of the Ghetto*, 80.

305 Ibid., 105.

306 Ibid., 172.

307 Purdy, '*British Road to Socialism* Discussion.'

308 Prior and Purdy, *Out of the Ghetto*, 58.

309 Ibid., 92.

310 Andrews, *Endgames*, 169.

311 'To carry through this gigantic task [establishing a new socialist state] the working people need a Communist Party to help lead and organise the struggle'; *British Road* (1968), 47; in the 1977 version the 'leading role' would have to be won, 'not imposed,' and the vision was of the party 'playing a leading, though not exclusive, role' (60).

312 In particular what was needed was 'the development of perspectives, policies, programmes which go beyond quantitative demands for more and begin to raise demands for qualitative changes which increase democratic control over the aspect of the life involved'; Pat Devine, Contribution to BRS discussion, *Comment*, 29 October 1977.

313 The role the party now assigned to itself was blurred, but concerned keeping the Labour Party, via the labour movement, as the principled core of the Broad

Democratic Alliance, a process that – in an optimistically projected renaissance – would in turn add lustre to the party, which would 'grow in numbers, influence and in the parliaments and local councils'; *British Road* (1978), 60.

314 Ibid., 25.

315 Miliband to Monty Johnstone, 7 February 1977, CP IND JOHN 5/1.

316 Deliberately remaining within the framework of the *British Road* debates, Prior and Purdy made much the same prescription, seeing the party's 'tradition of self-conscious Marxist theory' and 'capacity for strategic political analysis' as potentially equipping it to play an important mediating role between the new social movements and the labour movement; Prior and Purdy, *Out of the Ghetto* 189, 188.

317 More Gramsci was translated into English and published by Lawrence & Wishart in the late 1970s: Quintin Hoare, ed., and John Mathews, trans., *Selections from Political Writings 1910–1920* (London: Lawrence & Wishart, 1977); Quintin Hoare, ed. and trans., *Antonio Gramsci: Selections from Political Writings* 1921–26 (London: Lawrence & Wishart, 1978).

318 Roger Simon, *Gramsci's Political Thought: An Introduction* (London: Lawrence & Wishart, 1982), 122; Simon, 'Gramsci's Concept of Hegemony,' *Marxism Today* (March 1977): 78–86.

319 Cited in Andrews, *Endgames*, 194.

320 Ibid., 183.

321 Willie Thompson, letter, *Comment*, 27 October 1979.

322 Thompson, *Good Old Cause*, 218.

323 Halpin, *Memoirs*, 156.

324 Andrews, *Endgames*, 192–3.

325 Andy Croft, 'The Democratisation of Everything,' in Croft,: *After the Party*, 143.

326 Monty Johnstone to Francis King, 8 October 1983, CP IND MONT 1/1/7.

327 The stewards were George Hickman and Pete Carter; unsigned, 'The Great Male Cover Up,' *Comment*, 27 October 1979.

328 Mike Jackson to *Capital Gay*, 4 December 1984, LGSM 2/1, LHASC; Luke James, 'The Story behind the Film,' *Morning Star*, 17–18 January 2015.

329 LGSM were 'a group of perverts supporting the pits,' according to the *Sun*; Robinson, *Gay Men and the Left*, 164–9.

330 Martin Jacques, 'The Last Word,' *Marxism Today* (December 1991): 28; figures from Herbert Pimlott, 'From the Margins to the Mainstream: The Promotion and Distribution of *Marxism Today*,' *Journalism* 5, no. 2 (2004): table 1, 208.

331 Prior to Jaques's editorship, the ratio was very different: 44.7 per cent party officials as against 34.2 per cent academics in 1975; see, for instance. Pimlott, 'from the Margins,' table 2, 214.

332 Martin Jacques, 'Goodbye, and Thanks,' *Marxism Today* (December 1991): 3.

333 Eric Hobsbawm, 'The Forward March of Labour Halted?' *Marxism Today* (September 1978): 279–86; Hobsbawm, 'The Forward March of Labour Halted? – A

Response,' *Marxism Today* (September 1979): 265–8; Hobsbawm, *The Forward March of Labour Halted* (London: Verso in association with *Marxism Today*, 1981).

334 Stuart Hall, 'The Great Moving Right Show,' *Marxism Today* (January 1979): 14–20. 'Gramsci gives us, not the tools with which to solve the puzzle, but the means with which to ask the right kinds of questions'; Hall, 'Gramsci and Us,' *Marxism Today* (June 1987): 18; Hall, 'The Battle for Socialist Ideas in the 1980s,' reprinted in *Thatcherism and the Crisis of the Left: The Hard Road to Renewal* (London: Verso, 1988), 180.

335 Tony Lane, 'The Unions: Caught on the Ebb Tide,' *Marxism Today* (September 1982): 6–13.

336 Monty Johnstone, 'The CP, Marxism and Future Perspectives,' text of a talk given in 1986, CP IND JOHN 4/1/21.

337 Ruth was expelled in 1987 and Eddie terminated his membership at this point. Ruth Frow and Edmund Frow, *The Liquidation of the Communist Party of Great Britain: A Contribution to the Discussion* (Salford, UK: self-published, 1996).

338 Raphael Samuel, 'Re-opening Old Wounds,' *Marxism Today* (October 1986): 60–1; Samuel's two articles of this title, published in the *New Left Review* in the mid-1980s, were republished as Samuel, *The Lost World of British Communism* (London: Verso, 2006).

339 Halpin, *Memoirs*, 179.

340 The CPGB would receive just two brief and emphatically retrospective mentions in the *Manifesto*'s 460-page spin-off book, Stuart Hall and Martin Jacques, eds., *New Times: The Changing Face of Politics in the 1990s* (London: Lawrence & Wishart, 1989), 286, 231.

341 *Manifesto for New Times* (London: Communist Party, 1989), 59.

342 1,500 joined the new organization; membership was half that when Democratic Left disbanded in 2000; Andrew Pearmain, 'What Happened to the CPGB?' *Socialist History* 38 (2011): 64.

Conclusion

1 Immanuel Wallerstein et al., *Does Capitalism Have a Future?* (New York: Oxford University Press, 2013), 1.

2 Nouriel Roubini, one of the few economists to predict the 2008 financial crisis, considers that 'the best economic outcome that anyone can hope for is a recession deeper than that following the 2008 financial crisis'; online at https://www.project-syndicate.org/commentary/coronavirus-greater-great-depression-by-nouriel-roubini-2020-03?barrier=accesspaylog, accessed 11 April 2020. As I write, most economic forecasts for global gross domestic product in 2020 are for a 3–5 per cent contraction; Michael Roberts Blog, 6 April 2020, online at https://thenextrecession.wordpress.com/, accessed 11 April 2020.

3 Paul Mason, *Postcapitalism: A Guide to Our Future* (London: Penguin, 2015), 79–106.

4 Wolfgang Streeck, *How Will Capitalism End?* (London: Verso, 2016), 17.

5 Keir Milburn, *Generation Left* (Cambridge: Polity, 2019), 38.

6 In the United States, hourly wages increased by just 0.2 per cent between 1979 and 2019; Bhaskar Sunkara, *The Socialist Manifesto: The Case for Radical Politics in an Era of Extreme Inequality* (London: Verso, 2019), 192; Aaron Bastani, *Fully Automated Luxury Communism* (London: Verso, 2019), 26.

7 Bastani, *Fully Automated,* 26.

8 Ibid., *Fully Automated*, 87.

9 Randall Collins, 'The End of Middle-Class Work: No More Escapes,' in Wallerstein et al., *Does Capitalism Have a Future?*, 57.

10 Suzanne Jeffrey, 'Dirty Energy, Capitalism and the Working Class,' *International Socialism* 162 (Spring 2019): 93–111; The Intergovernmental Panel on Climate Change (IPCC) warns that thoroughgoing decarbonization must have begun before 2030 to prevent 'catastrophic' climate change above 1.5 degrees centigrade, unlikely amidst a system predicated on competition, single-use proliferation, and inherently resistant to regulation. Lola Seaton provides an overview of the debates the crisis has provoked on the Left in 'Green Questions,' *New Left Review* 115 (January–February 2019): 105–29.

11 Immanuel Wallerstein, 'Structural Crisis, or Why Capitalists May No Longer Find Capitalism Rewarding,' in Wallerstein et al., *Does Capitalism Have a Future?*, 33.

12 Susan Watkins, 'Out of Europe,' *New Left Review* 100 (July–August 2016): 5–31.

13 Bastani, *Fully Automated*, 19.

14 Streek, *How Will Capitalism End?*, 35

15 Wallerstein et al., *Does Capitalism Have a Future?*, 2.

16 Jeffrey Winters, cited in Streek, *How Will Capitalism End?*, 29.

17 Milburn, *Generation Left*, 37.

18 Ibid., 36.

19 Toby Helm, 'Austerity to blame for 130,000 "preventable" UK deaths – report,' *Guardian*, 1 June 2019, online at https://www.theguardian.com/politics/2019/jun/01/perfect-storm-austerity-behind-130000-deaths-uk-ippr-report, accessed 4 July 2019.

20 J.A. Smith, *Other People's Politics: Populism to Corbynism* (Winchester, UK: Zero, 2019), 19.

21 Bastani, *Fully Automated*, 25: 1.2 million people used foodbanks in Britain in 2017 (41,000 did so in 2010); use of foodstamps in the United States was up from 26 million in 2007 to 46 million by 2012 (24–5).

22 Ibid., 25; Milburn, *Generation Left*, 111.

23 Milburn, *Generation Left*, 117.

24 Paul Mason, *Postcapitalism: A Guide to Our Future* (London: Penguin, 2015), xiv.

25 Bastani, *Fully Automated*, 12.

26 Jeffrey, 'Dirty Energy,' 93–111.

27 Cedric Johnson, 'What Black Life Actually Looks Like,' *Jacobin*, 29 April 2019, online at https://www.jacobinmag.com/2019/04/racism-black-lives-matter-inequality, accessed 4 July 2019; Lorna Finlayson, 'Travelling in the Wrong Direction,' *London Review of Books*, 4 July 2019; key feminist manifestos include Cinzia Arruzza, Tithi Bhattacharya, and Nancy Fraser, *Feminism for the 99 Per Cent* (London: Verso, 2019); and Laboria Cuboniks, *The Xenofeminist Manifesto: A Politics for Alienation* (London: Verso, 2018).

28 Slavoj Žižek, *First as Tragedy, Then as Farce* (London: Verso, 2009), 147.

29 A widely reported US poll showing 33 per cent of 18–29-year-olds viewing the idea positively in 2016, more than double the over 65s; Milburn, *Generation Left*, 5.

30 Jeremy Gong et al., 'America's New Left,' *New Left Review* 116/117 (March–June 2019): 119–35.

31 Smith, *Other People's Politics*, 124–55; Robin Blackburn, 'The Corbyn Project,' *New Left Review* 111 (May–June 2018): 5–37.

32 Wary of vanguardism, leading thinkers eschew close engagement with the question of organization. Nick Srnicek and Alex Williams invoke the need for 'a counter hegemonic ecosystem of organisations'; *Inventing the Future: Postcapitalism and a World without Work*, rev. and updated ed. (2015; London: Verso, 2016), 169. Some concentrate on broad 'political cultures' (Mike Wayne, *England's Discontents: Political Cultures and National Identities* [London: Pluto, 2018], 23–9); some call for a new type of 'workers' party against work,' although say little about the characteristics of such a party (Bastani, *Fully Automated*, 194); others remain committed to the forms and functions of existing parties, seeing the way forward in social democratic electoral advance, trade union hegemony, mass mobilizations, and political strikes (Sunkara, *Socialist Manifesto*, 222).

33 Hoare and Nowell-Smith, *Selections from the Prison Notebooks*, 178.

34 Ibid., 181.

35 Ibid., 181, 129.

36 Ibid., 181, 147.

37 Raymond Williams, 'You're a Marxist, Aren't You? (1975), reprinted in *Resources of Hope*, ed. Robin Gale (London: Verso, 1989), 76.

38 The neoliberal project has now effectively dispensed with 'democratic' impediments to accumulation, including those mediating institutions and practices – 'reasonably free elections, government by established mass parties, strong trade unions and employer associations under a firmly institutionalized collective bargaining regime' – that simultaneously held capitalism in check through the Fordist years and lent it legitimacy; Streeck, *How Will Capitalism End?*, 38.

39 Ibid.

40 Mike Prior and Dave Purdy, *Out of the Ghetto: A Path to Socialist Rewards* (Nottingham: Spokesman, 1979), 21.

41 John Lewis, 'The Basis of Marxism,' *Marxism Today* (February 1960): 60.

42 William Davies, 'Bloody Furious,' review of Keir Milburn *Generation Left*, *London Review of Books*, 2 February 2020; Milburn, *Generation Left*, 117.

43 Ben Harker, 'Jack Lindsay's Alienation,' *History Workshop* 82, no. 1 (2016): 83–107.

44 Mason, *Clear Bright Future*, 140; positions provocatively developed in David Alderson and Robert Spencer, eds., *For Humanism: Explorations in Theory and Politics* (London: Pluto, 2017), especially 210–25.

45 Srnicek and Williams, *Inventing the Future*, 83.

Index

Aaronovitch, Sam, 83, 85, 108
Abercrombie, Patrick, 57
Abertillery Unity Male Choir, 41
Absolute Beginners (1959) (MacInnes), 139, 182
Ackland, Valentine, 33, 35, 90, 110
Action Program, 150. *See also* Prague Spring
Adam Smith Institute, 189
'Advanced Capitalism and Backward Socialism' (n.d.) (Warren and Prior), 174–9
Ainley, Ben, 184
Ainley, Ted, 152
Airlie, Jimmy, 171
Akamatsu, Toshiko, 106
Algeria, 128
Allen, Jim, 138
Allende, Salvador, 191
Alternative Economic Strategy, 172
Althusser, Louis, 152, 153, 180
Amalgamated Engineering Union (AEU), 48, 172
Amalgamated Union of Engineering Workers (AUEW), 172
'American Threat to British Culture' (1951) conference, 83
Angry Young Men, 119
Animal Farm (1945) (Orwell), 88
Arab Spring, 203
Aragon, Louis, 89, 91
Apartheid, 128
Army Bureau of Current Affairs (ABCA), 42, 62, 65
Army Bureau of Current Affairs Theatre Unit, 42
Army Education Corps, 42
Anderson, Perry, 10
Anglo-Soviet Friendship Committees, 41
Anglo-Soviet military alliance, 41
Anglo-Soviet weeks, 41
Angry Silence, The (1959), 137
Answers to Questions (1945) (Pollitt), 50, 71
Aprahamian, Francis, 129
Architects' and Technicians' Organisation (ATO), 32
Architectural Association School, 57
Arden, John, 122
Arena, 89–90, 108
Armed Forces Network, 95
Arnot, Robin Page, 17
Artists for Peace, 106
Artists International Association (AIA), 31, 42, 93
Arts Council, 67–8, 133, 184, 185
Ashton, Mark, 197

Associated Society of Locomotive Engineers and Firemen (ASLEF), 172
Association of Architects, Surveyors and Technical Assistants (AASTA), 32, 57
Association of Building Technicians (ABT), 57
Association of Cine Technicians' Union (ACT), 96, 137, 186
Association of Scientific Workers (AScW), 32, 54, 84
Association of University Teachers (AUT), 63
Aswad, 187
Attfield, John, 183
Attlee, Clement, 57–8, 65
Authors' World Peace Appeal, 96, 100

Badiou, Alain, 3
Baker, George, 90
Balibar, Étienne, 152, 191
Ball, Fred, 92
Ballads and Blues (1953), 103
Ballet Rambert, 43
Balzac, Honoré, 92
Bank of England, 201
Banner Theatre, 186
Barker, Clive, 133
Barlow Report, 56
Baron, Alexander, 92
Bart, Lionel, 132
base and superstructure theoretical model, 9, 19–20, 122, 135, 205–6
Bastani, Aaron, 202
Beatles, The, 141, 180, 181, 321n274
Beeching, Jack, 113, 114
Bellamy, Ron, 63, 66
Benn, Tony, 172
Benton, Sarah, 164
Berger, John, 106, 135, 136, 146
Bernal, J.D.: and Association of Scientific Workers, 32; and E.M. Forster, 88; housing work, 56, 58; influence on *For Soviet Britain* (1935), 28; influence on Labour Party, 129; influence on liberalization of Soviet science, 128; housing work, 56, 58; legacy of, 205; and 1956, 113; *Science in History* (1954), 129, 307n142; 'The Scientist and the World Today' (1933), 27; suffers stroke, 129; and University Teachers' Group, 63; wartime work, 54
Betteridge, Marie, 157
Bevan, Nye, 56–8, 128
Beveridge Report, 49
Beyond the Fragments: Feminism and the Making of Socialism (1979) (Rowbotham, Segal, Wainwright), 192
Black Dwarf, 154
Blenkinshop, Arthur, 134
Bloomfield, Jude, 183, 192, 206
Bloomsbury, 26, 67
Bond, Ralph, 96, 97, 133, 137
Book Society, 87
Boothman, Derek, 154
Borghini, Gianfranco, 166
Boughton, Rutland, 23, 94
Bow Street Runners, The, 141
Boyd, Andrew, 58
Bradshaw, Paul, 185
Brailsford, E.N., 26
Braine, John, 122
Brains Trust, 54
Brennan, Irene, 191
Briggs, Asa, 136
Britain for the People: Proposals for Post-War Policy (1944) (CPGB), 50, 52, 68–9, 80
Britansky Soyuznik, 42
British Association for the Advancement of Science, 54
British Broadcasting Company / Corporation: analysed in *Sunday Worker*, 24; *The British Road to Socialism* (1951), 82; Bernal on, 56,

84; 'The Challenge of Our Time' (1946), 88; exclusion of Communists during war, 42; Madge on, 31; MacColl and Lloyd work with, 103; 'Salute to Joseph Stalin,' 42; Third Programme, 71
British Drama League, 69
British Housewives' League, 99
British Political System, The (1954) (Gollan), 107–8
British Road to Socialism, The (1951) (CPGB), 12, 76, 80–2, 104, 106
British Road to Socialism, The (1958) (CPGB), 111, 115–18, 129, 134
British Road to Socialism, The (1968) (CPGB), 145, 147–8, 154–6, 165, 168, 173
British Road to Socialism, The (1977) (CPGB), 12, 149, 188–97
British Socialist Party, 13
Broad Left Journal, 168
Bronda, Antonio, 154
Bronksi Beat, 198
Brooks, Gladys, 157, 161–2
Broonzy, Big Bill, 100
Browder, Earl, 51, 52
Browne, Stella, 19, 216n41
Browning, Robert, 113
Burnham Committee, 132
Burns, Emile, 16, 116, 118, 125
Bush, Alan: and Army Education Corps, 41; cultural marginalization during Cold War, 94; and Edinburgh People's Festival, 105; intellectual formation of, 180; joins CP, 33; *Music and the People* (1939), 36; Music Group, 182; and 1956, 113; wartime work, 40
Butler, R.A., 59–60
Butler Act, 60
Butlin's Holiday Camp, Filey, 70
Butterfield, Herbert, 86
Cadogan, Peter, 115
Calder, Angus, 43
Calder-Marshall, Arthur, 90
Calendar of Modern Letters, 33
Callaghan, James, 129, 189
Cambridge Graduate Communist Party, 63
Cambridge Left, 27
Cambridge University Socialist Club, 32
Campaign for Homosexual Equality, 164
Campaign for Nuclear Disarmament (CND), 127, 139
Campbell, Beatrix, 10; background, 179; critique of reductive Marxism, 10, 206; and Smith Group, 154; *Wigan Pier Revisited: Poverty and Politics in the 1980s* (1984), 158; and WLM, 156; and Women's Advisory, 157, 163
Campbell, J.R., 111, 136, 144
Camus, Albert, 89
Cannon, Les, 112
Caribbean Labour Congress, 126
Carillo, Santiago, 166
Carr, E.H., 86, 136
Carritt, Bill, 154
Carter, Trevor, 125
Castle, Barbara, 172
Castro, Fidel, 138
Caudwell, Christopher, 36
Caudwell controversy, 90–1, 276n128, 277n130
Centre for Policy Studies, 189
Centre 42, 132–3, 182, 184
civil society, definitions of, 6, 7, 10, 20, 210n32
Challenge, 96, 139, 141, 185. *See also* Young Communist League
Challenge of Marxism, The (1963) (Simon ed.), 136–8
'Challenge of Our Time' (1946) (BBC), 88
Childe, Gordon, 63
Children's Sections (of CPGB), 16

Chance of a Million (1950), 96
Chaplin, Charlie, 24
Churchill, Caryl, 184
Churchill, Winston, 53, 56, 88
Cinema Action, 184
Clapham-Aston School, 86
'classlessness' debates, 121–2
Clinton, Hillary, 201
Cockburn, Claud, 30, 41
Cogito, 142
Cohen, Gerry, 162
Cohen, Jack, 32
Cole, G.D.H., 26
Cole, Sidney, 96, 185
Collins, Randall, 201
Cominform, 3, 76, 93, 105, 110
Comintern: creation, 13; conditions of membership, 4, 162; Second Congress (1920), 4; Third Congress (1921), 22; Fifth Congress (1924), 17; Seventh Congress (1935), 28; duration and dissolution of, 11, 38, 50; on newspapers, 22; on sexual division of labour, 18
Comment, 141, 165, 173, 179, 186
'Commission on the Middle Class' (1954), (CPGB), 107–8, 116, 121
Common Secondary School, The (1955) (Simon), 131
Common Wealth Party, 49
Communism and British Intellectuals (1959) (Wood), 115
Communist (newspaper), 21, 22
Communist Answer to the Challenge of Our Time (1947) (CPGB), 88
Communist Party of Great Britain: Africa Committee, 126; Agit-prop department, 16; and adult education, 19–21, 65–7; Artists' Group, 116, 135; Arts and Leisure Committee, 188; and Battle of Ideas, 9, 78, 85, 105, 112, 205; Bolshevization of, 15; and 'broad democratic alliance,' 192; and Broad Left Strategy, 144, 168, 170–3, 190; and 'broad popular alliance,' 82, 170–1, 195, 196; Building Bureau, 56; Built Environment Group, 183; on children's comics, 100; on cinema, 95; class against class line, 17, 29, 31, 114 (*see also* Communist Party of Great Britain: Third Period); commission to write party history, 114–15; creation of, 3, 13; on culture high, low, and middle, 43, 68–71, 86–7, 136, 180–1; cultural groups, 266n57; Cultural Groups Committee, 50; on dancing and dance halls, 95; on drugs 165; Economics Committee, 50, 78, 144, 173, 176; on economy as site of struggle, 47–8; Eighteenth Congress (1945), 72; and electoral performances of, 52, 55, 78, 144–5; Entertainment Industry Bureau, 40; Executive Committee, 54, 83, 118, 145; on the family, 158–61; on film and television, 99–100, 136–8, 144; finances of, 111; on folk music, 24, 140–1; on gender, 18–19, 156–63; Historians' / History Group, 36, 63, 85–6, 135, 182–3, 205, 311n196; historiography about, 11, 105, 188; and homosexuality, 163–4; on immigration, race, and empire, 78, 82, 117, 124–7; Industrial Department, 54; and intellectuals, 16–18, 151–4; International Department, 125; Literature group, 183; membership of, 30, 38, 43, 109–10, 127, 144, 149, 155, 173, 197, 207n4, 215n31, 224n111; Music Group, 135, 182; on national arts policy, 134; National Cultural Committee, 83–4, 107–8, 112, 118–19, 135–6, 152, 181, 182, 184; National Educational Advisory

Committee (NEAC), 59, 131; National Science Advisory, 54, 182; National Women's Advisory, 157, 162; and New Left, 112–15, 119–24; and newspapers, 19–21, 65–7; 1956 crisis, 109–12; nomenclature, 52, 246n106; and Popular Front period, 7, 9, 11, 17–18, 28–37; popular music, 138–44; post-war planning commission, 50; religion, 31, 145–6, 230n161; and school education 32, 59–60, 129–32; and scientists, 53, 84 (*see also* Engels Society); Sociology Group, 183; and sport, 25; and students, 53, 165–70; subgroups, 83; Theatre group, 184; Theory and Ideology Committee, 188; Third Period, 18; universities, 62–5; United Front line, 13, 18, 74; University Teachers' Group / University Staff Committee, 63, 107; Visual Arts Group, 183; West Indian Advisory Committee, 125; Writers' Group, 72, 120, 135; and youth culture, 111, 138–44, 181–2
Communist Review, 74, 108
Communist Unity Convention (1920), 13
Communist University of London (CUL), 152, 168, 170, 183, 186, 197
Congo, 128
Connolly, Cyril, 43, 54, 89
Cook, Arthur, 41
Cook, Dave, 168, 183
Co-operative Education Committee, 65
Cooper Clarke, John, 184
Corbyn, Jeremy, 203
Cornford, John, 36, 62
Cornforth, Maurice: and Caudwell Controversy; 91; closes CP cultural journals, 108; intellectual formation of, 180; on Marx, 123; in 1956, 113; and Philosophy Group, 183; on *Questions of Ideology and Culture* (1967), 146–7; on 'two camps' line, 90
Council for Educational Advance, 59
Council for Education and Music in the Arts (CEMA), 40, 133
Council for Proletarian Art, 23
Craig, David, 140
Crawfurd, Helen, 18, 24
Crimea Conference, 50. *See also* Yalta Conference
Crimea Conference: Safeguard of the Future (1945) (CPGB), 52
Criterion, 46
Croft, Andy, 197
Crossman, Richard, 129
Cuba, 128
culture: definitions of, 6, 210n37
Culture and Anarchy (1869) (Arnold), 71

Daily Express, 30
Daily Herald, 21, 24, 30, 98
Daily Mirror, 95, 98, 171
Daily Worker: ban of, 45; book page, 89, 135; and Cold War, 92; and cinema, 96; creation of, 24, 25; and *Declaration* (1957), 119; Farringdon Road premises, 57; fundraising for, 103; and 1956, 109; pop music, 139; during Popular Front period, 30; rebranded as *Morning Star*, 144; relaunch of, 49; sales, 38; sellers abused, 39; and television, 99
Dallas, Karl, 104, 141
Daly, Lawrence, 112, 172
Dance Band Director's Association, 40
Darnton, Christian, 40, 46
Davenport, Bob, 187
Davis, Mary, 183
Day Lewis, Cecil, 33, 34, 36
Daylight, 90, 108
Deacon, Bob, 164
Dean, Jodi, 8
Decision: British Communism (1978), 149, 188, 191

Declaration (1957) (Maschler ed.), 119
de Groot, Joanna, 157, 183
Delaney, Shelagh, 122
democratic centralism, 109, 162
Democratic Left, 200
Democratic Socialists of America, 203
Devine, Pat, 10, 178, 179, 195, 197
D'Eye, A.T., 66
Dickens, Charles, 92
dictatorship of the proletariat, 190–1
Dimitrov, Georgi, 28–30, 74, 83
Discussion, 30, 35
Dobb, Maurice: early 1930s victimization of, 26–7; intellectual formation of, 180; and 1956, 113; and party University Teachers' Group, 63; *Studies in the Development of Capitalism* (1946), 85; work across civil society, 26, 224n113; and working-class education, 23
Doctor Zhivago (Pasternak), 120
Donets Miners (1950), 97
Douglass, Stewart, 138
Dutt, Rajani Palme: background of, 17; and Bolshevization of CPGB, 17; and *The British Road to Socialism* (1958), 116–17; and Comintern, 50; on Communist newspapers, 21, 25; on intellectuals and professionals, 17, 53, 113; and *Labour Monthly*, 46; and New Left, 120; on Orwell, 99; on party's history, 115; post-war decline of, 72; and post-war planning commission, 50; retirement, 111, 144
dual power, 15, 28
Dylan, Bob, 141

Eagle, 100
Economic and Philosophical Manuscripts (1844) (Marx), 106, 123, 206
Edinburgh International Festival, 104
Edinburgh Peoples' Festival, 104–5, 205
Educational Bulletin, 62
Education Today and Tomorrow, 131
Electrical Trades Union (ETU), 129, 171
Eley, Geoff, 18
Eliot, T.S., 97, 100
Éluard, Paul, 89
Emergency Training Scheme (schoolteachers), 60
Engels, Fredrich, 157, 159
Engels Society, 63, 83–4, 129
Engineering Employers' Federation, 49
Entertainment National Services Association (ENSA), 40, 42, 133
Epstein, Sir Jacob, 106
Eurocommunism, 3, 188, 197, 207n4
Eurored, 188, 341n268

Family and Kinship in East London (1957) (Young and Wilmott), 122
Farrington, Benjamin, 63
Federation of Student Societies, 32
Felton, Monica, 56
Festa de l'Unità, 186
Festivals of Marxism, 187
Fête de l'Humanité, 186
Fighting the Bill, 184
Film Today, 95
Finsbury Council, 56
Fischer, Ernst, 136
Fore Publications, 36, 46, 89, 95
For Intellectual Liberty, 31
Forman, Stanley, 184
For Soviet Britain (1935) (CPGB), 28, 34, 52
Forster, E.M., 88
Foster, John, 183
Fowles, John, 180
Fox, Ralph, 23, 36
Frances, Hywel, 183, 198
Frankel, Benjamin, 94
Frankenburg, Ron, 183

Free Cinema, 122
French, Sid, 149, 190
From the City, from the Plough (1948) (Baron), 92
From Trotsky to Tito (1950) (Klugmann), 115
Frow, Eddie, 105, 199
Frow, Ruth, 199. *See also* Haines, Ruth
Fundamentals of Marxism-Leninism (1961), 123

Gagarin, Yuri, 129
Gallacher, Willie, 21, 32, 78, 137
Garman, Douglas, 65–6, 110
Garnett, Tony, 138
Gartside, Green, 185
Gaughan, Dick, 185
Gay Left, 164
Gay Liberation Advisory Committee, 164
Gay Liberation Movement, 157, 164
Gay News, 164
Gay Times, 164
Gibberd, Frederick, 56
Gibbes, Asquith, 125
Giles, G.C.T., 33, 113, 131, 132
Gill, Ken, 172
Golden Notebook (1961), (Lessing), 92
Goldfinger, Ernö, 57
Gollan, John: *British Political System* (1954), 107–8; on censorship, 135; and *Challenge of Marxism* (1963), 136; and commission to revise *The British Road to Socialism* (1951), 116; on CP industrial militancy, 171; and Malcolm MacEwan, 120; on political pluralism, 190; television appearance, 137
Goodbody, Buzz, 184
Good Old Cause (1949) (Hill and Dell eds), 86
Goodwin, Phil, 153, 166–7
Gorman, John, 110
Gramsci, Antonio: and civil society, 7; on crisis, 203; on Communist newspapers, 22; and hegemony, 8, 47, 175, 180; influence over Hamish Henderson, 104; influence over Party Group, 177–9, 193; influence over People's Jubilee (1977), 187; and intellectuals, 16, 21, 68; *Modern Prince & Other Writings* (1957), 123, 153; and 'national popular,' 187; and the party, 8, 196, 199, 204; and 'passive revolution,' 51, 67, 176; and 'Prison Letters,' 210n31; and 'Prison Notebooks,' 6, 12, 13, 30, 209n30; publication of *Selections from the Prison Notebooks* (1971), 153; on revolution, 8, 34; and Trotsky, 7; wars of position and wars of manoeuvre, 148; on writing history, 10
Grant, Andrew, 121
Gray, Robbie, 183
Great Tradition, The (1948) (Leavis), 92
Green, John, 184
Greene, Grahame, 88–9
Guardian, 92, 188
Guest, David, 27, 36
Guiding Lines on Question of Post-War Reconstruction (1942) (CPGB), 49
Guttuso, Renato, 91

Haines, Ruth, 105. *See also* Frow, Ruth
Haldane, J.B.S., 32, 53, 63, 84
Hall, Stuart, 12, 125, 180, 183, 199
Halpin, Kevin, 200
Hamilton, Patrick, 90
Handbook of English Freedom (1939) (Lindsay and Rickword), 37, 235n209
Hardy, Frank, 91
Hawthorn, Jeremy, 183
Heffer, Eric, 110
Heinemann, Margot, 90, 118
Henderson, Hamish, 104

Henry Cow, 186
Hibbin, Sally, 163
Hill, Christopher, 85, 109, 113, 115, 122
Hilliard, Christopher, 87
Hilton, Rodney, 63, 110, 122
Hindess, Barry, 183
Historical Novel, The (1962) (Lukács), 136
History of the Communist Party of the Soviet Union / Bolsheviks / Short Course (1939), 35, 74, 122, 123, 206
Hobsbawm, Eric: and Army Education Corps, 42; and Birkbeck, 63; and commission to write party's history, 114–15; 'The Forward March of Labour Halted' (1978), 12, 77, 199; and jazz, 140–1, 181; and Lukács, 92; and NCC, 118; and New Left, 119–20; and 1956, 109, 113; on Popular Front, 33; on twentieth-century periodization, 4; and wartime propaganda, 41. *See also* Newton, Francis
Hodgkin, Thomas, 66
Hogarth, Paul, 106, 110
Hogarth and English Caricature (1944) (Klingender), 42
Hoggart, Richard, 100, 107, 121, 122, 138, 180
Holland, Stuart, 172
Horizon, 46, 54, 88–9
Horner, John, 112
Horrabin, Frank, 20, 22
Horrabin, Winifred, 22
How to Win the Peace (1944) (Pollitt), 50
Hungary, 3, 109
Hunt, Alan, 167, 183
Hutt, Allen, 99

Ian Campbell Folk Group, 133, 185, 186
I'm All Right Jack (1959), 137
Independent Labour Party, 13
Indignados, 203
Industrial Relations Act, 172, 173
Information and Research Department (Foreign Office), 88
Institute for Public Policy Research, 202
Institute for Workers' Control, 174
Institute of Economic Affairs, 189
Intelligence Testing and the Comprehensive School (1954) (Simon), 131
'Internationale' (song), 42, 50
Internationale Arbeiter Reliefe, 24
International Marxist Group (IMG), 186
International Monetary Fund (IMF), 178, 189
Introduction to the English Novel I: To George Eliot (1952) (Kettle), 92
Inventing the Future: Postcapitalism and a World Without Work (2016) (Srnicek and Williams), 10
Iron Curtain (1948), 96
Iskra, 25

Jacks, Digby, 165, 168
Jackson, Mike, 198
Jackson, Tommy, 21, 23, 24
Jacobs, Julius, 69
Jacques, Martin: as academic, 184–5; on Althusser, 153; co-writes *The British Road to Socialism* (1977), 188, 192–3; election to Executive Committee, 151; on intellectuals, 154; and Radical Student Alliance, 167; on Rock Against Racism, 185; on shifting demographics, 179; on youth culture, 180–2
James, Selma, 162
James, Tony, 62, 168
Jameson, Fredric, 11
Jazz Scene (1959) (Newton), 140
John, Augustus, 106
John o' London's Weekly, 87
Johnson, Pamela Hansford, 90
Johnstone, Monty, 115, 149, 152–4, 196, 197, 199

Joint Production Committees, 48, 178
Joliot-Curie, Frédéric, 62
Jones, Claudia, 125–6
Jones, Jack, 172
Jones, Mervyn, 91, 92, 110

Kalla, Georgia, 184
Kerrigan, Peter, 111, 145
Kettle, Arnold: on aesthetics, 106; and *The British Road to Socialism* (1958), 116; and *Challenge of Marxism* (1963), 136; Cold War victimization of, 92; on *Doctor Zhivago*, 120–1; and Joan Simon, 132; and NCC, 118; and New Left, 124; and 1956, 113; and Raymond Williams, 122; and University Teachers' Group, 63
Keynes, John Maynard, 68, 121, 256n251
Key Poets book series, 89
Keyworth, Florence, 157
Khrushchev, Nikita, 109, 138
Kiernan, Victor, 63, 122
Kinks, The, 141
Kino Films, 31
Kitchen, The (1961), 137
Klingender, Francis: and Army Education Corps, 42; *Hogarth and English Caricature* (1944), 42; *Russia: Britain's Ally* (1942), 43; and socialist realism, 93; University Teachers' Group, 63; withdrawal from CP, 93, 110
Klugmann, James, 76, 115, 135, 146, 147
Koestler, Arthur, 88
Kondratieff, Nikolai, 5, 202

'Labour and the Affluent Society' (1960) (Crossman), 129
Labour Monthly, 46
Labour Party: and adult education, 65; and cinema, 96; and Edinburgh People's Festivals, 105; electoral focus of, 8; and Jeremy Corbyn, 203; membership, 3; relations with CP, 17, 39, 51, 172; and school education, 60–1; and wartime cultural energy, 71; on working-class cultural habits, 95; Young Socialists, 144
Labour Research Department, 26, 214n27
Lady Chatterley Trial, 135, 136
Laing, Dave, 185
Lawrence, Martin, 40
Lawrence & Wishart, 31, 91, 103, 106, 183, 228n151
Leavis, F.R., 67, 87, 92, 104
Lecercle, Jean-Jacques, 153
Leeson, Bob, 135
Left Bloc (Portugal), 203
Left Book Club, 31, 39, 46, 86, 205, 228n152
Left Review, 33, 34, 36, 39, 46
Lehmann, Beatrix, 46, 185
Lenin, Vladimir, on Britain, 6; *Collected Works*, 25; and Comintern, 3, 13; on Communist newspapers, 22; *Imperialism: The Highest Stage of Capitalism* (1916), 5; *Left Wing Communism – An Infantile Disorder* (1920), 5, 212n6; London memorial of, 41, 240n36; 'On Proletarian Culture' (1920), 34; *The State and Revolution* (1917), 6, 29; *What Is to Be Done?* (1902), 6, 25, 26; on world revolution, 13
Lennon, John, 175
Lesbians and Gays Support the Miners (LGSM), 198
Lessing, Doris, 90, 110, 119, 122
Levy, Hyman, 27, 32, 63, 84
Lewis, John, 89, 116, 120, 146–7, 153, 206
Liaison Committee for the Defence of Trade Unions, 172, 173
Liberal Party, 164

Lichtenstein, Roy, 180
Lindsay, Jack, 10; and ABCA Theatre Unit, 42; *All on the Never Never* (1961), 137; *Betrayed Spring* (1953), 59, 93; *British Achievement in Arts and Music* (1945), 39; *Byzantium in Europe* (1952), 85; critique of CP, 73–5, 80, 120; on Dagenham, 77; *England My England: A Pageant of the English People* (1939), 38; 'Fundamental Reconsiderations' (1946), 74, 260n291; *A Handbook of English Freedom* (1939), 37; *Hullo Stranger* (1945), 48, 95, 244n88; joins CP, 33; and *Left Review*, 33; *Live Now, Pay Later* (1962), 137; 'Man and the Alien Thing,' 123; *Marxism and Contemporary Science* (1949), 91; 'Marxist Theory of Culture' (1945), 73, 260n289; on Marx's 'Economic and Philosophical Manuscripts,' 106, 206; on Moscow Show Trials, 36; and NCC, 118; and New Left, 119–20; and 1956, 113; and *Our Time*, 46; 'Practice and Theory in Cultural Matters: Notes on a Basis for Discussion' (1945), 73, 259n288; on PCI and PCF, 83, 119; on Popular Front, 35, 41; and *Questions of Ideology and Culture* (1967), 146; on socialist realism, 91–2; *Time to Live* (1946), 69; on T.S. Eliot, 100
Ling, Arthur, 56
Listener, 54
Littlewood, Joan, 42, 185
Lloyd, A.L.: on commercial culture, 140; and folk music, 103, 141; removed from post at BBC, 42; stays in party after 1956, 113; works for Ministry of Information, 42; writes for *Picture Post*, 87
Loach, Ken, 138
Local History Bulletin / Our History (CP Historians' Group), 85
Local Party Committees, 16, 17
Lock, Graham, 153
Loftus, Maria, 159
Logue, Christopher, 133
Lomax, Alan, 103
London Caribbean Carnival, 126
London Labour Choral Union, 23
London Mercury, 46
London Philharmonic Orchestra (LPO), 40
London Trades Council, 69
London Youth Choir, 103
Long Cycles of the Conjuncture (1926) (Kondratieff), 5
Looking Ahead (1947) (Pollitt), 71, 76, 110, 116
Louzon, Robert, 20, 21
Lubetkin, Berthold, 56, 93
Lukács, Georg, 92, 136
Lysenko, T.D., 84, 129, 145
Lyttelton, Humphrey, 103

MacColl, Ewan (Jimmie Miller), 69–70, 103–4, 113, 140–1
MacDiarmid, Hugh, 105, 113, 185
MacEwen, Malcolm, 43, 113, 115, 120
MacInnes, Colin, 139
MacIntyre, Stuart, 183
MacLean, Sorley, 105
MacMillan, Nan, 33
Madge, Charles: analysis of mass culture, 31, 95, 181, 230n162; and *Cambridge Left*, 27; leaves CP 36; and Pilot Press, 61
Mairants, Ivor, 40
Maisky, Ivan, 43
Makin-Waite, Mike, 10
Mandel, Ernest, 166
Manifesto for New Times (1989) (CPGB), 200
Maoism, 141, 147, 157, 167, 320n271

Marcuse, Herbert, 152, 166
Marshall Plan, 78
Martin, Geoff, 167
Maruki, Iri, 106
Marx, Karl, 5, 106, 121, 123, 206
Marx House, 31, 65, 229n158
Marxism and Democracy (1980) (Hunt ed.), 183
Marxism Today (pamphlet series), 63
Marxism Today: on academic freedom, 185; and Christian-Marxist dialogue, 146; creation of, 114; on family, 158–61; James Klugmann's editorship, 135; John Gollan in, 190; Lewis-Althusser debate, 153; Martin Jacques' editorship, 199–200; and party splits, 189; on *Questions of Ideology and Culture* (1967), 145; on translations of Marx and Gramsci, 123
Marxist Quarterly, 108, 114, 297n31
Mass Observation, 27
Matthews, George, 116, 188
May Day Manifesto (1968), 170
McCaig, Norman, 105
McKibbin, Ross, 97
Mclean, J.A., 66
McLennan, Gordon, 187
McShane, Harry, 110
Meaning of Contemporary Realism, The (1963) (Lukács), 136
Meiksins Wood, Ellen, 7
Mercer, David, 138
Meredith, George, 92
Meynell, Francis, 21
Milburn, Keir, 202
Miliband, Ralph, 120, 196
Milligan, Martin, 104, 106, 123
Millions Like Us (1943), 95
Mind in Chains: Socialism and the Cultural Revolution (1937), 34–5, 233n191
Ministry of Information, 42
Ministry of Works Scientific Advisory Committee, 55, 56
Minority Report on Inner Party Democracy, 113, 115
Mitchison, Naomi, 105
Modern Quarterly, 31, 89, 96, 108
Monstrous Regiment, 186
Montagu, Ivor, 42, 95, 96, 97, 113
Montefiore, Dora, 18
Morning Star, 45, 145, 164, 188, 189. See also *Daily Worker*
Morris, Max, 131, 132, 190
Morris, William, 86, 93
Morrison, Herbert, 23, 55
Morton, A.L., 36, 85, 136, 268n76
Morton, Cyril, 190
Moscow Show Trials, 35, 41
Mouffe, Chantal, 4
Mountbatten, Lord, 54
Movement for Colonial Freedom, 124
Moving Left Show, 186
Mr Deeds Goes to Town (1943), 95
Mulhern, Francis, 67
Munby, Lionel, 113
Music and the People (1939), 36
Musicians' Social and Benevolent Council, 40
Musicians' Union, 40

Nairn, Tom, 166
National Association of Labour Teachers, 61
National Coal Board, 103
National Council of Labour Colleges (NCLC), 20, 22, 65
National Gay Rights Committee, 164
National Government, 29
National Left Wing Movement, 22
National Paul Robeson Committee, 124, 306n125

National Union of Mineworkers (NUM), 158, 172
National Union of Railwaymen (NUR), 172
National Union of Students (NUS), 32, 167
National Union of Teachers (NUT), 33, 61, 172
National Union of Women Teachers (NUWT), 33
National Viewers and Listeners Association, 138
Nature, 54
Neath, Dulais and Swansea Valley Miners Support Group, 198
Necessity of Art, The (1963) (Fischer), 136
New Communist Party, 149
New Era Film Club, 97
New Left Review, 123, 125, 152, 154, 167
New Musical Express, 103
New Propeller, 48
New Reasoner, 119, 120, 125
New School Tie (1946) (Giles), 61
News Chronicle, 98, 113
News of the World, 70, 98
New Statesman, 113, 128, 140
Newton, Francis, 140. *See also* Hobsbawm, Eric
New Town Committee, 56
New Trends in English Education (1957), 131
New Verse, 46
Nicholson, Fergus, 166–7, 168–9
Nicholson, Hubert, 90
Nineteen Eighty-four, 99
Niven, Barbara, 135, 180
'No Colour Bar for Britain' (1955) (CPGB), 107, 124
No Time to Be Young (1952) (Jones), 92
Notting Hill Carnival, 126, 205
Obama, Barack, 201
Observer, 58
Occupy, 203
OECD, 201
Old Vic, 43, 70
Olive, Paul, 186
Once a Jolly Swagman (1944) (Slater), 96
Origin of the Family, Private Property and the State (1884) (Engels), 157
Orwell, George, 36, 88, 99
Osbourne, John, 119
Osmond, Donny, 181
Our History, 183
Our Time, 46, 87–8, 90, 108, 199
Out of the Ghetto: A Path to Socialist Rewards (1977) (Prior and Purdy), 193
Owen, Alun, 138
Oxford Extra Mural Studies Delegacy, 66–7

Pankhurst, Sylvia, 16, 18, 212n6
Panter, Bernard, 190
Parti communiste française (PCF), 3, 33, 51, 145, 165
Partido Comunista Español (PCE), 197
Partito Comunista Italiano (PCI), 3, 51, 104, 154, 197
Party Group, 154–6, 165, 174. *See also* Smith Group
Pascal, Roy, 63
Past and Present (book series), 63
Past & Present, 85
Pasternak, Boris, 120
Paul, Cedar, 19, 22, 30
Paul, Eden, 19, 22
Paul, William, 13, 22, 30
Pearce, Brian, 113–15
Penn, Colin, 58
Pentonville Five, 171
People's Convention, 39, 40, 42, 47
People's Democracies, 51, 71, 100

People's History of England (1938) (Morton), 36, 85
People's Jubilee, 151, 187, 205
People's Republic of Mongolia, 4
Perks, Jeff, 186
Phillips, Van, 40
Picasso, Pablo, 62, 93
Picture Post, 24, 87, 100
Pilkington Report (1962), 138
Pilot Press, 62
Pindar, Winston, 125
Piratin, Phil, 59, 77
Pits and Perverts concert, 198
Planning and Building in the USSR (1943) (Ling), 57
Plato Films, 97, 137, 184
Plebs, 20, 21
Plebs League, 20
Plowden Committee, 131
Podemos, 203
Poetry and the People, 46
Polemic, 88
Politics & Letters, 89
Pollitt, Harry: on Americanization of Britain, 80; *Answers to Questions* (1945), 50; and formation of CP, 13; funeral footage, 137; *How to Win the Peace* (1944), 50; *Looking Ahead* (1947), 71, 76; and Marx House, 65; and post-war decline, 72; on post-war moment, 38; retirement, 110; and wartime production drive, 49
Postal Engineers' Anglo-Soviet Committee, 46
Poulantzas, Nicos, 183
Prague Spring, 149–50, 165
Pravda, 21
Presley, Elvis, 122
Pride (2014), 198
Priestley, J.B.: *Bright Day* (1946), 285; at Butlin's, 70; in *Daily Worker*, 73, 87; disowned by CP, 90; and Dutt, 237n224; on *A Handbook of English Freedom* (1939), 37; as middlebrow, 87, 270n85; and Unity Theatre, 69; and wartime music work, 40
Prior, Mike, 154, 165, 174–9, 193–7, 205
'Programme of the CPGB – A Critique' (1970) (Warren), 155–6
proletarian culture, 19, 34
Prokofiev, Sergei, 62
Purdy, David, 176–9, 193–7, 205

Quattrocchi, Angelo, 166
Questions of Ideology and Culture (1967) (CPGB), 145–8, 190

Radical Philosophy, 183
Radical Student Alliance (RSA), 167–8
Ragged Trousered Philanthropists (1914) (Tressell), 92
Ramelson, Bert: and *The British Road to Socialism* (1977), 191; Broad Left strategy, 144; and inflation, 176; and Institute for Workers' Control, 174; and seamen's strike, 171; and social contract, 174
Rank, Arthur, 96
Reasoner, 113, 115
Red Army, 41, 42
Redgrave, Michael, 69
Red Letters, 183, 189, 341n271
Red Rag, 161–3
Reed, John, *Ten Days that Shook the World* (1919), 36
Reid, Betty, 141, 152–3, 181, 182
Reid, Jimmy, 171, 173, 190
Reith, Sir John, 56
Report on Organization (1922) (CPGB), 15, 21
Revolutionary Socialist Student Federation, 167
Révolution prolétarienne, 20

Rickword, Edgell: 'Culture, Progress and English Tradition' (1937), 34; and *A Handbook of English Freedom* (1939), 37; joins CP, 33; leaves CP, 110; and *Our Time*, 46, 67, 87; praises Stalin, 36; pulls back from CP, 90
Ritchie, Jean, 103
Robbins Report, 165
Robeson, Paul, 36, 124, 306n125
'Robeson' party branches, 81, 125
Rock Against Racism, 185
Rothermere Press, 99
Rothstein, Andrew, 17, 115
Rowbotham, Sheila, 162
Rowe, Martha, 157
Rowsell, E., 136
Royal Academy, 43
Rudé, George, 113
Russell, Ralph, 124
Russell, Thomas, 40, 94, 106
Russians, The (Simonov), 43
Russia Today Society, 41

Samuel, Raphael, 120, 199, 268n75
San Carlo Opera, 70
Sandbrook, Jeremy, 138
Sanders, Bernie, 203
Sargent, Malcolm, 46
Sassoon, Donald, 4, 76
Saturday Night and Sunday Morning (1958) (Sillitoe), 122
Saville, John: and adult education, 66; and CP historians, 85; and CP theoretical weaknesses, 122; and 1956, 113–15; University Teachers' Group, 63
Scargill, Arthur, 158
Scott and Uthwatt Commissions, 56
Scritti Politti, 185
Scrutiny, 67–8, 87
Secondary School Selection (1957) (Vernon), 131
Second International Congress of the History of Science and Technology (1931), 27
Section of Intellectual Workers, 26
Seltman, Peter, 126
Selvon, Sam, 89
Seven: A Magazine of People's Writing, 46
Sex Pistols, The, 185, 187
Shakin' Stevens, 186
Sham 69, 185
Sharma, Vishnu, 125
Shop Stewards' National Council, 48
Short Course (1939). See *History of the Communist Party of the Soviet Union / Bolsheviks / Short Course*
Shrewsbury Pickets, 171, 186
Sillitoe, Alan, 122, 136
Simon, Brian: and *The Challenge of Marxism* (1963), 136; and *The Common Secondary School* (1955), 131; critic of streaming and intelligence tests, 106, 131; *Intelligence Testing and the Comprehensive School* (1953), 106, 131; legacy, 205; and Margaret Thatcher, 192; and NCC, 118, 131, 135, 152, 182; and NEAC, 132; and Plowden Committee, 131; publications in 1950s, 131; *Questions of Ideology and Culture* (1967), 145; stays in party after 1956, 113; as student activist, 32
Simon, Joan, 113, 131, 132
Simon, Roger, 153, 196, 335n169
Sinfield, Alan, 67
Sino-Soviet dispute, 154
Sitwell, Edith, 89
Slater, Montagu, 33, 42, 46, 95
Slipmann, Sue, 163
Small, Rosemary, 157–61
Smith Group, 154–6, 173, 193. *See also* Party Group
Snow, C.P., 128

social contract, 173, 174
Socialism and the Middle Classes (1958) (Grant), 121
Socialist Europe: Communist Party Journal of Soviet and East European Studies, 189, 341n271
socialist humanism, 106
socialist realism, 91–4, 106
Socialist Register, 196
Socialist Sunday Schools, 16
Society for Cultural Relations with the USSR (SCR), 41, 113
Society for the Study of Labour History, 120
Soviet Russia Pictorial, 24
Soviet Writers' Congresses, 106, 120
Soviet Union: British perceptions of, 41; films, 41; guidance over national Communist Parties, 11; 'Literature Controversy,' 88–90, 121; post-war scientific advancement, 128
Spare Rib, 157
Spencer, Stanley, 106
Spender, Stephen, 89, 92
Sprague, Ken, 184
Sputnik, 128–9
squatters' movement (1946), 58–9
Srnicek, Nick, 10, 206
Stalin, Joseph: on BBC, 42; and *The British Road to Socialism* (1951), 80; death of, 80, 105, 117; and execution of Kondratieff, 5; linguistics, 91; and *Short Course* (1939), 35; and show trials, 41; and *Ten Days that Shook the World* (1919), 36; tributes to, 90
Stalingrad, 43
Stalingrad Overture (1943) (Darnton), 46
Stalinism: in CP, late 1930s, 36; and *Decision: British Communism*, 191; definition, 4; New Left definitions of, 120; and 1956, 109; as orthodoxy, 8, 204; and 'two camps' line, 90
Stalin Peace Prize, 56
Stanley, Frank, 133
Starr, Mark, 22
Stevens, Bernard, 93, 110
Still, André, 91
Stockholm Peace Congress (1950), 84
Stone, Lew, 40
Strand, 87
Straw, Jack, 167, 168
Streeck, Wolfgang, 5, 205
Studies in the Development of Capitalism (1946) (Dobb), 85
Styles, Jean, 163
Sunday Worker, 22–5; 30
Swingler, Randall: analysis of CP, 70–1, 122–3; 259n282; and *Daily Worker*, 36; joins CP, 33; leaves CP, 110; *Music and the People* (1939), 36; and *Our Time*, 46; pulls back from CP, 90
Symphony of Liberation (1946) (Stevens), 93
Syriza, 203

Tanburn, Nigel, 187
Tanks for Russia, 43
Teachers' Anti-War Movement, 33
Tecton, 56
Tehran Conference, 50
Thatcher, Margaret, 192
That Was The Week That Was, 138
'Theatre and the People' conference (1946), 69
Theatre Workshop, 70, 103, 105, 132
Third International, 4, 6, 18. *See also* Comintern
This Week, 186
Thompson, E.P.: and adult education, 63, 66; and *The British Road to Socialism* (1951), 80; career post-1956, 110; and CP theoretical weaknesses, 122; on John Lewis, 116; and 1956, 113–15; on post-war affluence, 121; and

Thompson, E.P. (*continued*)
Short Course (1939), 35; on socialist humanism, 106; on Stalinism, 4, 36; *William Morris: Romantic to Revolutionary* (1955), 86
Thompson, Frank, 62
Thompson, Willie, 183, 197
Thomson, George, 63, 102, 113
Times, 109
Times Educational Supplement, 61, 106
Time to Change Course (1973) (Woddis), 173
Tocher, John, 190
Togliatti, Palmiro, 30, 83, 210n31
Topic Records, 42, 103, 112, 205
Torr, Dona, 85
Townshend, Pete, 141
Trades Union Congress (TUC), 46, 172
Transport and General Workers Union (TGWU), 172
Tribune, 36
Trotsky, Leon: and CPGB, 3; and culture and revolution, 6, 7, 20, 212n7; *Literature and Revolution* (1924), 23; and *Ten Days that Shook the World* (1918), 36
Trotskyism, 152, 157, 167
Twentieth Century Verse, 46
Two Cultures and the Scientific Revolution, The (1959) (Snow), 128
Tynan, Kenneth, 119

UK Uncut, 203
UNESCO, 55
Union of Construction, Allied Trades and Technicians (UCATT), 172
United Labour Federation (ULF), 32
United Nations, 50
Unity of Arts Society, 184
Unity Theatre: creation, 31; and Bristol Unity, 42; and Glasgow Unity, 70; and Leeds Unity, 42; and Lionel Bart, 132; and 1956, 112; Outside Show Group, 42; *Russia's Glory: The Red Army*, 42; post-war restructuring of, 69
Universities & Left Review, 119, 120
Upper Clyde Shipbuilders, 171, 182, 205
Uranium 235 (1945) (MacColl), 70
Uses of Literacy (1957) (Hoggart), 107
Utley, Freda, 10, 25–6, 34

Valentino, Rudolph, 24
Van Gyseghem, André, 42
Vickers, J., 66
Vietnam war, 167

Wainwright, Bill, 118
Wallerstein, Immanuel, 202
Warner, Sylvia Townsend, 33, 110
War Pictures (AIA Exhibition), 42
Warren, Bill, 10, 144, 154–6, 174–9, 197
Warren, Des, 171
Waterhouse, Keith, 122
Wat Tyler (1951) (Bush), 94
Wedgewood Memorial College, 66–7
welfare capitalism, 5, 11, 78, 121, 204
Wesker, Arnold, 122, 133, 136, 137
Westacott, Fred, 42
West, Alex, 92, 116, 118, 215n37
West Indian Gazette, 126
Whitehouse, Mary, 138
Whitworth, Geoffrey, 69
Who, The, 141
Wilkinson, Ellen, 22
Willett, John, 183
William Morris Music Society, 40
Williams, Alex, 10, 206
Williams, Raymond, 10; and Adult Education, 66–7; on Attlee government, 71; *Communications* (1962), 138; CP, critique of, 122; CP in dialogue with, 180; *Culture and*

Society 1780–1950 (1958), 100, 107, 108, 12; on J.B. Priestley, 89; and 'Marxism and the Mass Media' (1977), 186; and national arts policies, 133; on need for intellectual and educational work, 204–5; on Soviet Literature Controversy, 89
Williamson, John, 124, 306n125
Willis, Ted, 42, 132
Wilson, Alistair, 73
Wilson, Colin, 119, 122
Wilson, Elizabeth, 157, 163
Wilson, Harold, 171
Wintringham, Tom, 10, 33, 35, 36
Woddis, Jack, 165, 173
Woman Today, 31
Women's Committee Against War and Fascism, 31
Women's Liberation Movement (WLM), 156–63
Women's Parliaments, 12, 47, 48, 81, 205
Women's Social and Political Union, 19
Woolf, Virginia, 30
Woolton, Lord, 56
Workers' Dreadnought, 16
Workers' Educational Association (WEA), 65–7
Workers' Education Trade Union Committee, 65–7
Workers' International Pictorial, 24
Workers' Music Association: CP faction, 40; creation, 31; and folk music, 103; funding, 94; and legacy, 205; and Soviet culture, 42; wartime premises, 40
Workers' Socialist Federation, 16
Workers' Theatre Group / Movement, 23, 24
Workers' Weekly, 21, 25
Working Class Movement Library, 199
World Federation of Democratic Youth, 103
World Federation of Scientific Workers (WFSW), 55
World News and Views, 72–3
Worsley, Peter, 121
Writers' International (British Section), 33
Wyatt, Robert, 187

Yalta Conference, 50. *See also* Crimea Conference
Young Communist League: Bolshevization of, 16; fight at 1952 Congress dance, 103; membership, 127, 144, 186; and 1956 crisis, 109; and popular culture, 139–41

Zhdanov, A.A., 91, 135
Zhdanovshchina, 89
Zola, Émile, 92

www.ingramcontent.com/pod-product-compliance
Lightning Source LLC
LaVergne TN
LVHW040153080826
844660LV00014B/945/J

* 9 7 8 1 4 8 7 5 0 7 3 9 8 *